GASCONY
& THE PYRENEES

*'For an area scarcely larger than Belgium, Gascony offers an
amazing range of landscapes and climates. In the late spring, they'll
be surfing in Biarritz while in the Pyrenees climbers will still be
picking their way around patches of ice..'*

Dana Facaros & Michael Pauls

About the Guide

The **full-colour introduction** gives the authors' overview of the region, together with suggested **itineraries** and a regional **'where to go' map** and **feature** to help you plan your trip.

Illuminating and entertaining **cultural chapters** on history, food and drink, local people and activities give you a rich flavour of the region.

Travel covers the basics of **getting there** and **getting around**, plus entry formalities. The **Practical A–Z** deals with all the **essential information** and **contact details** that you may need, including a section for disabled travellers.

The **regional chapters** are arranged in a loose touring order, with plenty of public transport and driving information. The authors' top **'Don't Miss'** ⭐ sights are highlighted at the start of each chapter.

A **language and pronunciation guide**, a **glossary** of cultural terms, ideas for **further reading**, a comprehensive **index** and an eight-page **colour touring atlas** can be found at the end of the book.

Although everything we list in this guide is **personally recommended**, our authors inevitably have their own favourite places to eat and stay. Whenever you see this **Authors' Choice** (★) icon beside a listing, you will know that it is a little bit out of the ordinary.

Hotel Price Guide

Luxury	€€€€€	€230 and above
Very Expensive	€€€€	€150–230
Expensive	€€€	€100–150
Moderate	€€	€60–100
Inexpensive	€	€60 and under

About the Authors

Dana Facaros and Michael Pauls have lived all over Europe and written more than 40 books for Cadogan Guides. They currently live in an old *presbytère* near the Lot.

5th Edition Published 2007

INTRODUCING
GASCONY &
01 THE PYRENEES

Above: Biarritz, p.183; Col du Pailhères, near Ax-les-Thermes, p.357

For proof that France's southwestern corner is an exceptional place, one need look no further than the cartoon pictures in our children's old atlas: a graceful Basque *pelote* player dressed all in white, arching his long *chistera* at the ball, an izard perched atop a Pyrenean peak looking down at a mountain-climber, a mustachioed musketeer in a costume from the time of Louis XIII. For the Landes, there's an old-time shepherd on stilts, next to a stocky Gascon farmer in a beret with his geese. In short, this corner of France has character. And in a beautiful region that the disfiguring stresses of history and economics have passed over lightly, such character can be explored at leisure. Gascony is the perfect place for lazy touring, a place where nearly all the roads seem to be back roads, and where every village has its welcoming *auberge*; more likely than not this will include a restaurant where *madame* cooks up duck and game and other hearty dishes Parisians would die for. Besides the famous scenery and its multitude of other attractions, Gascony and the Basque lands, including the vibrant city of Toulouse, are home to some of France's finest cuisine *du terroir*, not to mention the seafood of the Bay of Biscay, and truly excellent wines.

The presiding angel of Gascony is Good King Henri – Henri IV – the Gascon who, three centuries ago, saved the country from its religious squabbling and taught Frenchmen, with a joke and a smile, to take it easy and enjoy life rather than slaughter each other over abstractions. The basis of Henri's policy is expressed in a quote that everyone still remembers: he wished every Frenchman to have a chicken in the pot on Sundays. The stories say he liked to sneak down to the palace kitchens to see how his own *poule au pot* was cooking, and didn't mind helping chop up the vegetables. Thanks to Henri, perhaps, that part of the Gascon mystique is still very present: the sense of contentment simple pleasures can bring.

Fashions in holiday playgrounds come and go. Nobody now remembers that France's southwestern corner was, a century ago, the most popular holiday destination in the land, that Queen Victoria came to Biarritz or that the English laid out the continent's first golf course at Pau. The relics of the joys that the Second Empire and the *belle époque* knew can still be seen on every side: gracefully ageing '*grands hôtels*' and gardens, and the fantastical architecture of the old casinos and bath establishments, along with mountain *refuges* that recall the memory of the great Pyrenean explorers such as Henry Russell. For a long time, the region was eclipsed by flashier upstarts, notably Provence and the Côte d'Azur. But the long hiatus gave the far southwest some breathing space, allowing it to perfect its charm while sparing it the overbuilding and overpopulation of so many other holiday centres. The time for rediscovery is at hand; few parts of France have so much to offer.

Above: Music festival, Foix, p.341; Atrium, Old Casino, Dax, p.118
Opposite: Place de la Trinité, Toulouse, p.314

Where to Go

For an area scarcely larger than Belgium, Gascony offers an amazing range of landscapes and climates. In the late spring, there will be surfing in Biarritz while in the Pyrenees climbers will still be picking their way around patches of ice.

Gascony below the mountains divides neatly into the separate worlds of the Landes and the Gers. The **Landes** is a distinctive and thoroughly peculiar place. What was once a sandy wasteland has become Europe's biggest forest – a man-made one, a vast flat carpet of pines planted in the time of Napoleon III. The face it turns to the sea is a solid line of beaches, backing up into heaps like the massive **Dune du Pilat**, 300ft (90m) tall and still growing; beach resorts such as **Arcachon** and **Hossegor-Capbreton** provide welcome breaks among the lonely expanses of sea, sand and pines. The neighbouring *département* of the Gers is the picture of southwest France most people carry around: rich lands and sweet rivers, a country of geese and *foie gras* and vineyards destined to provide fine armagnac. The **Gers** is the homeland of D'Artagnan and the Musketeers, and its landmarks have changed little since the Middle Ages: rugged castles, abbeys and *bastides*, as well as the Renaissance art of Auch's great cathedral.

Looking over the Pyrenees, from west to east, we begin with the **Basque Lands**, a world in itself. **Biarritz, St-Jean-de-Luz** and **Hendaye** make up France's biggest and best-known Atlantic resort strip, but behind this glittering façade stretches the timeless preserve of Europe's oldest nation, with its unique language and folklore. The Basques hold on to their culture with remarkable tenacity, and as you drive through the lovely, neat-as-a-pin villages of the green Labourdin or Soule, you'll see the locals performing their dances and peculiar sports on any summer weekend.

The Basque country shares the *département* of Pyrénées-Atlantiques with an equally distinctive land: **Béarn**. For centuries, Béarn was a proudly independent state, and it retains memories of the good old days at King Henri's castle at **Pau** and in medieval towns like Salies-de-Béarn. In southern Béarn begins the long stretch of parallel **Pyrenean valleys**, each of which will easily take you to a distinctive part of the mountains. The **Vallée d'Aspe** and **Vallée d'Ossau** come first, where Pyrenean bears and eagles live on in the shadow of the majestic Pic du Midi.

The mountains have always played a dominating role in the life of the Gascons, so much so that the Gascon words for north and south are *dessous* and *dessus* – down and up. The array of mountain valleys continues into the heart of the chain, in the *département* of **Hautes-Pyrénées**. **Lourdes** is here, along with

Above: Biarritz, p.183

Below: Lourdes, p.245

Opposite: Place St-Etienne, Toulouse, p.316;

famous sights like the **Cirque de Gavarnie** and the gracious old spa resorts: **Bagnères, Luchon, Cauterets**.

Then, lest anyone should forget, there is **Toulouse**. If there's one thing that keeps southwest France from nodding off in its vats of goose fat and wine, it is this big pink dynamo on the cutting edge of the 21st century.

There is another *département* in the centre of the chain, one not familiar to many, but increasingly popular with British house buyers looking for a life away from it all. The sparsely populated **Ariège** can show you surprises such as the wonderful Palaeolithic cave art at Niaux and the cloud-castle of Montségur, mystical last refuge of the medieval heretic Cathars. The individual little mountain principality of **Andorra** may be irresistible as a trip out from Ariège, or you may prefer to continue to the eastern edge of the Pyrenees, and visit the historic Catalan city of **Perpignan**.

01 Introduction | Where to Go

Chapter Divisions

Bay of Biscay

Arcachon

07 THE LANDES p.77

LANDES

Mont-de-Marsan

Dax

08 THE GERS p.77

GERS

Auch

TOULOUSE

ARRITZ

09 THE PAYS BASQUE p.167

PYRÉNÉES

10 BÉARN p.211

ATLANTIQUES

Tarbes

Lourdes

HAUTES-PYRÉNÉES

11 THE HIGH PYRENEES p.239

HAUTE-GARONNE

ARIÈGE

Foix

13 ARIÈGE, ANDORRA AND THE EASTERN PYRENEES p.323

PERPIGNAN

ANDORRA

PYRÉNÉES ORIENTALES

N

40 km
40 miles

CAFE des ARTISTES

Where's the Traffic?

It's the first thing many foreigners – and Parisians – notice when they come down here. It's clean, quiet, relatively inexpensive, and you can go where you like without any hassle. The charm of bygone days isn't only a matter of history and culture, but of a quality of life other places have lost; sometimes it will seem like you're in the 1950s here (and sometimes, maybe, the 1250s). The natural environment is in fine shape, and not just in the remote Pyrenees: forests are full of boar and deer, eagles soar overhead. The region is one of Europe's great highways for migrating birds. It is still largely a land of family farms, and these provide the elements of its famous cuisine.

Above: pine forest, The Landes, p.79; Old Peugeot, Bélesta, p.321

Clockwise from top: local flora and fauna, l'Ariège, p.325; landscape south of Mirepoix, p.350; barn

Red Wine, Ducks and Garlic

If you're averse to any part of this holy trinity of southwest cuisine, you might be in the wrong corner of France. Solid, hearty cooking is an essential part of the Gascon mystique, and has been since the days when Good King Henri promised to put a chicken in every Gascon pot. Most of France's *foie gras* comes from this region,

Above: garlic; cod in peppers

and most of its garlic too. Do not doubt, however, there is just as much skill as solidity in the southwestern kitchen, and more in the pantry than just quackers: plenty of *cèpes*, salmon and crayfish from the Adour, game dishes from the forests, and cheeses from the Pyrenean meadows. No one does seafood – and many other things – better than the Basques. And to wash it all down there are such up-and-coming wines as Jurançon, Madiran, Pacherenc and Irouléguy, not to mention the king of French spirits, armagnac.

Clockwise from top: oysters from Arcachon p.81; regional cheese; opening oysters at market, Toulouse, p.303

From Days of Old

Even in France, few places possess such panache, or such an unusual talent for making the past come alive. You can see it in its medieval monuments and half-timbered villages, and in the spectacle of its own style of bullfight, the *course landaise*. The Middle Ages live, too, in legends and memories: Charlemagne and Roland, and pilgrims trekking over the Pyrenees on their way to Compostela. Some of the best stories, however, come from the later centuries, the time of Henri II, the Gascon warrior who ended the Wars of Religion and won the throne of France. They'll tell you about Corisande, and Gaston Fébus, and the mysterious *cagots* of the Pyrenees, not forgetting, of course, d'Artagnan and the Three Musketeers – a lot of good Gascons could never be convinced these were really fictional characters.

Above: Château des Comtes des Foix, p.343; half-timbered detail, Mirepoix, p.350

Basques

Tucked away in a particularly soft and lovely corner of the mountains, there's a strange and special world where everything is painted red, green and white, where every village church has a *fronton* next to it for the kids to play *pelote*, where houses are covered in strings of red peppers drying on the walls. You couldn't be anywhere else but in the Basque lands, home of the oldest nation of Europe. Getting to know their ancient customs – and their cuisine – will be a treat, and the setting could not be more enticing. The Basque corner of France may be small, but it includes the swank resort of St-Jean-de-Luz, the beautiful Pyrenean foothills with their distinctive villages, and some of the choicest parts of the mountains.

Clockwise from top: Mijanès, p.359; pelote players, p.173; Basque gâteaux, Sare, p.198; Course Landaise, p.36; Col du Pailhères, near Ax-les-Thermes, p.357

Above: Tour du Castella, Tarascon-sur Ariège, p.352

Below: Calamari, Biarritz p.183; shoreline, St-Jean-de-Luz, p.192

Mountain Greenery

To many people, the Pyrenees are the most beautiful mountains of Europe, but there's a lot more to them than just scenery. Though hardly the biggest chain, they have always had an importance far out of proportion to their size. It was here that Europeans first discovered the wonders of nature two centuries ago, in the Romantic era. After that they initiated the habit of the mountain holiday – leaving elegant old spa towns and resorts such as Cauterets and St-Jean-Pied-de-Port for us to enjoy today. It's not just about skiing and hiking: the Pyrenees are an inexhaustible fount of folklore and curiosities, with sacred mountains at either end, one Basque, the other Catalan. Poke around in their inner fastnesses and you'll find prehistoric painted caves, medieval churches, Cathar castles, haunting legends and distinctive peculiarities like the little Ruritania of Andorra.

A Slice of Seacoast

It isn't the Côte d'Azur or the Amalfi Drive, but the Gascon/Basque stretch of seacoast does have its charms. For starters, you'll never run out of oysters, thanks to Arcachon at its northern tip. South of that there's plenty of sand to sit on, or climb, including Europe's biggest dune, the Dune du Pilat; not to mention river cruising nearby on the Leyre. Further south, there are quiet little hideaway resorts such as Mimizan, beloved of Winston Churchill, the delightful and colourful city of Bayonne, slightly faded grandeur in Biarritz, modern elegance at St-Jean-de-Luz, surfing on the Bay of Biscay, and all the best seafood you can eat.

Itineraries
The Best of the Pyrenees in Two Weeks

This is about as fast as it can possibly be done – but the Pyrenees are no place for hurrying; take this itinerary as a quick guide to seeing the best of what the mountains have to offer, and settle down for an extra day or two in whatever places strike your fancy.

Day 1 Starting from the Atlantic coast, tour the lovely villages of the Basque foothills: Ascain, Sare, Espelette, with a stop for stalactites at the Grottes de Istaritz or a tramway trip up the holy mountain of La Rhune. Finish in St-Jean-Pied-de-Port.

Day 2 After St-Jean, it's into the Haute-Soule for a walk through the Gorges de Kakouetta and the fascinating medieval church at Ste-Engrâce.

Day 3 Backtracking through Oloron-Ste-Marie, head into the Vallée d'Aspe. Serious mountain scenery begins here, with the Cirque de Lescun and the Pic du Midi. Cross over into the Vallée d'Ossau on the D918 or 924.

Day 4 A beautiful drive, the D918, leads into the heart of the mountains over the Col d'Aubisque. At the end, in the Val d'Azun, there's a lot to see in and around St-Savin and Cauterets.

Days 5–6 Using one of these as a base, take two days to explore the Cirque de Gavarnie and two other cirques, Europe's highest waterfall, and plenty of hiking opportunities, in an area that, for many, is the climax of the Pyrenees.

Day 7 Mostly a travelling day, through another scenic trans-valley road through the Col de Tourmalet, to see the old spa of Bagnères-de-Bigorre and the Vallée de Campan, with another stalactite cave to see, the Grotte de Médous.

Day 8 Today's valley is the Vallée d'Aure, for a look at the medieval villages of Sarrancolin and Arreau, and then on to St-Lary, major centre for the Parc National des Pyrénées.

Day 9 Around St-Lary there will be plenty of opportunities for hiking and sightseeing, especially around the Route des Lacs, in a secluded valley full of mountain lakes.

Day 10 Now backtrack to Arreau, and follow the Vallée de Louron, rich in Romanesque churches, and continue on to Bagnères-de-Luchon, another centre for mountain touring; you may dally here, or carry on north to see the great church at St-Bertrand-de-Comminges and the Grotte de Gargas with its Paleolithic cave paintings.

Day 11 From here, the D618 will take you back into the mountains and into the Ariège *département*. It's a greener, less

Above: St-Jean-Pied-de-Port, p.204; Cirque de Gavarnie, p.263

dramatic corner of the mountains, with many interesting old villages on the way to St-Lizier and its medieval monuments.

Day 12 Visit another fine medieval town, Foix, before heading southeast, with perhaps a detour to the famous last stand of the Cathars, the castle of Montségur. Continue to the spectacular cave paintings of the Grotte de Niaux, and finally the old spa of Ax-les-Thermes.

Day 13 Next stop is Andorra, for some wonderful scenery and maybe a little duty-free. Then past Latour-de-Carol and into the Cerdagne, a corner of the mountains full of exceptional medieval monuments and interesting things to see.

Above: Montségur, p.345

Below: Old Dax, p.120; Cathédrale Ste-Marie, Auch, p.155

Day 14 From the Cerdagne, follow the valley of the Conflent through the old fortress town of Villefranche, Prades and Serrabone with their Romanesque art, and on to Perpignan.

A Week with the Gascons

It isn't a region to overwhelm you with history and culture, but you won't be bored either. A week spent meeting this good honest nation, enjoying its cooking and exploring its sweet and pristine country, will be a week well spent.

Day 1 If you start from Toulouse, the sights on the way to Auch make a good introduction: the medieval villages of Gimont and L'Isle-Jourdain, Samatan and Lombez.

Day 2 Auch itself will take some time, for its cathedral and its stained glass windows. From here, head north through Fleurance and the old Roman town of Lectoure, towards the Abbey of Flaran and the medieval village of La Romieu.

Day 3 Now head into the Armagnac country, through Eauze and Labastide d'Armagnac. Buy a bottle or two, and continue on into the Landes, through Aire-sur-l'Adour and St-Sever, ending up at Dax.

Day 4 A day dedicated to water. You might take a river cruise on the Courant d'Huchet, or continue on to Capbreton-Hossegor or one of the smaller resorts for a day at the beach.

Day 5 Bayonne is more Basque than Gascon, but it's one of the most beautiful cities of France and well worth a look. For that matter, Biarritz is just down the road, part of the same urban agglomeration.

Day 6 Head eastwards into Béarn, for Orthez with its medieval bridge and Salies-de-Béarn with its canals. Continue on through Sauveterre and L'Hôpital-St-Blaise to Pau.

Day 7 After paying your respects to Good King Henri in Pau, you might head off for Lourdes, visit the Béarn wine country around Madiran, or take a dip into the Pyrenees around St-Bertrand-de Comminges on your way back to Toulouse.

CONTENTS

Contents

18

Maps and Plans

Contents

History

SPAIN

02

450,000–4000 BC

The dawn of history arrives in the Pyrenees, at a time when the rest of us are still snoring away

The Basques, the oldest nation of Europe, like to joke that when God created the first man, he got the bones from a Basque graveyard. No one knows for sure just how far back they go – only that someone, incredibly, must have been around even before them. For the areas around the Pyrenees are one of the oldest inhabited places on earth, and one of the cradles of human culture. The first European yet discovered, 'Tautavel Man', parked his carcass in a cave at the eastern end of the chain some 450,000 years ago. His possible successor, Neanderthal Man, was here too, as well as Cro-Magnon Man, who takes his name from the village in nearby Périgord where his remains were first discovered. The next and most spectacular human record begins with Mr Cro-Magnon's Palaeolithic era, c. 35,000 BC, and the first art in history. The most famous painted caves are in Périgord and northern Spain, but Gascony too has its share, at Niaux in the Ariège, Ustaritz in the Basque country, and several others. 'The infancy of art, not an art of infancy', as has been noted, Palaeolithic paintings combine masterful figurative drawing with a sophisticated turn of mind that often seems to share the aims and approaches of the art of our times.

Among the distinctions of the ancient artists in this area are the first known portrait, in the cave of Brassempouy in the Landes (Perigordian era, c. 35–30,000 BC), and the oldest work of sculpture ever found, a figurine of a goddess from Lespugue in the Haute-Garonne (Aurignacian era, c. 30–20,000 BC). This second period of Palaeolithic art was named after a Pyrenean village, Aurignac, where some of the first important finds were made. After a hiatus in the Solutrian era (c. 20–15,000 BC), when people concentrated more on perfecting stone tools and weapons, art made a great comeback in the fourth Palaeolithic period, the Magdalenian (c. 15–10,000 BC), represented in numerous Pyrenean caves (though few of them are open to visitors). The peoples responsible for this precocious art were probably largely nomadic, and as the last ice age slowly ended, they may well have gradually migrated northwards following the herds.

From then it's a long, dull wait until the next flowering of culture and Europe's first great civilization, in the Neolithic era. The result of a revolution in technology and culture that radiated outwards from the Middle East, the Neolithic world introduced agriculture, the domestication of animals, astronomy and building – their lasting monuments include dolmens, tumuli and menhirs. Neolithic peoples were great traders and liked to live near the sea or important rivers, and finds in the area of this book are limited to the Basque country in the far western Pyrenees. Their culture kept a remarkable unity across western Europe for some 3,000 years from 4000 to about 1000 BC. The metal-working cultures that replaced them often copied Neolithic forms, as in the small cromlechs (stone circles) found around the region, or the impressive burial tumuli in the Baronnies or near Bartrès, north of Lourdes. Both these sets of monuments lie close to one of Europe's oldest known roads, the 'Salt Road' that since Neolithic times connected the Atlantic with the Mediterranean, passing by way of Salies-de-Béarn, Pau, Lourdes and St-Bertrand.

Other important roads crossed the easiest passes of the Pyrenees: the 'Ténarèze', running from the Comminges up through the part of the Armagnac called by that name today, and another one passing through St-Jean-Pied-de-Port and up into the Landes.

4000 BC–AD 407

An agreeable people moves in to stay; the Romans muscle in and try to make serfs of them, with considerable success

Vascones, Gascons, Basques: the ways in which this simple name has been twisted about over the centuries provides a mirror for the obscure and often confusing history of this corner of France. It also provides a lesson in tenacity, with the intriguing suggestion by some French ethnologists that this region's history may have been unfolding with roughly the same cast of characters since the time of cave-painters.

'The Basques are like good women; they have no history.' So runs the old saying, but traces of habitation in the Basque lands go back at least 100,000 years, and somebody was painting on the walls of caves such as Ustaritz as early as 35,000 BC. Where did the Basques come in? The theories that they are related to the Palaeolithic people seem far-fetched; a more likely premise would be that they are the descendants of the Neolithic culture that arrived in these parts c. 4000 BC. Practically every word for common tools in Basque, Europe's oldest native language, comes from the ancient root *haiz*, meaning stone, even *haiztur*, scissors. The possibility of an identity between the Basques and the Iberians, the most ancient known inhabitants of Spain, is an open question.

About 800 BC, Celtic peoples started moving through the region, variously conquering or coexisting and intermarrying with the original peoples. When the Romans came, they found a nation they called Ouasconum or Vascones occupying much of the land between the rivers Ebro and Garonne, including almost all of the Pyrenees. Some of the names of the mixed Vascone-Celtic tribes are remembered in place names today: the Bigerriones (the Bigorre), the Auscii (Auch), Tarbii (Tarbes) and the Garunni (the Garonne River). Many of the outlandish names which so many Pyrenean villages have may also be of Basque origin, as far eastwards as the Mediterranean. If the *gaztelulak* are any evidence, the various tribes didn't always get along; the remains of these hilltop earthen forts are still a feature of the Basque country, which counts 242 of them.

The Roman conquest of Celts and Vascones did not happen all at once. Roman influence in southern Gaul was already felt in the 2nd century BC, following the Carthaginians, who probably stopped at Biarritz and other Atlantic harbours on their way up the important sea-trading route to Cornwall and its tin mines. In 71 BC, Roman control extended into the Comminges. Pompey passed through on a campaign against rebels in Spain that year and founded the city of Lugdunum Convenarum (St-Bertrand-de-Comminges), which was to be the metropolis of the northern flank of the mountains for centuries to come. For the final conquest, while Julius Caesar busied himself with stronger tribes to the north, his partner Crassus (a fantastically wealthy real-estate speculator who had gone into politics the Roman way, by purchasing a command, just as Caesar himself had done) was left with the job of subduing the southwest, which his legions managed without much fuss in 56, at a battle near Tartas in the Landes. Many of the Vascones escaped over the Pyrenees into the rugged country of northern Spain, where there was little the Romans could do about them.

For the next five centuries, the region made its way into classical civilization as Novempopulania, the 'land of nine tribes', organized as part of the Roman province of Aquitania. The old Salt Road became an even busier trading route, carrying the wine the Celts loved into the region, and then shipping it back the other way when Aquitanians found they could grow it themselves and undersell Provence and Italy. Most of the land fell into the hands of Roman speculators, or was parcelled out among the veterans of the legions, the usual Roman manner of pacifying and Romanizing new provinces in the west. Though Aquitania never became a prosperous, urbanized region like Italy or Provence, towns did appear and new technologies were introduced. The Romans, with their eternal obsession with taking the waters, developed nearly every thermal spring in Gaul, including Dax, Bagnerès, Luchon and a score of others. While most of the Celts seem to have easily assimilated into the new dispensation, the Vascones carried on in the Pyrenees, where the lack of roads made Roman control tenuous at the best of times, and so were able to resist Romanization and preserve their language and culture.

The average Aquitanian native might be excused for not appreciating Rome's contributions, for right from the beginning the Romans degraded most of their new subjects to the level of serfs. Rome's history, through Republic and Empire, is a story of the rich getting inexorably richer and everyone else losing what little they had, along with every last vestige of freedom and human dignity. By the 4th century AD, this process had reached its illogical extreme: nearly all the land in the province was owned by a handful of powerful families, who were able to build magnificent new villas for themselves, as at Montréal in the Gers and at Montmaurin in the Haute-Garonne, even while the Empire was in permanent economic crisis and the towns were rotting away. When the end came for Rome, much of the Gaulish countryside was already in the hands of the *bagaudae*, outlaw bands who waged guerrilla war against the system; these were especially strong in Aquitania.

407–1000

In which the Vascones move back to the old homestead, and take in a pair of ill-mannered boarders named Frank and Norman

The fatal invasions came after 407. Both Vandals and Visigoths passed through the region, the former especially welcome among the common people for their policy of gaining support by smashing up the great villas and burning the tax rolls. After 420 Aquitania found itself part of the new Visigothic kingdom, with its capital at Toulouse, but this was not to last. The Franks whipped the Visigoths at the Battle of Vouillé in 507, and gained, if not control of Aquitania, at least the right to try to collect a little tribute from it. The new bosses distinguished themselves mainly by the destruction of Lugdunum Convenarum, after a revolt in 586, while the Visigoths retreated into Spain, where their kingdom was to last right up till the Arab conquest.

Now, this is where all the linguistic confusion comes in. Those Vascones who had fled the Romans and settled in Spain so long before now came into conflict with the Visigoths, and either were pushed back over the Pyrenees, or decided on their own to retake their old homeland, by then largely a wasteland. They reappeared on the northern side in the 580s, and people began calling the area as far north as the Garonne 'Wasconia', which somehow later got turned into Gascony. Those Vascones who lived in the western Pyrenees had already lapsed into complete independence. There was little incentive for any of the barbarian kingdoms to trouble them, and they were fierce enough to put up a good fight whenever it was necessary, specialists in guerrilla warfare and the mountain ambush. They have been there ever since, and are the people we call the Basques today.

In 602, the king of the Franks appointed a 'Duke of Aquitaine' and 'Duke of Wasconie', military overlords charged with bringing the entire area under closer control. The chronicles of the next two centuries tell a tale of continuous and spirited resistance on the part of the Vascones. A big surprise for both parties came when the Arabs roared through the mountains in the early 700s after their rapid conquest of Spain. Charles Martel, the Frankish mayor of the place, beat them decisively at Poitiers in 732, but they continued to hold parts of the Pyrenees, including the castle of Lourdes, for a long time after. After that, the Franks under their new Carolingian dynasty – headed by Charles' son Pepin the Short – came south in strength. The rebellious Duchy of Aquitaine, along the Atlantic coast, was brought into line in 774 after a bloody war of three decades, while the Vascones of the plains were finally and completely defeated in 781.

For Pepin's son Charlemagne, who harboured imperial ambitions that looked beyond the Pyrenees, the Vascones, or Basques, who held out in the mountains were a mere nuisance. The minor episode of Roland's ambush and death at Roncevalles in 778, later to inspire one of the most popular romances of the Middle Ages, was merely a chance for the Basques to get a little revenge on their hated enemy. Charlemagne was still warm in his grave when his overextended empire started to disintegrate. The troubles of the Franks gave the Vascones south of the Pyrenees a chance to regain their independence, and they founded a little state that would grow into the Kingdom of Navarre. Though the people of Navarre gradually traded their Basque language and culture for Spanish, the Kingdom would remain a major actor in the region's history for centuries to come.

North of the mountains, they weren't so lucky. Aquitaine and Gascony suffered the visitations of the most destructive barbarians of them all, the Vikings, or Normans. From the 840s they came raiding nearly every year, wrecking Bayonne in 862 and Eauze a decade later. Not until 982 did Duke Guilhem of Gascony finally convince them they weren't wanted, by destroying a big Norman force near Dax. By this time, the feudal pattern was set. The king of the Franks was just a bad dream somewhere up north, and besides Aquitaine and Gascony, the lesser vassals the Carolingians had created – the counts of Bigorre and Armagnac and Foix, and the viscounts of Béarn, among others – drifted into near-total independence. The arrangement makes history messy, but it gave the southwest stability and some breathing space. After almost six centuries of terror, towns were growing again and churches began to spring up everywhere. By the magic year 1000, which everyone expected to bring the end of the world, medieval civilization was in fact well on its way.

1000–1259
Finally left in peace for a bit, Basques and Gascons tidy up the place and grow wealthy and happy in it

The dizzyingly rapid economic and cultural advances that created the medieval world are reflected even in this out-of-the-way corner of Europe. In the 12th century, new towns and villages were growing up everywhere around the castles (such places are called *castelnaux*; the Gers alone has over 200 of them), while monastic orders such as the Cistercians created new foundations and reclaimed land that had long lain waste. In the 1200s, expansion continued at an even faster rate. All over the south, forests were cleared and planned new towns, or *bastides*, were founded to house a burgeoning population that included many settlers from other regions, severely diluting the Basque element in Gascony north of the mountains and in the central Pyrenees. These areas joined the mainstream of the distinct, Occitan-speaking cultural world of the south. The busy traffic along the pilgrimage routes to Compostela gave an impetus to trade and cultural exchange, and the region benefited from proximity to culturally advanced Muslim Spain; influences from that direction ranged from the rediscovery of philosophy and learning to styles and methods in architecture. Most importantly, following the example of Spain, the troubadours of Provence and the southwest created modern Europe's first poetry.

Politically, the most important trend was the rise of the Duchy of Aquitaine. Under a long line of warlike dukes, all named Guilhem, Aquitaine grew to cover a fourth of what is now France, its dukes at most times more wealthy and powerful than the kings who were their nominal overlords. Guilhem VIII succeeded in adding the Duchy of Gascony to his dominions in 1058; Guilhem IX (1086–1127), who presided over Aquitaine at the height of its fortunes, was also one of the first troubadour poets. This Guilhem had a granddaughter, a beautiful and wilful woman whose life would be the stuff of romances, and whose career would change history: Eleanor of Aquitaine. Sole heir to the duchy, she married the French King Louis VII in 1137. The French thought they had picked the biggest feudal plum imaginable, but Eleanor's discontent with the cold, pious Louis led to a divorce and a more convivial marriage with Louis's mortal enemy: Henry Plantagenet, Duke of Anjou and soon to be Henry II, King of England. Along with Eleanor came the land, and for the next three centuries Aquitaine would be a possession of the English crown. Despite high taxes to pay for their incessant wars, the English proved capable rulers; usually sympathetic to local concerns, they won a high degree of loyalty from the people of Aquitaine while they battled the French on every front for more lands.

Béarn, another durable and well-organized feudal state, provides a good example of how history worked in this period. Like Armagnac, destined later to be its mortal enemy, Béarn first appears in history with its conquest by Charlemagne and the appointment of a Frankish viscount. The position became hereditary, and the viscounts gradually grew accustomed to doing as they pleased, acknowledging the suzerainty of France (or Navarre) only when it suited them, and keeping in shape with endless trivial wars against the counts of Armagnac to the north. Throughout the Middle Ages, Béarn changed dynasties as often as it changed capitals (Lescar, Morlaas, Orthez and Pau all held that honour). Viscounts tended to be named Gaston – they were numbered by dynasties, so there are a few Gaston IIs and Gaston IIIs. One of them once remarked that he was in the position of 'a flea between two monkeys' – Béarn in those days never seemed too intimidated by its powerful neighbours; maybe he was thinking he could always bite whichever one he chose. On the other hand, the viscounts often had trouble asserting their authority within their own borders. The long tradition of mountaineer independence found its expression in the *For de Morlaas*, a charter of rights that Viscount Gaston IV was forced to proclaim in the early 11th century, typical of the sophisticated, liberal constitutional arrangements that governed Pyrenean life at the time.

As for the Basques, the Middle Ages meant a degree of freedom, but also an inexorable decline. As the medieval states that claimed Basque property – Navarre and the other Spanish kingdoms, England, Béarn and France – grew in wealth and power, there was increasingly little chance that an event like Roncevaux could be repeated. This was a world dominated by a feudal aristocracy, one made up of foreigners, the descendants of Germanic invaders and Roman landowners, and it is not surprising that the Basques never coalesced into a nation. In this period the Basques are practically invisible, their language merely the patois of countrymen. All through the Middle Ages, in fact, the Basque boundaries shrank gradually, as the natives were either pushed out or assimilated by Spaniards, Gascons and Catalans. By the 1300s the Basque lands had contracted roughly to the boundaries of today.

1259–1530

In which the Gascons have fun and prosper through the Hundred Years War, and then find they have to pay a price

After the 1259 Treaty of Paris, which stabilized the borders between English- and French-controlled lands, the two sides dug in for an uneasy peace. In an age when national consciousness and nation-states were appearing, feudal logic could not last: as dukes of Guyenne (from the English mispronunciation of Aquitaine), the English kings owed homage to the kings of France, a fine situation to be in whenever the two nations' interests were in conflict. The inevitable showdown came in 1337, and went into the books as the Hundred Years War.

With England's early military successes, and Béarn's neutrality, the southwest was largely spared the terrors the war brought to France. By no means, though, did the Gascons care to keep out of the conflict. In his famous chronicles, Froissart echoed the prevailing opinion on the Gascons: *'Ils ne sont point estables'* – not a very stable lot, perhaps, but tremendous fighters when they were in the mood for it. With their own land relatively peaceful, Gascons picked up the habit of hiring themselves out as mercenaries for the English, the French or anybody else who could pay them, or who looked like a good bet for sacking towns and grabbing some swag. Gascons made up a majority in many of the *routier* bands that began terrorizing France in the 1350s – freebooters who went into business for themselves whenever the English and French had the effrontery to make a truce. Some of the Gascon captains were famous, such as Captal de Buch of the Landes.

Gascon mischief against the French was hardly limited to the *routiers*. In the early 1400s, just as it seemed that the long wars were dying down, France split up into factional conflicts, between the followers of the dukes of Burgundy and Orléans. Upon Orléans's assassination, leadership of his side fell to Count Bernard of Armagnac. 'Armagnacs' and 'Burgundians' spattered fresh blood all over France; by 1413 Count Bernard, allied with another Gascon, Constable of France Charles d'Albret, was in control of Paris and most of the country. A year later, Albret lay dead on the field of Agincourt; even after that climactic battle, though, the two factions continued to hate each other more than the English, permitting the occupation of Paris and the conquest of most of France by 1420. In the final phase of the war, however, the Gascons also contributed most of the troops that Joan of Arc inspired to victory – the English are recorded as calling her 'Jeanne l'Armagnacaise' in derision.

The departure of the English in the 1450s allowed France to extend its control over all of the southwest except Béarn. Only, this time, the French kings were not content with being mere feudal overlords. A typical example of the new policy was the destruction of the County of Armagnac in 1473. After unsuccessfully besieging the count at Lectoure, King Louis XI made an honorable peace with him – but when the gates were opened, the French sacked the town and slaughtered the count along with his family; soon after, Armagnac became part of the royal domain.

French rule proved a disaster for Gascony, as in the rest of the south. Travelling over most of the region today, you will see villages and towns that have barely grown or changed since the Middle Ages. Far from a glorious process of national unification, as French historians today portray it, the new possessions were treated as conquests to be exploited. In Gascony, as in the rest of the Midi, the heavy-handed authoritarianism of Paris brought with it economic stagnation that was to last for centuries, and the enforced death of a culture that had been one of the first and most promising of medieval times. The 1539 Decree of Villars-Cotterets mandated the use of the French language in all matters of law and government, the first step along the road to the eradication of the *langue d'oc*, a policy pursued with vigour until our own time.

1530–1815

As Protestant and Catholic gods smile down from separate heavens, the Gascons turn their military talents on each other and speed their country on its long decline

French control was solid, and with political opposition impossible the first wave of southwestern rebelliousness came in the form of religious dissent.

Protestantism found its way into the southwest from Calvin's Geneva, and found a warm welcome among the small middle classes. The first Protestant communities appeared in Béarn around 1532, notably at Oloron-Ste-Marie. At about the same time, the Béarnais dynasty was dying out, and its possessions eventually fell into the hands of Henri d'Albret and his wife Marguerite d'Angoulême. This ancient Gascon family had often been closely allied with the French kings. Henry II had given them the title of dukes over their lands in the Landes and Gers, and French assistance had been vital in allowing the Albrets to take over the throne of Navarre in 1481. Not that the title was worth much; at the time King Ferdinand of Aragon (soon to marry Isabella of Castile for the unification of Spain) had grabbed most of Navarre south of the Pyrenees by force, leaving a throne without much of a kingdom behind it. Henri and Marguerite presided over a refined Renaissance court, at Pau or at Nérac in the Agenais, where both Catholic and Protestant men of letters were welcome, but their daughter and heir, Jeanne d'Albret, turned out to be a grim Protestant bigot who forced all Béarn to accept her faith.

The southwest, along with the rest of France, was dividing into hostile camps. Even more than Jeanne, the kings and the Parlement of Bordeaux had started the fashion for intolerance by persecuting dissenters and occasionally massacring them wholesale. By 1560, it was outright civil war. Paris sent down Blaise de Montluc, a distinguished Gascon soldier, with the mission of ridding Gascony of Protestants. Montluc did the best he could, often stuffing village wells with all he could find of them. The Protestants, led by Jeanne and her captain, Montgomery, responded in kind. Montgomery's army roamed the southwest in the late 1560s, sacking monasteries and Catholic towns with a brutality to rival Montluc's.

As fate would have it, Jeanne's marriage to Antoine de Bourbon unexpectedly made her son the heir not only to Béarn and Navarre, but eventually to the throne of France. Henri of Navarre grew up to be a fierce and capable warrior in the Protestant cause, campaigning for two decades from one end of France to the other. When Henri III was assassinated in 1589, the Valois branch of the Capetian dynasty became extinct; next in line came the Bourbon branch, of which the senior member was Henri of Navarre – Henri IV. Hardline Catholics could never accept a Protestant king, and Henri had to fight on for a few years before deciding that Paris was worth a Mass. The historic compromise put an end to the wars, sealed by the 1598 Edict of Nantes decreeing religious tolerance, and the good Gascon soldier – *lou nouste Henric*, or 'our Henry' to the people of the southwest – became one of France's greatest and best-loved kings, under whose reign, as Gascons like to express it, 'France was annexed by Béarn'. Henri always had a special place in his heart for Béarn and especially Pau, his birthplace. He kept his royal titles of France and Navarre separate, and Béarn continued to be governed by its Sovereign Council, under its own system of laws.

Unfortunately, there were still plenty of fanatics loose in France. In 1610, one of them murdered Henri while his carriage was stuck in a Paris traffic jam. The religious peace held, though Henri's son, Louis XIII, and his minister Cardinal Richelieu had some very different ideas on how to treat the provinces. Louis marched down south with a big army in 1620 to put an end to Béarn's independence for ever. Richelieu, ever concerned with limiting the ability of the nobility to defy the king, determinedly set about demolishing castles not necessary for the national defence – a policy that has robbed Gascony of a good number of tourist attractions.

The early 17th century witnessed a series of conflicts between France and Spain; the Pyrenees saw a number of battles, and raids from both sides. The Treaty of the Pyrenees in 1659 put an end to these troubles, followed by the marriage of Louis XIV and the Spanish infanta, Maria Teresa, the following year at St-Jean-de-Luz. The *roi soleil*'s long reign was a miserable period for the southwest, as for the rest of France, combining oppressive absolutism and economic mismanagement with crushing taxes for Versailles and for endless aggressive wars. Worst of all, Louis's religious bigotry led him to revoke the Edict of Nantes. It was open season on Protestants once again, and the persecutions were especially severe in the southwest. Dissenters who escaped death or imprisonment emigrated in large numbers to the Americas or Germany; often these were the most progressive and industrious members of the towns and villages they fled.

By the 1700s the southwest was confirmed in its role as a forgotten, impoverished backwater, overseen by *intendants* appointed by the king. Good ones, such as Baron d'Etigny, *intendant* of Auch in the 1750s, often contributed important improve-ments: good roads (often lined with avenues of plane trees, as can be seen around France today), bridges, and new parks and public buildings in the towns. D'Etigny also built the spa at Luchon in the Pyrenees, in an age when 'taking the waters' first became fashionable among Europe's aristocrats.

All through this era, the Basques had adapted well to French rule. Unlike Gascony, French-controlled Euzkadi (the Basques' name for their own land) retained a substantial degree of self-government until the Revolution. In the Labourd, a kind of parliament called the *biltzar*, with elected representatives (but no nobles or clergy), met regularly to set tax rates and look after local business, and each small region or town possessed its *for*, its charter of rights and privileges, which the French usually respected. In return, the Basques remained stalwartly loyal to the French crown, and performed important services for it in time of war, especially on the seas, with the feared privateers of Bayonne. The Revolution marked a turning point, and brought with it the irony of this most democratic of peoples ranging themselves solidly on the side of reaction. It wasn't their fault. The Jacobins up in Paris abolished their self-government and traditional liberties, but even more resented than the Revolution's push for centralization and Frenchification, made worse under Napoleon, were the attacks on the church. The people who gave the church St Ignatius Loyola and St Francis Xavier were among the most devout Catholics you'll find (they still are).

1815–Present

The modern world dawns, bright with promise for every place except southern France

The only real result of the revolution for the southwest was a lasting economic depression, helped along by the British blockade and Napoleon's wars, the end of which found Wellington marching over the Pyrenees and besieging Bayonne on his way north. When the excitement was over, Paris-appointed prefects replaced Paris-appointed *intendants*, but few of the ephemeral governments in the 19th-century Gallic banana republic/monarchy/empire ever stirred themselves much to help the southwest. Nor did the region ever show much energy of its own. The railroad arrived at Bayonne and Tarbes in the 1850s, but this served mainly to help make it easier for young people to leave, and for imported goods to flow in and ruin the region's already hard-pressed farmers and manufacturers.

The southwest suffered more than any other part of France from rural poverty and depopulation. Young Gascons still went off to join the army, as they always had done; more simply emigrated to Paris or the colonies just to find a job. The Basque lands were as hard hit. Basques from the mountain uplands found their way in great numbers to the Americas, especially to Argentina and the United States, where the Basque connection goes back to the 1,500 sailors, many of them veterans of the privateers, who came to join Lafayette and fight for American independence. Simón Bolívar, liberator of Venezuela and Colombia, was of Basque descent. In the bayous of Louisiana and east Texas, as well as on the Argentine pampas, Basques became some of the New World's first cowboys in the 1840s, setting the model and contributing much to the image (*lariat*, among other cowboy terms, is a Basque word). There are still large Basque communities in Idaho, Utah, California and other states.

The only 19th-century regime that contributed much to the region, surprisingly, was the otherwise useless empire of Napoleon III. The Emperor himself had been conceived in a Pyrenean hotel (possibly with the help of a local shepherd), and he spent most of his frequent vacations in the region, helping to popularize both Biarritz and the mountains as holiday destinations. He also oversaw the reclamation of the empty Landes, transforming it into Europe's largest forest. Between the Pyrenees and the Basque coast, France's southwest corner developed into one of Europe's first holiday playgrounds. Thermal resorts such as Bagnerès-de-Bigorre and Salies-de-Béarn sprouted ornate grand hotels and casinos, while the English descended on Pau for its climate and gave the continent its first golf course.

In rural regions, though, the big story – the only story – was still abandonment and depopulation. The First World War contributed mightily to this trend; many villages lost a third or even a half of their young men, and everywhere you will see pathetic war memorials to remind you of France's greatest tragedy since the Black Death of 1348. Between the war and natural decline, the southwest lost over a quarter of its population between 1850 and 1950. In parts of the Gers the figure was almost two-thirds. Though the Second World War was less costly and destructive for France, it was still a miserable and dangerous time for the people of the southwest. From the beginning, the Germans seized a strip along the entire Atlantic coast as part of the occupied zone. The 'border' with Vichy-controlled territory was heavily guarded, and locals needed special papers to cross it. The Resistance was not particularly strong in Gascony, though the Basques and other mountain men did good work smuggling escapees over into Spain, and helping Allied agents coming the other way.

Many members of the Resistance in the area were Spaniards, part of the tens of thousands of republican soldiers and civilians who had escaped into France when Franco's troops conquered the Spanish Basque country in 1937–8. Most of these people remained in France after the war, and added some new blood and new energy to many towns and villages. More new arrivals came in the sixties: *pieds-noirs*, French settlers in Algeria forced to leave after Algerian independence; you'll meet them everywhere you go in the southwest. Politically, the only big change since the war has been the creation of regional governments under the Socialists' decentralization programme in 1981. So far it isn't much, but as the first reversal in five centuries of Parisian centralism, it at least gives provinces a start in reclaiming some control over their own destinies. The Basques, jealous of the complete autonomy their countrymen have won over the border in Spain, continue to be quietly assertive in trying to push decentralization even further. An informal council of mayors, heir to the old *biltzar*, meets regularly.

Culture

SPAIN

03

Dread and Delight: Romanticism in the Pyrenees

The Pyrenees may not be the highest mountains in Europe, but to many people they are the most beautiful. Until the end of the 18th century, however, few people imagined that mountains of any kind could be of any aesthetic interest whatsoever; the Pyrenees, a secretive, solitary world blasted by snow and storms, haunted by savage wolves and bears, were looked upon with horror, the Monts Affreux, a distant menace. No one in their right mind would have anything to do with them. Louis XIV, in fact, claimed to abolish the Pyrenees altogether.

These attitudes about altitudes only began to change when opinion-makers came into first-hand contact with the Monts Affreux in the 16th and 17th centuries. France's Classical Age was in full bloom and Greek and Roman models and mythologies were the chief references of the academies and salons, which controlled French culture with the same sense of authority to which the *ancien régime* pretended over every other aspect of life. Beauty was an ideal agreed upon by an academy, far removed from the individual. Society was highly organized and art and literature had to follow rules too. What brought Louis XIV's morganatic wife, Madame de Maintenon, down to Barèges in the Pyrenees was not the views, but something of which an ancient Roman would have approved: the curative waters. Enough fashionable people followed in Madame de Maintenon's footsteps, and even went on little expeditions into the Pyrenees, to discover they weren't as evil as their reputation.

By the mid-18th century, Louis Ramond de Carbonnières became the first man to climb and scientifically study the Pyrenees, publishing in 1759 his *Observations Faites dans les Pyrénées*. At the same time, Jean-Jacques Rousseau, the great dropout from the salons and Encyclopaedist circle, wrote *La Nouvelle Héloïse* (1761), introducing the idea of communing with nature, while Voltaire helped initiate a French fad for foreign authors (Shakespeare, Richardson and, later, Byron and Scott from Britain, and Goethe, Schiller and Lessing from Germany), writers not bound by the same academic rules as the French intelligentsia. The birth of French Romanticism, however, had to wait for the tightly controlled structures of the Classical Age to crumble like a house of cards in the Revolution. And when it did spring into bloom, French Romanticism proved essentially different from the earlier romantic movements in Britain and Germany, both of which were a return to national traditions; in France romanticism was a revolt against the rules. With the old system destroyed, the individual had become the only reality; opinions were free; careful classical symmetry, order and balance and rationalism were replaced by flights of fancy and the imagination; sincerity, emotion and inspiration were all that counted. Overbred French classicism was replaced by fiery, emotional novels by the likes of Victor Hugo.

The Romantic movement revealed the Pyrenees to the French nation; here nature, in the form of majestic snow-crowned peaks, misty abysses, mysterious caves, deep blue lakes, rushing streams and waterfalls, seemed to mirror the passion in each individual; awe and enchantment replaced fear and loathing. Old Pyrenean legends, tales of witches and sorcerers and travellers' accounts and picturesque albums were published throughout the 1860s and 1870s, partly in response to a new interest in folk tales, again inspired by the Germans; Gustave Doré's dramatic fairytale engravings of the *Voyage aux Pyrénées*, stories collected by an out-of-work mountain guide named Taine, fired the imagination and remains one of the classics of the region. It was the age of the first big-game hunts; as bears, izards (chamois) and wild boar fell to the Paris sportsman's bullet, high society filled the spas and went on jaunts with their mountain guides, dressed in soft hats, woollen stockings, breeches and braces, hobnobbing with royalty and the literati – not only Hugo but all the great names of French Romanticism: Chateaubriand, Vigny, Flaubert, Sand, Lamartine, Mérimée and Delacroix.

Even then, the great Romantic of the French Pyrenees was not altogether French. The legendary Count Henry Russell Killough (1834–1909) was born in Toulouse of an Irish father and Gascon mother, a volatile combination that resulted in the most enthusiastic and ardent of all the lovers of the Pyrenees. After spending his youth on adventures in the Rockies, the Andes, the Himalayas, the Gobi and Sahara, New Zealand and Siberia, Russell returned to Toulouse and decided to devote the rest of his life to exploring his own backyard. He was utterly fearless, the first to scale 16 peaks in the Pyrenees. His special passion was Mount Vignemale above Barèges, which he climbed 33 times; in 1869 he did it in the middle of winter, earning himself another first in Europe. His passion for Vignemale was so great that in 1882 he began excavating caves to live in near its peak; when his Villa Russell was devoured by a glacier, he excavated two others, including, lastly, one he called Villa Paradis just under the summit at 10,660ft (3,250m). When living on his own in his mountain 'villas', Russell was happy with a lambskin to sleep in; but when he entertained, no one did it with more style: Persian rugs, fine wines and food, candles and white tablecloths were spread on the glaciers. He wanted his guests to share his love for the mountains and would wake them at dawn to see the sunrise. Down in Pau, where he spent most of the winter with English expat society, he was famous for his love of mauve scarves. Author of the delightful *Souvenirs d'un Montagnard* (1908) and frequent contributor to the *Revue des Pyrénées*, he wrote of his beloved mountains with Romantic fire. 'My whole life has been a kind of challenge to civilization,' he once said, and wondered why people thought him eccentric.

Gascon Country Remedies

In 1881 Charles Lavielle, a Gascon country doctor, faithfully recorded all the 'alternative' cures he confronted in his practice and published them in his *Essai sur les erreurs populaires relatives à la médecine*. If nothing else, the remedies he found showed that a good deal of imagination over the centuries had accumulated on top of some fairly universal ancient beliefs. Among the errors the good doctor decried was a highly risky cure for eye diseases: touching the pupils nine times with the wedding ring of a new bride. This was sure to work, but only on the condition that the ring belonged to a woman of irreproachable virtue; apparently only purity in something invisible could counteract the blemish to make the world visible again.

Fortunately for the brides of Gascony, the main illness in the region, especially in the Landes, wasn't eye disease, but fever. One sure remedy for this was to cut the fingernails and toenails of the patient, gather up all the 20 clippings, stick them in a meatball and feed it to a dog. If that didn't work, it was necessary to take the membrane that encloses the white of a hen's egg and tie it tight with a silken thread around the left pinkie finger of the fever victim. The disease would thus be passed on to another object. Dogs, perhaps because they are the most susceptible to their owners' feelings, were likely targets; gouty people, for instance, could cure themselves by sleeping with a puppy. A branch of hawthorn, the most sacred tree of the indigenous Aquitaine peoples, was also good at absorbing fevers, but only if it was given an offering of bread and salt. It also warded off lightning.

From the night of time, when Neolithic shepherds blazed the 'salt route' in search of the mineral so essential for the health of their herds and flocks, salt has been a charmed substance; Dr Lavielle found that inflammations in the face, teeth and extremities were often attributed to the failure to carry a bit of salt on one's person when crossing water. A common preventative measure was always to carry three horse chestnuts in a trouser pocket (with reason: the substance between the outer shell of the conker and the kernel is essential for treating rheumatism). If the inflammation had already happened, it was necessary to fill a pot of water and drop in a handful of hay and nine pebbles; other people were to add dice, a comb and a pair of scissors. The pot was put on the boil, then the contents emptied into a vase while the inflamed part of the anatomy was exposed to the steam. The pain was supposed to be cut and combed away with the rising of the vapour. The nine pebbles may have in some way been related to the *esne harria* or 'milk stones' that many families in the Pyrenees used to heat up and drop in their hot milk every evening for the taste. The curious custom was preserved in 19th-century Toulouse café society, when *lait ferrat* was the rage: boiled milk with a stick of red-hot iron dropped in.

Giving birth in 19th-century Gascony had very little to do with the Lamaze and Leboyer techniques young mothers learn today. For an easy birth, the essential thing was to tie the mother's belt or girdle to the church bell and give it three good yanks; in some places, Dr Lavielle wrote, they tied the husband's knickers to the bell rope. Many Pyrenean valleys were far too remote for a doctor or midwife to assist the birth; mothers-to-be relied on old women who had proved their mettle by successfully bearing as many children as possible in the most trying circumstances. At the beginning of labour, it was important to eat a bowl of onion soup; throughout labour the old woman would ply the mother with wine and coffee. When the baby was about to be born, the mother would be helped to stand up and her assistant would catch the baby in a sieve. The umbilical cord would be cut as long as possible, to give the child a chance to have a beautiful voice, and it was important to wash the newborn in tepid, not hot, water, to keep the baby from turning brown. If the placenta was not expelled naturally, the old woman would put the husband's beret backwards on the mother's head. Some of this harks back to the ancient custom of *couvade*, noted by anthropologists in many cultures: immediately after birth the father takes the mother's place in bed with the child at his side, an old rite in the duel between matriarchy and patriarchy (i.e. the male desire to challenge the female even in her powers of reproduction) and one practised not so very long ago in Béarn and the Basque country. To this day fathers there seem to get most of the attention at birth celebrations.

If few of the remedies practised by Dr Lavielle's patients had any therapeutic value beyond that of trust and belief, the ancient treatment of shingles in the western Pyrenees is so effective that modern country doctors often refer their patients to village healers. *Lou cindré*, or the 'belt' as shingles is known, is an extremely painful viral disease. To be a healer, a person must already have had the 'belt' and been healed. This guarantees the necessary immunity, for what the healer does is 'take the belt' and 'return it to the earth' by hoisting the sufferer on his or her back and making ritual steps in two directions, tracing the form of a cross. The proper formulas are recited during this exercise, and the patient is asked the ritual questions: 'What are you wearing?' 'A belt.' 'I too had one, but Jesus took it away, and he'll take yours from you too.' If the healer is too old or frail to bear the weight, the patient has only to lay hands on his or her shoulders and follow the prescribed steps. The average doctor with all the products of modern medicine takes weeks and weeks to treat a shingles patient, but a healer in Béarn removes the symptoms in less than three days.

Mari, Mary

The apparition of the Virgin Mary to Bernadette at Lourdes may have been promoted into a global spectacle, but it was hardly the first. The Pyrenees are beyond doubt the most popular spot on the globe for Marian appearances; from the Atlantic to the Mediterranean over a hundred separate epiphanies have been recorded in as many different places since medieval times. Wherever you see a lone chapel in the mountains, the odds will be better than even it was built to commemorate a similar apparition, and usually the people of the nearest village will honour it with an annual pilgrimage procession.

Why does Our Lady choose to spend so much time in these mountains? Reaching back for the bits and shards of evidence that can be found on the beliefs of the earliest days, one finds that all mountains seem to be holy places – but the Pyrenees more so. There is no element of its landscapes, no chapter of its history and legend, that is not suffused with the otherworldly and the divine. One of the possible origins of the name Pyrenees is 'mountains of fire', for the ritual bonfires that shone from their peaks on the great holidays of the year (even today, the Catalans of the western Pyrenees surround their holy mountain, Canigou, with a ring of fires every Midsummer Day). Every Basque mountain had its attendant deity; some of these live on in folklore, such as Jauna Gorri, the 'Red Lord', who lives atop the Pic d'Anie (**Ahunamendi** in Basque) and sends the storms down to the valleys. Jauna Gorri tends a garden on the mountain top where the flowers of immortality grow, and he keeps his treasures there, guarded by hairy black giants called *pelutlak*. Beneath the mountains are the caves, sites of worship from the Palaeolithic era to the initiatory rituals of the Cathars.

Even more important than these are the region's many springs and *sources*. The Pyrenees are laced with them from end to end, including one of the world's largest concentrations of *sources* of medicinal value. The religion of Neolithic times seems to have been closely connected to the life-giving water that comes forth out of the earth, and here again, the tales of the Basques give ample evidence of a similar veneration. Nearly every source is associated with some spirit, inevitably female. In different localities they might be called *incantadas, senyoretas blancas,* or *daunas d'aygua* ('ladies of the waters'), and there are some charming stories attached to them. (If you ever see a thread floating up to the top of a fountain, be sure to pull it out to the end even if it seems there is no end. The thread is the life of an *incantada,* imprisoned in the water by a spell, and only if someone gathers up all the thread can she regain her human form.)

All the Pyrenees' wealth of folk and fairy tales give only teasing hints of the ancient rites and beliefs from which they are descended. Without much in the way of written records, trying to reconstruct the details of the old religions is difficult indeed. A large number of inscribed votive altars from Roman times have been dug up around the Pyrenees and, just to vex the archaeologists, nearly every one bears the name of a different god: Baicorrix, Aereda, Aherbelste, Exprecenn, Vaxus, Harauso, Abelio and so on. As with the Celts, religion for the proto-Basques was a local affair; the same deities, more or less, might go under a different name and carry different attributes in every valley or even every village.

But concerning the most important deity in the Basque pantheon, there is no confusion. Her name is Mari, of all things, and she is the Pyrenees' version of the transcendent Great Goddess that ruled the old religion throughout Europe before the coming of the Indo-European peoples. At once the queen of heaven and of the underworld, she sends thunder and storms down from the mountain tops, the places where her rites were always observed; all the other goddesses, spirits and fairies created by the pantheistic mind are just aspects of her. This Mari is no virgin; her consort, shocking as it must have seemed to the ears of the Christian proselytizers, was a great serpent, named Sugaar or Maju – the prototype for all the Pyrenees' many dragons, and according to legend the founding father of many of the oldest Basque families.

The Pyrenees, like many mountain regions, has always been conservative in terms of religion. Today the Basque country is the last corner of the world that will ever keep the Pope up at night worrying. Back in 1280, at the height of the 'Age of Faith' (to cite just one example), clerics in the Ariège were issuing furious decrees against ladies who insisted on staying out on the summits all night, enjoying the festivals of the goddess. Mari and Mary may bear the same name only by coincidence, but 1,400 years ago, when Christian missionaries began to expropriate the sacred sites, holidays and processions of the old religion to wean people gradually away from it, they probably did not realize they were helping maintain a religious continuity that goes back to the beginnings of time.

The Non-violent Bullfight: the *Course Landaise*

The very first civilization on European soil, that of the Minoans of Crete, was only rediscovered in the early 1900s. Ever since then, the archaeological evidence coming out of Crete has bewitched the world; the Early Minoan period, beginning in 2500 BC, not only offers a link between the great Neolithic cultures of Europe and historical times but seems to add substance to many Greek myths. The Minoans lived during the great age of the bull: the sun was in the constellation Taurus; myths tell of the Minotaur; Minoan palaces and temples are decorated with 'horns of consecration'. Most curious of all are the frescoes and ivory statuettes found at Knossos that show young men and women leaping over bulls. When Minoan archaeologists showed these bull-leaping frescoes to Spanish bullfighters, the toreadors replied that it looked, if not impossible, certainly fatal. The archaeologists have duly theorized that bull-leaping was an elaborate kind of human sacrifice.

Not in Gascony. Or at least the only difference is that the leaping, while formerly done over bulls, is now limited to the bull's slightly less dangerous wife – a black, long-horned Spanish breed, called the *vache landaise*. Bull sports in Gascony may not go back to Minoan times, but they're certainly nothing new. The first written records of bull running in the streets of St-Sever go back to 1457, but as in Spain the attachment is deeply ingrained and probably goes back at least to the Roman gladiators, who fought bulls as well as each other and every other beast imaginable.

In 1802 laws were passed that took the bulls off the streets and into the first wooden arenas. Now confined, rules for the game quickly evolved and achieved their final form in the Second Empire. This coincided with the introduction of the Spanish *corrida* in the south of France, hence much of the Spanish terminology in the *course landaise*: the team of *écarteurs* (the dodgers) is called a *cuadrilla* and all the cows, raised on *ganaderias*, or ranches in the Landes, are named Favorita, Paloma or Voluntaria. Each *ganaderia* fields a *cuadrilla* of six or seven *écarteurs* along with the 'men in white' – trainers, a lithe jumper or *sauteur*, and a rope man or *cordier*, whose existence often surprises many people attending their first *course landaise*. But there's reason: unlike the Spanish *corrida*, where the bull is killed, all the Favoritas and Palomas go back to the ranch after the show and over the years become cadgy old veterans in the ring. The job of the *cordier* is to let the cow get as close as possible to the *écarteur* without letting her actually touch him, and to prevent dangerous, vindictive turns of the head (the cows also wear rubber caps on their horns). The match is decided by points awarded by a jury, rather like figure skating; riskiness, as well as grace and art, are important factors in the scoring.

The *écarteurs* know each cow, and each cow knows all the tricks. The idea is to provoke her into charging, wait until the last minute, and like a dancer move just inches out of the way, or boldly leap over her. For spectators this is the most thrilling (and most Minoan) part of the show. There are two levels, the *courses formelles* where the individual or *écarteur* or *cuadrilla* is judged, and the less serious *courses mixtes* that include a classic programme followed by clowning around (the *charlottade*).

The Pariahs of the Pyrenees

Everywhere you go in this corner of France, you will see reminders of the Cagots. At the back end of a village, or set outside it, there will be a quarter that the locals call the *ancien Cagotérie*. Or a parish priest will show you the special door in the side of the church, the *porte des Cagots*, the only one they were allowed to use, or the *bénitier des Cagots*, the holy-water stoup reserved for them alone. Most of them were carpenters by trade, and wherever you see a really old market *halles*, or a wooden church steeple or a half-timbered house, chances are it was the Cagots who built it. The last full-blooded Cagot in Gascony died in the 1800s, though small communities of them were reported in obscure corners of the Basque country as late as 1902. But even as this mysterious people was fading away, French, Spanish and Basque writers and scientists were becoming interested in the strange story of these Gascon outcasts and who they really were.

The Cagots were peculiar to the territory covered in this book, along with Spanish Navarre. Under a number of different names, they are mentioned in documents dating back to the 11th century: Cagots, Crestias, Capots, Agots (in the Basque country), Ladres (Gascon for lepers), Gafets, Gézitains. People believed them to be lepers, and forced a stringent code of apartheid on them: Cagots could not farm, or enter a mill or a tavern, or drink out of public fountains save the ones reserved for them; they were kept at the back of the church, and served communion separately. Often they had their own church, and they were always buried in separate cemeteries. Though what remains of Cagot houses does not differ much from other dwellings, they were constrained to live apart, either in closed-off quarters of the towns or in separate hamlets on the outskirts. In some localities they were forced to wear distinctive clothing, such as a goose's foot pinned to their tunics. There was an elaborate etiquette in everyday life to stop them coming into close contact with anyone else, and Cagots by law always married amongst their own kind. Although exceptions are recorded, almost all Cagots worked with wood; besides the master carpenters, they chopped trees for firewood, and made furniture, wooden plates and utensils. Back then it was believed that wood did not transmit diseases (a notion oddly born out by scientific tests in recent times; bacteria survive much longer on plastic, for example).

One thing is certain; lepers they were not. Leprosy, though a continuing scourge in the Middle Ages, is not a hereditary disease, and the Cagots made up a sort of caste that lived its separate life for centuries, without any evidence of chronic ill health – though country people believed that even the touch of one would burn your skin. Plenty of imaginative guesses have been put forward as to their origins. Some held them to be descendants of Visigoths, caught behind after the Frankish conquests and reduced to servitude. Others claimed the first Cagots were Moorish slaves, brought back by the many Gascon lords who went to Spain to hire themselves out in the battles of the Reconquista. Miscellaneous conjectures include refugee Cathar heretics after the Albigensian crusade, Jews, religious excommunicates, or even gypsies.

The most reliable contemporary accounts of Cagots suggest they really didn't look much different from anyone else. And as for their origin, the correct answer might be 'all of the above, among others'. The most plausible hypotheses have the children of lepers still living apart, by habit or by force, in the old leper colonies that were once found all over the region. Over the centuries, they were possibly joined by any and every sort of vagabond and refugee. All the main pilgrimage routes to Compostela passed through Gascony – the last stop before the difficult crossing over the mountains – and a huge number of people made the trip each year (many of them forced to do it as penance or punishment for crimes); more than a few would be likely to stay. To these, add the people attracted by the huge land-clearing and *bastide*-building programmes of the 13th century (most of which welcomed criminals and anyone else willing to work) and it is easy to imagine all the loose ends of Europe piling up here on the Pyrenees' northern slopes. Neighbouring French-controlled Languedoc had no Cagots, but it did know several massacres of Jews and vagabonds in the 1300s (in medieval times, the lands of the king of France were never a very healthy place for minorities of any sort). Perhaps the stigma of a Cagot was a worthwhile trade for a peaceable life for some people. Still, the mystery of the Cagots will probably never be solved. Why, for example, were they called Crestias (Christians), and why, in the Middle Ages, were they exempt from civil law and taxes, subject only to Church laws and Church courts?

The end of the story is as remarkable as the beginning. The Cagots themselves seem to have undertaken an epic civil rights struggle, and incredibly enough, in the context of *ancien régime* France, they eventually won. In 1425, they complained about harassment by the consuls of the town of Lectoure, and won their case in the Count of Armagnac's courts. After losing another court battle in 1479, they appealed to the Parlement of Toulouse and obtained a medical inquest that concluded that they were not diseased in any way. Even so, it took until 1627 to get the Parlement to publish an ordinance prohibiting local officials from persecuting the *maîtres charpentiers* (as they evidently preferred to be known) – the Parlement also enjoined anyone from calling them 'Cagots'. From 1680 onwards, they are recorded fighting in Biarritz for the right to be buried in common ground; they won this, too, with the Bishop of Bayonne interceding in their favour. Also in Biarritz, the decades that followed saw the first recorded incidents of men marrying Cagot women, and finally a prototypical Rosa Parks, a Cagot named Michel Legaret, got fed up one Sunday and stepped right up to the front of the church. He got a hundred days in the local jail for that, an outrage that finally moved the Bordeaux Parlement to outlaw all segregation.

Winning in court proved much easier than raising the consciousness of their fellow men. That last decision caused riots in Biarritz, and Bordeaux responded with a decree written by Montesquieu himself demanding that order be restored, and that the new laws be enforced. Throughout the 18th century, Parlements and church officials had to intervene often in remote villages, where peasants resisted the new laws and sometimes resorted to violence. By then the Cagots' numbers were on the decrease, as men found they could take their skill and make a living in another part of France or the colonies where no one had ever heard of a Cagot. The definitive end of Gascon Jim Crow came with 1789 and the Declaration of the Rights of Man; in return, grateful Cagots signed up for the army in large numbers to defend the Revolution. After that, there were no more Cagots, only Frenchmen.

Our Good Henry

If the stories of kings and queens of yore, passed around the hearth on a winter's night, were to be the sole posthumous judge of character, some cads would get off pretty easy (Richard the Lionheart, who burned and slaughtered his way across his own duchy of Aquitaine, is one who springs to mind). Others, like those of the 7th-century Caliph Harun al-Rashid in the Arabian Nights, portray so many distinctive virtues and faults that one can't help thinking that they must contain some kernel of historical truth about the man's character. In France, no king can approach Henri IV for attracting good stories. The fact that he is a well-documented and a fairly recent historical character hasn't stifled storytellers in Gascony in the least. In some of the tales he plays the same benign role as Harun al-Rashid, as in one of the best, collected by Jean-François Bladé in 1886, called 'The Blacksmith from Fumel':

Henry IV was staying in his château at Nérac, on the northern edge of the Armagnac country, with his daughter Princess Sad Face, who never smiled, and his favourite white horse, which was far too high-spirited to let itself be shod. Fed up with both of them, Henry issued a decree: whoever could shoe his horse and make his daughter laugh could marry the princess and inherit his kingdom. A blacksmith from Fumel decided to try his luck, and took all the gold and silver he owned and melted them down to make horseshoes of gold and nails of silver, then set off for Nérac. When he stopped to rest he met a cricket, who offered to come along and help, and it rode along on the blacksmith's chin. He next met a rat munching its way through a field of tobacco, its favourite food; the rat offered to come along and rode on the young man's beret. On his last rest, the young man met the Mother of all Fleas; she offered to come along too, and sat on his nose. The blacksmith had scarcely arrived in Nérac when he met King Henry strolling with Princess Sad Face; she took one look at the man wearing a cricket, rat and flea and burst out laughing.

'Now I would try the second task,' said the blacksmith, and showed King Henry and his daughter the golden horseshoes and silver nails. 'Why, I've never seen the like!' exclaimed the king, and the blacksmith nonchalantly lied through his teeth, 'Oh, this is nothing. I've plenty of gold and silver back home.' Off he went into the stable where the wild white horse pranced and whinnied. 'Cricket, do your job!' he said, and the cricket jumped in the horse's ear and sang 'Cri Cri Cri!' so loudly that the horse was made deaf, and stood still. 'Rat, do your job!' the blacksmith then said, and the rat hopped under the horse's nose and, 'Pan Pan Pan Ft Ft Ft!', gassed him to sleep with smelly tobacco farts. The blacksmith then easily shod the horse, and Henry IV, who always kept his promises, married him straight away to his daughter.

But rather than make merry at the wedding feast, the blacksmith sat there, glum and worried, because he had lied about his wealth and knew he would soon be caught out. Just then a rich young man of the court took him aside: 'Blacksmith,' he confided, 'I have loved Princess Sad Face for years, but she would never have me. If you swear on your soul not to touch your bride in bed tonight, I will give you a big bag of gold doubloons.' The blacksmith agreed, and when he went to the bridal chamber, all he did was pace back and forth all night long and ask the princess every hour: 'Wife, do you realize how many gold doubloons fit in a big sack?' The next morning, King Henry went to his daughter and inquired about her first night of wedded bless. 'It was terrible! I slept alone, while my husband marched around the room asking me how many gold doubloons fit in a big sack.' 'Your husband has deeply offended you,' said the king. 'But I'm sure things will go better tonight.' But the rich young lord had another bag of gold doubloons to offer, and the same thing happened the next night. Then he had a third bag of doubloons, and the same thing happened the third night. By then the blacksmith figured he was wealthy enough. But it was too late, for after enquiring about his daughter's third night of marriage, and hearing an earful of the same, King Henry was furious. 'He will not offend you again! You don't want a capon for a husband, and I certainly don't want one for my son-in-law.' And he annulled the marriage, and remarried Princess Sad Face to the rich young man who had paid the blacksmith the three bags of gold.

The blacksmith was heartbroken, but the cricket, rat and Mother of Fleas offered to come to his aid one more time. When the newly married couple went to bed, the cricket and Mother of Fleas jumped on and bit the rich young man until he bled and hopped about as if he were possessed. When he finally collapsed in exhaustion, up popped the rat full of tobacco farts, and, 'Pan Pan Pan Ft Ft Ft!', knocked him out until the morning, when King Henry came in to ask his daughter how it went. 'Even worse! Just look at him,' she said. 'Give me back my blacksmith.' And the next night the blacksmith proved he was hardly a capon.

Another little story from Béarn about Henry IV, affectionately known as the *Vert Galant* or 'Gay Old Spark' for his many loves, tells how he once fell for a beautiful Cagote. 'You are a Cagote,' he said as he took her in his arms. '*Eh bien,* I'm going to tell you a secret: I'm one, too. But you mustn't tell.'

Pilgrims of the Milky Way

The bare facts of the story hardly account for the millions upon millions of pilgrims who have made the journey over the last thousand years to Compostela to pay homage at the tomb of St James the Greater. James, or St Jacques, or Santiago, the brother of St John the Evangelist, was one of the first disciples selected by Jesus, who nicknamed him Boanerges, the 'son of thunder'. In the year 44, he became the first of the twelve Apostles to be martyred when King Herod Agrippa had him decapitated. In faraway Spain, however, an apocryphal tradition stated that James had visited Zaragoza and converted the first Spaniards to the new faith. On the basis of that tradition, it seemed at least plausible that his followers just might have brought his body back to Spain after his death and buried it in the extreme north-west, in Galicia, a mystical land long sacred to the Celts and their Druid priests.

And that was the end of the story until the 9th century, when the Christian princes of Spain, chased by the triumphant Moors into remote pockets of northern Iberia, were desperately in need of divine aid to rally their forces. In 812, Pelayo, a monk of Galicia, duly saw a shower of stars and under it 'rediscovered' the tomb of St James, a find quickly authenticated by the Visigothic bishop Theodimir. By 844 Santiago had made his début as a ghostly knight, helping Ramiro I of Asturias defeat the Moors at the legendary Battle of Clavijo – the first victory of the Reconquista. By 950 the first French pilgrims, encouraged by the monks at Cluny, had blazed a trial to his tomb at the 'field of stars', or Compostela. Pilgrimages to Jerusalem or Rome were already something of a vogue; after the long centuries of the Dark Ages, the Church was keen on re-establishing the contacts across the old Roman empire it was determined to inherit for Christianity.

A vast network of major and minor pilgrims' routes descended through France like the veins on a maple leaf; pilgrims from Britain would sail down as far as the

English port of Bordeaux, and nearly all converged on the Pyrenees passes at Roncevaux in the Pays Basque or the Col du Somport (linking Béarn to Zaragoza), although other passes further east were used as well, usually marked by a hospice, hostel or hospital founded by the Knights of St John; many survive at least in name. Crossing the Pyrenees was the most dangerous part of the whole journey; the famous 12th-century travel guide, the *Codex Calixtinus*, written by French monk Aymeric Picaud, warned of wolves and bears, of 'false pilgrims' (bandits) and rather unfairly, of the Basques ('a barbarous people...strangers to any good sentiment, but raised to vice and iniquity'); better, wrote Aymeric, to avoid Roncevaux and take the Col du Somport. The main route that joined up in Spanish Navarre was known as the Camino Frances, for the majority were French pilgrims.

In the Middle Ages, an estimated two million pilgrims a year walked to Compostela. The flood was gradually reduced to a ripple from the 16th to the 19th century; the pilgrimage seemed a bit old-fashioned during the Renaissance and Reformation. The urge to travel and see new things had always been a part of the journey, and now there were whole new continents to visit. Symptomatic of this loss of interest, the monks in Compostela even misplaced Santiago's body; warned of an imminent attack by Sir Francis Drake, they hid the precious relic, and by some extraordinary attack of amnesia, forgot where they put it; in 1879, by chance, it turned up during restoration work on the cathedral.

Although the pilgrims' hospice at Roncevaux still served 30,000 meals a year to pilgrims in the 18th century, by the 1970s it looked as if the pilgrimage had dried up for good – just when it was about to undergo an extraordinary revival. In 1985, UNESCO designated the pilgrimage route as part of the World Patrimony of Humanity, helping to initiate the restoration of the superb Romanesque churches along the route (those at St-Sever, Aire-sur-Adour, and St-Bertrand- de-Comminges in this book offer a taste). The numbers have risen ever since: there were 4,918 pilgrims in 1990 and 9,734 in 1992, and at least triple that in 1993, a holy year (whenever 25 July, St James' day, falls on Sunday). The year 2000 saw an even greater increase as people made the pilgrimage to celebrate the millennium.

The renewal of Compostela is only part of the movement towards pilgrimages across Europe as church attendance falls off, as the brave new world of the Renaissance and Reformation seems tired, and there are no new places to go but within one's self. Pilgrims today speak of spiritual rather than religious reasons for making the arduous trek, seeking not indulgences or penitence, but the inner awareness, an alternative, something beyond what organized day-to-day life and church attendance can offer. Medieval pilgrims, who lived in the days of the totalitarian church, were no different, and were certainly better equipped than we are today to interpret the meaning behind the remarkable, unorthodox art in the medieval churches that lie along the way of initiation. The western quest appeals to something deep in the human soul, that resounds with poetic resonance. After all, it was a primordial Indo-European belief that a star appears in the Milky Way whenever a mortal is born, and 'shoots' towards the west when they die, towards the realm of the dead, towards Compostela (*campus stelae in finis terrae*), 'the field of stars at the world's end'.

Food and Drink

SPAIN

04

Regional Specialities

Intensely rural, sprinkled with small traditional family farms and overflowing with the good things of the earth, southwest France serves up a hearty cuisine of **fresh ingredients**, so delicious that eating and drinking are two of the most compelling reasons to visit. Each region has its own specialities, but they overlap quite a bit.

Gascon Cuisine

'*C'est le pays du bien vivre et du bon manger*,' say the Gascons of their fertile, generous country, and with good reason. In the face of modern dietary theory, it sticks to its age-old traditions, based heavily on **meat**. The Gers and the Landes rival one another in their annual production of ***foie gras***, the enlarged liver of either a goose (*oie*) or duck (*canard*). The Gers produces much of France's *foie gras d'oie*, generally said to be finer, while the Landes produces 60 per cent of the duck. *Foie gras* comes raw (*nature*) or half-cooked (*mi-cuit*) in a frying pan, with a bit of lemon or *verjus* (the tart juice of underripe grapes), salt and pepper and white grapes, and served with slices of toasted *pain de campagne*; a favourite Gascon way of serving it is *mi-cuit*, with grapes lightly sautéed in armagnac, or with apples fried in the fat. The remaining parts of the goose or duck hardly go to waste: thighs, legs or wings are preserved as *confits* (traditional potted meats), cooked and then put up in their own fat, and reheated in the oven. *Magrets* (that's a Gascon word; the French spell it *maigrets*) are halves of duck or goose breast, best simply grilled and served with a light cream sauce with parsley and garlic, or in the autumn, with fresh *cèpes*. The neck (*cou*) of the duck or goose is a delicacy, stuffed with truffle, minced pork and *foie gras*. Any meat that's left over is made into sausages, pâtés, terrines and meaty *rillons*, mixed with a bit of fat to make a smooth paste. *Gésiers* (gizzards) go into a *salade landaise*, along with slices of dried *magret* and *foie gras*. The fat is equally precious, and is used in a wide range of dishes instead of butter or olive oil. Even the fat-coated carcasses don't go to waste, but take the form of *demoiselles*, grilled on a wood fire, a traditional favourite that occasionally makes it onto restaurant menus.

Other poultry gets less of the limelight on restaurant menus. Gascony raises free-range **chickens** by the million; poulet de Loué from the Sarthe in the Gers is France's biggest producer, and the poulet de St-Sever in the Landes is second. Locally, much of it goes into soups. *Alicuit* is a traditional Gascon ragout of poultry giblets (even testicles), wings, potatoes, carrots and onions. Guinea fowl, capon, pheasant and partridge are often simply roasted in their own juices.

Game birds, 'gifts from heaven', are a veritable mania; quail, thrush, wild ducks, pheasants and woodcock (*bécassier*) appear on autumn menus, but the real favourite is wood pigeon, or *palombe*. All are served roasted and flambéed in armagnac, or cooked *en salmis*: roasted and flambéed and served in a rich sauce made from the giblets. The little *ortolan* (a kind of bunting), considered the greatest delicacy of all, has been hunted almost to extinction and is now protected by law.

Red meat – **beef**, **lamb** and **pork** – are certainly present, usually stewed or roasted (a *gasconnade* is a leg of lamb with anchovies and garlic); their sweetbreads, kidneys, brains, tongues and hearts star in a lot of dishes you'll never see back home. From the **rivers**, especially the Adour, come trout, pike (*brochet*) and crayfish (*écrevisses*), pike-perch (*sandre*), shad (*alose*) and salmon. Shad is one of the stars of local menus in the springtime: marinated in white wine and oil perfumed with bay leaves, then cooked on the grill over vine cuttings and served with diced ham and grapes; often it is stuffed with sorrel, which helps dissolve its many fine bones. Despite the Landes' long stretch of Atlantic coast, it only has one port, Capbreton, and **seafood** plays a correspondingly minor role in Gascon cuisine although you may find oysters on a menu, usully served raw with little grilled sausages called *crépinettes*.

A good deal of passion is reserved for **cèpes**. There are two kinds: the true *cèpe bordelais* (*cèpe de chêne*) and the less tasty *cèpe de pins*. They go into scores of dishes, from omelettes to *daubes*, or stews (usually pork in Gascony), cooked for hours in red wine, or grilled with garlic and served with ham. There are few strictly **vegetarian** dishes. Asparagus, both green and white, thrives in the sandy soil of the Landes and is often served as a starter; *soupe à l'oseille* (sorrel soup) is tasty, although it often has a dollop of goose fat in it. Fresh tomatoes are the main ingredient of *saupiquet*, stewed with white wine and onions.

Traditional Gascon **desserts** are somewhat rarer and invariably feature a nip of armagnac. Prunes are marinated in armagnac and orange blossom water and topped with paper-thin pastry called *pastis*, of one part butter to four parts flour, in a *tourtière*; sometimes apples replace the plums and it's called a *croustade*. Unique to Gascony, the slightly heavy cake *millasson* is made from cornflour and comes in a range of variations, often with apples and armagnac. Melons from Lectoure, apricots or cherries are served in armagnac and followed by a little glass of the same potion to close out a meal in style.

Béarnais and Pyrenean Cuisine

Like the rest of Gascony, Béarn is a region of **geese**, but there are a number of specific dishes that originated in the Béarn kitchen, among them *garbure*, a hotpot made from a quarter of a goose carcass, green cabbage, beans, sausage and salt pork, with thick slices of country bread in the broth. It's traditional, at the end of the bowl, to add a dash of red wine, a custom called *chabrot* (or *goulade*). Closely associated with Henri IV, who wanted every French family to have some once a week, the *poule au pot* is another classic; the chicken must first be stuffed with ham and breadcrumbs, then boiled with vegetables. A favourite Béarnais **soup**, *tourin*, made with lots of garlic, onions, tomato paste, a pat of duck fat and slices of country bread, is popular throughout the southwest. Most of the *jambon de Bayonne* – a raw **ham** similar to prosciutto – is actually made, salted and dried in Béarn. To receive the coveted label of authenticity (Marque Deposée Jambon de Bayonne), the pigs must have been raised in Béarn, the Basque country or Armagnac, and the salt must come from Salies-de-Béarn. Frogs' legs (*cuisses de grenouilles*) are popular in a variety of forms, as is *truit au Jurançon*, trout baked with mushrooms and crème fraîche. Unlike Gascony, Béarn is an important **cheese** producer, and most of it comes from sheep's milk (*fromages de brebis*): best known are Iraty, a mix of cow's and sheep's milk, and the pure sheep's milk cheeses from Sost and Laruns.

East of Béarn in the Pyrenees, you'll find much the same. Tarbes, however, is proudest of its **beans**, *haricots tarbais*, introduced in the 17th century and planted among the maize, which acts as poles to support the bean stalks; you'll often find them served in salads. This is also a good place to look for **cakes** and sweets: the conical layer cake *gâteau à la Broche*, chocolate-covered creamed chestnuts (*châtaignes*), *haricot tarbais* (a sweet that resembles the famous bean, made of nougat and fine chocolate), red and yellow *bigourdettes* (a variety of chocolates) and *hussardes* (chocolate-covered almonds).

Farther east, the Ariège has a few rustic specialities of its own. **Cabbage** is one of the favourite things local chefs feel compelled to include: if a dish is prepared *à la ariégeoise*, it will have cabbage, salt pork, potatoes and kidney beans with it. *Azinat*, perhaps the most famous Ariège dish, is a hearty cabbage soup cooked in an earthenware pot. Main courses often feature **lamb** (the leg, or breast, or on a spit, or en croûte, shepherds' style); other items you'll also see on the menus are frogs' legs, trout with ham, *cassoulet ariégeois* (with a ragout of mutton), *civet de sanglier* (boar stewed in a sauce of red wine, mushrooms, bacon, and onions), or the *tripes du Comte de Foix* which aren't as nasty as they sound. Meat dishes or even *azinat* may come with *rouzoule*, a kind of stuffing of ham, garlic and breadcrumbs. Like the other Pyrenean departments, the Ariège produces plenty of **cheese**: Moulis, Bethmale, Bamalou, Rogalais and Broussette are all strong and delicious, as well as *tomme* and *cabécou* – goat's milk cheeses.

Basque Cuisine

Basque cuisine is one of the spiciest in France, making liberal use of tasty dried red peppers called *piments d'Espelette*. They are a main ingredient in the essential Basque condiment **piperade**, made from red peppers, green peppers, tomatoes, garlic and whipped eggs, lightly fried and served with jambon de Bayonne; prepared minus the eggs, it is used as a relish. **Seafood** holds an important place in the diet: tuna, bonito tuna, and cod are caught on the high seas; special favourites are scallops (*coquilles St-Jacques*), lobster, small cuttlefish (*chiperones*, served stuffed or in a casserole in their own ink), big eels (served with parsley and garlic) and *pibales* (or *civelles*), baby eels that arrive in spring on the Basque coast straight from the Sargasso Sea, only to be drawn by the lights of night fishermen and tossed in the frying pan. At least once try the Basque fish soup *ttoro*, based on conger eel, gurnet and angler-fish, but with a hundred variations. In a land of shepherds, **lamb** is not surprisingly the favourite meat, especially lamb chops, sweetbreads and roast leg of lamb (*gigot*). The Basques are also known for their **charcuterie**, such as *tripotcha*, a kind of pudding (*boudin*) made from sheep's tripe, and *loukinkos* (also spelled *lukenques*), little garlic sausages. *Poulet basquaise*, stewed in a pot with peppers, tomatoes, mushrooms and wine, is universal, as is **sheep's cheese** (*Etorki* is sold everywhere in France). Finish a meal in grand style with an almondy **gâteau basque** topped with cherry sauce or some exquisite chocolate confection from Bayonne.

Catalan Cuisine

The Catalans in Andorra, Roussillon and the eastern Pyrenees have many sterling qualities, but display only the most modest ones in their restaurants. The totem fish of the *département* is the little **anchovy** of Collioure, which hardy souls from Spain to Marseille pulverize with garlic, onion, basil and oil to make *anchoïade*, a favourite apéritif spread on raw celery or toast. A popular starter is *gambas à la planxa*, **prawns** grilled and served on a 'plank', or anchovies with strips of red pepper, which is better than it sounds. Main courses include *roussillonnade*, a dish of bolet mushrooms and sausages grilled over a pine-cone fire, and *boles de Picolat*, Catalan meatballs with mushrooms cooked in sauce. The classic dessert is **crème catalane**, a caramel-covered trifle flavoured with anise and cinnamon.

Drinks

That venerable French institution, the **café**, is not only a place to drink but for many people a home away from home, a place to read the papers, play cards, write letters, read a book, meet friends, and just unwind. Prices are listed on the *Tarif des Consommations*: note that they go up depending whether you're served at the bar (*comptoir*), at a table (*la salle*) or outside (*la terrasse*).

French **coffee** is strong and black. If you order *un café* or *un express* you'll get a small black espresso; if you want milk, order *un crème*. If you want more than a few drops of caffeine, ask them to make it *grand*. For **decaffeinated**, the word is *déca*. The French only order *café au lait* (a small coffee topped off with lots of hot milk) when they stop in for breakfast. *Chocolat chaud* (hot **chocolate**) is usually good; if you order *thé* (**tea**), you'll get an ordinary bag. An *infusion* is a herbal tea – *camomille, menthe* (mint), *tilleul* (lime or linden blossom), or *verveine* (verbena).

Mineral water (*eau minérale*) comes either sparkling (*gazeuse* or *pétillante*) or still (*non-gazeuse* or *plate*). The usual international corporate soft drinks are available, and all kinds of bottled fruit juices (*jus de fruits*) and fresh lemon and orange **juices** (*citron* or *orange pressé*). **Beer** (*bière*) in most bars and cafés is run-of-the-mill big brands from Alsace, Germany and Belgium. Draught (*à la pression*) is cheaper than bottled beer. The strong **spirit** of the Midi is called *pastis*, first made popular in Marseilles as a plague remedy; its name comes from the Latin *passe-sitis*, or thirst quencher. A pale yellow 90° nectar flavoured with aniseed, vanilla and cinnamon, *pastis* is drunk as an apéritif before lunch and after work. The three major brands, Ricard, Pernod and Pastis 51 all taste slightly different; most people drink their '*pastaga*' with water and ice (*glaçons*), which helps make it taste more tolerable.

One of the pleasures of travelling in France is drinking great **wines** for a fraction of what you pay at home, and discovering new varieties that you've never seen in your local shop. However, smart restaurants are the last place to make your discoveries, with their prices marked up to triple or quadruple the retail. You can buy wine direct from the *vignerons* or the *caves coopératives*. In the text we've included a few addresses for each wine. Tours of wineries or *chais* are often possible, except during the grape harvest when everyone is busy. Don't neglect the wines with less exalted labels, especially those labelled VDQS (*vin de qualité supérieure*), such as Vin de Tursan or Côtes de St-Mont, or *vin de pays* – guaranteed to originate in a certain region – with *vin ordinaire* (or *vin de table*) at the bottom, which may not send you to seventh heaven but is usually drinkable and cheap. In a restaurant if you order a *rouge* or *blanc* or *rosé*, this is what you'll get, either by the glass (*un verre*), by the quarter-litre (*un pichet*) or bottle (*une bouteille*).

The Wines of Gascony and the Pyrenees

Because of its gentle climate, the region between the Atlantic and the Pyrenees has been making wine at least since Roman times. The mountains, rivers and valleys form a complex variety of micro-climates that protect the vines from frosts into November, allowing the grapes as much as an extra six weeks to ripen – hence the noble rot (*pourriture noble*) of the rich **Jurançons, Vic-Bilhs** and **Pacherencs**. After the Second World War the wines of the region began their current revival, thanks to their strong individual characteristics and the high quality of the chief vintages: the ruby red, highly tannic **Madiran** (perfect with *confits*, game bird dishes, red meat and Pyrenean cheeses), the reds and rosés of **Irouléguy** (good with chicken, or grilled or roast lamb), tangy sweet or dry Jurançon (the sweet is the traditional accompaniment for *foie gras*, while golden dry Jurançon and dry Pacherenc go well with both fresh-water fish and seafood) and the fruity whites and rosés of Béarn (ideal with mushroom dishes, omelettes, *garbure* and Bayonne ham).

The Basques distil their own liqueur, **Izarra**, which comes in a potent green, a mix of Pyrenean herbs with exotic spices that is sold in every bar in the land. Gascony, for its part, is practically synonymous with its mellow amber brandy, **armagnac**, made from a low-alcohol white wine fortified with *eau-de-vie*, distilled before being aged in special oak barrels for at least two or three years (*see* pp.142–3). Another high-octane Gascon speciality is *floc*, the 'Flower of Gascony', made by adding armagnac to stop the fermentation of the red or white wine, resulting in an apéritif ranging between 16° and 18° that is best when moderately chilled.

Restaurant Basics

Restaurants generally serve between 12 and 2pm and in the evening from 7 to 9pm, with later summer hours. In the southwest people tend to arrive early, to have a better choice of dishes and to get a crack at the specials or *plats du jour* – turn up at 1 for lunch or 8 for dinner and your choice may be very limited. All restaurants post menus outside the door so you'll know what to expect. If you have the appetite to eat the biggest meal of the day at noon, you'll spend a lot less money. Almost all restaurants have a choice of **set-price menus**, usually featuring three to four courses, and often with a few choices among the starters, main courses and desserts. Many expensive places offer a cheaper lunch special – the best way to experience some of the finer gourmet temples. Eating *à la carte* will always be much more expensive, in many cases twice as much. Menus sometimes include the house wine (*vin compris*); if you choose a better wine anywhere, expect a scandalous mark-up. If service is included it will say *service compris* or s.c., if not *service non compris* or s.n.c. Some restaurants offer a set-price gourmet *menu dégustation* – a selection of chef's specialities, which can be a great treat. On the other end of the scale, in the bars and brasseries, is the no-choice formula, which is more often than not steak and *frites*.

A full French meal may begin with an apéritif served with little savoury snacks called *amuse-gueule*; hors d'œuvres, a starter or two (soup, asparagus, *charcuterie*, pâté, *crudités* and so on); followed by the main course (or two), cheese, dessert, coffee and chocolates, and perhaps a *digestif* to finish things off. If you order a salad it may come before or after, but never with, your main course. In everyday eating, most people condense this feast to a starter, main course, and cheese or dessert.

If you're a vegetarian, you may have a hard time in the restaurants of Gascony and the Pyrenees, especially if you don't eat eggs or fish. But most establishments will try to accommodate you somehow.

Markets, Picnic Food and Snacks

In most villages, market day is the event of the week. Celebrated for their fresh farm produce, markets are fun to visit, and become even more interesting if you're cooking for yourself or are just preparing a picnic. In the larger cities they take place every day, while smaller towns and villages have markets but one day a week, and double as social occasions for the locals. Most markets finish up around noon. Other good sources for picnic food are the *charcuteries* or *traiteurs*: you can also find similar counters in the larger supermarkets. Cities are snack-food wonderlands, with outdoor counters selling pastries, *crêpes*, pizza slices, *frites*, *croque-monsieur* (toasted ham and cheese sandwiches) and a wide variety of sandwiches made from baguettes (long thin loaves of bread).

French Menu Reader

Starters and Soups
(*Hors-d'œuvre et Soupes*)
amuse-gueules appetizer(s)
assiette assortie plate of mixed cold hors-d'œuvre
bisque shellfish soup
bouchées mini vol-au-vents
bouillon broth
charcuterie mixed cold meats: salami, ham, etc.
potage thick vegetable soup
velouté thick smooth soup, often fish or chicken

Fish and Shellfish
(*Poissons et Coquillages*)
aiglefin little haddock
anchois anchovies
anguille eel
baudroie anglerfish
beurre blanc sauce of shallots and wine
   vinegar whisked with butter
blanchailles whitebait
brème bream
brochet pike
cabillaud cod
calmar squid
carrelet plaice
colin hake
coque cockle
coquillages shellfish
coquilles St-Jacques scallops
crabe crab

crevettes grises shrimp
crevettes roses prawns
daurade sea bream
écrevisse freshwater crayfish
éperlan smelt
escabèche fried fish, marinated and served cold
escargots snails
espadon swordfish
esturgeon sturgeon
flétan halibut
fruits de mer seafood
gambas giant prawn
gigot de mer a large fish cooked whole
grondin red gurnard
hareng herring
homard Atlantic (Norway) lobster
huîtres oysters
langouste spiny Mediterranean lobster
langoustines small Norway lobsters
limande lemon sole
lotte monkfish
loup (de mer) sea bass
maquereau mackerel
matelote d'anguilles eels in a wine sauce
merlan whiting
morue salt cod
moules mussels
omble chevalier char
palourdes clams
petit gris little grey snail
poulpe octopus
praires small clams
raie skate

rouget red mullet
St-Pierre John Dory
sandre zander or pike-perch
saumon salmon
sole (meunière) sole (with butter, lemon and parsley)
tellines tiny clams
thon tuna
truite trout
truite saumonée salmon trout

Meat and Poultry
(Viandes et Volailles)

agneau (pré-salé) lamb (grazed in fields by the sea)
aloyau sirloin
andouillette chitterling (tripe) sausage
biftek beefsteak
blanc breast or white meat
blanquette stew of white meat, thickened with egg yolk
bœuf beef
boudin blanc sausage of white meat
boudin noir black pudding
brochette meat (or fish) on a skewer
caille quail
canard, caneton duck, duckling
carré crown roast
cassoulet haricot bean stew with sausage, duck, goose, etc.
cervelle brains
chapon capon
chateaubriand porterhouse steak
cheval horsemeat
chevreau kid
chevreuil venison
chorizo spicy Spanish sausage
civet meat stew, in wine and blood sauce
cœur heart
confit meat cooked and preserved in its own fat
contre-filet sirloin steak
côte, côtelette chop, cutlet
cou d'oie farci goose neck stuffed with pork, foie gras, truffles
crépinette small sausage
cuisse thigh or leg
cuisses de grenouilles frogs' legs
dinde, dindon turkey
entrecôte ribsteak
épaule shoulder
estouffade a meat stew marinated, fried and then braised
faisan pheasant
faux-filet sirloin
foie liver
foie gras goose liver
frais de veau veal testicles
fricadelle meatball
géline de touraine rare black hen of the region

gésier gizzard
gibier game
gigot leg of lamb
grillade grilled meat, often a mixed grill
jambon ham
jarret knuckle
langue tongue
lapin rabbit
lard (lardons) bacon (diced bacon)
lièvre hare
maigret/magret (de canard) breast (of duck)
manchons duck or goose wings
marcassin young wild boar
merguez spicy red sausage
mouton mutton
navarin lamb stew with root vegetables
noix de veau/agneau topside of veal/lamb
oie goose
os bone
perdreau, perdrix partridge
petit salé salt pork
pintade guinea fowl
plat-de-côtes short ribs or rib chops
porc pork
pot au feu meat and vegetables cooked in stock
poulet chicken
poussin baby chicken
quenelle poached dumplings made of fish, fowl or meat
queue de bœuf oxtail
rillons pork pieces cooked in their fat, a speciality from Touraine
ris (de veau) (veal) sweetbreads
rognons kidneys
rosbif roast beef
rôti roast
sanglier wild boar
saucisse sausage
saucisson salami-like sausage
selle (d'agneau) saddle (of lamb)
steak tartare raw minced beef, often topped with a raw egg yolk
suprême de volaille fillet of chicken breast and wing
tournedos thick round slices of beef fillet
travers de porc spare ribs
tripes tripe
veau veal

Vegetables, Herbs, etc.
(Légumes, Herbes, etc.)

ail garlic
aneth dill
anis aniseed
artichaut artichoke
asperges asparagus
aubergine aubergine, eggplant
avocat avocado
basilic basil

betterave beetroot
blette Swiss chard
cannelle cinnamon
céleri celery
céleri-rave celeriac
cèpes ceps, wild bolet mushrooms
champignons mushrooms
chanterelles wild yellow mushrooms
chicorée curly endive
chou cabbage
chou-fleur cauliflower
choucroute sauerkraut
choux de Bruxelles Brussels sprouts
ciboulette chives
citrouille pumpkin
clou de girofle clove
concombre cucumber
cornichons gherkins
cresson watercress
échalote shallot
endive chicory (endive)
épinards spinach
estragon tarragon
fenouil fennel
fève broad (fava) bean
flageolet white bean
fleurs de courgette courgette flowers
frites chips (French fries)
galipette large round mushroom
genièvre juniper
gingembre ginger
haricots beans
haricots blancs white beans
haricots rouges kidney beans
haricots verts green (French) beans
jardinière mixed diced garden vegetables
laitue lettuce
lentilles lentils
macédoine diced vegetables
maïs (épis de) sweetcorn (on the cob)
menthe mint
mesclun mixed-leaf salad
morilles morel mushrooms
moutarde mustard
navet turnip
oignons onions
oseille sorrel
panais parsnip
persil parsley
petits pois small green peas
pied bleu wood blewit (type of mushroom)
piment pimento
pleurote type of mushroom
poireaux leeks
pois chiches chickpeas
pois mange-tout sugar peas, mangetout
poivron sweet pepper, capsicum
pomme de terre potato

potiron pumpkin
riz rice
romarin rosemary
roquette rocket
safran saffron
salade verte green salad
salsifis salsify
sarriette savory
sarrasin buckwheat
sauge sage
serpolet wild thyme
thym thyme
truffes truffles

Fruit and Nuts (*Fruits et Noix*)

abricot apricot
amande almond
ananas pineapple
banane banana
bigarreau black cherry
brugnon nectarine
cacahouète peanut
cassis blackcurrant
cerise cherry
citron lemon
datte date
figue fig
figue de Barbarie prickly pear
fraise (des bois) (wild) strawberry
framboise raspberry
fruit de la passion passion fruit
grenade pomegranate
griotte morello cherry
groseille redcurrant
mandarine tangerine
mangue mango
marron chestnut
mirabelle mirabelle plum
mûre sauvage blackberry
noisette hazelnut
noix walnut
noix de cajou cashew
pamplemousse grapefruit
pastèque watermelon
pêche (blanche) (white) peach
pignon pine nut
pistache pistachio
poire pear
pomme apple
prune plum
pruneau prune
raisin grape
raisin sec raisin
reine-claude greengage plum

Desserts

Bavarois mousse or custard in a mould
bombe ice-cream dessert in a round mould
bonbon sweet, candy

brioche light sweet yeast bread
charlotte sponge fingers and custard cream dessert
chausson turnover
compote stewed fruit
corbeille de fruits basket of fruit
coupe ice cream: a scoop or in a cup
crème anglaise egg custard
crème Chantilly sweet whipped cream
crème pâtissière thick pastry cream filling made with eggs
crémets fresh cream cheese, normally from Anjou and mixed with fresh cream and sugar
gâteau cake
gaufre waffle
glace ice cream
macaron macaroon
madeleine small sponge cake
miel honey
mignardise same as petits fours
œufs à la neige floating islands/meringue on a bed of custard
pain d'épice gingerbread
parfait frozen mousse
sablé shortbread
savarin a filled cake, shaped like a ring
truffe chocolate truffle
yaourt yoghurt

Cheese (*Fromage*)

chèvre goat's cheese
doux mild
fromage (plateau de) cheese (board)
fromage blanc yoghurty cream cheese
fromage de brebis ewe's milk cheese
fromage frais a bit like sour cream
fromage sec general name for solid cheeses
fort strong

Cooking Terms and Sauces

bien cuit well-done (steak)
à point medium (steak)
saignant rare (steak)
sanglant rare (steak)
bleu very rare (steak)
à l'anglaise boiled
à la bordelaise cooked in wine, bone marrow and diced vegetables
à la diable in a spicy mustard sauce
à la périgourdine in a truffle and *foie gras* sauce
à la provençale cooked with tomatoes, garlic and olive oil
à la vapeur steamed
au four baked
barquette pastry boat
broche roasted on a spit
chasseur cooked with mushrooms and shallots in white wine

en croûte cooked in a pastry crust
en papillote baked in buttered paper
épices spices
flambé set aflame with alcohol
frais, fraîche fresh, cold
frappé with crushed ice
galantine cooked food served in cold jelly
garni with vegetables
(au) gratin topped with melted cheese and breadcrumbs
grillé grilled
haché minced, ground
marmite casserole
médaillon round piece
mijoté simmered
mornay cheese sauce
pané breaded
pâte brisée shortcrust pastry
pâte à chou choux pastry
pâte feuilletée flaky or puff pastry
paupiette rolled, filled slices of fish or meat
poché poached
salé salted, spicy
sucré sweet
timbale pie cooked in a dome-shaped mould

Drinks (Boissons)

bière (pression) beer (draught)
bouteille (demi) bottle (half)
brut very dry
café coffee
café au lait white coffee
café express espresso coffee
chocolat chaud hot chocolate
citron pressé freshly squeezed lemon with sugar and jug of water
demi a third of a litre
doux sweet (wine)
eau water
  ...gazeuse sparkling
  ...minérale mineral
  ...plate still
eau potable drinking water
eau-de-vie brandy
glaçon ice cube
infusion/tisane herbal tea
jus juice
lait milk
moelleux semi-dry
orange pressée freshly squeezed orange with sugar and jug of water
sec dry
thé tea
verre glass
vin (blanc, mousseux, rosé, rouge) (white, sparkling, rosé, red) wine

Planning
Your Trip

SPAIN

05

When to Go

Climate

Gascony's climate is that of the Aquitaine Basin, shielded from intemperate continental influences by the Massif Central. It is a fairly balmy, humid climate, strongly influenced by the Atlantic, with long hot **summers** broken by moist winds off the ocean. Early **spring** and late **autumn** usually get the most rainfall – and it can rain for weeks or even months at a time. The lush green western Pyrenees get masses of precipitation, on average over 200 days a year all along the Spanish border, including some 50 or so days of snow. **Winters** along the Atlantic coast are fairly mild, with fewer than 40 days of frost a year, while the inland valleys and the great forest of the Landes are usually a few degrees warmer or colder; the pocket around the Basque coast and southern Côte d'Argent enjoys something of a micro-climate, with winters as warm as the Mediterranean coast, although a good deal wetter.

Unless you're coming to the region to ski or learn about the intricacies of preparing foie gras, winter is the bleakest time to visit; accommodation, restaurants and sights simply close down, and the skies are often cloudy all day. Up in the Pyrenees, unless it's an exceptional year, the ski season doesn't really start properly until Christmas or reach its full stride until February. No matter how lovely the weather is, nothing under the snow line really opens up until the first tourist rush of the year – Palm Sunday and Easter week. The weather from March into May is wonderfully inconsistent: it can be hot enough for a dip in the pool or so cold that you need a heavy coat, and can vary from week to week. May and June are often good months to come: usually summer has set well in, and it's hot enough for swims in the coastal lakes, the sights are open, hotel rates are still low. Hot July and August are French school holidays, when everything is packed, prices are high, and the Pyrenees are apt to be pummelled by sudden and very violent thunderstorms. On the bright side, there are scores of village fêtes, fairs, festivals, concerts and races. The region often looks its best in September and

Average Maximum Temperatures in °C/°F

	Jan	April	July	Oct
Dax	11/52	17/63	27/81	20/68
Bayonne	13/55	18/64	28/82	24/75
Tarbes	12/54	16/61	29/84	24/75

October, when most of the tourists have gone home (although late August–October are excellent months for surfing); the scenic mountain trails are empty, while down in Armagnac and the other wine regions everyone is concentrating on the *vendange*. November and December can be dismal, but wild mushrooms, game dishes and masses of holiday oysters and foie gras offer some consolation.

Festivals

Every single village or town in this book puts on a party at least once a year, usually in honour of its patron saint. The pronounced Spanish influence in Gascony and the Pyrenees, added to the inhabitants' natural panache, tends to make these **fêtes** among the liveliest in France. Many are accompanied by **bullfights**, either Spanish *corridas* or the bloodless *course landaise* (*see* p.36–7), while the Basques have a *pelote* match and perform astounding feats of strength running races with 100lb weights in each hand, for instance; the local *bandas* (brass bands of 20 or 40 local musicians in dashing costumes) play Basque or Navarrais tunes all night long in the streets, and there are usually firework displays too. Larger villages will host a visiting circus or funfair. There is invariably plenty of what the French call *animation* (everything from a local merchant chattering away on a portable microphone to jumping motorcycles, or dogs pulling sleds on wheels) and plenty of dancing, from performances of the local folklore societies to *bal musette*, accordion tangos for the older generation and loud local rock bands for the young. Nearly all of the really goofy festivals listed above happen in the Gers.

National Holidays

See p.72.

Calendar of Events

Please note that exact dates can vary from year to year: contact the local tourist office to confirm. *Départements* are abbreviated as follows: Gers 32, Landes 40, Basques 64, Béarn 64B, Hautes-Pyrénées 65, Haute-Garonne 31, Ariège 09. For information on festivals in Midi-Pyrénées (depts 32, 65, 31 and 09) refer to *http://festivals.midipyrenees.fr.*

January

Last Tues and Wed *Foire aux Pottoks*, Basque horse fair, Espelette 64

2nd half Comedy festival throughout Haute-Pyrénées 65

February

Early Feb Violet festival and market, Toulouse 31; Cinemà festival, Luchon 31

Sometimes Dogsled races and ice sculpture competitions, Arrens 65

March

Mid-month International organ competitions, Biarritz 64; Festival of Latin-American film, Toulouse 31

April

Good Friday–Easter Sacred music festival, Lourdes 65

1st Sun after Easter *Coupes de Pâques*, auto races, Nogaro 32; Easter Fair, Tardets 64

Mid-month Ham fair, Bayonne 64

Last Sun Flower market, Fourcès 32

Dates vary Hesteyade, Occitan choir festival, at Ibos 65

End month Flamenco festival, Toulouse 31

May

1 *Fête de Mer*, Mimizan 40

2nd Sun Festival of *Bandas y Peñas*, Condom 32

Sometime Onion festival, Trebons 65

Ascension Day *Fête des Fleurs*, Riscle 32

Pentecost Bullfights and festivities at Vic-Fézensac 32

End month World Cricket Trainers' Championship, Lavardens 32

Throughout month Festival of religious music at St-Lizier and the Couserans 09

June

1st Sun after Pentecost Battle of Saracens and Christians, Martres-Tolosane 31

2nd Sun after Pentecost *Processions de la Fête-Dieu*, Bidarray 64 and Iholdy 64

2–6 *Fêtes patronales*, Grenade-sur-l'Adour 40

Early in month *Fête de Mer*, Capbreton 40; *Fêtes locales*, Boucau 64, Urcuit 64; Jazz Altitude festival, Luz 65

2nd Sun Cherry festival, Itxassou 64

2nd week *Fêtes locales*, Arcangues 64

Mid-month Surf championship, Biarritz; Aire-sur-l'Adour fête, with *courses landaises* 40

21 and last week in June Fire festival for St-Jean, at St-Lizier and other villages in Ariège, Landes and Pyrénées-Atlantiques; summer equinox gatherings and fireworks

25 St-Sever 40, big fête with a celebratory *course landaise* 40

Last week *Fêtes locales*, St Pierre-d'Irube 64, Hasparren 64

Last Sun World Well-Water Drawers' Championship, Pavie 32

Last week/early July *Festival de Pau* 64B with theatre, dance and music

Throughout month Music Festival, Auch and throughout Gers 32; photography and visual arts festival, Toulouse 31

July

Early July *Festival d'Art Flamenco*, Mont-de-Marsan 40; *fêtes locales* St-Pée-sur-Nivelle, St-Jean-Pied-de-Port and Lahonce 64; *fêtes patronales*, Eauze 32; Tursan wine festival, Geaune 40

July–Aug *Festival du Comminges*, concerts at St-Bertrand-de-Comminges 31; Concerts and exhibitions at Abbaye de l'Escaladieu, Bonnemazon 65

2nd Sun Tuna Festival, St-Jean-de-Luz 64

Mid-July–mid-Aug *Nuits Musicales en Armagnac* and International Folklore Festival of Gascony, Condom 32

13 *Fête du Chipiron*, Hendaye 64

13–14 Big Bastille Day celebrations at Arcachon 40, Mimizan 40, Nogaro 32, Eugénie-les-Bains 40, Castets 40

15 Re-enactment of a Basque wedding, St-Etienne-de-Baïgorry 64

Mid-month Jazz festival and medieval market, Bayonne 64; sheep festival, Lannemezan 65; Jazz Altitude festival, Luz 65; Festival de Germ, Vallée du Louron 65; Medieval Days in Foix 09 (music, medieval markets, jousts); Big festival of country music, Mirande 32; Latin and World music, Pamiers 09; Piano festival in Hautes-Pyrénées 65

3rd week *Fête de la Madeleine*, Mont-de-Marsan 40

23 Tuna festival, Hossegor 40

25 *Fêtes locales*, Gotein-Libarrenx 64

End of month *Fête de la Madeleine*, with a competition of the unusual, St-Palais 64; *Fêtes locales*, Lasbastide-Clairence 64 and Arbonne 64; Lou Gran Marcat, an old-fashioned market, Rabastens-de-Bigorre 65; *Festival Equestria*, Tarbes 65

Last week in July Festival of Salsa, Vic-Fézensac 32; Jazz in Foix 09

29 July–3 Aug *Fêtes patronales*, Montfort-en-Chalosse and Peyrehorade 40

Last week July–1st week Aug Fantasia, classical music festival at St-Lizier 09

End July–mid-Aug Photos and visual arts, Lectoure 32

Throughout month Sculpture and marble festival, St-Béat 31

August

1 Sheepdog competitions, St-Jean-Pied-de-Port 64; *Foire de Garris*, cattle fair, St-Palais 64

Early Aug Festival of wheat and good bread, Sarlabous 65; cheese fair, Loures-Barousse 65

3–8 *Fête*, with fireworks and *courses landaises*, Hagetmau 40

1st Wed Beginning of huge 5-day *Fêtes de Bayonne*, Bayonne 64

4–9 *Fêtes patronales*, Amou 40; Basque sport finals, Biarritz 64

1st Sun Pastorale, shepherds' festival, Gotein Libarrenx 64

1st week in Aug *Festival de la Marionnette*, Mirepoix 09; folklore festival, Sentein 09

Early Aug Traditional dance and music festival, Sarrant 32

2nd weekend *Fêtes Basques*, Hendaye 64; crafts fair, Mauléon Soule 64

2nd week *Fêtes locales*, St-Etienne-de-Baïgorry 64, Cambo-les-Bains 64; world pig-snorting championship, Trie-sur-Baïse 65; sardine festival, Ustaritz 64

1st half Musical evenings, Cologne 32; in even-numbered years, *Festival des Pyrénées*, with dancers from around the world, Oloron 64B

Mon after 2nd Sun World Snail Speed Championship, Lagardère 32

12–17 *Fête patronale* at Dax, with *courses landaises* 40

Mid-month Big jazz festival at Marciac 32; World Championship of Melon Eaters, Lectoure 32; astronomy festival, Fleurance 32; mountain-climbing race, Auzat-Vicdessos 09; International professional Cesta Punta finals, St-Jean-de-Luz 64

13 Basque shepherd hollering contest, Hasparren 64; sardine festival, Ustaritz 64

13–25 Assumption Day fête, Bayonne 64, Moliets 40, Ainhoa 64, Anglet 64

14 Festival of Basque song, Garindein 64

15 Re-enactment of a Basque wedding, St-Etienne-de-Baïgorry 64; *Nuit Féerique* and fireworks, Biarritz 64; Espadrille festival, Mauléon Soule 64; crafts fair of the Val d'Aran, St-Béat 31; Madiran Wine Festival, 65; *Fête de Mer*, Arcachon 40

1st weekend after 15 Aug Big flower festival, Bagnères 65

18–23 *Fêtes patronales*, St-Julien-en-Born 40

19 Cheese fair, Tardets 64

3rd week Rip Curl Pro, World Surfing Championships at Hossegor/Seignosse 40

3rd Sun Smugglers' cross-country race, Sare 64; Force Basque festival, St-Palais 64

Last week *Fêtes locales*, Bassussarry 64; Tango festival, Tarbes 65

Throughout month Le Houga 32 hosts three Gascon world championships: dove-cooing, *quilles à l'Escabeilhe* and eating *demoiselles* – fat-coated duck carcasses

September

1st two weeks Local *fête*, Foix 09

1st half Quiksilver Surf master championships and *Musique en Côte Basque*, big name recitals, Biarritz and throughout Basque country 64; *corridas*, Bayonne 64; *Fêtes patronales*, Urrugne 64

3 World lark whistling contest and other events, Vieux-Boucau 40

1st Sat *Fêtes du ttoro*: best Basque fish soup competition, St-Jean-de-Luz 64

1st Sun Famous pilgrimage at Sarrance 64B; local *fête*, Le Mas-d'Azil 09

2nd Sun *Fêtes de Sare*, Sare 64

Mid month Fiesta at Ordino, Andorra; International piano recitals, St-Jean-de-Luz 64

19 *Fête des Corsaires*, St-Jean-de-Luz 64

3rd Sat *Foire aux côtelettes*, lamb chop fair, Arrens 65

End month International Festival of Latin American cinema and culture, Biarritz 64; world champion fishing from boats competition, Anglet 64; *Foire aux côtelettes*, Luz-St-Saveur 65; Surfing competitions, Biarritz 64

Most of month International piano festival, Toulouse, 31

October

Early month Formula III Grand Prix at Nogaro 32; every 3 years, the *Championnat de France des Ecarteurs (courses landaises)*, Mont-de-Marsan 40

2nd week Antiques fair, Mont-de-Marsan 40

1st half of month International organ festival, Toulouse 31

Mid-month Important international theatre festival, Bayonne 64; *Haricot Tarbais* festival, bean *fête*, Tarbes 65

Last weekend Kite-flying contest, Hossegor 40; horse fair, Aspet 31

Last Sun *Fête du Piment*, Espelette 64

Throughout month Festival of Occitan culture, Toulouse 31

November

8–12 *Fêtes du St-Martin*, Biarritz 64

2nd weekend St-Martin's Fair, Aurignac 31

30 Ste-Catherine's Fair, Aspet 31

End of month Circus festival, Auch 32; apple fair, Montbrun-Bocage 31

December

Throughout month *Marchés de gras* – foie gras, fattened ducks and geese markets – are held in most towns

4–5 *Fêtes patronales*, Guéthary 64

Tourist Information

A little **preparation** will help you get much more out of your precious holiday. Check the list of events (*see* above) to help you decide where you want to be and when, and book your accommodation early; if you are planning to base yourself in just one or two areas, write ahead to the local tourist offices (*syndicats d'initiative* or *offices de tourisme*) listed in the text for complete lists of self-catering accommodation, hotels and campsites in their areas (many of these have their own websites). Alternatively, contact one of the many agencies in the UK or USA. For more general information about your holiday, get in touch with a French Government Tourist Office:

UK: French Government Tourist Office, 178 Piccadilly, London W1V 0AL, **t** 09068 244 123, *www.franceguide.com*.

France: Maison de la France, 20 Av de l'Opéra, 75041 Paris, **t** 01 42 96 70 00.

USA: 16th Floor, 444 Madison Av, New York, NY 10020, **t** (212) 838 7800; Suite 715, 9454 Wilshire Bd, Beverly Hills, Los Angeles, CA 90212, **t** (310) 271 6665.

Canada: 1981 Av McGill College, No.490, Montreal, Quebec H3A 2W9, **t** (514) 288 4264.

Useful Web Addresses

There are a large number of excellent websites that provide information on the area. In addition to those listed throughout the book, try *www.tourisme.fr* or *www.france.com*.

Embassies and Consulates

Foreign Embassies in France

The only consulates in the region are:

UK: 353 Bd de Président Wilson, Bordeaux, **t** 05 57 22 21 10.

USA: 25 Allée Jean-Jaurès, 31000 Toulouse, **t** 05 34 41 36 50.

Embassies and consulates in Paris include:

Australia: 4 Rue Jean-Rey, 15th, **t** 01 40 59 33 00, Ⓜ Bir-Hakeim.

Canada: 35 Av Montaigne, 8th, **t** 01 44 43 29 00, Ⓜ Franklin D. Roosevelt.

Ireland: 4 Rue Rude, 16th, **t** 01 44 17 67 00, Ⓜ Charles de Gaulle/ Etoile.

New Zealand: 7 Rue Léonard de Vinci, 16th, **t** 01 45 01 43 43, Ⓜ Victor-Hugo.

South Africa: 59 Quai d'Orsay, 7th, **t** 01 53 59 23 23, Ⓜ Invalides.

French Embassies Abroad

UK: 58 Knightsbridge, London SW1X 7JT, **t** (020) 7073 1000, *www.ambafrance-uk.org*; 21 Cromwell Rd, London SW7 2EN, **t** (020) 7073 1200, *www.consulfrance-londres.org* (*for visas*); 11 Randolph Crescent, Edinburgh EH3 7TT, **t** (0131) 225 7954 – recorded visa information only, *www.consulfrance-edimbourg.org*.

Ireland: 36 Ailesbury Rd, Ballsbridge, Dublin 4, **t** (01) 277 5000, *www.ambafrance.ie*.

USA: 4101 Reservoir Rd NW, Washington, DC 20007-2185, **t** (202) 944 6195, *www.ambafrance-us.org*; 205 North Michigan

Avenue, Suite 3700, Chicago, IL 60601, t (312) 327 5200, *www.consulfrance-chicago.org*; 10990 Wilshire Bd, Suite 300, Los Angeles, CA 90024, t (310) 235 3200, *www.consulfrance-losangeles.org*; 934 Fifth Av, New York, NY 10021, t (212) 606 3600, *www.consulfrance-newyork.org*. There are also French consulates in Atlanta, Boston, Houston, Miami, New Orleans and San Francisco.

Australia: 6 Perth Av, Yarralumla ACT 2600, t (02) 6216 0100; Level 26, St Martins Tower, 31 Market St, Sydney; NSW 2000, t (02) 9268 2440, *www.ambafrance-au.org*.

Entry Formalities

Passports and Visas

Holders of **EU**, **US** and **Canadian** passports do not need a visa to enter France for stays of up to three months, but everyone else does. Apply at your nearest French Consulate; the usual visa is the *visa de circulation*, allowing for multiple stays of three months over a three-year period. If you intend staying longer, you need a *visa de long séjour* and eventually a *carte de séjour*, neither required by EU citizens. On the other hand, non-EU citizens had best apply for an extended visa at home, a complicated procedure requiring proof of income, etc. For further information refer to the French government website: *http://vosdroits.service-public.fr*.

Customs

EU nationals over the age of 17 can now import a limitless amount of goods for their personal use. Arrivals from **non-EU** countries have to pass through French customs.

Duty-free allowances have now been abolished within the EU. For people entering the EU from outside, duty-free limits are 1 litre of spirits or 2 litres of liquors (port, sherry or champagne), plus 2 litres of wine, 200 cigarettes and 50 grams of perfume. Larger quantities – up to 10 litres of spirits, 90 litres of wine, 110 litres of beer and 3,200 cigarettes – bought locally and provided you are travelling between EU countries, can be taken through customs if you can prove that they are for private consumption only and taxes have been paid in the country of purchase.

Residents of the USA may each take home US$400-worth of foreign goods without attracting duty, including the tobacco and alcohol allowance. Canadians can bring home $300 worth of goods in a year, plus their tobacco and alcohol allowances.

Disabled Travellers

When it comes to providing access for all, France is not exactly in the vanguard of nations; many Americans who come over are appalled. But things are beginning to change, especially in newer buildings.

Access and facilities in 90 towns in France are covered in *Touristes Quand Même! Promenades en France pour les Voyageurs Handicapés*, a booklet usually available in the tourist offices of large cities, or write ahead to the **Centre Technique National d'Etudes et de Recherches sur les Handicaps et les Inadaptations**, 236 bis Rue de Tolbiac, 13th, Paris, t (01) 53 80 66 63. The **Association des Paralysés de France**, 22 Rue du Père-Guérin, 13th, Paris, t (01) 44 16 83 83, *www.apf.asso.fr*, publishes *Où Ferons-Nous Étape?* listing French hotels and motels accessible to those with limited mobility. Hotels with facilities for the handicapped are listed in Michelin's Red Guide to France.

The **Royal Association for Disability and Rehabilitation (RADAR)**, Unit 12, City Forum, 250 City Rd, London EC1V 8AF, t (020) 7250 3222, *www.radar.org.uk*, can give specialist advice and has publications for every stage of a holiday including transport and accommodation.

If you wish to visit Lourdes, **Tangney Tours**, Pilgrim House, Station Court, Borough Green, Kent TN15 8AF, t (01732) 886 666, *www.tangney-tours.com*, organize travel by ambulance carriages in special trains.

The Channel Tunnel is a good way to travel to France by car from the UK, since disabled passengers can stay in their vehicles. By train, Eurostar gives wheelchair passengers first-class travel for reduced fares. Most ferry companies will offer facilities if contacted beforehand. Vehicles fitted to accommodate disabled people pay reduced tolls on *autoroutes*. For further information contact the **Ministère des Transports**, 246 Boulevard St Germain, 75700 Paris, t 01 40 81 21 22.

Disability Organizations

In the UK

Access Ability, *www.access-ability.org*. Information on travel agencies catering specifically for disabled people.

Holiday Care Service, The Hawkins Suite, Enham Place, Enham, Alamein, Andover SP11 6JS, t 0845 124 9974, *www.holidaycare.org.uk*.

Royal National Institute of the Blind, t (020) 7388 1266, *www.rnib.org.uk*. The RNIB Holiday service offers information on a range of issues for the blind and visually impaired and will answer any queries.

Royal National Institute for the Deaf (RNID), 19–23 Featherstone Street, London EC1Y 8SL, Infoline t 0808 808 0123, textphone t 0808 808 9000, *informationline@rnid.org.uk*, *www.rnid.org.uk*. Call their information line for help and advice.

In the USA and Canada

Alternative Leisure Co, 165 Middlesex Turnpike, Suite 206, Bedford, MA 01730, t (718) 275 0023, *www.alctrips.com*. Organizes vacations abroad for disabled people.

American Foundation for the Blind, t (212) 502 7600, *www.afb.org*. An excellent information source for visually impaired travellers.

SATH (Society for Accessible Travel and Hospitality), t (212) 447 7284, *www.sath.org*. Advice on all aspects of travel for the disabled.

Mobility International USA, 132 East Broadway, Suite 343, Eugene, OR, 97401, t/TTY (541) 343 1284, *www.miusa.org*. Information on international educational exchange programmes and volunteer service overseas for the disabled.

In Australia and New Zealand

Australian Council for Rehabilitation of the Disabled (ACRODS), PO Box 60, Curtin, ACT 2605, Australia, t/TTY (02) 6283 3200, *www.acrod.org.au*. Information and contact numbers for specialist travel agents.

Disabled Persons Assembly, PO Box 27–254, Wellington 6035, New Zealand, t (644) 801 9100, *www.dpa.org.nz*. All-round source for travel information.

Insurance and EHIC Cards

Citizens of the EU who bring along their **European Health Insurance Card** (EHIC – apply online at *www.ehic.org.uk*, or pick up a form from a post office) are entitled to the same health services as French citizens. This means paying up front for medical care and prescriptions, of which costs of 75–80 per cent are reimbursed later – a complex procedure for the non-French. As an alternative, consider a **travel insurance** policy, covering theft and losses and offering 100 per cent medical refund; check to see if it covers extra expenses if you get bogged down in airport or train strikes. Beware that accidents resulting from sports are rarely covered by ordinary insurance. Canadians are usually covered in France by their provincial health coverage; Americans and others should check their individual policies.

Money

The currency of France is the **euro**, divided into 100 **cents**. There are seven banknotes, in denominations of 5, 10, 20, 50, 100, 200 and 500, and eight coins, in denominations of 1 and 2 euros, and 1, 2, 5, 10, 20 and 50 cents.

Travellers' cheques are now available in euros and are the safest way of carrying money. Major international **credit cards** are widely used in France. Visa (in French, Carte Bleue) is the most readily accepted, although for the French, Carte Bleue is a direct-debit bank card. American Express is often not accepted, however. French-issued credit cards have a special security microchip (*puce*) in each card. The card is slotted into a card reader, and the holder keys in a PIN to authorize the transaction. New UK cards have gone over to the same system so transactions should be easy.

In case of credit card loss or theft, call the 24-hour services, which have English-speaking staff:

American Express, t 01 47 77 79 28 (the office in Bordeaux is t 05 56 00 63 36).

Diners Club, t 08 10 31 41 59.

MasterCard, t 01 45 67 84 84.

Visa, t 08 00 90 11 79.

Under the Cirrus system, withdrawals in euros can be made from bank and post office automatic cash machines (**ATMs**), using your UK PIN. The specific cards accepted are marked on each machine, and most give instructions in English. Credit card companies charge a fee for cash advances, but rates are often better than bank rates.

05 | Planning Your Trip | Money

Banks are generally open 8.30–12.30 and 1.30–4; they close on Sunday, and most close either on Saturday or Monday as well. Exchange rates vary, and nearly all take a commission of varying proportions. Places that do nothing but exchange money (and hotels and train stations) usually have the worst rates or take out the heftiest commissions, so be careful. It's always a good bet to purchase some euros before you go, especially if you are planning to arrive during the weekend or late at night.

Getting There

By Air

From the UK and Ireland

The big international airports in the region are at **Bordeaux** and **Toulouse**. There are smaller airports at Lourdes/Tarbes, Agen, Pau, Biarritz and Carcassonne. Lourdes/Tarbes is the second biggest charter airport in France, and 80 per cent of passengers are pilgrims; travel organizations and Catholic organizations can fill you in on pilgrim charters.

From North America

The only direct flights to southwest France are from Montreal on Air-Transat, which in summer flies direct to Bordeaux and Toulouse. Otherwise, your best bet is to find a cheap flight to a European hub like London or Paris (KLM, by way of Detroit and Amsterdam, is often the cheapest to Toulouse, or by Lufthansa to Munich and then on to Toulouse) and continue on from there.

Air France (*www.airfrance.us*) also has summer flights from various US airports to the southwest.

Airline Carriers

From the UK and Ireland

Air France, UK t 0870 142 4343, *www.airfrance. co.uk*. Connecting flights from Paris Orly daily to Biarritz, Pau, Bordeaux, Toulouse and Lourdes/Tarbes. Also from Dublin to Toulouse.

Aerocondor, *www.aerocondor.fr*. Flights to Agen from Paris Orly.

British Airways, UK t 0345 222 111, France t 08 02 80 29 02, *www.british-airways.com*. Bordeaux and Toulouse from London Gatwick.

easyJet, *www.easyjet.com*. London Gatwick and Bristol to Toulouse and Luton to Bordeaux.

Flybe, *www.flybe.com*. Toulouse from Bristol and Birmingham, and Bordeaux from Bristol and Southampton.

Ryanair, t 08701 569 569, in France t 05 59 43 83 93, *www.ryanair.com*. Biarritz and Carcassonne from various UK and Irish airports.

From the USA and Canada

Air Canada, Canada/USA t 888 247 2262, *www.aircanada.ca*.

Air France, USA t 800 237 2747, *www.airfrance.us*; Canada t 800 667 2747.

Air-Transat, t (1877) 872 6728, *www.airtransat.com*.

American Airlines, t 800 433 7300, *www.aa.com*.

British Airways, USA/Canada t 800 247 9297, *www.ba.com*.

Delta, t 800 221 1212, *www.delta.com*.

KLM, USA represented by North West Airlines, t 800-225 2525, *www.nwa.com*.

Lufthansa, USA t 800 645 3880, Canada t 800 563 5954, *www.lufthansa.com*

Charters, Discounts and Special Deals

UK and Ireland

Trailfinders, 194 Kensington High St, London W8 7RG, t 0845 050 5940, *www.trailfinders.com*.

Budget Travel, 134 Lower Baggot St, Dublin 2, t (01) 631 1100, *www.budgettravel.ie*.

United Travel, Stillorgan Bowl, Stillorgan, County Dublin, t (01) 215 9300, *www.unitedtravel.ie*.

Also try websites such as *www.cheapflights.co.uk* and *www.lastminute.com*.

USA and Canada

Air Brokers International, USA t (800) 883 3273, *www.airbrokers.com*.

Last Minute Travel Club, USA t (877) 970 3500; Canada t (877) 970 3500, *www.lastminuteclub.com*. Payment of an annual fee gets you cheap standby deals, special rates for the major car rental companies and train tickets.

www.traveldiscounts.com, USA t (408) 813 1111. Members get special rates on flights, hotels and tours.

Student Discounts

Students equipped with relevant ID cards are eligible for considerable reductions, not only on flights, but on trains and on admission fees to museums, concerts and more. Agencies specializing in student and youth travel can help you in applying for the cards, as well as filling you in on the best deals.

STA Travel, 117 Euston Rd, London NW1 2SX, **t** 0870 166 2603, *www.statravel.co.uk*. Many other branches in the UK, including; Bristol **t** 0870 166 2609; Leeds **t** 0870 168 6878; Manchester **t** 0870 166 2622; Oxford **t** (01865) 262 300; Cambridge **t** 0870 166 2591. In the **USA**, New York City **t** (212) 627 3111. In **Australia**, Sydney **t** (02) 9212 1255.

Europe Student Travel, 6 Campden St, London W8, **t** (020) 7727 764; non-students as well.

Travel Cuts, 187 College St, Toronto, Ontario M5T 1P7, **t** (416) 979 2406, *www.travelcuts.com*. Canada's largest student travel specialists; branches in most provinces. In the USA refer to *www.travelcuts.com/us*

For help in France contact:

CIDJ (Centre d'Information et de la Documentation Jeunesse), 101 Quai Branly, 75740 Paris, Cedex 15, **t** (01) 44 49 12 00, *www.cidj.com*.

UFCV (Union Française des Centres de Vacances et de Loisirs), 10 Quai Charente, 75019 Paris, **t** (01) 44 72 14 14, *www.ufcv.fr*. Cultural, sporting and leisure holidays for young people 4 to 18.

By Train

Air prices and the sheer brain-mushing awfulness of airports make travelling by high-speed train an attractive alternative. **Eurostar** trains, **t** 08705 186 186, *www.eurostar.com*, leave from London Waterloo or Ashford International in Kent, and there are direct connections to Paris (Gare du Nord; 3 hours) and Lille (2 hours). Fares are cheaper if booked at least 7 days in advance and you include a Saturday night away. You need to check in at least 20 minutes before departure, or you will not be allowed onto the train.

France's high-speed **TGVs** (*trains à grande vitesse*) shoot along at an average of 180mph when they're not breaking world records. The journey from Paris Gare de Montparnasse on the TGV Atlantique to Bordeaux takes 2hrs 58mins, and continues on to Toulouse in slightly under 5hrs; branches race to Tarbes in about 6hrs, and to Dax, Bayonne and Biarritz. Travel costs are only minimally higher on a TGV than on slower trains; some weekday departures require a supplement and all require **seat reservations**, which you can make when you buy your ticket or at the station before departure. Another pleasant way of getting there is by overnight **sleeper** (the slower trains for the southwest all depart from the Gare d'Austerlitz in Paris).

People aged under 26 are eligible for a discount on fares (see the travel agencies listed above) and there are other **discounts** if you're aged over 65 available from major travel agents.

You can **book tickets** for through-journeys from outside France. In the UK tickets can be booked from any British Rail station or travel centre, or from the **International Rail Centre, Victoria Station**, **t** (020) 7834 2345. You can also visit the **Rail Europe Travel Shop**, 179 Piccadilly, **t** 08702 41 42 43, or book on-line at *www.raileurope.co.uk*. or *www.sncf.fr*.

SNCF central reservations and information is available on **t** 08 36 35 35 35, 7am–10pm daily. If you reserve by phone or Minitel (3615 SNCF), you must pick up and pay for your ticket within 48 hours.

If you plan on making several long train journeys, look into the variety of **rail passes**; note that France has now pulled out of the Eurodomino scheme. Visitors from North America have a wide choice, including Eurail pass, Flexipass and Saverpass, which can all be purchased in the USA; call **t** (877) 257 2887, *www.raileurope. com/us/index.htm*. A variety of passes and discounts are available once within France (*see* p.63).

You must always '*composter votre billet*' (**date-stamp your ticket** in the orange *composteur* machine at the station) before starting your journey.

For long-distance train travel, **bicycles** need to be transported separately, and must be registered and insured. Trains marked with a bicycle symbol on the timetable let you put the bike in the luggage van. They can be delivered to your destination within 3 days for €49. On Eurostar you need to check in your bike at least 24 hours before you travel, or wait 24 hours at the other end.

By Ferry

Two ferry companies make the journey from Britain to northern Spain, from where it's a short car journey to the Pyrenees.

Brittany Ferries, t (08705) 561 600, *www. brittanyferries.com*, sail from Plymouth to Santander, and offer excellent standards including air-conditioned en suite cabins, a choice of restaurants, cinemas, swimming pool and sauna.

P&O Ferries, t (0870) 129 6002, *www. poferries.com*, sail from Portsmouth to Bilbao; their *Pride of Bilbao* is the UK's largest ferry, with accommodation for 2,500 passengers and 600 cars; it offers several restaurants, a cinema, sauna, swimming pool, and has cabins for all passengers.

If you prefer to cross the Channel, Brittany Ferries sail from Portsmouth to Caen and St-Malo, Poole to Cherbourg and St-Malo, and Plymouth to Roscoff; P&O can transport you from Dover to Calais and from Portsmouth to Le Havre and Cherbourg.

By Coach

The cheapest way to get from London to southwest France might be by **National Express Eurolines** coach, **t** 08705 80 80 80. *www.eurolines.co.uk*, in the UK; tickets are available from any National Express office. There are at least three journeys a week from London to Bordeaux and down the Landes to the Pays Basque and San Sebastian (26hrs) and to Toulouse (22hrs). The trip is long and slow but has an open return and saves you the hassle of crossing Paris to change trains. On the other hand the cheap flights offered by Ryanair, Flybe and easyJet often beat the coach hands down, especially out of season.

By Car

A car entering France must have its **registration** and **insurance papers**. If you're coming from the UK or Ireland, the dip of the headlights must be adjusted to the right. Carrying a warning triangle is mandatory, and it should be placed 50m behind the car if you have a breakdown. All cars in France are required to have rear seat belts and these must be worn by rear seat passengers. Drivers with a valid licence from an EU country,.

Canada, the USA or Australia don't need an international licence. If you plan to hire a car, look into air and holiday package deals to save money, or consider leasing a car if you mean to stay three weeks or more. Prices vary widely from firm to firm, and beware the small print about service charges and taxes.

If you're driving down from the UK you may face going through or around Paris on the abominable *périphérique*, a task best tackled on either side of rush hour. To avoid it, seasoned travellers favour the Portsmouth–Caen ferry, offering a direct and not too frenetic drive via Le Mans, Tours and Poitiers. Caen (360 miles to Périgueux) and Le Havre (390 miles to Périgueux) are the closest Channel ports to the southwest. From Caen or Le Havre take the N158/N138 to Le Mans and Tours, and continue on the N10 to Poitiers, from where you can branch off for Bordeaux, via Angoulême.

Another Bordeaux alternative is the *autoroute* A10 from Tours. If you're visiting the west end of the region, you might also consider sailing to St-Malo and taking in Rennes, Nantes, La Rochelle and Saintes, and picking up the A10 there towards Bordeaux. Another option is taking the ferry from Plymouth to Bilbao, which will leave you only a three- to four-hour drive to Biarritz.

The **Channel tunnel** is another option. Eurotunnel carries cars and their passengers from Folkestone to Calais on a simple drive-on-drive-off system (journey time 35mins). Payment is made at toll booths (which accept cash, cheques or credit cards). Prepaid tickets and booked spaces are available, but not necessary. Eurotunnel runs 24 hours, all year round, with a service at least once an hour through the night. **UK Terminal**, PO Box 2000, Folkestone, Kent CT18 8XY, **t** (01303) 282 222, *www.eurotunnel.com*.

Getting Around

By Train

SNCF general information: t 08 36 35 35 35, *www.sncf.com*.

The southwest has a decent network of trains, although many of the smaller lines have only two or three connections a day, making it rather difficult to see much of the

Discount Rail Fares

Découverte discounts are free, but only available on tickets booked in advance. The annual *cartes* must be paid for. Ask about extra perks with the *cartes*, such as Avis car hire, discounts on hotels, and on Corsica ferries.

Découverte Séjour Return journeys of at least 200km, comprising one night's stay-over at the weekend, entitle you to a 25% discount if you depart during a *période bleue*.

Découverte à Deux If two people (related or not) make a return trip together, including a one-night minimum stay-over at the weekend, they are eligible for a 25% discount on first or second class for journeys begun in blue periods.

Découverte Enfant+ A 25% discount for one child under 12 accompanied by up to 4 people.

Découverte 12–25 Young people are eligible for a 25% discount if they buy their ticket in advance and begin travel in a *période bleue*.

Carte 12–25 Young people 12–25, travelling frequently, can purchase this card for €49; it's good for a year and gives a 25–50% discount on all trains and 2% reduction on Avis car hire.

Carte Enfant+ This card is issued in the name of a child under 12, costs €65 and allows the child and up to 4 people who travel with them up to a 50% discount on TGVs and other trains. It is valid for one year and entitles you to a discount on Avis car hire. Travel is free for under-4s.

Carte Sénior People over 60 can purchase this for €53. Valid for a year, it entitles you to 25–50% discounts on travel, plus 25% when travelling by train abroad if the railway adheres to Rail Plus, and a 25% discount on Avis car hire and Mercure hotels, among other offers.

Senior Découverte Eligibility for 25% off the journey for those over 60, travelling in *périodes bleues*, plus a discount on Avis car hire.

Grand Voyageur A €30 card valid for 3 years for those travelling at least twice a month, and offering various services to make travel easier.

Carte Escapades A card for 26–29-year-olds, costing €85 a year, giving 25–40% reduction on travel covering at least 200km (return) and a stay-over at the weekend, plus a 20% reduction on Avis car hire.

country by rail; in places SNCF buses have taken over former train routes. Prices, if not a bargain, are still reasonable, and **discounts** are available especially if you travel off-peak in a *période bleue*. *See* box, above.

Tickets must be **stamped** in the little orange machines by the door to the tracks that say *Compostez votre billet* (this puts the date on the ticket, to keep you from using the same one over and over again). Any time you interrupt a journey until another day, you have to re-*composter* your ticket.

Long-distance **Trains Corails** can be utterly delightful when they aren't too crowded. They have snack trolleys and bar/cafeteria cars (the food isn't bad), and some offer play areas for small children.

Nearly every station has banks of mechanical **lockers** (*consignes automatiques*) that spit out a slip with the lock combination when you use them; they take about half an hour to puzzle out the first time you use them, so plan accordingly.

By Bus

Do not count on seeing any part of rural France by public transport. The bus network is barely adequate between major cities and towns (places often already well-served by rail) and rotten in rural areas, where the one bus a day fits in with the school schedule, leaving at the crack of dawn and returning in the afternoon; more remote villages are linked to civilization only once a week or not at all.

Buses are run either by the SNCF (replacing discontinued rail routes) or private firms. **Rail passes** are valid on SNCF lines and they generally coincide with trains. Private bus firms, especially when they have a monopoly, tend to be a bit more expensive than trains; some towns have a *gare routière* (coach station), usually near the train station, while in others the buses stop at bars or any other place that catches their fancy. Stops are hardly ever marked, while on the other hand in some areas there are conspicuous bus stops everywhere, where in fact no service exists. The posted schedules are not always to be trusted. The tourist office or shops near the bus stop may have a more accurate instinct for when a bus is likely to appear.

By Car

Unless you plan to stick to the major towns, cycle, or walk, a car is regrettably the only way to see the southwest. This too has its drawbacks: relatively high rental car rates and quite expensive petrol, and an accident rate higher than that of the UK (and much higher than the USA). Recent government crackdowns to reduce deaths on the road have improved driving standards but it is still true to say that the vaunted French logic and clarity breaks down completely on the asphalt. Go slowly and be careful; never expect any French driver to be aware of the possibility of a collision.

Roads are generally excellently maintained, but anything of less status than a departmental route (D road) may be uncomfortably narrow. **Petrol stations** are rare in rural areas and they are closed on Sunday afternoons, so consider your fuel supply while planning any forays into the back country. The scoundrels will expect a tip for oil, windscreen-cleaning or air. The price of petrol (*essence*) varies considerably, with motorways always more expensive.

France used to have a rule of giving priority to the right at every intersection. This has largely disappeared, although there may still be intersections, usually in towns, where it applies – these will be marked. Watch out for the *Cédez le passage* (Give way) signs and be careful. Generally, as you'd expect, give priority to the main road, and to the left on roundabouts. If you are new to France, think of every intersection as a new and perilous experience. Watch out for byzantine street parking rules (which would take pages to explain: do as the natives do, and be especially careful about village centres on market days).

Unless sweetened in an air- or holiday-package deal, **car hire** in France can be an expensive proposition. Try ADA, *www.ada.fr*, which has cars from €55/day up to 200km, cheaper if you reserve 2 weeks ahead and for longer hire periods.

Speed limits are 130km/80mph on the *autoroutes* (toll motorways); 110km/69mph on dual carriageways (divided highways); 90km/55mph on other roads; 50km/30mph in an 'urbanized area': as soon as you pass a white sign with a town's name on it and until you pass another sign with the town's name barred. Fines for speeding, payable on the spot, can be astronomical if you flunk

Car Hire Offices in France
(from Toulouse airport)
ADA, t 05 61 30 00 33, *www.ada.fr*.
Avis, t 08 20 61 16 78, *www.avis.fr*.
Budget, t 05 61 71 85 80, *www.aplbudget.com*.
Europcar, t 08 25 82 55 14, *www.europecar.fr*.
Hertz, t 08 25 80 10 31, *www.hertz.fr*.

the breathalyzer. The French have one admirably civilized custom of the road; if oncoming drivers unaccountably flash their headlights at you, it means the *gendarmes* are about.

If you wind up in an **accident**, the procedure is to fill out and sign an official report called a *constat amiable*. If your French isn't sufficient to deal with this, hold off until you find someone to translate for you so you don't accidentally incriminate yourself.

If you have a **breakdown** and are a member of a motoring club affiliated to the Touring Club de France, ring the latter; if not, ring the police, **t** 17.

By Bicycle
Tour de France champions pump straight up the steepest Pyrenees, but if you're looking for something a bit less to a lot less challenging, you'll find it along the plethora of tiny rural roads in Gascony and foothills of the Pyrenees. French drivers, not always courteous to fellow motorists, usually give cyclists a wide berth.

Maps and info are available from the **Fédération Française de Cyclotourisme**, 12 rue Louis Bertrand, 94207 Ivry-sur-Seine, **t** 01 56 20 88 88, *www.ffct.org*; in Britain information on cycle-touring in France is available from the **Cyclists' Touring Club**, Parklands, Railton Rd, Guildford, Surrey GU2 9JX, **t** 0870 873 0060, *www.ctc.org.uk*.

Getting your own bike to France is reasonably easy: Air France and British Airways carry them free from Britain. From the USA or Australia most airlines will carry them as long as they're boxed and are including in your total baggage weight. In all cases, it is wise to telephone ahead. Certain French trains (marked with a bicycle symbol in the timetable) will carry bikes for free and you may be able to set them on a TGV or

Corail if they are folded, wrapped and the wheels removed.

Bike Hire

The French are keen cyclists, and if you haven't brought your own bike, the main towns and holiday centres always seem to have at least one shop that hires **mountain bikes** (VTT) or **touring/racing bikes**; local tourist offices have lists. Be prepared to pay a fairly hefty deposit on a good bike and you may want to enquire about theft insurance.

You can also hire bikes of widely varying quality (most of them 10-speed) at most SNCF stations and in major towns. The advantage of hiring from a station means that you can drop it off at another, as long as you specify where when you hire it. Rates run at around €10 a day.

On Foot

A network of long-distance paths, the *Grandes Randonnées*, or GRs for short (marked by distinctive red and white signs), take in some of the most beautiful scenery in Gascony and the Pyrenees, and the Pyrenees make up some of the most gorgeous walking territory in Europe. Each GR is described in a Topoguide, with maps and details about camping sites, *refuges*, *gîtes d'étape* and so on, available in area bookshops or from the **Federation Française de la Randonnée Pédestre**, 64 Rue du Dessous des Berges, 75013 Paris, t 01 44 89 93 93, *www.ffrp.asso.fr*. A good source in the UK is **Stanford's International Map Centre**, 12–14 Long Acre, London, WC2E 9LP, t (020) 7836 1321, *www.stanfords.co.uk*.

The most popular trail is the **GR 10**, which goes straight across the Pyrenees, passing through many villages, and is accessible to any fit walker; also the more difficult **Haute Randonnée Pyrénéenne**, higher up and more or less following the French-Spanish frontier, and passing through fewer villages.

In the Pyrenees, the best maps and trail guides and much of the mountain accommodation is administered by the **Randonnées Pyrénéennes**, and there are a number of places that can give you all the details, among them the **Centre d'Information sur la Montagne et les Sentiers**

(CIMES), 4 rue Maye Lane, 65420 Ibos, t 05 62 90 09 92. In the Ariège, pick up *L'Ariège à Pied* (€14.50) from the **Comité Départemental Ariègeois de la Randonnée Pédestre**, 17 cours Irénée Cros, 09000 Foix, t 05 34 09 02 09, *www.cdrp09.com*.

Where to Stay

Hotels

Like most countries in Europe, the tourist authorities grade hotels by their facilities (not by charm or location) with **stars** from four to one. There are even some cheap but adequate places undignified by any stars at all. Some places with good facilities have no stars at all, simply because the hotel owners have not applied to be graded.

Almost every establishment has a wide range of rooms and prices – a very useful and logical way of doing things, once you're used to it. In some hotels, every single room has its own personality and the difference in quality and price can be enormous; a large room with antique furniture, a television or a balcony over the sea and a complete bathroom can cost much more than a poky back room in the same hotel, with a window overlooking a car park, no antiques, and the WC down the hall. Some proprietors will drag out a sort of menu for you to choose what sort of price and facilities you would like. Most two-star hotel rooms have their own showers and WCs; most one-stars offer rooms with or without. The following guide will give you an idea of what prices to expect from the different star ratings. Throughout the guide, we state the price ranges of hotels according to the list below, and give the star rating as well.

Although it's impossible to be more precise, we can add a few more generalizations. **Single** rooms are relatively rare, and usually two-thirds the price of a double, and rarely will a hotelier give you a discount if only doubles are available (again, because each room has its own price); on the other hand, if there are three or four of you, triples or quads or adding extra beds to a double room is usually cheaper than staying in two rooms. **Prices** are posted at the reception desk and in the rooms to keep the management honest.

Hotel Price Ranges

Note that prices listed here and elsewhere in this book are for a double room in high season.

luxury	€€€€€	€230+
very expensive	€€€€	€150–230
expensive	€€€	€100–150
moderate	€€	€60–100
inexpensive	€	under €60

Flowered wallpaper, usually beige, comes in all rooms at no extra charge – it's an essential part of the French experience. Breakfast (usually coffee, a croissant, bread and jam for €4–6) is nearly always optional: you'll do as well for less in a bar. As usual rates rise in the busy season (holidays and summer, and in the winter around ski resorts), when many hotels with restaurants will require that you take **half-board** (*demi-pension* – breakfast and a set lunch or dinner). Many hotel restaurants are superb and described in the text; non-guests are welcome. At worst the food will be boring, and it can be monotonous eating in the same place every night when there are so many tempting restaurants around. Don't be put off by obligatory dining. It's traditional; French hoteliers think of themselves as innkeepers, in the old-fashioned way. In the off-season board requirements vanish into thin air.

Your holiday will be much sweeter if you **book ahead**, especially from May to October. July and August are the only really impossible months; otherwise it usually isn't too difficult to find something. Phoning ahead a day or two is always a good policy, although beware that hotels will usually only confirm a room on receipt of a cheque covering the first night (not a credit card number). Tourist offices have lists of accommodation in their given areas or even *départements*, which come in handy during the peak season; many will even call around and book a room for you on the spot for free or a nominal fee.

Chain hotels (Climate, Formula One, etc.) are in most cities, but always dreary and geared to the business traveller more than the tourist, so you won't find them in this book. Don't confuse chains with the various umbrella organizations like Logis et Auberges de France, Relais de Silence, or the prestigious Relais et Châteaux, which promote and guarantee the quality of independently owned hotels and their restaurants. Many are recommended in the text. Larger tourist offices usually stock their booklets, or you can pick them up before you leave from the French National Tourist Office.

Bed and Breakfast

In rural areas, there are plenty of opportunities for a stay in a private home or farm. *Chambres d'hôtes*, in the tourist office brochures, are listed separately from hotels with the various *gîtes* (*see* below). Some are connected to *ferme-auberge* restaurants, others to wine estates or a château; prices tend to be moderate to inexpensive. Local tourist offices will usually provide you with a list if you ask them.

Youth Hostels, *Gîtes d'Etape*, and *Refuges*

Most cities have **youth hostels** (*Auberges de Jeunesse*) which offer dormitory accommodation and breakfast to people of any age for around €12 a night. Most offer kitchen facilities as well, or inexpensive meals. They are the best deal going for people travelling on their own; for people travelling together a one-star hotel can be just as cheap. You should also bear in mind that most are in the most ungodly locations – in the suburbs where the last bus goes by at 7pm, or miles from any transport at all in the country. In the summer the only way to be sure of a room is to arrive early in the day. To stay in most hostels you need to be a member of Hostelling International, which you join by becoming a member of your national YHA organization. Contact the following for more information:

Fédération Unie des Auberges de Jeunesse (FUAJ), 27 Rue Pajol, 75018 Paris, **t** (01) 44 89 87 27, *www.fuaj.org*.

Youth Hostels Association (YHA), Trevelyan House, Dimple Rd, Matlock, Derbyshire, DE4 3YH, **t** (01629) 592600.

American Youth Hostelling International, 733 15th St NW, Suite 840, Washington, DC 20005, **t** (202) 783 6161, *www.hiayh.org*.

Another option in cities are single sex dormitories for young workers, **Foyers de Jeunes Travailleurs et de Jeunes Travailleuses,** which rent out individual rooms if available for slightly more than a youth hostel.

A *gîte d'étape* (www.gite-etape.com) is a simple shelter with bunk beds (but no bedding) and a rudimentary self-catering kitchen set up by a village along GR walking paths or scenic bike routes. In the Pyrenees, the *gîtes d'étape* are administered by the *Randonnées Pyrénéennes*. Again, lists are available for each *département*; the detailed maps mentioned on p.65 mark them as well. In the mountains similar rough shelters along the GR paths are called *refuges*; most of them are open in summer only. Both charge around €10–18 a night.

Camping

Camping is a very popular way to travel, especially among the French themselves, and there's at least one campsite in every town, often an inexpensive, no-frills site run by the town (Camping Municipal). Other campsites are graded with stars like hotels from four to one: at the top of the line you can expect lots of trees and grass, hot showers, a pool or beach, sports facilities, and a grocer's, bar, and/or restaurant, and prices rather similar to one-star hotels (although these, of course, never have all the extras). Camping on a farm is especially big in the southwest, and is usually less expensive than organized sites. If you want to camp wild, it's imperative to ask permission from the landowner first, or you risk a furious farmer, his dog and perhaps even the police.

Tourist offices have complete lists of campsites in their regions. If you plan to move around a lot, the *Guide Officiel Camping/ Caravanning* is available in most French bookshops. Also see *www. campingfrance. com*. A number of UK holiday firms book camping holidays and offer discounts on Channel ferries: **Canvas Holidays, t** 0870 192 1154, *www.canvasholidays.co.uk*; **Eurocamp**

Travel, t 0870 901 9410, *www.eurocamp.co.uk*; **Keycamp Holidays, t** 0870 700 0740, *www. keycamp. co.uk*. The French National Tourist Office has complete lists. The Michelin Green Guide: *Camping/Caravanning France* is very informative and also lists sites with facilities suitable for disabled visitors. In the UK, a couple of useful organizations are **Camping and Caravanning Club**, Greenfields House, Westwood Way, Coventry CV4 8JH, t 0845 130 7631; and **Caravan Club**, East Grinstead House, East Grinstead, Sussex RH19 1UA.

Gîtes de France and Other Self-catering Accommodation

Southwest France offers a vast range of self-catering accommodation, from inexpensive farm cottages to history-laden châteaux and fancy villas, or even on board canal boats. The **Fédération Nationale des Gîtes de France** is a French government service offering inexpensive accommodation by the week in rural areas. Lists with photos for each *département* are available from the French National Tourist Office, from most local tourist offices, or in the UK from the official rep: **Maison de la France**, 178 Piccadilly, London W1J 9AL, t 09068 244 123. In France, contact the **Maison des Gîtes de France**, 59 Rue St-Lazare, 75009 Paris, t 01 49 70 75 75. Prices range from €250–1,000 a week, depending very much on the time of year as well as facilities; nearly always you'll be expected to begin your stay on a Saturday.

Many *départements* also have a second (and usually less expensive) listing of *gîtes* in a guide, *Clévacances, www.clevacances.com*.

The Sunday papers are full of options, or contact one of the firms listed below. The accommodation they offer will nearly always be more comfortable and costly than a *gîte*, but the discounts holiday firms offer on the ferries, plane tickets or car rentals can make up for the price difference.

Specialist Tour Operators

There are a number of ways to combine a holiday with a special interest. For more information, contact the **Cultural Services of the French Consulate**, 23 Cromwell Rd, London SW7 2DQ, t (020) 7073 1300, or at 4101 Reservoir Rd NW, Washington, DC 20007, t (202) 944 6400.

In the UK

Bike and Sun Tours, 42 Whitby Ave, Guisborough TS14 7AN, t (01287) 639 739, *www.bikeandsuntours.co.uk*, arranges two-week guided motorcycle tours in the Pyrenees.

Erna Low Consultants, 9 Reece Mews, London SW7 3HE, t (0207) 594 0290, *www.ernalow. co.uk*, provides spa holidays in Biarritz.

Exodus Travel, 9 Weir Rd, London SW12 0LT, t (020) 8675 5550, *www.exodustravel.co.uk*, arranges easy to strenuous trekking, skiing, snow-shoeing and riding in the Pyrenees.

French Expressions, 13 McCrone Mews, Belsize Lane, London NW3 5BG, t (020) 7431 1312, plans tailor-made tours to the Basque country.

Headwater Holidays, The Old School House, Chester Rd, Castle, Northwich, Cheshire CW8 1LE, t (01606) 720 033, *www.headwater.com*, organizes unescorted walking in the Pyrenees.

Inntravel, Hovingham, York YO60 7JU, t (01653) 617 949, *www.inntravel.co.uk*, arranges walking holidays in the Pyrenees.

St Peter's Pilgrims, 87A Rushey Green, London SE6 4AF, t (020) 8244 8844, *www.stpeter.co.uk*, organizes pilgrimages to Lourdes by air for three, four or seven nights.

In the USA/Canada

Du Vine Adventures, 124 Holland St, Suite 2, Somerville, MA 02144, USA, t (617) 776 4441, *www.duvine.com/bordeauxhotels.html*. Tours and holidays focusing on châteaux and wine.

Self-catering Operators

Companies are springing up offering information and on-line booking only. Try *www.francedirect.co.uk*, who have a large selection of cottages and villas.

In the UK

Allez France, Cutters House, 1560 Parkway, Solent Business Park, Fareham, Hants PO15 7AG, t 0845 330 2056, *www.allezfrance.com*, offers a wide variety of accommodation, from apartments to *gîtes*, villas and cottages.

Bowhills Holidays, Mayhill Farm, Mayhill Lane, Swanmore, Southampton SO32 2QW, t 0870

235 2727, *www.bowhills.co.uk*, arranges accommodation from simple two-bed cottages to 12-bed luxury.

Dominique's Villas, The Plough Brewery, 516 Wandsworth Rd, London SW8 3JX, *www.dominiquesvillas.co.uk*, has several large châteaux around Auch.

French Life Holidays, Spring Mill, Earby, Barnoldswick, Lancs BB94 0AA, t 0870 197 6675, *www.frenchlife.co.uk*, offers quality self-catering accommodation throughout the region.

Gascony Secret, The Stonehouse, Windsor Green, Cockfield, Suffolk IP30 0LY, t (01284) 827253, *www.gascony-secret.com*, *gîtes*, cottages and châteaux in Gers, Hautes-Pyrénées and Ariège.

Just France, Gemini House, 10–18 Putney Hill, London SW15 6AX, t (020) 8780 4480, *www.justfrance.co.uk*, self-catering villas and cottages in the Landes.

VFB Holidays, Normandy House, High St, Cheltenham GL50 3FB, t (01242) 240340, *www.vfbholidays.co.uk*, arranges accommodation from rustic *gîtes* to luxurious farmhouses.

In the USA

France by Heart, PO Box 614, Mill Valle, CA 94942, t (415) 331 3075, *www.francebyheart.com*. More than 200 properties throughout the country.

Hideaways International, 767 Islington St, Portsmouth, NH 03801, t (603) 430 4433, *www.hideaways.com*. Villas, farmhouses and châteaux throughout France.

At Home Abroad, 405 East 56th St, New York, NY 10022, t (212) 421 9165, *www.athomeabroadinc.com*.

Practical A–Z

SPAIN

06

Imperial–Metric Conversions

Length (multiply by)
Inches to centimetres: 2.54
Centimetres to inches: 0.39
Feet to metres: 0.3
Metres to feet: 3.28
Yards to metres: 0.91
Metres to yards: 1.1
Miles to kilometres: 1.61
Kilometres to miles: 0.62

Area (multiply by)
Inches square to centimetres square: 6.45
Centimetres square to inches square: 0.15
Feet square to metres square: 0.09
Metres square to feet square: 10.76
Miles square to kilometres square: 2.59
Kilometres square to miles square: 0.39
Acres to hectares: 0.40
Hectares to acres: 2.47

Weight (multiply by)
Ounces to grams: 28.35
Grams to ounces: 0.035
Pounds to kilograms: 0.45
Kilograms to pounds: 2.2
Stones to kilograms: 6.35
Kilograms to stones: 0.16
Tons (UK) to kilograms: 1,016
Kilograms to tons (UK): 0.0009
1 UK ton (2,240lbs) = 1.12 US tonnes (2,000lbs)

Volume (multiply by)
Pints (UK) to litres: 0.57
Litres to pints (UK): 1.76
Quarts (UK) to litres: 1.13
Litres to quarts (UK): 0.88
Gallons (UK) to litres: 4.55
Litres to gallons (UK): 0.22
1 UK pint/quart/gallon =
1.2 US pints/quarts/gallons

Temperature
Celsius to Fahrenheit:
multiply by 1.8 then
add 32

Fahrenheit to Celsius:
subtract 32 then multiply
by 0.55

France Information

Time Differences
Country: + 1hr GMT; + 6hrs EST
Daylight saving from last weekend in March
to end of October

Dialling Codes
Note: omit first zero of area code
France country code 33
To France from: UK, Ireland, New Zealand 00 /
USA, Canada 011 / Australia 0011 then dial 33
and the full number without the initial zero
From France to: UK 00 44; Ireland 00 353; USA,
Canada 001; Australia 00 61; New Zealand 00
64 then the number without the initial zero
Directory enquiries: 118 000
International directory enquiries: 00 33 12

Emergency Numbers
Police: 17
Ambulance: 15
Fire: 18
Car breakdown: 0870 737 5720

Embassy Numbers in France
UK: 05 57 22 21 10; **Ireland** 01 44 17 67 00;
USA: 05 34 41 36 50; **Canada** 01 44 43 29 00;
Australia 01 40 59 33 00; **NZ** 01 45 01 43 43

Shoe Sizes
Europe	UK	USA
35	2½ / 3	4
36	3 / 3½	4½ / 5
37	4	5½ / 6
38	5	6½
39	5½ / 6	7 / 7½
40	6 / 6½	8 / 8½
41	7	9 / 9½
42	8	9½ / 10
43	9	10½
44	9½ / 10	11
45	10½	12
46	11	12½ / 13

Women's Clothing
Europe	UK	USA
32	6	2
34	8	4
36	10	6
38	12	8
40	14	10
42	16	12

Crime and the Police

Police t 17

Southwest France isn't exactly a high crime area. Isolated holiday homes get burgled, as anywhere else; cars are occasionally broken into or stolen. Generally the police are more annoying than the crooks, especially the customs officers; these can turn up anywhere in the interior, and they have nothing better to do than arbitrarily stop cars from outside their department and give them the once-over. Report **thefts** to the nearest *gendarmerie*: not a pleasant task but the reward is the bit of paper you need for an insurance claim. If your passport is stolen, contact the police and your nearest consulate for emergency travel documents. By law, the police in France can stop anyone anywhere and demand ID; in practice, they tend only to do it to harass minorities, the homeless, and scruffy hippy types. If they really don't like the look of you they can salt you away for a long time without any reason.

The **drug** situation is the same in France as anywhere in the West: soft and hard drugs are widely available, and the police only make an issue of victimless crime when it suits them (your being a foreigner may just arouse them to action). Smuggling any amount of marijuana into the country can mean a prison term, and there's not much your consulate can or will do about it.

Eating Out

The French tend to eat quite early, often at 12 or 12.30 for **lunch**, and generally between 7 and 9pm in the evening, with slightly later summer hours for **dinner**. Brasseries and cafés are flexible and open long hours, but restaurants don't often like serving late. Most restaurants recommended in this book offer a choice of set-price menus, and these are the prices we provide to give a rough idea of cost. Most places post their menus outside the door so you know what to expect. If service is included it will say *service compris* or s.c.; if not, *service non compris* or s.n.c.

For more on eating in the Gascony and the Pyrenees, including specialities, wines and a menu decoder, *see* **Food and Drink**, pp.44–52.

Electricity

The electric current in France is 220 volts. British and Irish visitors with appliances from home will need two-pin European plug adaptors (readily available in supermarkets if you don't bring one), and North Americans with 110v equipment will normally need a voltage transformer as well.

Health

Ambulance (SAMU) **t 15**
Fire t 18

Local hospitals are the place to go in an **emergency** (*urgence*). Doctors take turns going on duty at night and on holidays even in rural areas: pharmacies will know who to contact or else telephone the local **SOS Médecins** – if you don't have access to a phone book or Minitel, dial directory assistance t 118 000. To be on the safe side, always carry a phone card (see 'Post Offices', p.72; 'Telephones', p.76). If it's not an emergency, pharmacies have addresses of local doctors (including those who speak English), or outpatient clinics (*Centres Hospitaliers*). **Pharmacists** themselves are trained to administer first aid, and dispense free advice for minor problems. In cities pharmacies open at night on a rotating basis; addresses are posted in their windows or in the local newspaper. In most rural pharmacies you can ring the doorbell after hours and roust out the pharmacist on duty.

For information on EHIC cards and health insurance, *see* p.59.

Internet

The old saying that it doesn't pay to be first certainly applies to France with its national

Restaurant Price Categories

The Toulouse section of this guide divides restaurants into the categories shown below (for full meal, per person, but not including wine); *à la carte* is normally more expensive. Prices for restaurants in other regions are shown within the individual listing.

very expensive	€€€€	over €60
expensive	€€€	€30–60
moderate	€€	€15–30
inexpensive	€	below €15

computer system, the Minitel, which was distributed to every phone subscriber in the 1980s. Next to the Internet it seems a Neanderthal, but its presence considerably slowed French interest in the Internet. This is changing fast; most cities and towns now have **cybercafés** (the tourist office will give you a list), and most hotels have their own websites with online booking.

Opening Hours, Museums and National Holidays

Most, though not all, **shops** are closed down on Sunday and some Mondays. In many towns Sunday morning is a big shopping period. **Markets** (daily in the cities, weekly in villages) are usually open mornings only, although clothes, flea and antique markets run into the afternoon. In the summer you may find evening markets.

Museums, with a few exceptions, close for lunch as well, and often on Mondays or Tuesdays, and sometimes for all of November or the entire winter. Hours change with the season: longer summer hours begin in May or June and last until September – usually. Some change their hours every month. We've done our best to include them in the text, but don't be surprised if they're not exactly right. Most close on national holidays and give discounts if you have a student ID card, or are an EU citizen under 18 or over 65 years old; most charge admission.

National Holidays

Banks, shops and businesses close on national holidays; some museums also close, but most restaurants stay open. These holidays are:

1 January
Easter Sunday
Easter Monday
1 May
8 May (VE Day)
Ascension Day
Pentecost and the following Monday
14 July (Bastille Day)
15 August (Assumption)
1 November (All Saints')
11 November (First World War Armistice)
Christmas Day

Churches are usually open all day, or closed all day and only open for Mass. Sometimes notes on the door direct you to the *mairie* or priest (*presbytère*) where you can pick up the key. If not, ask at the nearest house – they may well have it. There are often admission fees for cloisters, crypts and special chapels.

Post Offices

Known as the PTT or Bureau de Poste and marked by a kind of blue bird on a yellow background, French **post offices** in the cities are open Mon–Fri 8am–7pm, Sat 8am–12. In villages offices may not open until 9am, close for lunch, and close at 4.30 or 5. You can receive mail *poste restante* at any of them; the postal codes in this book should help your mail get there in a timely fashion. To collect it, bring some ID. You can buy stamps in tobacconists as well as post offices.

Post offices offer free use of a **Minitel** electronic directory; they've done away with printed directories, and using these slow, cumbersome and complicated technological marvels can be a major nuisance. Offices usually have at least one telephone booth with a meter – the easiest way to phone overseas.

Sports and Activities

The great outdoors is one of the main reasons for visiting this corner of France, with its rare combination of ocean, lakes, rivers and mountains. Below is a far from all-inclusive listing of possibilities.

Bicycling

For doing it yourself, *see* 'Getting Around', p.64. Any mountain resort of any size will rent out **VTT**, or mountain bikes. In the summer throngs come down to watch the Tour de France, which usually tackles at least the near-vertical Col de Peyresourde.
Fédération Française de Cyclotourisme, 12 rue Louis Bertrand, 94207 Ivry-sur-Seine, t 01 56 20 88 88, *www.ffct.org*.

Bullfights

Aficionados call the *corrida* an art, not a sport, and it's big in Dax, Mont-de-Marsan, Bayonne, Estang and Vic-Fézensac. Many people in the region prefer the bloodless *course landaise* (*see* pp.36–7).

Bungee-jumping

According to the Académie Française, this is called *saut à l'élastique*. You can do it at Le Mas-d'Azil in the Ariège from the Pont Napoléon in Luz-St-Sauveur (Hautes-Pyrénées) and Pont de la Baillanouse, Prats-de-Mollo-la-Preste (Pyrénées-Orientates), *www.saut-elastique.com.*

Canoeing and Kayaking

The **Fédération Française de Canoë-Kayak** is at 87 Quai de la Marne, 94340 Joinville-le-Pont, t 01 45 11 08 50, *www.ffck.org.*

In the Hautes-Pyrénées, contact **Le Relais d'Isaby**, Villelongue, t 05 62 92 20 77, *www.isaby.asso.fr.*

The Leyre, in the **Parc Naturel des Landes de Gascogne**, offers genteel five-day canoe trips (*see* pp.86 and 93).

Canyoning

Outings and all the necessary equipment are provided by **Loisirs Aventures** at St Lary (*see* 'white-water rafting, p. 75); **Adrénaline Passion**, at Sarrancolin, t 05 62 98 73 25; and, for Luz and the Gavarnie, with the **Bureau des Guides**, Luz-St-Saveur, t 05 62 92 87 28, all in the Hautes-Pyrénées.

Car-racing

You can get a taste for this at Nogaro in the Gers, in a Clio RS21 Renault Sport or a Formule Renault, *www.circuit-nogaro.com.*

Caves

Speleology, potholing, spelunking – whatever you want to call it, it's very popular. Options include **Sports Aventure in St Girons**, Ariège, t 05 61 96 08 22 or **Cocktail Aventure** at Herran, Haute-Garonne, t 05 61 97 52 74.

Fédération Française de Spéléologie, 28 rue Delandine, Lyon, t 04 72 56 09 63, *http://ffspeleo.fr.*

Comité de Spéléologie Régionale Midi-Pyrénées, 7 Rue André-Citroën, 31130 Balma, t 08 73 18 03 28, *http://comite.speleo.midipy.free.fr.*

Deep-sea Diving

The Côte Basque has a number of schools and hires out equipment: try the **Union Sportive de Biarritz**, *http://union.sportive.free.fr*, Allée des Passereaux, t 05 59 03 29 29.

Fédération Française d'Etudes et de Sports Sous-Marins, 24 Quai de Rive-Neuve, 13284 Marseille, t 04 91 33 99 31, *www.ffessm.fr.*

Fishing

You can fish in the sea without a permit as long as your catch is for local consumption. Freshwater fishing (extremely popular in this region of rivers and lakes) requires an easily obtained permit from a local club; tourist offices can tell you where to find them. Often the only outdoor vending machine in a town sells worms and other bait. Ocean-fishing excursions (for tuna and other denizens of the deep) are organized by the day and half-day, arranged in advance; contact local tourist offices for details.

Gambling

You'll find casinos with at least slot machines at the main coastal and mountain resorts or you can do as the locals do and play for a side of beef, a lamb or a VCR in a Loto, in a local café or municipal *salle de fêtes*. Loto is just like bingo, including the way some of the numbers have names: 11 is *las cambas de ma grand* (my grandmother's legs) and 75, the number of the *département* of Paris, is *los envaïssurs* (the invaders).

Golf

This is one of the prime golfing regions of France, with the oldest and most beautiful greens and fairways; the very first course in France is in Pau, and between Bordeaux and Biarritz you'll find 20 courses open to the public year-round; summer green fees for 18 holes are between €42 and €50. There are also courses in the mountains at Montrejeau and Luchon (Haute-Garonne), and La Bastide de Serou (Ariège), Laloubère, near Tarbes, and Lourdes (Hautes-Pyrénées), Auch, Eauze, L'Isle-Jourdain, Fleurance and Masseube.

Fédération Française de Golfe, 68 rue Anatole France, 92300 Levallois-Perret, t 01 41 49 77 00, *www.ffgolf.org.*

Horse-riding

Each tourist office has a list of Centres Hippiques or Centres Equestres that hire out horses. Most offer group excursions, although if you prove yourself an experienced rider you can usually head off down the trails on your own.

Fédération des Randonneurs Equestres, 10 route de St Gaux, 33340 St Germain d'Esteuil, **t** 06 70 07 39 02, *www.fref-france.com*.

Parachuting

Lessons for beginners (minimum age 15), jumps and gear are available from the **Centre Ecole de Parachutisme du Bassin d'Arcachon**, Aérodrome de Villemarie, La Teste 33260, **t** 05 56 54 73 11.

Paragliding, Hang-gliding and Microlites

Paragliding (*parapente*), a cross between parachuting and hang-gliding, has become quite popular in the Pyrenees year-round: the *parapente* itself weighs only 3 to 5kg and folds into a backpack; you ski or run down a slope until lifted off the ground, and with a good updraft sail several miles before gently descending. Because of the volatile winds near the coast, paragliding is restricted to the higher Pyrenees. Learn how to do it at **Les Aigles de Montcalm** at Auzat, Ariége, **t** 05 61 04 87 53, or you can try **Gypaetes** in Foix **t** 06 78 55 39 26, *www.gypaetes.com*. In the Hautes-Pyrénées, try **Air Aventures Pyrénées**, Luz, **t** 05 62 92 91 60; or **Comme Un Oiseau**, Aucun, **t** 05 62 97 47 63.

For Microlite clubs (ULM in French), in the Pays Basque, try **Planet'Air**, chemin de Brané, Navarrenx, **t** 05 59 66 23 37.

Pelote and Basque Sports

See pp.173–4.

Pétanque

Like *pastis* and a twangy lilting accent, *pétanque* is one of the essential ingredients of the whole south of France, and even the smallest village has a rough, hard court under the plane trees for its practitioners – nearly all male, although women are welcome to join in. It's similar to *boules*: the object is to get your metal ball closest to the marker (*bouchon* or *cochonnet*). Tournaments are frequent and well attended.

Rock-climbing (*Escalade*)

The French love to dress up in bright colours and climb and dangle up vertical rock faces. If you want to join them, a place to try with rock faces of varying levels of difficulty is the **Bureau des Guides**, 66 allées d'Etigny, Luchon, **t** 05 61 79 69 38; there's also the **Maison de Montaigne** at Luz-St-Sauveur, **t** 05 62 92 87 28, in the Hautes-Pyrénées.

Rugby

Since 1900 rugby, perfectly adapted to the Gascon temperament and broad-shouldered physique, has been the national sport of the southwest, the cradle of most of the players on the national team. There's a women's version without tackling called *barette*.

Sailing and Windsurfing

The *étangs*, or lakes, just along the inner edge of the sand dunes along the Côte d'Argent are ideal for easy sailing and windsurfing, or just learning how. The coast is framed on the north and south by ocean pleasure ports: Arcachon in the north and Guéthary, Hendaye and St-Jean-de-Luz in the south.

Skiing

The Pyrenees don't get as much of the white stuff as the Alps but in recent years snow cover has been good and snow canons help. The mountains in this book, the western and central Pyrenees, generally have the most snow. Besides skiing down pistes, the relative lack of avalanches and crevices make the Pyrenees perfect for off-piste, cross-country and mountaineering skiing. The ski station websites mostly post information about conditions and you can go down to the mountains and ringing around to see who has the best snow. Besides February, the busiest month (when French schools take their two-week ski holidays), finding accommodation on the spot usually isn't a problem. Just don't expect much

Alpine cuteness. For information on skiing in the French Pyrénées see *www.pyrenees-online.fr*. Resorts in this book from east to west are:

Ariège (*www.ariegepyrenees.com*): Ascou-Pailhères (1,500–2,000m), t 05 61 64 28 86; Ax-Bonascre (1,400–2,400m), t 05 61 64 60 60; Guzet (1,100–2,100m), t 05 61 96 00 11; Monts-d'Olmes (1,500–2,000m), t 05 34 09 86 28; Goulier-Neige (with a ski stadium, 1,500–2,000m), t 05 61 64 88 99; Mijanès-Donezan (downhill and cross-country, 1,530–2,000m), t 05 68 20 40 44; Chioula (cross-country only, 1,240–1,650m), t 05 61 64 20 20; Etang de Lers (cross-country and ice skating, 1,300–1,615m), t 05 61 04 91 13; Tour Lafont (cross-country, 1,250–1,500m), t 05 61 64 53 53; Plateau de Beille, the biggest cross-country station in the Pyrénées (1,800–2,000m), t 05 34 09 35 35. For general information, contact **Comité Departmentale du Tourisme**, 31 bis Ave du Général de Gaulle, Foix 09004, t 05 61 02 30 70.

Haute-Garonne (*www.cdt-haute-garonne.fr*): Bourg d'Oueil (1,200–1,600m), t 05 61 79 34 07; Luchon-Superbagnères (1,440–2,260m), t 05 61 79 11 23.

Hautes-Pyrénées (*www.pyrenees65.com*): La Mongie/Barèges, the biggest in the Pyrenees (1,250–2,500m), t 05 62 91 94 15; St-Lary-Soulan (1,700–2,400m), t 05 62 39 50 81; Gavarnie-Gèdre (one of the best for downhill and cross-country, bobsleighing and ice skating, 850–2,400m), t 05 62 92 48 05; Hautacam (1,500–1,810m), t 05 62 97 10 16; Cauterets (1,350–2,300m), t 05 62 92 50 50; Piau-Engaly (the most futuristic, 1,420–2,400m), t 05 62 39 61 69; Luz-Ardiden (with cross-country trails, 1,800–2,500m), t 05 62 92 30 30; Payolle/Campan (good cross-country), t 05 62 91 70 36; Val d'Azun-Arrens Marsous (cross-country, 1,350–1,600m), t 05 62 97 49 49; Nistos Cap Nestes (cross-country, 1,600–1,800m), t 05 62 39 74 34; Peyragudes (1,600–2,400m), t 05 62 99 69 99; Val Louron (1,450–2,200m), t 05 62 99 92 00.

Pays Basque/Béarn: Iraty (cross-country, 1,200–1,500m), t 05 59 28 51 29. For other ski stations in Pyrénées Atlantique see *www.pyrenees-atlantiques.com/stations-de-ski/stations-bearn.htm*.

Fédération Française de Ski, 50 Av des Marquisats, 74000 Annecy, t 04 50 51 40 34, *www.ffs.fr*.

For skiing in **Andorra**, *see* p.363.

Skittles

In some places in the area, especially Armagnac and the Chalosse, 6- or 9-pin skittles, or *jeu de quilles*, the ancestor of bowling, is more popular than *pétanque*; tourist offices in the Gers and Landes have a complete calendar of tournaments.

Surfing

Surf bums from all across Europe flock in late summer to ride the big rollers that hit the Côte d'Argent from the Bay of Biscay. Hendaye, Anglet, Guéthary, Biarritz, Hossegor-Seignosse, Mimizan-Plage and Biscarrosse are the main centres, where there are schools to learn and world championships to watch, but you'll find plenty of small clubs in between that hire out both surfboards and body-boards.

Walking

See 'Getting Around', p.65. The Salies-de-Béarn tourist office organizes a 2-day and 2-night trek from farm to farm accompanied by a Basque *pottok* pony carrying the luggage and/or children, t 05 59 38 32 82.

Fédération Française de Randonnée Pédestre, 14 Rue Riquet, 75009 Paris, t 01 44 89 93 93.

Water-skiing and Jet-skiing

These are practised on the larger coastal *étangs* and at St-Jean-de-Luz and Ciboure.

White-water Rafting/Hydrospeed

From early April to the end of September, you can go white-water rafting down the rivers shooting out of the Pyrenees – the Gaves, the Noguera Pallareasa (the mightiest river in the Pyrenees, just over the border in Spain) and the Neste d'Aure; spring is the most thrilling time to go, while summer is recommended for beginners.

Contact **Loisirs Aventures** in St Lary, t 05 62 39 44 79, *http://loisirs.aventures.chez-alice.fr*, or the **Relais d'Isaby** at Villelongue, both in the Hautes-Pyrénées. In Béarn, try **Rafting Eaux-Vives**, Place des Casernes, 64190 Navarrenx, **t** 05 59 66 04 05.

Telephones

British and Irish **mobile phones** work in France if they have a roaming facility; check with your service provider. If you're going to be in France a while and using your mobile a lot, and as long as your mobile is not locked to a UK network, avoid high charges (both outgoing and incoming) by temporarily replacing your UK SIM card with an international one (sold, for example, at *www.0044.co.uk*). or buying a pay-as-you-go phone from a large supermarket or communications shop.

Nearly all **public telephones** have switched over from using coins to *télécartes*, which you can purchase at any post office or newsstand at €7.41 for 50 *unités* or €14.74 for 120 *unités*. The easiest way to **reverse charges** is to spend a few euros ringing the number and giving your number in France (always posted by public phones). For **directory enquiries**, dial **t** 118 000, or see *www.pagesjaunes.com* (the French *Yellow Pages* online) or try your luck and patience on the free, slow, inefficient Minitel electronic directory in post offices.

The French have eliminated area codes, giving everyone a 10-digit telephone number.

If you're ringing France from abroad, the **international dialling code** is 33, then drop the first 'o' of the number.

For international calls from France, dial 00, wait for the change in the dial tone, then dial the **country code** (UK 44; US and Canada 1; Ireland 353; Australia 61; New Zealand 64), then the local code (minus the initial 'o') and number.

Time

France is one hour ahead of UK time and six hours ahead of North American EST. French summer time runs from the last Sunday in March to the last Sunday in October; clocks change on those days.

Tipping

Many people leave a tip if they're happy with their meal and the service; if you eat *à la carte*, you might consider adding a gratuity of around 10% (service is included in the price of set menus; *see* p.71 and **Food and Drink**, p.48).

Toilets

The hole-in-the-ground lavatory is still surprisingly common in France. Bars and cafés normally don't mind you using their facilities, but it's polite to make a small purchase at the same time.

If you're driving, it makes sense to head for the nearest (free) service station facilities, and it's wise to keep a stock of emergency toilet paper with you at all times. There are some public toilets for which you have to pay, either to get into – those funky, modern oval-shaped street facilities – or to get out of, when there's a caretaker (you should leave them a small tip).

The Landes

In French 'Landes' means moors or heaths, but the moors that take up most of this, the second-largest département in France, are the 'Desert of France', swept by the legendary storms off the Bay of Biscay. In the old days, they say, you could hear the sea from 30 miles away, and the winds were powerful enough to lift hay wagons right off the ground. The storms sped dunes inland from the coast, burying villages in their wake and stopping up the rivers with sand, creating insalubrious marshlands.

This all started to change over 100 years ago, when France's desert was transformed into Europe's largest forest. With the establishment of a major nature park and development of the coast into the 'Côte d'Argent', there is plenty to keep visitors entertained.

SPAIN

07

Don't miss

⭐ Europe's biggest sandpit
Dune du Pilat **p.83**

⭐ France's top thermal spa
Dax **p.118**

⭐ Boating under the willows
Courant d'Huchet **p.124**

⭐ The fascinating church of Ste-Quitterie
Aire-sur-l'Adour **p.107**

⭐ Views and vineyards
Mugron **p.116**

See map overleaf

The Landes

GIRONDE

BORDEAUX

Don't miss

⭐ Dune du Pilat **p.83**

⭐ Dax **p.118**

⭐ Courant d'Huchet **p.124**

⭐ Aire-sur-l'Adour **p.107**

⭐ Mugron **p.116**

These landes are sandy tracts covered with pine trees, cut for resin. Historians report, that when the Moors were expelled from Spain, they applied to the court of France [...] to settle on [...] these landes; and that the court was much condemned for refusing them. It seems to have been taken for granted, that they could not be peopled with French; and therefore ought rather to be given to the Moors, rather than be left waste.

Arthur Young, *Travels in France*, 1790

In the 18th century the only inhabitants of the Landes were 'uncouth' Tartars, who lived a miserable life walking about on stilts, raising sheep for their manure, which was essential to grow their miserable crops of rye, as the land was too poor for wheat. Life was so hard that the Landais were 'condemned never to grow old'.

It was Napoleon himself who first had the idea of doing something with the Landes: 'I will turn this country into a garden for my old guard,' he declared, although neither he nor most of his old guard survived to see any sign of a garden. Having heard the Landes region was a desert, he introduced dromedaries, which all perished from the excessive humidity in winter; he then brought in buffalo, which died from the excessive dryness in summer. In general discouragement, the Landes were relegated to the back burner until one summer day in 1856, when the little emperor's equally imperial nephew, Napoleon III, was changing trains at Labouheyre and was inspired to act on his uncle's idea (the fact that Napoleon III had acquired 7,400 hectares in the Landes naturally had nothing to do with it). He stoutly told everyone that he considered the Landes a kind of local Algeria, his mission not to colonize but to promote business and capital first through drainage and irrigation schemes, followed by 'scientific exploita-tion' – not of timber, but of resin. On 19 July 1857, Napoleon III ordered the plantation of maritime pines across the Landes de Gascogne. At first the locals feared that the shade of the pines would make them ill, but it wasn't long before they found that the life of a lumberjack or resin-gatherer suited them just fine.

Although the invention of new solvents and foreign competition has cut into the Landes' resin revenues, the trees continue to thrive and supply a good portion of France's lumber, its paper and the 'pâte fluff' for its disposable nappies. Planted in a vast triangle between Bordeaux, Bayonne and Nérac, the forest covers 11,000sq km, an area equal to two average French *départements* or a third of Belgium. The once plaguesome sand dunes of the coast have been converted into a holiday playground with big breakers, all polished and renamed the Côte d'Argent, the Silver Coast. The distinctive wide Landaise farmhouses or *bordas*, made of beams and white plaster, with a low sloping roof that often runs all the way to the ground on the west side (as protection from the mighty blasts from the Bay of Biscay), are being restored and converted into holiday *gîtes*. And the northern part of the Landes is now a Natural Park, determined to prove that the region is hardly dull, no matter what travellers down the straight, eternal A10 tunnel through the pines to Spain may say (in fact, the very first tourists to explore the area were English milords, who came down in the 1850s, a full half-century before any French tourists set foot in the Landes).

A note on the way this chapter is arranged

We begin with Arcachon and its Bassin in the southern Gironde, which marks both the northern limits of the Parc Naturel des Landes de Gascogne and the beginning of the Côte d'Argent. The Park follows, and then the northern Côte d'Argent; then it's down to the departmental capital of Mont-de-Marsan, the villages along the Adour and the pretty Chalosse region south of the river.

Note that the part of Bas-Armagnac that is in the Landes is included with the rest of the Armagnac region in **The Gers**, *see* p.132.

If nothing else, a look at the map may tempt you to explore. Although Gascon is the age-old language of the Landes, many place names have been traced back to the Celto-Iberians (mostly names endings in 'os'), the Romans (those ending in 'an' or 'acq') or Visigoths ('enx'). This helps in part to explain the piquant names of many Landais villages, which often look as if they came straight out of the Scrabble bag: Boos, Gaas, Buglose, Pissos, Stuc, Hinx, Arjuzanx, Bats, Uchacq, Yzosse, Goos, Le Barp, Le Bun and Gassies. Just try to pronounce them.

Arcachon and its Bassin

Gascony's inland sea and favourite playground, the 250sq km Bassin d'Arcachon, not only sounds like something in your bathroom, but like a bathroom fixture the actual amount of water in it varies greatly, when the tide sweeps through twice a day – at low tide large sections turn into sandy mud pies.

Despite its location near Bordeaux, the Bassin managed to stay out of history most of the time; the Romans and Rabelais wrote admiringly of its oysters, and in the Middle Ages it belonged to the redoubtable Capitals de Buch, English allies in the Hundred Years War. In the 18th century Louis XVI thought to make the Bassin into a military port and sent down an engineer of the Ponts et Chaussées, Brémontier, to fix the shifting sands. Brémontier built tall palisades 80 yards (88m) in from the high tide, halting the wind-borne sand to create barrier dunes between 30 and 40ft (11–14m) high, which he anchored with a long-rooted grass called *oyat*. To stop the dunes from wandering inland, he spread a mix of seeds of gorse, broom and maritime pines under a network of branches. The gorse sprouted up quickly, and helped hold down the soil as the slower pines established themselves. For all that, the Revolution intervened before the military port project ever got under way, leaving the Bassin to daydream to the ebbs and flows of its tides until the mid-19th century, when it discovered its double destiny as a massive nursery for oysters and a summer resort for the Bordelais; these days the gargantuan Dune du Pilat, just south of Arcachon, alone attracts a million visitors a year. Yet many corners have been left untouched by mass tourism: the little

Getting to and around Arcachon

There are **trains** nearly every hour from Bordeaux to Arcachon and, in the summer, TGVs direct from Paris Montparnasse (Bd du Général-Leclerc, t 36 35).

Several CITRAM **buses** a day from Bordeaux (from 8 Rue Corneille, t 05 56 43 68 43, or from the station coinciding with the TGVs, *www.citram.fr*) serve Andernos, Arès, Cap Ferret, Pyla-sur-Mer and Pyla-Plage. Autobus d'Arcachon, t 05 57 72 45 00, runs tourist trips of the area.

For a **taxi**, t 06 08 00 23 24.

Bicycles are a convenient way to get around, and the Bassin has many cycle-tracks; you can hire bikes in all the villages, and in Arcachon at Locabeach, 326 Bd de la Plage, t 05 56 83 39 64, *www.locabeach.com*; and Dingo Vélo, Rue Grenier, t 05 56 83 44 09, *www.dingo-velo.com*.

There's a **tourist train** that leaves from in front of the tourist office in summer.

villages in the back Bassin could be part of a 17th-century Dutch landscape painting, with their ports sheltering the Bassin's small, shallow-keeled sailing boats called *pinasses* (or *pinassayres*, in Gascon), painted the colour of the owner's house, usually green, light pink or straw yellow.

Arcachon

Arcachon was a small fishing village until 1841, when its life was turned upside down by the building of a railway line from nearby La Teste de Buch to Bordeaux. This new link neatly coincided with the new fashion for sea-bathing launched by the Duchesse de Berry. Private villas went up here and there, but the resort really took off after 1852, when a pair of brothers, Emile and Isaac Pereire, took over the railway line and extended it to Arcachon. The Pereire brothers were descendants of Spanish Jews who had found a safe haven in Bordeaux during the Inquisition; their grandfather, Jacob, was famous for inventing the first sign-language alphabet for deaf-mutes in the 1700s. The Pereire brothers proved just as inventive, but as property speculators, and laid out their new resort with cute winding lanes according to the Anglophile tastes of Napoleon III. They divided the residential sections into four subdivisions, each named after one of the four seasons. Although Spring and Autumn never really caught on, the **Ville d'Hiver**, the area best sheltered from the ocean winds and always 3°C/5°F warmer than the rest of Arcachon, attained full fashion status by the 1860s – Gounod, Debussy, Alexandre Dumas, Napoleon III, Marie Christine of Austria and her future husband Alfonso XII of Spain (who came incognito) were all habitués. For a centrepiece, the Ville d'Hiver has the **Parc Mauresque**, named after its fabulously outlandish pseudo-Moorish casino (1864), inspired by the Alhambra and the Great Mosque of Cordoba – but tragically destroyed by a fire in 1977. Inspired by its fantasy, the usually staid 19th-century Bordelais who built second homes in the Ville d'Hiver let their hair down, indulging in neo-Gothic, Tyrolean, Tudor, pseudo-medieval and other fond fancies; some 200 of these lacy gingerbread villas survive, many now owned by wealthy retirees. Don't miss the fine overall view of the Bassin from the Parc Mauresque gardens, its **Passerelle Saint-Paul** (over adjacent Allée Pasteur), built by Eiffel in 1862, and the observatory. A lift links Ville d'Eté with Ville d'Hiver arriving at Parc Mauresque.

The **Ville d'Eté**, facing the Bassin and cooler in the summer, has most of Arcachon's tourist facilities, seaside promenades, sheltered sandy beaches and the **Musée-Aquarium**, with a pretty collection of local sealife, tropical fish, tortoises, seashells and shark skeletons. The Ville d'Eté's most notorious resident was Toulouse-Lautrec, who had a house by the ocean and liked to swim in the nude, offending the sensibilities of his neighbours. To pacify them, he erected a fence between his house and the beach – then mischievously covered it with obscene drawings. The furious neighbours eventually bought the house and gleefully burned the fence. Their descendants have never really forgiven them. (They should consider the chagrin of the heirs of the young man in the Marquesas Islands, charged with tidying up Gauguin's hut after the painter's death. Finding it cluttered with sculptures and paintings, he loaded everything on to his boat and dumped the lot into the Pacific.)

Since 1950, a new crop of villas has gone up along the ocean front in Parc Pereire, overlooking Arcachon's best beach, **Plage Pereire**. As incredible as it seems, in 1922 someone had the chutzpah to drill for oil right in the middle of the park, but instead of black gold discovered, at 500m (1,600ft) down, a natural spring of mineral water, known as **Les Abatilles**, which is exploited and bottled in the spa. Further south, along Boulevard de la Plage, a casino has been installed in the more Disneylandish than out-landish **Château Deganne**, with a congress centre, the Palatium, to keep it company.

Musée-Aquarium
*Rue Professeur-Jolyet,
t 05 56 54 89 28, open
mid-Mar–early Nov
and Feb school hols
9.45–12.15 and
1.45–6.30; June–Aug
9.45–12.15 and 1.45–7*

Excursions

Two companies, **Les Bateliers Arcachonnais** (t 05 57 72 28 28, *www.bateliers-arcachon.asso.fr*) and **Digue Ouest Le Marin Independant** (t 06 08 16 32 25) make excursions to the Ile aux Oiseaux.

The Bassin's only island, the Ile aux Oiseaux, is government-owned and given over to sea birds as well as oyster farms and sailing boats. In the old days, herdsmen in boats would have their horses swim over to the sweet islet pastures. The Ile aux Oiseaux's landmarks are its picturesque *cabanes tchanquées*, huts perched on stilts.

In July and August both companies also offer day-trips to the shadeless, hot and sandy Banc d'Arguin, a wildfowl refuge at the entrance to the Bassin; in June sandwich terns by their thousands nest here (bring a picnic). Guided tours of the oyster beds are available, and four-hour trips up the cool, forested River Leyre (*see* p.86). Both also offer cruises up the coast and to the dune. The Bateliers also run painting cruises – bring your ownbrushes.

The Dune du Pilat

🌟 Dune du Pilat

As the afternoon draws to a close in Arcachon, the thing to do is drive or cycle 8km south, through the resorts of **Moulleau, Pyla-sur-Mer** and **Pyla-Plage**. In the pine trees, there's a pay car park where you can leave your vehicle, and, beyond that, the awesome, terrible, extraordinary sight of the Moby Dick of dunes, the **Dune du Pilat**, at 347ft (105m) the highest pile of sand in Europe, at 2.7km the longest, and at 550 yards (500m) the widest. Excavations in this little chunk of the Sahara have found that Pilat began to form 8,000 years ago, and more or less reached its present dimensions in the 17th century. Like all dunes, it's in a constant state of flux, and every year it inches about 15 yards (14m), consuming the pines and forcing the campsites and cafés at its rim (see 'Where to Stay', p.84) to move a bit further inland. A wooden stair with 190 steps helps you get to the top of the steep behemoth for an unforgettable view – especially at sunset. If you can't resist the urge to roll and slide and scamper down the ocean-side slope, be prepared to face the torturous return trip back up the slippery sands. Often included in the sundown view are schools of bottlenose dolphins and porpoises, who like to frolic just offshore.

South of the sand-monster there's **Le Petit Nice beach**, and beyond that a naturist beach, both with lifeguards and snack bars.

07 The Landes | Arcachon and its Bassin

Market Days in Arcachon

Daily, in the covered market in Place de Gracia during the summer; closed Mon out of season.

Where to Stay in and around Arcachon

ⓘ Arcachon >

Esp Georges Pompidou, **t** *05 57 52 97 97, www.bassin-arcachon.com and www.arachon.com; open July–Aug daily 9–7; Jan, Feb, Nov, Dec Mon–Sat 9–6; Mon, Wed, Fri and Sat from April to early Nov, they offer hour-and-a-half-long guided tours of the Ville d'Hiver*

Arcachon ✉ 33120

Hotels in fashionable Arcachon are in general more expensive than anywhere else in this book. You will need to book months in advance for anything in July or August. All the places below have rooms in both price categories; rates rise considerably for a sea view.

****Arc-Hôtel sur Mer, 89 Bd de la Plage, **t** 05 56 83 06 85, *www.arc-hotel-sur-mer.com* (€€€€–€€€). A stylish hotel where the rooms, all with balconies, overlook either water or garden; a pool, sauna and a 'Californian' Jacuzzi are among the

other amenities, and there is direct access to the beach. *Open all year.*

***Grand Hôtel Richelieu, 185 Bd de la Plage, **t** 05 56 83 16 50, *www.grand-hotel-richelieu.com* (€€€). An old-fashioned hotel dead in the centre of town, right across from the beach. *Closed Nov–mid-Mar.*

***Les Vagues, 9 Bd de l'Océan, **t** 05 56 83 03 75, *www.hotel-les-vagues.com* (€€€). You can't stay much closer to the ocean. Decorated with a fresh, light touch. *Open all year.*

Le Dauphin, 7 Av Gounod, **t 05 56 83 02 89, *www.brubers.com/dauphin-arcachon* (€€). A typical 19th-century Arcachon villa, close to the beach. The bedrooms are small but comfortable and there is a pool. *Open all year.*

Les Mimosas, 77 bis Av de la République, **t 05 56 83 45 86, *contact.hotel @wanadoo.fr* (€€). Tidy if somewhat bland rooms not far from the sea in the Ville d'Eté. *Closed Jan and Feb.*

Le Nautic, 20 Bd de la Plage, **t 05 56 83 01 48, (€€). A hotel with a Spanish touch. *Open all year.*

Le Provence, 106 Bd de la Plage, t 05 56 83 10 78 (€€). Only 50m from the beach, a simple, family-run inn, with a restaurant. *Closed Nov and Dec.*

Saint-Christaud, 8 Allée de la Chapelle, t 05 56 83 38 53 (€). If you book early you can get a room near the beach at this family-run, friendly place; half-board required in July and August. *Open all year except Christmas.*

Des Abatilles, t 05 56 83 24 15. The municipal campsite; nothing fancy, there are pools and a restaurant and it's clean and cheap. Camping club d'Arcachon. 1.8 km from beach and town. Chalets to hire. *Closed mid-Nov–mid-Dec.*

Pyla-sur-Mer ✉ 33115

**La Corniche, 46 Av Louis-Gaume, t 05 56 22 72 11, *http://chez.com/corniche* (€€€). By the beach and at the foot of the mighty dune, a neo-Basque wood and brick hotel built in 1932, with spacious balconies and a stairway down to the beach. The restaurant is good too. *Menus from €17. Restaurant closed Wed.*

**Côte Sud, 4 Av de Figuier, t 05 56 83 25 00, *www.cote-du-sud.com* (€€€). In a 1940s villa in the pines, a 5-minute walk from the beach; the restaurant offers a good value €22–28 menu, with plenty of seafood and game dishes in season. *Closed Dec and Jan.*

**Ttiki-Etchea, 2 Pl Louis Gaume, t 05 56 22 71 15 (€). Basque-style, charming, set among the tall pines next to the sea. *Open Easter–mid-Oct.*

There are several excellent campsites south of the dune although beware that they are often packed cheek by jowl in the summer. Many offer activities suitable for all the family: **Camping La Dune**, t 05 56 22 72 17, *www.campingdeladune.fr*; **Pyla Camping**, t 05 56 22 74 56, *www.pyla-camping.com*, closer to the beach; and **Camping Panorama**, Rte de Biscarosse, t 05 62 22 10 44, *www.camping-panorama.com*. Also try **Camping du Val de L'Eyre**, 8 Route de Minoy, 33770 Salles, t 05 56 88 47 03, *www.valdeleyre.com*. Family camp site.

For information and bookings for all campsites to be found in the surrounding area see *www.campingbassinarcachon.com*.

ⓘ **Pyla-sur-Mer** ›
2 Av Ermitage, t 05 56 54 02 22 and at the Dune t 05 56 22 12 85, www.pyla-sur-mer.com; open July–Aug daily 9–1 and 2–7; Sept–June Mon–Fri 9–1 and 2–7

Eating Out in and around Arcachon

Fresh seafood in all its forms is one of the reasons the French flock to Arcachon.

Restaurant Le Chipiron, 69 Bd Chanzy, t 05 57 52 06 33. An authentic little Spanish bistro near to the marina, serving tapas, delicious baby squid and other offerings with a good value set menu at lunchtimes. *Weekday menu €11, à la carte €30. Closed Wed all year and Mon eve, Tue eve Sep–April.*

Gérard Tissier, 35 Bd de l'Océan, Pyla, t 05 56 54 07 94, *http://restaurant-tissier.com*. A good restaurant on the roadside with a pleasant terrace, serving traditional dishes including fish. Try *turbot sauvage roti* or *pigeon-neau aux épices*. There is a fireplace for the winter. *Menus €29–49.*

Aux Mille Saveurs, 25 Bd Général-Leclerc, opposite Arcachon Station, t 05 56 83 40 28, *www.auxmillesaveurs.com*. Lacks a view, but makes up for it with its cuisine, notably the *noisette de filet de bœuf aux poivres différents, jus infusé au gingembre*. Lovely desserts. *Menus (lunch) €15–31. Open daily July and Aug; closed Tues eve and Wed.*

Le Patio, 10 Bd de la Plage, t 05 56 83 02 72. Surrounds diners with vines, a waterfall and delicious aromas from specialities such as lobster salad and oysters in flaky pastry. *Fixed menu €28. Closed Tues.*

Diego Plage, Bd Veyrier Montayneres, t 05 56 83 84 46. Enjoying a prime location overlooking the beach, with generous helpings of fresh fish and seafood platters. *Menus €19–28. Open daily.*

Chez Yvette, 59 Bd Général Leclerc, t 05 56 83 05 11. More formal, with an enviable reputation for its superbly fresh seafood for the past 30 years, and a cellar of white Bordeaux wines to go with it. Expect to pay around €30 à la carte or try the set menu at €18.50. *Open all year.*

Chez Pierre, 1 Bd Veyrier-Montagnères, t 05 56 22 52 94. In the waterfront pedestrian zone, offering a well-prepared variety of seafood and luscious desserts in its cosy interior or out on the terrace, with excellent views of the Bassin. *Menus from €16. Open all year.*

Entertainment and Nightlife in and around Arcachon

After dark, much of Arcachon's life gravitates around the glamorous **Casino d'Arcachon**, 163 Bd de la Plage,

t 05 56 83 41 44, where the roulette and blackjack tables open after 9pm; the complex includes bars, a restaurant, and a disco, **Disco Le Scotch**, t 05 56 83 41 43. *Open from midday.*

The local discos put on a number of special nights in the high season: in Arcachon, try **Le Cotton Club**, 4 Bd Mestrézat, t 05 56 54 87 69; and **L'Escorida**, 177 Bd de la Plage, t 05 56 22 55 07.

Around the Bassin

Ten *communes*, picturesque little ports with wooden oyster shacks, beaches, a river delta and a bird sanctuary, and a score of rather more commercial amusements wait to be savoured around the rim of the Bassin. Try at least once to cross the water the traditional way, in a *pinasse* – *promenades* are offered from the ports of Arcachon, Andernos and Lège-Cap-Ferret.

La Teste de Buch

East of Arcachon, pines line the Bassin at La Teste de Buch. Its name recalls the Captals de Buch who lorded it over the Bassin in the Middle Ages, although in those days pine resin rather than oysters was the cash crop. La Teste has some handsome houses dating back to the 18th century, and includes in its boundaries not only the Dune du Pilat and a race track, but also the **Lac de Cazaux**, the second largest in France. There's also a **zoo** with big cats, bears and other animals, also combining a farm and activities park.

Zoo
Rte de Cazaux, t 05 56 54 71 44; open April–Sept daily 10–7, Oct–Mar 2–6

La Hume

In the same area, La Hume has sprouted two other roadside attractions to keep mom and dad in the poorhouse: a 'zoo' of domestic and farmyard animals, the **Parc Animalier La Coccinelle**, where children can feed lambs and goats; **Aqualand**, for a day splashing in rivers, pools with waves, and every kind of waterslide imaginable.

Parc Animalier La Coccinelle
t 05 56 66 30 41; open July and Aug daily 10–7.30; June and early Sept daily 10–7

Aqualand
t 08 92 68 66 13; open June–mid-Sept daily 10–7; adm

Gujan-Mestras

Next to La Hume, the Bassin's oyster capital, Gujan-Mestras, has seven little ports crowded with *oustaous* (oyster huts), which provide the perfect backdrop for ordering a plate of oysters *à déguster*, as the French say. The critter on Gujan's coat-of-arms, however, is the ladybird beetle, the *barbot* in Gascon, a name that goes back to the early days of the phylloxera epidemic, when the locals noticed that their infected vines invariably swarmed with ladybirds. They accused those helpful insects of spreading the

The Oyster's their World

Oysters from the Bassin were popular among rich Romans of Burdigala, who would set up relays to have them brought to their tables in a few hours, where they would slurp them raw with garum, the prized and mysterious fish-gut sauce that culinary archaeologists guess was something similar to Vietnamese *nuoc nam*. By the Middle Ages, when the old Roman roads were full of mud and potholes, tastes turned to dried oysters stored in barrels, eaten in a sauce or fried. The Bassin's industry remained small and local, however, until 1850, when once again speedy transport, in the form of the railway, allowed the tasty bivalves to chug post-haste to Bordeaux, and then on to Paris in 1857 – at a time when restaurant diners thought nothing of beginning a meal with 10 or 15 dozen. Twice, however, Arcachon's bread-and-butter industry was devastated by oyster parasites; the first, in 1922, wiped out Arcachon's flat, native *gravettes*. These were replaced by *portugaises*, which in turn fell prey to a new parasite in 1970. Since 1972, the oysters farmed in the Bassin belong to two different species – a new *gravette*, a flat hybrid of Charente and Breton oysters, and a parasite-resistant, elongated Japanese oyster, the *huître creuse*, or *gigas*. There are still problems, however, from time to time.

Today the Bassin d'Arcachon is the fourth-largest oyster producer in France, but the first in Europe to 'trap' microscopic oyster embryos and larvae swishing about the sea in search of a home – they simply can't resist stacks of Roman roof tiles, bleached in a mix of lime and sand. After eight months clinging to a tile, the baby oysters are moved into calm nurseries in flat cages; the next year, they are moved once more to oyster parks, in fresh plankton-rich waters, where the oyster farmers defend them the best they can against greedy starfish and crustaceans, who will nevertheless devour 15 to 20 per cent of the crop over the next three years. In the parks, the oysters are constantly turned, to encourage them to develop a nice shape and a hard shell. When at long last they're ready to go on the market, they are placed for up to four days in special pools that trick them into no longer trusting the tide, so that they remain sealed tight while they are shipped and sold by size, from 6 (the smallest) to 0 (the largest and best).

'Now if you're ready, Oysters dear/We can begin to feed,' as the Walrus said. To prepare the little rascals *à la mode d'Arcachon*: count on a dozen oysters per person (or more if you're really greedy), four (or more) *crépinettes* (small flat sausages cooked in white wine), plenty of thinly sliced rye bread and butter and glasses of dry white Graves, properly chilled at 6–8°C (44°F). Open the oysters and keep cool, fry or barbecue the sausages just before serving and eat – slurp down a cold oyster, take a bite of hot sausage with a bit of buttered bread and wash it down with a swallow of wine.

plague, while in fact they were gobbling down the real culprits as fast as they could; the priest at Gujan even held *barbot* exorcisms in the vineyards. When the real, much tinier lice-like pests were discovered, the villagers of Gujan became the butt of jokes from their neighbours, who called them the *barbots*. By the 1920s, Gujan had learned to laugh at itself, and adopted the ladybird bug as its own, even naming its rugby team the Barbots.

Le Teich: the Delta of the Leyre

At Le Teich, the Leyre (or L'Eyre), one of the most important rivers of the Landes, drains into the Bassin d'Arcachon, forming the kind

Excursions

The Leyre delta is an especially fun part of Gascony to explore by canoe or kayak, especially if you are a keen birdwatcher, and there are several places to hire one by the day or half-day from June to September: the park's **Maison de la Nature** (book in advance, t 05 56 22 80 93); **Villetorte Loisirs**, 30 Rue du Pont Neuf, Le Teich, t 05 56 22 66 80; or **Club du Pont de Lamothe**, D650, Le Teich, t 05 56 22 67 57.

The Bassin d'Arcachon

10 km

5 miles

N

Lège-Cap-Ferret

Arès

Claouey

Andernos-les-Bains

Bassin

Ile aux Oiseaux

Taussat

Lanton

Audenge

d'Arcachon

Cap Ferret

Le Moulleau

Arcachon

Gujan-Mestras

Parc Ornithologique

Biganos

Pyla-sur-Mer

Pyla-Plage

Le Teich

Banc d'Arguin

Dune de Pilat

LaTeste

Dunes de Ginestras

Eyre

Dune des Places

Sanguinet

Belin-Béliet

Biscarrosse-Plage

Etang de Cazaux et de Sanguinet

BORDEAUX

106

250

A63

07 The Landes | Around the Bassin

Parc Ornithologique
*t 05 56 22 80 93,
www.parc-
ornithologique-du-
teich.com; open winter
daily 10–6, summer
daily 10–8; adm; bring
binoculars, or rent them
on the site*

Maison de la Nature
*t 05 56 22 80 93,
www.parc-landes-de-
gascogne.fr*

of marshy delta beloved of migratory waterfowl flying between Africa and Scandinavia. In 1972, Le Teich was set aside as the **Parc Ornithologique**. The delta is the nesting ground for several species, especially grey herons, black cormorants, white storks, black and white oystercatchers, egrets, kingfishers, dabbling garganeys and spoon-billed shovelers. Altogether some 280 different species have been sighted. One of the big success stories has been the return of the mute swan, which vanished from France at the time of the Revolution. For general information, visit the park's **Maison de la Nature** (*see* p.89).

The Parc Ornithologique is divided into four sections, and by taking the marked 3.5km (2-hour) path from the Maison de la Nature you can visit them all. The largest section, the vast **Parc de Causseyre**, has several hides and observation posts where you can watch a score of different year-round residents; the **Parc de la Moulette** is where the geese, swans and ducks are concentrated; the small **Parc des Artigues** has a collection of ducks from around the world, at liberty, and large aviaries; and the inaccessible **Parc Claude Quancard** is for wading birds (although there are two observation posts). There's a fine viewpoint over the entire delta from the **Observatoire du Delta de Leyre**.

Tchanquayres: Why the Landais Wore Stilts

If maritime pines are synonymous with the Landes today, in the past the region's symbol was something straight out of Monty Python: shepherds on stilts, dressed in fleecy sheepskin coats and boots and black berets. Introduced only in the 16th century under somewhat mysterious circumstances, the traditional Landais stilts, or *tchanques*, are about a yard high and strapped three times around the calves; the foot rests on a shelf, the *paouse pé*, and the leg of the stilt, the *escasse* (hence the French word for stilt, *échasse*) ends in a point made of horn or hard wood. The stilts were handy for walking quickly through marshy land (wet on top, but with a solid sand base below), but woe to the *tchanquayres* who met a mole hill, far from the perches they had at home to hoist themselves up onto the stilts. Because of the flat terrain, the higher altitude provided by the *tchanques* was all a shepherd required to keep track of straying lambs. The last piece of essential gear for a shepherd was his little knitting bag, or *braguète*, which occupied many a weary hour high over the moors. Once they had mastered their stilts, the shepherds (and shepherdesses) took to dancing on them as well.

Although the stilts have become as obsolete as the sheep, some twenty societies in the Landes keep up the lofty tradition today, dancing high at local fêtes, or running races like drunken flamingos. Stilt-racing enjoyed something of a fad in the 1890s, and no one has yet topped the feat of Sylvain Dornon, the *échassier national* who, in what the French like to term their 'world-record-breaking spirit', climbed up to the second platform of the Eiffel Tower on stilts, and topped it off by running on his *tchanques* from Paris to Moscow and back again in 1891.

The Back Bassin, Around to Cap Ferret

At **Biganos**, north of the Leyre delta, many of the old picturesque oystermen's *cabanons* have been converted into pretty holiday homes, while the poor old oystermen, one presumes, now work in the local paper mill. The Roman town of **Boios** is being unearthed nearby and the tourist office organizes **guided visits** showing historical sites throughout the area. At **Facture-Biganos** is the **Moulin de la Cassadotte** where they raise trout and sturgeon and produce caviar. The next town, **Audenge**, is a sleepy fishing village where the day's catch is trapped in reservoirs left by the retreating tide – a method of fishing that inspired someone to dig similar tide-fed reservoirs for humans; if the tide is out you can join the locals for a refreshing dip in the public seawater pools. There are paths around the wonderful saltwater marshes of **Les Domaines de Certes** and **Graveyron**. Next to the north is **Lanton**, which has a long beach and a 12th-century church, the oldest to be found on the Bassin. **Andernos-les-Bains** is a lively summer resort with splendid views across the water and the longest jetty in France. There are also the remains of a fourth-century Gallo-Roman villa, finds from which can be seen in a small museum at the Maison Louis David, along with art exhibitions. Andernos, like the next village **Arès**, has safe beaches for children.

The northwestern curve of the Bassin is sprinkled with little oyster-port resorts set between the calm waters and rough Atlantic. All belong to the *commune* of **Lège-Cap-Ferret**. The prettiest of these ports is L'Herbe, an intimate hamlet of wooden houses on tiny lanes founded in the 17th century. The *commune's*

Boios guided visits
book through Biganos tourist information, Rue Jean Zay,
t *05 57 70 67 56*

Moulin de la Cassadotte
t *05 56 82 64 42; open mid-July–mid-Aug, Wed–Mon*

21 miles of ocean beaches culminate in the sandy tail of **Cap-Ferret**, which has long been doing its damnedest to close off the mouth of the Bassin; long before anyone had even heard of global warming the sea was nibbling away at the land and in the past 200 years the cape has grown 4km (2½miles) and gobbled up several fashionable villas in its wake.

A path leads around to the tip of the cape, with splendid views of the Dune du Pilat, most breathlessly from the top of the 255 steps of the **lighthouse**. The cute little **Tramway du Cap-Ferret** links the end of the road to the ocean beaches, where surfers ride the big rollers expedited by the Bay of Biscay.

Lighthouse
open July and Aug daily 10–7.30; April, June and Sept 10–12.30 and 2–6; Oct–Mar Wed–Sun 2–5; closed mid-Nov–mid-Dec

Tramway du Cap-Ferret
t 05 56 60 60 20; open April–early Sept

07 The Landes | Around the Bassin

ⓘ **La Teste >**
Pl Jean Hameau, t 05 56 54 63 14, www.latestedebuch.fr; open Mon–Sat 9–12 and 2–5

ⓘ **Biganos >>**
t 05 57 70 67 56, www.villedebiganos.fr

ⓘ **Gujan-Mestras >**
41 Av de Lattre de Tassigny, t 05 56 66 12 65, www.ville-gujanmestras.fr; open Mon– Sat 8.30–12 and 1.30– 5.30, Sun 9.30–12.30

ⓘ **Andernos-les-Bains >>**
Esp du Broustic, t 05 56 82 02 95, www.andernoslesbains.fr; open Mon–Sat 9.30–12.30 and 3–5.30

ⓘ **Lège-Cap-Ferret >**
1 Av Gén. de Gaulle, Claouey, t 05 56 03 94 49, www.lege-capferret.com; open July and Aug 10–1 and 3–6.30; June and Sept Mon–Sat 10–1 and 3–6

ⓘ **Le Teich >>**
Pl du Souvenir, t 05 56 22 80 46, office-de-tourisme-le-teich@wanadoo.fr; open July and Aug Mon–Sat 10–1 and 2.30–7, Sun 10–1; Sept–June Mon–Fri 10–12.30 and 2.30–5.30

Market Days around the Bassin

La Teste de Buch: near the church every day July and Aug, covered market daily exept Mon.

Where to Stay and Eat around the Bassin

Gujan-Mestras ✉ 33470

***La Guérinière, Rte Bordeaux-Arcachon, **t** 05 56 66 08 78, *www.lagueriniere.com* (€€€). The most elegant place to stay here, with airy modern rooms set around a garden and pool. There's also an elegant restaurant (menu €30–100). Exotic garden terrace. *Open all year.*

L'Escalumade, 8 rue Pierre Dignac, **t** 05 56 66 02 30. Overlooking the oyster farms, a good fish restaurant with meat dishes too. *Menus €22–46. Closed Sun eve out of season and Mon all year.*

Les Viviers, Port de Larros, **t** 05 56 66 01 04. The light-filled dining room and terrace restaurant offers a wide selection of shellfish and other denizens of the deep, as well as a tasty beef *brochette* with *cèpes. Menu €19–25. Closed Tues eve, Wed all day and Thurs eve, out of season.*

Le Teich ✉ 33470

The Maison de la Nature, t 05 56 22 80 93, doubles as a hostel, with 36 beds, communal kitchen and bikes and canoes for hire by groups.

Ker Helen, near the port on the D650, **t** 05 56 66 03 79, *www.kerhelen.com.*

A good campsite, with caravans or bungalows to hire. *Open Mar–Nov.*

Biganos ✉ 33380

*Hôtel de France, 99 Av de la Libération, **t** 05 56 82 61 08, *www.parc-landes-de-gascogne.fr* (€). A good choice if you are on a tight budget. *Closed Sept.*

Andernos-les-Bains ✉ 33510

L'Esquirey, 9 Av Commandant-Allègre, **t** 05 56 82 22 15. A haven for oyster-lovers – the freshest of bivalves served in a real *cabanon* at friendly prices – along with the freshest, tastiest fish the Bassin has to offer. *A la carte only, approx €25–30. Closed Mon and mid-Dec–mid-Jan.*

Lège-Cap-Ferret ✉ 33970

Cap-Ferret is the trendiest spot on the Bassin these days, and there are plenty of bars, restaurants and camp-sites, but only a handful of hotels; quite a few people sleep out under the stars.

***Des Dunes, 119 Av de Bordeaux, Cap Ferret, **t** 05 56 60 61 81 (€€€€). This hotel down at Cap-Ferret is a dune-side, seaside place that has recently been renovated and upgraded. Facilities now include a sauna, and rooms have TV, mini-bar and safe.

La Frégate, 34 Av de l'Océan, Cap Ferret, **t 05 56 60 41 62, *www.hotel-la-fregate.net* (€€€€€–€€). Modern hotel complete with a pool. There are 28 renovated rooms and 2 apartments. *Closed Christmas and Jan.*

Hotel des Pins, 23 Rue des Fauvettes, Cap-Ferret, **t 05 56 60 60 11 (€€).

ⓘ Arès
Esp G Dartiguelongue,
t 05 56 60 18 07,
www.ares-tourisme.
com; open July and Aug
Mon–Sat 8.30–1 and
2–7; Sept–June Mon–Sat
8.30–12.15 and 4–7

A good small hotel with a decent restaurant, set in a 1920s house with garden. *Open Mar–Dec.*

Hotel de la Plage 1, Rue des Marins–L'Herbe, **t** 05 56 60 50 15 (€€). A delightful, simple 8-room wooden hotel by the beach, with a good restaurant, although the menu is rarely committed to paper. *Menu €18. Closed Jan.*

Chez Hortense, Av du Sémaphore, Cap-Ferret, **t** 05 56 60 62 56. The best restaurant in this corner of the area (especially known for its mussels) offers a good selection of seafood, prepared in a wide variety of styles. *Around €36 for à la carte. Open Easter to early Sept.*

Chez Pierrette, 9 Impasse des Sternes, Piraillan, **t** 05 56 60 50 50. In a traditional Basque house, with a good reputation for dishes, based on the market and the day's catch, but there are meat specialities as well. *Menu €28 or à la carte.*

Rond-Point, **t** 05 56 60 51 32, Port de l'Herbe. An equally simple décor but more pretensions in the kitchen, preparing abundant portions of seafood (*tartare de thon rouge poêlé*, for instance) as well as land food, served inside or out on the terrace. *Menu €13–47.*

Chez Auguste, Le Petit Piquey, **t** 05 56 60 52 12. The local oyster bar to see and be seen in, with a terrace overlooking the sandy Dune du Pilat. *Closed Oct–Easter and Tues in season.*

Pat-à-Chou, Le Grand Piquey, **t** 05 56 60 51 38. The best home-made ice cream on the whole Bassin. *Open 7–1 and 3.30–8; closed Mon.*

Auberge de Jeunesse, 87 Av de Bordeaux, Cap-Ferret, **t** 05 56 60 64 62. So many customers that many end up under tents.

Parc Naturel Régional des Landes de Gascogne

The Parc Naturel des Landes de Gascogne (which includes the Parc Ornithologique of Le Teich, *see* above) was created in 1970, with the same goal as other natural parks in France, to both safeguard and promote an underpopulated region with a distinct environment and traditions. Managed by landowners, local business people and regional politicians, the park made one of its main goals to suck in excess visitors from the coasts and create jobs through tourism.

The park covers 290,000 hectares, including large swathes of two *départements*, the Gironde and the Landes, stretching between the Bassin d'Arcachon in the north and Brocas in the south. There's no finer place to take your first steps in the secret world of the Landes: the park encompasses the delta of the Leyre (also spelled l'Eyre: there are two intransigent orthographic camps) and the lovely rivers of the Grande and Petite Leyre, immersed in lush greenery and perfect for canoeing. A network of walking paths and little rural roads will get you into the pinewoods, passing by villages and medieval churches from the days when most visitors in the Landes were pilgrims en route to Santiago de Compostela. Several museums, especially the excellent Ecomuseum at Marquèze, offer insights into life in this unique region.

Getting to the Nature Park

Trains from Bordeaux pass through Labouheyre, **t** 36 35.

Belin-Béliet

Located both on the Leyre and the N10 from Bordeaux to Biarritz, Belin-Béliet is a modest place, best known today as the seat of the Parc Naturel administration. Until the 11th century, however, Belin was the capital of old kings of Gascony and a fierce rival of Bordeaux; it was the birthplace of Eleanor of Aquitaine in 1122, and (some say) of her second and favourite son, Richard the Lion-Heart. The castle where the most fascinating woman of the Middle Ages first saw the light of day is now little more than a low mound, marked by a stele, located just west of the village centre.

The church of **St-Pierre-de-Mons** on the outskirts of Belin was built during Eleanor's reign, although its bell tower was only fortified a century later, during the Hundred Years War – that time bomb left behind by her French and English marriages. Inside are four archaic capitals, carved with scenes of mysterious import; pilgrims to Compostela would stop to pray by the scented sepulchre of Charlemagne's paladins, whose bodies were miraculously brought here after Roncevalles (*see* p.205; Saint-Seurin in Bordeaux and the Alyschamps in Arles had similar tombs, but perhaps there were enough bodies to go around). The local **Musée d'Histoire** has a number of curiosities, including two megaliths, ancient sarcophagi, Iron Age vases, local costumes, items related to traditional Landais industries, and *grimoires* – old books of magic.

Musée d'Histoire
t 05 56 88 00 06;
open July–Aug daily 3–7

The Queen from Belin

Eleanor's father was the powerful Count of Aquitaine, her mother an heiress from the House of Toulouse; her grandfather, Count Guillaume IX of Aquitaine, was the very first troubadour of them all and a rascally adventurer. As the sole heiress to Aquitaine and Poitou, she was the marriage prize of the century; after wedding the cold, pious Louis VII in 1137, accompanying him on a crusade to the Holy Land and bearing him two daughters, she had had enough by 1152 and insisted on dissolving the marriage. Even more galling to Louis was her re-marriage, only two months later, to his arch-rival Henry Plantagenet, heir not only to the throne of England but of the counties of Anjou and Brittany. One of his first acts, and one that did much to make the English popular from the start, was to grant the common people of Aquitaine the right to hunt – 600 years before the rest of feudal France won the same right in the Revolution.

Like her son Richard, whom she made her heir as Count of Aquitaine, Eleanor spent as little time as possible in England, preferring to rule over her court of love at Poitiers, where her eldest daughter, Marie of Champagne, helped to write much of the code of courtly love. Yet her later years were bitter. Henry imprisoned her in England for her political intrigues, invariably in favour of her beloved Aquitaine, and as she lived to the then incredibly ripe old age of 82 she saw much of her hard work and travels come to nought as three of her four sons by Henry predeceased her, leaving only John Lackland, the one she loved least and the baddie in the Robin Hood legends, to try to fit into the shoes of his extraordinary parents.

From Belin-Béliet, take the D110 west and turn right just before the A63 for the abandoned village of **Vieux Lugos**. In 1869 it was moved to higher, healthier ground further west, leaving behind the fortified Romanesque church of Saint-Michel, now isolated in a clearing, of interest for its frescoes dated *c.* 1500 of the *Seven Deadly Sins being led off to Hell* on the right wall, and *Works of Mercy* on the left.

Up the Petite Leyre

Moustey stands at the confluence of the Grande Leyre and the Petite Leyre. Unusually, its central square has not one but two churches side by side, both from the end of the 1200s: one, Saint-Martin, was built as the village parish church; the other, Notre-Dame, with a handsome bell tower rising directly from the

Excursions

Few rivers in France are as ideal for rowing gently downstream as the Grande Leyre and the Leyre, whether you want to spend a day's outing or a week going the whole distance from Mexico (no kidding) on the Grande Leyre to Le Teich. Lined with white sandy cliffs, little beaches and lush foliage (willows, ferns, alders), the water is perfectly clear, albeit with a slight orange tint from iron oxide in its sandy bed. And life can seem to be but a dream: no motorboats intrude, and glimpses of civilization are limited to the rare village or small nautical bases where you can spend the night camping out or in a *gîte*. The season runs from May to September. In July and August be prepared to share the river; with Arcachon nearby it's no secret. The slow, tranquil waters of the Leyre/Eyre make it the perfect place for beginner canoeists and children. The only qualification is knowing how to swim. The bases along the river hire out canoes at around €21 a day for two people and tents, and can arrange to pick you up downstream (you pay by the kilometre). This list starts with the furthest upstream and gives distances and times from the previous base.

Base de Mexico, on the D626, 3.5km from Commensacq, **t** 05 58 07 05 15, *www.mexicoloisirs.com*, has a *gîte* and campsite. *Open all year.*

Halte Nautique, at Trensacq, 5km/2hrs downstream, **t** 05 58 07 04 41, with a *gîte* and a *gîte d'étape*. Open July and August only. For horseriding see *www.ranch-elvire.com*.

Base de Testarouman, Pissos, 21km/7hrs downstream, **t** 05 58 08 91 58, with camping and a group *gîte*. *Open all year.*

Base de Saugnac, Saugnacq-et-Muret, 15km/5hrs downstream, **t** 05 58 07 73 01, the main centre on the river, with *gîtes* and camping. *Open all year.*

Centre de Graoux, Belin-Béliet, 15km/5hrs downstream, **t** 05 57 71 99 29, *gîtes*. *Open all year.*

Salles, 10km/3hrs downstream, **t** 05 56 88 20 53. Canoes and kayaks for hire. *Open June–Sept.*

Mios, 9km/3hrs downstream, **t** 05 56 26 63 00, with a campsite. *Open mid-June–mid-Sept.*

Maison de la Nature du Bassin d'Arcachon, Le Teich, 10km/3hrs from Mios, **t** 05 56 22 80 93, with *gîtes collectives* for groups of 15 or more; booking essential. *Open all year.*

Musée du Patrimoine Religieux
not open in 2006; call **t** *05 58 07 71 26*

Attelages des Vallées de la Leyre
t *05 58 07 75 60*

façade (a typical feature of southwestern Romanesque churches), was the chapel of a pilgrims' hostel-hospital, demolished in 1870. Notre-Dame now houses the Parc Naturel's **Musée du Patrimoine Religieux et des Croyances Populaires**, with two changing exhibits on popular beliefs and superstitions. For carriage rides through the forest and walking tours with a donkey, call **Attelages des Vallées de la Leyre**.

From Moustey the D120 follows the valley of the Petite Leyre. Unlike the Grande Leyre, the Petite is not kept clear of dead trees and vegetation, but its waters, rich in eel and pike, are specially reserved for fishermen – and otters, if you're lucky enough to see one. The first village up the Petite Leyre is **Belhade** (Gascon for 'beautiful fairy'), set in an old oak forest and the seat of the oldest barony of the Landes. The château with its moat and three towers is on the edge of town, built over a prehistoric camp, while in the centre of the village is a little 11th-century Romanesque church with a *clocher-mur* and a portal adorned with very curious sculpted capitals on its columns: a mermaid pulls a boat with two sailors, a serpent eats a man, birds ride animals.

The Petite Leyre has a **Sore** on one of its elbows – a village founded in the Middle Ages. Of the Albrets castle that once stood

Liquid Diamonds

When American imports were cut off during the Civil War (1861–5), the price of resin, 40 francs a barrel back in the 1850s when Napoleon III first planted the pine forests, soared to 245. This began a golden era in the Landes; at the beginning of the 20th century, when the stuff was in great demand for making turpentine and rosin, there were 30,000 *gemmeurs*, or resin-tappers, employed in the giant forest; today there are a mere 50. It's hard, seasonal labour; the average *gemmeur* works between 12 and 15 hours a day between April and October (the heat makes the pines 'bleed' more easily), collecting the resin from 1,000 to 1,500 trees. Since 1960, new techniques using sulphuric acid have doubled the yield; now, instead of 1,000, the *gemmeur* only has to visit 500 trees in five days to fill a 200-litre barrel. Pines are first tapped when they're between 17 and 20 years old. Some specimens have been tapped for 200 years; others, destined for the chop, are bled dry. In the old days the *gemmeurs* used stilts to tap high up the trunk, using a little reversible container called a *pot Hugues*; now even these have been replaced by plastic sacks.

Atelier de Produits Résineaux
t 05 58 08 31 31; open April–May and mid-Sept–Oct daily 2–6; June–mid-Sept daily 10–12 and 2–7; adm

Maison de l'Estupe Huc
t 05 58 08 06 18; open July and Aug 2–6.30

here, only the moat and a gate survived the Wars of Religion; there's a 12th-century fortified mill and a church from the same period, with an unusual arcaded bell tower. **Luxey** is a sweet little village and site of the **Atelier de Produits Résineaux**, in an old resin distillery behind the church, where you can learn all about the sticky liquid diamonds that were the forest's first cash crop. The **Maison de l'Estupe Huc** explains how the forest has been, and is, protected against fire.

Up the Grande Leyre to Sabres

South of Moustey, **Pissos** provides a popular base with its 20 *gîtes forestiers*. Its church, St-Jean-de-Richet, has a Romanesque apse, decorated with pretty modillons, and inside, 14th-century frescoes rediscovered in 1969. To the south, at Trensacq, turn west 6km on the D45 for **Commensacq** and its 11th-century church of St-Martin. The vaults are decorated with 15th-century paintings of Adam and Eve, and there's a pretty baldachin and altar that somehow survived the usual depredations of French churches. Best of all, the central pillar has a carved frieze of musicians, including a pig playing the bagpipes, a rabbit playing the violin and a wonderfully sensual mermaid. Mermaids, or sirens, turn up with some frequency on Romanesque churches, often spreading their tails to display the entrance into the womb. It is a symbol steeped in medieval mysticism, perhaps not entirely inaccessible to the modern imagination. Some scholars believe the sirens represent desire and act as intermediaries by which nature's energy and inspiration are conducted into the conscious world. Others claim that they betray the existence of an ecstatic cult, based on music and dance and descended from ancient Dionysian rituals.

Further west on the D45 is **Labouheyre**, an important market and *gîte* centre that first grew up along a Roman road, then along the pilgrimage road, and then along the N10; the old town gate and the church of Saint-Jacques, with a 15th-century portal, are its chief monuments. A narrow road south of Labouheyre leads to **Solférino**, founded as a model village around a model estate by Emperor Napoleon III in 1863, just as his great forestation project was proving a success. It was to be something of a social laboratory as well; remembering his vaguely progressive politics from his exile in London, the emperor constructed cottages for his 'colonists' which they could eventually own with two hectares of land by working for free for 75 days a year for 10 years. In 1905, Empress Eugénie sold Solférino to another family, the Schneiders.

Sabres to the east attracts plenty of tourists on their way to the Eco-musée, but don't neglect a glance at its 11th-century church, with a towering triangular *clocher-mur* and richly carved portal, decorated with saints and imaginary flowers and beasts. Even in the 20th-century Sabres was so cut off from the rest of the world that when the first German soldiers in their long black coats marched through the village in 1940, some old women were heard to cry in terror that the Huguenots were back in town. Six kilometres southwest of Sabres on the D77 you can visit one of the best dolmens in the Landes, the Pierre de Grimann.

Marquèze and the Ecomusée de la Grande Lande

Marquèze and the Ecomusée de la Grande Lande
t 05 58 08 31 31; open April, May and Nov Mon–Sat

The only access to Marquèze, the pride of the Parc Naturel, is, if you are lucky, by a delightful old steam train that chugs 5km from Sabres in 10 minutes (*see* over). There's a snack bar and mediocre restaurant on the site, or you can bring a picnic lunch. Optional guided tours (in French) last an hour and a half; a brochure is available in English so you can wander about on your own.

Until about 50 years ago, the Landes were divided into agricultural *quartiers*. Each *commune* had between 6 and 12 *quartiers*; the most important was the site of the church and cemetery and, over the years, of the school, *mairie* and shops. The other *quartiers* were all more or less alike, little islands of civilization in the desert of the Landes: in the centre would be the *maison du maître*, or landowner's house, along with the servants' house, the shepherds' houses, the miller's house, and the *maisons des métayers*, or farm labourers' houses (although '*métayer*' means sharecropping in French, in the Landes the word refers to any kind of farming). Other houses belonged to the *brassiers*, who lived only from the strength of their *bras*, or arms. Around the houses were buildings that look remarkably like smaller versions of the houses: barns, sheds, pigsties, mill, ovens, sheepfolds, hives and chicken coops (on stilts, to protect them from the foxes), located on a lawn known as the *airial*, planted with oaks and chestnuts. Inside the houses are furniture and exhibitions.

Getting to Marquèze

The **steam train** from Sabres runs 1 June–15 Sept, 10 departures daily, 10.10–5.20. Last return from Marquèze 7pm. On Sun and hols, nine run, the last leaving at 4.40pm; in April, May and mid-Sept–Oct, five trains run in the afternoon only, starting at 2pm; adm: discount combination tickets available.

Marquèze was an abandoned *quartier* of Sabres, rescued in 1978 by the board of the Parc Naturel to become the first *eco-musée* in France. Most of the buildings to be seen on the site date from the end of the 19th century; a few come from other *quartiers* and have been reconstructed on the *airial*. Marquèze's surroundings have been meticulously maintained as well, including the orchard and stream, the fields and forests and Landais sheep chomping in the meadow; one goal of all *eco-musées* is to conserve old varieties of seeds, trees and domestic animals in danger of being lost for ever.

South of Sabres

There are only a few points of interest between the Parc Naturel and Mont-de-Marsan. Southeast on the N134 from Sabres, in **Garein**, the 11th-century church has frescoes of the coronation of the Virgin, rediscovered in 1900 when parts of the plaster crumbled off. There is now, beside the N134, the **Graine de Forêt** on flora and fauna in the forest, human interaction with the forest environment and how the forest is commercially exploited.

Graine de Forêt
*t 05 58 08 31 31,
www.grainedeforet.
com; open April–June
and Sept–Oct, Sat 2–6,
Sun and hols 10–1 and
3–6; July and Aug 10–1
and 2–6*

Labrit, east of Sabres, was the humble cradle of, and gave its name to, the d'Albrets, the most influential and powerful of all Gascon families, who out of this little Landais nowhere blazed like a comet across the history of 15th- and 16th-century France. Their rise to riches, fame and royal favour was no mere accident: they were faithful agents of the French Crown, at a time when Gascony/Aquitaine had few natural ties to France, but was a patchwork of regions accustomed to a fair amount of independence under English sovereignty and the feudal anarchy that preceded it. In return, the kings of France showered every sort of prize on the d'Albrets, not the least of which were advantageous marriages. With their help Henri d'Albrets became king of Navarre and husband of François I's sister, the talented Marguerite d'Angoulême; their hellcat daughter, Jeanne, grew up to be one of

---

Omelette aux Cèpes

In a frying pan, brown a handful of sliced fresh *cèpes* in a little oil; add salt and pepper. Drain off and keep the oil and set the mushrooms aside; return the frying pan to the heat and stir up a spoonful of freshly chopped parsley with a bit of garlic (what the French call a *persillade*), and set it aside as well. Then heat up the oil from the mushrooms in a large frying pan. Whip seven or eight eggs with a little salt, pepper, a spoonful of oil and one spoonful of *crème fraîche*. Pour the egg mixture into the very hot oil, add the mushrooms and parsley and cook at as high a temperature as you dare. *Serves four.*

the most fanatical leaders of the Protestant camp in the Wars of Religion. Jeanne's Protestant son in turn became king of France as Henri IV, who converted to Catholicism ('Paris is worth a Mass') and put a truce to religious bigotry in his Edict of Nantes. But what remains of the d'Albrets in Labrit? Not much, although the Maison Landaise in Labrit has a permanent exhibition on the finds made at the mounds and ditches which are all that remain of an 11th-century castle that once belonged to the family. You can take a guided tour of the site. Southwest of Sabres, in **Arengosse**, the feudal motte of Bezaudun marks the home of the ancient kings of Gascony, though it was occupied until the 1840s by the Cagots (*see* **Culture** pp.37–9). **Morcenx** grew up around the railroad and owes its big spot on the map to the fact that it's the only town for miles around and a lunch stop en route to Dax.

Market Days in the Nature Park

Labouheyre: Thursdays.
Morcenx: Wednesdays and Saturdays.
Belin: Fridays.

Where to Stay and Eat in the Nature Park

ⓘ **Belin-Béliet >**
Parc Régional, 33 Rte de Bayonne, t *05 57 71 99 99, www.parc-landes-de-gascogne.fr Hotel de Ville,* t *05 56 88 06 14, http://site.voila. fr/belin-beliet; open summer only*

ⓘ **Moustey >**
Mairie, t *05 58 07 71 26; open July and Aug Mon–Fri 9–12 and 2– 5.30; Sept–June Mon– Wed 9–12 and 2.30– 5.30, Thurs–Fri 9–12*

ⓘ **Sabres >>**
Eco-Musée, t *05 58 08 31 31; open April–Oct*

⭐ **Auberge des Pins >>**

Bélin-Beliet ✉ 33830
Madame Clements, 11 Rue du Stade, t 05 56 88 13 17 (€). A *chambre d'hôte* in the centre of the village, a 19th-century house surrounded by a garden with lovely views from the rooms. *Open all year, call first.*

Moustey ✉ 40410
Le Haut Landais, Pl des Platanes, t 05 58 07 77 85, *www.lehautlandais. com*. A 17th-century *auberge* in Moustey. Some of the best cooking in the area. Run by a friendly Dutch woman. *Menus €20–25, main dish €15. Closed Mon, and Mon–Fri eves Oct–June.*

Sore ✉ 40430
The commune operates nine woody cottages, or *gîtes forestiers*, and a campsite with a pool; to book, ring the *mairie*, t 05 58 07 60 06.

Pissos ✉ 40410
To rent one of Pissos' 20 economical *gîtes forestiers*, ring the *mairie*, t 05 58 04 41 40, see *www.pissos.fr*. Gîtes for 4 from €384 per week.

Café de Pissos, on the edge of village, t 05 58 08 90 16. For a typical country feast packed with Landais delights, from *salmis de palombe* and *foie gras* to salmon. Speciality is *mignons de canard au foie frais poelé sauce porto*. Five rooms (€). *Menus from €12–38. Closed Nov–early Dec; restaurant closed mid-Nov–mid-Dec, Sun, Tues eve and Wed all day, out of season.*

Labouheyre ✉ 40210
*****Hôtel Brémontier**, 110 Rue des Hauts-Fourneaux, t 05 58 07 01 13, *www. bremontier.fr* (€). Very simple hotel. *Menu €12–27. Closed Sun eve and Mon except Aug and mid-Sept–mid-Oct.*

Chambres d'Hôte Loustau, in a park 5km west of Labouheyre at Lüe, t 05 58 07 11 58 (€). Lovely Landais *maison du maître. Open May–mid-Sept.*

L'Auberge Landaise, Lüe, t 05 58 07 06 13, *www.auberge-landaise.com*. A traditional half-timbered farmhouse with a terrace, serving up heaped portions of *confits*, roast pigeon, roast lamb, *foie gras*, game dishes, and other delights. Eight *set menus from €10–32. Closed Sun eve, Mon, and Oct.*

Sabres ✉ 40630
******Auberge des Pins**, Rte de la Piscine, t 05 58 08 30 00, *www.aubergedes pins.fr* (€€). The complete Landais experience: renovated rooms in a country house, set in a pretty park, with an excellent restaurant; English spoken. *Menus €18–64. Closed Jan and Sun eve and Mon out of season.*

Down the Côte d'Argent

Nearly dead straight and practically endless, the 'Silver Coast' as it was dubbed by a Bordeaux newspaperman in 1905, is the biggest beach in Europe, some 140 miles of pale sand between the deep green forest and the bracing blue Atlantic. It stretches from Médoc's Pointe de Grave at the mouth of the Garonne and, after a momentary interruption at the mouth of the Bassin d'Arcachon, continues all the way down to Bayonne, offering broad vistas of empty space rare in Europe. Backing the beach is a long chain of carefully tended, artificial dunes (which you should only cross at the specially arranged points); the first task when sowing the pine forest was to follow Brémontier (*see* p.80) in planting tufty *oyat* grass to anchor the moving sands into dunes, breaking the winds and sheltering the first pine saplings.

The Golfe de Gascogne, or Bay of Biscay, sends so many big rollers special delivery to the coast that the Côte d'Argent is up in the same league as California, Australia, Hawaii and Tahiti for surfing; the sport was introduced to France in 1955 when a Californian student visiting the area was impressed enough to have his board shipped over. If that's not enough, just on the other side of the dunes are a score of freshwater lakes and ponds formed by the numerous streams that crisscross the Landes' forests. Lined with sandy beaches, not only are they ideal for calmer swimming and sports like windsurfing and sailing, but they also happen to lie on one of the continent's major flyways for migratory birds. The whole is one of France's largest outdoor playgrounds: the pleasures of surfing, *char à voile* (land yachting), windsurfing, sailing, fishing, bird-watching, hang-gliding, golfing, cycling, or just building sand castles on the beach see nearly 3 million summer visitors and 600 tonnes of sunscreen lotion every year.

**Musée Historique
de l'Hydraviation**
332 Av Louis Bréguet,
t *05 58 78 00 65,*
*www.asso-hydraviation.
com; open July and Aug
daily 10–7; Sept–June
Wed–Mon 2–6; closed
hols in winter; adm*

**Biscarrosse
museum**
216 Av Louis Brégnet,
t *05 58 78 77 37; open
July–Aug daily 9.30–7
except Sun am; June
and Sept Tues–Sat 10–12
and 2–6*

Biscarrosse, Biscarrosse-Plage and Sanguinet

Biscarrosse is a big town but a fairly dull one, and owes much of what panache it has to its land-of-lakes setting. Just north is the vast Etang de Cazaux et de Sanguinet, while the town itself is set between the Petit Etang de Biscarrosse and the vast Etang de Biscarrosse et de Parentis. And when the lakes seem too tranquil, the thumping waves of the Atlantic are only 10km away.

For years Biscarrosse was an important seaplane port, a past remembered at the **Musée Historique de l'Hydraviation**, stocked with models, mementoes and photos. Although it's a while since a seaplane landed here, rockets sometimes blast off from the Centre d'Essai des Landes, which keep a large slab of the Côte d'Argent – between Biscarrosse-Plage and Mimizan-Plage – strictly off limits. There's a **museum** on the town's history, traditions and people.

Getting around the Côte d'Argent

You need a **car** to get around, as public transport is pretty thin on the ground. **Buses** (line 611) link Arcachon to Biscarrosse in the summer; contact Autobus d'Arcachon, 47 Bd Général-Leclerc, for information, **t** 05 57 72 45 00.

Biscarrosse's other claim to fame revolves around its centuries-old elm in the main square. The story goes that the unfaithful wives of Biscarrosse would be brought here under its shade, so that their guilt would be publicly exposed. One day, however, one of the women was innocent, a fact the elm recognized by forming a white crown of leaves over her head. The elm has re-created the curious white crown every year since. Antoine de Saint-Exupéry, who besides writing *Le Petit Prince* was one of France's star pilots in the early days of airmail, loved to sit in its shade when he was in Biscarrosse on a mission. Nearby, the town church hides a fine 14th- to 15th-century Gothic interior.

The prettiest part of Biscarrosse is up around the three tiny pleasure ports on the clear waters of the **Etang de Cazaux et de Sanguinet**, just north of Biscarrosse town: Ipses, Navarosse and Port-Maguide, the latter with a pretty beach and windsurfing.

Boat trips
t 05 56 66 87 28;
May–Sept

There are **boat trips** around the lake from Port Navarosse.

Sports and the casino are what bring most summer visitors to Biscarrosse and its seaside annexe, Biscarrosse-Plage, a rather characterless, purpose-built resort that sprouted up in the 1970s by the beach; one of the best things to do is take the coastal road north towards Arcachon for the magnificent views of coast and dunes. In August and September, white sea daffodils (*Pancratium maritimum*) scent the dunes so sweetly that many people unfortunately cannot resist picking them, although they play a vital role in anchoring the dunes. Little by-roads, some drivable, lead down to the beach, where no one cares if you've brought your bathing costume or not.

If the Atlantic is too rough for a satisfying swim, the lakes around Biscarrosse, especially the Etang de Cazaux et de Sanguinet, have sandy beaches as well. Before the dunes blocked off its mouth, this lake was one of the Landes' many rivers, or *courants* as they're called. In 1977, archaeologist-divers found signs of ancient settlements 22ft (7m) under the lake, dating from the Bronze Age to the Gallo-Roman period, when the Roman Via Antonina passed here. Canoes, ceramics, coins, jewellery and other artefacts are now displayed in the **Musée des Sites Lacustres**, in the Place de la Mairie in Sanguinet, 13km up the lake shore. Sanguinet itself stands over the Gallo-Roman village of Losa, located along the Roman road from Bordeaux. Its submerged stone temple can be seen some 12ft (3.6m) under the surface of the lake.

Musée des Sites Lacustres
t 05 58 82 13 32; open July and Aug daily 10–12.30 and 2.30–7; otherwise by appt

07 The Landes | Down the Côte d'Argent

In between Biscarrosse and Sanguinet is an old **forest** of pines and oaks growing atop ancient dunes; ferns and heather cover the lower regions, a prime area for finding wild mushrooms in the autumn, especially *cèpes, chanterelles*, and the orangish-yellow *bidaou*, or *tricholome équestre*.

Parentis-en-Born

Here is a village where life flows like honey

Saint-Exupéry

If Biscarrosse has had something of its tourist potential compromised by the adjacent rocket-testing area, Parentis-en-Born and its lake have been more dismally undermined, since 1955, by the presence of petroleum derricks – the first lake platforms in Europe, busily sucking up the contents of France's biggest oil field and sending them down the pipeline to refineries on the Gironde. Parentis is proud of its turn-of-the-19th-century arena and its restored 15th-century church; during the restoration, some medieval muskets were found from the days when the church was fortified.

The 'Born' in Parentis refers to the surrounding region, for a long time beyond the *bornes* or boundaries, a kind of end of the world. Besides the lakes, there isn't a whole lot to see in the Born. Along the D652 towards Mimizan, **Gastes** makes a nice stop for a lake swim; Ste-Eulalie-en-Born, with its statue of St-Eutrope by a fountain that once enjoyed a certain renown for healing lame children, lies on the river or *courant* of the same name, linking the Etang de Parentis with that of Aureilhan, one of the prettiest of all the Landes's lakes.

Market Days in the North of the Côte d'Argent

Biscarrosse: Fridays and Sundays.
Parentis: Thursdays and Sundays in summer.

Where to Stay and Eat in the North of the Côte d'Argent

Biscarrosse ✉ 40600

***La Forestière, Av du Pyla, Biscarrosse-Plage, **t** 05 58 78 24 14, *www.hotellaforestiere.com* (€€€). The nicest place on the sea, and also has a pool. Half-board obligatory in July and August. *Menus €18–38. Open from April until mid-Oct.*

La Caravelle, at Ispe (5314 Rte des Lacs), **t 05 58 09 82 67, *www.*

lacaravelle.fr (€€). Near the golf course, a lovely, quiet place, right on the Etang de Cazaux et de Sanguinet; but the food is so good that many non-guests drop in for a meal. *Menus €16–38. Closed Nov–mid-Feb.*

La Transaquitain, 15 Rue des Parterres. Navarrosse, **t 05 58 09 83 13, *www.hoteltransaquitain.com* (€€). Also overlooks the lake and has a swimming pool besides. *Open April–mid-Sept.*

Auberge Regina, 34 Av de la Libération, Biscarrosse-Plage, **t** 05 58 78 23 34, (€€). A couple of minutes' walk from the beach, this pretty *auberge* run by a gay couple is the trendiest place to stay in Biscarrosse-Plage. Bedrooms are chalet-like with a distinct Mediterranean feel. All bedrooms have Internet access – cyber-café meets beach house. *Menus from €15. Open daily mid-Feb–Dec.*

Atlantide, in Pl Marsan, **t 05 58 78 08 86, *www.hotelatlantide.com* (€).

ⓘ **Sanguinet**
Mairie, t 05 58 78 67 72, www. sanguinet. com; open July and Aug Mon–Sat 9.30–12 and 2–7, Sun 9–12; Sept–June daily 9.30–12 and 2–5.30

⭐ **Auberge Regina >>**

ⓘ **Biscarrosse >**
55 Pl G. Dufau. t 05 58 78 20 96, www. biscarrrosse.com; open Oct–Mar Mon–Fri 9–12 and 2–5, Sat 10–12; April–June and Sept Mon–Fri 9–6, Sat and Sun 10–12 and 2–5; July and Aug daily 9–8

ⓘ **Parentis >**
Pl du Général-de-Gaulle, **t** *05 58 78 43 60, www.parentis.com; open July and Aug Mon–Sat 10–1 and 3–7, Sun 9–1; Sept–June Mon–Sat 9–12.15 and 1.45–5.30*

33 pleasant, modern rooms with all the usual facilities. *Open all year.*
Chez Camette, 532 Av Latécoère, **t** 05 58 78 12 78. For a good, honest meal. *Lunch menu €10. Menus €15–23. Open daily July and Aug, the rest of the year closed Fri eve and all Sat.*

Parentis-en-Born ✉ **40160**
Cousseau, 11 Rue St-Bartélémy, **t** 05 58 78 42 46. Long the place to dine in

Parentis, with a typical French provincial atmosphere but serving up tasty sea and land food, sometimes deliciously combined as sole prepared with *girolle* mushrooms; also *foie gras* prepared in a variety of ways and a wide choice of wine. *Daily changing menu €10–41. Closed Fri eve and Sun eve, and mid-Oct–mid-Nov; open daily in July and Aug.*

Middle Côte d'Argent: Mimizan to Léon

Mimizan and Mimizan-Plage

May God keep us from the song of the Siren, the tail of the whale, and the bell tower of Mimizan.
Old Gascon sea-dog saying

With all these pine trees, there has to be a paper mill somewhere, and Mimizan, at the mouth of the *courant* that flows through Sanguinet, Parentis and Aureilhan lakes, won the prize; its Papeteries de Gascogne claims to be the largest producer of brown paper in the world. But don't let the threat of a change in wind and the occasional gust of stink put you off: unlike Biscarrosse, which is similarly endowed with the combined pleasures of ocean and lake, Mimizan, the 'Pearl of the Côte d'Argent', has some history and character. Once the Roman port of Segosa, it had a **Benedictine abbey**, built in the 12th century, of which only the UNESCO World Heritage-listed brick *clocher-mur* and beautifully carved Gothic portal have survived the usual vicissitudes, not the least of which was being half buried in sand, along with the rest of the town, in 1342. In the old days, the abbey and town were granted the right of asylum, or *sauveté* (the four stone pillars marking the boundaries still stand). Not only could any fugitive from justice find safe refuge within the magic square, but the inhabitants of Mimizan enjoyed salvage rights that made them the dread of sailors; whenever a ship was seen to be floundering, the abbey bell would toll and the village would pounce on the cargo, free to drink as much of the alcohol they could hold and cut off bolts of cloth to make clothes.

Musée d'Histoire de Mimizan
t 05 58 09 00 61; open 15 June–15 Sept Mon–Sat 10.30–7; guided tours 11–6

Across from the remains of the abbey is the modest little **Musée d'Histoire de Mimizan**, with a few bits on local geography, and ancient and medieval history. Phone ahead for a combined guided tour of the abbey and museum that includes a virtual visit of the abbey intact.

North of Mimizan, the sweet verdant banks of the **Etang d'Aureilhan** have been planted with exotic trees, flowers and shrubs, making for a lovely lakeside promenade. This lake enchanted the Duke of Westminster, who in 1910 built himself a Tudor-style manor called Wolsack. King Gustav II of Sweden, Coco Chanel and Winston Churchill were frequent guests between the wars; today only the façade and two wings are intact, along the D87. The big wide beach, **Mimizan-Plage**, is divided by the *courant* running into the ocean, and has four areas with lifeguards, both to the north and south of the bridge.

South of Mimizan

This is the least populated stretch of France's Atlantic coast. There are a number of small villages with road access to the beaches: **Bias** (with Maison de l'Airial, an information and discovery centre on wood and the forest) is one and **St-Julien-en-Born** is another, located near the *courant* leading down to **Contis-Plage**. Contis-Plage has a couple of hotels and a **lighthouse** with 196 steps you can climb for the view. Just inland from St-Julien, **Mézos** is a pretty village with a good 14th-century church, built by the Knights of Malta in the local stone, called *garluche*. Further south, there is access from Lit-et-Mixte, with its old wooden bullring, to **Cap-de-l'Homy Plage** ('Man's Head Beach') with a summer lifeguard. The coastal route, the D652, continues south from Lit-et-Mixte to **St-Girons**, with a road to the beach of the same name.

Inland, **Uza** overlooks a pretty little man-made lake, dammed back in the 18th century to supply water power for the local iron forges. The owners of the forge built themselves a little Italianesque loggia to live in as well as the village church, which contains three painted wooden Renaissance-era statues. Further inland through the forest, **Lévignacq** is just as picturesque, an old village with an old *lavoir*, a watermill and a remarkable church. Built and fortified in the 1200s, the church tower is topped by a pointed roof and a curving steeple; inside the wooden ceiling is covered with paintings from 1715, and frescoes from the 15th century were found in the choir during the recent restoration. For Léon and the southern Côte d'Argent, *see* p.124.

Contis-Plage lighthouse
t 05 58 51 31 08; open July and Aug Tues and Thurs 10–12.30 and 2.30–4.30

Tourist Information in Mimizan

Mimizan tourist office organizes informative guided tours of the forest, natural sites, and a number of industries using wood.

Where to Stay and Eat in Mimizan

Mimizan ✉ 40200
***Le Patio, 6 ave de la Côte d'Argent, t 05 58 09 09 10, *www.le-patio.fr* (€€€€€). If you are staying awhile consider this complex of duplex, studios and bungalows (10 in total). Some rooms have an ocean view from the balcony, others have terraces facing the garden. Out of high season you can stay on a nightly basis. *Closed Nov–mid-Jan.*
***Au Bon Coin du Lac, right on the lake at 34 Av du Lac, t 05 58 09 01 55, *www.auboncoindulac.com* (€€€). If your pockets are deep enough or you want to splash out, this peaceful and stylish place is hands-down the most delightful place to sleep and eat in Mimizan. There are only 4 luminous, elegant rooms and 4 apartments; tables from the equally attractive restaurant spill out along the lakeside terrace, where you won't go wrong

ⓘ **Mimizan**
38 Av Maurice-Martin, Mimizan-Plage, t 05 58 09 11 20, www.mimizan-tourisme.com; open July and Aug Mon–Sat 9–7, Sun 10–12.30 and 4–7; April–June and Sept Mon–Fri 9–12 and 3–6, Sat 10–12 and 3–5; Oct–Mar Mon–Fri 9–12 and 3–6, Sat 9–12

★ **Au Bon Coin du Lac >>**

① **Mézos**

*Av du Born. t 05 58 42
64 37, www.ot-mezos.fr;
open July and Aug
Mon–Sat 10–12 and
4–7; June and Sept
Mon–Sat 10–12 and 5–7,
Oct–May Tues and Sat
3–5, and in school hols
Mon–Sat*

① **Vielle-Saint-
Girons**

*Rte de Linxe, t 05 58
47 94 94, www.
tourisme-vielle-
st-girons.com*

trying one of the house specialities. The desserts, prepared by a special pastry chef, are out of this world, and the cellar offers a magnificent array of wines. *Menus €18–30 and à la carte. Note: it is possible that the hotel may close in 2007 so call first.*

Hotel de la Foret, 39 Av Maurice Martin, Mimizan-Plage, t 05 58 09 09 06 (€€€–€€). Pleasant Logis de France opposite tourist office. Pretty terrace and garden. Half-board obligatory in July and Aug. *Menus €15–23. Open all year.*

L'Emeraude des Bois, 68 Av du Courant, t 05 58 09 05 28, *www. emeraudedesbois.com* (€€). Set among lofty old trees a few minutes from the centre of Mimizan, an attractive old house, with a range of rooms in a range of prices; the restaurant is excellent and serves many old French

favourites. *Menus €16–35. Restaurant closed lunchtimes and Oct–Mar, restaurant closed Oct–end April.*

Hôtel de France, 18 Av de la Côte d'Argent, Mimizan-Plage, t 05 58 09 09 01 (€€). Bright, welcoming rooms with bathrooms, some overlooking a courtyard and some the sea. *Closed mid-Oct–Mar.*

Hôtel du Centre, 2 Rue de l'Abbaye in Mimizan-Bourg, t 05 58 09 37 70, www.hotelducentremimizan.com. Similar fare is served at similar prices in this hotel's pretty dining room; also has rooms (€). *Menus €12–24. Open all year.*

Camping Municipal de Mimizan-Plage, t 05 58 09 00 32, *www. mimizan-camping.com*. There are plenty of campsites around Mimizan: one of the nicest is this one, nearest the sea. *Open May–Oct.*

Mont-de-Marsan

Birthplace of former French prime minister Alain Juppé and the biggest town in the Landes with all of 32,000 souls, Mont-de-Marsan isn't exactly cosmopolitan and urbane – except for six days during the last two weeks of July when it explodes in honour of the Magdalene, with *corridas*, *courses landaises* and a megaton of fireworks. Located where the rivers Douze and Midou meet to form the Midouze, an important tributary of the Adour, the site was inhabited in prehistoric times, although the traces of these first settlers were bulldozed in 1980. One apocryphal text claims the medieval town was founded by Charlemagne, but the real founders were the abbots of St-Sever, who built a priory dedicated to the Magdalene here, and a certain Pierre de Lobaner, the lord of Marsan, who founded a *castelnau*, or new town, nearby in 1140. The town prospered by transporting the wines and wheat of Armagnac down the Midouze to the Adour and the sea. Made departmental capital in the Revolution, it owes much of what character it has to the neoclassical administrative buildings erected under Napoleon. During the Second World War, the Germans enlarged the airport, making it one of the most important in France in terms of size; it is now used as a testing ground for the newest Mirages and other military aircraft.

Around Town

In the narrow confines between the Douze and Midou, the fortified *ville médiévale* is the most interesting part of Mont-

Getting to and around Mont-de-Marsan

Although Mont-de-Marsan owed its importance in the last century to rail, few **trains** on the Bordeaux–Tarbes line pass through its little station at the south end of town. For information on the *département's* bus network and schedules, you can contact RDTL, 99 Rue Pierre Benoit, **t** 05 58 05 66 00.

de-Marsan. The walls were built in the 14th century by Gaston Fébus. There are a pair of 13th-century houses along Rue Maubec, and in the centre, along Rue Victor Hugo and its extension, Rue Dulamon, a cluster of First Empire public buildings and mansions. To create a harmonious ensemble, the creators of the new departmental capital demolished the Gothic church of the Magdalene and replaced it with the nondescript current neo-classical model; its marble high altar is by the Mazetti brothers from Avignon, who travelled across the Landes in the 18th century and created works in a number of churches. Every now and then they were even inspired.

Musée Despiau-Wlérick
6 Pl Marguerite-de-Navarre, just south of Rue Victor Hugo, t 05 58 75 00 45; adm, free on Mondays

Lacataye donjon
open Wed–Mon, 10–12 and 2–6, closed hols; adm

But the main attraction is the **Musée Despiau-Wlérick** installed in 1968 in the 14th-century **Lacataye donjon**. It is dedicated to two sculptors born in Mont-de-Marsan. The more important, Charles Despiau (1874–1946), was the son of a local plasterer who became Rodin's assistant from 1907. In 1914, Despiau reacted against Rodin's romanticism and left his workshop to develop his own, far more classical style; he is best known for his sensitive, psychologically penetrating female portrait busts. The second, Robert Wlérick (1882–1944), had a Belgian father and belonged, like Despiau, to the group of Independent Sculptors, but concentrated more on genre works until he got the commission to sculpt half of all the Monuments aux Morts in the Landes (or so it seems); his greatest claim to fame is having carved large parts of the equestrian statue of Maréchal Foch on the Trocadéro Esplanade in Paris. The museum prides itself on being the only one in France solely devoted to modern figurative sculpture. The ground floor is devoted to works by Despiau, the first floor to sculptures by Wlérick, while the second and third floors have works by their contemporaries; along the stair are pretty 18th-century ceramic works from Samadet. Don't miss the view over the town from the donjon's terrace. In 1988 Mont-de-Marsan decided it was time to give some of the museum's bronze and marble inhabitants a breath of fresh air and you can see them standing around the town's streets, waiting for something to happen. The tourist office produces a leaflet with a walk to discover them.

North of the Douze and the *ville médiévale* is a pleasant garden, the **Parc Jean Rameau**, decorated with sculptures by Despiau; nearby Place Francis Planté is named after another son of Mont-de-Marsan, one of the great virtuoso pianists of the 19th century.

During the Feria de Ste-Madeleine, the action takes place down by the train station at the **Arènes du Plumaçon**, built in 1889.

The east end of Mont-de-Marsan, the **Quartier Saint-Médard**, is named after the church of Saint-Médard, first built in the Middle Ages, although its chief glories are from the 17th and 18th centuries, especially its carved wooden door and retable. Nearby, the **Parc de Nahuques** is Mont-de-Marsan's biggest recreation area; part of it is home to swans, donkeys, Tibetan goats and other small animals, who live at liberty. West of town, **St-Pierre-du-Mont** has been absorbed by the capital, and is the site of the Romanesque church of St-Pierre, part of the priory founded by the abbots of Saint-Sever in the 10th century. It has a fine wooden door similar to Saint-Médard, and a marble altar and stucco decorations by the Mazetti brothers.

Parc de Nahuques
open July and Aug Mon–Fri 9–12 and 3–7; Sat, Sun and hols 3–7; Sept–June 2–6; adm

07 The Landes | Mont-de-Marsan

Northeast of Mont-de-Marsan, towards Roquefort

In its heyday in the 11th and 12th centuries, the abbey of Saint-Sever founded a string of churches and priories this way, along a branch of the **Compostela pilgrimage route** that descended from Langon through Mont-de-Marsan, now followed by the D932. The first church, **Ste-Marie**, is in Bostens, and has an interesting bell tower decorated with carvings as well as sculpted modillons. The second is in **Sarbazan**, defended by a massive tower and containing a few carved capitals inside. A **Gallo-Roman villa** with mosaics was excavated nearby. The third is up in **Roquefort**, where the fortified church of Notre-Dame dates from a 12th-century priory; much of it was rebuilt in the Gothic period.

East of here the pretty region of Armagnac touches the Landes: *see* p.132.

Market Days in Mont-de-Marsan

ⓘ **Mont-de-Marsan >**
6 Pl du Général-Leclerc, t 05 58 05 87 37;open Mon–Sat 9–12.30 and 1.30–6, summer 9–6

Comité Départemental, 4 Av Aristide Briand, t 05 58 06 89 89, www. mont-de-marsan.org; open July and Aug Mon–Sat 9–6.30; Sept–June Mon–Sat 9–12.30 and 1.30–6

Food market: Tuesdays and Saturdays.
Flea market: The first Wednesday of each month, all day in Place Saint-Roch – a bustling local market with plenty of colour and not a few bargains.

Where to Stay and Eat in and around Mont-de-Marsan

Mont-de-Marsan ✉ 40000
Book early for the Feria de Ste-Madeleine.

**Richelieu, Rue Wlérick, t 05 58 06 10 20 (€). The Richelieu (a Citotel hotel) has recently been refurbished in a retro Art Deco style, but still has the air of the old classic. Very comfortable. Restaurant is lacking in ambiance but makes up in cuisine; the chef has come from the same family for three generations. *Menus* €17–35. *Open all year. Restaurant closed Sat and Sun eve.*

**Sablar, Place Jean-Jaurès, t 05 58 75 21 11, www.hotelsablar.fr (€). Usually has a simple room not occupied by a travelling salesman. *Open all year.*

Around Mont-de-Marsan ✉ 40000
For more luxurious lodgings, look on the periphery.

***Abor**, on the Grenade Road, t 05 58 51 58 00, www.aborhotel.com (€€). Clean and modern. Set in the forest, air-conditioned, with a pool and a good restaurant, L'Airial, with a garden terrace and generous regional cuisine. Menus €20–30. Open all year.

***Le Renaissance**, Rte de Villeneuve, t 05 58 51 51 51, www.le-renaissance. com (€€). Neoclassical in spite of its name, a handsome manor house set amid verdant lawns, with a pool. The rooms are large and comfortable and the bathrooms totally luxurious. The restaurant draws in hungry clients from all over the area with delicately prepared dishes based on regional products; try the magret de canard with peas. Menus €11–49. Restaurant closed Sat lunch plus Sun eve.

Hotel-Restaurant Zanchettin, 1565 Av de Villeneuve, t 05 58 75 19 52 (€). Just outside Mont-de-Marsan en route to Villeneuve, a small family hotel-cum-bar and tabac, which has cheap rooms and menus in its tiny terrace and restaurant. Menus €11–20. Closed mid-Aug–early Sept and Christmas and New Year.

Didier Garbage, due west of Mont-de-Marsan on the N134 in Uchacq-de-Parentis, t 05 58 75 33 66, may have a name that sounds rather unappetizing in English, but the food here is just the opposite; try the flambéed pigeon. Menus €35–45 but start at €12 in the bistro; closed Sun eve and all Mon.

Auberge de Lapouillique, Mazerolles 40090, t 05 58 75 22 97, 4km east of Mont-de-Marsan (signs will guide you; book in advance). A big old inn under the oaks, serving Landais specialities. Menus €19–33. Closed Sun eve, Mon and Tues eve.

Down the Adour

South of Mont-de-Marsan the very first toes of the foothills of the Pyrenees embrace the Adour, one of the most important rivers in southwest France, its green-blue waters rich in salmon, shad, pike, eel and other tasty fish. The Adour is so prone to flooding in the winter and early spring that once it reaches the Landes it forms for itself an extra-wide river bed, a swampy muddy prairie of islets and canals known as the barthes. The barthes are one of the secret ingredients that make the spa of Dax so popular; they are also a special environment, host to some 130 species of bird, a little 8-inch (20cm) terrapin the French call the cistude d'Europe, and 50 or so little poneys barthais (or landais), the last members of a native species living in semi-liberty along the Adour. It's not only their survival that is in doubt, but that of the barthes themselves, threatened especially west of Dax, where the demands of civilization are drying the barthes for suburban plots, industrial areas or farmland.

The fertile hills south of the Adour are divided into three small regions, the Tursan, Chalosse and Pays d'Orthe. All three offer a striking contrast to the dreamlike infinity of flat pine forests to the north. Here the main tree is oak, standing in groves amid rolling fields of grain and vineyards, pastures and spring vegetables. Everything is more self-contained, plumper, richer, glossier, more solid (especially the houses, which are made out of stone). The one out of every five Landais who is a farmer lives south of the Adour, and like their brethren in Armagnac they prefer to play 6- or 9-pin *quilles*, or skittles, rather than the more traditional *pétanque*. And there are other surprises, too.

Aire-sur-l'Adour and the Tursan

Aire-sur-l'Adour, 'Capital of *Foie Gras*'

⭐ Aire-sur-l'Adour

Aire is a hoary old town, founded by the Tarusates, a Celtic tribe. Crassus conquered it for Rome in 50 BC and it went on to become the occasional capital of the Visigothic kings of Aquitaine in the 5th century. The Visigoths were Arians – heretics according to the Church – and they weren't above tormenting the Catholics in their realm. Their most memorable deed during their stay in Aire involved a young Catholic princess named Quitterie. Quitterie had refused to marry a local Visigoth lord and took refuge in Aire, where she performed a number of miracles. Eventually the rejected suitor found her, and when Quitterie still refused him he cut off her head. In the age-old tradition of decapitated saints, her trunk picked up her head and walked up the hill, choosing the site of her tomb; a miraculous fountain at once gushed forth. In the obscure associative logic of religion, Quitterie and her fountain were soon performing miraculous cures of headaches and mental illness. She is the patron saint of Gascony, and her cult is widespread on both sides of the Pyrenees.

Eglise Ste-Quitterie
mairie: t 05 58 71 47 00 except at weekends; open mid-May–early Sept Mon 2.30–6.30, Tues–Fri 9–12 and 2.30–6.30, Sat 9–12 and 2–5.30; early Sept–mid-May call the mairie

The **church of Ste-Quitterie**, a not unpleasant mix of Roman-esque, Gothic and 18th-century, presides over the upper level of Aire, known as the Quartier du Mas. In the old days, a constant stream of pilgrims and the faithful (it served as a cathedral from the 12th to the 18th centuries) assured that it was always open; today opening hours are restricted (*see left*). The main western façade dates from the 14th century and presents a rather sad, forgotten face to the world, with much of its original decoration chewed away by Huguenots, Revolutionaries and the weather. However, the portal, tucked under the the square brick bell-tower porch, is still mostly intact and decorated with an impressive Gothic tympanum showing scenes from the Last Judgement. The righteous are given robes to wear by an angel, the damned are led off in a chaingang into the maw of hell in the form of a monster, while those doomed to purgatory are stewed in a big pot. The whole is set in luxuriant floral motifs, with the ranks of angels, apostles and prophets in attendance.

The interior was reworked in reheated Baroque by the Mazetti brothers; their choir in coloured marbles remains intact, while the Romanesque capitals that were long masked have been uncovered, some carved with biblical scenes, others with plants, animals or

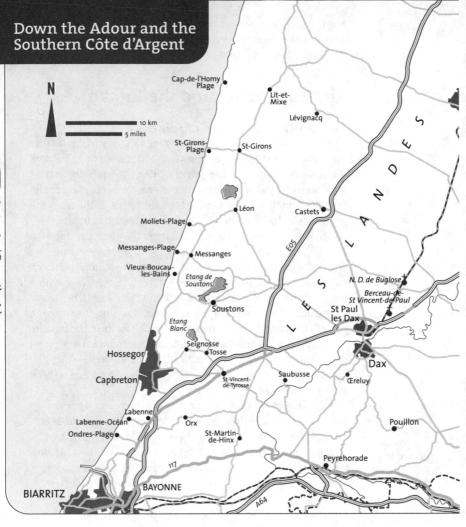

Down the Adour and the Southern Côte d'Argent

monsters. The crypt was originally part of a Roman temple to Mars;
it had a miraculous spring where the baptistry is now. In the old
days there were cells nearby, where the mentally ill were locked up
in the hope of a cure. The magnificent 3rd- or 4th-century white
marble sarcophagus of Ste-Quitterie is carved with scenes from the
Old and New Testaments: God, dressed in a Roman toga, is seen
creating man, the 'Synagogue' is symbolized by a veiled Roman
woman, Daniel is in the Lions' Den, Lazarus comes back to life. On
the sides Jonah is sleeping under a tree, thrown into the sea
and vomited forth by the whale, and Tobias battles the fish. A
sacrificial altar, probably from the Roman temple, is in the small
chapel opposite; test the chapel's bizarre acoustics by speaking
towards the altar.

The palace of Alaric II, the king of the Visigoths, occupied the same spot as the nearby privately owned **Château du Mas**. In the lower town there are a few buildings of note: the 17th-century **Hôtel de Ville**, originally the Bishops' Palace, with a fine stone stair and, tucked below it, a few mosaics and other minor archaeological finds. The adjacent cathedral, rebuilt and reworked from the 12th to the 19th centuries, lost its title to Dax in 1933. In the Place du Commerce is a handsome **covered market** built in 1860, converted into a theatre and abandoned: nowadays Aire's lively fruit and vegetable market and winter Marché de Gras, 'Fat Market', spilling over with geese and ducks (alive or dead), takes place under a roof along Rue Henri-Labeyrie. The 15th-century **Maison de l'Officialité**, at 6 bis, was originally the seat of the local court.

Vin de Tursan and Coteaux de Chalosse

The Tursan and Chalosse had their golden age in the 17th and 18th centuries, when they imported wine down the Adour to Bayonne, and from there to England and Holland, at a time when Bordeaux controlled all the production up its own river, the Garonne, and did everything it could to stifle competition. Neighbouring on the prestigious Madiran growing region, the hills around Geaune have grown vin de Tursan since the 12th century. The reds, made of tannat, cabernet and égiodola, have a pleasant supple quality, a wine for bons vivants that goes well with the regional duck and goose cuisine, while the whites, made from an unusual medieval variety called baroque, as well as chasan and aribola, are fruitier and excellent with asparagus dishes. Vin de Tursan was granted the *appellation* VDQS in 1958, and most of it is produced through Geaune's co-operative, the **Caves des Vignerons Landais** (open for tours and tastings, Mon–Fri 9–12 and 2–5.30, until 6.30 in July and Aug; but ring ahead on t 05 58 44 51 25, to let them know you're coming). Ask about the new *route des vins*.

To the west, the Vin de Pays Coteaux de Chalosse is made from similar varieties, but suffered a dire setback in the 1860s when the vines were ruined by oïdium. Replanted last century and commonly regarded as a 'petit vin', the vintners have been striving to improve the quality and structure in their wines. You can see, or rather taste, how they're doing in Mugron, down the Adour from St-Sever, at the **Caves des Vignerons des Coteaux de Chalosse** (Av Réné-Bats, open for visits same hours as above, t 05 58 97 70 75).

Grenade-sur-l'Adour and Our Lady of Rugby

The first town of importance down river, Grenade-sur-l'Adour is a pretty *bastide* town founded in 1322; its *cornières* are still intact, and the church conserves a pretty flamboyant Gothic retable. Grenade is better known, however, for its unusual chapel just across the river at La Rivière, **Notre-Dame-du-Rugby**. Dedicated to the 'Virgin supporter of teams from the Landes', it is hung with the jerseys of players who came to leave their prayers inscribed in the 'golden book'. The stained glass and other art is what stays with you, however, especially the statue made by an old rugby captain of a young Jesus handing off the ball to his Mother.

Notre-Dame-du-Rugby
turn left up the narrow road

To the north of Grenade on the D406, in **Bascons**, the Virgin supports another local craze in the chapel of **Notre-Dame-de-la-Course-Landaise**, set in the midst of cornfields, but don't come looking for statues of Jesus or the Apostles dodging bulls. There's a small **museum** dedicated to the sport.

Bascons museum
t 05 58 52 91 76; open Wed–Fri 2–7

The Tursan

An agricultural region of uneven, broken valleys south of Aire and Grenade, the Tursan is the source of most of the geese and ducks in the Fat Market, as well as the corn that feeds them, dairy cattle and wine. It also has a spa, **Eugénie-les-Bains**, named after its godmother, the Empress Eugénie, wife of Napoleon III, although by rights it should be renamed Michel-Guérard-les-Bains after the famous chef who put it on the map when he transformed the dowdy baths into a health-orientated *nouvelle cuisine* pleasure dome (*see* p.112). Eugénie's waters are used for treating obesity and digestive troubles – hence the *Premier Village Minceur de France*, 'France's Top Slimming Village'.

To the south, **Geaune**, the capital of the Tursan, was founded as a *bastide* in 1318 by a *sénéchal* from Genoa, who named it after his home town (*Gênes* in French). It has a 15th-century southern Gothic church with an enormous bell tower and porch, and is the centre of local wine production.

Samadet

West of Geaune, Samadet is a pleasant hilltop village synonymous with the lovely dinnerware made by the **Manufacture Royale de Fayance de Samadet**, in business for just over a century (1732–1840). Founded when the Marquis and Abbé of Rochépine, Charles Maurice de Bouzet, obtained the necessary royal work permit, the industry is remembered in the **Musée de la Faïencerie**, near the church.

After Louis XIV bought his first faïence (after having had to melt down all his gold and silver plates to pay for his endless wars), it became fashionable on the tables of French aristocrats, and various factories were set up to meet the new demand. Made from the excellent local clay, sand and marl, Samadet table services are characterized by their delicate, highly stylized animal and floral *motives* or hunting scenes, painted in rich pure colours. Often imitated, Samadet has rarely been equalled, and pieces sell for small fortunes today. Besides a display of 250 plates and bowls, a workshop has been recreated in the museum to show how it was done; other artefacts evoke traditional rural life in the Tursan and a room is dedicated to table settings. Near the museum, a new atelier has been set up to recreate Samadet pieces – at almost affordable prices.

Musée de la Faïencerie
t 05 58 79 13 00, www.museesamadet. org; open Tues– Sun Jan–Mar 2–6; April–Oct 10–12.30 and 2–6.30; Nov–Dec 2–6; closed hols; adm

Market Days in Aire-sur-l'Adour and the Tursan

Aire-sur-l'Adour: Tuesdays and Saturdays; from November to February, goose and duck market, also on Tuesdays.

Grenade-sur-l'Adour: Mondays.

Geaune: Thursdays (every other week).

Where to Stay and Eat in Aire-sur-l'Adour and the Tursan

Aire-sur-l'Adour ✉ 40800

Chez l'Ahumat, 2 Rue Pierre-Mendes-France, t 05 58 71 82 61 (€). On a quiet lane near the centre of Aire, with some of the nicest low-price rooms around. The restaurant features delicious *cuisine landaise* at exceptional prices as well, served with local wines. *Menus €11–27. Open all year except 15–30 Mar and 1–15 Sept. Restaurant closed Wed.*

Maison Crabot, t 05 58 71 91 73 (€). Some of the best places are a short drive away from Aire-sur-l'Adour. Five km from Aire, signs will guide you to this peaceful hilltop farmhouse with pretty views. Summer kitchen and fridge available to guests. Dinner by reservation only. *Open all year.*

Ferme Auberge Lacère, Bahus-Soubiran, 6km west on the D2, t 05 58 44 40 64. Serves satisfying regional duck dishes, *poule au pot* and warm *foie gras* served in the traditional

ⓘ Aire-sur-l'Adour >
Pl Charles-de-Gaulle, B.P. 155, t 05 58 71 64 70, otsi.aire@wanadoo.fr; open Sept–May Mon–Fri 9–12 and 2–5; June Mon–Sat 9–12 and 2–5; July–Aug Mon–Fri 9–12.30 and 2–6, Sat 2–5

⭐ **La Maison Rose >>**

ⓘ **Grenade-sur-l'Adour >**
1 Pl des Déportés, t 05 58 45 45 98, www. tourismegrenadois.com; open summer Mon, Tues and Thurs 8.30–12; winter 4–6 on Mon, 2–4 Tues and 3–5 Thurs, Fri 8.30–12

ⓘ **Eugénie-les-Bains >**
Rue René Vielle, t 05 58 51 13 16, www.ville-eugenie-les-bains.fr; open Mon–Fri 9.30–12 and 2–6, Sat 10–12 and 2.30–4

ⓘ **Geaune**
Route de la Chalosse, t 05 58 44 42 00; open Mon–Thurs 8.30–12.30 and 1.30–5.30, Fri 8.30–12.30 and 1.30–4.30

Landais fashion, with apples or grapes. *Menu €13–25. Open year-round Sat eve and Sun lunch, and in summer every day by reservation. Closed mid-Dec–mid-Feb.*

Grenade-sur-l'Adour ✉ 40270

***Pain Adour et Fantaisie, Pl des Tilleuls, **t** 05 58 45 18 80, *www.chateauxhotels.com/fantaise* (€€€€–€€). Set in a handsome old house in the arcaded heart of the *bastide*, with comfortable rooms overlooking the river and a celebrated restaurant, where Philippe Garret prepares excellent, aromatic dishes prepared from a wide variety of ingredients, many local (home-smoked salmon from the Adour, asparagus from the Landes), followed by luscious desserts (the €35 menu is tremendously good value; the other menu is €82). *Closed Sun eve and Mon and Wed lunch, exc in July and Aug; it's a good idea to reserve. Hotel open early Dec–end of Nov.*

Hôtel de France, 3 Pl des Tilleuls, **t** 05 58 45 19 02. One room only (€). There's a bistro and restaurant, bistro menus starting at €10, restaurant at €12–36. *Restaurant closed Sun eve and Mon.*

Eugénie-les-Bains ✉ 40320

Eugénie-les-Bains is the fief, or rather little paradise, created by Christine and Michel Guérard. Set in a beautiful 30-acre wooded park full of rare trees and flower gardens, there are a number of excellent eating places to choose from:

***Les Prés d'Eugénie, **t** 05 58 05 06 07, *www.michelguerard.com* (€€€€€) is one of the dreamiest small hotels in all France; romantic rooms with wrought-iron balconies occupy the main neoclassical wing, while others, exquisitely furnished with antiques, are in a 19th-century convent near the herb garden. A gymnasium, billiards hall, spa, sauna, beauty centre, tennis courts, heated pool and thermal slimming centre are on the grounds, and guests can join in courses on *nouvelle cuisine*. *Closed Dec–28 Mar.* Christine Guérard has also refurbished and redecorated

La Maison Rose (same phone), a charming country inn in the estate grounds (€€€€–€€€), where some rooms come with kitchenettes. The restaurant to the *Prés d'Eugénie* attracts visitors from around the world to this remote corner of the Landes, is best known by the name of the legendary sorcerer of saucepans, Michel Guérard. After installing himself in Eugénie-les-Bains in the early 1970s, Guérard hit the world of *haute cuisine* like a comet, earning a constellation of stars and *toques* from the guides. He has remained firmly at the summit ever since that time, continuously improving and adding new imaginative dishes to his repertoire, which is based on using only the finest natural ingredients and especially products from the Landes – many of them, like the herbs, are picked fresh the same day. The wonderful Baroque dining room provides an exquisite stage setting for each exquisite dish, which is every bit as beautiful to look upon as it is to taste, with Guérard's flawless combination of flavours and textures. The wine list covers most of the great vineyards of the southwest, and includes the excellent white Baron de Bachen vin de Tursan that Guérard produces in his own vineyard (for a table, book as far in advance as possible, **t same number as hotel). *Menus €135–185. Closed Mon eve except July and Aug.* Jan–Mar the restaurant to **La Maison Rose** specializes in healthy eating.

Another recent Guérard acquisition, **La Ferme aux Grives**, at Les Charmilles, is an old Landais farm and specializes in the kind of delicious food that the original owners may well have dined on themselves. Among the delicious items on the menu are some wonderful country hams, melt-in-your-mouth roast suckling pig, and magnificent desserts that will send you waddling over to make an urgent appointment at the slimming centre. *One menu at €34. Closed Tues eve and Wed in low season and Jan–mid-Feb.*

St-Sever and the Chalosse

St-Sever, site of the Landes' most important abbey in the Middle Ages, enjoys a superb setting, high on a balcony between the gently rolling hills of the Chalosse and the endless sea of pine forests to the north. The Chalosse, a region even lusher than the Tursan, is known as the 'Secret Garden of the Landes'. Good food is a near-Pantagruelian obsession in its little hilltop villages; the excellent quality of the corn grown here gives the *foie gras* from the Chalosse its national prize-winning finesse and fattens a unique race of beef cattle.

St-Sever, the 'Cap de Gascogne'

Naturally defensible, St-Sever has been inhabited since the dawn of time; since the Middle Ages it has been divided into two districts. One, the lofty plateau of Morlanne, was the site of the Roman *castrum*, where the Pope's emissary St Severus converted the 5th-century Roman governor Hadrian (before the Vandals lopped off his head). Not a stone remains of this, but you can drive up to the Belvedere for the view, shared by a statue of General Lamarque, a patriotic stalwart of the Revolution born in St-Sever in 1770, whose funeral in Paris in 1828 ignited a bloody riot (see Victor Hugo's account in *Les Misérables*). Below stretches the formerly walled Cité of St-Sever – the centre of the modern town – that grew up around the Benedictine abbey, an important pilgrimage stop on the Limousine branch of the Compostela road. Although for centuries the French believed the Landais were really Tartars, St-Sever hosted the only authenticated Tartars to cross through the area: the emissaries of the Khan Argoun, who stayed in St-Sever in 1287 on their way to the court of the Black Prince in Bordeaux. Since the mid-19th century, St-Sever has been the goose-feather capital of the Landes, stuffing the downy by-product of the regional *foie gras* industry into duvets, sleeping bags and jackets.

Although a handful of 18th-century *hôtels particuliers* survive in the centre of St-Sever (among them, the building housing the tourist office), the star attraction is the **Benedictine abbey** founded in 988 by the count of Gascony, Guillaume Sanche. It reached its golden age under the reign of Abbot Grégoire de Montaner of Cluny (1028–72), who rebuilt the abbey on a grand scale, with seven staggered apses, here and there reusing Gallo-Roman marble columns. Work proceeded throughout the 12th century: the floor was covered with a splendid mosaic (of which some fragments remain behind the choir), and several different workshops of sculptors carved the capitals. Heavily damaged in the Hundred Years War, the nave was rebuilt with Gothic arches in the 14th century; the cloister and monastery buildings date from this period.

Benedictine abbey
http://abbatiale.
saint-sever.fr; open
Oct–Mar Mon–Sat 8–6 ,
and April–Sept Mon–Sat
8–7, Sun 8–12

07 The Landes | St-Sever and the Chalosse

Worse was yet to come: the Protestants in 1570, some statue-guillotining Revolutionaries and, to top it off, 19th-century restorers from the *Monuments Historiques* whose leaden neo-Romanesque touch destroyed much of the abbey's charm. Fortunately, the restorers left the capitals alone. Those from the 11th century have simple, decorative floral designs. Sculptors from the early 13th century added (in the south apses) figures amid the leaves and stems: birds, grinning lions, and Daniel in the Lions' Den (definitely the favourite subject of 12th-century sculptors in the Midi – but no one really knows why). The finest capitals of all, in the north tribune (at the end of the transept), are believed to have been carved by the vigorous School of Toulouse, with the Feast of Herod and Beheading of St John the Baptist. Also note the sculpted wooden case of the organ (1711).

Couvent des Jacobins
t 05 58 76 34 64, http://jacobins.saint.sever.fr; open July–Sept 2.30–6; phone ahead for guided tours

In 1280 Eleanor of Castile, wife of Edward I of England, founded another monastery in St-Sever, the Dominican **Couvent des Jacobins**. Restored after the Wars of Religion, it did duty as a school and agricultural college after the Revolution until 1970; since then the town has been slowly restoring it bit by bit as a cultural centre. The church, its plan strict and plain compared to the elaborate apses of the Benedictines, has a Gothic portal and rose window; the chapterhouse, entered through the right, has retained some of its murals from the 14th and 15th centuries; the adjacent refectory has a painting of a monk kneeling before St Dominic and a cardinal. The cloister was completely rebuilt in the 17th century and now houses the little **Musée des Jacobins**, with Gallo-Roman and medieval artefacts, items relating to the pilgrimage route, old postcards and a display devoted to the

School of painting
http://beatus.saint.sever.fr

Gallo-Roman mosaics
guided tour organized by tourist office, t 05 58 76 34 64; June–Sept Tues–Sat

celebrated illuminated 11th-century *Apocalypse of St-Sever* (now in the Bibliothèque National in Paris), a creation of the wonderfully inventive **school of painting** founded by Grégoire de Montaner. On a guided visit organized by the tourist office (June–Sept Tues–Sat) you can also visit the house of Doctor Sentex in Place de Verdun in the historic town centre, with **gallo-Roman mosaics** covering the ground floor.

Salade Landaise

You'll see this *salade composée* listed as a starter on many menus throughout southwest France, and it's easy to prepare, especially if you're self-catering: the average supermarket carries all the ingredients. The following serves six people. First, mix a dressing using a tablespoon of hazelnut oil and two tablespoons of sunflower oil, a tablespoon of wine vinegar, pepper and a bit of salt. Wash and drain whatever lettuce is in season. In a frying pan, heat up 6 sliced *gésiers confits* (gizzards preserved in fat), 12 thin slices of dried duck breast (they come ready in packages from the *charcuterie* counter, labelled *aiguillettes de magret séché*), and 12 thin slices of fresh *magret de canard*; put them on paper towels to soak off any excess fat, and let them cool. Meanwhile place the lettuce around six plates, embellish with the meat slices, dress the salad and place a medallion of *foie gras de canard* in the centre of each plate; serve preferably with a dry Jurançon.

South of St-Sever

After St-Sever, pilgrims en route to Compostela passed through **Audignon**, 5km southwest, where there was a hospital and a gem of a Romanesque church to receive them, with a beautiful apse decorated with carved modillons and capitals. The bell tower doubled as a donjon, and the doorway, decorated with masks, dates from the 14th century. Inside, there's a superb 15th-century stone retable with frescoes from 1550, and stone blocks cut with distinctive masons' marks (open 8–8). Two kilometres to the south of Audignon on the D21, **Aulès** has another good Romanesque church with carved capitals on its exterior.

Further south, **Hagetmau** means 'bad beech tree' in Gascon (there must be a story there somewhere, but we don't know it) and takes no little pride in being 'The Chair Capital of Europe', producing everything from the straw-seat country farm chair to Louis XV armchairs – but don't expect any factory outlets. Instead, Hagetmau offers more Romanesque art in its atmospheric **Crypte de St-Girons**. This is all that remains of a Benedictine abbey, built over the 4th-century tomb of St Girons, evangelist of the Chalosse. Although the vaults of the crypt are more recent, the 14 elaborately sculpted capitals are fascinating: there's a *tête à tête* between a man and a dragon, the story of Lazarus, and the Deliverance of St Peter from prison.

On the Hagetmau–Mugron road (the D18) you can visit a modern pilgrimage site: **Maylis**, the 'Mother of Lilys', where the Olivetan **Abbaye Notre-Dame de Maylis** has Romanesque and Gothic elements in its old church and a 12th-century statue of the Virgin. The monks cultivate a special plant used in treating liver and kidney ailments and run a shop (*www.boutiques-theophile.com*).

Brassempouy, southwest of Hagetmau, is famous as the source of the unique Venus of Brassempouy, or the *Dame à la Capuche*, 'the hooded lady'. Carved in mammoth ivory and measuring 3.5cm – about an inch – this is the oldest known human portrait, going back 23,000 years. It was discovered in 1894 in the Grotte du Pape just outside the village, where excavations continue apace in the summer. Current finds are in the new **Maison de la Dame**. Although the original was whisked off to Paris' Museum of St-Germain-en-Laye, the museum has a copy of the *Dame à la Capuche*; note that her so-called 'hood' could just as easily be an elaborate corn-row hair style. There is also Le Jardin de la Dame where you can learn how our ancestors lived and how their environment looked then. Also worth a look is Brassempouy's fortified 12th-century church of **St-Sernin**; you can climb the slightly dangerous stairs to the top of the bell tower for an excellent view.

Abbaye Notre-Dame de Maylis
t 05 58 97 72 81

Maison de la Dame
t 05 58 89 21 73, http:// maisondeladame.chez-alice.fr; open Tues–Sun June–Sept 11–12 and 2–7; Feb–May and Oct–Nov 2–5.30

Le Jardin de la Dame
http:// lejardindeladame. site.voila.fr

07 The Landes | St-Sever and the Chalosse

> ### Capcazal
> *Capcazal*, 'first house', is the local word for a place occupied and cultivated since the beginning of time, or almost. Owners of such houses, who occupied a midway point between the nobility and the commoners, enjoyed a variety of privileges, such as the right to own a dovecote and complete freedom from the feudal system.

Château de Gaujacq
t 05 58 89 01 01; open July and Aug 11–6, otherwise call; closed mid-Dec–mid-Feb; botanical garden: www.thoby.com

West of Brassempouy, the 17th-century **Château de Gaujacq** (or de Sourdis), standing on the ruins of a Roman *castrum* just outside the village of the same name, is open for guided tours. The de Sourdis family were so fond of the Carthusians that they built their home in the form of a Charterhouse, complete with an interior cloister; here the Marquis de Montespan came to retire and die after his wife became the mistress of Louis XIV. The rooms are noted for their lovely panelling and furnishings from the 17th to 19th centuries. The colourful **botanical garden** is used to propagate endangered species and heath and moorland varieties.

Another road from Brassempouy, the D21, leads southwest to the happy little town of **Amou**, a town originally called Amor by the Romans, hence the town's motto '*Amor que so*', or 'I am Love'. Set on the banks of the Luy de Béarn and surrounded by orchards, its Romanesque church boasts a colourful rococo altar, and its 17th-century château, built to the designs of Mansart, offers a rare look at French Classicism in this neck of the woods. West of Amou, **Pomarez** is the 'Mecca of Bullfighting' (in this case, the *course landaise*), which it loves so well that it built the first covered arena in France, with seats for 3,000 – more than the village itself can begin to fill.

Back along the Adour

The Adour is most scenic between St-Sever and Mugron, where the *villages perchés* sit on natural terraces over the water. Here **Montaut** has been a stronghold since the Middle Ages, and as such was destroyed by the Huguenots in 1569. The village **cultural centre** displays tools and explanations from the nearby Solutrean-era *gisement d'Arcet*, where flint tools were manufactured between 20,000 and 15,000 BC. There are also paintings by Olga Olby, sculpture by Lydia Luzanowski and information on the history of the village. **Brocas**, 5km south of Montaut, has a fine 12th-century church, Saint-Pierre, all that remains of an **abbey**. During the 19th century Brocas was the site of an important iron works and in an old **foundry** you can learn about the techniques employed, and see examples of the items created. There is still the original blast furnace. **Mugron**, the 'Belvedere of the Chalosse', enjoys a wonderful view (especially from its church) of the great forest to the north. The centre of the Chalosse wine production (*see* p.110), Mugron's old *chais* can still be seen along the river,

Cultural centre
t 05 58 76 05 13; call to visit

Brocas abbey
open May–Sept 9–7; Oct–April 9–5

Foundry
t 05 58 51 64 05; open mid-June–mid-Sept 3–7; adm

 Mugron

Moulin de Poyaller

t 05 58 97 95 72, www. moulin-poyaller. com; open July and Aug Sun–Thurs 12–7, mid-Mar–June and Sept–early Nov 2.30–6.30; adm

Musée de la Chalosse

t 05 58 98 69 27; open April–Oct Tues–Sun 10–12 and 2–6.30; Nov–Mar Tues–Fri 2–5:30

where the wine was stored before shipment to Bayonne. You can also visit a 400-year-old water mill, the **Moulin de Poyaller** where you can also take a boat ride and visit the wallabies and deer. Just north, the pretty 11th-century church at **Nerbis** was another foundation of Saint Sever.

An interesting museum can be found in the 13th-century *bastide* of **Montfort-en-Chalosse**, which was founded by the king of England and remains one of the prettiest villages in the Chalosse. The **Musée de la Chalosse** is contained in the Domaine de Carcher, a master's house preserved and furnished as it was at the end of the 19th century, complete with barns and outbuildings and an exhibit on wine. The church of Montfort is equally worth a look, a charming combination of Romanesque and Gothic, heavily fortified in the 15th century; but as with many villages in the Chalosse, many people come to Montfort just to eat.

Market Days in St-Sever and the Chalosse

St-Sever: Saturdays.
Hagetmau: Wednesdays and Saturdays.
Amou: Sundays.
Pomarez: Mondays.
Mugron: Thursdays and Saturdays.
Montfort-en-Chalosse: Wednesdays.

Where to Stay and Eat in St-Sever and the Chalosse

St-Sever ✉ 40500

Le Relais du Pavillon, Quartier Péré (at the crossroads of the D924 and D933), **t 05 58 76 20 22 (€). A peaceful haven in a garden with pool, where the chef prepares an excellent *magret de canard à la ficelle* and other tasty delights. *Menus €11–45 with lots of foie gras. Restaurant closed Sun eve and Mon; hotel closed 1st two weeks in Jan.*
Camping des Rives de l'Adour, t 05 58 76 04 60. A pleasant site on the river, near the canoe and kayak base. *Open July and Aug.*

Hagetmau ✉ 40700

*Le Jambon, 245 Rue Carnot, **t** 05 58 79 32 02 (€). You can check in here at the

'Ham', a good standard provincial hotel, and feast by the fireplace on Chalosse beef steaks, *soufflé de St Jacques aux écrevisses. Menus €15–45. Closed Jan.*

Mugron ✉ 40250

Ferme-Auberge Marquine, t 05 58 97 74 23. Good fills, with a meaty menu – country ham, *rillettes de canard, foie gras*, a choice of duck *magrets* or *confits*, with a traditional *tourtière* to finish off. *Menus €12–31. Open daily all year, but ring ahead. Closed Mon.*

Maylis ✉ 40250

Ferme-Auberge Caoubet, t 05 58 97 91 74. Colette Laborde's restaurant has both set menus. and an *à la carte* menu featuring *foie gras*, quails stuffed with *foie gras* and capon *confits*, as well as the more common duck *magrets* and *confits. Menus €15–30. Call first for a reservation.*

Montfort-en-Chalosse ✉ 40380

Aux Tauzins, on the D2 towards Hagetmau, **t 05 58 98 60 22 (€€). This cosy old family-run country inn has been open for decades, with comfortable rooms, set in a garden with a pool. The restaurant makes excellent use of the good things from the Chalosse, as in *foie frais aux raisins* or *tournedos landais. Menus €21–40. Closed Sun eve and Mon out of season, late Jan–mid-Feb, and first 2 weeks Oct.*

ⓘ **St-Sever >**
Pl du Tour-du-Sol, t 05 58 76 34 64, www.saint-sever.fr; open Mon–Fri 9–12 and 2–5.30, Sat 9–12

ⓘ **Hagetmau >**
56 Pl de la République, t 05 58 79 38 26; open Mon–Sat 9–12.30 and 2.30–6.30

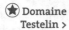 **Domaine Testelin >**

Domaine Testelin, Baights, t 05 58 98 61 21, *www.domaine-de-testelin.fr* (€€). Twelve lovely rooms in a magnificent, warm friendly *maison de maître*, set in a park; the food is equally lovely, featuring succulent *magrets* and other regional specialities, washed down with *vin du Tursan*. Menus €14–36. Closed Sun eve and Tues eve, late Jan and end of Sept–early Oct.

Dax

 Dax

With five deep wells bored into the left bank of the Adour pouring out over 7 million litres of hot water steeped in sodium chloride, calcium and magnesium sulphates every day, Dax easily makes its living as France's top thermal spa. It's a busy, pleasant town of 50,000 – a metropolis by Landais standards – full of flowers, mimosa and minivans transferring patients to and fro between the hotels and the baths. If you're aching, scores of doctors are on hand to prescribe a cure; if you're French, it's a bargain – a fat section of the prospectus the tourist office sends out is devoted to analysing all possible Social Security reimbursements for soaking in the water or getting plastered in mud. And all cures seem to last three weeks. If you fancy some pampering you can visit the pools and Jacuzzi paying leisure rates by the hour at **Thermes Borda**.

Thermes Borda
30 Rue des Lazaristes,
t 05 58 74 86 13,
www.thermes-borda.fr,
Mar–Dec Mon–Sat 3–8

The first known Dacquois were the Tarbelli, a tribe of Gauls defeated by Caesar's lieutenant Crassus in 56 BC. A Roman garrison town, Aqua Tarbellica, was set up next to the Gaulish village. It owed its first fame to a shaggy dog legend: one of the centurions stationed in the garrison had an old dog that was stiff with rheumatism, so he left it behind when he was sent over the Pyrenees to crush a Spanish revolt. When he returned, he was amazed to see old, infirm Fido frisking about like a pup. No one could explain the change, but the centurion was curious enough to follow the dog one day on his rounds. To his surprise, the dog went

Dax Facts

Back in the 19th century, a visiting doctor caused a stir when he accused Dax of lax hygiene for mixing something that looked like cow dung into the Fontaine Chaude. An inquiry revealed that the stuff was really algae, and although you won't see it floating around the Fontaine Chaude any more (thanks to a cement bottom added in 1961), it is one of the keys to Dax's fame as '*La Première Station de Pélothérapie*', which translates something like 'First in Hot Mud Pie Cures'. The earliest thermal mud installations were pits dug along the banks of the river; whenever the Adour overflowed, the mud from the *barthes* oozed into the pits where everyone could wallow to their heart's content. These days, the mud is scientifically gathered, filtered and mixed with hot water from the fountain, and spread out to ripen for four to six months in large solar basins – artificial *barthes*. Here greenish algae and bacteria incubate in the mud mix (it looks like the picture of proto-evolutionary primordial soup in your biology schoolbook) which contribute in some mysterious way to the anti-inflammatory, soothing effect when the sticky, plasticky grey mud, now called *peloïde de Dax*, is heated and applied to aching joints and bad backs. The spas apply 1,000 cubic metres of the stuff every year, by prescription only; if you'd like to try a bath, however, the **Thermes Borda**, 30 Rue des Lazaristes, t 05 58 74 86 13, is open Monday to Saturday from 3–8; closed Jan and Feb.

Getting to and around Dax

The tourist office can arrange for a **taxi** to collect and return you to Bordeaux or Biarritz airports. You need to phone and then send a refundable deposit of €72, cheque payable to Navette d'Dax, giving details of the flight and passenger numbers.

The **train** station (on the TGV Atlantique route from Paris) is on the north bank of the Adour, half a kilometre north of the centre. (The Bordeaux–Dax track is almost dead straight after Arcachon and there are never any cows on it: the French make use of it whenever they're trying to break speed records with a new TGV engine.)

For local and regional **bus** information (RDTL), call **t** 05 58 56 80 80, *www.rdtl.fr*.

For a **taxi**, call **t** 05 58 91 25 25, 06 08 53 77 89 or 06 08 53 39 20.

---

mucking through the shallow *barthes* along the Adour and jumped into a pool of hot mud. The centurion, who had a few aches and pains himself from a winter spent in the Pyrenees, joined his dog in the mud, enjoyed the experience and quickly spread word of a miraculous cure.

The good news of the mud's therapeutic qualities reached all the way to Rome, where Julia, the man-eating daughter of Augustus, was also afflicted with rheumatism. Not wanting to miss out, she became the first celebrity to take the muds and in gratitude renamed the garrison Aqua Augustus after her dad. By the 2nd century AD, the garrison had grown into a proper town with at least one temple; in the 4th century it was walled in as its name gradually contracted on Gascon tongues to Dax. In the 12th century Richard the Lion-Heart gave it a castle, but it was razed to the ground in 1891. Its current career as a full-time spa took off after the construction of the railway from Bordeaux in 1854.

A Walk through Old Dax

From the 4th century to the mid-1800s, Dax was corseted in its town walls on the left bank of the Adour; only a part of these and eight of the original 49 towers have survived near the river. It has the perfect centrepiece for a spa town, the neoclassical arcaded **Fontaine Chaude**, built in 1818 around the steaming source. Known by the Tarbelli Gauls and the Romans as the fountain of the naiads, or La Néhe, this is the most generous of the 50 hot springs in France, pumping out 2,400 cubic metres of water a day at 64°C (147°F); in Gascon it's called *Lou Bagn Bourren*, the Boiling Bath, and was an old favourite of housewives for cooking hard-boiled eggs, dipping chickens for easy plucking and washing the sheets.

Musée de Borda
t 05 58 74 12 91,
www.dax.fr;
open Tues–Sat 2–6;
closed hols

From the Fontaine Chaude, Rue Cazade leads to the **Musée de Borda**, housed in the 16th-century Hôtel de St-Martin-d'Agès, where Mazarin lived while arranging the marriage of Louis XIV (*see* p.193). The collection was founded as a cabinet of curiosities by Dax's most famous son, Jean-Charles de Borda (1733–99), a member of the Académie de Sciences who did much to improve the technology of the French fleet and invent new navigational instruments at the time of the American War of Independence. The museum houses an important collection of engraved ivories from the Upper Palaeolithic era and another cast of the famous *Dame à la Capuche*, from Brassempouy (*see* above). There's a large collection of Roman votives from Dax and Aire, some impressive bronzes found under Dax's *halles* in 1982 (note especially the Mercury, with a little goat, and the cockerel that became the symbol of Gaul) as well as Gallo-Roman mosaics and a statue of *Sleeping Eros* discovered embedded in the town walls when they were levelled in 1850.

In the medieval section are a pair of Merovingian sarcophagi from St-Vincent de Xaintes, the first church in the Landes, founded in the 4th century, and a stone where debtors who couldn't pay up were made to sit in Rue du Mirailh; every time someone passed by they had to receive three smacks on the behind. The coin collection ranges from the ancient Greek to the curious ceramic pennies minted by the Weimar Republic in the 1920s, and a display tells the history of the *course landaise*. Opposite the museum, you can see the foundations of a Roman temple and house, the **Crypte Gallo-Romaine**, discovered in 1979 .

Crypte Gallo-Romaine
guided visits only, meet at the Musée de Borda at 4pm; call the museum for information

Rue Cazade continues south to Rue Saint-Pierre, site of the new Hôtel de Ville and the 4th-century city gate; beyond the gate is another section of walls, repaired in the 19th century by the *Monuments Historiques*. West of the Hôtel de Ville towers the ponderous bulk of the **Cathédrale Notre-Dame** completed in 1894, the third church built on the site. The original Romanesque cathedral was bombed to bits by the English in 1295; its splendid Gothic replacement collapsed in 1645. St Vincent de Paul convinced Anne of Austria, Louis XIV's mother, to raise a special tax for its rebuilding, but it still took 275 years to complete. The resulting mongrel Baroque-classical interior is morose and frumpy, but there's an impressive organ case from the 17th century, said to be carved from the chestnut trees that were once used by Dax's hangman.

From the Gothic cathedral were salvaged 80 choir stalls from the mid-16th century, lovingly carved with a Renaissance lunatic asylum of bizarre figures twisting about the seats like circus contortionists. Best of all is the 12th- or early 13th-century **Portal of the Apostles** installed inside the left transept in 1890 to protect it from the elements. One of the few southern Gothic portals to escape the Revolution, the 19th-century wrecking ball and the grasp of American museum collectors (only because it was forgotten, wedged into a wall between 1642 and 1890), its tympanum depicts a favourite medieval subject, the Weighing of Souls. Over the centre pillar Christ holds the book of the Seven Seals, while around him stand expressive life-size statues of the twelve Apostles with their various emblems. Along the lintel, the dead rise from their graves, the blessed from smart tombs on the right, while on the left the reprobates are pursued and chewed by devils, monsters and Deadly Sins.

Behind the cathedral, pedestrian-only Rue Neuve has some of Dax's finest buildings from the 17th century; at the top of the street, turn left into Cours de Verdun to see the handsome **Atrium Casino**, built in 1929 and thanks to recent renovation mainstains its Art Deco style. Up the Adour, in the riverside Parc Théodore Denis, the rather elegant white **Arènes** with its domed towers is the busiest arena in the Landes, with both *courses landaises* and Spanish *corridas* from June to October.

On the west side of Dax, the former village of **St-Vincent-de-Xaintes** was annexed to Dax in 1950. A church from the 1890s stands on the site of the 4th-century church of St-Vincent (although it conserves a Gallo-Roman mosaic in the choir), while the old oak forest belonging to the parish is now the attractive public park of the **Bois de Boulogne**, a great place for a picnic, pony rides, fishing in the pond or whacking a golf ball on the driving-range. Other attractions in Dax include Le Pavillon du Foie Gras, where you can tour the factory, see how it's made and buy direct; and the **Musée de l'Aviation Légère**, with a collection of old fighter planes, 'Bananes' helicopters and their prototypes. Dax also has the **Musée Georgette-Dupouy**, with 62 paintings by the artist who lived in Dax and died there in 1992; and the Parc du Sarrat with more than 1,200 trees and 1,500 shrubs, some of which are rare; note that you can only visit as part of a guided tour, just contact the tourist office.

Le Pavillon du Foie Gras
t 05 58 56 73 21; open May–Oct Mon–Fri 10–12 and 3–6

Musée de l'Aviation Légère
58 Av de l'Aérodrome, t 05 58 74 66 19; open July and Aug Tues–Sun 2–6; Mar–Jun and Sept–Nov Tues–Sat

Musée Georgette-Dupouy
25 Rue Cazade, t 05 58 56 04 34, open 2–6, http:// ass.gdupouy.free.fr

Around Dax

Just over the Adour from Dax, **St-Paul-lès-Dax** is worth a visit for its 12th-century church, in particular for the eleven sculpted capitals and niches around the exterior of its apse, beautifully carved in white and coloured marble with floral designs, monkeys, musicians and fantastic animals. The white marble niches show a curious mix of biblical scenes – Samson and the Lion, St Veronica wiping Christ's face with a handkerchief, the Last Supper, the Crucifixion, two Angels at the Tomb, the Resurrected Christ, and flame-spitting monsters.

Six kilometres northeast of Dax, the village of Ranquine was renamed **St-Vincent-de-Paul** after the saint born here in 1581. In a small complex known as **Le Berceau de St-Vincent-de-Paul**, run by the Sisters of Charity, his half-timbered house has been restored with original furnishings; a neo-Byzantine chapel of dubious taste was plumped next door, and in the grange you can watch a video on the life of the saint, who as a young shepherd kept the family flock in the shade of the huge oak tree nearby. His family, noting his piety, sent him off to study with the Franciscans in Toulouse, and he was ordained at the age of 20. In 1605 he was captured by Barbary pirates and enslaved, an experience that gave him a deep empathy with the world's outcasts. When he managed to escape to Paris, he devoted his life to charity, during a time when it was common for poor parents to drop unwanted babies off at hospitals, which commonly sold them for a few pennies to beggars who would break their limbs to incite the pity of passers-by. Vincent de Paul formed an institute known as the Priests of the Mission, or Lazarists, in 1625, and in 1633 founded the Sisters of Charity to help him in his work. His reputation was so great that Louis XIII summoned him to his deathbed to perform the last rites; one of his last tasks was chaplain to galley slaves. He died in 1660 and was canonized in 1737, declared the patron saint of all charitable societies.

Nevertheless, the chief pilgrimage destination in the Landes is the ornate 19th-century **Notre-Dame de Buglose** just north, where the towers have a 66-bell carillon and a 900lb painted stone Virgin holds pride of place. Note, from a less ambitious era, the 17th-century reliefs showing the Sisters of Charity in the chapel of St-Vincent-de-Paul, just left of the choir.

Market Days in Dax

The big Saturday market by the cathedral, established in 1356 by order of the Black Prince, is especially colourful and packed with geese and ducks.

Flea market: first Thursday of each month, Pl Camille-Bouvet.

St-Paul-lès-Dax: Thursdays.

Where to Stay in Dax

ⓘ Dax >
11 Cours Foch, t 05 58 56 86 86, www.dax.fr. and www.dax-tourisme. com; open July and Aug Mon–Sat 9–7, Sun 10–1; April–Oct Mon–Sat 9.30–12.30 and 2–6.30, Sun 10–1; Nov–Mar Mon–Fri 9.30–12.30 and 2–6, Sat 9.30–12.30

Dax ✉ 40100

An unusual feature of Dax is that many of the town's 58 hotels are directly connected to thermal establishments. High season is September and October, when it can be hard to find a place that will take you in for just one or two nights. Note that at least demi-pension is obligatory in nearly every hotel.

***Hôtel Splendid, 2 Cours Verdun, **t** 05 58 56 70 70 (€€€); a Mercure hotel. If you can afford the experience, check into this renovated hotel, built in 1928, with its enormous lobby, Art Deco furnishings and grand old bathrooms intact; along with a spa cure there's a health centre on the premises, and lounging about in white bathrobes is *de rigueur. Menus €26–32. Closed Jan and Feb.*

Hôtel de la Paix, 18 Rue Fontaine Chaude, **t 05 58 90 16 46 (€€€). Near the pedestrian-only centre, and linked by a lift to the Thermes Romains. Special rates for 3-week stays and discounts to a second person. Full board available if you are taking cures, by arrangement with a local restaurant. *Open Mar–Nov.*

***Grand Hôtel, Rue Source, **t** 05 58 90 53 00, *www.thermes-dax.com* (€€). Large, well-lit rooms, each individually furnished, and its own baths, the Thermes-Adour. There are also 7 apartments. *Menus from €17. Closed for Christmas.*

Beausoleil, near the centre at 38 Rue du Tuc-d'Eauze, **t 05 58 56 76 76, *www.hotel-beausoleil-dax.fr* (€€). This white, old-fashioned hotel oozes charm and comfort, peace and quiet and offers lots of personal attention. *Menus from €12. Closed Mon eve plus Dec–early Mar.*

Miradour, Av Eugène Milliès-Lacroix, **t 05 58 56 77 77 (€€; half-board only for stays of 4 days and over). Overlooking the river, modern and very pleasant, with direct access to its own bath. *Menus €8–15. Open all year.*

Le Richelieu, 13 Av Victor-Hugo, **t 05 58 90 49 49, *www.le-richelieu.fr* (€€). Centrally located and renovated, with a pleasant patio for sunny days and a restaurant that tries harder than most; there is also a 'Club Rétro' on Rue St Eutrope where for a €5 cover charge you can dance and sing to French golden oldies. *Menus €12–36. Open Wed–Sun 9.30pm–5am.*

*Hôtel de la Nehe, Rue de Fontaine Chaude, **t** 05 58 90 16 46 (€€). Like the **Paix**, linked by a lift to the Thermes Romains, and offering special rates for 3-week stays and discounts to a second person. *Closed late Nov–early April.*

Auberge des Pins, 86 Av Francis-Planté, **t 05 58 74 22 46 (€). A charming little inn with a large garden just outside the centre; traditional *landaise* meals. *Menus €11–18. Closed mid-Dec–mid-Jan.*

*Au Fin Gourmet, 3 Rue des Pénitents, **t** 05 58 74 04 26 (€). Right in the centre of town by the Fontaine Chaude, this hotel has rooms ranging from the very basic to others with private bathrooms and TVs as well as studios. The food is very good with many *landais* recipes on the menu (make sure you try the delicate *cèpe* omelette) served in a choice of pretty little rooms. *Menus €15–32. Closed mid-Dec–mid-Jan and Sun in Feb and Mar.*

Hôtel Loustalot, 60 Pl Joffre, **t** 05 58 74 04 13 (€). Just over the bridge from the centre of Dax on the right bank of the Adour; the décor inside is more modern than the exterior might suggest, and there is a good chance of finding a room with a bathroom for only one or two nights. *Open all year.*

Chênes, just west of Dax in the Bois de Boulogne, **t** 05 58 90 05 53, *www.camping-les-chenes.fr.* An extremely good campsite with spotless showers, a range of facilities and very reasonable rates. *Open late Mar–late Oct.*

Eating Out in Dax

L'Amphitryon, 38 Cours Gallieni, **t** 05 58 74 58 05. As most guests dine in their hotels, Dax has relatively few restaurants. Besides the **Au Fin Gourmet** mentioned above, try this friendly place for constantly changing menus that feature plenty of delights from Amphitryon's watery realm. *Menus €20–38. Closed Sun eve plus all day Mon.; closed first half of Jan and end Aug.*

Auberge La Chaumière, Rte de Bayonne, Quartier Hardy, St-Paul-lès-Dax (3km west of Dax), **t** 05 58 91 79 81. There aren't many restaurants that can say they've been in business since 1868, but this one can. The excellent menu offers a Basque-Landaise gastronomic journey with full use of regional and seasonal produce. Try the *gratin de tourteau* or the lamb with sweet peppers and *cèpes. Menus €25 and à la carte. Closed Mon and Tues.*

Le Moulin de Poustagnacq, Saint-Paul-lès-Dax, **t** 05 58 91 31 03, *www. moulindepoustagnacq.com.* When the Dacquois dine out, they usually get in their cars and head out of the centre. This popular place overlooks a forest and pond; the kitchen uses local ingredients to create imaginative dishes such as *le homard en casse croûte, caviar d'aubergine au citron confit, coulis de crustacé,* served with a wide choice of wines. *Menus €29–67. Closed Sun eve plus Mon and Tues lunch.*

Restaurant du Bois de Boulogne, Allée du Bois-de-Boulogne, **t** 05 58 74 23 32. With a cool and shady summer terrace overlooking the Adour, this is another good bet for fish-lovers, but the chef also does good regional meat dishes. *Menus €17–30. Closed Sun eve.*

Ferme Auberge de Thoumio (6km south) 40180 Saint Pandelon, **t** 05 58 98 73 41, offers *landaise* specialities using their own farm produce; plenty of local *foie gras* and duck. *Menus €12–26. Open Mar–mid-June and mid-Sep–mid-Dec at weekends by reservation only; mid-June–mid-Sept open daily exc Sun eve and Wed.*

The Southern Côte d'Argent

The playground continues; one thing not to miss is the descent down the Huchet, where Landais gondoliers will punt you through semi-tropical lushness worthy of the sets in *The African Queen*. *See* map pp.108–09.

Léon, its Lake and the Courant d'Huchet

Traditional houses give the old village of Léon its tone, while the most lush and beautiful river in all the Landes, the **Courant d'Huchet**, brings it visitors from far and wide. The Huchet flows 12km down to the sea, passing under a canopy of alders, pines and willows hung with garlands of ivy and creeper, through giant tamarisks, majestic ferns called *osmondes royales*, wild hibiscus and waterlilies. Apparently it was something of a secret until 1911, when Gabriele d'Annunzio among others discovered it while hurtling through the Landes on a cross-country car race. Throughout April to the end of October, the flat-bottomed boats of **Les Bateliers du Courant d'Huchet** make the trip, lasting up to four hours.

The region south and west of the Etang de Léon has been set aside as a nature reserve, a good place to observe the local water-loving birds. The nearest beach is **Moliets-Plage**, the seaside extension of **Moliets-et-Maa**, best known for its golf course. Just down the coast, **Messanges** was long famous for its *vin des sables*, where vineyards planted in the hollows of the dunes yield a now-rare red wine with the perfume of violets. You can find *vin du sable* at the **Bergerie de Camentron**.

The next town south has a double-double-barrelled name, **Vieux-Boucau-Port-d'Albret**. Just Port d'Albret back in the Middle Ages, it marked the spot of the sometime mouth of the mighty Adour; so great was the force of the river's waters that the sandy soil of the Landes could not begin to contain it in a proper bed, and when huge Atlantic storms battered the coast and stuffed its mouth with sand, the Adour would change direction. For a long time its mouth was at Capbreton; it moved to Port d'Albret in 907; in 1164 it went south to Bayonne, and then to back to Capbreton; in the 14th century it went back to Port d'Albret, which prospered – until 1578 when the Adour once again curled to the south. But this time, Bayonne, distressed at seeing its own port silt up with sand, asked King Charles IX for help, and he sent down an engineer who dug a canal for it to ease into. And there it has stayed – thanks to constant dredging. These days Port-d'Albret, spread around the banks of a salt-water lake, is the name of a purpose-built holiday resort annexe of the pleasant old village of Vieux-Boucau ('Old Mouth').

⓶ **Courant d'Huchet**

Les Bateliers du Courant d'Huchet
http://bchleon.free.fr;
2hr trips daily
April–Sept 10am and
2.30, morning only July
and Aug; €11.50; 3–4hr
trips daily 2.30pm,
€4.50–18.50; book
ahead – up to two
weeks ahead in Aug –
on t 05 58 48 75 39

Bergerie de Camentron
Rte des Lars,
Messanges,
t 05 58 48 99 08

Getting to and around the Southern Côte d'Argent

No trains pass through here; the nearest stations are in Dax and Bayonne, and from there buses travel to the main points on the coast.

Inland from Vieux-Boucau-Port-d'Albret, **Soustons** manufactures corks for Bordeaux wines and is the most important market town for the region. It has its own lake, the Etang de Soustons. A *bergerie* that once belonged to former president François Mitterand is nearby and there's a bronze statue to him – the town is very proud of its presidential connection.

To the south lie two more small lakes, now part of a nature reserve: the Etang Noir (named after its thick black mud) and the Etang Blanc (named after its fine sandy bottom). Near them, **Tosse** has a lovely 11th-century church with an apse decorated with exterior carvings. **Seignosse** is an old village just south of the Etang Noir, while all the beach action as usual happens a few kilometres away in **Seignosse-le-Penon**, which grew up in the 1960s as one of the major surfing capitals of the coast. The sea-water pools have been incorporated into the water-leisure complex **Atlantic Park**, full of water slides, pools, and there's a spa for the grown-ups. If you play golf, don't forget to take your clubs as there's also a popular 18-hole **golf course**.

Atlantic Park
t 05 58 49 89 89,
open mid-May–early
Sept

Seignosse golf
course
t 05 58 41 68 30,
www.golfseignosse.com

Capbreton-Hossegor

Two separate *communes*, divided by the Bourret Canal, are responsible for this booming resort's name, and a unique setting with the Pyrenees hovering on the horizon has made it the biggest holiday centre between Arcachon and Biarritz: besides the usual ocean beach, it has a warm, sandy tidal lake (another former mouth of the Adour), two rivers and a canal. The older town, Capbreton, was an important whaling and fishing port before the 14th century, when the Adour graced it with its presence. When the Adour moved and the port silted up, Capbreton rapidly declined; the few people who stayed around grew table grapes. It began to perk up again in the 18th century, when Napoleon III built a long jetty and it began to farm oysters. In the early 1900s, artists and writers from Biarritz set up a colony around the Lac d'Hossegor, with the idea of living fraternally together in a cultural milieu. It did produce one painter of interest, Roger Sourgen (1883–1979), son of a Landais customs officer, who learned enough of his father's trade to become a successful smuggler as well as a naïf artist, painting the lakes and pines around Hossegor. In the 1930s the property developers followed (see the luxurious villas near the golf course) and ever since the resort has grown, sacrificing any old-world charm the centre of

Hossegor once had. However, it's not without some style – and plenty of boutiques for shoppers. Besides all the usual beach things, climb up the high dune known as **Super-Hossegor** for the view. There is an 18-hole golf course and cycle-paths criss-cross the town.

Capbreton has been filled to the hilt with new building, preserving only a few old houses in the very centre that somehow escaped the developers. One feature of Capbreton that may never be exploited is its unique underwater canyon, or the **Fosse de Capbreton**, 2km offshore, an abyss plunging 100m down, ten times deeper than anywhere nearby. Louis XIV's great engineer Vauban back in the 17th century was the first to propose it as a deep-water port. It's still an idea that crops up every now and then; for the time being the resort contents itself with a marina – the only one between Arcachon and Bayonne – named *Mille Sabords* (translated as 'Blistering Barnacles!' whenever Captain Haddock says it in *Tintin*), and the **Ecomusée de la Pêche et de la Mer**, in the municipal casino with a great view across the ocean and port, an aquarium, ships' models, fossils, shells and films. (Note that in March 2007 the Ecomusée is due to move into a new home next to the Capitainerie.) Along the ocean beach, you should only swim in the designated areas, protected by lifeguards; the big rollers that bring champion surfers to Capbreton hit the coast just to the north, towards Seignosse. There are many **boat trips** and other sporting activities on offer – contact the tourist office for further information.

Ecomusée de la Pêche et de la Mer
Av G. Pompidou,
t 05 58 72 40 50,
www.ecopeche.fr; open
July and Aug daily
2–6.30; April–Sept
daily 2–6

Boat trips
contact Bateau
Jean B, t 05 58 72 33 36

South of Capbreton-Hossegor

There are two more small resorts along the coast before you reach Bayonne: **Labenne-Océan** and **Ondres-Plage**. Labenne is just west of the Marais d'Orx, a favourite nesting marsh of migratory birds, especially a number of species of ducks and geese, which has been purchased by the WWF and the **Conservatoire du Littoral**. The marsh was drained by Napoleon III and given as a present to his cousin, Count Walewsky, the natural son of Napoleon I. Over the years it filled up with water again, much to the delight of more than 200 species that stop here throughout the year. You can have a guided visit by appointment. Labenne also has a **reptile house,** with approximately 150 slippery specimens, where you can get very close to the crocodiles and alligators. Opposite there's a **zoo and a mini-farm** to please younger members of the family.

Between here and the Adour to the east, the villages have interesting churches (especially **St-Martin-de-Hinx** and **Biarrotte**) and the occasional château.

Conservatoire du Littoral
t 05 59 45 42 46;
www.reserve-naturelle-
marais-dorx.org

Reptile house
on N10, t 05 59 45 67
09, www. reptilarium.fr

Zoo and mini-farm
t 05 59 45 43 93,
www.parc-animalier-
labenne.com

Market Days in the Southern Côte d'Argent

Soustons: Mondays and Thurs, in July and Aug.

Capbreton: Saturdays, but daily in the summer.

Hossegor: Monday, Wednesday and Sunday mornings, June–Sept.

Labenne: Tuesdays and Fridays in July and Aug.

Where to Stay and Eat in the Southern Côte d'Argent

Léon ✉ 40550

**Hôtel du Lac, t 05 58 48 73 11, *www.hoteldulac-leon.com* (€€–€). The only hotel here, but it's simple and nice enough. *Closed Nov–Mar.*

Moliets ✉ 40660

Hotels here are built around the golf course.

***Green Parc Océan, Rue des Croquillots, t 05 58 48 57 57, *www. maeva.com.* Maeva-Green Parc (€€€). Large, attractive and well-run; there are pools, tennis courts, kids clubs, and a disco; rented by the week in high season; minimum 2 nights out of season. *Closed mid-Sep–Mar.*

**Hotel de l'Océan, Av de l'Océan, t 05 58 48 51 19, *www.hotelocean-moliets.com* (€). For something cheaper in Moliets, this place fits the bill; most rooms have sea views. *Menus from €18. Closed for renovation at time of writing, due to reopen Spring 2007.*

Soustons ✉ 40140

***Relais de la Poste, t 05 58 47 70 25, *www.relaisposte.com* (€€€€€–€€€). The very best place to eat and stay, 10km east of Soustons, at Magescq, with comfortable rooms set in a park with huge pines, a heated pool, hammam, Jacuzzi, massage and tennis court. But it's the exquisite *landaise* cuisine, prepared by Bernard and Jeanne Coussau and then by sons Jean and Jacques, that has made it renowned: the pigeon with *girolle* mushrooms, the *foie gras*, duck fillets,

and potatoes sautéed in goose fat that melt in your mouth, accompanied by warm, crisp bread made in the Relais' special oven, a superb list of wines from Bordeaux and Burgundy as well as the finest armagnacs, not to mention perfect desserts as full of rich flavours as all the other courses. *Menus €55–100. Closed early Nov–mid-Dec and Mon and Tues from Oct–April; restaurant closed Mon, Tues lunch, Thurs lunch May–Oct, except Aug.*

Saint Christophe, 15 Pl Sterling, t 05 58 41 15 16 (€). A good but unexciting option. *Open all year.*

Seignosse ✉ 40510

***Golf Hôtel de Seignosse, Av du Belvédère, t 05 58 41 68 40, *www.golfseignosse.com* (€€€). Built in the style of a Louisiana plantation house, in the heart of the golf course, with a pool and pretty terrace and *restaurant gastronomique*; rooms are well equipped with satellite TV, mini-bars, etc. *Menus €28–36. Closed mid-Dec–mid-Feb.*

Du L'Etang Blanc, t 05 58 72 80 15, *www.hotel-restaurant-charme-hossegor.com* (€€€–€€). A quiet little inn by the Etang Blanc with regional cuisine. *Restaurant (menus €28–45). Closed Jan–early Feb.*

Campeiole Les Oyats, Rte des Casernes, t 05 58 43 37 94, *www.campeole.fr.* A camp site near the sea with lots of shade and a pool for the small fry. *Open mid-May–mid-Sept.*

Restaurant le Cottage, 1 Av Jean Moulin, Campéole, Fond du lac d'Hossegor, t 05 58 43 10 65. A pretty restaurant with a lovely terrace set in its own woods back from the road. The chef spent time in Provence where he discovered an ancient Provençal cookbook, and some of his wonderful recipes have been adapted from this. The use of fresh herbs is ambitious and refreshing. Most of the options focus on local favourites, using both meat and fish. *Menu €19 for lunch only; €39 plus à la carte.* The €39 menu includes plenty of *foie gras* and scallops. Charming and efficient service. *Closed Jan–early Feb and Mon and Tues.*

ⓘ **Léon >**
Pl Jean-Baptiste Courtiau, t 05 58 48 76 03, www.ot-leon.fr; open July and Aug Mon–Sat 9–1 and 3–7, Sun 10–1; Sept–June Tues–Fri 9–12 and 2–5

ⓘ **Seignosse >>**
Av des Lacs, t 05 58 43 32 15, www.tourisme-seignosse.com; open mid-June–mid-Sept Mon–Sat 9–7, Sun 10–1 and 3–7; rest of year Mon–Sat 9–12 and 2–6

ⓘ **Moliets >**
Rue du Gén. Caunègre, t 05 58 48 56 58, www. moliets.com; open Oct–Mar Mon–Fri 9–12.30 and 2.–5.30; July and Aug Mon–Sat 9–12.30 and 2–6.30, Sun 10–12.30 and 1.30–5.30; April–June and Sept Mon–Sat 9–12.30 and 2.30–5.30

ⓘ **Vieux-Boucau-Port-d'Albret**
Le Mail 11, t 05 58 48 13 47, www.ot-vieux-bocau.fr; open Mon–Sat 9–12 and 2–6

ⓘ **Soustons >**
Grange de Labouyrie, t 05 58 41 52 62, www.soustons.fr; open July and Aug Mon–Sat 9.30–1 and 2.30–7, plus Sun am; Sept–June Mon–Fri 9.30–12.30 and 2–6, Sat 9.30–12.30

Hossegor ›

Pl des Halles, t 05 58 41 79 00, www. hossegor.fr; open July and Aug Mon–Sat 9–12 and 2–6, Sun 10–1 and 3–7; Sept–June Mon–Sat 9–12 and 2–6

Capbreton ››

Av Georges Pompidou, t 05 58 72 12 11, www.capbreton-tourisme.com; open July and Aug 9–7 plus Sun 10.30–12.30 and 4–7; Sept–June Mon–Sat 9–12 and 2–6

Hossegor ✉ 40150

Of the two linked towns, Hossegor has the nicer places to stay, many set back in the trees.

****Les Hortensias du Lac, Av du Tour du Lac, t 05 58 43 99 00, *www. hortensias-du-lac.com* (€€€). Between ocean and lake, built in the local style, and friendly and comfortable, too. Heated pool. No restaurant but champagne breakfast served until midnight.

***Le Mercedes, Av du Tour du Lac. t 05 58 41 98 00, *www.hotel-mercedes. com* (€€€–€€). A white and blue Art Deco exterior, sparkling on the edge of the lake, and the best place to stay in town. The rooms are spacious and decorated in pastels. *Open April–Oct.*

**Les Acanthes, Av du Touring Club, t 05 58 43 78 09 (€€). At the end of the lake and an easy walk from the ocean. Apartments are available for 2–5 people on a nightly, weekend or weekly basis. Rooms are kept in good clean condition and there's a terrace for eating outside if you choose to prepare meals in the kitchenette. The hotel can provide breakfast, drinks and ice cream. There's a garage for storing bikes which is ideal if you have children.

**Hotel la Tetrade, 1187 Av du Touring Club, t 05 58 43 51 48 (€€). Owned by a family of oystermen, on the main lake road. Rooms are pleasant and immaculate; be sure to reserve one with a view. The restaurant naturally features oysters and other seafood, and is good. Southwest meat dishes served too. *Menus €18–33. Open all year.*

Dégustation du Lac, 1830 Av du Touring Club, t 05 58 43 54 95. Besides the hotel restaurants, Marianne

Lamoliate's restaurant is worth trying for its exquisite seafood platters and fish soup at very reasonable prices. *Menus start at €16. Closed Sun exc July and Aug and Oct–Mar.*

Le Pizzaïol, Av du Touring Club, t 05 58 43 57 04. The décor with all the Chianti bottles may be a bit corny, but it has the best pizza in town. *Open til 1am in July and Aug.*

Amigo, 579 Bd de la Dune, t 05 58 43 54 38. For *gambas*, sardines or tapas. *Open daily mid-Mar–mid-Nov and weekends in Jan and Feb.*

Capbreton ✉ 40130

***L'Océan, a big white hotel near the port at 85 Av G-Pompidou, t 05 58 72 10 22, *www.hotel-capbreton.com* (€€). One of the nicest here, with large, comfortable soundproofed rooms. Two restaurants, one specializing in seafood, the other Italian. *Open all year.*

**Bellevue, Av G-Pompidou, t 05 58 72 10 30, *www.cafe-bellevue.fr* (€). Twelve refurbished rooms and a delightful restaurant. Traditional southwest favourites and seafood. *Menus €16–30. Closed Nov–Jan.*

Regalty, Port de Plaisance, t 05 58 72 22 80. In the fishermen's quarter, head for where the nautical style is a backdrop to excellent fish dishes. *Menu €25; lunch €19.50. Closed Sun eve, all Mon, and Nov.*

Pêcherie Ducamp, 4 Rue du Port d'Albret, t 05 58 72 11 33. Pescophobes should stay away from this fishmonger's which has been converted into a restaurant. Waitresses in plastic boots and aprons serve nothing but the freshest fish and shellfish. *Menu €24–48.*

The Gers

Whether in town or country, you will notice the Gers seems strangely empty, as if all the people were taking a siesta. In fact, the people simply aren't there; they all went off to Paris or Toulouse long ago. Today there are only 174,000 Gersois left, and only one town of more than 8,000 (Auch, with 22,000). But the département *has genuine attractions: the great art of Auch cathedral, a number of medieval abbeys, such as La Romieu and Flaran, and a surprisingly large number of gracious châteaux. Above all the Gers is a land of* bastides *— over a hundred of them, ranging from Mirande, which has almost grown into a town, to little arcaded squares lost in the woods that never got more than half built in the Middle Ages and have been declining genteelly ever since.*

SPAIN

08

Don't miss

⭐ **Roman-style luxury**
Séviac p.138

⭐ **Touring the armagnac estates**
Labastide d'Armagnac p.141

⭐ **A historic hilltop town**
Lectoure p.147

⭐ **Renaissance stained glass**
Cathédrale Ste-Marie, Auch p.155

⭐ **Medieval mysteries**
La Romieu p.134

See map overleaf

10 km
5 miles

N

LANDES

932

933

Meylan

656

Cueyze

Sos   Poudenas

Mézin

Francescas

Estrebouy

Moncrabeau

Ste-Maure-de-Peyriac

Villeneuve-de-Mézin

Liatores

Sarbazan

656

La Romieu

Bostens

St-Justin

Fourcès

Castelnau-sur-l'Auvignon

Pouydesseaux

Labastide
d'Armagnac

933

Barbotan-les-Thermes

Condom

Lac d'Uby

Séviac

Montréal

Larressingle

Abbaye de
Flaran

Cazaubon

Lamothe

Mouchan

Maignaut-
Tauzia

Villeneuve-
de Marsan

Ravignan

Eauze

931

Valence-sur-
Baïse

Mont-de-
Marsan

Perquie

Lagardère

Pardeilhan

124

Estang

939

Grenade-sur-
l'Adour

Panjas

Manciet

Vic-Fezensac

Eugénie-les-
Bains

Nogaro

G E R S

Gallo-
Roman
Towers

p.78

Aire-sur-l'Adour

Aignan

Gallo-
Roman
Tower

Biran

Geaune

Ségos

St-Mont

Termes
d'Armagnac

Tasque

Plaisance

Maumusson

946

Diusse

Aydie

Castelnau-
Rivière-Basse

Bassoues

Monclar-sur-
Losse

Arzacq-
Arraziguet

Madiran

Marciac

Mirande

Taron-Sadirac

Monlezun

Laas

PYRÉNÉES
ATLANTIQUES

Sévignacq

Lembeye

Maubourguet

Tillac

Belloc-
St-Clemens

13

Miélan

Lagujan

p.212

SPAIN

Don't miss

p.241

You've seen the Eiffel Tower and Mont Blanc, but have you been to the *département* that produces more garlic than any in France? No doubt everyone knows the Gers as home of the World Championship Snail Races (in Lagardère) and the World Championship Melon-Eating Contest (in Lectoure), but beyond these, *département* number 32 may seem a bit obscure. Its own tourist literature proudly claims it as the 'most discreet province of France'; the Gersois are probably aware that jokes are made at their expense in sophisticated, up-to-date metropolises like Pau and Agen.

Most of the Gers is serious farmland and, not surprisingly, the *département* is one of the stoutest strongholds of *Coordination*

Rurale (based in Auch), the militant group that is always in the news for dumping tons of manure on a local *préfecture* or truckloads of potatoes across a highway, or splattering politicians with fresh, home-produced eggs. They are capable of sticking a sharp Gascon rapier into nearly anybody's political career, so places like the Gers are very well taken care of. Since it's your EU tax money, you might as well come down and enjoy it.

Besides the garlic, the Gers is an enormous producer of *foie gras*, *confits* and such – it's probably the only *département* in France with more geese than people, not to mention the ducks, and a few million free-range chickens (the *département* has lots of room). In some parts of the *département*, hedgerows have been cleared for industrial-style grain agribusiness (mostly corn to stuff into the geese). But most of the Gers looks much as it did in the time of its most famous son, the semi-fictional musketeer d'Artagnan; in some places lavender is grown, adding a gratifying Provençal touch when it blossoms in early summer.

More by chance than any other factor, the Gers has neither the resources nor the strategic location to attract any kind of industry whatsoever. But what's bad news for the tourist offices may be good in the long run for the Gers, and for now, at least, it makes the heart of Gascony the perfect place for anyone who wants a dip into *la France profonde* at its unspoiled best.

The Armagnac

This is more of a fond old expression than a term with any precise geographical meaning. 'Armagnac' can mean the old territories of the counts of Armagnac, the big bosses in the heart of Gascony before the French rubbed them out and gobbled up their lands in 1473. But to people today it is more likely to mean the area where little-a armagnac is produced, the finest of French brandies (cognac? they've never heard of it). This area, roughly, includes everything west and north of Auch, and Armagnac is still its name and its fame. Touring it can seem truly civilized; where else in the world can you stop in at a château for a shot of eau-de-vie every five minutes?

Condom

With such a name, what's a town to do? The natural instinct of the Gascon, of course, would be to flaunt it, as with the fellow on France's national rugby side who called himself 'Condom' after his home town, and proudly carried the name into international combat until his retirement a few years back, no matter what the

Getting around the Gers

By Car

You aren't going to get very far here without a car. Even more than the rest of the southwest, public transportation in the Gers is rudimentary at best. Remember that this is a very sparsely settled region, and petrol stations are few and far between.

By Rail and Bus

From Auch, there are rail connections to Agen (via Fleurance and Lectoure), and to Toulouse; the *Ville Rose* is only 1½ to 2½ hours away (via Gimont and l'Isle-Jourdain).

Auch is also the centre of what bus service there is (ring **t** 05 62 05 76 37 in Auch): daily runs to Tarbes, Bordeaux, Toulouse and Mont-de-Marsan; slightly more frequently to Mirande, Condom, Vic-Fézensac, Fleurance, Lectoure and nearby villages.

By Bicycle

On the other hand, the Gers is excellent country for bicycling: just hilly enough to be scenic without too many steep gradients, and plenty of shade along the back roads.

08 The Gers | Condom

Musée des Préservatifs
Rue Sénéchal, t 05 62 28 11 22; open June–Sept daily 10–12 and 3–7; adm

nasty Britons were mumbling in the scrum. Lately, the whole town has decided that they might as well make the best of it and recently opened the **Musée des Préservatifs**. If you're hoping for some grisly examples of our rubber friends down through the ages, no such luck – the museum places its emphasis firmly on the modern context. They have the first machine ever to produce them *en masse*, and three rooms extolling the virtues of condoms against AIDS.

Nobody knows where the name came from. The best guesses imagine some Roman place name, such as *Condatum* or *Condominium*. As a town, though, Condom did not appear until the Middle Ages, when it grew up around a Benedictine monastery, now long disappeared. Ask any of the farm boys, slouching in the bars on a Saturday evening, and they may well tell you that the name is entirely deserved; one senses they feel the bright lights of Auch or Agen calling them away.

Condom's one sight is its **Cathédrale St-Pierre**, begun in 1507 (the same year that the archbishops of Auch began the ambitious decorative programme in their cathedral; the armagnac business must have been thriving). This is a magnificent building, though it has taken its bumps over the centuries, from Montgomery's Protestants in the Wars of Religion, to the mobs of the Revolution and the 19th-century restorers. The most decorated portal, on the southern door, was finished in 1531, and Montgomery's men smashed it up only 38 years later. An excellent example of the southern approach to the flamboyant Gothic of the era, the church's interior features complex vaulting and big gallery windows. A few of the stained-glass windows are original, though most were installed in the 19th century, done in the style of Arnaut de Moles's windows at Auch. About the same time, the stone

134

Musée de l'Armagnac
t 05 62 28 47 17; open April–Oct 10–12 and 3–6; winter 2–5; closed Mon, Tues, hols and Jan

Château Cugnac-Armagnac
Rue Daunou, t 05 62 28 08 08

Boat trip
Gascogne Navigation, Quai de la Bouquerie, t 05 62 28 46 46, www.gascogne-navigation.com

Aqualudiques
Av des Mousquetaires, t 05 62 29 17 48; open July–early Sept 10–8

 La Romieu
www.la-romieu.com

enclosure was added around the choir. Outside there is a simple 16th-century cloister, now used as offices by the *mairie*.

Nearby on Place Lannelongue, the bishops' stables have been converted into the **Musée de l'Armagnac**, with a collection of farm bric-a-brac and exhibits on making armagnac the old-fashioned way. At the same time you can visit the Ryst-Dupeyron cellars at **Château Cugnac-Armagnac** with its early 20th-century *chais* (cellars) and actors in period dress. If you miss these two, don't worry – there are plenty more opportunities to learn about armagnac in the *département*.

Another summer activity for tourists is a **boat trip** up the Baïse, taking in 14th- and 15th-century bridges, mills, the towpath and a lock. You can also hire a houseboat. Children will also like the pools and waterslides of **Aqualudiques**.

La Romieu

The nearby abbey of Flaran (*see* p.152) gets most of the tour buses, but La Romieu, east of Condom on the D41, would be a much more rewarding place to visit if you only have time for one. On the way, you can take a short detour to **Castelnau-sur-l'Auvignon**, for a look at the simple Templar commandery there. The Templars, along with the other orders of crusading knights, had buildings like this throughout Europe, local headquarters from which to oversee the vast lands they owned. The building isn't special, but it is one of the few such buildings to survive intact.

La Romieu itself, with its towers dominating a wide panorama of farmland, makes a memorable sight, one that has changed little over the centuries. The name means 'pilgrim', one who has been to Rome; a pilgrim named Albert founded a monastery here in 1082, acting on behalf of the powerful Abbey of St Victor in Marseilles, the force behind scores of new foundations in the Midi.

It was not until the 14th century, though, that La Romieu grew into the lavish complex we see today. From the village that grew up around the abbey came a young nobleman named Arnaud d'Aux, whose luck it was to see his friend and cousin become pope – Clement V, the Gascon elected with the connivance of the king of France, who moved the papacy to Avignon and began the 'Babylonian Captivity' (as the Italians call it).

Thanks to his family connections, Arnaud was named a cardinal, serving as the papal chamberlain, and occasionally as ambassador to Edward II, King of England and Duke of Aquitaine, while piling up plenty of absentee bishoprics, and plenty of revenues from them. Interestingly, he also presided over the trial of the Templars in 1307, and must have picked up lots of confiscated loot from them too (perhaps the lands around Castelnau). In 1312, he began spending much of the booty on the enlargement of the abbey in his home town, along with a palace for himself and his family.

Tour de Cardinal
t 05 62 28 86 33; open June–Sept Mon–Sat 10–7, Sun 2–7; May Mon–Sat 10–6.30, Sun 2–6.30; Oct–April Mon–Sat 10–12 and 2–6, Sun 2–6

The palace is mostly gone, leaving only the **Tour de Cardinal**. Together with the two larger towers of the adjacent **Collegiate church**, it dominates La Romieu's impressive little skyline. All three towers are very good examples of the showy, sophisticated architecture that was spreading at the time from the papal court at Avignon. The church's bright and airy interior, full of flowers, is a delight, but the real treasure here is the adjacent building called the **sacristy**, on the ground floor of the larger of the towers.

Most likely, this octagonal hall was originally intended as a tomb for Arnaud d'Aux and his family. The entire interior is covered with well-preserved frescoes: beautiful angel musicians on the vaulted ceiling, and portraits of family members and biblical personalities on the walls. Along with these is a real puzzle, a set of peculiar, carefully painted designs. They might be simply abstract decoration, or perhaps some sort of symbol of esoteric significance (there are hints of such intent in the architecture of the church). If they do have some kind of religious significance, no one so far has even managed a good guess at what they might represent; nothing like them appears anywhere else. If you can find someone around who has the keys, ask to see the unusual double-spiral staircase, an architectural trick with separate flights for ascending and descending wound together. Outside, there is a fine Gothic **cloister**, which was heavily damaged in the Wars of Religion. At the entrance to La Romieu is the award-winning **Gardens of Coursiana** with 700 types of trees and shrubs from around the world, including a garden of medicinal plants and an English garden.

Gardens of Coursiana
t 05 62 68 22 80, www. jardinsdecoursiana.com; open mid-April–Oct Mon, Tues and Thurs–Sat 10–8, plus first Sun of the month; joint ticket available with Collegiate

The picturesque village that grew up around the abbey was a *sauveté*, a place under the protection of the Church and off limits to all armies and fighting. Parts of its fortifications survive, as a reminder that the arrangement didn't always work out well in practice. The village was built around an arcaded square; like the *bastides*, many of these *sauvetés* were planned foundations.

Around La Romieu

North of La Romieu, delightful back roads like the D41/D266 and its continuations will take you through an odd little *pays* called the **Fimarcon**, after the medieval lords who owned most of it. Caught in one of the worst places to be during the Hundred Years War, these barons and their people made almost every one of their villages into little fortresses. Fragmentary remains of their work – castles, fortified churches, defensive trenches and such – are everywhere, especially around the villages of **Berrac**, **St-Mézard** and **Estrépouy**. **Liatores**, west on the D267, has a fine Romanesque church.

08 The Gers | La Romieu

Market Days in Condom

Condom: Wednesdays.

Where to Stay and Eat in Condom and La Romieu

ⓘ **Condom >**
Pl Bossuet, **t** 05 62 28 00 80, www.tourisme-tenareze.com; open July–mid-Sept Mon–Sat 9–7, Sun 10.30–12.30; mid-Sept–June Mon–Sat 9–12 and 2–6

Condom ✉ 32100

***Hôtel des Trois Lys, right in the centre on Rue Gambetta, **t** 05 62 28 33 33, www.les-trois-lys.com (€€€–€€). Occupying an 18th-century mansion, this hotel has a warm, welcoming atmosphere and is well kept and comfortable. It has just enough room at the back for a small swimming pool. Menus €22–32. Restaurant closed all Sun, Mon lunch, and Thurs lunch.

Logis des Cordeliers, Rue de la Paix, **t 05 62 28 03 68, www.logisdescordeliers.com (€€). Has a pool but no restaurant.

Hôtel le Continental, 20 Av Maréchal Foch, **t** 05 62 68 37 00, www.lecontinental.net (€€–€). Pleasant enough if nondescript hotel next to the bridge overlooking the Baïse and near the aquatic centre. The modern restaurant is brightly decorated with local artists' work. The menu is regional – plenty of beans and duck. Menus €20–32; lunch €13.

Camping Municipal, across from the centre, on the river on Av des Mousquetaires, **t** 05 62 28 17 32. An inexpensive site, bungalows and chalets available for rent. Open April–Sept.

Moulin du Petit Gascon, on the D931 towards Eauze, **t** 05 62 28 28 42. Foie gras and duck, of course, but you might wish to choose the filet aux morilles when there are morels to be had. Good desserts. Menus €15–28. Closed in winter, Sun eve and Wed.

La Romieu ✉ 32480

Hameau de Capuran, Blaziert, **t** 05 62 28 48 76, http://perso.orange.fr/gites-de-capuran (€€–€). Five gîtes for 2–8 people and 2 rooms.

Camp de Florence, just outside the village, **t** 05 62 28 15 58, www.lecampdeflorence.com (€). Bungalows and mobile homes available. Pool, tennis, a few rooms, and a restaurant. Snack bar and pizzas too. Restaurant closed Nov–Mar.

West of Condom

The countryside is green and delicious, though you might find it somewhat disfigured by the signs for the armagnac estates that pop up at every crossroads. The main route west, the D15, passes **Larressingle**, the 'Carcassonne of the Gers' – a wonderful specimen of rustic Gersois hyperbole, but just the same this medieval fortified village (the smallest one in France) makes a striking sight. Its walls, built in the 13th century, are almost intact, and the village tucked inside seems to have changed little since then; the unusual church is partly Romanesque, with some carved capitals. Playing the medieval card, there is a reconstructed **siege camp** with arms and weaponry and a **museum of medieval village life**. South of Larressingle, there is another medieval church at **Mouchan**, built as a stop for pilgrims along the route to Compostela; it has some of the earliest Gothic vaulting in the south. The **Château du Busca Maniban**, 5km from Cassaigne on the D229 at Mansencome is a beautiful 17th-century castle boasting the oldest distillery still in use, dating back to 1693. The guided tour includes a free

Siege camp
t 05 62 68 33 88, http://larressingle.free.fr; open daily April–Sept 10–7; Oct, Nov and Mar 11–5

Museum of medieval village life
t 05 62 28 08 08; open May–Sept

Château du Busca Maniban
t 05 62 28 40 38, www.buscamaniban.com; open April–Oct daily except Sun and hols 2–6; adm

Château de Cassaigne
t 05 62 28 04 02, www. chateaudecassaigne.com; open July and Aug daily 9–12 and 2–6; Sept–June Tues–Sun 9–12 and 2–6

Château d'Ensoulès
t 05 62 68 49 87, www.museeartnaif. com; open May–Oct Wed–Sun 10–1 and 2–5; Feb–April, Nov and Dec 10–1 and 2–5

tasting of some very fine Armagnac. The **Château de Cassaigne**, further up the D208, was the residence of the bishops of Condom. The 16th-century building is open for visits, offering a look at its old-fashioned kitchens and armagnac cellars. The *floc* is divine. Just east at Béraut the **Château d'Ensoulès** has an exhibition of naïve art with more than 500 colourful paintings from around the world.

East from Larressingle on the D15, the next village is **Montréal**, a sleepy balcony of a town that seems almost forgotten on its hilltop. Montréal is an English bastide, founded in 1289, though the site was occupied even in Celtic times. The village's immediate ancestor, however, lies down on the plain at Séviac, one of the most important Roman-era finds in southwest France.

A Little Place in the Country

The way we learned it in school, the Roman age was a wonderfully civilized time when everyone wore togas and recited Latin verse in the Forum – until those malodorous barbarians barged in to spoil the party. But for a moment, try and imagine a place like the Gers in the 4th century AD, as it really was. Grass is growing in the streets of Augusta Auscorum (Auch) and the other towns. Trade is rotten, the currency's worthless, and crushing imperial taxes are forcing what's left of commerce into extinction; legions of bureaucrats wait to squeeze out every last *denarius*, while telling you what you can and can't do, according to the emperor's restrictive and increasingly bizarre edicts on economic planning. Everything belongs to a small handful of colossally wealthy families: all the land, all the money, and even most of the people. There have always been armies of slaves on the big estates, but beyond these, the majority of free citizens have already become serfs, giving up their lands and selling themselves into bondage with the big landowners, just to get off the tax rolls and avoid prison and torture when they couldn't pay. Anyone with any nerve, an increasingly scarce commodity in the Roman twilight, has gone off to the woods to join the *bagaudae*, the guerrilla bands that haunted Gaul and Spain in the last two centuries of Roman rule.

Despite the advantages that accrued to them under the imperial system, landowners had by this time completely abandoned the decomposing state, avoiding all taxes and contributing no time or talent to saving the Empire or trying to reform it. They had also abandoned the cities, preferring to spend their time at their country villas far from crime, decay and the other troubles of the day. With their owners' monopoly of wealth, these villas often grew into full-sized towns in themselves – private towns replacing public ones, devoted to the pleasure and wellbeing of a single family, and staffed by hundreds or even thousands of slaves, as well as private armies, when necessary to keep the *bagaudae* at bay. The complexes were built around one or a number of courtyards, and included elaborate baths and temples.

The landowning families were never too seriously inconvenienced by the barbarian invasions; for a while, after the Empire collapsed, they formed a committee at Arles and ran southern Gaul for themselves. After that, they easily reached an accord with the new Gothic and Frankish overlords. The old and new groups gradually intermarried, and over the generations metamorphosed into something new – the feudal aristocracy of medieval Europe. But history has had its way with these villas, as with all vanities. While their owners were turning into feudal barons, their homes made a parallel transition into feudal castles. Especially after the invasions of the Vikings and Arabs, defence was all-important, and hilltop sites came into favour. The villas, often built in lovely natural settings near water, were abandoned (such as Montmaurin, east of Lannemezan) or, more often, turned into villages, housing the descendants of Roman slaves and serfs. The villagers recycled the stone for their own houses, and the foundations and the mosaics just disappeared, under the dirt floors of the peasants the villa's builders had oppressed for so long. Undoubtedly, there are some that have not yet been re-discovered.

The Roman Villa of Séviac

1 Séviac

The first to call attention to this site was a local boy named Lannelongue, who went up to Paris and became an Academician, and personal physician to Sarah Bernhardt. No one bothered to start digging, however, until 1961. The site, as with so many of the mega-villas of Roman Gaul, was hidden well enough. Now it has been completely excavated, and the foundations exposed under plastic-roofed pavilions. Like most Roman villas, this one was built on a peristyle plan, meaning that it has a central rectangular courtyard around which the rooms were arranged. The most impressive of the ruins are the **baths** and **pool**, the former with vestiges of proper Roman hypocaust central heating – a space under the floor propped on columns, where heat from a fire in another room could circulate. There are also some well-preserved **mosaics** with floral and geometric motifs, and an especially good one with a goldfinch among vines. The excavators found two skeletons from the 6th or 7th century, and they have named them 'Les Amants' and put them under glass for your inspection. More finds from Séviac can be seen in the small **museum** at the tourist office in Montréal: mosaics, jewellery, potter, sculptures and so on. A second villa is currently being excavated and remains from the Merovingian period are nearby.

North of Séviac

North of Montréal on the D29, **Fourcès** is worth a detour if you have the time. It was one of the few medieval *bastides* laid out in the form of a circle, with a castle at the centre that was a frequent bone of contention in the Hundred Years' War. The castle was demolished long ago, leaving a pretty circular square shaded by plane trees. The people of Fourcès today haven't been shy about taking advantage of it; they've tarted it up as cute as can be – it could be a village in a model train layout. Parts of the wall remain, along with the 15th-century Tour de l'Horloge, overlooking the little River Auzoue. You'll also find a small museum on the 'how we used to live' theme.

Beyond Fourcès, the D29 will take you to a little corner of the Bas-Armagnac district currently in the *département* of Lot-et-Garonne. **Mézin**, the biggest village, was the home of Armand Fallières, president of France from 1906 to 1913. Fallières's presidency caused no embarrassment to Mézin, and the villagers have named their main square after him. There is a small **museum**, with exhibits on Fallières' life and on corks – cork oaks being one of the area's traditional crops – and also a Roman statue of Jupiter. Mézin grew up around an important Cluniac abbey, and it retains the **abbey church of St-Jean** – Romanesque in the apse while the rest is

Mézin museum
t 05 53 65 68 16; open June–Oct Tues–Sat 2–6, Sun 3–5.3; July and Aug Tues–Sun 10–12.30 and 2–6.30; Sept Tues–Sat 10–12.30 and 2–6.30, Sun 3–5.30

graceful Gothic. On the vault over the altar, note the whimsical carving of a grimacing giant and a pot of flowers. The tympanum on the north door must have been destroyed in the Revolution; replacing it you can still make out part of some painted revolutionary slogan about the 'Supreme Being'. These are common enough in French village churches; the radicals in Paris were telling the peasants it was still all right to believe in God, though not necessarily the God of the Christian Church.

You could get lost for a long time in the lush countryside around Mézin and never mind it. On the stretch of the D656 that follows the valley of the Gélise, you'll pass things like a pretty country chapel and a traditional *pigeonnier* on stilts, and plenty of farmers hang out signs to sell you asparagus and *cèpes, foie gras* and *floc*. At **Poudenas** there is a fine Italianate château to visit; built largely in the 17th and 18th centuries, it has some period furniture and paintings. There are Romanesque churches at **Sos** and **Gueyze**, and a fortified church from the 13th century at **Villeneuve-de-Mézin**, south of Mézin. **Meylan**, just inside the pine forest of Les Landes, is a tiny village that seems to consist of a swing set, a *mairie* in a shed, a picnic table and a war memorial, yet it contains so many curiosities that the Meylanais have drawn out a little itinerary of them, posted in front of the *mairie*. The circuit includes the château and unusual Romanesque church of **St-Pau**, a small cromlech hidden in the pine woods, called Las Naous Peyros, and **Lac Sans-fond**. As the name implies, no one has yet found the bottom of this mysterious little lake. There are a number of legends: about the phantom that haunts it, and about the church that once stood on its bank; the lake swallowed it up one Sunday morning, parishioners and all.

Château at Poudenas
t 05 53 65 78 86; open to groups only by appointment; adm

⭐ **Château de Fourcès >>**

ⓘ **Montréal >**
Pl de la Mairie, t 05 62 29 42 85, www.montrealdugers.com; open Tues–Sat 10–12 and 2–6

⭐ **Chez Simone >**

Market Days West of Condom

Montréal: Fridays.

Where to Stay and Eat West of Condom

Montréal ✉ 32250
Chez Simone (opposite the church), t 05 62 29 44 40. This fine old building decorated with frescoes shelters a superb restaurant. It is well known in the area for its duck and *foie gras* though the truffle omelettes and old armagnacs are pretty good too. The lunch menu is a bargain (€15), otherwise menus are €25 and upwards. *Closed Sun eve and all Mon.*

Fourcès ✉ 32250
★★★Château de Fourcès, t 05 62 29 49 53, www.chateau-fources.com (€€€). A superbly restored château on the edge of this *bastide* village, with some fine spacious rooms, a ravishing garden and a swimming pool. The food here is also a treat, professional and inventive, and service is friendly. *Menus €29–47. Open Mar–Oct. The restaurant is closed Wed and Thurs and lunchtimes.*

L'Auberge, t 05 62 29 40 10. This restaurant on Fourcès's circular square offers simple, good-value warming local food such as cassoulet and duck breasts. There's a terrace in summer and roaring fire in winter. *Menus €14–25. Closed Tues, Sun eve and Mon eve except July and Aug.*

Sos ✉ 47170
*Le Postillon, Pl Delbosquet, **t** 05 53 65 60 27 (€). This hotel-restaurant is in a restored smithy, with a few simple rooms and nice fat *magrets* and *confits* with *cèpes* out on the terrace. *Menus €10–20. Closed Feb.*

Eauze and the Bas-Armagnac

South of Montréal, on the way to Eauze, on the D29, you'll pass **Lamothe** and its landmark, a three-storey medieval defence tower called the Tour de Lamothe. Everyone in the Bas-Armagnac comes to the Thursday morning market at **Eauze**. A true *gros bourg*, as the French like to say, Eauze is the centre of the armagnac trade and the biggest agricultural market of the eastern Gers. Originally the capital of a Celtic tribe called the Elusatii, it was an important town in Roman and Merovingian times, with its own bishops. The Vikings trashed it thoroughly in one of their bold inland raids in the 840s, and nothing but *eau-de-vie* has come out of it since. The market takes place on the edge of the old town, in a delightful open place where the branches of the plane trees have been tied together to make a roof. A few blocks away in Place d'Armagnac, the tall brick church of **St-Luperc** dominates the centre, a rugged work of the 15th century. Facing it, a 15th-century half-timbered building bears a plaque marking it as the **Maison de Jeanne d'Albret**. Half the towns in Gascony have a house where Jeanne once slept, though it's a wonder they care to remember the nasty old bag; if she hadn't been Henri IV's mother they probably would have knocked the place down long ago. Today it houses the convivial Café Commercial, with a rugby mural on the wall. The other noteworthy thing about Eauze is its **war memorial**, which won fourth prize in a contest in the 1920s, back when every town and village in France was erecting one.

Eauze Treasure
Place de la République, **t** 05 62 09 71 38; open June–Sept Wed–Mon 10–12.30 and 2–6; Feb–May and Oct–Dec Wed–Mon 2–5; closed Jan and hols plus 1st weekend in July; adm, but free first Sun of the month

The big news these days is the **Eauze Treasure**, housed in a new museum of its own on Place de la République. Discovered in 1985, this is the only ancient treasure in France saved in its entirety. Excavated from a prosperous Roman colony dating from the 1st to the 4th centuries, the treasure consists of 28,003 coins and about 50 precious objects, including jewellery and statues. From time to time the important site of **Elusa**, just outside Eauze, is open to the public for guided tours: contact the museum for details.

Château du Tariquet
www.tariquet.com

Eauze is also the centre of the *vin de pays* region Côtes de Gascogne, long dismissed as the plonkiest of plonk. No longer. In answer to a decline in armagnac sales in the 1970s, Yves Grassa, proprietor of Eauze's **Château du Tariquet**, the largest family-owned vineyard in France, went abroad to learn New World wine-making techniques (to the chagrin of the wine establishment). He has made colombard and ugni-blanc into what has become top-selling white wine from southwest France, with dozens of awards.

ⓘ **Barbotan-les-Thermes >>**
Pl Armagnac, t 05 62 69 52 13, www.barbotan-cazaubon.com; open Mar–Nov Mon–Sat 9–12 and 2–6, Sun 2–6; Dec–Feb Mon–Thurs 9–12 and 1.30–5.30, Fri 9–12 and 1.30–4.30

ⓘ **Eauze >**
Pl de la Cathédrale, t 05 62 09 85 62; open last week of June–Aug Mon–Sat 9–12.30 and 2–6.30, Sun 10–12,;Sept–third week of June Mon–Sat 9–12 and 2–6; closed first week in Jan

Market Days around Eauze

Eauze: Thursdays, goose and duck market in winter.
Barbotan: Wednesdays.
Cazaubon (near Barbotan): Fridays.

Where to Stay and Eat around Eauze

Eauze ✉ 32800
Municipal Campground, just outside town at Moulin de Pouy, t 05 62 09 86 00. This campsite has a pool.
Café de France, Pl d'Armagnac, t 05 62 09 80 31. The place to go for an inexpensive 3-course lunch.
Auberge du Moulin de Pouy, Moulin de Pouy, t 05 62 09 82 58. A pretty terrace and home cooking on menu makes this a good choice. *Menus €12–42. Closed 1st two weeks of Sept plus Sun eve and all Mon.*

Barbotan-les-Thermes and Cazaubon ✉ 32150
***Château Bellevue, Rue Joseph-Cappin, Cazaubon, t 05 62 09 51 95, *www.chateaubellevue.org* (€€). 25 rooms in an old mansion, with a pool and excellent restaurant. *Menus €19–29. Closed Jan and 1st week Feb, restaurant also closed Sun eve and Mon.*

Manciet ✉ 32370
**La Bonne Auberge, Pl du Pesquerot, t 05 62 08 50 04 (€€). Right in the centre of the town, with a restaurant that people come all the way from Auch and even Bordeaux to visit. Many game dishes, including a wonderful roast pigeon with apples. *Menus €14–43. Closed Sun eve.*
**Le Moulin du Comte, north in hamlet of Bourrouillan, t 05 62 09 06 72 (€). Hotel-restaurant in a restored old mill by the river, with spacious and comfortable rooms and a big pool. *Menus €19–46. Open daily all year.*

Head west from Eauze and you will be entering one of the real empty quarters of the southwest. The scenery is pleasant enough, a typical Gersois landscape of oak forests and rolling hills, but there is nothing to detain you long in any of the area's scores of humble villages, or in its humble spa and casino town, **Barbotan-les-Thermes**, where there is plenty of mineral-rich mud to help you with your rheumatism, varicose veins and gout; of course the Romans sojourned here, too, though remains are few. Just outside the village, the **Lac d'Uby** is a small man-made lake with a sandy beach built in, along with water sports facilities. Barbotan has a simple Romanesque church, St-Pierre, and there are others to be seen in the neighbourhood, at **Panjas**, **St-Cane** and **Estang**.

② **Labastide d'Armagnac**
ⓘ **Labastide d'Armagnac**
t 05 58 44 67 56, www.labastide-d-armagnac.net, open summer Mon–Sat 9.30–12.30 and 2–6.30, Sun 10–12 and 3–6; winter Mon–Sat 9.30–12.30 and 2–6.30

A Dip into Les Landes: Labastide d'Armagnac

One little piece of the Bas-Armagnac has been left out in the cold, in the *département* of Les Landes; even so, the armagnac brandy produced around here is rated among the very best. At its centre, **Labastide d'Armagnac** is a *bastide* of considerable charm, one that has changed little since the Count of Armagnac, Bernard VI, and his liege lord, Edward I of England, got it started in 1291. There's little more to it than the central Place Royale, with its

All For One and One For The Road: Armagnac and Floc

The vines in the Gers date back at least 1,000 if not 2,000 years, but until the Middle Ages the 10° white wine they produced had the reputation of barely being able to travel across the table, let alone to other parts of France. The main variety of grape, *folle blanche*, was nicknamed *picquepoul*, 'tingle-lips', for the extremely dry, acidic sensation it gave the unwary.

Turning tingle-lips into a fine amber brandy was an idea introduced in 1285 by Arnaud de Villeneuve, a medical student at the University of Salerno, who joined the University of Montpellier and went on to become the personal doctor of the first Avignon pope, Clement V of Bordeaux (whom he inadvertently killed by prescribing a plate of ground emeralds for a stomach upset). In 12th-century Salerno, the Arab-Italian faculty had perfected the ancient Egyptian art of distilling the essences from plants and fruits, and the first record of the Gascons applying this fine art to grapes dates from 1411 (upstart cognac, armagnac's arch rival, dates only from the early 17th century). As far as anyone knows, armagnac is the oldest eau-de-vie distilled from grapes in the world, and to give you some idea how closely the brandy is intertwined with the Gascon mystique, one of the larger producers stores his in three great barrels known as Athos, Porthos and Aramis.

Although Gascony's first guild of *vinaigriers-distillateurs* dates from as far back as 1515, it wasn't until the 17th and 18th centuries that armagnac was produced on a wide scale. The first market was Dutch; before setting out on a long voyage, Dutch ships were fitted out with a large barrel of '*vin brûlé*' or brandy, and as most ships made a final call at Bordeaux or Bayonne before crossing the Atlantic, Dutch shipowners encouraged the production of armagnac.

By the late 19th century, armagnac was so successful that 100,000 hectares of vines were planted – just in time for the disastrous phylloxera epidemic, which devastated nearly the entire lot. The vines were replanted with resistant varieties (ten different kinds of white grapes are allowed, the main ones being bacco 22-A, a resistant hybrid of folle blanche and noah – although its days are probably numbered, as after 2010 the AOC board will no longer allow hybrids – ugni blanc and colombard) although they were hardly replanted on the same scale: today fewer than 20,000 hectares are under production, in an area strictly limited in 1909 by Armand Fallières, the Gascon vintner from Mézin who also happened to be president of France.

The production of armagnac isn't exactly coterminous with the boundaries of the Gers. AOC armagnac can be made as far north as Agen, as far west as Mont-de-Marsan and in the south almost to the Pyrenees; it hardly ever crosses the Adour. There are three sub-regions: limestone Haute-Armagnac or 'Armagnac Blanc' which includes almost everything east of the River Baïse, with Auch as its centre, although only 500 hectares are under vines; Ténarèze, in the middle, a mix of limestone and sandy soils stretching south from Condom (8000 hectares); and Bas-Armagnac or 'Armagnac Noir' (10,000 hectares) on fawn-coloured sand amid deep oak forests around Eauze, Nogaro and Aire-sur-l'Adour. Some experts consider armagnac from Ténarèze to be the finest, especially a well-aged Ténarèze with its perfume of violets, while the majority stand behind Bas-Armagnac, plummier in the nose and quicker to mature, though any controversy of this sort is liable to lead to fisticuffs.

What all armagnac has in common, however, is the use of acidic, low-alcohol white wine (the humid Atlantic air currents are mostly responsible for this), which makes it perfect for distillation. The essential technique for making armagnac hasn't changed since 1818, when the Marquis de Bonas patented an armagnac still that permitted a single-pass distillation process as opposed to the two-step process formerly used (the two-step process is still used to make cognac).

Some time between December and April, when the wine has finished fermenting, it is distilled. This is a delicate process and two specialists known as *brûleurs* are called in to watch over the still day and night to maintain a constant temperature. If the temperature becomes too hot then the brandy will taste harsh. If the temperature is too low then the brandy will be uneven (these days, however, gas burners have been installed to replace the wood fires, making the *brûleurs*' job much easier).

It is during distillation that the distinctive armagnac aromas are formed in their most embryonic forms, depending on the quality of the soil, wine and distillation. Fresh from the still, the armagnac is a rough brandy with an alcohol content ranging from 58 to 63°. To soften it up, it is put in a 400-litre cask made from the dried heart of black oak from the forests around Monlezun and shut away in a darkened store-room at a constant temperature. In the first ten years of ageing some 6 per cent of the brandy is lost every year through evaporation ('the angels' share') and is carefully replenished by distilled water; it's also at this time that the brandy receives its distinctive burnished golden hues, by dissolving the tannins of the wood. The tannins make the brandy bitter, although after three to ten years the bitterness gives way to the natural armagnac fragrance. After ten years it is transferred into old casks that no longer have any tannin. As no additives of any kind are permitted at any stage from grape to bottle, armagnac is advertised as the 'most natural brandy in France'.

To be sold as genuine 'armagnac' the brandy has to spend at least two years ageing in the oak cask; anything less is sold as an *eau-de-vie de vin du pays gascon* which is often ideal for the many recipes that call for dishes flambéed in armagnac, or served well-iced with smoked fish instead of vodka or schnapps, or drunk between courses of a meal as a *trou gascon*. The finest brandies are aged in oak barrels for up to 40 years, demanding continual attention and checking. When the head magician or *maître de chai* decides that the armagnac has at last reached its quintessential apogee of taste and finesse, further evolution is stopped by transferring it to glass vats or bottles.

Everywhere that armagnac is produced, you'll also find *floc de Gascogne*, the 'Flower of Gascony', an aperitif that has been made here since the 1500s and has become popular once more.

Essentially, *floc* is grape juice mixed with armagnac, but don't sniff – it has been strictly AOC since 1989, divided into the same three regions as armagnac. It follows similarly strict rules: after the addition of armagnac (which prevents the fresh juice from fermenting), setting the alcoholic content at 16 to 18°, the *floc* is aged for a year in oak casks. Fresh and fruity, it goes down quite well properly chilled in the hot months; *floc rosé*, made from merlot, cabernet sauvignon and cabernet franc grapes, is an especially good accompaniment to melons from Lectoure and sheep cheeses from the Pyrenees, while *floc blanc*, made from colombard, ugni blanc (saint-émilion) and gros manseng, is a favourite apéritif or dessert wine, especially good with a *tourtière* or slice of Roquefort cheese. Uniquely in France, *floc* owes its revival and success almost exclusively to women, who in 1980 formed the only French female wine confraternity (perhaps consorority is the proper word), the Dames du Floc de Gascogne. Their symbol is a bouquet of violets, roses and plum flowers – the traditional perfumes of armagnac. For more information contact *www.floc-de-gascogne.fr*.

typical arcaded buildings, and a small grid of streets with many half-timbered houses; Henri IV spent some time here before he became king, and the locals claim their square provided the inspiration for the famous Place des Vosges Henri built in Paris. Labastide became a Protestant stronghold in the Wars of Religion, and where the D626 passes through the village stands the **Temple** (all Protestant meeting houses were called temples). This one, built in the 1600s before Louis XIV revoked the Edict of Nantes and put an end to religious tolerance, looks more like a barn. Today it houses a small **museum** dedicated to *bastides*, the 'new towns' of the Middle Ages, and their role in building the southwest. Labastide also has the **Ecomusée de l'Armagnac**, dedicated to vines and spirits, naturally, but they also arrange nature trips around the surrounding countryside.

Just east of the village on the D626, bicycle fans will want to make a pilgrimage to **Notre-Dame-des-Cyclistes**, a small country chapel that is the official sanctuary for France's bicycle racers.

Some of the other attractions in this region include **St-Justin**, a *bastide* only a decade older than Labastide, and **Villeneuve-de-Marsan**, the biggest village in the region, known for its *foie gras*

Temple museum
t 05 58 44 81 06, call mairie to visit; adm

Ecomusée de l'Armagnac
t 05 58 44 88 38; open Mon–Fri 9–12 and 2–6, April–Oct also Sun and hols 3–6; adm free

Notre-Dame-des-Cyclistes
open July and Aug Mon–Sat 10–12 and 3–7, Sun 10–12; May, Jun and Sept daily 3–6

Château de Ravignan
t 05 58 45 28 39; open for guided visits April–Oct Mon–Fri 4–5.30; Nov–Mar Fri and Sat 3–6; call first

markets in winter and for its restaurants. Anyone who ever gets just a little nostalgic for the *ancien régime* will enjoy a trip to the **Château de Ravignan**, near Perquie. Begun in the time of Louis XIII, the château has a collection of court costumes from the 18th century, period furniture and paintings. It's still in the family, but they offer tours of the house, formal gardens and *chais*.

Not to be outdone by the cyclists, the serene toreros of the Landes have created a chapel and museum dedicated to their art at Bascons, just southeast of Mont-de-Marsan, the **Musée de la Course Landaise**, with exhibitions on the history of the sport and costumes.

Musée de la Course Landaise
t 05 58 52 91 76, www.bascons.fr; open Wed–Fri 2–7, and the first weekend of the month, June–Sept

Nogaro to Miélan: the Pays d'Artagnan

The biggest village in the eastern end of the Armagnac, **Nogaro** has plenty of brandy and *foie gras*, but likes better to dress up in racing colours and expound on the joys of speed – heady stuff, for a place where every day seems like Sunday and dogs are wont to sleep in the middle of the street. Nogaro started out as the Roman city of Nogarolium, but its current pride is its race track, the **Circuit Paul Armagnac**, which hosts a full schedule of events in summer. There's a school of race driving attached, with courses for beginners, and also a small airport where you can learn to pilot gliders and sailplanes. If that isn't why you came to the Gers, visit the town's entirely sedentary church, originally part of the monastery around which Nogaro grew up. Begun in the 11th century, it has some lively capitals (*Daniel in the Lion's Den*, *David Playing a Rebec*), delicately carved arcades in the courtyard, and a colourful window of the *Coronation of the Virgin*, claimed to be a work of Arnaut de Moles.

Circuit Paul Armagnac
t 05 62 09 02 49, www.circuit-nogaro.com

Espagnet and **Toujouse**, west of Nogaro, also have Romanesque churches; the people of the latter village have assembled a collection of old farm gear, furniture and such, called the **Musée du Paysan Gascon**. South of Nogaro, you're heading towards the **valley of the Arros**. The landscapes are wilder and emptier here, the villages fewer and smaller. From any height, you'll be able to see the taller peaks of the Pyrenees to the south; the further you go, the grander the panoramas. Most of this area produces armagnac, but it is also part of the Madiran AOC wine region (*see* pp.230–1) – some vintners make both.

Musée du Paysan Gascon
t 05 62 09 67 33; open May–Oct daily 10–12 and 2–6; Mar, April and Nov Sun 2–6; otherwise by appt

Termes-d'Armagnac takes its name from the Latin *terminus*; this village was the boundary between those Kilkenny cats, the Dukes of Armagnac and Viscounts of Béarn. Termes sits under a commanding height with a tremendous view, and naturally it had a strong castle, partly built by Thibaut de Termes, who fought alongside Joan of Arc. Only one tower remains of it now, a striking

ⓘ **Termes-d'Armagnac**
t 05 62 69 25 12, www.tourdetermes.com; open June–Sept daily 10–7.30; Oct–May Mon–Fri 2–6

Musée du Panache Gascon
www.tourdetermes. com; open June–Sept daily 10–7.30; closed Tues am; Oct–May daily 2–6

Cave Cooperative Plaimont
t 05 62 69 62 87, www.plaimont.com

ⓘ **Aignan**
t 05 62 09 22 57, http://mairie.orange.fr/ aignan; open July–Aug Mon–Fri 10–12 and 2–6, Sat 9–12; Sept–June Mon–Fri 10–12 and 3–5, closed Wed pm

Chapelle Notre-Dame
t 05 62 09 24 09; open July and Aug Tues–Sun 10.30–7; Sept–Dec and mid-Feb–June Tues–Sun 2–6

Exotic garden
t 05 62 09 01 17, http://palm-sarthou. ifrance.com; open daily 9.30–12 and 2.30–7

landmark outside the village, and they have kitted it out as the **Musée du Panache Gascon**, with dioramas of historical scenes .

Just down the D3, **Tasque** had an important Benedictine monastery, until Montgomery's Protestant raiders torched it on Christmas Eve, 1570. The church remains, with a Romanesque portal portraying Christ in a mandorla. Inside is a weird, Celtic-looking cross, probably from as far back as Charlemagne's time. Note the old mechanical clock with its heavy weights. Though no longer working, it's one of the last survivors of its kind.

West of Termes on the River Adour, **St-Mont** has another old church worth a look, with some early, strangely carved capitals and scanty fragments of medieval painting. St-Mont is better known for its petit vin (VDQS), produced by the **Cave Cooperative Plaimont** (*see* p.231). **Aignan**, set in the middle of some delicious countryside east of Termes, must be one of the most attractive villages in the Gers, and a major producer of armagnac, with plenty of old-fashioned cellars to visit in the hinterlands. The original seat of the counts of Armagnac, Aignan was wrecked by the Black Prince in 1355, but it retains its arcaded square and a good 12th-century church. Charles de Batz, the legendary D'Artagnan, was born at the **Château de Castelmaure** (privately owned) north of nearby Lupiac. At the **Chapelle Notre-Dame** in **Lupiac** there is a museum dedicated to him at the Centre d'Artagnan, with an audio presentation in English. North of Aignan at **Betous** is a **garden** of palm trees, banana trees and other exotic plants.

Plaisance and Bassoues

South and east of Termes, the countryside gradually rumples into the contorted topography of the Vic-Bilh (*see* p.229). **Plaisance-du-Gers**, the little capital of the 'Pays d'Artagnan', hasn't done much for itself since the Black Prince burned it down on his 1355 tour. It's nice enough, but besides a few old half-timbered houses Plaisance's only monument is a ghastly Victorian Gothic church by one of the architects of Lourdes.

Just south of Plaisance, the D946 branches eastwards for Auch. It's a beautiful drive, a natural balcony with views of the Pyrenees in many places. At the end of the best part of the drive stands **Bassoues**, one of the most interesting of the Gers's many *bastides*. Bassoues was a strategic possession of the archbishops of Auch, who laid it out in the 1280s to accompany their strong castle, much of which remains today, including a stout 140ft (43m) **donjon**.

Donjon
t 05 62 70 97 34, http://bassoues.free.fr; open July and Aug daily 10–7; April–June, Sept and Oct 10–12 and 2–6; closed Tues all of Jan; Nov–Mar Sat, Sun and Wed 10–12 and 2–5

Bassoues also has a 15th-century church, the old archbishop's palace, a wooden *halle* and, out by its cemetery, the **Basilique St-Fris**. The crypt contains the relics of this obscure saint who defeated the Arabs in a battle near Bassoues in 732, when the invaders were in retreat after the great battle of Poitiers.

Marciac, Monlezun, Tillac and Miélan

Continuing south from Plaisance, the D3, the main drag of this corner of the *département*, takes you to the busy village of **Marciac**, a late 13th-century *bastide* that now stands the Gers on its ear each August with one of France's biggest jazz festivals. You can learn about the history of jazz, accompanied by some great jazz sounds, at **Les Territoires du Jazz** in the tourist office. Marciac is also known for furniture-making, and for the tallest **tower** in the Gers, the 293ft (90m) steeple of its church, a glorious 14th-century building with some good sculptural work inside.

Les Territoires du Jazz
www.jazzinmarciac.com

The imposing landmark that is clearly visible from the D3 at **Monlezun** is that village's ruined **castle**, yet another casualty of the Hundred Years War. It belonged to a certain Count Géraud of Pardiac, who was the brother of the powerful Count Bernard IV of Armagnac who after 1407 was the leader of the 'Armagnac' faction, siding with the king against the English. Suspecting Géraud of intrigues against him, he attacked the castle by surprise one night, capturing the unfortunate Géraud and his family. Bernard then razed the place and starved all the Pardiacs to death. The locals like to joke that the surviving tall tower, sticking up like a finger, is Géraud's last, eternal gesture of defiance.

Next along the route comes **Tillac**, a little medieval jewel consisting of a pretty single arcaded street of half-timbered buildings and a 15th-century church, unfortunately partially destroyed by fire. Tillac grew up around a castle, of which only two defence towers remain. Just up the D16, **Laas** is nothing but a few houses on the site of a long-demolished château. The house was abandoned because it was haunted, but the ghosts stayed – and they've been puttering around at night for the last 300 years or so.

Miélan is another typical *bastide* founded by the Sénéchal de Beaumarchais, who planted scores of them around the southwest for the king of France, and who liked to name them after famous places. Just as Fleurance is named after Florence, Miélan was after Milan (the Sénéchal also founded Cologne and a Pavie – Pavia – near Auch). West of here on the N21 there is a famous viewpoint where you can enjoy a tremendous panorama over the Pyrenees, the **Puntous de Laguian**.

Market days in the Pays d'Artagnan

Nogaro: Wednesdays and Saturdays.
Riscle (near Termes): Fridays.
Plaisance: Thursdays.
Miélan: Thursdays.

Where to Stay and Eat in the Pays d'Artagnan

Nogaro ⊠ 32110
**Hôtel du Commerce, in the village centre, t 05 62 09 00 95 (€). Basic but reasonably priced accommodation. *Closed Fri eve and Sat lunch.*

ⓘ **Nogaro >>**
81 Rue Nationale, t 05 62 09 13 30, www.nogaro.fr; open Mon–Sat 10–12 and 2–6

(i) Plaisance-
du-Gers >
10 Rue Adour, t 05 62
69 44 69; open mid-
June–mid-Sept Tues–Sat
10–1 and 2.30–6.30;
mid-Sept–mid-June
Tues–Fri 9.30–12.30 and
2–6, Sat 9.30–12.30

(i) Marciac >>
Place du Chevalier,
t 05 62 08 26 60,
www.marciactourisme.
com; open April–Sept
daily 9.30–12.30 and
2.30–6.30; Oct–Mar
Mon–Fri 9.30–12.30 and
2.30–6, Sun 11–1

Plaisance-du-Gers ✉ 32160

Ripa-Alta, Pl de l'Eglise, **t** 05 62 69 30 43 (€€). In this small hotel in the village centre there's also a restaurant that's been a favourite in the area for decades, with complex cuisine. *Menus* €15–38. *Closed mid-Jan–early Feb; restaurant closed Sun eve.*

Ségos ✉ 32400

****Domaine de Bassibé**, **t** 05 62 09 46 71, *www.bassibe.fr* (€€€). If you really want to get away, you couldn't get farther than this hamlet in the western corner of the Gers, and the 10 lovely rooms set in the various buildings of a former estate, all restored with taste and style. It's a bit expensive, but they have a regular clientele that doesn't seem to mind.

The restaurant, set in what were once the estate's *chais*, serves up a very sophisticated cuisine with imaginative *foie gras* starters; good wines from nearby Madiran and Bordeaux. *Menu à la carte €46. Except for July and Aug restaurant closed all day Tues and Wed, and lunchtime Mon, Thurs and Fri.*

Marciac ✉ 32230

La Petite Auberge, on the arcaded square, **t** 05 62 09 31 33. This is a popular spot for lunch, with a simple and filling four-course meal at a reasonable price. Go for the pricier menus if you want the duck. *Menus €11–36. Closed Wed eve and Thurs and mid-Oct–mid-Nov.*

The Valley of the Gers: Lectoure and Fleurance

The eastern end of the Gers is a *pays* called the **Lomagne** that extends eastwards into the *département* of Tarn-et-Garonne. It is a country of knobbly hills where both the roads and the little rivers such as the Arrats and the Auroue meander around, not in much of a hurry to get anywhere. The Lomagne is known for wheat and garlic (a third of all the garlic in France!) and not much else, but it does the best with what it has.

Lectoure

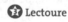 Lectoure

The French were often unkind to Lectoure. First they burned it down, and then they took away its ancient distinction as a capital by creating the *département* of the Gers and moving the seat of authority to Auch. Today the town (a population of 4,000 is enough to qualify as a town around here) has an aristocratic and somewhat forlorn air about it, sitting up on its lofty cliff with its monuments and its memories.

History

Lectoure occupies a strategic spot; an easily defensible site overlooking the Gers, it has always been the military key to Gascony. A Celtic tribe called Lactoratii, the first recorded residents, were famous for being one of the very few Celtic tribes to sit out the Gallic Wars, even going so far as to sign a treaty with the Romans. Collaboration paid off; the Lactoratii were the only Gauls to retain control over their affairs, forming a little republic under

Roman protection with the blessing of Julius Caesar. Roman Lactora was one of the important cities of the southwest in Roman times, spreading down onto the plain from its original site; the old Celtic *oppidum* served as a kind of acropolis, with temples to Jupiter and Cybele.

Lectoure retreated back to the hilltop during the invasions that followed, but still suffered some rough handling from both the Visigoths and the Normans. During the Middle Ages, it became the capital of the counts of Armagnac, and remained so until 1473. At that time, France was beginning to recover from the Hundred Years War, and King Louis XI took the opportunity to assert greater control over the south. His army attacked Lectoure, defended by Count Jean V in person. After a long siege, the two sides agreed on a peace by which the Armagnacs would recognize the authority of the king, and in turn the rights of both the Armagnacs and the town would be confirmed.

The French, unfortunately, were not being entirely truthful, and when Jean V opened the gates they immediately poured in, then sacked and burned the town. Their soldiers treacherously murdered the gullible count, and most of the population along with him. That put an end to the Armagnacs once and for all and, as a result, to the independence of Gascony.

Louis XI rebuilt the city, and in the Wars of Religion Lectoure had the good sense to side with Henri of Navarre – the future Henri IV. As king, Henri and his son Louis XIII favoured Lectoure, but with the Revolution, and the dividing of France into *départements*, Lectoure lost out to Auch, and has dwindled in importance ever since.

The Musée Lapidaire

Musée Lapidaire
t 05 62 68 70 22; open daily Mar–Sept 10–12 and 2–6; Oct–Feb Wed–Mon 10–12 and 2–6; closed hols

Lectoure's *mairie* occupies the old episcopal palace; underneath, in the bishops' cellars, the town has an excellent, recently redesigned museum. The collection was begun more than a century ago, when workmen excavating underneath the cathedral discovered a score of Gallo-Roman *tauroboles* – funeral monuments in the form of altars, decorated with bulls' heads. These are remarkable, in that they are dedicated not to the usual gods of the classical world, or even those of the Celts, but to Cybele, the Great Goddess of Asia Minor whose cult became widespread in Gaul and the rest of the Western Empire in the first three centuries AD. Translations (into French) of the inscriptions on the monuments have been posted, giving a fascinating insight into life in ancient Lactora.

Along with them is an early Christian marble sarcophagus carved with vine leaves, typical of the fine work that was still being turned out in Aquitaine throughout the twilight of the Roman Empire. The museum also has on display an interesting collection of jewellery from Roman and Merovingian times, as well as bits of mosaics found around the town, including one labelled *Ocianus* – a very strange face, full of foreboding.

Upstairs in the *mairie*, you can ask to see the two rooms of memorabilia of Lectoure's two famous sons: Maréchal Lannes, who fought in the Napoleonic Wars, and Admiral Boué-de-Lapeyrère, navy minister during the First World War (he tried, unsuccessfully, to talk Winston Churchill out of the Gallipoli landings). Another room houses a restored 19th-century pharmacy.

Centre de Photographie
t 05 62 68 83 72, www.centre-photo-lectoure.fr; open Mon–Sat July and Aug 2–7, Sun 3–7; Sept–June Tues–Sat 2–6

Nearby on Rue Ste-Claire is the **Centre de Photographie** with a wide variety of summer exhibitions.

Lectoure's **cathedral** is dedicated to St Gervais and St Protais, a very obscure pair of 4th-century martyrs in Milan; this suggests this church was around at a very early date, though most of its present incarnation was begun in 1488, as part of Louis XI's rebuilding programme. There is little of note inside the cathedral, only a small collection of religious paraphernalia – but if the sacristan is around, ask if you can go up the bell tower, for a view that takes in half the Gers and, on a clear day, the Pyrenees.

Failing that, the view from the **Bastion** on the eastern edge of the town is almost as good. Lectoure's old neighbourhoods, trailing on the slopes of the hill, are peaceful and lovely for walking, especially around **Rue de la Barbacane**. This quarter will show you a number of old convents, half-timbered houses and the 13th-century **Tour d'Albinhac**, part of a fortified town residence, of the sort that was more common in Italian cities at that time. There's a very interesting **museum** dedicated to woad (*pastel*) where you can learn how the precious blue dye was produced in the 15th and 16th centuries. *Pastel* created enormous wealth for merchants in and around Toulouse and Albi (in the Tarn) and many of the impressive buildings in these towns are thanks to the local cultivation of woad (*see* p.308).

Woad museum
Bleu de Lectoure, t 05 62 68 78 30, www. bleu-de-lectoure.com; open summer daily 10–12.30 and 2–7; winter 9.30–12.30 and 2–6.30

Into the Lomagne: Villages and Châteaux

Northeast of Lectoure, the D23/D953 is a pretty road for an aimless ramble; it passes through **Miradoux**, the first *bastide* founded in the Gers (1252), and **Flamarens**, a very picturesque village that has been saved from decrepitude by a number of private restoration projects in recent years. A perfect example of this is Flamarens's magnificent **château** that was destroyed by a fire and has just undergone a long programme of restoration. Some other villages of note in the vicinity are **Ste-Mère**, west of Miradoux, with a well-preserved medieval castle and, just to the north at **Rouillac**, a château built by another of the relatives of Pope Clement V (*see* La Romieu, p.134); and another *bastide*, **Dunes**, with a richly decorated 15th-century church. At **Plieux** the château

Château de Flamarens
t 05 62 28 68 25; open July and Aug Wed–Mon 10–12 and 3–7

Contemporary Art Museum
t 05 62 28 60 86, www.chateaudeplieux. org; open July and Aug Mon and Wed–Sun 3–7; Sept–June Sat and Sun 3–7

has been superbly restored by the celebrated local writer Renaud Camus and it is now open as a **contemporary art museum**.

There are quite a few interesting châteaux that can be visited in this out-of-the-way region: the **Château de Lacassagne**, just outside Lectoure on the N21, was built by a grand prior of the Knights of Malta; the place is still in the family, and they occasionally open it up (*ask at the Lectoure tourist office*). Some of the rooms are reconstructions of halls at the Knights' headquarters in Valletta, Malta, decorated with a series of big paintings of famous episodes in the Order's history.

Château de Gramont
t 05 63 94 05 26; open May–Sept Tues–Sun 10–12.30 and 2–6; Oct–April Tues–Sun 2–6; adm

At **Gramont**, where the D25 crosses the River Arrats, the lovingly restored château is a fine example of a Gascon nobleman's house of the 17th century, complete with period furniture and tapestries.

Château de Terraube
t 05 62 68 93 85; call for opening times

And at **Terraube**, west of Lectoure on the D42, there is a mostly 16th- to 18th-century château that once belonged to a renowned warrior of the Hundred Years War, Hector de Galard. This fine fellow lives on as the Jack of Diamonds in the French pack of cards (in France, all the face cards are representations of historical personages). Terraube also has a famous (or infamous) well – it was into this that Blaise de Montluc's merry men bundled all the local Protestants, in one of the opening atrocities of the Wars of Religion.

For another Lomagne excursion, take the little unnumbered road south from Lectoure that follows the valley of the Gers. The road is marked for the Lac des Trois Vallées, a popular recreation area. Eventually it turns into the D45 and takes you to **St-Clar**, the garlic capital of the area. This singular village is actually made up of two separate *bastides*, each with its own arcaded square (one was laid out in the 14th century, but nobody could be bothered to build on any of the lots until five centuries later), as well as an original *castelnau*, which has a 13th-century church and a crumbling feudal castle as well as a later *faubourg*. There is a **museum** on public schools from the late 18th to the mid-20th century which includes the reconstruction of a 1930s classroom. To the north, the little church in **St-Créac** preserves some very early, Byzantine-style medieval frescoes. Just south of St-Clar, **Avezan** has a striking castle, the restoration of which is nearly complete, overlooking the Arrats.

Musée de l'Ecole Publique
t 05 62 66 32 78, www.musee-de-lecole-publique.com; open June–Sept Wed–Sun 3–7, May and Oct 2–6

Fleurance

Yet another *bastide*, one of the earlier ones (1272), Fleurance was also one of the few to grow into a real town. From the time of its prosperity, in the 18th century, there is an elegant ensemble of buildings around the central **Place de la Halle**, including the *mairie*, a market and fountains with allegories in bronze of the Four Seasons, one at each corner. The real reason for stopping, though, is three more stained-glass windows by Arnaut de Moles, as good as the ones in Auch cathedral and perhaps even more colourful. They are found in the **Eglise de Notre-Dame**, a Gothic church of brick and stone built mostly in the 14th-century – how they got it up in the middle of the Hundred Years War is something of a mystery. The windows, in the apse, catch the eye as soon as you enter the church: on the left, St Lawrence, Mary Magdalene and St Augustine; in the centre, the Virgin with the Trinity; and on the right a wonderful 'Tree of Jesse' (a common subject in medieval glass, a genealogical tree showing the descent from Jesse of Mary and Jesus).

South of Fleurance, the N21 follows the River Gers closely on the way to Auch. Near Miramont Latour, at **Latour**, on the same site, is a 13-century castle with a **museum** on rural life, a 17-century convent chapel and a *pigeonnier*. The only other distractions along the way are another restored 17th-century château, the **Château de Rieutort** near Roquelaure, and **Montaut-les-Crénaux**. This fortified village has only fragments of its walls and castle, but its 12th-century church of St-Michel survives intact, one of those rare Romanesque jewels you can find in out-of-the-way French villages. Not much has been changed in 800 years; the church still has its original stone altar, along with some fragments of Roman mosaics that were found in the vicinity and set up for safekeeping here.

Latour Museum
t 05 62 62 27 99; open July and Aug Thurs–Sun 3–7; June and Sept Sun 3–7

ⓘ **Fleurance >**
112 bis Rue de la République, t 05 62 64 00 00, http://tourismefleurance.free.fr; open July and Aug Mon–Sat 9–6.30, Sun 9.30–12.30; Sept–June Mon–Sat 10–12 and 2–5.30

ⓘ **Lectoure >**
Mairie, Pl de la Cathédrale, t 05 62 68 76 98, www.lectoure.fr; open Mon–Sat 10–12 and 3–5, Sun 3–50

★ **Hotel de Bastard >**

ⓘ **Miradoux**
t 05 62 28 63 08, www.citaenet.com/miradoux; open Tues–Fri 9–12 and 3–6

Market Days in the Valley of the Gers

Fleurance: Tuesdays and Saturdays.
Lectoure: Fridays.
St-Clar: Thursdays.

Where to Stay and Eat in the Valley of the Gers

Lectoure ✉ 32700

**Hôtel de Bastard, Rue Lagrange in the centre, t 05 62 68 82 44, *www.hotel-de-bastard.com* (€€–€). The best thing about staying in this hotel is of course sending a card home from it. The nobleman who built this stately town mansion in the 1700s may well have been a real bastard, but the current owners are actually quite amiable. The atmosphere is conservative French provincial and the rooms airy and tasteful. There is also a fine terrace with a pool looking out over the rooftops of Lectoure and even room for a small garden. In the restaurant, along with traditional Gascon fare on offer, the cooking takes some welcome detours, usually in the direction of Italy, with dishes such as aubergine cannelloni with duck. *Menus €15–60. Closed Sun eve and Mon and also at Christmas and in Jan.*

Auberge des Bouviers, Rue Montebello, t 05 62 68 95 13. This is a happy place where the windows are full of flowers and the traditional southwest cooking is first class. *Menus €22–38. Closed Sun eve, Mon all day and Sat lunch.*

Bellevue, 55 Rue Nationale, t 05 62 68 80 06. This restaurant has a good menu with the accent on honest regional cooking. *Menus €12–18. Closed several days in Oct.*

Le Gascogne, 121 Rue Alsace Lorraine, t 05 62 68 77 57. This is a classic French establishment, with a pretty terrace, specializing in fish and wood-fire grillades. *Menus from €18. Closed Tues and Wed eve.*

From Condom to Auch

The Abbaye de Flaran

Abbaye de Flaran
t 05 62 28 50 19; open July–Aug daily 9.30–7; Feb–June and Sept–Dec daily 9.30–12.30 and 2–6; closed Jan and hols; guided tours; adm

Just south of Condom on the outskirts of the village of Valence, the Abbaye de Flaran was founded by the Cistercians in 1151. The great leader of this order, St Bernard of Clairvaux, never tired of preaching how beauty in architecture or decoration was nothing but worldly vanity, and this substantial complex is less remarkable for these than for the fact that nearly all of the monastic buildings have survived intact. The *département* has recently done a thorough restoration, and operates the complex as a cultural centre.

Though Cistercians did not care to dress up their buildings, they were hardly a lot of otherworldly mystics. Following the lead of St Bernard, one of the most mean-spirited ayatollahs in history, they did have two little weaknesses: money and power. In the order's golden age, the 12th century, they acquired vast lands across Europe, and used the most up-to-date agricultural methods to exploit them, while their leaders meddled in political and moral affairs everywhere. Bernard was the great enemy of Abelard and the universities, and Cistercians dedicated themselves especially to stamping out free-thinking wherever they could find it.

As such, they weren't welcomed in the south and, though Cistercians founded hundreds of monasteries across Europe, this is one of their few colonies in what was then Aquitaine. The **church**, begun in 1180, shows the elegance common in the best Cistercian buildings, with simple arcading, and just a touch of stonecarving around the cornices and windows for decoration. It is always interesting to see how the medieval master masons responded to the Cistercian beliefs – a 'less is more' approach to architecture that many minds of that fertile age must have found wholesome and satisfying. Among the other buildings are an equally austere cloister, the main halls, a lovely **chapter house** built with some reused Roman columns, the refectory (dining hall) and library.

Around the Abbey

Château-Monluc
t 05 62 28 94 00; open June–Sept Mon–Sat 10–12 and 3–7, Sun/hols 3–7; Feb–May and Oct–Dec Tues–Sat 10–12 and 3–7; closed Jan

The Cistercians usually chose their sites well. The little River Baïse is navigable along most of its length, and this was an important trade route in medieval times. As another testimony to this, the area is littered with **castles**, usually in varying stages of ruination. Some of the better ones are at **Tauzia**, only a few kilometres from Flaran, across the D930, and further south at **Pardeilhan** and **Lagardère**. One of the largest can be seen at **Herrebouc**, overlooking the Baïse.

If you're passing by Tauzia you might also wish to stop in at the **Château-Monluc** at St-Puy, which is some 8km further east. This was the home of Blaise de Monluc, Maréchal de France under Henri II and less a fierce Catholic bigot than a simple soldier following orders. His spree in the 1550s, massacring Protestants wherever he could find them, contributed as much as anything to setting the tone for the Wars of Religion. Today the château is better known for the liqueur it produces: *Pousse-Rapier*, based on armagnac with an orange flavour; the vaulted *chais* from the 1500s are worth a visit.

Vic-Fézensac isn't exactly on the way to Auch. It isn't really on the way to anywhere, and seems to know it. The biggest village and market of the area, it comes alive twice each year and only twice: for its bullfights, which take place around Pentecost, and for its popular Sulsa festival on the last weekend in July.

A Roman Mystery: the *Tourasses*

Rather than detour to Vic-Fézensac, you might wish to take a ramble through the countryside between **Biran** and **St-Lary**, to seek out the *tourasses*. These unusual towers, built of neat masonry and usually about 30ft (9m) tall, are a speciality of the Gers; the *département* has over a dozen of them, and the greatest concentration is here, on or around the Roman road that once ran up the valley of the Baïse. Nobody knows exactly what purpose the *tourasses* (as the locals call them) originally served. They may have been trophies, erected to commemorate some military feats, like the famous trophy of Augustus at La Turbie in Provence, or more likely they served some religious purpose. Nearly all of them have a niche for a statue, but since all the statues are missing we'll never know; Christians turned them all into shrines long ago. There is one on the opposite side of the D930 from St-Lary, off on a side road, and two others further west on the road to the hamlet of Lat Roque. Perhaps the best-preserved and easiest to find is just south of Biran, on the road to Le Mas on the eastern bank of the Baïse. Biran, built around its ruined castle, is an attractive village; its church has an enormous marble altarpiece, in the cold style of the age of Louis XIV.

If you're out looking for towers, though, you might bypass a genuine attraction on the other side of the D930. **Lavardens** looks to have been a serious and busy place long ago, a densely built fortified village on a lofty site. The **château** attatched to it was a stronghold of the counts of Armagnac. Henri of Navarre captured it from the Catholics and destroyed it, but a century later a local nobleman rebuilt it as a residential château. For a while this château belonged to the Marquis of Mirabeau, father of the famous Revolutionary orator; after falling into decay it has been completely restored and is open for visits. The best feature is the intricate pavements, done in patterns of different kinds of stone.

Château de Lavardens
t 05 62 58 10 61, www.chateaulavardens. com; open daily June–Sept 10.30–7; April, May, and Oct 10.30–12.30 and 2–6; Nov–mid-Dec and mid-Feb–Mar 10.30–12.30 and 2–5; closed mid-Jan–mid-Feb; adm

(i) **Vic-Fézensac** >
t 05 62 06 34 90,
www.vic-fezensac.com;
open July and Aug
Mon–Sat 9–12.30 and
2–6, Sun 9–12.30;
Sept–June Mon–Sat
9–12.30 and 2–6

(i) **Valence** >
t 05 62 28 59 19,
www.citaenet.com/
valence-sur-baise; open
Mon–Fri 9–12 and 2–6

(★) **Ferme**
de Flaran >

(i) **Jegun**
t 05 62 64 54 62,
www.coeurde
gascogne.com

08 The Gers | Auch

Market Days from Condom to Auch

Vic-Fézensac: Fridays.
Valence: Wednesdays.

Where to Stay and Eat from Condom to Auch

Valence ✉ 32310
**Ferme de Flaran, t 05 62 28 58 22, *www.fermedeflaran.com* (€€). This restored farmhouse stands just off the D930 south of Condom, within easy walking distance of the abbey. There is a pool, and friendly management who are very dedicated to Gascony and its traditions, going out of their way to help visitors discover the region. This dedication also extends to the restaurant, where

all the southwestern favourites you would expect turn up. *Menus €20–38. Closed Sun eves and Mon exc for mid-July–mid-Aug and hotel closed end of Oct–early Nov.*

Castéra-Verduzan ✉ 23410
Hôtel Ténarèze, t 05 62 68 10 22, *www.hotel-tenareze.com* (€). Halfway between Condom and Auch. This old, family-run hotel has 24 pleasant rooms but may close at the end of 2006, so call first. The restaurant is called **Auberge Le Florida, t 05 62 68 13 22. Both the lunch and dinner menus have a good range of fish choices, some game (when in season) and of course the duck and *foie gras*. There is a good selection of local wines on the menu, too. *Menus €13–50, starting at €27 on Sun. Restaurant closed Sun eve and Mon, exc summer.*

Auch

Auch could be a lovely little town, if it wanted to. The metropolis of the *département*, with its 23,000 people, has all the ingredients: a pretty setting overlooking the River Gers, and an elegant core of monuments and squares inherited from the days when the town was run by its archbishops. Unfortunately, Auch seems to have no ambitions to be anything more than an overgrown farmers' market. The centre looks dowdy and uncared for, and every open space without exception has been pressed into service as a car park. Too bad for that: visitors will just have to settle for two of the greatest artistic achievements France has ever produced: Arnaut de Moles's spectacular stained-glass windows, and a set of choir stalls that have to be seen to be believed. Both are in the cathedral.

History

The records say that this town was originally called Elimberris, an odd name that suggests a Basque origin. When it first appears in history, though, it was inhabited by a Celtic tribe called the Auscii, and consequently it became known in Roman times as Augusta Auscorum (the Augusta, as in so many towns across the Empire, denotes a special sign of favour from Augustus or one of the later emperors; there would have been a ceremonial 'refounding' and renaming, perhaps accompanied by a new temple or amphitheatre or some such work, which would have been financed from Rome). Auch survived the Dark Ages by retreating up to the high ground around the cathedral and building a set of walls. After the Vikings had their way with Eauze in the 870s, the archbishops moved from there to Auch, and the town began to grow again. Though nominally under the suzerainty of the counts of Armagnac, it was the archbishops, and the town's elected consuls, who made most of the decisions during the Middle Ages. In fact the situation was far more complicated than that; in typically intricate and balanced medieval fashion, Auch was a schizophrenic three cities in one. The archbishops looked after the centre, around the cathedral; the counts and their vassals, for their part, took care of the settlement that grew up around their castle of Fézensac, now demolished; while a third nucleus appeared to the north, which was owned by the Priory of St-Orens – all three contained in an area of less than a square mile.

After the French crushed the Armagnacs and put an end to their dynasty in 1473, they wasted little time in occupying Auch. For the next three centuries it was ruled by *intendants* appointed by the king, and these added some gracious embellishments, including the Allées d'Etigny, a grand promenade of plane trees off central Place de la Libération. Since then Auch's destiny has mirrored that of the Gers as a whole: no economic activity to speak of besides farming and government, and probably about the same population as it had in the 14th century.

Cathédrale Ste-Marie

⭐ **Cathédrale Ste-Marie**

'A cathedral like this should be put in a museum!'
Emperor Napoleon III

At first sight this wonderful building is a bit disconcerting, with its strange façade looming over central Place de la République. This is one of the last cathedrals in France to be completed – not surprisingly, for such an ambitious work in such a small town – and the west front was not added until the 17th century.

The French would call the façade's style *classique*, which means lots of bits and pieces from Italian Renaissance style books pasted together every which way. The bits go together harmoniously enough; there isn't another façade quite like this one anywhere in the south of France. The façade has been recently cleaned, which has brightened up Auch substantially. Walking around the sides, you can see the flamboyant Gothic intent of the original architects, with impressive ranks of buttresses and arches, and an elegant apse.

Auch began its cathedral in the 14th century, but the work didn't really get rolling until 1463, under an archbishop named Jean de Lescun. Thus, despite its Gothic form, built on a plan inspired by the great cathedrals of the Ile-de-France, this cathedral is essentially a child of the Renaissance. When Renaissance ideas and styles really took root in France, in the early 1500s, Auch was fortunate to have another forceful archbishop, one who had travelled in Italy – and one who had access to some serious money; Cardinal Clément-Lodève was the brother of Georges d'Amboise, who at different

mise au tombeau

7–9

10–12

4–6

13–15

3

16

2

17

1

18

choir

The Stained Glass (*see* plan, opposite)

Nobody knows much about Arnaut de Moles, except that he came from St-Sever in the Landes, and that he started his work here in 1507. If he hadn't chosen to work in the obscure medium of stained glass, and to leave practically all of his life's work here in the middle of the Gers, he might have gained the renown he deserves as one of the greatest artists of his time.

New advances in technique helped him achieve incredible colour effects. A stain made from silver nitrite or silver chloride created the brilliant golds and yellows, something medieval stained-glass artists did not have at their disposal. In all, Arnaut's work, in which he engraved details directly onto the glass with acid, much more than medieval artists did, is an art that seems much closer to painting.

The 18 windows, in the ambulatory chapels surrounding the choir, make a complete account of the Christian story of fall and redemption. Old and New Testament figures are mixed together according to the medieval idea of typology, in which everything in the Old prefigures something in the New. Their complex symbolism makes a fascinating progression from Genesis, through the Crucifixion (which is at the centre as the turning point of history) through to the Resurrection in the last window.

It begins in the left aisle with:

1   The Creation, Adam and Eve (note the Creation in the upper panel, with the concentric circles of the cosmos, the 'celestial spheres', opposite a scene of the creation of Eve). At the bottom you can see the expulsion from paradise and Cain and Abel.

2   God the Father with Angelic choir, Noah, the Annunciation. The female figure is a sibyl, one of the oracular priestesses of the ancient world; in Christian legend each of these in some way foretold the birth of Christ. Other sibyls appear in succeeding windows. Note also the coat of arms of the archbishop who hired Arnaut, Cardinal Clermont-Lodève.

3   Graceful figures of Abraham and Melchizidek, St Paul and the Sibyl of Samos; below, sacrifice of Isaac, Nativity.

4   The Virgin Mary with Old Testament prophets; in a medallion, portraits of the cathedral architect, Pierre de Beaujeu, and his wife.

5   Jacob, Jonah, St Mark; below, Jonah and the whale; a medallion portrait of Jean V, the last count of Armagnac.

6   Moses, a sibyl, Enoch; below, the burning bush, the sibyl of the Capitoline Hill with Emperor Augustus.

7   Joseph, St Andrew, Joel; below, Joseph sold by his brother.

8   Some charming angel musicians; above, Joshua, a sibyl, Amos; below, the flight into Egypt.

9   Caleb, Bartholomew, Abdias; above, the 'Holy Women' including Mary Magdalene.

10 Isaiah, St Philip, Micah.

11 The central window: Crucifixion, with St John and Mary Magdalene. This window, like the two flanking it, displays big *fleurs-de-lys* in honour of the King of France.

12 David, St James the Greater, in the costume of a pilgrim to Compostela, Azarias. The next chapel was originally the entrance to the sacristy, and hence has no window. It does, however hold a remarkable work of Renaissance sculpture, a *mise au tombeau* (entombment of Christ, a common subject in the 15th century); Joseph of Arimathea and Nicodemus hold the body, while St John, the three Marys and Mary Magdalene look on. Note the figures of the soldiers on the side, dressed in typical military costume of the 1500s. This work too is traditionally attributed to Arnaut de Moles, who was also a sculptor; no one knows for sure.

13 Jeremiah, a sibyl, Nahum; below, the flagellation of Christ.

14 Daniel, a sibyl, St Matthew; below, Daniel in the lions' den.

15 Sophonias, Elias, Uriah.

16 Esdras, Habbakuk, and an exceptionally lovely Tiburtine Sibyl. Here too are portraits of King Louis XII and former archbishops including Jean de Lescun.

17 More portraits, including the king's son, the future François I; Elisha, Judas and a sibyl; below, the crown of thorns.

18 Christ, flanked by a doubtful-looking Thomas and a believing Magdalene; below, the Last Supper. At the end, the artist signs off: 'On the 25 June 1513 these present works were completed for the honour of God and Our Lady. *Noli me tangere*. Arnaut de Moles.'

times filled the offices of chief minister to King Louis XII, and papal legate to France. Under him, the most important features of the interior were begun, the choir and the stained glass.

The Choir Stalls

The choir is an unusual feature, completely enclosed as in a Spanish cathedral. It is usually locked, but someone is sure to be around with the key. Though worth seeing, the stalls are badly lit and you might find it handy to bring a torch. The entire space is filled with a set of 113 choir stalls, in which the monks of the cathedral chapter would celebrate the Mass. Made of heart of oak, soaked in water for fifty years to harden it and permit carving of the tiniest of details, this ensemble is one of the masterpieces of Renaissance woodcarving. It is also one of its most ambitious projects; two centuries ago, a monk of Auch tried to count all the figures on the stalls, and came up with over 1,500.

Elaborate sets of choir stalls such as this one were common enough in Europe in the 15th to the 18th centuries, but this one would be hard to beat. At first glance, expending so much time and talent on a locked-up place for monks to plant their behinds might seem a mad obsession, somewhat like making a model battleship out of toothpicks. But take this rather as an eccentric but glorious example of that Renaissance innovation: art for art's sake. These choir stalls took over fifty years to make, and many hands assisted in the work.

One theory has it that this was a special project of the *compagnie des sculpteurs* (like the masons, every other art and craft in medieval times was organized into a self-governing brotherhood); journeyman woodcarvers would make a trip as a kind of artistic pilgrimage, a *devoir de liberté*, and contribute some work to the whole. This would explain the wide range of styles in the work, and also the great freedom of subject matter. Unlike Arnaut's windows, and entirely contrary to the encyclopaedic, carefully thought-out decorative plans in earlier cathedrals, there is no grand scheme here, reflecting the truth of scripture and the organization of the cosmos. Rather, within limits each artist seems to have done as he pleased. Some of the works mirror the figures in the stained glass, which was under way at the same time; others represent other biblical personages or vignettes. Mythology is represented – even Hercules makes an appearance, slaying the giant Antaeus – and others are pure flights of fancy.

Unfortunately, none of the artists added much to their works that would clear up exactly who all these figures really are. Perhaps this was by design; certainly, this is one of the first – if not the first – great works executed for the Church in France where religious symbolism takes a back seat to pure artistic expression. The same monk who tried to count all the figures also attempted to identify them all. Though he did his best, the result is probably extremely unreliable. You can get a brochure with his guesses from the caretaker. At any rate, the main panels, above the seats, echo a motif of the windows, with pairs of male and female figures, beginning with Adam and Eve and continuing through sibyls, saints and Old Testament figures.

The vast majority of the figures, however, are concealed among the magnificent carved Gothic traceries, on the arms or under the seats; you'll find something beautiful in every corner, or at least something that will surprise you or make you laugh. It will take two hours or so to look the thing over carefully. This is a wonderful place to bring your children, and even for adults the endless details of the stalls make one of the best treasure hunts you could imagine. See if you can find the *camel*, the *winged bulldog*, the *skeleton*, the *baby snake*, the *saw*, the *two-headed monk*, the *unicorn*...

The man with the keys will also let you down to see the **crypt**, where there is a 7th-century sarcophagus and a number of other relics from local saints, as well as the cathedral treasure, with plenty of old church bric-a-brac and busts of Henri IV and Marguerite of Valois. A different generation of woodcarvers, Parisians this time, contributed the cabinet for the great **organ**, a work of architecture in itself (1694).

The Monumental Stair

Auch turns its back towards the River Gers, as you will see if you come from Mirande or Comminges; just the same, this is its best face, with a quiet river-front boulevard (Avenue Sadi Carnot) and the **monumental stair**, built in the 1860s, leading down from the apse of the cathedral. There are 370 steps if you're going that way, and landings with a **statue of d'Artagnan** (Charles de Batz never would have dreamed...) and a bizarre modern work that consists of the story of Noah, in Latin, engraved in the pavement.

Also behind the cathedral you can see the striking 14th-century tower called the **Tour d'Armagnac**, one of the landmarks of the city and a proud monument for all Gascons. Unfortunately, the tower and the building to which it is attached, the Palais de l'Officialité, never belonged to the Armagnacs or had any connection with them whatsoever. Rather, they served as the offices of the archbishops of Auch, and their prisons.

South of the stair and the cathedral is one of the oldest neighbourhoods of Auch, the **Quartier du Caillou**, a forbidding tangle of narrow hillside street alleys that often turn into claustrophobic stairways. The locals call these old streets the '*pousteries*', a fittingly strange setting for a place that briefly was the home of Nostradamus. The wizard spent some time in Auch in the 1540s, and taught at the old Jesuit College on Rue de la Convention.

There's more life on the streets north of the cathedral. In Rue Dessoles, just off Place de la République, stands the lovely half-timbered **Maison Fedel** from the 15th century, which now houses the tourist office; one of the oldest houses in Auch, it leans in so many directions at once that it seems to be made of pastry. Rue Dessoles is the main street of the old town; at its opposite end are some walls and a tower, relics of the **Priory of St-Orens**, once one of the most powerful monasteries in Gascony.

Musée des Jacobins

Musée des Jacobins
Place Louis-Blanc,
t 05 62 05 74 79; open
Tues–Sun 10–12 and
2–6; closed hols exc July
and Aug; adm

From here, heading down towards the river, find your way to Rue Daumesnil and the Musée des Jacobins, housed in a monastery that dates mostly from the 17th century. Founded in the middle of the French Revolution, in 1793, this is one of the best-run little provincial museums in France, even if the collections are a bit like grandma's attic; everything is atractively presented and good fun. The small archaeological rooms display some 1st-century frescoes from a Roman villa near Auch (in the 'late Pompeiian style', meaning still good, though the inspiration is wearing a bit thin), and a scant few relics from Augusta Auscorum, including a big statue of Emperor Trajan with a big Roman nose (any archaeo-logical museum worth its salt has one of these: it's paradoxical, though, that one of the greatest and most intelligent of emperors should have been the most enamoured of financing statues of himself everywhere, all bigger than life). The epochs that follow offer a grab-bag of items: a number of medieval tombs and tombstones, including a fine Renaissance *gisant* of Cardinal Jean d'Armagnac, and some beautifully made musical instruments, such as a harpsichord from the time of Louis XV.

Holding pride of place among the museum's paintings are the works of a local boy named Jean-Marie Roumeguère, who seems to have specialized in sunrises, sunsets and burning houses. The upstairs holds a large collection devoted to traditional Gascon crafts, with furniture, costumes, lace and samplers, an exhibit on the life of d'Artagnan, and a room with some lovely 18th-century faïence – Auch and Samadet in the Landes were ceramic centres at the time.

The museum is laid out to save the best and most surprising for last: a fascinating collection of pre-Colombian and colonial **Latin-American Art**, gathered by an Auscitain named Pujols who travelled over the continent for most of his life and then came home to run this museum. He brought back pottery, figures and fabrics from Teotihuacan and the other Mexican cultures, from

Peru (including a statue of Manco-Capac, founder of the Inca dynasty) and from the Caribbean Indians. Some of the best of these works are 19th-century fakes, of which every collector must have picked up a few; here they have been proudly given a display case of their own. From after the Spanish conquest there is mostly naïve religious art and folk crafts, such as some wonderful carved stirrups and a bolo from Argentina. There's also a section on Egyptology including several funerary artefacts and some interesting Coptic pieces discovered by local archaeologist Charles Palanques.

Market Days in Auch

Saturday is the big market, but also Thursdays.

⭐ Jardin des Saveurs >>

ⓘ Auch >
1 Rue Dessoles, t 05 62 05 22 89, www.auch-tourisme.com; open mid-July–mid-Aug Tues–Sat 9.30–6.30, Mon 10–6.30, Sun 10–12 and 3–6; May–mid-July and mid-Aug–Sept Tues–Sat 9.15–12 and 2–6.15, Sun 10–12.15; Oct–April Tues–Sat 9.15–12 and 2–6, Mon 10–12 and 2–6

Where to Stay in Auch

Auch ✉ 32000

***Hôtel de France**, Pl de la Libération, t 05 62 61 71 71, www.hoteldefrance-auch.com (€€€–€€). Few hotels in all of France have as many stories to tell as this one. As the Armes de France it was a noted establishment 200 years ago. The Auscitains claim that no less a personage than the son of Louis XVI, the poor Dauphin Louis, was smuggled out of Paris during the terror and ended up here, working as a stable boy (until recently, his descendants still lived in the area, though no one took their claim to the throne very seriously outside the Gers). For all that, it is a thoroughly modern hotel, with luxurious rooms and amenities including a sauna. No pool, but they will arrange sports such as riding and golf out in the nearby countryside. Open all year.

Le Robinson, just south of Auch, t 05 62 05 02 83, www.hotelrobinson.net (€). In a beautiful forest setting, this hotel has clean and stylish modern rooms with balconies and television.

*Hôtel de Paris**, Av de la Marne near the train station, t 05 62 63 26 22 (€). This is a family-run, well-cared-for hotel. Closed Nov and Sun eve.

Camping Ile St-Martin, on the N21 towards Tarbes, t 05 62 05 00 22. This site is well equipped and municipally run. Open mid-April–Sept.

Eating Out in Auch

Jardin des Saveurs, in the **Hotel de France** (see left), t 06 62 61 71 71. This famous hotel also claims the highest-rated restaurant of the département, with new chef Roland Garreau as accomplished as his legendary predecessor, André Daguin. The lunch menu goes for €19 with wine; otherwise you'll find menus for €27–52 in the restaurant. And for that, they lay it on thick: the very best foie gras, perhaps with a hint of truffles, along with all the other natural delights of the southwest. Some of the dishes on offer are traditional favourites (it's a surprise to find cassoulet on the menu in such a place), others inspired flights of fancy. For accompaniment, they have probably the best cellar in the southwest. Closed Sun eve except July and Aug.

Relais de Gascogne, 5 Av de la Marne, t 05 62 05 26 81. This hotel-restaurant delivers good local cuisine such as daube à l'armagnac, cassoulet, duck and fish. Menus €15–26. Closed end Dec–mid-Jan.

Hôtel de Paris, Av de la Marne, t 05 62 63 26 22. This hotel (see left) has an acceptable if less than exciting restaurant. Menus €10–24. Closed Sun eve and Nov.

Café Gascon, Rue Lamartine, t 05 62 61 88 08. After visiting the cathedral nearby, a good light lunch can be had here. Closed Wed out of season and Mon and Tues eve.

East from Auch: More *Bastides*, Castles and *Foie Gras*

Mauvezin, on the D928, grew into a town in the 13th century and has been dwindling ever since. A stronghold of Protestantism in the Wars of Religion, the town was known as 'Little Geneva' but still somehow managed to survive. Mauvezin's landmark is its *halles*, a stone and timber construction that has lasted since the 14th century. The town is St-Clar's redoubtable rival in garlic, and tries to keep its name in the headlines with the annual Garlic Festival, and the beauty pageant to select the Garlic Queen. **Cologne**, 10km to the east, doesn't have such an impressive market, but the centre of this *bastide* of the 1280s is one of the prettiest sights in the Gers: a typical square, surrounded by an ensemble of comfortable-looking old houses of brick and half-timber. The *halles* here may be smaller, but it is another fine example of traditional carpentry, built also in the 14th century; note the old standard measures, carved into the stone pillars that support it.

Château de Laréole
t 05 61 06 33 58; open May and June Wed, Sat and Sun 10–6; July and Aug daily 10–7; Sept Sat and Sun 10–6, free guided visits

Just 5km east of Cologne, just over the border in the Haute-Garonne, you can visit the grand Renaissance **Château de Laréole**, recently restored and opened to the public. Begun in 1579 by Pierre de Cheverry, son of a great Toulouse *pastel* merchant who went on to fame and fortune as the treasurer of France, it was finished in only three years thanks to the tremendous sums at his disposal. The Wars of Religion were raging, so defence was an important consideration – hence the four towers and moat – yet style wasn't overlooked, either, most strikingly in the stone and brick stripes that decorate both the exterior and central courtyard. Unfortunately the original furnishings are long gone, but there's an exhibition on the history of the château and its owners over the centuries. You can now go upstairs and also visit the surrounding park, laid out in the 18th century according to the geometric theories and perspectives of Le Nôtre; although neglected in the last century, it too is being restored to its original form.

The N124 stretches from Auch into the furthest eastern reaches of the Gers, passing through **Gimont**, another distinctive *bastide* and one of the centres of the *foie gras* trade. The village's church of Notre-Dame possesses a Renaissance triptych of the cruci-fixion. East of here, both the countryside and the villages begin to change. We're entering the valley of the River Save, whose waters flow almost to Toulouse before they find their way into the Garonne. Toulouse isn't far away, and the Ville Rose shows its influence in the predominantly brick churches and buildings of villages like **L'Isle-Jourdain**, the biggest centre of the region. L'Isle's history is wrapped up with the ancient family of the same name,

It Looks Potentially Wonderful, But What Does One Do With It?

Such is the common reaction of the uninitiated to a *foie gras* in its natural splendour. So we'll tell you. Wherever you get a chance to purchase a fresh *foie gras* (goose or duck), at a market or even better, from a farmer, look for one that is firm, and light in colour with a touch of pink to it – not yellowish. Don't worry about the size. Once you've got it home, carefully cut out all the blood vessels and bile ducts as well as you can, along with any greenish bits. Then soak it overnight in water with a bit of vinegar (¼ cup).

The next day, dry it well, and sprinkle it all over with salt and pepper (and maybe a little armagnac). If you want it *au naturel*, now wrap the *foie* up tightly in a thin cloth, cover with foil and put it in the refrigerator (very cold, but not freezing) for 3–5 days. Some people like it just like this, sliced into very thin medallions and served well chilled. Others cook it in a sealed jar immersed in boiling water; one hour per kilo, or proportionately less according to weight. *Mi-cuit* ('half-cooked') seems to be the favourite way throughout the southwest. This can mean roasting it in a medium oven in a sealed container with a half-inch of water in it, for a half-hour or maybe more (don't overcook it; as soon as the inside is good and hot it's done). Or else, get yourself a mess of goose fat (*graisse d'oie*, which the same farmer can probably supply), melt it down and cook the *foie* gently in it for about ten minutes. This way, you can store the cooked *foie* in a canning jar, covered with the fat used in cooking. It keeps for a long time in the refrigerator, and you can use the fat to make a *tourin* or fry potatoes.

The great chefs of the southwest worry themselves endlessly, thinking up clever new recipes for *foie gras*. But hardly anyone else here does; they're perfectly happy to eat it on toast, or to put it in a proper *salade composée* with thin slices of *magret* (or *magret séché*) or *gesiers* (gizzards), or maybe all three, along with lettuce, oil and vinegar – and, most importantly, a sprinkling of hazelnut oil. Everybody has their own variation and their own name for this kind of salad; throw in what you like. Another simple and traditional way of doing *foie gras* is to slice it (before cooking) into thin escalopes, dust with flour and fry gently in oil. Then put aside and use the same pan to fry some sliced potatoes. If the grease from the *foie gras* isn't enough to do this, add some *graisse d'oie*. (Face it; if you mean to get serious about southwestern cooking, you're going to be keeping a jar of goose fat in the back of the refrigerator. The family will eventually get used to it.) Serve the potatoes with the *escalopes de foie gras* arranged on top. Or instead of potatoes, after the *escalopes* are cooked add some white grapes to the pan (with a little armagnac), and cook for about 5 minutes, and then serve with the *foie* – this is a favourite in the Landes.

Musée Campanaire
t 05 62 07 30 01; open mid-June–mid-Sept Wed–Mon 10–12 and 2.30–6.30; mid-Sept–mid-June until 5.30; closed hols and first half of Jan

Château de Caumont
t 05 62 07 94 20; open May, June, Sept and Oct Sat, Sun and hols 3–6; July and Aug daily 3–6

who took on the 'Jourdain' because one of their members was baptized in the Jordan, while his parents were off in the First Crusade. Cardinal Richelieu, who made the guidebook writer's job considerably easier by knocking down hundreds of castles around France (to decrease the chances of rebellion among their noble owners), got rid of L'Isle's, but one of its towers suvives as the bell tower of the brick church of **St-Martin**. The *halles* is brick too, and now houses the **Musée Campanaire**, devoted to bell-ringing. There is a handsome bridge over the Save, built just outside town in the 12th century.

Twelve kilometres southwest on the D39, the **Château de Caumont** was built in the late 16th century by a favourite of King Henri III. Outside, the château looks all business – the memory of the Wars of Religion was still warm when it went up – but inside you'll find one of the most luxurious mansions in the southwest, complete with some wonderful rooms redone in the mock-medieval style of the Victorian era.

At Caumont, you are already halfway to the next village, **Samatan**, the real *foie gras* capital of the Gers and there's a museum to it at the tourist office. Nothing much here is very old, partly because the Black Prince smashed up the place in 1355, and partly because Samatan is really only the successor to a truly old and somewhat peculiar place, **Lombez**, just 2km down the D632. Lombez was an important settlement for a very long time. Remains from the Celts and even earlier have been found here, and the town enjoyed prosperity as the Roman Lumbarium. From the Middle Ages until 1789 it was the seat of a bishopric; Petrarch stopped in to visit a cleric friend of his in the 1330s. From then, it has all been downhill. Lombez today is left with some 1,200 people, and the brick **Cathédrale Ste-Marie** topped by an attractive bell tower in the style of Toulouse's St-Sernin. Inside, copying Auch's cathedral, there is a fine set of stained-glass windows, said to have been done by followers of Arnaut de Moles, and a set of carved wooden choir stalls to match. The church *trésor* has some items that go back to the 13th century.

Cathédrale Ste-Marie
for info call Lombez tourist office, t 05 62 62 37 58

Market Days East from Auch

Both Samatan and Gimont are famous for their *marchés au gras*, which are held from mid-Oct–Mar, every Monday morning in Samatan and Nov–April Sunday morning in Gimont. Samatan's may well be the biggest *foie gras* market to be found anywhere in the world, and it can be particularly frantic, especially in December. Half the *foie gras* in France disappears in the week between Christmas and New Year's Day; Paris alone gobbles up a staggering 2,000 tons of the stuff during the festive period.

Though great fun to watch, these markets are mostly intended for the pros – including some of the great chefs of the southwest, who send somebody to get the best right at the source – but if you happen to be around, you can pick one up too.

As for the regular weekly markets:
Mauvezin: Mondays.
Cologne: Thursdays.
Gimont: Wednesdays.
L'Isle-Jourdain: Saturdays.
Samatan: Mondays.
Saramon: Saturdays.

(i) Mauvezin >>
t 05 62 06 79 47; open July and Aug Mon–Sat 9–12 and 2–6, Sun 9.30–12.30; Sept–June Mon–Sat 9–12 and 2–5.30, Sun 9.30–12.30

(i) Gimont >>
83 Rue Nationale, t 05 62 67 77 87, www.ot-gimont.com; open Tues–Fri 10–12.30 and 3–7, Sat 10–1

(i) Cologne >
t 05 62 06 99 30; open Tues–Thurs 9–12 and 2–5, Fri 10–12

(i) Samatan >
t 05 62 62 55 40; open July and Aug Mon–Sat 10–12 and 3–6, Sun 10–12; Sept–June Mon and Wed–Sat 10–12 and 3–5

Where to Stay and Eat East from Auch

Mauvezin ✉ 32120
Auberge Cheval Noir, t 05 62 06 83 94, *www.auberge-chevalnoir.com*. Typical country inn serving regional cuisine with a little twist. *Cassoulet de Cabecou* (goat's cheese). *Menus €16–24. Lunchtimes Mon–Fri only.*

Gimont ✉ 32200
★★★**Château de Larroque**, just east of the village on the N124, t 05 62 67 77 44, *www.chateau-larroque.com* (€€€€–€€). The château is a stately country house of a century ago, set in an enormous park. A Relais du Silence member, it offers plenty of peace and quiet, a pool and tennis, and an excellent restaurant (but it's one of the most expensive places in the Gers). The kitchen is fittingly distinguished. In the capital of *foie gras*, you can be sure of getting the best, and the restaurant here does quite a lot of it, in salads, or in unusual combinations with *cèpes* or even oysters. There's also a memorable *daube* with scallops and crayfish. The cellars are more than well stocked. *Menus €24–55. Oct–April closed Mon and Tues eve.*

ⓘ L'Isle-Jourdain ›
t 05 62 07 25 57,
www.mairie-
islejourdain.fr; open
mid-June–mid-Sept
Mon–Sat 9.30–12.30
and 1.30–6.30;
mid-Sept–mid-June
Mon–Sat 9.30–12.30
and 1.30–5.30

L'Isle-Jourdain ✉ 32600

*Hôtel du Centre, t 05 62 07 00 23 (€).
A venerable choice. *Closed Oct.*

Puits Saint-Jacques, Pujaudran, 7km
along the N124, **t** 05 62 07 41 11,
http://lepuitsstjacques.fr. Set in a
restored medieval stable with a
pleasant terrace, this restaurant is
very good for fish (*les tronçons de thon*
roulé aux herbes* and roast lobster).
There's also plenty of meat and *foie
gras*. *Menus €22–75. Closed Sun eve
and Mon and Tues.*

Hostellerie du Lac, near to the lake,
t 05 62 07 03 91 (€). Pretty bedrooms,
a swimming pool, and a restaurant
with a huge shady terrace. *Menus
€12–36. Closed Sun eve Sept–June.*

South of Auch: the Astarac

In this homespun *pays*, the landscapes are a continuation of the
jumbly valleys just to the south. A row of eight rivers, each about
5km from the next where they enter the *département*, flow in from
the mountains, spreading out like a fan across the Astarac; the
roads from east to west go up and down like rollercoasters.

Mirande, the little capital of the Astarac, is a rarity in the Gers: a
bright little metropolis of 4,000 souls with an evident civic pride –
a place that, though not in any hurry, seems to be going somewhere. In 1994 the women's basketball team were French
champions. The town is now becoming famous for its country
music festival. Yet another typical *bastide*, with its straight streets
and arcaded square, Mirande is a lovely place to stroll. The main
street is closed to traffic; here you will see the town's most notable
embellishment, the spire of the Eglise Ste-Marie, supported by a
flying buttress and arch that crosses over the street. Inside, there
are some good stained-glass windows from the early 16th century.
Just around the corner, Mirande has proudly opened a tiny **Musée
des Beaux-Arts**, with a collection of paintings and ceramics.

**Musée des
Beaux-Arts**
13 Rue de l'Evéché,
t 05 62 66 68 10;
open Mon–Fri 9–12 and
2–6, Sat 10–12 and 3–6;
closed hols; adm

If you like Mirande you may be inspired to press further into this
region of narrow, exasperating roads, minuscule villages and
forests; there are some modest but beautiful surprises, such as
Montclar-sur-Losse, on the D159 just west of Mirande, just a
château and church lost in the trees, but a corner of France that
sticks in the memory. Everything further west is described above
(*see* pp.144–6); if you're going east, get out the magnifying glass
and look on the map for **Belloc St-Clamens**, where there is a rare
early Romanesque church, substantially unchanged in 900 years.
Seissan, another *foie gras* village, is south of Auch along the River
Gers; the two windows in the old church are attributed by the
locals to Arnaut de Moles, but we have our doubts. There are better
ones from the same period at **Simorre**, where the very interesting
church of the early 1300s was once part of a Benedictine abbey.
Viollet-le-Duc, the famous restorer of Paris's Notre-Dame and
Carcassonne, fixed up Simorre too, and it is to him we owe the
leering gargoyles and much of the other sculptural detail.

Market Days South of Auch

Mirande: Mondays.
Seissan: Fridays (also a big *marché au gras* from October to April).

Where to Stay and Eat South of Auch

Mirande ✉ 32300
**Hotel du Prince, 15 Ave d'Etigny,
t 05 42 54 10 34,
www.hotelduprince.com (€€). Well-equipped rooms in an attractive house with garden, pool and terrace.
Brasserie des Arts, **t** 05 62 66 50 27, *www.brasseriedesarts.fr* (€). There are 4 colourful rooms available at this restored 19th-century brewery in the centre of the village. There's a patio and bar. Meals available (€15). The brasserie also organizes art exhibitions and concerts.

Europ-hôtel Maupas, at the northern edge of town, **t** 05 62 66 51 42 (€). There are nice rooms and a more than ample €18 menu, which may include duck or possibly grilled salmon. *Open daily all year.*

Camping de l'Isle du Pont, just outside town on the N21, **t** 05 62 66 64 11, *www.camping-gers.com*. *Gîtes* and chalets plus a number of activities. Canoes, pool, tennis and kids' club. Tent and caravan park. *Open mid-May–mid-Sept; chalets and park open all year.*

Pizzeria La Squadra, 7 Pl Astarac. Decent and inexpensive pizza and pasta dishes.

ⓘ **Simorre**
Rue de la Mairie,
t 05 62 65 36 34

ⓘ **Mirande** ›
13 Rue de l'Evêché,
t 05 62 66 68 10,
www.ot-mirande.com;
open July and Aug
Mon–Fri 9–12 and 2–6,
Sat 10–12 and 3–6, Sun
10–12; Sept–June
Mon–Fri 9–12 and 2–6,
Sat 10–12 and 3–6

The Pays Basque

Of all the départements of France, number 64 is the one with the most remarkable split personality. Béarn, occupying the eastern half of the département, is a resolutely Gascon province redolent of garlic and castles and good Jurançon wine; it has personality enough of its own. But cross the Gave d'Oloron, a national boundary that does not appear on any map, and you enter an entirely different world: specifically, the land of the Basques, Euzkadi, the oldest nation of Europe.

SPAIN

09

Don't miss

⭐ **A delicious medieval town**
Bayonne **p.176**

⭐ *Belle époque* **and beaches**
Biarritz **p.183**

⭐ **Sun, sand and seafood**
St-Jean-de-Luz **p.192**

⭐ **The high mountain gateway to Spain**
St-Jean-Pied-de-Port **p.204**

⭐ **Isolation and tradition**
Ste-Engrâce **p.208**

See map overleaf

The Pays Basque

p.233

LANDES

Pouillon

St-Martin-de-Hinx

Peyrehorade

Hastingues

Sorde-l'Abbaye

Bellocq

Orthez

Abbaye d'Arthous

Château de Gramont

Bidache

Salies-de-Béarn

Maslacq

117

Athos

Sauveterre-de-Béarn

Laàs

Mour

Labastide-Clairence

Hasparren

BIARRITZ

BAYONNE

A64

E80

117

Côte Basque

Bidart

Guéthary

St-Jean-de-Luz

Corniche Basque

Arcangues

Ciboure

Urrugne

Hendaye

Ascain

Ustaritz

Larressore

St-Pée-sur-Nivelle

Espelette

Cambo-les-Bains

Grottes d'Istaritz et d'Oxocelhaya

P A Y S

St-Esteben

PYRÉNÉES

St-Palais

Navarrenx

Sare

Ainhoa

B A S Q U E

ATLANTIQUES

Gurs

Grottes de Sare

Artxamendi

Bidarray

Ossès

Larceveau

Mauléon

L'Hôpital-Saint-Blais

St-Etienne-de-Baïgorry

St-Jean-Pied-de-Port

St-Jean-de-Vieux

Ordiarp

Aussurucq

Tardets

Aramits

Arette

Forêt des Arbailles

Ahusquy

Alçay

Etchebar

Larrau

Ste-Engrâce

Pic d'Anie

Lescun

Forêt d'Iraty

Gorges de Holçarté

Gorges de Kakouetta

113

918

9

SPAIN

SPAIN

Don't miss

 Bayonne p.176

 Biarritz p.183

 St-Jean-de-Luz p.192

 St-Jean-Pied-de-Port p.204

 Ste-Engrâce p.208

10 km

5 miles

N

You'll know you're in the Pays Basque when you find a village with a *fronton* (*pelote* court) in the middle, one where the shop signs are packed full of 'z's and 'x's, and where everything except the dogs and cats is painted red, white and green. Those are the eternal colours of the Basque flag, which waves proudly over the autonomous Basque provinces across the border in Spain, but is discouraged by the authorities over here. Three of the seven traditional provinces of Euzkadi are in France, laid out in vertical stripes across the western half of the Pyrénées-Atlantiques *département*: first, the coastal Labourd (from Lapurdum, the Roman name of Bayonne), a delightful land full of beautiful villages, which also includes Bayonne and Biarritz where Basques have long been a minority; next, inland, the Basse-Navarre, with Pyrenean valleys in the south and hardworking farmers in the humble lowlands; and finally the even humbler Soule, around Mauléon.

One doesn't visit the Basque country to see the sights, which are few and far between. The real attraction is the Basques themselves, a taciturn though likable lot, and their distinctive culture and way of life. The setting also helps to make the trip worthwhile, emerald landscapes that have been well tended by the same people for millennia (and well they should be emerald; the Basque country gets as much rain as the west of Ireland). The Basques' tremendously long but thoroughly uneventful history is covered in **History**, pp.19–30, but to really appreciate this world-in-itself, here is a brief primer in things dear to Basque hearts, from *ttoro* to tombstones.

The Basques

Language

Want to impress your hosts with a few words of Basque? Just try it! The Basques point out with great pride that their language is not only Europe's oldest, but by far the most difficult. There are four distinct dialects, and in each the grammar is Kafkaesque, to put it mildly. Verbs, for example, can vary according to the gender of the person you are addressing. The vast number of grammatical tenses includes not only a subjunctive, but two different potentials, an eventual and a hypothetical. But grammatical complexity permits beauty and economy; you can express anything in Basque in far fewer words than in most other languages.

Basque is maddeningly, spectacularly indirect. For example, to say 'I am spinning', comes out *Iruten ari nuzu*, or literally, 'In the act of spinning doing you have me!' Or try out this proverb: *Izan gabe eman dezakegun gauza bakarra da zoriona*. 'Having without, give (*Izan gabe eman*), we can (*dezakegun*), one thing only is (*gauza bakarra da*), happiness (*zoriona*)' – 'happiness is the only thing we can give without having'. Pronunciation, thank God, is not such a problem; it's phonetic, and there are only a few letters you need to know: **e**, as long 'a'; **u**, as 'oo'; **j**, as 'ee'; **s**, as something halfway between 's' and 'sh'; **tz** or **z**, as 's'; and **x**, as 'sh'. Pronounce all the vowels, and don't make any soft consonant sounds; practise on the village of Azcoitia (ahsko-IT-ee-ah). One of the peculiarities of the language is its habit of doubling words for effect, unknown to any European tongue but common among the Polynesians. In Basque, something very hot is *bero-bero*; a glutton makes *mauka-mauka*, and when a Basque walks on all fours this is called *hitipiti-hatapata*. Like eskimos, who know no generic word for 'ice', the Basques have no word for 'tree' or 'animal'. And being the democratic folk they are, there is no word for 'king' either – they had to borrow one from the French and Spanish potentates to whom they were forced to pay taxes.

In all the Basque lands, on average only a third of the inhabitants still speak their language. Owing to the severe cultural oppression in Spain under Franco, the percentages are much higher on the French side: 72 per cent in Basse-Navarre and 60 per cent in the Soule. But following the example of the Catalans in Spain, Basques on both sides of the border are actively promoting their own language in the schools, with some success. It's important to remember that Basque is a living literary language, the centrepiece of a living culture. The plays known as *pastorales*, possibly descended from medieval mystery plays, are still written and produced at festival times, and Basques pay great reverence to the *bertsulari*, poets who have memorized a vast repertoire of traditional pieces and who are also skilled at improvisation.

Basque Cuisine

Basques know how to eat. Go into a village restaurant at nine in the morning on a market day, and watch the boys tuck into their three-course breakfasts – soup, tons of meat, fish and potatoes, with a gallon or so of wine for each. Fortunately for them, the Basques also know how to cook. Their distinctive cuisine will be one of the delights of your visit to the Basque country, and your one chance for something piquant in France, a nation pathologically disdainful of anything too spicy. Like the Greeks, the well-travelled Basques took their culinary skill with them everywhere. Basque restaurants turn up in unlikely places all over France, and it isn't unusual to drive through a dusty, one-horse town out in the American west where the only restaurant serves up good Basque home cooking.

Not surprisingly, Basque cooks exert most of their talents on seafood. Marseille has its *bouillabaisse*, among a score of other exotic and treasured fish stews of southern Europe, but the Basques stoutly maintain that their version, called *ttoro* (pronounced 'tioro'), is the king of them all; naturally there is a solemn *confrérie* of the finest *ttoro* chefs. A proper one requires a pound of mussels and a mess of crayfish and congers, as well as the head of a codfish and three different kinds of other fish. They say the cooks of St-Jean-de-Luz and Hendaye make the best ones; St-Jean holds an annual *ttoro* festival with a competition and *dégustation* in early September. Currently, a very popular dish is *piquillos à la morue*: skinned red peppers stuffed with a purée of cod, potatoes, butter, parsley and a little garlic. Other seafood delights include *thon basquaise*, fresh tuna cooked with tomatoes, garlic, aubergine and spices.

Another icon of the kitchen is the red pepper, the *piment d'Espelette*; Basque housewives still hang strings of them on the walls of their houses for drying (and for decoration). Some of these go into *piperade*, the relish of pepper, tomato, egg, ham and garlic that can accompany almost any Basque dish. Milder peppers turn up everywhere: in omelettes, or in the common stewed chicken, *poulet basquaise*. Other treats, made the old-fashioned way, include the *pur brebis* sheep's milk cheese from the Pyrenees, the best in France, and the famous Bayonne ham, which is hung for over a year; it has a strict set of rules and an *appellation contrôlée* status like fine wines. You can find out how it's done at Jambon Pierre Ibaialde in Bayonne.

Jambon Pierre Ibaialde
41 Rue des Cordeliers,
t 05 59 25 65 30

As for drinks, there is AOC Irouléguy wine from the Pyrenean foothills, and plenty of special herb liqueurs, from home-made specialities you'll find in restaurants to Bayonne's famous green Izarra. The Basques are also fond of good hard cider. They claim to have taught the more famous cider-makers of Normandy and Asturias their secrets long ago, and back in the 1500s Basque fishermen used to trade the stuff to the American Indians for furs.

Folklore

The Basques are not alone. In fact, their long intimacy with their land has forced them to share it with an unreasonably large number of gods, demons, spirits and fairies, creatures of one of the richest mythologies of Europe. Many tales are connected to the dolmens and other Neolithic monuments that grow so thickly on the mountains here; often their names connect them to Mari, the ancient Basque great goddess. The dolmens were built by the *jentillak*, the race of giants that once lived side by side with the Basques. The *jentillak*, often a great help to their neighbours, invented metallurgy and the saw, and introduced the growing of wheat. One day a strange storm cloud appeared from the east, and the wisest of the *jentillak* recognized it as an omen and interpreted it as the end of their age. The giants marched off into the earth, under a dolmen (still visible in the Arratzaran valley in Spanish Navarre). One was left behind, named Olentzero, and he explained to the Basques: 'Kixmi [Jesus] is born and this means the end of our race.' Olentzero lives on today, as the jolly fat doll or straw figure prominent in the Basques' celebrations of Christmas and New Year's Day.

Other familiar creatures include the *laminak*, originally small female fairies with a capacity to help or harm, now a sort of leprechaun that gets blamed for everything that goes wrong. And where mythology fades off into nursery-lore we have the 'man with the sack' who comes to carry off naughty children, and a large bestiary with jokes like the elusive *dahu*, a kind of lizard with legs shorter on one side – the better to walk the Pyrenean slopes. Along with the myths goes a remarkable body of pre-Christian religious survivals, including rituals that lasted well into the 20th century; many old Basques in isolated villages can remember festivals with Midsummer bonfires in their childhood. If you'd like to learn more about this bottomless subject, an excellent introduction is the *Petit Dictionnaire des Mythologies Basque et Pyrénéenne* by Olivier de Marliave (Editions Entente).

Basques are passionately fond of music, whether it's choral music at Mass (which they do extremely well), Basque rock (rare, perhaps fortunately), or traditional tunes played on the *dultzaina*, a primitive bagpipe, and a flute called the *txistu*. Dozens of traditional dances are still current, and small groups in many villages keep them up; you'll have a chance to see them at any village fête.

Basque Accessories

No old Basque gentleman would be complete without a beret (most of which are made in Béarn), and a walking stick, or *makila*. These are taken very seriously. Made out of seasoned and dried medlar wood, they are exquisitely carved and decorated with silver trim. By tradition, there is always a coin built into the *makila*, and each one will usually carry an inscribed motto, such as *hitza hitz* – 'one's word is one's word'. If you want one to take home, the best place is the 200-year-old family firm of **Ainciart-Bergara**, in the village of Larressore, or else the **Fabrique de Makilas** on Rue de la Vieille Boucherie in old Bayonne – but they don't come cheap. With a striking, healthy inclination for combining beauty and utility, Basque artisans excel at the simple things of everyday life: furniture and woodcarving, and especially embroidered linens. *Linge basque*, whether factory-made or woven on an old wooden loom, may be your best bet for a beautiful and practical souvenir.

Basques have their own distinctive style of 'discoidal' or round-headed tombstone. Archaeologists have dug up some models

Ainciart-Bergara
www.makhila.com

4,500 years old, and they've been using them ever since. The earliest ones often had human figures, sun symbols or other symbols carved on them; since the coming of Christianity the stones usually show crosses. You will see them in any churchyard, usually turned south so that the sun shines on the carved face all day.

One thing the Basques are very good at is houses. There's nothing in the southwest as pretty, simple and functional as a traditional Basque *etche*, or cottage, with its distinctive long, low gable along the façade, and half-timbering and shutters – inevitably painted deep red or green, of course (really more maroon than red, a colour called 'bull's blood'). Originally this was a simple farmhouse, where the lower storey was a wine cellar or given to other farm business; examples of these, some 300 or 400 years old, can still be seen in many villages. One particularity of the older houses, here and in neighbouring Béarn, is the carved lintels over the main door, with the year and name of the builder, accompanied by odd symbols or a sententious inscription. In the 19th century these houses evolved into the modern Basque villa. The style became extremely popular throughout France in the 1920s and '30s, and you'll see versions of it with a bit of Art Deco trim in suburbs everywhere. To learn about houses in Bayonne visit the **Boutique du Patrimoine et l'Habitat**.

Boutique du Patrimoine et l'Habitat
42 Rue Poissonnerie, t 05 59 25 60 83; open Mon–Fri 2–5

Sporting Life

The real national sport, of course, is smuggling. But the Basques love to play, and over the millennia they have evolved a number of unique outlandish games. Many of these are based on pure brute strength, the celebrated *force basque* that provides a major element of the national mystique. One can imagine them, back in the mists of time, impressing each other by carrying around boulders – because that's what they do today, in a number of events generally called the *harri altxatzea*, literally stone-lifting. In one, contestants see how many times they can lift a 500lb (225kg) stone in five minutes; in others, they roll round boulders around their shoulders. Related to this is the *untziketariak*, in which we see how fast a Basque can run with 100lb (45kg) weights in each hand. They're fond of the tug-of-war too; they probably invented it. Besides these you will see them at village festivals pulling loaded wagons, racing with 200lb (90kg) sacks on their shoulders, or chopping huge tree trunks against the clock. Don't fool with these people.

The miracle is that at the same time they could develop a sport like *pelote*, the fastest ball game in the world. Few sports in the world can offer an image as beautiful and memorable as the *pelotari* in his traditional loose, pure white costume, chasing down the ball with a long, curving *chistera*. Pelote takes a wide variety of forms, but the basic element is always the ball: a hard core, wrapped tightly with string and covered with hide – like a baseball, only smaller and with more bounce; in a serious match this ball can reach speeds of 150mph. The oldest form of the game is *rebot*, played without a wall. This is done bare-handed; other versions, played in an outdoor *fronton* (court), may be bare-handed, with a leather glove (*pasaka* or *joko garbi*), or with the *chistera*, made of leather and osier, which enables a player to scoop up the ball and fling it back in the same motion. Whatever the game, it usually requires teams of two players each. The ground in front of the wall is marked off in *cuadros* every 4m (13ft) from it; to be in, a ball bounced off the wall must usually hit between the 4th and 7th *cuadros* if it is not returned on the fly

Every Basque village has a *fronton* as its principal monument, usually right in the centre. On some village churches from as far back as the 1600s you can see how the architects left one smooth blank wall to accommodate the game. Besides the *fronton*, the game may be played in a covered court (*trinquet*), or one with another wall on the left side, a *jaï-alaï*, in which case the game is called *cesta punta*, the fastest and most furious form of *pelote* (thanks to Basque emigrants this has become a popular sport around the Caribbean).

If you want to get in a little action yourself, you might try to talk your way into it at any village *fronton* when they're practising (they'd be charmed), or else contact the **Fédération de Pelote Basque** in Bayonne; they set up training courses in summer for beginners. As for getting in on the gambling aspect of *pelote* – go ahead and throw your money away if you want to. A list follows of towns where you're likely to see a match in summer; matches take place at least once a week, but times and days change, so ring the local tourist office to ask for the most up-to-date schedule. Towns include: Anglet, Ascain, Biarritz, Bidart, Cambo-les-Bains, Guéthary, Hasparren, Mauléon, St-Etienne-de-Baïgorry, St-Jean-de-Luz, St-Jean-Pied-de-Port, St-Palais, St-Pée-sur-Nivelle and Sare. In addition, there are games indoors year-round in the *trinquets*: at Bayonne, in the Trinquet St-André; at St-Jean-Pied-de-Port, in the Trinquet Garat; and usually at weekends in St-Jean-de-Luz.

Fédération de Pelote Basque
Trinquet Moderne, Bayonne, 60 Av Dubrocq, t 05 59 59 22 34, www.ffpb.net

Most of the big championships are held in July and August, often in Biarritz or St-Jean-de-Luz. *Force basque* competitions are usually held in July and August; many villages put something on for Basque Sports Week, the second week in August; the big festivals are at St-Palais (late August) and St-Etienne-de-Baïgorry (mid-July and early August). Bayonne has a bullfight season in August and September.

Nationalism

Basque nationalism is hardly a recent phenomenon. In its modern version, it started in the 18th century, with a community of liberal bourgeois in Bilbao and the other outward-looking port cities of Basque Spain; these supported Enlightenment thinkers such as Manuel de Larramendi, who developed a concept of Basque nationhood based on language and tradition. Throughout the 19th century, nationalist thought and the development of Basque culture proceeded apace in Spain, while at least on the political side it ran into a stone wall in the much more repressive climate of France. French Euzkadi thus became a sideshow to main events, while in Spain, the PNV, the first Basque nationalist party, controlled a majority of the region's parliamentary seats from 1917 on. Franco's rule was a catastrophe for the Basques: over 100,000 prisoners and 200,000 exiles after the Civil War, including the entire intelligentsia and political leadership. Resistance groups did not start forming until 1952. ETA (Euzkadi ta Askatasuna, or Basque Homeland and Liberty) was founded in 1959. Its bombing campaign near the end of Franco's reign was singularly effective – notably when they blew the car carrying Franco's successor, Carrero Blanco, over the roof of a Madrid church. In the new Spain the Basques got all they wanted: full autonomy and the right to their language and culture; this left ETA out in the cold as a band of die-hards demanding total independence. That did not keep them from continuing their terror tactics up until the present day, with help of and safe havens among the Basques over the border in France.

A few years ago, when the French government started cracking down on ETA operatives and sympathizers, the organization responded by bombing Renault dealerships around Spain. They've stopped that, which suggests somewhere a deal has been cut. France may be a democratic country, but in affairs like this we know as little of what goes on as we do about political factions in China. ETA does seem to be on its last legs – widespread disgust among Spanish Basques at terrorist tactics have made them pariahs in many circles, and the organization was conspicuously silent in Spain's magic year of 1992.

Though most French Basques decided long ago that being French wasn't so bad after all, there are in fact plenty of nationalists; hang around for a while and you'll meet them. The police watch over them and manipulate them silently and skilfully. This is something at which the French have had centuries of practice – all over the Midi, as well as in Brittany, Corsica and the colonies – and they're extremely good at it, probably the best in the world. Basque nationalism within France, such as it is, is also not an issue that the media are often permitted to emphasize. We met one nationalist supporter, a young mechanic on his way to a ping-pong tournament. With an earnest look in his eyes, he told us: 'They'll never let the Basque lands unite, because together we would be stronger than either France or Spain.' A marvellous people, bless them.

Bayonne

⭐ **Bayonne**

Arthur Young, the famous English traveller of the 1780s, called it the prettiest town he'd seen in France. Young had a good eye; even today, Bayonne is as attractive and lively an urban setting as you'll find in the southwest. Despite a remarkable history, a majestic cathedral and a delicious medieval centre full of brightly painted old half-timber buildings, Bayonne doesn't attract much attention

Bayonne

Getting to and around Bayonne

Bayonne is a stop along the main **rail** line from Paris through Bordeaux and down to the Spanish border. There are plenty of trains along this run; most of them also stop at Biarritz. There will be a few TGVs each day; and these also stop in Biarritz (contact SNCF information on t 36 35 and *www.voyages-sncf.com*). Other lines from Bayonne go up the Gaves to Orthez and Pau in Béarn, and down the valley of the Nive to St-Jean-Pied-de-Port.

There is a parallel and equally convenient **bus** service down the coast run by the ATCRB line, t 05 59 08 00 33, *www.autocars-atcrb.com* – about a dozen a day from Bayonne and Biarritz to St-Jean-de-Luz and Hendaye, and several buses for San Sebastian, Spain, a week.

Public transportation in the Bayonne-Biarritz area is run by an aggressive-sounding line called STAB (info and tickets: Bayonne, Pl du Général de Gaulle, t 05 59 59 04 61; Biarritz, Av Louis Barthou, t 05 59 24 26 53. The very useful website *www.bus-stab.com* has information and plans of all routes. Regular STAB buses connect the two cities, from the Hôtel de Ville in Bayonne to the Hôtel de Ville in Biarritz – line 1. Biarritz's SNCF station is far from the city centre; the no.2 bus terminates here and links with the station at Bayonne. There is a free bus that goes around the town Mon–Sat 7.30am–7.30pm; ask at the tourist office.

The no.6 bus from Biarritz goes to the city **airport**, the Aérogare de Parme, t 05 59 43 83 83, *www.biarritz.aeroport.fr*, with four or five flights a day from Paris Orly with Air France, t 08 20 82 08 20, and three a day from Charles de Gaulle. Ryanair, t 05 59 43 83 93, flies daily from London Stansted, and there are regular flights to Dublin and Shannon, *www.ryanair.com*. If you want to discover the Adour there's a 2-hour or all-day **boat** trip with the Bateau Le Bayonne, leaving from the *quai* near Allées Boufflers, t 06 80 74 21 51.

---

these days, lost as it is in the sprawling conurbation that includes Biarritz, the ports and industry of Boucau and the bedroom community of Anglet. Nevertheless, if you enjoy good cities or if you need a break from the beaches, spend a day in Bayonne.

History

Bayonne began in the 3rd century AD as a Roman *castrum* called Lapurdum, home to the cohort that guarded Novempopulania. Nothing, however, is heard from it until the booming 12th century, when it adopted its present name and grew into an important port town. From the beginning, Bayonne was not Basque but in fact a predominantly Gascon town; the two peoples have been getting on well enough ever since. From 1151 until 1452, the English ruled Bayonne. As in Bordeaux, it was an arrangement enjoyable to both sides; Bayonne gave the Plantagenets a strong base at the southern end of their continental empire, and the town enjoyed considerable privileges and freedom, not to mention a busy trade with Britain. At the same time, the intrepid Basques began sailing around the Atlantic in (as any reader of *Moby Dick* knows) the world's first whale fishery. They taught whaling to the Dutch, who taught the English, who, in turn, taught the Massachusettsans.

All that ended when King Charles VII marched in at the end of the Hundred Years War. Not long after, an even bigger disaster hit – the River Adour suddenly picked itself up and moved to a new bed, leaving the port high and dry. But Bayonne, close to the border with Spain, was important to the French; in 1578 they sent down engineers to dig a canal and redirect the Adour, and the port was back in business. A century later, Louis XIV dispatched his famous military engineer, Vauban, to make Bayonne an impregnable stronghold; the sprawling, state-of-the-art fortifications he designed, along with the Citadelle, are a striking feature of the cityscape even today.

Bayonne's military vocation flourished during the 18th century. An armaments industry grew up and gave the world the word 'bayonet', while Basque and Gascon corsairs, with letters of marque from the king, sallied out to snatch what they could from the Spanish, the English and North Africans. Besides weapons, the city's other passion was sweets. Jewish refugees from Spain introduced chocolate to Bayonne in the 1600s, and Louis XIV and his courtiers spread it across France when the king passed through on his way to marry the Spanish infanta in 1659. Bayonne's *chocolatiers* gradually built up a reputation as the best in France – there are still quite a few in the old town who keep up the tradition. Two of the best are Daranatz and Cazenave, both in Rue Port Neuf. (Back in the 17th century, incidentally, chocolate was thought of only as a drink, and a century later a Basque pirate captain named Sopite thoughtfully provided something to sprinkle on top – bringing the first cinnamon to France from Sumatra in a daring trip ordered by royal command in the middle of a war; his ship, *La Basquaise*, met five English vessels on the way home and beat them all.)

Bayonne lost its status as a free port, and most of its trade, with the Revolution, and there were more troubles to come. Vauban's walls proved their worth in the Napoleonic Wars. Coming up from Spain, Wellington's army twice besieged the city, in 1813 and 1814; they took it on the second try, by stringing a bridge of ships across the Adour and dragging artillery across it to bombard the city from both sides. Recovery came only with the arrival of the railway from Paris in 1854. Industrialization proceeded apace after that, and now Bayonne's little jewel of a historic centre is wrapped in the 'BAB' (Bayonne, Anglet, Biarritz), a metropolitan area of over 100,000 people, counting Biarritz and smaller towns.

Grand Bayonne and the Cathedral

Bayonne's main street is a river, the little Nive, and it is one of the most delightful centerpieces a city could ask for, lined on both sides with busy quays and old tall houses with trim painted in bright colours (mostly red and green, but no prizes for guessing that). The Nive also marks the division between the two old quarters of the walled town, Grand Bayonne and Petit Bayonne. The former is the business and retail end, jammed with animated, pedestrian-filled shopping streets. Right in the heart of Grand

Choco-Musée
Puyodebat
*t 05 59 59 48 42;
open Tues–Fri 3–6,
call first*

Cathédrale
Ste-Marie
*t 05 59 59 17 82; open
Mon–Sat 10–11.45 and
3–5.45, Sun and hols
3.30–6; no visits
during services*

Bayonne, on Rue des Gouverneurs, you can learn more about chocolate at the Choco-Musée Puyodebat.

Cathédrale Ste-Marie

One of these, narrow Rue Argenterie, will take you from the quays to Bayonne's landmark and symbol, the **Cathédrale Ste-Marie**. It is also a symbol of the coming of French control – one of the few examples of the northerners' Gothic style in the southwest, and certainly one of the best. Begun in the 12th century, most of the work was done in the 13th. Some was still going on in the 1500s, when the south tower went up, and the arms of the King of France were added to the sculptural decoration of the portal in honour of Bayonne's new rulers. Throughout, the building was largely financed by Bayonne's whalers. The bishops exacted a tenth of the profits from them, also claiming 'by divine right' the most prized parts of each whale for themselves – the tongue and the fat; nobody really knows what they did with them. Despite all the city's loot from cetaceans, piracy and chocolates, however, the cathedral still wasn't finished until the 1800s, when followers of Viollet-le-Duc oversaw a thorough restoration and added the matching north tower.

So far from the Ile-de-France, and so long in building, it isn't surprising that there are no unusual stylistic departures here. What is surprising is how well it all fits together. Best of all, it still enjoys the sort of setting a Gothic cathedral should have – among narrow streets and tightly packed tall buildings, where its presence and verticality make exactly the impression its designers intended.

Individual details worth calling attention to are few; this cathedral was thoroughly trashed in the Revolution. Inside, there's no need for detail; the rise of the slender pilasters that carry the rib-vaulted nave permit a lofty interior that no church in the southwest save the Jacobins in Toulouse can match. There is some good Renaissance stained glass in the nave windows, heavily restored a century ago. Note the scene of Adam and Eve, where the serpent (with a female head) wears the bonnet of a medieval doctor of philosophy – just to show what a subtle argument she was capable of. In the left aisle, the **Chapel of St Jerome** has one of the best windows (1531), a scene of the Canaanite woman (from Matthew, 15:22), crowned by a salamander, the symbol of King François I. The **sacristy** shelters the only original 13th-century sculptures that survived the Revolution: one tympanum of the *Last Judgement*, with the Devil boiling a king and a bishop in his cauldron, and another of the *Virgin Mary*, surrounded by angel musicians. This leads to a lovely cloister, also much damaged in the Revolution.

Château-Vieux

Just behind the cathedral, on Rue des Gouverneurs, the **Château-Vieux** was the city's stronghold and the seat of its governors: first the English (parts of what you see are from the 12th century; one of the governors was the Black Prince), and then the French (the outworks were added in the time of Louis XIV to guard against revolts by the Bayonnais).

Though usually closed to visitors, some of the tours organized by the Syndicat d'Initiative will take you through here, and through the amazing expanses of underground chambers that underlie much of the city, some of them as properly vaulted as the cathedral's aisles. In medieval times they were used for storing wine.

Petit Bayonne

The smaller but livelier side of Bayonne, this is a *rive gauche* on the right bank of the Nive. The narrow back streets of Petit Bayonne are crowded with popular neighbourhood bars and restaurants – you won't see the likes of an old, unspoiled city neighbourhood like this in many places in southwest France. Right in the middle, on the Quai des Corsaires, is the **Musée Basque**. This 16th-century building facing the Nive started out as a convent, and later did long service as a customs house. In 1922 the city of Bayonne took it over as a museum that gradually turned into the largest collection of objects on Basque culture and folk life anywhere. Recently modernized and reopened after a long absence, the collection includes over 100,000 items covering every aspect of Basque life with interactive displays, from agriculture to seafaring, with special sections on the old Basque talent for wood and stone carving, religious and folklore traditions, and modern Basque art.

Musée Basque
t 05 59 46 61 90, www.musee-basque.com; open May–Oct Tues–Sun 10–6.30; Nov–April Tues–Sun 10–12.30 and 2–6; daily in July and Aug; closed hols

Musée Bonnat

Bayonne's own Léon Bonnat was one of the best-known salon painters of late 19th-century France, the sort of happy Philistine who got rich painting celebrity portraits, collected prizes and sneered at the Impressionists when he served as a judge in the Salon competitions. When he died, in 1922, Bonnat left his own considerable collection of art to Bayonne, and it has become the nucleus of one of the finest museums in the southwest.

Some of Bonnat's work takes pride of place in the museum's main hall: portraits of shiny bankers and blooming society ladies in corsets – another world. There's a portrait of Puvis de Chavannes, by Bonnat, and one of Bonnat himself – done by Degas, of all people. If you want to do the museum chronologically, however, start upstairs, with the late medieval and early Renaissance works the French, ignorantly and infuriatingly, still call 'primitives'. Besides works of *quattrocento* masters Domenico Veneziano and Maso di

Musée Bonnat
5 Rue Jacques Laffitte, t 05 59 59 08 52; www.musee-bonnat.com; open July and Aug daily 10–6.30; May, June, Sept and Oct Wed–Mon 10–6.30; adm

Banco, there are some obscure delights: a Christ and Virgin of the Toulouse school, better than most of their work you'll see in any churches, and a number of Catalan-Aragonese paintings from the same age, with the Catalan love of extreme stylization and rich gold backgrounds. As always with this art, the works range from the really excellent, such as the *St Martin* of the unknown 'master of the Musée Bonnat', to some that are almost naïve – a bit of precocious Diego Rivera with halos and gold leaf.

There is a fine Madonna by Botticelli, from the late period when the artist renounced his magical mythological works and lapsed into extreme piety. It didn't always work; this one, despite the Christian trappings, is still plainly Botticelli's *Venus*. From the late Renaissance and Baroque there are some good Flemish tapestries, two El Greco portraits, and an entire room devoted to Rubens.

Almost all the great schools of 17th- and 18th-century painting are represented here. Standouts include a bit of chilly militarism from the time of the Thirty Years War in Jan Bronkhorst's portrait of *General Octavio Piccolomini*; a Murillo, *Daniel in the Lions' Den*, and an equally disturbing, untitled painting by Ribera of a distraught girl combing her hair. This work, in its weird intensity, seems to prefigure Goya, and there are some Goyas here in the museum to compare it with, including a fascinating self-portrait.

There's no telling whose face is going to turn up on the walls of this museum. Among the English paintings you will see Lawrence's portraits of the composer *Karl Maria von Weber* and *Johann Heinrich Füssli* – better known as Henry Fuseli, crazy painter and friend of William Blake. Ingres, one of the spiritual fathers of salon painting, was understandably a favourite of Bonnat's; among ten of his works here is an unspeakable portrait of the unspeakable last Bourbon, *King Charles X*.

An important part of Bonnat's collection were the 36 works by his friend Antoine Barye, the most popular sculptor of his day. Nearby, not always open, is the *cabinet des dessins*, a collection of almost 2,000 drawings and prints from the Renaissance up to the 20th century. Down in the basement is the museum's archaeological collection. Many of these works were Bonnat's: Greek pots and Roman glass, votive reliefs, and lovely statuettes of various goddesses that caught the painter's fancy.

Château-Neuf

Château-Neuf
ramparts open access

On the eastern edge of the walls, the Château-Neuf looms over the town, a stronghold begun in 1460 by the French to consolidate their control over the city. The adjacent parts of Vauban's walls, however, were tidied up by the city and opened to the public a decade ago. On these **Remparts de Mousserolles** you can see what was going through Vauban's mind, and what war was like in the late 17th and 18th centuries. To defend a city properly, it was usually necessary to destroy at least half of it for the fortifications. Baroque fortifications are notable for the space they take up: one or two rings of low-slung, zig-zagging ramparts, with a complex of earthen salients and trenches beyond them, all designed to counter artillery rather than repulse a direct attack, which with the improved firearms of the age would have been suicidal.

Today the Mousserolles ramparts are an attractive city park, with a lagoon and open-air theatre.

Quartier St-Esprit

The third district of Bayonne, cowering under Vauban's haughty Citadelle and half-demolished 150 years ago for the railway station, is the Quartier St-Esprit, reached by the long bridge across the Adour. At the end of the bridge, the **St-Esprit** church was a gift of Louis XI, that most excellent monarch who wore old clothes and kept a troupe of dancing pigs to entertain him. This 15th-century Gothic building retains from its original decoration an unusual wood sculptural group of the *Flight into Egypt* in the left aisle.

On the other side of the Citadelle, the working end of Bayonne, an impressive stretch of docks and factories follows the wide Adour down to the sea. At the northern edge of town, off Avenue Louis de Foix, is the **English cemetery** from Wellington's campaigns; Queen Victoria and other members of the royal family always came to visit when they were in Biarritz.

Market Days in Bayonne

ⓘ **Bayonne >**
Pl des Basques, t 05 59 46 01 46, www. bayonne-tourisme.com; culture website www.ville-bayonne.fr; open July and Aug Mon–Sat 9–7, Sun 10–1; Sept–June Mon–Fri 9–6, Sat 10–6

Markets are held on Monday to Saturday mornings in Les Halles and all day on Friday. Place des Gascons holds a market on Wednesday and Saturday mornings; and Place de la République on Friday and Sunday mornings; Rue St-Catherine has one on Friday and Sunday mornings; and Polo Beyris holds one on Friday morning.

Where to Stay in Bayonne

Bayonne ✉ **64100**

If you're not too concerned about being very close to a beach, the animated streets of Bayonne might make a nice, cheaper alternative to staying in Biarritz.

***Best Western Grand Hôtel, 21 Rue Thiers, t 05 59 59 62 00 (€€€). All the

city can offer in terms of luxury; it is bland but stately.

Hôtel Loustau, 1 Pl de la République, t 05 59 55 08 08, *www.hotel-loustau. com* (€€€). Comfortable, well-run hotel, overlooking the Pont St-Esprit and the Adour. *Menus €17–25. Restaurant closed Sun eves in winter.*

**Hôtel Ibis, 44–50 Bd Alsace-Lorraine, Quartier St-Esprit, t 05 59 50 38 38 (€€). A functional chain hotel with a small garden and a restaurant. *Open all year.*

*Hôtel des Arceaux, 26 Rue du Port-Neuf, t 05 59 59 15 53, *www.hotel-arceaux.com* (€€–€). One of the best reasonably priced options, near the cathedral. *Open all year.*

*Monbar, 24 Rue Pannecau, t 05 59 59 26 80 (€). Well-kept little hotel on a lively street in Petit Bayonne, across the Nive. *Open all year.*

Hôtel Paris-Madrid, Pl de la Gare, t 05 59 55 13 98 (€). A little bit different: a family-run hotel with most rooms looking over a quiet courtyard, creating a little haven of peace in the middle of Bayonne. The decor is a bit worn but the place is clean and reasonably comfortable. *Closed for Xmas and weekends in winter unless you phone well in advance.*

Eating Out in Bayonne

Like other cities of the coast, Bayonne does much better with restaurants than with hotels. Many of the best inexpensive places can be found in Petit Bayonne, either on the quays along the Nive or in the back streets behind them.

The Bayonnais, 38 Quai des Corsaires, **t** 05 59 25 61 19. Traditional Basque restaurant in the old town, with décor dedicated to local sporting heroes. *Closed Mon, and Sun in winter.*

(★) Le Cheval
Blanc >

Le Cheval Blanc, Rue Bourg Neuf, just round the corner from the Musée Bonnat, **t** 05 59 59 01 33. At the top of the heap, by popular acclaim. Even though the Tellechea family has been running this place for a long time, they never get tired of finding innovative twists to traditional Basque cooking: salmon from the Adour or *poulet basquaise* with *cèpes*. *Menus €27–57. Closed Sun eves and Mon except in Aug, one week in summer and two weeks in Feb.*

Francois Miura, 24 Rue Marengo, **t** 05 59 59 49 89. A stylish small restaurant with modern furniture and contemporary paintings, specializing in fish dishes but there are meat options too. *Menus €20–31. Closed Sun eves and Wed.*

Le Petit Chalut, **t** 05 59 25 54 60. A hole-in-the-wall on Quai Galuperie. It offers fresh seafood on a set menu: grilled fish or *thon basquaise* when the catch is in. *Menus €16–24. Open daily all year, with electro music on Thurs eve.*

Biarritz

(⚿) Biarritz

For their 1959 season, the designers at Cadillac came up with something special: a sleek and shiny convertible, nearly 25ft (7.5m) long, with the highest tailfins in automotive history (22 inches/ 56cm). They called it the *Biarritz*, a tribute to the Basque village that was chosen by fortune, for a few decades at the end of the 19th century, to become the most glittering resort in Europe. Nowadays, there's still enough Ritz in Biarritz to support six luxury hotels (among 65 more modest establishments). But, freed from the burden of being the cynosure of fashion, the resort has become a pleasantly laid-back place, where anyone, wealthy or not, can have an unpretentious good time.

A recent article by the economic journal *Les Echos* confirms that the population of BAB is growing rapidly thanks to workers following the companies moving in and the influx of retired people from across France. There are also many holiday homes in the area. The Mayor of Biarritz, Didier Borotra, is quoted as saying that out of 23,000 houses 8,000 are second homes. After September, Biarritz seems to decline into an overgrown village. Then everybody knows everyone else; they shake hands and exchange pleasantries on street corners, or lounge in the bar talking about how nice and quiet it is.

09 The Pays Basque | Biarritz

Biarritz

History under the Palms

Local historians claim that both Biarritz and its landmark, the Atalaya, are names bestowed by the ancient Phoenicians, who may well have used the port as a stage on their trade routes to Britain. Biarritz is said to mean something like 'safe harbour', and Atalaya a kind of tower (like the *talayots* of Minorca), an important landmark visible to the early, coast-hugging sailors.

Before the 1860s, Biarritz was never more than a simple fishing village. But in the Middle Ages, even more than Bayonne it was the heart of the Basque whaling fleet. Cachalots and other species of whales were once common in the Bay of Biscay. A permanent watch was kept on the Atalaya, and whenever one was sighted, the entire village would row out and try to nab it; the Biarrots were probably the inventors of the harpoon, and a harpooner once figured on the village's coat of arms. When the whales caught on and started avoiding the area, the Biarrots and the other Basque whalers bravely sailed out into the open sea after them.

There doesn't seem to be any conclusive evidence for it, but the Basques will tell you they discovered Newfoundland in the 14th century, and probably other parts of the Americas as well (Columbus did after all take a Basque along to be his navigator). By 1800, Basque whalers couldn't keep up with the British and

Americans, but Biarritz was beginning to make part of its living from a new and unprecedented phenomenon, the desire of northerners to come and spend a holiday beside the sea.

Eugenia Maria de Montijo de Guzmán, to whom Biarritz owes its present status, came from a minor Spanish noble family a bit down on its luck. But even as a young girl, fortune-telling gypsies and nuns forecast a brilliant future for her; 'an eagle will carry you to the heavens and then drop you,' one of them supposedly said. Eugenia also had a scheming, social-climbing mother, who got her daughter as far as the court of the new Emperor Napoleon III in Paris in 1852. This striking 26-year-old was more than capable of doing the rest of the job herself. A brilliant horsewoman who liked to smoke a cigar now and then, she made quite an impression. But there was a cold, unapproachable side to her too, and she used it to win the Emperor's heart by being the only girl in Paris the old rogue couldn't have. It is claimed he found his way into her bedroom one night; meeting a chilly reception, he asked the way to her heart. 'Through the church,' she replied.

As Empress Eugénie, she helped inaugurate the cult of fashion in Paris, making the fortune of Worth, the first of the celebrity couturiers. With a political outlook somewhat to the right of Attila the Hun, and a near-total control over Napoleon, she was able to exert a tremendous influence over the policies of the government, presiding gloriously over the orgy of greed, corruption, décolletage and waltzes that was the Second Empire. It took a woman historian, Edith Saunders, to notice this strangely significant bit of the world's secret history. In her book, *A Distant Summer*, she wrote:

...Eugénie had risen like a brilliant star, to create not only new fashions but a new taste in beauty, a new type of woman. The old type, which had lingered on in England and was represented in the pages of Dickens, belonged to Europe's Romantic period and was open-mouthed, angelic and mawkish. The new type, with its prediliction for blonde hair and its hard expression, is still with us. The Empress set the modern standard of highly polished perfection which is maintained today by Hollywood film stars and mechanically transmitted to entranced millions who follow in the measure allotted by their circumstance. To look like a film star is the dream of the present day woman of the industrial age; in 1855 everyone dreamed of looking like Eugénie.

As a girl, Eugénie and her mother had often vacationed at the 'just-discovered' village of Biarritz. As Empress, she dragged Napoleon back down with her and established the summer court on the beach. Having invented the new woman, Eugénie now made some great contributions to the modern concept of the seaside resort. The imperial couple didn't stay in a hotel; Eugénie had a palace – the Villa Eugénie – built on the most prominent spot along the beach in 1854. Everybody who was anybody in Paris soon followed, along with grand dukes, *petit* dukes, every sort of count and baron, and plenty of factory owners with marriageable daughters. The royal families of Spain and Belgium came; the English were already here, laying out golf courses, while Count von Bismarck canoodled with the wife of the Russian ambassador.

The Fall of France in 1870 put an end to the Second Empire, and to Eugénie's fairy-tale. In 1881, the government of the Third Republic demolished the Villa Eugénie after a fire, and divided the estate into building lots. But you can't keep a good princess down; Eugénie lived a romantic if somewhat melancholy life in exile, an object of fascination wherever she travelled. She died in Madrid in 1920, at the age of 94.

Even without her, Biarritz carried on. More Russian princes and even Queen Victoria came to visit (in 1889); the Prince of Wales left so much money in the casino that they named two different streets after him. The *belle époque* brought a tidal wave of building: grand hotels, the casino, a salt-water spa and acres of wealthy villas in every imaginable style. It wasn't a wild scene like the Côte d'Azur in the 1920s. The swells followed a respectable and rather bland daily schedule, starting with a morning promenade past the shop windows on Rue Mazagran at 10, followed by an hour on the beach, dressing for lunch at 11.30, and so on. The First World War started Biarritz's fall from fashion; in the 20s everybody started shifting to Nice and Cannes where life promised more excitement.

Biarritz has begun to shake off its dusty image with dramatic refurbishment of its hotels and fine buildings, in architectural styles ranging from *belle époque* to Art Deco and Art Nouveau. These include the splendid Municipal Casino, which dominates the Grand Plage, with its restored casinos, entertainment centres and an old-style grand café overlooking the beach.

Despite its hordes of retirees, Biarritz is hardly behind the times. France Telecom has made it the experimental city for the communications of the future, wiring up the town with a single fibre optic cable to provide cable TV, telephone, '*visiophone*', '*télétel*', 'interactive communications' and God knows what else. And plenty of young people still come in the summer for one unexpected reason – surfing. Stuck in its odd angle of coastline, Biarritz provides what many claim are the only perfect waves on the Atlantic; French hot-doggers and surf bunnies have made it the modest Malibu Beach of Europe. And lots of good Frenchmen who have never heard of surfing, and who would never dream of sitting on a beach, know Biarritz for its crack rugby squad – the great Serge Blanco played here until his retirement in 1992 (now the local hero runs a thalassotherapy centre down in Hendaye, *see* p.196).

The Atalaya

Here, on the tip of old Biarritz's little peninsula, is the height where in the old days the watch would send up smoke signals when whales were sighted. To the right, the Port des Pêcheurs now holds only pleasure craft. To the left is the old fishing port, long ago unusable and filled up with the beach of Port-Vieux, and also the best place in Biarritz for a stroll, the **Rocher de la Vierge**. Napoleon III and Eugénie are responsible for this system of causeways and tunnels, connecting a number of crags and tiny islands into a memorable walk just above the pounding surf; the biggest rock carries a marble statue of the Virgin Mary.

Up on top of the Atalaya, the **Musée de la Mer**, in a clean Art Deco building, contains an imaginatively decorated old aquarium for a look at what's down below the surface of the Bay of Biscay, along with exhibits on the natural history of the sea, whales and whaling, navigation, etc. Audio-guides are available in English.

Descending eastwards from the Atalaya, the Bd Maréchal Leclerc takes you to the church of **Ste-Eugénie**, another modest contribution from the Empress; the big organ inside won a prize at the 1900 Paris World's Fair. It faces one of the centres of resort life in the old days, the beautifully restored Casino Bellevue, now converted to residences and exhibition and conference rooms.

Not far away, by the city marketplace on Rue Broquedis, is the **Musée de Vieux Biarritz**; set in a former Anglican church, this is a small exhibition of photos and mementos of the good old days. There is also an interesting museum of oriental art, **Asiatica**, with a collection which includes jades, bronzes and porcelain from China, Nepal and India, and many Tibetan *thangkas* (paintings on silk) and an audio-guide to the collection available in English. Finally, if you didn't get your fill in Bayonne, there is a **chocolate museum**, including tastings.

Beaches and Villas

Below this, the shore straightens out northwards into the long, luscious expanse of the Grande Plage, which before Eugénie was called (for reasons not entirely clear) the Plage des Fous, dominated by the magnificent casino. Farther up the beach, behind the wrought-iron fences, is Biarritz's stately landmark, the sumptuous Hôtel du Palais. This is the spot where Eugénie built her palace, destroyed by fire in 1881. The present hotel, begun in 1905, is the successor to an even grander one that also burned down. Across the street, the Russian aristocrats built their onion-domed church of St-Alexandre-Nevsky (1908).

Avenue Edward VII, which becomes Avenue de l'Impératrice further on, was the status address of *belle époque* Biarritz, lined with ornate hotels and residences now largely converted to other

Musée de la Mer
*t 05 59 22 75 40,
www.museedelamer.
com; open daily July
and Aug 9.30am–12am,
Easter, June and Sept
9.30–7; rest of year
9.30–12.30 and 2–6;
closed Mon Nov–Mar
plus most of Jan; adm*

**Musée de
Vieux Biarritz**
*t 05 59 24 86 28; open
Tues–Sat 10–12.30 and
2–6.30; adm*

Asiatica
*1 Rue Guy Petit, t 05 59
22 78 78, www.
museeasiatica.com;
open Mon–Fri 10.30–
6.30, Sat and Sun 2–7*

Musée du Chocolat
*Av Beaurivage, t 05 59
41 54 64, www.
lemuseeduchocolat.com;
open July and Aug
Mon–Sat 10–12 and
2.30–6*

09

The Pays Basque | Biarritz

uses. In the shady streets behind them, all originally part of the imperial estate, scores of wealthy villas still survive, in a crazy quilt of styles ranging from Art Nouveau to neo-Moorish to Anglo-Norman. Some of the best can be seen on and around Avenue Reine Victoria. Also in this area, you can have a look at what passed for piety in the Second Empire – another creation of Napoleon and Eugénie, the 1864 **Chapelle Impériale**, on Avenue Reine Victoria at Rue Pellot. The lavish neo-Byzantine interior is now open, following major renovations.

Chapelle Impériale
open mid-July–mid-Sept Mon–Sat 3–7; mid-April–mid-July and mid-Sept–mid-Oct Tues, Thurs and Sat 3–7; mid-Oct–Dec 3–5

There is an enjoyable walk along the Plage Miramar to the most visible landmark on this stretch of the coast, the 143ft (43m) **Phare St-Martin**, a rare example of an old-fashioned lighthouse: built in 1834, and little changed since. It has only 249 steps to climb; at the base there is a giant sundial.

Phare St-Martin
t 05 59 22 37 00; open July and Aug Tues–Sun 10–12 and 3–7; mid-April–June Sat, Sun and hols, 3–7

As for beaches, there is a wide choice of places to plant your towel, and you should be able to find a spot that's not too crowded even at the height of summer. From south to north: at Biarritz' southern limits is the broad expanse of the Plage de la Milady, Plage Marbella and the Côte des Basques, a favourite of the surfing set. Under the old town is the tiny but pleasant Plage du Port Vieux. The Grande Plage and Plage Miramar, the centre of the action, are lovely if often cramped, but further out, stretching miles along the northern coast in the suburb of Anglet, there are plenty more. When the beach traffic's too terrific in summer take the special **Navette des Plages** bus from Place Clemenceau or Av de l'Impératrice to the above-mentioned beaches, or go north and take your pick among the Plage de la Chambre d'Amour, the Plage des Corsaires, de la Madrague, de l'Océan, des Dunes, and Plage des Cavaliers. The first one takes its name from a number of caves, now mostly submerged, that served as lovers' trysts long ago. Plenty of different stories have grown up around the place – about pairs of lovers who took refuge here and were tragically drowned with the tide – but the notorious French witch-hunter de Lancre, who wrote a report on witchcraft in the Labourd in 1609, said that this was known locally to be none other than the birthplace of Venus, where the goddess rose up from the foam of the sea.

Navette des Plages
t 05 59 52 59 52; summer only

Around Biarritz: Arcangues

For a break from the city, in 10 minutes you can drive from the beach to Arcangues, a lovely village on a height south of Biarritz. In the centre, a fine 16th-century church shares space with the *fronton* and a bust of Arcangues's son Luis Mariano, celebrated singing star of some really excruciating French film musicals of the 1940s and 50s.

Sports and Activities in Biarritz

ⓘ **Biarritz >**
*Place d'Ixelles,
Javalquinto (next to the
town hall), t 05 59 22
37 00, www.biarritz.fr
and www.ville-
biarritz.fr; open July and
Aug daily 8–8;
Sept–June Mon–Sat
9–6, Sun 10–5*

Golf thrives in Biarritz. There are 10 courses around the town and several more in St-Jean-de-Luz, ranging from lush, professional-length links with an ocean view to dinky par-3 places to practise your iron shots. At least one important tournament is held in Biarritz each season. Serious courses include the **Golf de Chiberta** in Anglet, Bd des Plages; **Golf d'Arcangues** in Arcangues, south of Biarritz; **Golf de Chantaco**, Rte d'Ascain, St-Jean-de-Luz; and **Golf de la Nivelle**, Place Sharp, Ciboure. For more information contact the **Association Golf Côte Basque–Sud Landes** at Moliets on **t** 05 58 48 54 65.

If you should feel a sudden desire to take up **surfing**, there are more than a dozen schools in Biarritz and Anglet, and plenty of places to rent equipment. Some useful contacts are **Biarritz Surf Training**, 102 Rue Pierre de Chevigné, **t** 05 59 23 15 31, *www. surftraining.com* and **Ecole de Surf Moraiz**, 4 Pl Bellevue, **t** 05 59 41 22 09, *www.jomoraiz.com*.

You may not have heard of **thalassotherapy**, the use of sea water for aiding stress, fitness or recovery from diseases – but in France it is big news; Biarritz has two of the most up-to-date establishments, the **Institut Thalassa**, 11 Rue Louison Bobet, **t** 05 59 41 30 01, and **Les Thermes Marine**, 80 Rue de Madrid, **t** 05 59 23 01 22, *www.thalassa.com*.

For other water sports, you might do better in some of the smaller resorts down the coast. St-Jean-de-Luz has plenty of places that offer deep-sea fishing excursions or rent sailing boats, including the **Ecole Nationale de Voile**, at Socoa, Ciboure, **t** 05 59 47 06 32, which also offers courses in windsurfing and such. Or else, back at Biarritz, you can fritter away your money on the *tiercé*, *quarté* and *quinté* at the **Hippodrome des Fleurs** on Av du Lac Marion, still one of France's premier racing venues. To see around Biarritz there's a tourist train that leaves from near the casino (**t** 06 07 97 16 35, *www.petit-train-biarritz.fr*, runs April–Oct).

Where to Stay in Biarritz

Biarritz ✉ 64200

Don't let Biarritz' past fool you into thinking there's no place for the likes of you and me here. In fact the vast majority of people who come these days are looking for a bargain, and they have little trouble finding it, although Biarritz is somewhat lacking at the lower end of the scale – if you arrive without a reservation in July or August you might get pushed up into the higher brackets. The tourist office on Place d'Ixelles can help you find a suitable room.

Luxury (€€€€€)

****Hôtel du Palais**, 1 Av de l'Impératrice, **t** 05 59 41 64 00, *www.hotel-du-palais.com*. Probably the most prestigious address on France's west coast. Built in Biarritz's glory days on the site of Napoleon and Eugénie's villa, this compound on the beach has a circuit of old wrought-iron fences to separate you from the rest of the world. For a while in the 1950s, the Palais was closed, but the city got it fixed up and reopened, under a determined mayor who had campaigned under the simple slogan: 'No Palace, No Millionaires.' Some of the rooms are palatial, many with period furnishings. Since July 2006 there is now also a spa with pool, gym, sauna and beauty treatment centre. The dining room sparkles with bejewelled chandeliers. *Menus* €55–90.

****Miramar**, 13 Rue Louison Bobet, **t** 05 59 41 30 00, *www.thalassa.com*. The younger contender for the luxury prize. Modern and up-to-date, this hotel may not have the panache of the Palais, but compensates with very high standards in every respect: one of Biarritz' best restaurants and another serving simpler meals, two pools, sauna and even its own thalassotherapy centre. *Menus* €52–70. *Open all year.*

***Plaza**, Av Edward VII, **t** 05 59 24 74 00, *www.groupe-segeric.com*. Built in 1928, recently renovated, with a touch of restrained Art Deco elegance.

It has retained much of its original decoration, with a quiet sense of decorum to match. *Open all year.*

Expensive (€€€)

***Maison Garnier**, 29 Rue Gambetta, t 05 59 01 60 70, *www.hotel-biarritz. com*, is set in a 19th-century Basque house. There are seven exquisitely restored rooms, all with antique furniture.

Moderate (€€)

***Château du Clair de Lune**, 48 Av Alan Seeger, t 05 59 41 53 20, *www.chateauduclairdelune.com*. An alternative far from the centre. It's in a *belle époque* villa in a delicious park, with tranquillity assured, and lovely rooms, though it's a bit expensive. Special deals with some of the golf courses nearby.

***Louisiane**, Rue Guy Petit, t 05 59 22 20 20, *www.louisiane-biarritz.com*. Worth a try despite its unprepossessing modern exterior. This is a conveniently located, well-managed chain hotel with its own swimming pool, a boon for those who want to swim rather than surf.

Inexpensive (€)

****Hôtel du Rocher de la Vierge**, 13 Rue du Port-Vieux, t 05 59 24 11 74. At the centre of the action in the old town. *Open all year.*

****Hostellerie Victoria**, 11 Av Reine Victoria, t 05 59 24 08 21, is in a delightful villa with garden from the old days, close to Grande Plage. *Closed mid-Oct–1 April.*

****Palacito Hotel**, 1 Rue Gambetta, t 05 59 24 04 89, *www.hotel-palacito. com*. A traditional small hotel right in the middle of town.

***Palym**, 7 Rue du Port-Vieux, t 05 59 24 16 56. A family-run, old-style place popular with surfers.

Camping

While every other town on the coast has a huge choice of places to pitch your tent, Biarritz doesn't. You'll do better looking in nearby Bidart, which has 9 of them.

Biarritz Camping, 28 Rue Harcet, t 05 59 23 00 12, *www.biarritz-camping.fr*. Mobile homes available. *Closed mid-Sept–early May.*

Eating Out in Biarritz

Expensive (€€€)

La Rotonde, Hôtel du Palais, t 05 59 41 64 00, may be the southwest's ultimate trip in luxurious dining: a magnificent domed room with its original decoration, and views over the beach and sea. There is a formidable wine list. *Menus €55–90.*

Le Relais, Miramar Hotel, t 05 59 41 30 00. Without the posh ambience of the former, but you can eat as well for a bit less. Seafood is the main attraction, cooked with a delightful lightness and savour: a *fricassée* of sole and langoustines, or lobster ravioli with *cèpes*. *Menus €52–70.*

Les Jardins de l'Océan, Hôtel Régina et Golf, 52 Av de l'Impératrice, t 05 59 41 33 00. Good for a slightly more modest seafood extravaganza. Prices are reasonable but you may be tempted to splurge for the *grand plateau de fruits de mer*, including lobster. *Menu €34 plus à la carte.* There's also a bar for lighter meals. *Closed lunchtimes.*

Campagne et Gourmandise, 52 Av Alan Seeger, t 05 59 41 10 11, *www.campagneetgourmandise.com*. In a Basque farmhouse in the grounds of the Château du Claire de Lune (*see* 'Where to Stay', above). You can dine on a terrace with breathtaking panoramic views of the Pyrenees. Typical dishes include *fricassée de champignons en cappuccino d'herbes, queue de bœuf à la tranche de foie gras*, and pigeon tart. *Menu about €43, but changes regularly.*

Moderate (€€)

Chez Albert, Port des Pêcheurs, t 05 59 24 43 84, *www.chezalbert.fr*. This may at first glance look like a typical tourist restaurant, but it's popular year round with visitors and Biarrots alike for quality seafood at reasonable prices, including paella, grilled lobster and sardines. There are meat choices too. *Menu €36. Closed for several weeks in winter.*

Goulue, 3 Rue E. Ardouin, t 05 59 24 90 90. A *belle époque*-style restaurant with attentive service of classic local dishes; try a plateful of baby squid or monkfish cooked with bacon. *Menus* *from €11 at lunch; €24 in the evenings. Closed all Mon, and Tues lunch out of high season*.

Le Clos Basque, 12 Rue Louis Barthou, **t** 05 59 24 24 96. An authentic little bistro with stone walls and Spanish tiles inside, and a charming terrace outside. Local specialities such as squid with peppers are served. *Menu €23. Closed Sun eve exc July and Aug and Mon all year*.

Café de la Grande Plage, 1 Av Edouard VII, **t** 05 59 22 77 88, *www.lucienbarriere.com*. 1930s-style brasserie-café, facing the ocean and overlooking the Grand Plage. Part of the casino, it has a range of drinks and light meals. *Open daily all year*.

Le Surfing, 9 Bd Prince de Galles, **t** 05 59 24 78 72. Overlooks the Plage des Basques and is the place for fashionable surfers to peel off their wetsuits and enjoy a décor of surfboards and Hawaiian shirts. It specializes in fish but serves lots of good salads too. *Menu €21. Closed Sat, Sun eve and Mon lunch*.

Blue Cargo, Villa Itsasoan, Av Ibarritz, **t** 05 59 23 54 87, *www.bluecargo.fr*. In a villa perched right on the beach of Ibarritz, on the outskirts of Biarritz. It's perfect for sunset-over-the-sea drinks or simple seafood meals. *A la carte only, €25–30. Becomes a nightclub later. Open April–Sept*.

Bistrot des Halles, Rue du Centre, **t** 05 59 24 21 22. Usually crowded for lunch and dinner. As in any French town, you won't go wrong looking around the market, and you won't do better than the daily special (usually a grilled fish or steak). *Menu €17. Closed Sun exc for hols, plus 15–31 Oct*.

Inexpensive (€)
The Players, Esplanade du Casino de Biarritz, **t** 05 59 24 19 60. Can't be beaten for good cheap fish and vast pizzas. It's right next to the Grand Plage, with views out to sea. *A la carte €20, pizza €8–10. Closed Nov and 1st week Dec*.

Bar Jean, 5 Rue des Halles, **t** 05 59 24 80 38. A Biarritz classic; the place to go for superb fresh tapas, oysters and a good choice of wines in a traditional Spanish tiled bodega. *Closed Tues and Wed from Oct–April plus Jan and Feb*.

El Callejon, 15 Pl Georges Clemenceau, **t** 05 59 24 99 15. A good tapas bar. *Open eves only exc Sat and Sun*.

Pâtisserie Miremont, Pl Clemenceau, **t** 05 59 24 01 38. Port des Pêcheurs is the site of several tapas places. This is the place to go while you're waiting for dinner: today, as in the *belle époque*, an essential Biarritz experience is to drop in at 4pm for a coffee and a little pastry. The *pâtisserie* retains its original décor, with rooms overlooking the sea.

The Côte Basque

If Biarritz is too big and cosmopolitan, there's St-Jean-de-Luz down the coast, and if St-Jean is still too frenetic, you've got two very amiable choices in between, Bidart and Guéthary. Both are perfect Basque villages, with church, *mairie* and *fronton* right in the middle, and both have good beaches. If they do get a bit crowded at the height of summer, it's much too early to call them spoiled yet. Leaving Biarritz on the coastal N10, **Bidart** comes first, with a grand view across the coast from the pilgrimage chapel of Ste-Madeleine. Bidart's parish church, in the centre, has some painted altarpieces and a quite unusual Slavic baptismal font – a gift of Queen Natalie of Serbia, who spent a lot of time here before the First World War, in a palace called the Pavillon Royal above the beach. You can visit an 18th-century flour mill in **Bassilour**, where they make gateau Basque. Sleepy **Guéthary** has been a resort as

Bassilour mill
t 05 59 41 94 49,;closed Tues mid-Sept–June

ⓘ **Guéthary >>**
*Rue du Comte
Swiecinski,* **t** *05 59 26
56 60, www.guethary-
france.com; open
summer Mon–Sat
9–12.30 and 2–6.30;
winter Mon–Fri 9–12.30
and 2–5.30, Sat 9–12.30*

★ **Hotel Villa
Catarie >>**

Where to Stay and Eat in Bidart and Guéthary

Bidart ✉ 64210

Elissaldia Hotel, Pl de la Mairie, **t** 05 59 54 90 03, *www.hotel-elissaldia.com* (€€). A cheap, authentic place to stay within a *pelote* ball's throw of the church and *fronton* court. It's a snip with sea views thrown in. There's also a bar and restaurant. *Menus €17–38. Open daily all year.*

Table des Frères Ibarboure, Chemin de Italiénèa, **t** 05 59 54 81 64, *www. freresibarboure.com.* One of the region's most celebrated restaurants. It's a family establishment, but the cuisine is predictably perfect and abstrusely soignée, from the *foie chaud de canard aux agrumes* to the rich and extravagant desserts. *Menus €34–98.* There are 8 rooms, too, part of the Relais du Silence. *Restaurant closed Sun eves plus Mon lunch in July.*

Also closed mid-Nov–mid-Dec and three weeks in Jan.

Guéthary ✉ 64210

***Hotel Villa Catarie**, Av du Géneral de Gaulle, opposite the *Mairie* and *fronton*), **t** 05 59 47 59 00, *www.villa-catarie.com* (€). This old Basque villa has been beautifully restored. Comfort, romance and luxury classically done. A bit pricey but a lovely place to stay and feel pampered.

Restaurant Madrid, right in the village centre on Av du Général de Gaulle, **t** 05 59 26 52 12, is cheery and homey and serves mostly seafood. *Menus €17–25. Closed early Nov–early Dec plus Jan.*

Kandela, t 05 59 47 77 57, also in the centre, is a tiny restaurant with a terrace, specializing in grills, fish and seafood, with a good local wine list. *Menus €18–24. Closed mid-Nov–mid-Mar.*

Musée Guéthary
*http://musee.
guethary.free.fr; open
May–Oct Mon and
Wed–Sat 2–6, July and
Aug 2–6.30*

long as Biarritz, though it never made it big. It has a Basque-style *mairie*, which must get a window broken every now and then from the *fronton* in front of it, along with a tiny port and a beach. In an early 20th-century house in the village'ss park the **Musée Guéthary** is full of sculpture by Polish artist George Clément de Swiecinski and there are temporary exhibitions across a range of genres.

🔢 **St-Jean-de-Luz**

St-Jean-de-Luz

For those who do not naturally gravitate towards the sun and fun of the beach, a seaside resort needs a certain special, intangible quality. Like the theatre, a good resort must be able to make one suspend one's disbelief. In all of southern France, there are very few places that can do this: one is Collioure on the Mediterranean, another St-Jean-de-Luz. The name is perfect. Light and colour can be extraordinary here, illuminating an immaculately white Basque town and acres of glistening rose-silver seafood that its restaurants roll out on tables to lure in customers. Even in the Basque lands, St-Jean's cooks are renowned for their skill and imagination. The beaches are fine and, best of all, this is not the sort of town to have entirely succumbed to the tourist tide; the fishermen on the quay still strut around as if they own the place. What more could you ask?

Unfortunately, the name really has nothing to do with light (*luz* in Spanish). Gradgrind etymologists have traced it back to a Celtic

Getting around St-Jean-de-Luz

There is a **tourist train** that leaves from the Rond Point du Port, **t** 05 59 41 96 94.

or Latin word *louth* or *lutum*, meaning mud, the same as Paris's original name, Lutetia – Mudville. St-Jean, or rather Donihane Lohitzun, as the Basques know it, grew up in a swampy nowhere that just happened to have a good harbour. It began to thrive as a fishing port when the River Adour started silting up the harbour of Bayonne in the Middle Ages. The Luziens shared fully in the French Basques' whaling and buccaneering adventures until the Revolution. It's tuna and sardines they're after now, and tourists.

The Port

A casual visitor could walk around St-Jean all day and never notice it had a beach, but it's a good one, long and deep, tucked away on the northern side of town; the beach is protected by a jetty, and very safe for swimming. At its centre is the lavish **casino**, built in 1924.

St-Jean naturally turns its face to the port, lined with blue, red and green fishing boats, and a broad quay where the fishermen spread their nets; St-Jean is home to the biggest tuna fleet in France. There will be boats offering excursions around the area, or to the Spanish coast. Some, like the *Nivelle III*, also offer deep-sea-fishing trips. Behind the port is the town hall and the adjacent

Nivelle III
t 06 09 73 71 81

St-Jean – Petit Paris

It was a party to remember, and without its tourists St-Jean would be left only with the memory of that one glorious month when it seemed the centre of the world. In 1659, Spain and France signed the Treaty of the Pyrenees, putting an end to a century and a half of almost continuous hostility. To ice the deal, a marriage was arranged between Louis XIV and the Spanish infanta, Maria Teresa. Preparations went on for a year, and this obscure whaling and fishing port, roughly halfway between Paris and Madrid, was chosen as the venue. In May 1660, *everybody* came to St-Jean, including nearly the entire French court. 'Monsieur' (Louis's neurotic uncle) and Cardinal Mazarin were there; the 'Grande Mademoiselle' (Louis's flamboyant cousin) and her lover floated down, and all the dandies and popinjays of Versailles followed in their wake. Louis himself arrived last, in a gilded carriage. One observer, Madame de Motteville, marvelled at how everyone was covered in lace and feathers and tassels. So were the horses. It reminded her of King Cyrus and ancient Persia.

Years before, a gypsy fortune-teller had predicted that peace between France and Spain would finally come 'with a whale'. And on the day that Maria Teresa and the Spaniards arrived in St-Jean, a great whale was sighted just off the harbour. The courtiers rushed to the shore to watch the town's seamen give chase. Young Louis, however, took the opportunity to barge in on his future bride in her chambers; he surprised her *en déshabillé* and they had an intimate lunch together. For the wedding, there were Basque dancers, mock naval battles offshore, a bullfight and a grand ball in the main square, now Place Louis XIV, illuminated with thousands of candles and torches. Louis and his bride lived happily ever after (though the France Louis ruled suffered greatly); when the queen died, Louis remarked that her death was 'the only chagrin she ever caused me'. The peace with Spain has lasted up to the present, save for the unfortunate interlude of Napoleon. As for the whale, they caught it, and the bishop of Bayonne, who performed the wedding ceremony, took the tongue and fat of it back to Bayonne.

194

09 The Pays Basque | St-Jean-de-Luz

**Maison de
Louis XIV**
*Pl Louis XIV, t 05 59 26
01 56; open June– Sept
daily 10.30–12 and
2.30–5.30; July and Aug
daily 10.30–12 and
2.30–6.30; adm*

**Pavillon de
l'Infante**
*Pavillon visits mid-
June–mid-Oct Mon–Sat
11–12.30 and 2.30–6.30;
closed Mon am*

Maison de Louis XIV, where the Roi Soleil stayed for his wedding. It is a typical Basque townhouse, built in 1643. You can also visit the nearby Pavillon de l'Infante, where the Infanta stayed.

From the port, the main stem, pedestrian Rue Gambetta, takes you to **St-Jean Baptiste**, largest and greatest of all the Basque churches to be found in France, where Louis XIV and Maria Teresa were married. The church is a lesson in Basque subtlety, plain and bright outside, and plain and bright within; any Baptist or Methodist would feel at home here. The aesthetic is in the detail, especially the wonderful wooden ceiling formed like the hull of a ship, and the three levels of wooden galleries around both sides of the nave, carved with all the art and sincerity the local artisans could manage.

The church was begun in the 1300s, but such wooden galleries do not last for ever, no matter how well made; this latest version, probably much like those that preceded it, was completed in the 1860s. Another feature, also typical of Basque churches such as this, is the ornate gilded altarpiece, dripping with Baroque detail. The main door of the church was sealed up after Louis and Maria Teresa passed through it on their wedding day.

Ciboure

Right across the port from St-Jean, over a little bridge, this is the less-touristy, working member of these twin towns. Ciboure is the home of the composer Maurice Ravel, who was born at No.12 Quai Ravel, and who once started a concerto based on Basque themes and rhythms (called *Zaspiak Bat*), but never finished it. At the

Berrain farm
*t 05 59 51 06 06; open
April–Oct*

farm Berrain on the N10 there is an ecomusée on Basque life, traditions, crafts, sports and music.

The town has a mirror-image of St-Jean's picturesque port, though this side is mostly used by pleasure boats. Behind the port, there are pretty streets of old Basque houses such as **Rue de la Fontaine**, and the simple St-Vincent, a 16th-century fortified church with an octagonal tower. On the northern end of town, facing the coast, is the quarter of **Socoa** with its **castle**, begun by Henri IV which today houses a surfing and windsurfing school.

(i) **St-Jean-
de-Luz >**
*Pl Maréchal Foch, t 05
59 26 03 16, www.saint-
jean-de-luz.com; open
Sept–mid-Nov and
Feb–June Mon–Sat 9–12
and 2.30–6.30; July and
Aug daily 9–7.30*

Market Days around St-Jean-de-Luz

St-Jean-de-Luz: Markets are held on Tuesdays, Fridays, and also Saturdays in summer. There are also markets all year round in Les Halles from Monday to Saturday, and on Tuesday, Friday and Saturday in summer there are local producers around Les Halle.
Ciboure: Sundays.

Where to Stay around St-Jean-de-Luz

St-Jean-de-Luz ✉ 64500
If St-Jean has one unfortunate drawback, it's finding a reasonably priced place to stay – rates here are even higher than in Biarritz – although, unexpectedly, the top spots are not by the beach.

****Chantaco**, Route d'Ascain, t 05 59 26 14 76, *www.hotel-chantaco.com* (€€€€€–€€€). The emphasis is on golf, with Chantaco golf course, the area's most famous, next door. The hotel, in a 1930s-style Andalucian villa, with a patio covered in vines, is set in a lovely park, and offers tennis courts and a pool in addition to golf. Here you'll find deluxe rooms and service, with prices to match. There's a restaurant and 24-hour room service. *Closed Nov–April.*

***Hôtel de la Plage**, 33 Rue Garat, t 05 59 51 03 44, *www.hoteldelaplage.com* (€€€). As its name suggests this hotel just a 3-minute walk from the beach. Spacious, bright, modern bedrooms. The owner's brother has a restaurant next door (*see* below). A comfortable hotel. *Closed late Oct–early Feb but open Christmas and New Year.*

****Parc Victoria**, 5 Rue Cèpe, t 05 59 26 78 78, *www.parcvictoria.com* (€€€). A gracious mansion on the outskirts of town set in large luxuriant gardens. It's a beautifully decorated, intimate place (18 rooms and suites). It has a pool and a shady terrace. *Menus* €38–78. *Closed mid-Nov–mid-Mar.*

***Hôtel les Almadies**, 58 Rue Gambetta, t 05 59 85 34 48, *www.hotel-les-almadies.com* (€€€–€€). A lovely hotel in the heart of town in the main pedestrian zone. Seven good-sized bedrooms with balconies. The hotel has been renovated and has a clean, crisp and modern design. Very light and airy. The owners are friendly and helpful.

***De la Poste**, 83 Rue Gambetta, t 05 59 26 04 53, *www.grandhoteldelaposte.com* (€€). Right in the centre of town (with the added bonus of its very own snooker table). *Open all year.*

Bakea, 9 Pl Camille Julian, across the harbour in Ciboure, t 05 59 47 34 40, *www.hotelbakea.com* (€€). Eight rooms. *Closed Dec–Jan.*

Ohartzia, Rue Garat, t 05 59 26 00 06, *www.hotel-ohartzia.com* (€€). Very pretty, family-run hotel, situated in the middle of St-Jean, with a lovely terrace and garden on the first floor. Neat as a pin. *Closed Dec–Jan.*

Eating Out around St-Jean-de-Luz

St-Jean-de-Luz ✉ 64500

Everyone knows St-Jean as the capital of Basque cuisine in France, and there is a marvellous collection of restaurants around the centre. Competition keeps the quality high. Rue de la République, just off main Rue Gambetta near the port, must be counted among the sights of the Basque coast no one should miss. It's almost entirely lined with seafood restaurants, each one with its beautifully arranged table of *fruits de mer* out front.

Auberge Kaiku, 17 Rue de la République, t 05 59 26 13 20. The oldest house in St-Jean (1540) rolls out one of the most sumptuous tables; but you can negotiate your way to a fine marine repast. *Menu* €35–50 plus *à la carte.* Service can be slow when busy. *Closed lunchtimes Sept–June.*

Bakea, 9 Pl Camille Julian, across the harbour in Ciboure (*see* 'Where to Stay', t 05 59 47 34 40, has outside tables right on the port. It is a local favourite for *ttoro* and grills. This is also a charming hotel. *Menus from* €18. *Closed first half of Dec and Feb, and Sun and Mon except July and Aug.*

Chez Pantxua, Port de Soccoa, t 05 59 47 13 73. A long-established local favourite decorated with Basque paintings, serving *fruits de mer* and fish according to the catch of the day. *A la carte only, around* €40–50. *Closed Mon eve and Tues out of season, plus first two weeks of Dec, Jan and Tues eve only July and Aug.*

Pasaka, 11 Rue de la République, t 05 59 26 05 17. A cosy interior and two terraces, where you can feast on freshly caught local grilled sardines, or *ttoro*, a satisfying Basque fish soup with potatoes and saffron. *Menus* €17–23. *Closed Mon and Tues out of season plus a week in Mar, Nov and Dec.*

Le Peita, 21 Rue Tourasse, t 05 59 26 86 66. All the Basque seafood favourites; full meals *à la carte* average around €23. *Open evenings only Wed–Mon.*

Le Portua, 18 Rue de la République, t 05 59 51 01 12. Oysters, salmon for starters, a satisfying *ttoro* and grills. *Menu €20–30. Open daily all year.*

Restaurant le Brouillarta, Rue Garat, t 05 59 51 29 51. A busy brasserie next door to the **Hôtel de la Plage**. Decorated with bright Basque paintings, it is a popular lunch spot. *Menus up to €27, less at lunchtime, dish of the day €8.50. Open daily in July and Aug; closed mid-Nov–mid-Dec and Jan.*

Restaurant Chez Maya, 2 Rue St Jacques, St-Jean, t 05 59 26 80 76. This place is very popular with the locals and tourists alike for its simple and authentic Basque cuisine. Good value. *Menus from €19. Closed Thurs lunch, and Wed only in summer.*

Vieille Auberge, 22 Rue Tourasse, t 05 59 26 19 61. For a filling Basque meal in the company of Luziens that usually include grilled fish and sometimes paella. *Menus €16–24. Closed Tues, Wed and Jan–Mar.*

Urrugne and Hendaye

To get to Hendaye, you have a choice of either the coastal road, the scenic Carniche Basque (the D912), or else the more inland N10 or the motorway; these two pass through **Urrugne**, where the church of **St-Vincent** has a Renaissance portal with some excellent reliefs, which were damaged somewhat by English artillery in 1814. Note the famous, if somewhat gloomy, inscription on the tower's sundial: *vulnerant omnes*, *ultima necat*, referring to the hours – 'each one wounds, the last one kills'. Inside, there is more good sculptural work, notably on the bishop's chair, supported by a figure the locals call 'Samson'; they say if you pull his nose you will grow strong, and you can bet all the aspiring Basque barrel-lifters and wagon-pullers stop in to visit. The **Château d'Urtubie** was the home of the medieval viscounts of the Labourdan. The castle in its present incarnation dates from the 1340s, though each century until the Revolution added its bits and pieces; Wellington made it his headquarters briefly in 1814. The interior has some impressive 17th- to 18th-century furnishings, and a fine set of Flemish tapestries.

Château d'Urtubie t 05 59 54 31 15, www.chateaudurtubie. net; open mid-Mar–Oct daily 10.30–12.30 and 2–6.30; mid-July–Aug daily 10–30–6.30

From the village, a winding road leads up to the pilgrimage chapel of **Notre-Dame-de-Socorri**, with views over the mountains; it's a lovely spot for a picnic (though it may be disconcerting to know that nearly all the souls sleeping in the chapel's oak-shaded cemetery were victims of cholera epidemics).

A booming resort and the border crossing-point into Spain, **Hendaye** is divided into two distinct units, the old town and **Hendaye-Plage** on the coast. Hendaye's border location on the River Bidassoa puts it in the news every century or so. There is a small, uninhabited island in the Bidassoa called the **Ile des Faisans** (also known as Ile de la Conférence) that belongs to neither country; a traditional meeting place for kings and ministers since the 1400s, it is still under an unusual joint administration – the Spanish watch over it from February to July, the French the rest of the year. Here in 1526, King François I was returned after a year of imprisonment, when he was captured in battle at Pavia, Italy, by the Spanish King and Holy Roman Emperor Charles V. In 1659, the Treaty of the Pyrenees was signed here, and the following year representatives of both sides came back to plan the marriage of Louis XIV and Maria Teresa. A special pavilion was erected for the occasion and decorated by Velázquez – who caught a bad cold doing the job, which eventually killed him. In October 1940, Hendaye's train station was the scene of the famous meeting between Hitler and Franco. Hitler had come down in his private rail car to bluster the Caudillo into joining the war; later he said he would rather have his teeth pulled out than talk to such a stubborn character again.

The **beach** is long and broad, though as a resort Hendaye can't match the charm of the other towns along the Côte Basque. The old town offers nothing particularly special to draw you out of your way, and the beach area is a bland place lined with old villas, gradually being replaced by concrete hotels, the preserve of family vacations. Occasionally, tours are offered at the **Château Antoine d'Abbadie**, an eccentric Disneyland-Gothic castle set on a hill at the southern end of the beach. It was built by Viollet-le-Duc for an Irish-born traveller son of a Basque family named Antoine d'Abbadie who spent a lot of time in Ethiopia; there's a large collection of mementoes from that country, an observatory and **Le Domaine**, an exotic 110-acre park. The villa is covered with inscriptions in Amharic and Gaelic.

Looking over into Spain, you can practise rolling your Spanish 'r's on the town of Fuenterrabia. Spain announces itself even before you get there, with the striking Baroque bell tower of the town's church, visible from the beach at Hendaye. It's a beautiful village, full of flowers and brightly painted houses, and if you want to press on further the big resort of **San Sebastián**, the Spanish Biarritz, is just down the coast.

Château Antoine d'Abbadie
t 05 59 20 04 51; open for guided visits Feb–May and Oct–mid-Dec Mon–Sat 2–5; June–Sept Mon–Fri 10–11.30 and 2–6; unaccompanied visits at lunchtime and weekends 2–6; adm

Le Domaine
www.academie-sciences.fr/abbadia.htm

Market Days in Hendaye

Hendaye: Wednesdays and Saturdays.

Where to Stay and Eat around Urrugne and Hendaye

Urrugne ⊠ 64122
Chez Maïté, Pl de la Mairie, t 05 59 26 14 62. Try fish, *poulet basquaise* and a choice of very special home-made desserts. There are cheap set menus, but it's worth paying a little more for the specialities *à la carte*. Menus €25–33 and à la carte for €35–40. Closed Sun eve, and Mon mid-Sept–April.

Hendaye ⊠ 64700
Rather less attractive than Biarritz or St-Jean, Hendaye is correspondingly less posh.
***Hôtel Serge Blanco, Bd de la Mer, t 05 59 51 35 35, *www.thalassoblanco. com* (€€€€–€€€). Named after the famous Basque rugby star who is the

(i) **Hendaye >>**
12 Rue des Aubépines, t 05 59 20 00 34, www.hendaye.com; open July and Aug Mon–Sat 9–7.30, Sun 10–1; Sept–June Mon–Fri 9–12 and 2–6

proprietor and whose empire features a thalassotherapy centre, gym, pool and restaurant on the beach. *Closed most of Dec.*

**Lafon, 99 Bd de la Mer, t 05 59 20 04 67, is a hotel (€) that serves menus at €17–23. There's also a snack bar. *Open Easter–Oct.*

**Santiago, 29 Rue Santiago, t 05 59 20 00 94 (€). One of the least

expensive hotels with a garden, bar and restaurant. *Open Mar–Oct.*

Hondarribia (Spain)

Parador El Emperador, Plaza de Armas del Castillo, Hondarribia, Spain, t 00 34 943 64 55 00, *www.parador.es* (€€€€). An option over the border. This *parador* is lovely, though expensive, and in a 16th-century castle, the Palacio de Carlos Quinto.

The Labourd Interior: Around La Rhune

The name of La Rhune, westernmost monument of the Pyrenean chain, comes from the Basque *larrun*, or pastureland. It's full of cows and sheep all right, just as it has been for the last few millennia. The tracks around its slopes have been one of the main Basque smugglers' routes for centuries. A Basque tale has it that La Rhune was once covered in gold. Some evil men came to take it away; they cut down the trees and burnt them to get at it, but the gold all melted and flowed away. The mountain's summit also had a reputation as an *akelarre*, a ritual ground for witches and sorcerers; up until the 18th century the mayors of the villages around it always paid a monk to live on top as a hermit for a term of four years, to keep the witches away and to pray for good winds.

Ascain and Sare

Coming in from Hendaye or St-Jean, the first of the villages below La Rhune is **Ascain**, with its landmark three-arched medieval bridge over the Nivelle, and a 16th-century church on its lovely square. You can also learn about cider-making with tastings and visits to the cellars at **Cidrerie Txopinondo**. From here a hiking trail leads up to the 892m/2925ft summit of La Rhune, or else you can take the D4 up to the Col de St-Ignace, where there is another trail and also an old, open tramway to the top, the **Petit Train de la Rhune**.

In Neolithic times, La Rhune was a holy mountain, as evidenced by the wealth of monuments around its slopes. The rites of the ancient Basque religion were usually celebrated on mountain tops, hence their reputation in Christian times as haunts of sorcerers. You'll need a *série bleue* map and a day's hiking (at least) to find the monuments; there are eight small stone circles around a place called the **Crête de Gorostiarria**, and several dolmens and circular tumuli on the northern and western slopes. On the slopes of La Rhune towards Sare, the easiest to find are the four dolmens at a farm called **Xominen**, just off the Col de St-Ignace; further away at

Cidrerie Txopinondo
t 05 59 54 62 34, www.txopinondo.com,; open mid-June–mid-Sept Tues–Sat 10–12 and 3–7

Petit Train de la Rhune
t 08 92 39 14 25, www.rhune.com; open mid-Mar–Sept daily, Oct–early Nov Wed–Sun; closed hols. Departs every 35 mins in July and Aug from 8.30am, at 10am and 3pm, otherwise in accordance with numbers and the weather

the **Aniotzbehere** farm are two more. The northern side of the
Pic d'Ibanteli has four of them.

Just beyond the pass lies **Sare**, one of the true capitals of the
Basque soul. For its isolation and its traditionally independent
ways, people jokingly call it the 'Republic of Sare'. Since the 1400s,
the republic was one of the main centres for what the Basques call
gabazkolana, or 'night work' – smuggling. Folks on both sides of the
border never really saw the logic of paying duties on moving their
flocks around to French and Spanish foreigners. Smuggling sheep
and cows gradually led to other things too. The French authorities
usually treated all this with commendable humanity. The story is
still told of a zealous customs man, just arrived from Alsace in the
1920s, who shot a local man in the leg while he was taking some
cows over the slopes of La Rhune. His superiors went to the mayor
of Sare and to the man's family to explain the situation and
express their regrets, and then sent their officer over to the hospital to make his apologies. In 1938 and 39, Sare's night workers
found a more rewarding if less lucrative business – helping their
countrymen from the Spanish side escape Franco's troops; a few
years later, they were doing great work smuggling Allied pilots and
spies back the other way.

Sare's **church** is a wonderful example of the traditional Basque
style, with its three levels of wooden balconies; memorials inside
include the tombs of one of the early figures of Basque literature,
the 17th-century Pierre Axular. More than most villages, Sare has
retained a number of fine **town houses** with carved lintels, both in
the village and in the *quartier* of Lehenbizkai to the south – in the
Basque country, outlying hamlets are considered as 'quarters', or
neighbourhoods of the main village.

South of town, a side road off the D306 takes you to the **Grottes
de Sare**, with Palaeolithic drawings largely destroyed by vandals in
1918; it's said that you can go in here and find your way out at the
Cuevas de Bruja, across the border in Spain, but no one has tried it
lately. There's also a museum on site with mostly prehistoric finds,

Grottes de Sare
*t 05 59 54 21 88; open
Feb school hols–Mar
2–5; April–June and
Sept 10–6; July and Aug
10–7; Oct 10–5; Nov and
Dec 2–5; closed
Christmas Day and Jan;
adm; guided tours and
sound and light show*

The *Pottok*

It has a face that would make you suspect there was a camel somewhere in the family tree – but a
sweet face just the same, with big soft eyes and a wild shaggy mane. It is quite shy, hiding out on the
remotest slopes of the western Pyrenees, but it's not afraid of you; come too close and you'll get a
bite to remember. The *pottok* is the wild native pony of the Basque country. They've been around for
a while; drawings of *pottoks* have been found in the prehistoric caves up in the Dordogne.

Though they're hard to catch, people have been molesting the poor *pottoks* for centuries. A century
ago, they were shipping them to Italy to make salami, or to Britain to pull mine cars, a dismal task for
which their strength and small size made them perfectly adapted. Annual horse fairs took place in
the villages of Espelette and Hélette. Business was so good that the unfortunate *pottoks* were on the
road to extinction only a few decades ago. Then, a famous mayor of Sare, the late Paul Dutournier,
stepped in, and got the government to set up a reserve for them on the slopes of La Rhune.

Animal park
t 06 15 06 89 51,;
open Easter–October
daily 10–7

**Museum on the
gâteau Basque**
t 05 59 54 22 09,
www.legateaubasque.
com; open Easter–Sept
afternoons

Basque house
t 05 59 85 91 92,
www.ortillopitz.com

and outside there are reconstructed dolmens, cromlechs and tumuli. Sare also offers a domestic **animal park** for the kids; a **museum on the gâteau Basque** – learning how it was made then and now including tastings; and a traditional **Basque house** presenting the history and traditions of the Basque people . The D306 continues on to the Col de Lizarrieta and the Spanish border on its way to Pamplona.

Saint-Pée-sur-Nivelle and Ainhoa

In the late 1500s many gypsies and converted Muslims fleeing from Spanish persecution took refuge in the Labourd. In that most credulous of ages, all manner of stories about sorcerers and heathen rituals started circulating. The trouble began in 1609, started not by the Church's Inquisition, but by the Parlement de Bordeaux. A lawyer named de Lancre was sent, and like most professional witch-hunters this one revealed himself as a murderous psychotic. De Lancre installed himself in **Saint-Pée**'s château, and soon accused the baroness herself of forcing him to participate in a black Mass, where the Devil himself was present. With authority from the king, de Lancre started a reign of terror that lasted three years. Relying largely on the testimony of children and tortured women, he had several hundred people condemned to the stake over the next three years. When he started barbecuing parish priests, too, the Bishop of Bayonne finally put an end to it.

Ainhoa, one of the southernmost of all *bastides*, was founded in the days when the English were fighting against the Navarrese for control of this disputed region. A 13th-century Navarrese baron started it, not only to keep the English out, but with the intention of charging tolls and otherwise making money off pilgrims to Compostela. Despite the straight streets, Ainhoa is another lovely *Labourd* village with many old houses – note the lintel over the door of the **Maison Gorritia** on the main street, telling how a mother built it in 1662 with money sent home by her son in the West Indies. For a pleasant if steep walk, take the path up to the pilgrimage chapel of **Notre-Dame-de-Aranzazu**, with panoramic views over the valley.

Espelette
www.espelette.fr

From either St-Pée or Ainhoa, the next step is **Espelette**, the village famous for its red peppers; in the late summer you'll see them hanging everywhere. You can learn all about them at a permanent exhibition in the Chateau. Here too are many attractive old houses, a church with a Baroque altarpiece, and an interesting cemetery full of discoidal stones; you might note an odd modernistic one, marking the tomb of a local girl, Agnes Souret, who became the first Miss France. There is now an exhibition to her, again at the Château, and also one to local naturalist Père Armand David, a regular traveller to China.

(i) **St-Pée-sur-Nivelle**
Pl du Fronton, t 05 59 54 11 69, www.saint-pee-sur-nivelle.com; open summer Mon–Sat 9.30–12.30 and 2–6

(i) **Ascain** >
Rue Ernest Fourneau, t 05 59 54 00 84, out of season t 05 59 54 68 34, www.ascain-tourisme.fr; open Sept–June Mon–Fri 9–12.15 and 2–5.15; July and Aug Mon–Sat 9.30–12.30 and 2.30–7, Sun 10.30–1

(i) **Sare** >
mairie, t 05 59 54 20 14, www.sare.fr; open Jan–June and Sept–Dec Mon–Fri 9.30–12.30 and 1.30–5.30; July and Aug Mon–Fri 9.30–12.30 and 1–6.30, Sat 3–6.30

(★) **Euzkadi** >>

(★) **Arraya** >

Where to Stay and Eat around La Rhune

Prices for both rooms and meals in the Labourd will be a relief after the coast. And you'll never be disappointed with the quality of either – in fact the modest joys of an old Basque country inn may be one of the major reasons for coming here.

Ascain ⊠ 64310

**Du Pont d'Ascain, Route de St-Jean-de-Luz, t 05 59 54 00 40, www.charmehotel.com (€€). Rooms overlooking the Nivelle and its bridge and a delightful restaurant with a garden terrace: piperade and other dishes. Menus €18–35. Open daily mid-Mar–mid-Nov.

*Achafla Baïta, Route d'Olhette, t 05 59 54 00 30 (€). Out in the peaceful countryside. There is also a good restaurant with lots of fish in a variety of sauces, from cèpes to beurre blanc. Menus €11–33. Closed Sun eve, Mon eve and Tues eves in winter plus mid-Nov–mid-Dec.

Sare ⊠ 64310

In the Labourd, hotels tend to be sweet and simple, with immaculate rooms in white traditional buildings with red shutters and oak beams. Sare provides a bewildering choice of these, all wonderfully inviting.

***Arraya, Place du Village, t 05 59 54 20 46, www.arraya.com (€€€–€€). Quite expensive for the area, but with a memorable restaurant. Menus are reasonable; might want to surrender a little more for specialities such as fried trout with ham and garlic vinegar and crab ravioli. Menus €21–31. Closed Nov–March.

**Pikasseria, just outside Sare at Lehembiscay, t 05 59 54 21 51 (€). Also has a good restaurant. Restaurant closed early Nov–Mar and Wed, except July and Aug.

Col de St-Ignace, at the pass on the D4 near the Rhune cable car, t 05 59 54 20 11, is a simple restaurant. Menus €13–25. Open 1 April–11 Nov.

Les Trois Fontaines, Col de St-Ignace, t 05 59 54 20 80. A country auberge near the cable car. There's a charming terrace and garden, serving Basque specialities. Menus €12–23.

Ainhoa ⊠ 64250

***Ithurria, Place du Fronton, t 05 59 29 92 11, www.ithurria.com (€€). A large Basque house with pool, sauna and gym, and a celebrated restaurant, featuring dishes such as pigeon with garlic, and local foie gras. Menus €32–48. Restaurant closed Wed plus Thurs lunch except July and Aug. Closed Nov–Easter.

**Oppoca, Place du Fronton, t 05 59 29 90 72, www.oppoca.com (€). On the main street of this pretty village, in a restored 17th-century post house. Lovely rooms, some furnished with antiques. There is also a fine restaurant with a terrace, serving seafood and meat. Menus €18–50. Closed mid-Nov–20 Dec; restaurant is also closed Sun eve and Mon.

Espelette ⊠ 64250

**Euzkadi, 285 Karrika Nagusia, t 05 59 93 91 88, www.hotel-restaurant-euzkadi.com. Worth travelling out of your way for, even in an area that is so rich in good restaurants. There are pleasant rooms with a small pool and tennis courts, and a remarkable restaurant where the chef is passionate about traditional Basque recipes and traditions. Some of the house specialities are things you won't see anywhere else, such as axoa, a stew of veal and peppers, and tripoxa, a black pudding in a pepper and tomato sauce. Menus €17–33. Closed Nov–mid-Dec; restaurant also closed Mon and Tue except July and Aug.

The Valley of the Nive

The little river that comes to such a handsome end among the quays and half-timbered houses of Bayonne has a long way to go before it reaches that city. Starting in the Spanish Pyrenees, it opens out into a narrow valley that cuts a diagonal swath across the Basque country. The D932/D918 that follows it is the high street of the Labourd and Basse-Navarre.

Hasparren to St-Etienne

From Bayonne, an alternative route to the D932 into the heart of the Basque country is the D22, the **Route Impériale des Cimes**, a beautiful road over the hilltops that was built in the time of Napoleon. It will take you to Hasparren, a grey, hard-working town where there is an unusual Roman altar behind the church. Nearby La Bastide-Clairence was founded by the king of Navarre in 1314; settled by Gascons, it long remained an ethnic enclave among the Basques. Just outside the village is a Jewish cemetery, from the community of Spanish refugees that formed here in the 1600s.

Southeast of Hasparren, near the village of St-Esteben, the

Grottes d'Isturitz et d'Oxocelhaya
*t 05 59 29 64 72,
www.grottes-isturitz.
com; open Mar– May
plus Oct and Nov daily
2–5; June–Sept daily
11–12 and 2–5; July and
Aug daily 10–1 and 2–6;
guided tours and
workshops on Wed for
adults and children*

Grottes d'Isturitz et d'Oxocelhaya are one of the most important prehistoric sights of this region; tools, paintings and other relics, including a musical instrument, have been found here going back some 40,000 years. Most of these have been spirited off to museums though, and visitors will have to content themselves with a look at the underground stretch of the River Arbéroue, and some exceptional cave formations.

On the main road, the D932 up the Nivelle valley, the first big village is **Ustaritz**, once the meeting place of the Biltzar. Next comes **Larressore**, known for the manufacture of *makilas*, and then the biggest village of the interior, **Cambo-les-Bains**. The name of this genteel spa seems to come from a Roman army camp; locals called the site 'Caesar's camp' long ago. The spa grew up in the 16th century, and became briefly fashionable when Napoleon III and Eugénie visited from Biarritz. The Prince of Wales (Edward VII) also liked to drop in during his Biarritz holidays to see a legendary *pelote* star named Chiquito de Cambo play. Cambo's attraction is the **Villa Arnaga**, the home of dramatist Edmund Rostand, who came here in the 1900s to treat his pleurisy at the baths . The

Villa Arnaga
*t 05 59 29 83 92,
www.arnaga.com; open
April–Sept 10–12.30 and
2.30–7; Oct 2.30–7; Mar
Sat and Sun 2.30–6;
guided tours of garden
in July and Aug, Mon
4.30 and Tues 11*

Irouléguy

From the sunny Palaeozoic Basque highlands come the red, rosé and white wines of Irouléguy, the wine that 'makes girls laugh'. Tucked in sheltered pockets in the mountains, and trained on vertical espaliers to protect the vines from frost, the once vast number of grape varieties has been limited since 1952, when Irouléguy was given its AOC status: cabernet (or *acheria*, 'fox' in Basque) and *tannat* for reds, and *courbu* and *menseng* for whites. Try the generous, sombre red Domaine de Mignaberry, the leading label produced by the co-operative **Maîtres Vignerons du Pays Basque** in St-Etienne-de-Baïgorry (**t** 05 59 37 41 33, open Mon–Sat 9–12 and 2–6, Sun also in summer) or the co-operative's fine fresh rosé, Les Terrasses de L'Arradoy. Of the independent growers, **Domaine Brana**, 3 bis Av du Jaï Alaï, St-Jean-Pied-de-Port (**t** 05 59 37 00 44, *www.brana.fr*, open July–15 Sept daily 10–12 and 2.30–6.30), has bottled some excellent, peppery reds; **Domaine Ilarria**, in Irouléguy (**t** 05 59 37 23 38, call ahead to visit) produces a lovely rosy rosé.

house contains mementoes from his life; the real attraction how-ever is the splendid 18th-century-style French garden.

After Cambo, the foothills begin rising steadily. Nearby off the D918 is the sweet tiny village of **Itxassou**, famous for cherries. From here, through the hamlet of Laxia, a steep and difficult road can take you to the summit of 918m/3,010ft **Artxamendi** on the Spanish border, another ancient holy place. Besides a number of natural wonders, including waterfalls, small herds of *pottok* and rock needles, this 'mountain of the bear' has evidence of occu-pation ranging from long-abandoned iron mines and shepherds' huts to Neolithic dolmens and cromlechs.

From here, you cross the ancient boundary from the Labourd into Basse-Navarre. The next villages down the valley are **Bidarray** and **Ossès**, centres of a rich rolling country known for its *pur brebis*. Their prosperity 300 years ago has given both a number of fine houses, many with 17th-century inscriptions. Bidarray has a grace-ful medieval bridge, the Pont d'Enfer, and a rare 12th-century church. If medieval churches are rare in these parts, it is only because of Basque tidiness; just as families rebuild their houses every few centuries on the same site, so they cannot stand to see an old church or any other building looking frowzy. Ossès's church, St-Julien, was rebuilt by the villagers in the 1500s, with a built-in *fronton*, a later Baroque façade and a rich interior decoration. The hills around the nearby village of **St-Martin-d'Arossa** offer three examples of another peculiarity of the Basque country, the *gaztelu*. This is an earth- and rock-built hilltop fortress dating from the Iron Age; no one knows if the locals or invading Celts built them.

St-Etienne-de-Baïgorry, the principal centre for the production of Irouléguy wine, is really a collection of villages around the Nive and its branch, the Nive des Aldudes. St-Etienne, the centre, has another lovely humpbacked medieval bridge, and the château of the feudal *seigneurs*, the Etxauz.

09 | The Pays Basque | The Valley of the Nive

Market Days in the Valley of the Nive

Hasparren: Every other Tuesday, and Saturday for farm produce.

Where to Stay and Eat in the Valley of the Nive

Cambo-les-Bains ✉ 64250

***Domaine de Xixtaberri, Quartier Hegala in the hills above Cambo, t 05 59 29 22 24 34, www.

xixtaberri.com (€€). Bright colourful rooms. A *ferme-auberge* with stunning views. Meals reserved for guests, usually organic produce. *Menu €22.*

**Bellevue, Rue des Terrasses, t 05 59 93 75 75 (€€). An old, pleasant establishment with a view, near the top of town. The restaurant serves menus costing €18–32. *Closed Mon and Sun eve plus early Jan–mid-Feb.*

**Hostellerie du Parc, Place de la Mairie, t 05 59 93 54 54, www.hotels-basque.com (€€), in the lower part of town, offers 10 pretty rooms, a little garden, and a reasonable restaurant.

ⓘ **Cambo-les-Bains** ›
Av de la Mairie, t 05 59 29 70 25, www.cambo-les-bains.net; open Mon–Sat 8.30–12.30 and 2–5; mid-July–mid-Sept also Sun 10–12.30

★ **Domaine de Xixtaberri** ›

ⓘ **Hasparren**
2 Pl St Jean,
t 05 59 29 62 02

⭐ **Hotel
Barberaenea >>**

ⓘ **Ustaritz**
Centre Lapurdi, t 05 59
93 20 81, www.ustaritz-
tourisme.com; open
daily 9–12 and 2–5.30

There is outside dining in summer.
Menus €17, only offered to guests.

****Chez Tante Ursule**, Bas Cambo, t 05
59 29 78 23 (€). Small rustic hotel with
a modern annexe. There is also an
excellent restaurant. Try the
pimentoes stuffed with *morue* or
salads with *foie gras* or *boudin noir.*
*Menus from €15. Closed last two weeks
in Nov, and mid-Feb–mid-Mar.*

Itxassou ✉ 64250

****Fronton**, Place du Fronton, t 05 59
29 75 10, www.hotelrestaurantfronton.
com (€€). The hotel of choice in the
village. The restaurant has a room
with a view, and specialities include
pipérade and *filets de canard aux
cerises. Closed Wed, plus Jan–mid Feb
and a week in Nov.*

Txistulari Hotel, direction St-Jean-
Pied-de-Port, t 05 59 29 75 09 (€).
Traditional Basque villa that has been
modernized. Well run and neat as a
pin. Nice terrace plus pool with lovely
views. Regional cuisine, popular with

the locals. *Menus €17–28 plus à la
carte; lunch weekdays €11. Closed Sun
even and Sat lunch in winter, and mid-
Dec–early Jan.*

****Etchepare Sallaberia**, Place de la
Mairie, t 05 59 29 75 14. *Menus €13–23.
Closed mid-Nov–Mar.*

Bidarray ✉ 64780

Hôtel Barberaenea, Place de L'Eglise,
t 05 59 37 74 86, www.hotel-
barberaenea.fr (€). Bidarray offers a
perfect setting, nestled in rolling hills
with mountain views, nothing but the
odd bleat or sheep's bell to break the
quiet. The hotel is at the top of the
village in the square opposite the
12th-century church. There are three
leafy terraces and the interior is a step
back in time; flagstone floors and
antique Basque furniture. The same
family has run an inn here since 1875.
Bedrooms are a good size,
comfortable and clean. The restaurant
serves traditional fare. *Menus €16–22.
Closed Nov–Feb.*

St-Jean-Pied-de-Port

⭐ **St-Jean-
Pied-de-Port**

This town's real name, in Basque, is Donihane Garazi. The French
name is even more curious, but port is an old mountain word for a
pass, and St-Jean, or Donihane, stands at the foot of the pass of
Roncevaux, the 'Gate of Spain' of medieval French legend and
poetry. The location has made it a busy place. From the 8th century,
Arab armies must have passed this way many times on their way
to raid France; Charlemagne and Roland came back the other way
to raid Spain, and pass into legend along the way. Pilgrims from all
over Europe came through on their way to Compostela, and
another famous visitor, Richard the Lion-Heart, put the original
town – now nearby St-Jean-le-Vieux – to siege in 1177. When he
took it, that most pitiless and destructive of warriors razed it to the
ground; the kings of Navarre refounded St-Jean on its present site
soon after.

Though it still holds four big fairs each year, just as in medieval
times, St-Jean today makes more of its living from visitors; it's the
main centre for mountain tourism in the Basque lands, and in
summer it can be quite a crowded place. Bars, restaurants and
souvenir shops pack the centre, along the D933 and the picturesque streets around the **Vieux Pont** over the Nive. Old houses
with wooden balconies hang over the little river, and facing the
bridge stands the church of **Notre-Dame**, originally built by Sancho

the Strong of Navarre in commemoration of the battle of Navas de Tolosa (1212), where the Christian Spaniards finally put an end to Muslim dominance of the peninsula. The current building is Gothic, rare in these parts, though it has been much reworked since. The old streets climb up from here to the house which the St-Jeanais have called the **Prison des Evêques**, and turned into a tourist attraction with art exhibitions and so on. The house in fact seems to have belonged to a merchant, and the unusual vaulted underground chamber may have been for storing his wares, like the similar cellars in Bayonne. The bishops who lived in the mansion above it *c.* 1400 weren't exactly kosher – supporters of the Antipope at Avignon during the great Schism – and the chains and shackles in the cellar wall were probably used by local authorities

Prison des Evêques
41 Rue de la Citadelle,
t 05 59 37 00 92; open
Easter–Oct daily
10–12.30 and 2–6.30

Roland the Rotter

All over the south of France, the very mountains and rocks carry the memory of Roland – the Brèche de Roland in the High Pyrenees, hewn with a mighty stroke of the hero's sword Durandal, or a cleft in a great boulder it was touched by the hoof of his horse. From France, his fame spread across Europe, remembered in everything from Ariosto's Renaissance epic *Orlando Furioso* to the ancient, mysterious statue of 'Roland the Giant' standing in front of the city hall in Bremen. But who is this Roland really?

Outside the *Chanson de Roland* and the other versions of the legend, information is scarce. The chronicler Eginhardt, writing *c.* 830, mentions a certain Roland, Duke of the Marches of Brittany, who perished in the famous ambush in the Pyrenees in the year 778, without according him any particular importance. Two hundred years later, this obscure incident had blossomed into one of the great epics of medieval Europe. Here is the mighty hero, with his wise friend and companion in arms, Oliver. He is the most *puissant* knight in the army of his uncle Charlemagne, come down from the north to crusade against the heathen Muslims of Spain. Charlemagne swept all before him, occupying many lands south of the Pyrenees and burning Pamplona to the ground before coming to grief at an unsuccessful siege of Zaragoza. On their return, Roland and Oliver, with the rearguard, are trapped at the pass of Roncevaux, the 'Gate of Spain', thanks to a tip from Roland's jealous stepfather Ganelon. Numberless hordes of *paynims* overwhelm the French; though outnumbered, they cut down Saracens by the thousand, like General Custer or John Wayne against the savage Injuns. Finally Roland, cut with a hundred wounds, sounds his horn Oliphant to warn Charlemagne and the main army, alas too far away to rescue them. In vain the dying Roland smites his sword against the rock to break it, meaning to keep it from the hands of the infidels. As he dies, the angels Michael and Gabriel appear to carry his soul to heaven (and as for his sword, though it isn't mentioned in the *Chanson de Roland*, he throws Durandal into the air and it lands in the rock of Rocamadour, an important pilgrimage site in the Lot).

History says it wasn't a Muslim horde at all, but rather the Basques who did Roland in. And why shouldn't they get their revenge on these uncouth Franks who were invading and devastating their lands, trying to force this democratic nation to kneel before some crowned foreign thug who called himself their king? We might excuse a people who did not even have a word in their language for 'king', if they were not much impressed either with Charlemagne or his duke. The exact process by which this affair metamorphosed into an epic will never be known, but tales and songs in the oral tradition must have spread and refined themselves constantly over those two centuries, until the caterpillar Roland of history re-emerged into the written word as the mythological butterfly of the *Chanson*. As in many epics from Virgil to *El Cid*, a modicum of political propaganda is involved. For the French, up in Paris, glorification of Carolingian imperialism provided poetic justification for the expansionist dreams of the medieval Capetian kings. And replacing the embattled Basque farmers with bejewelled infidel knights for an enemy makes perfect sense: the time of the *Chanson* also witnessed the beginning of the Crusades.

in the 18th century to lock up poor peasants who didn't pay their salt tax. If you climb to the top of the town for the view, you'll find the **citadel**, a castle last remodelled in the 17th century by Vauban.

Just east on the D933 stands St-Jean's original, **St-Jean-le-Vieux**. The town destroyed by the Lion-Heart has only the Romanesque tympanum of its church to remind it of its former importance. There are also scanty remains of a large Roman camp, including baths. There is a museum on site with items found during excavations. North of St-Jean-le-Vieux, on a height above the D933, a venerable stone pillar with a cross on top is known as the **Croix de Ganelon**, supposedly the spot where Roland's treacherous step-father was pulled apart by wild horses on Charlemagne's command.

South of St-Jean, the D933 leads down to the Spanish border and 16km beyond that, the cold, misty pass of Roncevaux itself. For an alternative, if you want to get really lost, take the D301 from St-Jean down to the pretty village of **Estérençuby**, hub of a wild maze of steep narrow roads and hiking trails around the border. With a good map, you can find your way to the abandoned **Château Pignon**, a battered old castle last rebuilt by Ferdinand of Aragon that saw trouble in every conflict up to the Napoleonic wars. Even better, take the D428 up to the Col d'Arnostéguy, passing the primeval beeches of the **Forêt d'Orion** in one of the remotest parts of the region; exactly on the border stands the mysterious **Tour d'Urkulu**, a circular platform of huge, well-cut stone blocks some 65ft (20m) in diameter. Some historians, for lack of a better explanation, suppose it to be the remains of a Roman victory monument, like the ones set up on the Mediterranean at La Turbie and Perthuis. It is just as likely, though, that it is far older; the surrounding slopes are littered with dolmens, cromlechs and other Neolithic remains, and arrowheads dated from the Bronze Age have been found on the site. Some have speculated that the name Urkulu, which has no meaning in Basque, might have something to do with Hercules.

Museum at St-Jean-le-Vieux
t 05 59 37 91 08; open mid-June–mid-Sept Mon–Thurs 2.30–6

Market Days in St-Jean-Pied-de-Port

Mondays.

Where to Stay and Eat around St-Jean-Pied-de-Port

St-Jean-Pied-de-Port ✉ 64220
Being a popular tourist base, St-Jean's hotel prices are substantially higher than the other villages nearby.

(i) **St-Jean-Pied-de-Port** >
Place Charles-de-Gaulle, t 05 59 37 03 57, www.terre-basque.com; open July and Aug Mon–Sat 9–7; Sept–June Mon–Sat 9–12 and 2–6; free guided tours of the town Mon and Fri am

***Les Pyrénées, Place Général de Gaulle, t 05 59 37 01 01, www.hotel-les-pyrenees.com (€€€–€€) has a restaurant that is one of the most esteemed culinary temples in all the Basque country. Hotel is a member of Relais and Châteaux and has a pool and Jacuzzi. People come from miles around for cooking that, while not notably innovative, brings the typical Basque-Gascon repertoire of duck, *foie gras* and game dishes to perfection; they're especially noted for their desserts. A gratifying menu (*exc* Sun) puts Les Pyrénées within the reach of most. *Menus €40–85. Closed Tues exc July–Sept. Closed 20 Nov–just before Christmas and most of Jan.*

Hôtel Central, Place Charles de Gaulle, t 05 59 37 00 22 (€€). Old family hotel and restaurant with views over the River Nive, which according to the fishing season yields such delights as salmon and eels for the table. *Menus €19–44. Closed Dec–Feb.*

**Ramuntcho, 1 Rue France, t 05 59 37 03 91 (€€–€). One of the nicest places to stay in the old town, just inside the Porte de France. Rooms have balconies and a view. The restaurant serves good simple dishes. *Menus €13–31. Closed Tues and Wed except July and Aug, and mid-Nov–after Christmas.*

**Hôtel des Remparts, Place Floquet, t 05 59 37 13 79, *www.touradour.com/hotel-remparts.htm* (€). A historic building dating from 1643 offering less expensive rooms. *Menus €14–19.*

Closed weekends Oct–April and Nov–mid-Jan.

Pecoïtz, t 05 59 37 11 88, in Aincille, just south of St-Jean-le-Vieux on the D118 (€). Rooms cheaper than anything in the town, a quiet and lovely setting, and a very good restaurant that does game dishes in season, *pouler basquais* and *confits. Menus €15–34. Closed Thurs eve–Sat lunch out of season and Jan–Mar.*

Estérençuby ✉ 64220

**Sources de la Nive, t 05 59 37 10 57 (€), is in Estérençuby, 11km south of town. Set among the mountain forests, next to the river, it offers all the calm you can stand, as well as a restaurant that serves *salmis de palombe* (don't ask where the dove came from), and other rural treats. There is a swimming pool. *Menus €14–30. Closed Tues in winter, and Jan.*

The Haute-Soule

By now, the mountains are getting taller and so are the roofs: steep slate ones become more common than the Roman tiles of the coast. From St-Jean-le-Vieux, the D18 will take you deeper into the remotest corner of the French Basque country, the beautiful, seldom-visited Haute-Soule, a 50km stretch of Pyrenees with scarcely more than 1,000 inhabitants. From the village of Mendive, an alternative route is the D117, narrow but marvellously scenic, passing near several peaks of over 910m/3,000ft. The only settlement it passes is **Ahusquy**, a former spa; from here trails lead into one of the largest of Pyrenean forests, the **Forêt des Arbailles**.

The D18/D19 is just as good, though more difficult, crossing three mountain passes before it arrives at **Larrau**, the closest thing to a village the Haute-Soule can offer. The GR 10, the hiking trail that runs the length of the Pyrenees, passes nearby, among many other trails, and if you have some time to spare there are a number of attractions: west of Larrau is a small ski station called **Les Chalets d'Iraty**, set amidst another lovely beech forest, the **Forêt d'Iraty**. This area is a major transit point for many kinds of migrating birds; serious birdwatchers come from all over to see them in autumn. Hunters come too, and some of them still follow the practice of trapping doves by the thousands in great nets – remarkably this is still legal in France. Netting birds is turning into a hot issue, and considerable hostility surfaces each year between hunters, birders, environmentalists and the local authorities.

Gorges d'Holcarte
t 05 59 28 51 28

Gorges de Kakouetta
t 05 59 28 60 83; open mid-Mar–mid-Nov daily 8am until dark

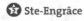 **Ste-Engrâce**

East of Larrau, the GR 10 leads you to the wild and spectacular **Gorges d'Holcarte,** a series of canyons explored for the first time only in 1908; now a trail runs along the top, with a cable footbridge across the gorge. Further east the GR 10 meets another, similar sight, the **Gorges de Kakouetta**, also accessible by car on the D113. Here too a trail has been laid out; there's a lovely waterfall at the end. The D113 continues to a dead end in the mountains, passing tiny **Ste-Engrâce**. This is one of the most isolated and tradition-bound of all Basque villages; the twisting road up to it was only built a decade ago. It is also the unlikely setting for one of the most fascinating medieval churches in the Pyrenees. Built in the 12th century, this cockeyed church sits on a slope, tilted and asymmetric; pilasters added a century ago keep it from sliding away. The Romanesque tympanum shows the chrism, the monogram of Christ, in a circle supported by two flying angels – a remarkable example of the persistence of symbolism. Replace the chrism with a laurel crown and you have the emblem of the Roman Imperium from the time of Augustus. The carved capitals inside are painted in detail, as Romanesque sculpture was meant to be. One shows a pair of lovers; for lack of a better explanation they are said to represent Solomon and Sheba, accompanied by a medieval European's idea of what an elephant might look like; others seem to show Salome's dance and the three Magi. Behind the church is an old cemetery with some strange discoidal tombstones.

Heading north from the Haute-Soule, the D26/D918 follows the valley of the Saison (or Gave de Mauléon, depending to whom you're talking), a stream popular with canoeists. The valley is a rich land, thick with tiny villages of which the largest is **Tardets**. The

Musée Agro-Pastoralisme
t 05 59 28 74 62; open July and Aug

Musée Agro-Pastoralisme at Tardets focuses on local rural life and its shop sells regional produce. **Ordiarp** has an interesting Romanesque church and cemetery in a pretty setting. There are caves with prehistoric paintings around Ossas and Camou, but they are currently closed to the public. The peculiarity of this area is its large number of *gaztelu*; good examples can be found near the villages of Aussurucq, Ideaux-Mendy, Etchebar (an especially impressive one with three circuits of fortifications), Alçay and Ordiarp; this must have been as hot a border region in the Bronze Age as it was in the time of Louis XIII. The **Centre Interactive d'Evocation des Chemins de St Jacques** tells pilgrims' tales, has information on Romanesque architecture, and initiates visitors into Souletine legends, dances and songs.

Centre Interactive d'Evocation des Chemins de St Jacques
t 05 59 28 07 63; open mid-June–mid-Sept Mon–Fri 10.30–12.30 and 4–7

East of Tardets, the D918 takes you to the villages of **Aramits** and **Arette**. The former is the home of Dumas's musketeer Aramis; there have always been some people here who won't admit he's a fictional character. The latter is largely new, rebuilt after a surprise earthquake in 1967. At Aramits you can visit a reconstructed

Shepherd's hut
t 05 59 88 95 38, July and Aug Thurs 5–7

Moulin d'Arette
t 05 59 88 90 82, www.valleedebaretous.com; guided visits July and Aug Wed 6pm,;otherwise call

shepherd's hut and see how he spent his time in the mountains. Then at the tourist office in Arette there is a permanent exhibition on a shepherd's life and the forest and at the **Moulin d'Arette** you can learn what the miller got up to.

The Inner Reaches of the Soule: Mauléon

At first glance, the temptation to leave this grey industrial town immediately might be irresistible. But hang around a while; Mauléon, the town of the evil lion (*mauvais lion*), has character. They make furniture, sheep's milk cheese and fabrics here, too, but everyone knows Mauléon as the world capital of the espadrille. And even though most of these classic French summer sandals may be produced in Asia these days (what isn't?), Mauléon's little factories still do their best to keep competitive. The capital of the Soule is a proper Basque village with its working clothes on, that's all.

Château d'Andurain du Maytie
1 Rue Jeu de Paume, t 05 59 28 04 18; open 1 July–20 Sept Fri–Wed, visits 11–12 and 3–5.30; closed Sun am; adm

Château Fort
for information call tourist office, t 05 59 28 02 37; open 15 June–15 Sept daily 11–1.30 and 3–7; adm

To prove its Basqueness, there is the busy and famous *fronton* right in the centre, on the park called Les Allées. Mauléon's château faces it, the **Château d'Andurain du Maytie**, also known as the Hôtel du Maytie. This stern yet graceful building was erected in the early 1600s by a local boy who became bishop of Oloron-Ste-Marie in nearby Béarn. It is still in the original family; highlights are the Renaissance fireplaces and the grand oaken carpentry that holds up the steep roof, designed by a shipwright. Old Mauléon climbs precipitously up to the town's other castle, the **Château Fort**. There has probably been a castle on this site for at least 3,000 years; this latest version dates from the 1300s, rebuilt after Richard the Lion-Heart chased out the French viscount and wrecked the place in 1261. Mauléon and the castle remained English until 1449, when the viscount of Béarn seized it. In 1642 Richelieu ordered it destroyed, but before the work was done he changed his mind and ordered it rebuilt, and sent a bill for 130,000 livres to the Mauléonais, causing a fierce but short-lived fracas called the Revolt of Matalas. A tour of the castle may be wonderfully evocative, but watch your step – parts of it could collapse at any minute.

St-Palais

The northeastern corner of the Basque lands is a humble country, where you'll see plenty of livestock and farming paraphernalia and little else. Its only centre is an equally humble though quite pleasant village with a memorable Friday morning market, St-Palais (*San Pelayo* in Basque). Once St-Palais had a viscount and a mint, and the village disputed with St-Jean-Pied-de-Port the honour of capital of Basse-Navarre; today it's best known as host to the annual *Festival de Force Basque* each August (and a lot of the

(i) **Mauléon >**
10 Rue J. B. Heugas,
t 05 59 28 02 37,
www.valleedesoule.
com; open Sept–June
Mon–Fri 9–12.30 and
2–6; July and Aug 9–1
and 2–7

(★) **Bidegain >**

(i) **St-Palais >>**
Pl Charles de Gaulle,
t 05 59 65 71 78,
www.tourisme-
saintpalais.com

Musée de Basse Navarre
Pl Charles de Gaulle,
t 05 59 65 71 78; open
Mon–Sat 9.30–12.30
and 2–6, Sun 10–12.30

Atelier de Tissage Ona Tiss
23 Rue de la Bidouze,
t 05 59 65 71 84; open
July and Aug Mon–Sat
9–12 and 2–5; Sept–
June Mon–Thurs 9–12
and 2–5

Market Days in the Haute-Soule

Tardets: Every other Monday, and every Monday in July and August.
Mauléon: Tuesday and Saturday mornings.
St-Palais: Fridays.

Where to Stay and Eat in the Haute-Soule

Mauléon ✉ 64130

Bidegain, Rue de la Navarre, **t 05 59 28 16 05 (€). This friendly, immaculate hotel across from the château is highly praised in a guidebook from the 1920s that we chanced upon at an old book sale. The praise is still deserved, and what's more the place doesn't seem to have changed all that much in 80 years. The restaurant is a real winner, with tables set in a sweet covered terrace looking out on to the delightful gardens. *Menus €11–33 plus à la carte.*

Barcus ✉ 64130

***Chilo, t 05 59 28 90 79, *www.hotel-chilo.com* (€€). Way out in the middle of nowhere, some 15km east of Mauléon, and it's worth the detour. This hotel has been in the same family for generations. Some rooms are fancy and furnished with antiques and there's a lounge with an open fire for colder evenings. There is also a pool where you can relax and enjoy views of the hills. There's a fine restaurant, with a garden terrace, which is especially good for fish, along with starters like a salmon terrine and a wide range of tempting desserts. *Menus €18–68. Closed Sun eve plus Mon and Tues lunch in winter, and 2 weeks in Jan and 2 in Mar.*

St-Palais ✉ 64120

Hôtel de Trinquet, t 05 59 65 73 13, *hoteltrinquet.saintpalais@wanadoo.fr* (€). Traditional hotel in the central square of this market town, with a classic wood-beamed restaurant. *Menus €12–28.*

farmers you'll see walking around on market day look as if they could be competitors).

From the old days all that survives is the mansion called the **Maison des Têtes** across from the chapel of St-Paul on Rue du Palais-de-Justice. A 17th-century house of a noble family, its façade is decorated with odd 'heads' including those of Henri IV and Jeanne d'Albret. Nearby, in the courtyard of the *mairie*, you can mull over St-Palais's history in the small **Musée de Basse Navarre**. You can see how Basque cotton and linen is made and buy some at the **Atelier de Tissage Ona Tiss**.

Béarn

From the earliest times, this isolated region of mountains and foothills has been above all a grazing land, its calendar punctuated by the annual descent and return of the shepherds and cowherds from the Pyrenean Vallée d'Aspe and Vallée d'Ossau. A cow is the proud device on Béarn's coat of arms, the symbol of this stalwart Pyrenean Ruritania. There isn't much else that is really distinctive about Béarn – what gives the region its identity is its long history as an independent state.

10

Don't miss

1 Roman mosaics
Sorde l'Abbaye **p.214**

2 'Salt City'
Salies-de-Béarn **p.216**

3 A king's castle and cliffs
Pau and the Boulevard des Pyrénées **p.224**

4 A Romanesque portal
Oloron Ste-Marie cathedral **p.232**

5 Spying birds of prey
Falaise aux Vautours **p.237**

See map overleaf

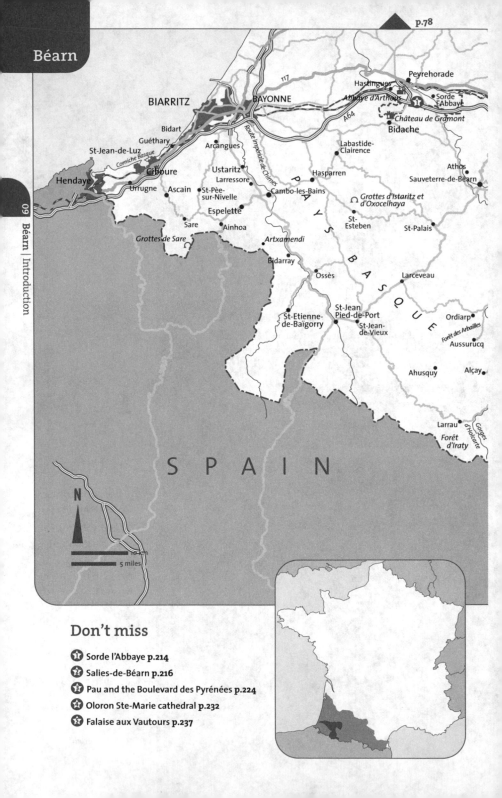

Béarn

117

BIARRITZ   BAYONNE

A64

Peyrehorade

Hastingues
Abbaye d'Arthous   Sorde
                            l'Abbaye
                    Château de Gramont
                    Bidache

Bidart
Guéthary   Labastide-
St-Jean-de-Luz   Clairence
        Corniche Basque Arcangues
                                        Athos
Ciboure   Ustaritz   Hasparren   Sauveterre-de-Béarn
           Larressore
Hendaye Urrugne Ascain St-Pée-   *Grottes d'Istaritz et*
                  sur-Nivelle Cambo-les-Bains *d'Oxocelhaya*
              Espelette   St-
              Sare   Ainhoa   Esteben   St-Palais
Grottes de Sare *Artxamendi*

                    Bidarray
                                Larceveau
                        Ossès

                                        Ordiarp
                St-Etienne- St-Jean   *Forêt des Arbailles*
                de-Baigorry Pied-de-Port   Aussurucq
                             St-Jean-
                             de-Vieux
                                          Ahusquy   Alçay

P A Y S   B A S Q U E

                                              Larrau
                                              Forêt   *Gorges*
                                              d'Iraty   *d'Holçarte*

S P A I N

N

5 miles

Don't miss

09

Béarn | Introduction

Route impériale de Chênes

Amou

Maumusson

Diusse

Aydie

Castelnau-Rivière-Basse

Madiran

Bellocq

Orthez

Morlanne

Arzacq-Arraziguet

Taron-Sadirac

Salies-de-Béarn

E80

Maslacq

Lacq

Sévignacq

Lembeye

9

13

134

943

Laàs

Mourenx

Navarrenx

Monein

Lescar

Pau

Morlaàs

Gurs

Lucq-de-Béarn

Lacommande

Mauléon

117

E80

117

Tarbes

L'Hôpital-Saint-Blais

B
E
A
R
N

PYRÉNÉES

Oloron-Ste-Marie

Gan

Bœil-Bezing

Nay-Bourdettes

Pontacq

ATLANTIQUES

Coarraze

Ossun

918

Tardets

Asasp

E07

937

Lestelle-Bétharram

Bartrès

Etchebar

St-Christau

Arudy

Grotte de Bétharram

St-Pé-de-Bigorre

Lourdes

113

Sarrance

Ste-Engrâce

Pic du Pibeste

Gorges de Kakouetta

Bedous

Laruns

Falaise aux Vautours

Accous

Eaux-Bonnes

918

Aucun

Argelès-Gazost

Pic d'Anie

Cette

Vallée d'Aspe

918

Lescun

Etsaut

Arrens

Borce

Pic de Gen

Gabas

Artouste

Cauterets

Gave d'Aspe

Pont-d'Espagne

Pic du Midi d'Ossau

Balaïtous

Marcadau

Parc National des Pyrénées

Vignemale

The scenery of Béarn is generally terrific, not only in the Pyrenees, but looking at them from the intensely green rolling foothills that make up most of the region. Most of Béarn is contained in the valleys of two gravelly, impetuous rivers, the Gave d'Oloron and the Gave de Pau; there is the thoroughly delightful spa town of Salies-de-Béarn; fine medieval monuments at Sorde, l'Hôpital-St-Blaise, Lescar, Oloron-Ste-Marie and elsewhere; and Jurançon and Madiran wines to sample. Pau, the resort of the Victorian British, has grown into one of the liveliest cities of the southwest. From

Pau's famous balcony, the Boulevard des Pyrénées, you can see natural wonders like the Cirque de Lescun and the wonderful region of mountain lakes and gorges around the Pic du Midi.

Along the Gaves de Pau and d'Oloron

Peyrehorade and Around

For centuries, this river town on the borders of Béarn, the Basque country and the Landes was Béarn's window on the world. As the point furthest inland at which the Gave de Pau is navigable, it was an important port until the 19th century. Now it's something of a time capsule, a peaceful and contented village that tourists pass through on their way to Biarritz or the mountains. Its **Château de Montréal**, whose particularly nasty noble family wrung every last penny out of the peasants until the Revolution, now houses the *mairie*. Peyrehorade has a pretty riverfront boulevard (boat excursions around the river in summer), and another castle, the ruined 13th-century **Château d'Aspromonte**, above the village.

Just west of Peyrehorade, the *bastide* of Hastingues was founded by Edward I when he passed through in 1289, and named after his seneschal of Gascony, John de Hastings. The seneschal's house, now in ruins, remains along the Rue Principale. South of Peyrehorade, off the D19, the department has restored the **Abbaye d'Arthous**, a once-wealthy foundation, begun in 1167, that spent most of the time after the Revolution in use as a barn. The church has some good carved capitals and modillons, along with a tympanum, recently restored; it shows an unusual subject, the *Adoration of the Magi*. It also houses a local museum.

Further south, on the borders of the Basque lands, is **Bidache**. By some quirk of history this village's lord owed no feudal allegiance to the viscount, the king of France, or anyone else, and Bidache remained practically independent up to the Revolution. Today, it offers the visitor the romantic ruined **Château de Gramont**.

Sorde-l'Abbaye and its Roman Villa

For one of the surprise attractions of this region, take the D29 east from Peyrehorade to Sorde, a tiny village on the Gave d'Oloron. The place has always been inhabited; prehistoric traces have been discovered in nearby caves, and Neolithic peoples added some curious earthworks outside the village at La Redoute. A wealthy Roman villa here metamorphosed into a **Benedictine abbey** during the Dark Ages. By the 12th century it was a major power in the area,

Abbaye d'Arthous
t 05 58 73 60 20; open 9–12 and 2–6; closed Tues and Jan; adm

Bidache
www.bidache.org

Château de Gramont
Currently closed for renovations, due to reopen in 2008

⭐ **Sorde Abbey**
t 05 58 73 09 62; open April–Oct Tues–Sun 10.30–12 and 2.30–6.30, guided tours; early Jan–Mar and Nov–mid-Dec Mon–Fri 9–11.30 and 1–5

Corisande

Diane d'Andouins, Comtesse de Guiche, was the daughter of the royal seneschal of Béarn. As a girl, she loved reading the chivalric romances popular in the 16th century, the sort of books parodied by *Don Quixote*. So much was she taken with these fond medieval fantasies that she began calling herself 'Corisande', after the heroine of one of the most famous romances, *Amadis de Gaule*.

As this Corisande grew up to become one of the celebrated beauties of the age, she never lost her sense of chivalric virtue. Up at court in Paris, she was pressed into service by Catherine de' Medici for her famous *bataillon volant* of charmers, girls sent to seduce the notables of France and influence them to support the queen's endless political intrigues. It didn't work out; the accounts suggest Corisande wasn't up to the ultimate sacrifice the job occasionally required.

When her husband, Philibert de Gramont, was killed in the Wars of Religion, Corisande retired to his castle at Bidache. Already celebrated for her virtue in Catherine's court, as well as for her considerable intelligence and grace, she now became something of a legend, sitting up in her castle like the Lady of Shalott. It proved irresistibly attractive to young Henri of Navarre, the young firebrand who had already put in a night's wenching in every town between Flanders and the Pyrenees. Henri polished up his manners and came to Bidache to court Corisande. Although perhaps never consummated, it was a relationship that changed history. French historians credit Corisande with civilizing the Gascon warrior, with giving him some lessons in tenderness and courtesy. The two became friends for life, and Corisande contributed sympathy, good advice – and a good deal of cash – all through the campaigns that brought Henri IV to the throne of France.

owning vast lands, mills, forts and villages all around the Pays d'Orthe and beyond. The huge **church**, begun in the late 13th century, is as rough and crumbly as an oyster shell outside. Inside, there is no pearl, but a strange confusion of styles. While building was under way, in about 1290, this part of Aquitaine came under the control of the French king – meeting the threat of the English and their new settlement at Hastingues. The style of the church also changed, from southern Romanesque (as in the chapel to the right of the altar) to northern Gothic (the chapel left of the altar).

In the jumble of buildings behind the church there are two things to see. First, the half-ruined **abbey buildings**, in a picturesque state of dilapidation; and secondly, the separate **abbot's residence**. The clues to what's hidden inside are in the old abbot's gardens – walls and pavements carefully excavated, along with fragments of mosaic. The abbot's residence, in fact, occupies the central part of the ancient Roman villa. Such historical continuity is not unusual; through the end of the Empire and the onset of the Dark Ages, the Roman élite gradually and gladly put much of its wealth and property in the hands of the Church, a Church of their creation, and in which the élite's younger sons held the positions of power. Some of Sorde's abbots may well have been lineal descendants of the Roman family that built the villa. The guided tour includes the **baths** that have been excavated, along with the villa's residential quarters. Some contain mosaics with geometric and floral motifs, some with hunting scenes. Excellently preserved, they are some of the best **Roman mosaics** discovered in southern France.

Salies-de-Béarn

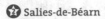 Salies-de-Béarn

'Salt City', they call it, and ever since Roman times an endless supply of the ever-popular NaCl has made this town's fortune. Salies may be the loveliest town in Béarn, a picture-postcard vision of steep-gabled houses overlooking the River Saleys. A mighty underground source, seven times saltier than the sea, once poured out enough water to make the whole area a saline swamp. Unsung engineers of the Bronze Age drained it for farmland, but it was probably the Romans who first found a way to put the waters to good use. Back at that remote date, life in Salies was probably much the same as documented in the 1500s: then nearly everyone lived from salt, collecting the water in great kettles, boiling it down, and carting the precious mineral off to the warehouse for their pay. Undercut by competition from Languedoc sea-salt in the 19th century, Salies found new life from the spring by becoming a spa. From the 1850s until the Second World War, Salies was in fashion with the Parisians; grand hotels, a Moorish-style bathhouse and even a casino were built.

Today the spa still does good business. And the Salies tourist office still extols the virtues of its waters, with their 'excitative, but non-aggressive' properties, especially good for arthritis, gynaeco-logical matters and underdeveloped children. Besides the sodium and chlorine they contain more magnesium than any other known spring in the world, a heavy load of sulphur, potassium and calcium, as well as bits of nickel, strontium, carbon, rubidium, boron, bromium, gallium and nearly everything else on the Periodic Table. There are veterinarians who will arrange a thermal cure to get your dog back into shape, or help its recuperation after surgery. The boosters have come up with a slogan for Salies tourism that might have been penned by Gertrude Stein: 'It's here; it's there ... it isn't anywhere else!'

From the Boar to the Baths

A walk through the old town, bordering the D933 that runs through Salies, is a delight. Start at the central Place du Bayaa, with the bronze boar's head of the salty **Fontaine du Sanglier**. An old legend of the founding of Salies had hunters on the track of this boar, who led them to the yet-undiscovered spring, where he was cornered and killed. The boar's motto is inscribed around the Salies coat of arms: *Si you nou y eri mourt arrès nou y bibéré* ('Had I not died here, none of you would live').

Near the fountain are two small museums: a folkloric **Musée des Arts et Traditions Locales** on Place du Bayaa and, on Rue des Puits-Salants, a 17th-century house that has been restored as the **Musée du Sel** where you can learn everything you ever wanted to know

Musée des Arts et Traditions Locales
t 05 59 38 00 33; open mid-May–mid-Oct Tues–Sat 3–6

Musée du Sel
same number and hours as above, shared ticket

about salt-making in the old days. Many of the old half-timbered houses on the surrounding streets still have the outdoor basins called *coulédés*, where they kept their salt.

The spa area is set in a park on the northern edge of town. Besides the *parfait*-striped Moorish bathhouse, there is the old casino, now a library, a Victorian bandstand, and the **Hôtel du Parc**, worth a look inside for its spectacular lobby, a tall skylighted court surrounded by mahogany-panelled galleries. Salies keeps its visitors busy: there is a miniature golf course in the park, a salt-water swimming pool at the bathhouse, and opportunities for riding, tennis and other sports; some of the streams in this area are good for trout and salmon fishing; the tourist office has all the details. There is also a 12-hole golf course, at the Hôtel Hélios.

Around Salies

Bellocq, north of Salies, is the oldest *bastide* in Béarn; its rugged castle, under restoration, was built in the 1200s and hardly changed after that. South of Salies, **L'Hôpital d'Orion** was a commandery of the Knights of St John (the Knights Hospitaller) and a stop along the pilgrims' route to Compostela. From this survives an unusual 13th-century church. Gaston Fébus stopped at an inn here in 1391, after hunting the woods around Sauveterre. While cleaning up for dinner, a servant poured cold water over his hands. The count turned white and fell into his chair; he died half an hour later, probably from a cerebral haemorrhage.

Sauveterre-de-Béarn

A *sauveterre*, in the Middle Ages, was supposed to be a place of peace, exempt from all the terrors of feudal warfare; all the local barons, counts and dukes would promise faithfully to leave it alone. To show just how successfully this worked in practice, here is Sauveterre-de-Béarn, with the most imposing fortifications of any town in the region.

Viscount Centulle IV gave this *sauveterre* its charter in 1080, and for the next two centuries it prospered greatly, as evidenced by the ambitious Romanesque church of **St-André**. There is some good sculpture here: a portal with Christ and the symbols of the Evangelists, and a few carved capitals.

Much of the walls survives, along with the gates and the huge bastion called the **Tour de Montréal**. The real attraction of Sauveterre, however, is its lovely setting on the wooded banks of the Gave d'Oloron, where you can see the town's landmark, a fortified, half-demolished medieval bridge called the **Pont de la Légende**. In 1170, the wife of Viscount Gaston V of Béarn, a Navarrese princess named Sancie, was charged with aborting her child. A trial by ordeal was decided, and Sancie was thrown from this bridge, tied hand and foot. She popped up like a cork and washed up on the bank 'three arrow shots downstream', as the chroniclers put it, and the judges were satisfied. There's a model of the village made from thousands of stones and animated by a sound and light show at the **Chapelle de Sunarthe**.

Chapelle de Sunarthe
t 05 59 38 58 65; call for times

Around Sauveterre-de-Béarn

Laàs, 9km up the Gave from Sauveterre on the D27, has an 18th-century castle set in a gorgeous park; it was meticulously restored by a gentleman named Serbat, who was president of the French antique dealers association. Part of it is now open as a **museum** containing a rich collection of tapestries and furnishings from the 16th to the 18th centuries. There is also a good number of historical curiosities: a beautiful 14th-century book of hours that belonged to the Dukes of Burgundy, Mary Queen of Scots' sewing scissors, and the bed Napoleon slept in the night after Waterloo. **Athos**, just northeast of Sauveterre along the Gave, is – could you doubt it? – the home of the first of the Three Musketeers; the village also has a pretty Gothic church.

Laàs museum
t 05 59 38 91 53; open July and Aug daily 10–7; May, June and Sept Wed–Mon 10–12 and 2–7; April and Oct Wed–Mon 2–7; adm

Another village on the Gave d'Oloron, **Navarrenx**, has fortifications as good as Sauveterre's. These, however, aren't medieval, but the first modern anti-artillery walls in France. An Italian engineer named Fabrizio Siciliano designed them in 1521; the last word in military architecture for their day, a century and a half later not even the great Vauban, Louis XIV's chief fortress-builder, could find anything to improve here. The walls were only tested once, when Protestant refugees gathered here and held off a Catholic army for two months in 1569. You can learn about the town's history at the **Arsenal**.

Arsenal
t 05 59 66 14 93; open all year

L'Hôpital-St-Blaise and its Moorish Church

Continuing down the Gave d'Oloron, you'll pass **Gurs**. This honest village has no touristic pretensions whatsoever; the big sign it has erected along the D936 spells out facts and figures – 'so that we remember'. In 1939, 30,000 Spaniards fleeing Franco's final victory were interned at a camp here; among them were many members of the International Brigade. A few years later, under the occupation, the camp held 30,000 Jews, most of them refugees from Germany. Most were shipped eastwards in 1944; those that died here are buried, along with many Spaniards, in the cemetery on the southern edge of town. It may be a discordant note in this serene countryside, but it is a memorable place to visit.

L'Hôpital-St-Blaise may be little more than a few houses in a forest clearing south of Gurs, but it is well worth a detour for one of the most unusual and beautiful churches in the southwest.

Built in the 12th century, **St-Blaise** was attached to a hospice for pilgrims going to Compostela. At first sight, the Greek plan with its central dome is enough of a surprise, but then you notice the delicate stone latticework that fills some of the windows, an art that was popular in Islamic Spain and North Africa. Inside, the Muslim influence is striking. Doubtless the architects came from Spain, working in the Mudejar style common there throughout the Middle Ages. They skilfully wove Andalucian elements into the Byzantine plan: lobed arches in the apse, and a wonderful dome made of four pairs of round arches, interlaced to form an eight-pointed star; this was probably inspired by the one in the mihrab of the Great Mosque of Córdoba. Among the few carved decorations, note one very un-Christian symbol, the Pythagorean pentagram on the left transept; the church seems to be designed according to the proportions of this figure. The people of the village have cobbled together an endearingly screwy home-made *son et lumière* to entertain you; just drop a coin in the box by the door.

Son et lumière
http://perso.orange.fr/
hopital-saint-blaise

From St-Blaise, you can follow the D25 across the Gave d'Oloron to the attractive village of **Lucq-de-Béarn**, which takes its name from a holy grove (*lucus*) of ancient times. Another 12th-century church here, St-Vincent, has some carved capitals bizarre even by Romanesque standards. The altar is a 4th-century sarcophagus, with reliefs of *Adam and Eve*, *Daniel in the Lions' Den*, the *Sacrifice of Abraham* and the *Raising of Lazarus*.

(i) Salies-de-Béarn >>
Rue des Bains, t 05 59 38 00 33, www.bearn-gaves. com; open Oct–May 10–12. and 2.30–5; June– Sept 10–1 and 3–7; July– Aug daily 10–1 and 3–7

(i) Peyrehorade >
Mairie, 147 Av des Evadés, t 05 58 73 00 52, www.peyrehorade.info; open Sept–June Tues–Sat 9.30–12.30 and 2–5.30; July and Aug until 6

Market Days in the Northern Gaves

Peyrehorade: Wednesdays.
Navarrenx: Wednesdays.

Where to Stay and Eat in the Northern Gaves

Peyrehorade ✉ 40300

***Central, Pl Aristide Briande, t 05 58 73 01 44, *www.hotel-le-central.fr* (€€). Opposite the village church; this well-kept hotel also has a restaurant – a simple, unpretentious room with nothing to offer but exceptional cooking, with treats like *pot-au-feu* with foie gras. *Menus €15–37. Open daily July–Sept. Other times closed Fri and Sun eves and Mon plus Xmas and 3 weeks in Feb/Mar.*

Restaurant La Pasta, on the road to Bidache, t 05 58 73 02 40. A good but basic pizzeria.

Salies ✉ 64270

Salies is the place to stay in this area, and there are plenty of choices.
**Hôtel du Golf, t 05 59 65 02 10, *www.hotel-restaurant-du-golf.com* (€€). A posh-looking place with reasonable rates, a golf course, pool and a good restaurant. *Menus €15–24. Closed 3 weeks over Christmas.*

*Hélios, Domaine d'Hélios, t 05 59 38 37 59, *www.golf-salies.com* (€). In the same complex as the **Hôtel du Golf**, renovated but less expensive, with a garden setting and use of the golf course. *Open all year.*

Municipal camp site, Camping. Mosqueros, t 05 59 38 12 94. Set in a lovely park with all the amenities. *Open April–mid-Oct.*

La Terrasse, Rue du Saleys, across from the church on Rue l'Oumé, t 05 59 38 09 83. For confits and suchlike, on a pleasant terrace overlooking the Saleys. *Menus €15–20. Closed Tues eve and Feb.*

(i) **Sauveterre-de-Béarn >**

Place Royale, t 05 59 38 32 86, http:// sauveterre.de.bearn. free.fr; open Nov–Mar Tues–Sat 10–12 and 2.30–5; April, May and Oct Mon 2.30–6, Tues–Sat 10–12.30 and 2.30–6; June–Sept Mon 3–7, Tues–Sat 10–1 and 3–7

(★) **La Belle Auberge >>**

(i) **Navarrenx >**

Pl des Casernes, t 05 59 38 32 85; same hours as Sauveterre-de-Béarn

Sauveterre-de-Béarn ✉ 64390

Municipal campsite, t 05 59 38 53 30. Pleasantly situated under the trees by the river.

L'Hôpital-St-Blaise

*Auberge de Lausset, opposite the church, **t** 05 59 66 53 03 (€). For a rural retreat amidst some delightful countryside, make sure that you stop at this little-visited hamlet. Or at least stop for lunch at this modest family-run inn; it offers real country cooking where trout, agneau and other local favourites hold a prominent place on the menu. *Menus €12 (weekday lunch), €15–26. Closed Mon and 3 weeks Oct plus 2 weeks Jan.*

Navarrenx ✉ 64190

***Hôtel du Commerce, Place des Casernes, **t** 05 59 66 50 16, *www.*

hotel-commerce.fr. This traditional Béarnaise house stands right in the heart of the town. The interior is modern and comfortable whilst keeping its rustic charm. *Menus €16–29. Closed from just before Christmas to Jan.*

Castagnede ✉ 64270

La Belle Auberge, 7km from Salies on D27, **t** 05 59 38 15 28 (€). This simple *auberge* has the best reputation in the area. There is a very pleasant annexe containing bedrooms, a large pool and garden but the real reason that people travel for miles to the middle of nowhere is to enjoy the wonderful food. Excellent value. *Menus €12–22. Closed Sun and Mon eves plus mid-Dec–31 Jan and 1–15 June.*

Orthez

After seeing half a medieval bridge in Sauveterre, you might like to have a look at a whole specimen. Orthez, capital of Béarn when Pau was still a mere village, is the place to go. Orthez owed its medieval prominence to Viscount Gaston VII (1229–90), who made it his capital. Gaston Fébus, who built up Pau, nevertheless spent much of his time here; Froissart, the chronicler of the Hundred Years War, came for a visit and wrote a glowing account of Fébus's wealthy and sophisticated court, with 'knights and squires coming and going, talking of arms and love'. Orthez was wakened from its medieval dream with a start in 1569, when Jeanne d'Albret's Protestant soldiers under Montgomery burned the place to the ground. Nothing has come along to disturb its peace since, and Orthez today with its 12,000 souls is as cheerful and contented a town as you'll find anywhere.

The Pont Vieux

Orthez's centre having moved away from the riverfront over the centuries, this beautiful fortified bridge is now hard to find – go to the end of Rue du Bourg-Vieux from the tourist office, and take a right into Rue des Aiguilletiers. Gaston Fébus built it, *c.* 1370, though what you see now was heavily restored a century ago; the bridge had been seriously damaged by Wellington's army in 1814. In medieval times, criminals were often tossed off this bridge. Note also the little window in the side of the central tower; this was medieval Orthez's garbage disposal system – everything was

Feasts and Terrors of Gaston Fébus

The viscount cuts a dashing figure in French history; perhaps his greatest virtue was to embody better than anyone else the strong and hearty medieval spirit that has nourished so many legends. A great and flawed character, born to fight and hunt and lord it over meaty banquets in the hall with troubadours and dogs lurking around the tables, Gaston Fébus was made for Hollywood. His honorific, from Phoebus Apollo, was conferred early on for his long blond hair, which flowed in battle or the chase like the rays of the sun. His Pyrenean domains of Foix and Béarn felt his strong hand for 48 years (1343–91), and even though Fébus abrogated the charter, the *For de Morlaas*, not even the commoners grumbled too much; the viscount quite capably maintained the peace and liberties of his lands in a bad time, playing off the French, the English and his treacherous brother-in-law on the throne of Navarre, and keeping the troubles of the Hundred Years War at bay.

Froissart, in Orthez, had a hard time finding out what had happened to the younger Gaston, the viscount's son. An 'old and distinguished squire' finally told him the story, how the viscount's wife had become estranged from him in a quarrel over money, and how she had gone to live with her brother, King Charles the Bad of Navarre. Young Gaston went to visit his mother, and when he was ready to return the king gave him 'a very fine little purse filled with a certain powder', explaining that it was a love potion – just sprinkle a little on the count's food, and he will have one desire only: to have his wife – your mother – back with him again. The youth believed everything, but back in Orthez his half-brother, the bastard Yvain, became curious about the purse and informed the viscount. Froissart recounts the scene in the great hall.

'Gaston, come nearer. I have something to say in your ear.' The young man came up to the table. The count gripped him by the chest and undid his tunic, then took a knife and cut the strings of the purse and held it in his hand.

Fébus sprinkled the powder on some bread and gave it to one of his greyhounds, which immediately rolled over and died. The viscount was barely prevented from slaying his son; instead he locked him up in the dungeon of the Tour Moncade.

Young Gaston was the viscount's only heir, and the barons of Béarn begged him to be merciful; even the pope at Avignon sent a cardinal to plead Gaston's case. Gaston, for his part, depressed and confused, said nothing, and refused to take the meals brought to him. One night the angry Fébus went down to the dungeon and touched the point of his dagger to his son's throat, saying 'Ha, traitor, why don't you eat?' He left the cell, not knowing that he had accidentally pierced a vein.

Gaston Fébus was never the same man after that; his last task on earth was to write a grim book of penitence and prayers called the *Livre des Oraisons*. When he died at l'Hôpital d'Orion, 11 years later in 1391, the first thought of every man present was for the continuity of the state – and for the vast treasure that was kept in the Tour Moncade. It was the loyal Yvain who took the initiative, seizing the viscount's ring and riding back to Orthez to take control of the fortress and the treasure. Yvain, who could not inherit either, ended up in Paris. Not long afterwards, dressed as a chained savage at a masque, his costume caught fire and he died a flaming torch before the eyes of the king and the court.

Museum of Protestantism in the Béarn
t 05 59 69 14 03, www. museejeannedalret. com; open July and Aug daily 10–12 and 2.30–6.30; rest of the year 10–12 and 2–6

simply tossed out into the Gave de Pau. The Protestants of 1569 expanded on the concept, using the window to dispose of all the town's priests and nuns.

In the centre of Orthez, a passageway off Rue du Bourg-Vieux leads to the tourist office, in the **Maison de Jeanne d'Albret**, a restored 15th–18th-century mansion built around a typical Béarnais *pigeonnier* and courtyard. Whether or not the countess actually did stay here is open to debate. As well as the tourist office, you'll find a museum of Protestantism in the Béarn. Beyond this, Rue du Bourg-Vieux changes its name to Rue Moncade, with

(★) **Auberge St-Loup** >>

(ⁱ) **Orthez** >
Maison Jeanne d'Albret, Rue du Bourg-Vieux, t *05 59 38 32 84,* www.marie-orthez.fr; *open June–Sept Mon 3–7, Tues–Sat 10–1 and 3–7; April, May and Oct Mon 2.30–6, Tues–Sat 10–12.30 and 2.30–6; Nov–Mar Tues–Sat 10–12 and 2.30–5*

Where to Stay and Eat in Orthez

Orthez ✉ 64300

**Auberge du Relais, just west of Orthez, on the D933 at Berenx, t 05 59 65 30 56, www.auberge-du-relais.com (€). In a rustic setting with a park and swimming pool; the restaurant has an outdoor terrace. *Menus €10–14. Closed Sat exc July and Aug plus Xmas and 3 weeks in Feb.*

**La Reine Jeanne, behind the tourist office on Rue du Bourg-Vieux, t 05 59 67 00 76, www.reine-jeanne.fr (€). Pleasant, simple air-conditioned rooms; the same can be said of the

restaurant. *Menus €16– 34. Closed 2 weeks Feb–Mar; restaurant closed Sun eve Oct–April.*

Auberge St-Loup, 20 Rue du Pont Vieux, t 05 59 69 15 40. Orthez's long-time favourite restaurant has had its cuisine revitalized by a new young chef. Duck is the star of the menu – as *confits, aiguillettes*, in pies and everything else you could do to a quacker; also some interesting seafood dishes and *côte de bœuf*. Summer dining is in a pretty garden courtyard; it's just across the river near the medieval bridge. *Menus €21–45. Closed Sun eve and Mon plus Nov.*

some of Orthez's oldest buildings, including the charming **Hôtel de la Lune**. A block away on Place St-Pierre, the town's main church, **St-Pierre**, barely survived the depredations of the Protestants. Most of what you see, including the bell tower, is 19th-century restoration, though some good original Gothic carvings remain on the capitals and portal.

The Tour Moncade

Further out, on the eastern edge of Orthez, Rue Moncade becomes the spine of another medieval bourg, one that grew up around the castle of the Béarn viscounts. All that's left of it, besides some bits of the outer wall, is the tall, five-sided keep, the Tour Moncade, along with the adjacent residence of the counts, including the *tinel* or great hall of Gaston Fébus.

The Tour Moncade is haunted, though not by Gaston or any of his family. The ghost is the Princess Blanche of Navarre; caught up in a dynastic struggle in the 1450s, she was imprisoned here until her death – some say she was poisoned. Today, from May–Sept, you can climb up it for a view of the green undulating countryside.

Up the Gave to Pau

If you follow the river, along the N117 or the A64 motorway, you'll run smack into an unexpected smear of industry around **Lacq**. The discovery of natural gas deposits here in 1951 sparked a little industrial boom that continues today. The earth might consider swallowing up nearby **Mourenx**, an industrial town laid out in 1957 and a good example of French planning at its most gruesome. A much prettier road, though slower, is the D9 through Maslacq, Mourenx and **Monein**, a village that still glories in the compliment of Henri IV, who called it the 'Paris of Béarn'. It isn't easy to see why, though you might stop to look at its Renaissance church. There are guided visits throughout the year; contact the tourist office at Pau.

From Monein, another lovely country road, the D34, leads up into the valley of the River Bayse. **Lacommande** was another foundation of the medieval knightly orders, like l'Hôpital d'Orion, a hospice for Compostela-bound pilgrims. The hospice and commandery survive here, along with their **church of St-Blaise**, a Romanesque building with rich carvings and a Moorish-vaulted chapel in the transept.

Lescar

Any time someone digs a hole in Lescar, something Roman turns up; the most important city of the region in Roman times, Civitas Beneharnum was razed to the ground by Norman raiders in the 800s, and only reappeared under its modern name two centuries later when a monastery was founded on the site. From mid-June to September the tourist office organizes a 5km walk evoking the Gallo-Roman period. Today, strikingly sited on a height over the valley of the Gave de Pau, Lescar is almost a suburb of Pau, though it is an island of grace and tranquillity in a built-up part of the valley.

Lescar's monument is its **cathedral**, begun as the abbey church in 1141. Much of the building has suffered changes, but the apse contains as complete a gallery of stone curiosities as any: lions and pussycats, a mermaid, serpents and many characters that can't be identified. Before 1569, this was the Westminster Abbey of Béarn, and notables of the Foix-Béarn house buried here include Henri II d'Albret and Marguerite d'Angoulême. In that year, Montgomery's Protestants made a shambles of the place, wrecking the tombs and stealing anything of value. For 40 years after, this was a Protestant temple; fortunately, the real treasure was sleeping under plaster, not to be discovered until 1837: unique **mosaics**, odd hunting scenes featuring boars, fanciful lions, and a man with a wooden leg. Some of the capitals are Corinthian, recycled from Roman buildings. The tourist office organizes guided visits. Across from the church is a **museum of local archaeology** from 3000 BC to antiquity.

Museum of local archaeology
t 05 59 81 06 18; open mid-April–early Nov 10.30–12 and 3–7

Market Day in Lescar

Tuesday mornings.

Where to Stay and Eat in Lescar

Lescar ✉ 64230
Lescar, only 8km from the centre of Pau, makes a quiet alternative to staying in the city.

**La Terrasse, 11 Rue Maubec, t 05 59 81 02 34 (€). Pleasant enough rooms and a reasonable restaurant, with a menu beginning at approximately €26. *Closed 1st 3 weeks of Aug, 2 weeks Dec–Jan, Sat lunch and Sun.*

ⓘ **Lescar**
Place Royale, t 05 59 81 15 98, www.marie-lescar.fr; open all year Mon–Sat 10–12 and 2–6

10 Béarn | Up the Gave to Pau

Pau

 Pau

Perhaps your great-grandparents vacationed here, back in the 19th century when the Pyrenean air made Pau so popular. But resorts go in and out of fashion, and few outside Gascony have heard of Pau now, although the airport with flights to Stansted is starting to bring back the British tourists and house-hunters. It comes as a surprise to find such a big, up-to-date city so close to some of the choicest, most unspoiled parts of the mountains.

History

The modern bridge just to the east of Pau's castle marks the site of a far earlier one, a wooden bridge that existed even in the Dark Ages along Gascony's high road – the route shepherds took to move their flocks from the Pyrenees to winter pasture in the Landes. The high cliffs over the Gave de Pau also made it the logical spot to control the river. Though a castle and a small village stood on the site in the Middle Ages, it was Gaston Fébus in the 1370s

Jurançon and Béarn

Jurançon, Henri IV's favourite wine, is like Henri himself one of the most distinct products of Gascony. Grown on the hillside lining the south bank of the Gave de Pau, these white wines made from petit manseng, gros manseng and courbu grapes owe their striking individuality to a combination of factors: a gentle moist climate, buckets of sunshine, and dry, warm autumn winds that allow for a late harvest in November – essential for the overripened sweet vintage. The earth itself is sweet and clayey, laced with iron with an underpinning of siliceous or limestone rock. The vineyards themselves are rarely visible; most are tiny and tucked away on family farms, behind the trees and shrubs that help anchor down the slippery clay.

There are two AOC Jurançons. Golden sweet Jurançon offers a rarefied balance of the sumptuous, rich qualities of the finest *vin moelleux* with a fresh, tangy acidity. It never tastes heavy, nor can many wines match its astonishing fragrance, reminiscent of the exotic fruits that Carmen Miranda loved to stick on her head – guava, pineapples, lychees, passion fruit or mangoes – each estate has its own individual taste; all are delicious with desserts or foie gras prepared with wild mushrooms. Their longevity is legendary; buy a few bottles now to serve at your grandchildren's baptisms.

Straw-coloured Jurançon Sec, with a similar exotic bouquet and aftertaste, is one of France's great white *vins de garde*. In the past few years, three growers in the village of Monein ⑤ (*see* map p.230) have consistently produced wines that are a class apart: **Clos Uroulat** at Quartier Trouilh, t 05 59 21 46 19, *www.uroulat.com*; phone ahead to visit, the highest property in the appellation; **Domaine Cauhapé**, t 05 59 21 33 02, *www.cauhape.com*; open Mon–Fri 8–6, Sat 10–6, closed Sun and hols, whose vintner, Henri Ramonteu, is a student of Bordeaux's star œnologue, Dubourdieu; and the traditional **Domaine Bru-Baché**, t 05 59 21 36 34.

Part of the growing area for white, red and rosé AOC, Béarn touches the northwestern edge of Jurançon, although the larger portion stretches west of Orthez. Béarn is an ancient vintage that was once part of the Bayonne wine trade, especially after the 17th century, when nostalgic Protestant émigrés created a demand abroad for the wines of the Pyrenees. The whites make use of the same grape varieties as Jurançon, with the addition of lauzet, camarelet, rafflat de mocade and sauvignon; reds and rosés can be no more than 60 per cent tannat, with cabernet franc, cabernet sauvignon, fer, black manseng and black courbu. Bellocq ⑥ (*see* map p.230) is the main centre, where you can visit the cooperative **Les Vignerons de Bellocq** on the outskirts of town, t 05 59 65 10 71.

Getting to Pau

The airport has daily **flights** from Paris and Stansted.

Getting around Pau

Pau is the centre for all transportation in this stretch of the Pyrenees.

By train: The rail station, with connections to Bordeaux, Tarbes and Lourdes, is down by the river, underneath the Boulevard des Pyrénées on Av Jean Biray.

By bus: For the coast and the mountain villages, there are plenty of buses, most leaving from central Place Clemenceau. The TPR line (**t** 05 59 82 95 85) has frequent services (four or five a day) to Salies-de-Béarn, Bayonne, Biarritz, Nay-Lourdes, Mauléon, Monein, Mourenx and Orthez (via Lescar). There are also services to Tarbes, Mont-de-Marsan, Oloron and up the Gave d'Ossau to Laruns and Gourette.

who first realized the potential of the site; he expanded the castle and built a wall, intending to make Pau the capital of his domains. It was a popular residence with most of the later rulers of Béarn, including Henri d'Albret and Marguerite d'Angoulême, who brought down the latest Renaissance tastes from Paris and made the castle a showplace. Their grandson, Henri IV, was born there, giving Pau its enduring claim to fame. While young Henri was off travelling and campaigning, his dour mother Jeanne d'Albret spent much of her time here, putting an end to the brilliant court life of the old days and turning most of the Palois into good Calvinists. After Louis XIII and his army seized Béarn, Pau dwindled, a medieval relic that would not reawaken until the 1840s.

In Pau's hotels and shops, you'll occasionally see old hunting and racing prints, a reminder of the city's days as the Gascon outpost of the British Empire. The trend started with some of Wellington's veterans, who liked the country and came back in their retirement. The real impetus, however, came with a Scottish doctor named Taylor, who in 1869 wrote a book called *The Climate of Pau*, extolling the benefits of the area for just about any affliction. After this, Pau rapidly became one of the star resorts of Europe. With few sights to see, the British (and a good number of Americans) had to bring their own amusements with them. They built the first golf course on the continent, along with a racetrack and a casino; they established cricket and hunting clubs. The centre of the town filled up with milliners' shops, travel agents and even tearooms, while wealthy foreigners lined the outskirts with luxurious villas. Fashion moved on to Biarritz after 1890, following the example set by Queen Victoria – by that time the seaside, not the mountains, was the place to see and be seen in. For a while, Pau struggled on as a resort, as Parisians and other northern Frenchmen replaced the Anglo-Saxons; they kept the clubs going, and some even learned to play cricket and drink tea.

On 3 February 1909 Wilbur Wright put on a demonstration of his latest aircraft in Pau for an audience that included the kings of

Great Britain and Spain. Soon after that, France's first school of aviation was started here. Not much else happened until the 1950s, when the discovery of gas deposits at nearby Lacq fuelled a modest boom that continues today. Though most of the aeronautics has moved on to Toulouse, the training school is still here, specializing in parachuting. There is a **museum to French parachutists**, from the days of the Second World War up to recent times, and visitors can ask at the tourist office about a range of air-sports such as paragliding. The chemical and agro-food industries are important to Pau and the town has a new university, a busy, rebuilt centre, a convention hall, an inexplicably large number of lingerie shops, a few nightclubs, and and a tandoori restaurant.

Musée des Parachutistes
*Rte de Bordeaux,
t 05 59 40 49 18,
http://museepara.free.fr*

King Henri's Castle

King Henri's Castle
*t 05 59 82 38 02,
www.musee-château-pau.fr; open daily
for guided visits
mid-June–mid-Sept
9.30–12.15 and
1.30–5.45; rest of year
daily 9.30–11.45
and 2–5*

Pau's restored old centre, the quarter called the Hédas, is a delightful place that any French city might envy. Only a few medieval half-timbered buildings survive in out-of-the-way places, but the streets around Nouste Henric's castle have become a pedestrian zone full of lively restaurants and cafés. The castle itself, rising behind its moat, is a stunning vision of Renaissance turrets and gables. Not all of them are original, though – the pretty **tower** on the end of the right wing, facing you, was done in the time of Louis Philippe after long centuries of neglect. The grim brick **donjon** on the left dates from the time of Gaston Fébus. Between these is a beautifully carved marble **triple arch**, part of the 19th-century restorations but good enough to fool you into thinking it a Renaissance work.

Before 1620, this must have been one of the most lavishly decorated palaces in the south. Louis XIII, who had come down personally to oversee the conquest of Béarn, carried most of the furnishings back to Paris with him. For the next two centuries, the castle saw duty as a royal prison. In 1791, the revolutionaries in Paris declared it the 'property of the nation' but refrained from selling it off out of respect to the memory of Good King Henri. Nevertheless, it remained a prison until Louis Phillippe ordered restorations in the 1830s. The works continued through the reign of Napoleon III,

King Henri's Cradle

As every Gascon schoolboy knows, this is the star attraction. In 1553, the pregnant Jeanne d'Albret was up in the north, keeping her husband Antoine de Bourbon company while he warred with Emperor Charles V. Both parents thought that the heir to Gascony should have his birthplace there, and Jeanne had to rush back home. Henri was born ten days after her arrival in Pau, and the affair was so hurried that no one could find a proper cradle for the baby – so instead Jeanne used a big tortoise's shell, which little Henri found quite cosy. This odd relic was preserved ever after – a loyal Gascon officer saved it from the revolutionaries by hiding it and putting another tortoise shell in its place. Now it is displayed here in a charming sort of shrine, along with Henri's helmet, an arch-Renaissance tapestry of the *Apotheosis of Henri IV*, and banners with the royal arms of France and Navarre.

who took a personal interest in the place and often came for visits in Pau's heyday as a resort. They were overseen by Viollet-le-Duc, famous restorer of Paris' Notre-Dame and so many other important buildings in France. It is to his workshop that we owe most of the fine sculpted detail around the courtyard. Since that time, enough of the original furnishings have been reassembled to make the excruciatingly detailed guided tour worth the trouble.

In the castle's other rooms, you will see a fine collection of **Gobelin and Flemish tapestries**, as well as a notable 16th-century series on the story of Cupid and Psyche, in the Salle Marquet de Vasselot, and another, the oldest in the castle, with scenes of the months and seasons.

Just east of the castle on Place des Etats stands a plain building dear to the hearts of Gascon patriots, the old **Parlement de Navarre**. Before the French kings installed their Parlement in 1620, this served as home of the Sovereign Council, Béarn's last independent government (*parlements*, in old France, were not legislative bodies, but judicial councils). Another two streets east, stately **Place Royale** was laid out in the 18th century, a classically simple bit of town design from the Age of Enlightenment. Once lined with '*grands hôtels*' and cafés, it was the centre of the town's life, and the site of the evening promenade, in the days when the English came to Pau. The swells of the *belle époque* built the impressive neo-Gothic **St-Martin**, nearby on Rue Henri IV.

The Boulevard des Pyrénées

Pau is an Occitan word for rampart or palisade, and the cliffs above the Gave de Pau that once made it an excellent place for a fortress now give the city its most memorable embellishment, the Boulevard des Pyrénées. Running from Henri's castle to the Parc Beaumont, it skirts the city centre, providing a panorama over a 50-mile (80km) stretch of mountains and the wooded foothills in front. The Palois never get tired of it. They come to mull over the view in the morning, they walk their dogs there in the afternoon, and they come back in the evening for the sunsets. The odd conical mountain rising just a bit higher than the rest is the Pic du Midi.

The Boulevard's charms can be dangerous. Charles Maurras, the writer and politician, had a kind of mystical experience here in the 1880s, when he first realized what he later called 'the natural necessity of submission for the order and beauty of the world'. Maurras went on to found the fascist Action Française, and he ended his life in prison as a Vichy collaborator.

At the eastern end of the Boulevard, **Parc Beaumont** was laid out as an English garden a century ago. At its centre, the old **casino** has been restored and converted into a convention and recreation centre; part is still a casino.

Casino
t 05 59 11 20 00,
www.paucc.com

10

Béarn | Pau

Musée des Beaux-Arts

This surprisingly good collection is kept just north of the park on Rue Lalanne. The majority of the paintings are 18th- and 19th-century French, with Pyrenean landscapes naturally well represented, but there are also some choice works of the Italians, Flemish and Spaniards: an odd night scene by Luca Giordano, better known for painting Baroque ballroom ceilings, an unexpected *Last Judgement* from Rubens, even an El Greco, the *Ecstasy of St Francis*. Perhaps the best-known work is a classic of Degas, the *Cotton Brokers' Office in New Orleans*. The artist painted it on an American visit with his businessman father. There is also a collection of modern art, and a section with medieval and ancient coins.

There isn't much else in Pau. Most of the city's churches were wrecked or turned into Protestant temples by Jeanne d'Albret, but there is another museum, a little house on Rue Bernadotte dedicated to the remarkable career of Pau's other favourite son, Jean-Baptiste Bernadotte. A soldier who worked himself up through the ranks to become a marshal and confidant of Napoleon, Bernadotte fell out with the emperor and was forced into retirement. The heirless king of Sweden made him an adopted son, and Bernadotte wound up leading troops against Napoleon in the Russian campaign. In 1826 he assumed the Swedish throne, and ruled for 26 years as Charles XIV, ancestor of the modern royals. The **Musée Bernadotte** contains personal relics, paintings and period furniture. In the same neighbourhood, some of the villas of the English survive on the side streets off Rue Montpensier.

Where to Stay in Pau

Pau ✉ 64000

While none of the *grands hôtels* of Pau's glory days survives, there are over 40 hotels around the city in all price ranges to ensure you have a pleasant stay.

****Parc Beaumont, 1 Av Edouard VII, t 05 59 11 84 00, *www.hotel-parc-beaumont.com* (€€€€€). This modern, upmarket hotel is beside the park and some of the rooms have views onto the Pyrénées and terraces. The restaurant **Jeu de Pomme** is excellent with mouth-watering options such as *filet de bœuf cuit au beurre, poêlée de mini legumes, jus au tamarin*.

***Bristol, 3 Rue Gambetta, t 05 59 27 72 98 (€€). At the posher end of the scale, the Bristol is as old-fashioned as its name, but comfortable, quiet and reasonably priced, with good courteous service. *Open all year.*

**Grand Hôtel du Commerce, 9 Rue Maréchal Joffre, t 05 59 27 24 40 (€€). A traditional hotel close to the castle, with a decent restaurant. A good choice for sightseeing. *Menus €15–26. Open daily all year.*

**Regina, 18 Rue Gassion, near the castle, t 05 57 27 29 19 (€). One of the nicest budget choices in the area, though it's on a busy street and some rooms can be noisy. *Open all year.*

*Hôtel Matisse, 17 Rue Mathieu-Lalanne, near the Musée des Beaux-Arts, t 05 59 27 73 80 (€). A simple place, but a good choice in this price range. *Open all year.*

Logis des Jeunes, Base de Plein Air, Gelos, t 05 59 35 09 09. Youth hostel. *Open all year.*

Eating Out in Pau

Also try the places with outside tables in the streets around the castle.

Au Fin Gourmet, 24 Av Gaston-Lacoste, down below the Boulevard des Pyrénées, t 05 59 27 47 71, *www.restaurant-aufingourmet.com*. Try here for a rather more ambitious dining experience. The fish is particularly good. *Menus €18–58. Closed Sun eve, and Mon; plus 2 weeks July–Aug and 2 weeks in Feb.*

Chez Pierre, 16 Rue Louis-Barthou, t 05 59 27 76 86. A firm favourite, considered '*très* British' with its golf clubs over the bar, but serving southwest French cuisine, notably foie gras and *béarnais cassoulet*. *Menus €31. Closed Mon and Sat lunch and all Mon.*

Restaurant La Brochetterie, 16 Rue Henri-IV, t 05 59 27 40 33. Popular for its grilled duck and spit-roasted pig and lamb. *Menus from €11 at lunch, à la carte €20–30. Closed Mon.*

Le Viking, 33 Bd Tourasse, t 05 59 84 02 91, *www.restaurant-chez-pierre.com*. Rustic and intimate, treating local produce with flair and not a little style; try their *croustillant de suprème de pigeonneau aux girolles de foie gras. Menus change regularly, €25–56). Closed Sat and Sun lunch.*

North of Pau: the Vic-Bilh

Looking at a relief map, you'll see how the tremendous run-off from the well-watered Pyrenees creates wild landscapes of narrow, closely packed parallel valleys, each with its rushing stream or rocky *gave*. Nowhere is this more pronounced than between Pau and Aire-sur-l'Adour, the tract of deepest Gascony people call the Vic-Bilh, the 'old country'. There are no trains, few buses, and no main routes through it. Trying to get across its tangle of winding back roads is utterly exasperating. The landscapes, though clean and pretty, are generally unexceptional (though you'll usually get a view of the Pyrenees while crossing the crest of the roller coaster from one valley into another). The villages often have piquant names like Boueilh-Boueilho-Lasque and Coslédaa-Lube-Boast that are longer than their main street. They get such names from being consolidated after rural depopulation over the last century.

There are a few medieval churches, as at **Taron-Sadirac** and **Diusse**, but the only one worth a detour is the 11th-century church in the village of **Sévignac**. The local baron, the story goes, built it in expiation for a couple of murders. To remind himself and others just how easy it is to go astray, he had the artists embellish the portal with a full array of personified vices: a glutton patting his belly, another one vomiting, a merchant with a money-box, a pair of fellows arguing, and a man and a woman displaying parts of their anatomies not often seen on church portals.

At the western edge of the Vic-Bilh, in a little *pays* called the Saubestre (from the Latin *sylvestrensia* for its extensive forests) stands the village of **Morlanne**. The castle here, like Pau's and most of the others in this *département*, is the work of Sicard de Lordat, Gaston Fébus's personal architect. Half ruined by the 20th century, it was purchased by a historian named Raymond Ritter (he wrote,

Morlanne castle
t 05 59 81 60 27; open July and Aug Wed–Mon 10–7, April–June and Sept and Oct 2–7

among other things, a biography of Corisande), who spent the last decades of his life restoring it.

Morlaas, on the borders of the Vic-Bilh just northeast of Pau, was the capital of Béarn for two centuries starting from the 10th century. Not much is left to testify to the town's medieval prominence, only the church of Ste-Foi. The exterior has suffered from fires and renovations over the centuries, though a wonderful portal survives: a tympanum of *Christ and the Four Evangelists*, surrounded by scenes of the *Massacre of the Innocents* and the *Flight into Egypt*, and a border of the 24 *Apocalyptic Elders*.

On the northern edge of the Vic-Bilh, just over the border in the *département* of Hautes-Pyrénées, **Madiran** gives its name to the region's singular AOC wine district. The centre of the wine trade in the area, Madiran has plenty of opportunities for *cave* visits, but little to see except for the remains of the village's Benedictine abbey (the monks here introduced vine-growing to the area in the Middle Ages). There is a big, barn-like abbey church, with an unusual crypt, made for the veneration of holy relics and carved with some unusual, primitive capitals.

A Wine Tour of Vic-Bilh

Madiran and Pacherenc du Vic-Bilh are two AOC wine areas that share the same frontiers in the hilly Vic-Bilh with the villages of Madiran ① and Maumusson ② in the centre. Here the climate is drier than anywhere elsewhere in Beárn and the hard clay soil isn't good for growing anything else. Two 11th-century abbeys, Madiran and Ste-Foy, each developed their own wine-making traditions – the former made a deep, dark, full-bodied red wine from tannat and cabernet, while the monks of Ste-Foy created a white wine from ruffiac grapes known as Pacherenc. Originally Pacherenc was dry, with a refreshing coarseness, although in recent years a sweet variety in the Jurançon mould has been developed as well.

Madiran is a class apart. The most tannic wine in France, powerful enough to drink with jugged game, strong mountain cheeses and *entrecôte béarnaise*, it is also one of the great success stories of recent years. For years, Madiran suffered a dark age so dark that the few wine drinkers who even knew its name shuddered to recall that astringent red toothpaint. Enter, in the 1970s, a new breed of wine-growers led by Alain Brumont, who by hard work, inspiration and a dollop of public relations transformed the old wine into a drink so elegant, robust and full of flamboyant Gascon character that he was showered with awards as the *vigneron* of the 1980s. Headquartered in Maumusson ②, Brumont bottles his inky nectar under three labels: at the top of the line, made from 100 per cent tannat are **Château Bouscassé** Vieilles Vignes, and the even more expensive **Château Montus** Prestige. The Montus Pacherenc Sec and Moelleux are equally superb. To mention just a few of the many other excellent estates in the district: **Château d'Aydie**, a handsome, jagged-towered Béarnais manor in Aydie ③ run by the Laplace family, who also played a major role in the rebirth of Madiran (also try their Pacherenc Moelleux, especially the 2001 and 2002); **Château Lafitte-Teston** in Maumusson, which produces another pure tannat Madiran; and the **Cooperative de Plaimont**, at Plaimont in St-Mont ④, one of the largest in France, producing consistently fine Madirans under its Collection label, but also Pacherenc du Vic-Bilh Moelleux under the St Albert label. It is also the most important bottler of Côtes-de-Saint-Mont, the adjacent *appellation* squeezed between in Madiran and Bas-Armagnac. Red Côtes-de-St-Mont are similar to Madirans in their high tannic quality; Plaimont's very best wear the label of the 17th-century Château-de-Sabazan. For Jurançon Sec visit Monein ⑤, and for red, white and rosé Béarn wines Bellocq ⑥; *see also* wine box, p.224.

Château Bouscassé and Château Montus
Madiran, t 05 62 69 74 67

Château d'Aydie
Aydie, t 05 59 04 08 00; open Mon–Sat 9–12 and 1.30–6

Château Lafitte-Teston
Maumusson, t 05 62 69 74 58

Cooperative de Plaimont
St Mont, www.plaimont.com; open July and August 9–7, Sept–June Mon–Sat 8.30–12 and 2–6.30

Oloron-Ste-Marie

Oloron, the gateway to the Béarnais Pyrenees, began as the Celtiberian Illuro, 'city of the waters'. Burned down by the Normans at about the same time as Lescar, it gradually reappeared as twin towns, Oloron on its high hill and Ste-Marie, a new medieval *bourg* across the river; they only merged in 1858. Since the Pyrenees' first hydroelectric plant was built here in the 1870s, Oloron has been a centre of manufacturing. Today, sprawling over hills and valleys, it looks uncannily like a Pennsylvania mill town – though the only real industries in Oloron make berets and Lindt chocolates.

Ste-Marie Cathedral

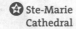 Ste-Marie
Cathedral
*open 8–8, guided
visits June–Sept 10–12
and 3–6, contact the
tourist office*

This is a typically bastard French church: Romanesque in front, Gothic behind and a little of everything else mixed in. Located in the *bourg*, near the river, it was begun in the 12th century and largely completed by 1500. The **portal** is one of the finest in the southwest, a flight of medieval fantasy in the style of Moissac that includes two remarkable *voussures* around the tympanum, one carved with the 24 Elders of the Apocalypse playing their rebecs and viols; the other recalling the parable about the preparations for a wedding feast. The joys awaiting us in heaven are described in terms any true Gascon would appreciate: they're hunting the boar, fishing for salmon, bringing in the wine and cheeses, killing the fowls. At the top of the arch, a hellish demon serves to underline the parable's point that 'many are called but few are chosen'.

On the tympanum, by a different artist, is the *Descent from the Cross* with the Virgin, John the Evangelist and Joseph of Arimathea in attendance. On the right, the statue on horseback is Constantine, representing the true faith (some say he's really Gaston IV of Béarn); the wretch being devoured by a lion on the left reminds us of the passage through death to a new life. The *trumeau* (column between the doors) shows two Saracen captives carved in Pyrenean marble; they may be an allusion to Gaston IV's successes in the Crusades.

Inside, the choir and apses are quite impressive flamboyant Gothic work, rare in these parts. Gothic sculptors of the 1300s also added some fine capitals and an unusual baptismal font. There is a *trésor* containing some Italian Renaissance items. If it's near Christmas, you can see the cathedral's elaborate crêche, carved in about 1700. Surprisingly the Pyreneans always neglected this widespread folk art, and this is one of the few examples; some of the figures wear berets.

Quartier Ste-Croix

Modern Oloron spreads along three valleys, where the Gave d'Aspe and Gave d'Ossau come together to make the Gave d'Oloron. The Gave d'Ossau bridge is a 13th-century original, while the Pont de Ste-Claire over the Gave d'Aspe was an early iron work of engineer Gustave Eiffel; this leads to a delightful **Jardin Public** with a Victorian bandstand and statuary.

Ste-Croix
*open 8–8; guided
visits by appointment
with the tourist office*

Between the two bridges, you can take the formidably steep Rue Dalmais up to the Quartier Ste-Croix, the acropolis of ancient Illuro and medieval Oloron. At the top, the square around **Ste-Croix** was the site of the annual fair that made Oloron's prosperity in the Middle Ages; parts of the covered market hall that once surrounded the building can still be seen. Various restorations disfigured much of the church's exterior, though there is some good Romanesque carving on the apses. The interior has a splendid Moorish dome in

Tourist Information in Oloron-Ste-Marie

(i) Oloron-
Ste-Marie >
*Allées du Comte de
Treville,* **t** *05 59 39
98 00; www.tourisme-
oloron.com; open
summer Mon–Sat 9–7,
Sun 10–1;
winter Mon–Sat
9–12.30 and 2–6.30*

For €10 you can buy a pass that gets you into four sites and a bracelet that activates information points around the town.

Where to Stay and Eat in Oloron-Ste-Marie

Oloron-Ste-Marie ✉ 64400

Rancèsamy, Quartier Rey, 64290 Lasseube. About 2km out of Lasseube, which is 11km from Oloron on the D24 towards Pau, **t** 05 59 04 26 37, *www. missbrowne.com* (€€). Isabelle and Simon Browne welcome you to their little oasis of tranquillity in a beautiful setting, with views of the verdant Vallée d'Ossau with mountains in the distance. It's an old stone house, lovingly restored and decorated throughout with *objets d'art* and furniture collected from all over the world. Bedrooms are spacious and comfortable and most have a view over the Mediterranean style courtyard. There's a lovely garden and

pool. Two evenings a week, Mrs Browne gets creative in the kitchen, using local and home-grown produce; she offers regional and international cuisine (€32, including wine and coffee). There is also a lounge and kitchen for communal use. *Open all year, on reservation.*

Bristol, 9 Rue Carrerot, **t 05 59 39 43 78 (€). Even cheaper than the above. *Menus €12–20. Closed Sun Oct–May and Christmas and New Year.*

Hôtel de La Paix, Avenue Sadi Carnot, by the SNCF station, **t 05 59 39 02 63, *www.hotel-oloron.com* (€). One of the least expensive, with a garden. No restaurant.

Château de Boués, just outside town on the D919, **t** 05 59 39 95 49 (€). A lovely château with several guest rooms and a pool. *Open May–end Sept.*

La Promenade, 64290 Lasseube, **t** 05 59 04 26 24. Locally popular, family-run auberge where the Brownes may send you when not serving dinner. No frills, regional fare and a good wine list. *Menus €15–22. Closed Mon, exc July and Aug.*

Tour de Grède
*visitors can climb it
mid-June–mid-Sept
10–12 and 3–6*

**Maison du
Patrimoine**
t *05 59 36 12 05, open
daily; open Tues–Sun
10–12.30 and 3–7
July–Oct; adm*

the form of an eight-pointed star, like the one in l'Hôpital-St-Blaise. Carvings on the capitals include a picture-book of biblical scenes.

Rue Dalmais was the main street of the medieval town; along it you'll see the old town hall, the 15th-century **Maison du Sénéchal** and a 13th-century tower called the **Tour de Grède**, with an adjoining mansion of the 1700s. This houses the **Maison du Patrimoine**, a museum with archaeological finds, paintings, and an exhibition on the concentration camp at nearby Gurs (see p.218). Stroll along the Promenade Bellevue for a great view of the town.

The Vallée d'Aspe

The N134 follows the Gave d'Aspe up towards the Spanish border. Footsore Roman legionaries once trod this path and the Romans gave the border pass, the Col du Somport, its name: Summus Portus, the highest gate.

South of Oloron, the first place of interest is off on a side road, the D918 from Asasp. The source at **St-Christau** has been known since ancient times, its waters a sure cure for skin diseases. One of

Vallées d'Aspe and d'Ossau

Navarrenx

Monein

Lescar

Pau

943

E80

Gurs

Lucq-de-Béarn

Lacommande

L'Hôpital-
Saint-Blais

Gan

Bœil-Bezing

Oloron-
Ste-Marie

Nay-
Bourdettes

937

Lestelle-
Bétharram

E07

Grotte de Bétharram

Asasp

St-Christau

Arudy

Défilé
d'Escot

Plateau
de Benou

Vallée d'Ossau

Sarrance

Bilhères

Lourdios-Ichère

Bielle
Béon

Vallée d'Aspe

Aste-Béon

Bedous

Assouste

Laruns

Col d'Aubisque

Accous

Eaux-Bonnes

918

Aucun

918

Pic d'Anie

Cette

Gourette

Arrens

Lescun

Pic de Gen

Etsaut

Gorges du
Bitet

Borce

Gave d'Aspe

Gabas

Artouste

Fort du Portalet

Lacs
d'Ayous

Lac d'Artouste

Pic du Midi
d'Ossau

Balaïtous

Marcadau

Col du Somport

Forges d'Abel

S P A I N

N

10 km

5 miles

the first spas of France, it was also one of the first to be forgotten. A park, two mouldering hotels of the 19th century, and a stately building called the **Rotonde** built over the source in the 1630s are all that remains. A large number of Celtiberian relics, jewellery and figurines were found near the fountain, along with a grim mustachioed bust of a Celtic god, which is still on display in the Rotonde.

From here the serious mountains begin; your last chance to leave the valley is the D294, following a beautiful but lonely route through forests and up to the 1,026m/3,364ft Marie-Blanque pass, before finishing in the Vallée d'Ossau. The N134, meanwhile, continues south through a dramatic gorge, the **Défilé d'Escot**, and then skirts the picturesque village of **Sarrance**. The chapel here was built to house an image of the Virgin that was found at a fountain by a shepherd; Sarrance has been a place of pilgrimage since the 1400s. Sarrance is also home to part of the **Ecomusée de la Vallée d'Aspe** which, across four sites in the valley, evokes the landscape, valley life and traditions. The site here has water and stone for its theme and through documents, videos and artefacts, tells the history of the village and its pilgrims. Another of the museum's sites is at the mountain village of **Lourdios-Ichère**, where the village of last century is recreated through the writings of a teacher/secretary at the *mairie*.

Ecomusée de la Vallée d'Aspe
Sarrance: t 05 59 34 57 65, http://ecomusee. vallee-aspe.com; open July–Sept 10–12 and 2–7; rest of year 2–6

Lourdios-Ichère:
t 05 59 34 57 65; open July–Sept 10–12 and 2–7, rest of year Sat, Sun and hols 2–6

The Cirque de Lescun and the Pic du Midi

Around **Bedous**, the green hills give way to stark grey cliffs, and there may be a distinct chill in the air even in summer; Bedous isn't much, but it's proud to be the birthplace of the explorer Pierre Laclede, founder of St Louis, Missouri. **Jouers** and **Cette** have the only Romanesque churches in the valley, both with unusual carved modillons on the apses. At **Accous** another part of the **Ecomusée de la Vallée d'Aspe** tells you about cheeses made in the valley and you get to taste some. **Lescun**, high above the valley, offers the greatest natural attraction of the area, the **Cirque de Lescun**. Though not quite as large as the Cirque de Gavarnie, it is nevertheless a spectacular sight. The arch of peaks rising above the green valley includes the 2,482m/8,138ft **Pic d'Anie**. The GR 10 from Lescun climbs right to the top of this peak, and there are plenty of other hiking trails.

Ecomusée de la Vallée d'Aspe
Accous: t 05 59 34 76 06; open Mon–Fri 9.30–12 and 2.30–6, Sat 10–12 and 2.30–6

Back on the N134, south of Cette at the tiny village of **Etsaut** is the **Maison du Parc**, information centre for this part of the Parc National des Pyrénées, and a good place to get acquainted with the nature and traditional civilization of the valley. From here you can take part in an organized nature tour. Etsaut also has another nature centre, the **Museum of the Bear**. Just across the main road from Etsaut, an equally tiny place called **Borce** merits a short detour. The one hamlet in this part of the Pyrenees that never

Maison du Parc
www.parc-pyrenees.com

Museum of the Bear
t 05 59 34 88 30; open daily 9.30–12.30 and 2–6.30

suffered from fires or wars, Borce retains its medieval appearance, with some interesting buildings including a hospice for pilgrims on their way to Compostela. The restored chapel here is another part of the Ecomusée: it tells the history of the chapel and the pilgrims.

The most curious stretch of the GR 10, the **Chemin de la Mâture**, meets the highway a little further south. Back in the age of wooden ships, Pyrenean pines made the longest and straightest masts France could get. The Chemin, built in the 1860s, was nothing more than a long steep slide, down which the trunks would go to the valley on rollers. Some parts of it are paved, and over a kilometre is cut out of solid rock. Following the GR 10 this way will bring you to a barren but striking area of mountain lakes, the **Lacs d'Ayous**, all in the shadow of the mighty 2,920m/9,573ft **Pic du Midi d'Ossau**, the pyramidal landmark of the western Pyrenees. The geologists believe the Pic and the area around it to be the caldera of a volcano that collapsed 240 million years ago. For the Béarnais, the Pic is an old friend; people call it 'Jean-Pierre'.

Overlooking the N134, just beyond the Chemin, the grim fortress on the hill is the privately owned **Fort du Portalet**. Following on the fall of France in 1940, Marshal Pétain sent a number of political leaders here after the famous show trial at Riom, including former prime ministers Paul Reynaud, Edouard Daladier and Léon Blum. After the Liberation, the new government found it a fitting lock-up for Pétain himself.

Close to the new tunnel under the Col du Somport into Spain is an old ironworks called **Les Forges d'Abel**. The property used to belong to a local boy named Pierre Loustaunou, born in 1754. As a young shepherd, he was taking somebody else's flock down to summer pasture when he had the inspiration to sell them; the money financed a huge adventure, culminating in a career as general to an Indian maharajah. Pierre eventually returned with a bag full of rubies, and bought the forge and many other things; ruined in the troubles of the French Revolution, he was last seen as a mendicant dervish preaching somewhere in the Levant.

ⓘ **Bedous**

Office de Tourisme de la Vallée d'Aspe:
Pl Francois Sarraille,
t *05 59 34 57 57,*
www.vallee-aspe.com;
open mid-June–mid-Sept Mon–Sat 9–6.30,
Sun 2.30–5.30; rest of year Mon–Sat 9–5.30

⭐ **Au Bon Coin >**

Market Days in the Vallée d'Aspe

Bedous: Thursdays.

Where to Stay and Eat in the Vallée d'Aspe

St-Christau ✉ 64660
***Au Bon Coin, on the D918 (Route des Thermes), **t** 05 59 34 40 12, *www.thierry-lassala.com* (€€). A modern hotel in a lovely forest setting. In this perfect isolation, there are pretty rooms at reasonable rates, a pool, gardens and an excellent restaurant serving both simple Béarnais favourites and some surprising seafood dishes – from peppers stuffed with crabmeat to lobster lasagne. *Menus from €26. Closed Sun eve, Mon and Tues lunch out of season.*

The Upper Aspe Valley

There are more interesting places to spend a night in these mountains than just a plain old hotel, including the mountain refuges at L'Abérouat, near Lescun, and Arlet (t 05 62 44 36 60, summer only), both of which provide an opportunity to savour the mountain scenery.

Auberge Cavaliere, on the trails above Accous (✉ 64490), t 05 59 34 72 30, www.auberge-cavaliere.com (€). Accommodation and meals for hikers and riders.

Camping des 4 Saisons, Asasp, near St-Christau, t 05 59 34 43 10, www.aspe-4saison.com (€). There are caravans and mobile homes available. *Open June–Sept.*

Maison de l'Ours, Etsaut, t 05 59 34 86 38, http://giteours.club.fr (€). Rooms and meals, along with nature walks and activities. *Open all year.*

Le Châlet Restaurant, Urdos, near the Spanish border, t 05 59 36 00 60. No accommodation. *Open daily.*

Youth hostel, Lourdios ✉ 64570, t 05 59 34 46 39. *Open all year.*

10

Béarn | The Vallée d'Ossau

The Vallée d'Ossau

Closer to the heart of the Pyrenees, this valley is a little wilder than the Aspe, with peaks crowding in against the road. The people who live here, a self-governing community of shepherds, in the old days thought of themselves as set apart; indeed they claimed not to be Gascon at all, and some have speculated that they are direct descendants of the Celtiberians, maybe with a little Moorish blood mixed in. Some smaller villages, like Assouste, still manage their affairs by the ancient *jurat*, a council of the heads of families.

Coming from Oloron or Pau, the entrance to the valley is the village of **Arudy**, centre of the Pyrenean marble trade. Here the **Maison d'Ossau**, in a restored 17th-century house, provides a good introduction to the valley, including exhibits on nature, history and traditions of the area. From Arudy, the D934 leads into the valley, passing under the ruined medieval castle at **Castet**, and the beautiful white twin villages of **Bielle** and **Bilhères**. Bielle's name betrays its ancient origins – from a Roman villa the village gradually replaced. From its greatest period of prosperity in the 16th century, it has an attractive late Gothic church, St-Vivien, and an ensemble of houses to match, many with Béarnais carved lintels, the only decoration the austere Béarnais ever allow on their homes. Above Bilhères, on the **Plateau de Benou**, a hiking path will take you near three small **Neolithic cromlechs** (stone circles). There are many natural springs on the plateau, and this must have been an important religious site.

Further south, around Béon and Aste, you can see the steep winding roads that lead up to the marble quarries; here you can also visit **La Falaise aux Vautours**, an educational and observation centre (with cameras hidden on the cliffs and interactive computers) for the many species of birds of prey that live around the mountain-tops: kites, eagles, Egyptian vultures, and especially various species of buzzard; if you're lucky in these parts, you may

Maison d'Ossau
t 05 59 05 61 71; open July and Aug daily 10–12 and 3–6; Jan–June and Sept Tues–Fri 2–5, Sun 3–6; Oct–Nov Sun 3–6; adm

⭐ **La Falaise aux Vautours**
t 05 59 82 65 49, www.falaise-aux-vautours.com; open June–Aug daily 10.30–12.30 and 2–6.30; May and Sept, 2–6 plus school hols 2–5

get to see the biggest of all in Europe, the rare and fearsome lammergeyer. **Laruns**, the little capital of the Ossau, won't detain you long, unless you come on 15 August when everyone's out in traditional costume for the valley's big festival. **Assouste**, above Laruns, has a good Romanesque church.

The Col d'Aubisque

From Laruns you can detour eastwards on the marvellous, tortuous D918 (*completely open only from June to November*). It is 36km of Pyrenean scenery at its best, passing the little spa of **Eaux-Bonnes** and the modern ski resort at **Gourette**. Empress Eugénie, wife of Napoleon III, visited occasionally at Eaux-Bonnes; it was she who ordered this improbable road to be made. Eaux-Bonnes, like its matching book-end spa Eaux-Chaudes, back on the D934, still has a Second Empire look about it from the days when the Empress made it briefly fashionable. After Gourette, the D918 passes through the weird landscapes of the **Crêtes Blanches** before reaching the 1,694m/5,554ft Col, with spectacular views just under the summit of the peak called **Soum de Grum**. Carry on further and you'll be in the Vallée d'Arrens (see p.257).

ⓘ **Arudy** ›
Mairie, t 05 59 05 77 11, www.ot-arudy.fr; open July–Aug daily 10–12 and 2–6; rest of year Mon–Sat 10–12 and 2–4

ⓘ **Laruns** ›
Maison de la Vallée d'Ossau, t 05 59 05 31 41; open all year Mon–Sat, 9–12 and 2–6, Sun 9–12; July and Aug daily 9–12.30 and 2–6.30

Market Days in the Vallée d'Ossau

Arudy: Tuesdays.
Laruns: Saturdays.

Where to Stay in the Vallée d'Ossau

Laruns and Environs ✉ 64440

Laruns is not a resort town, and there are only simple places to stay.

**Hôtel de France, Ave Gare, t 05 59 05 33 71 (€). *Closed Thurs, except summer and school hols.*

**Hôtel de la Poste, Eaux-Bonnes, t 05 59 05 33 06, *www.hotel-dela-poste.com* (€). Ten nice rooms and a restaurant (*see below*). *Open May–mid-Oct.*

*Le Glacier, t 05 59 05 10 18, *www.leglacier.fr.st* (€). The ski station at Gourette, high up at the Col d'Aubisque, can be a pain to reach but it promises some memorable scenery. Le Glacier is the least expensive.

Barthèque camp site, Laruns, t 05 59 05 38 88. Well equipped and with a swimming pool. *Open all year.*

Refuge d'Embaradere, Laruns, t 05 59 05 41 88, *www.gite-embaradere.com.* Cheap dormitory accommodation with meals for €12–16. *Closed for several weeks in Nov and May.*

Eating Out in the Vallée d'Ossau

Auberge Bellevue, Rue de Bourguet, Laruns, t 05 59 05 31 58. One of the best places in the mountains, where you can have a fine Béarnais *garbure* or a *confit* at very reasonable prices. Some lighter more modern alternatives too. *Menus €13–22. Closed Mon eve and Tues out of season, plus Jan and June.*

Hôtel de la Poste, Eaux-Bonnes, t 05 59 05 33 06, *www.hotel-dela-poste.com.* They put on a delicious €17.50 menu at this hotel including *truite pochée sauce hollandaise, fricassée d'agneau de lait*, plus dessert. *Menus up to €31.*

Pic du Midi, Gabas, t 05 59 05 33 00, *www.vallee-ossau.com/restaurant/turon.* Hearty *garbure* and *confits.* They also produce and sell cheese. *Menus €9–11. Closed Nov.*

The High Pyrenees

The big mountains of the Pyrenees make getting around difficult, and this has always been a rather poor and isolated part of France. But do not suppose that there's nothing to do but close the book and get out the skis or binoculars. On the contrary, these valleys harbour Neolithic mysteries and Roman relics, fine medieval churches and Renaissance paintings (especially in the valleys to the east), elegant old spa resorts such as Bagnères and Luchon, plenty of cable cars to ride, and caves to explore (one with Palaeolithic art inside). Each valley has its own history and traditions, and in a dozen or so villages the proud Gascon highlanders have set up little museums of folk life to show you what it was like in the old days.

SPAIN

11

Don't miss

⭐ **Miracles and crowds**
Lourdes p.243

⭐ **Viewing vertiginous peaks**
Cirque de Gavarnie p.263

⭐ **Gothic beauty and Roman remains**
St-Bertrand-de-Comminges p.287

⭐ **A majestic mountain spa**
Luchon p.292

⭐ **France's biggest Gallo-Roman villa**
Montmaurin p.298

See map overleaf

nees

943

Lagujan Miélan

Vic-en-
Bigorre

Rabastens-
de-Bigorre

St-Sever-
de-Rustan

Morlaàs

E80

117

Tarbes

21

Bœil-Bezing

Nay-
Bourdettes

937

Pontacq

Ossun

Tournay

HAUTES-

ande

Arudy

Lestelle-
Bétharram

Bartrès

PYRÉNÉES

Plateau
de Benou

Bilhères

Bielle

Vallée d'Ossau

St-Pé-de-
Bigorre

Capvern-les-Bains

Mauvezin

938

Lourdes

Bagnères-de-
Bigorre

Lahitte

Pic du
Pibeste

Campan

Esparros

†Assouste

Col d'Aubisque

Arras-en-
Lavedan

Argelès-Gazost

Vallée de Campan

Laruns

918

Arcizans-Avant

Ste-Marie-
de-Campan

Eaux-Bonnes

Gourette

Aucun

918

Arrens

St-
Savin

Beaucens

Hautacam

Pierrefitte-Nestalas

Cádeac

p.213

Pic de Gep

Barèges

La Mongie

Ancizan

Gorges du
Bitet

Gabas

Artouste

Cauterets

Luz-St-Sauveur

l'Arbizon

Vielle-
Aure

Lac d'Artouste

St-Sauveur

Massif de Néouvielle

Soulan

Espiaube

Sailhan

St-Lary

Pic du Midi
d'Ossau

Balaïtous

Pont-d'Espagne

Lac de Gaube

Gorge de Luz

Tramezaigues

Marcadau

Fabian

SPAIN

Parc National
des Pyrénées

Gèdre

Aragnouet

Notre Dame d'Héas †

Plau-Englay

Port de
Boucharo

Gavarnie

Sarradèle

Cirque de
Gavarnie

Marboré

Rioumajou

Monte Perdido

SPAIN

Don't miss

⭐ Lourdes **p.243**

⭐ Cirque de Gavarnie **p.263**

⭐ St-Bertrand-de-Comminges **p.287**

⭐ Luchon **p.292**

⭐ Montmaurin **p.298**

Belloc-St-Clemens
Masseube
Simorre
Lombez
L'Isle-en-Dodon
632
Trie-sur-Baise
Péguilhan
Boulogne-sur-Gesse
Ciadoux
Galan
Montmaurin
Lespugue
Aurignac
Cazères
E80/117
Larroque
St-Marcet
Martres-Tolosane
St-Placard
St-Martory
Ausseing
Lannemezan
Belbèze-en-Comminges
La Barthe-de-Neste
Montréjeau
St-Gaudens
Montsaunes
Salies-du-Salat
Labastide
COMMINGES
Sauveterre-de-Comminges
St-Lizier
St-Bertrand-de-Comminges
Barbazan
Sarrancolin
St-Pé d'Ardet
St-Girons
Luzenach
627
929
St-Lary
Argein
Castillon-en-Couserans
Arreau
Lançon
Bethmale
Bordères-Louron
Sentein
125
Vieille-Louron
618
Loudenvielle
Mont Valier
Vallée de Louron
Val d'Oô
Bagnères-de-Luchon
Granges-d'Astau
Lac d'Oô
Hospice de France
Lac du Portillon
N
10 km
5 miles

The current border between France and Spain was laid out in the Peace of the Pyrenees of 1659; both sides sent out surveyors to determine once and for all a line across the highest peaks in the middle. Three-quarters of the Pyrenees mountains may be in Spain, but the French side can certainly claim more than its share of scenic wonders. It wasn't just after Franco's death that Spain wanted to become part of Europe. The reasons for this go back to the long, slow epochs of continental drift. The loose island that is now the Iberian peninsula began snuggling desperately up to the continent a few million years ago. At the line of impact, the Pyrenees were slowly thrown up, and the highest points naturally grew up near the northern edge, as if on the crest of a wave.

And that crest, including the famous *cirques* and the tallest peaks of the chain, Monte Perdido and Aneto, is the subject of this chapter: the centre of the Pyrenees, with the grandest panoramas and the greatest opportunities for walking and winter sports. It includes the Hautes-Pyrénées and part of the Haute-Garonne, an ensemble of valleys, each offering its own sights and attractions. Before the Revolution, most of this region belonged to the Counts of Bigorre, a little fief that caused its neighbours little trouble and was finally swallowed up by the Viscounts of Béarn in 1425.

Into the Mountains: from Pau to Tarbes

Musée de Beret
Pl St-Roch, **t** *05 59 61
91 70, www.
museeduberet.com;
open July and Aug
Mon–Sat 10–12 and 2–7,
Sun 10–12; April–June
and Oct Tues–Sat 10–12
and 2–6; Nov–Mar
Tues–Sat 2–6*

**Kangaroo and
animal park**
t *05 59 71 03 34.;
open daily*

Coarraze château
t *05 59 61 10 27; open
mid-July–mid-Aug
2.30–6*

Passing through the eastern edge of Béarn, on the way into the mountains, the D937 passes first the most onomatopoetic village in the southwest, **Bœil-Bezing**, and then the most negative, **Nay**. This busy village lives mostly from making berets – before Atatürk's infamous Hat Law of 1925, Nay had a thriving business selling fezes to the Turks. There's a **museum** to the famous titfer in Place St-Roch. Nay is a *bastide*, laid out in the usual grid by the viscounts of Béarn in 1302; despite a certain discreet charm, it has nothing much else to detain you, except perhaps a wonderfully ferocious war memorial on the *place*, with a First World War *poilou* about to hurl a grenade into the knitting shop across the way. Across the Gave de Pau from Nay, at **Asson**, south of Nay, there's a **kangaroo and animal park**. **Coarraze** will show you its castle, begun in the Middle Ages and converted into a proper château in the 18th century. You can visit the park, landscaped garden and some of the interior.

Next, as a prelude to Lourdes, there's **Lestelle-Bétharram**, one of the most peculiar holy sites anywhere. A chapel stood here from the earliest times, but not until the 1600s, after Montgomery's Protestants sacked it in the Wars of Religion, was it promoted into a major pilgrimage site. Legends and miracles were concocted, and even the name of the place was changed, from Gatarram to Bétharram, supposed to mean 'the House of the Most High' in Hebrew. Soon thousands of pilgrims were pouring in, and a major building programme was begun. The result, crowded on a hillside just south of the village, is an epitome of the religious architecture and religious sensibility of 17th-century France – weird, and a little sinister. The gloomy buildings lining the Gave de Pau belong to a religious college; behind them stands the chapel, packed with paintings and dripping with gilt woodwork. Oddest of all is the **Calvary**, trailing up the hillside, a series of small stone chapels built in the 1800s that look like mausolea in Victorian cemeteries.

Just south of the village off the D937 is a series of caves, the **Grottes de Bétharram**. So close to Lourdes, it isn't surprising they are so well laid out for tourists. Everyone rides a little train past the colourful stalactites; there's a boat ride across the underground lake, and commentary in nine languages.

Grottes de Bétharram
*t 05 62 41 80 04,
www.betharram.com;
open 25 Mar–25 Oct
daily 9–12 and
1.30–5.30; early Jan–
25 Mar Mon–Fri visits at
2.30 and 4*

Getting ever closer to Lourdes, the village of **St-Pé** had one of the biggest abbey churches of the southwest before Montgomery and the Protestants wrecked it in 1569. Over the next two centuries it was almost completely dismantled, though some good carved capitals survive in what's left. St-Pé (Peter) must really have stopped here – they've got his key in the village parish church.

Lourdes

🟠 **Lourdes**

Even a century ago, honest souls like Emile Zola were shocked and disgusted by the holy circus of Lourdes; the writer J. K. Huysmans found the place '...a gigantic Saint-Louis Hospital'

Getting to and around Lourdes

The main roads are lined with cars for miles before you even reach the town limits and **parking** is a problem. The no.1 **city bus** will be useful to all footsore pilgrims, shuttling between the rail station and the Grotte (**t** 05 62 94 32 96 for information on town bus services).

Lourdes has plenty of **travel firms** that organize **day trips** or half-day trips out to the mountains and even to the Basque country. Most of these go for about €20 (full day); for details, see the two Gares Routières d'Excursions on Bd du Lapacca and Av du Paradis.

Lourdes also has good **bus** connections to the Pyrenean valleys: there are at least eight buses a day up the valley to Argelès and Cauterets.

(famous Paris madhouse), 'the essence of horror dripping from a barrel of gross joy'. Today, at any of the town's endless souvenir stands, you can purchase a little plastic bottle in the shape of the Virgin Mary to fill up with water from the sacred *source*, and then simply put a stamp on it and mail it home – they're approved by the French post office. But in our times, when you can see vulgarity and commercialism crasser than Lourdes on the television any night of the week, being shocked isn't so easy. And it's hard to be dismissive about a place that means so much to so many sincere people – millions of them, who have come from every continent to the world's most popular Christian pilgrimage site. The pilgrims themselves put on quite a show, by far upstaging anything in Lourdes itself: coachloads of chattering Italian housewives on their dream holiday, youngsters with guitars who have hitched from Ireland or Spain; youth groups from Missouri or Japan, with earnest leaders constantly counting heads. It's not uncommon to hear them singing in the streets – and where else in Europe can you see that?

History

Long before Bernadette, Lourdes was an important town. With a strategic location at the edge of the mountains, the site was occupied all through prehistoric times. The ancient Pyrenean Basques were here, and also the Celts, though the Romans were probably the first to fortify the heights overlooking the Gave. In the 8th century, Lourdes was briefly a stronghold of the Moors, invading from Spain, and after that it served for centuries as the chief bastion of the vassals Charlemagne appointed to keep the Moors out, the counts of Bigorre. Just the same, no one would ever have heard of the place were it not for a 14-year-old girl named Bernadette Soubirous (St Bernadette, since 1933), who saw the Virgin Mary and discovered the miraculous spring in 1858.

Apparitions of the Virgin are as common as sightings of izards in the Pyrenees, and it isn't likely that Bernadette's would have made much of a stir but for two factors. First, the spring early on developed a reputation for curing hopeless cases. Far more important, though, was active and heavy promotion by the Church, which historically has been inclined to look at apparitions and miracles with a sceptical eye. For Rome, Bernadette's visions couldn't have come at a better time. Only a decade earlier, the pope had briefly been toppled from his throne in the revolution of 1848. Anti-clericalism and free thinking were in the ascendant, and such a simple country miracle proved the perfect tonic for increasing the faith. As an added bonus, in the fourth of Bernadette's visions the Virgin declared to her, 'I am the Immaculate Conception.' Just at that time, the popes were promulgating the controversial dogma of the divine birth of Mary and, whether or not a little clerical prompting had a hand in it, Bernadette's word helped greatly in swaying pious opinion.

Massive promotion of the Lourdes pilgrimage did not really begin, though, until the 1870s or so, after the Paris Commune and the end of papal rule in Rome. The Church saw itself and society in deep crisis, and Lourdes was part of the response – the centre-piece, in fact, of the conservative Catholic reaction against modernism. Within a few years, Lourdes had become what it is now: the biggest (although perhaps not the most dignified) Christian pilgrimage site anywhere. Six million people visit in an average year – about 300 for every inhabitant. Although pilgrims will be in evidence all year round, most people come on the important Church holidays, when organized groups arrive from around the world.

The Town Centre

Place Peyramale, the centre of Lourdes, is dominated by the tourist information centre, a very sharp work of modern archi-tecture, and a huge McDonald's, which after the Grotte itself may be the busiest place in town. From here, Rue Basse and Boulevard de la Grotte, lined with souvenir stands, head west for the pilgrimage sites, while Rue St-Pierre bears south, towards the workaday Lourdes of the Lourdais, with its lively market – two worlds, giving the impression that they like to keep a certain distance from each other.

Above it all, atop the hill overlooking the town, is the **château**. The site has been occupied at least since Roman times. Legend states that the castle was occupied by Moors from Spain, who seized it on their retreat home after the Battle of Poitiers. Later, under a chief named Mirat, the Muslims were besieged by Charlemagne. During the fighting, a salmon fell miraculously from the sky at Mirat's feet; he sent it as a present to the Frankish king, saying that he had no worry about holding out indefinitely, since heaven itself was providing provisions for him. The siege dragged on and on, and only ended when the bishop of Puy-en-Velay, who was with Charlemagne, suggested a compromise – the Muslims all converted to Christianity, swore fealty to

AVENUE ANTOINE BEGUERE

ROUTE DE PAU

Basilique Ste-Bernadette

Gave de Pau

PONT ST-MICHE

Grotte de Massabielle

Fontaine

Basilique du Rosaire

ESPLANADE DES PROCESSIONS

Basilique
Souterraine Pius X

RUE MONSEIGNEUR THEAS

BOULEVARD PERE

Ω Grotte

DU

CALVAIRE

CHEMIN

RUE STE-MARIE

AVENUE BERNADETTE SOUBIROUS

PONT VIEUX

Musée Grévin

RUE MASSABIELLE

PLACE DE
LA MERLASSE

RUE

PARADIS

AVENUE PEYRAMALE

DU

AVENUE MONSEIGNEUR RODHAIN

Gare Routière
des Excursions

L'ARROUZA

DE

RUE

N

Gave de Pau

Musée du Petit Lourdes

150 metres

150 km

Station

AVENUE DE LA GARE

AVENUE HELIOS

RUE DE PAU

BOULEVARD DU LAPACCA

BOULEVARD DE LA GROTTE

Aquàrium

RUE BERNADETTE SOUBIROUS

PLACE JEANNE D'ARC

Gare Routière des Excursions

Musée de la Nativité

RUE MAUPAS

QUAI ST-JEAN

CHAUSSEE MARANSIN

RUE BASSE

RUE SOUBIES

Château/ Musée Pyrénéen

RUE DU BOURG

RUE DES 4 FRERES SOULAS

RUE DE LANGELLE

PLACE PEYRAMALE

RUE DES PETITS FOSSES

RUE BARON DUPRAT

RUE ST-PIERRE

Sacré Couer

Police

Cachot de Bernadette Musée Christi

RUE DU FORT

RUE DE BAGNERES

RUE BARTAYRÈS

Musée du Gemmail

RUE DE LA GROTTE

PLACE DU MARCADAL

DE L'EGALITE

RUE DES PYRENEES

RUE DU GARNAVIE

RUE DE LAPAIX

RUE LAFITTE

AVENUE JOFFRE

Musée de Lourdes

Halles

PLACE DU CHAMP COMMUN

PLACE CANDEVIELLE

Bus Station

JUIN

PLACE DES PYRENEES

CHEMIN DES ROCHERS

AVENUE MARECHAL

AVENUE ROGER

AVENUE DU MARECHAL FOCH

AVENUE

BOULEVARD D'ESPAGNE

CAZENAVE

Grottes des Sarrazins

To Pic du Jer and Funicular ↓

Musée Pyrénéen
t 05 62 42 37 37; open
July and Aug daily
9–6.30, April–June and
Sept 9–12 and
1.30–6.30, Oct–Mar
Sat–Thurs 9–12 and
2–6, Fri 9–12 and 2–5;
closed hols

Charlemagne and the bishop, and got to keep the castle (unfortunately, like so many other similar legends, it seems this one was invented in the later Middle Ages to support the Church's claim to part of the castle's rents). Throughout medieval times, the castle was a stronghold of the counts of Bigorre: in fact most of what you see today dates from around the 1590s, after a rebuilding ordered by Henri IV. Today it houses the **Musée Pyrénéen**, with old farm paraphernalia and objects of everyday life from the time of Bernadette Soubirous, along with a stuffed bear and exhibits on the Pyrenees and mountain-climbing.

Bernadette

That we know nearly everything about the beginnings of the Lourdes phenomenon, in great detail, is thanks to the indefatigable Inspector Jacomet of the police, who was charged with investigating it. It starts out simply enough. Bernadette Soubirous was 14 years old, a sickly, asthmatic girl in a very religious family that had come down in the world. Her father, François, had once owned a mill, but by 1858 he and his family were reduced to living in penury in a tiny hovel that had once been a prison cell, the famous *cachot* shown to Lourdes visitors today. On 11 February of that year, Bernadette, her sister Antoinette and a friend, Jeanne Abadie, went out to the 'old cave', Massabielle, to gather scraps of wood for the family fire. To reach the spot, a shallow canal had to be crossed. Bernadette, worried about an asthmatic attack, stayed behind while her sister and friend went across. There, at about 1pm, she felt a warm, strange breeze that seemed to caress her face. Then the vision manifested itself. A 'girl', as Bernadette first described her (later '*une dame*'), spoke kindly to her in Gascon, telling her 'three secrets', and directing her to dig with her hands in the soil of the cave, where the miraculous spring came forth.

Bernadette's talkative sister soon spread the word around, and the news caused quite a stir. Crowds began gathering around the spring. The Virgin appeared three more times to Bernadette and, as Jacomet noted, to many others as well. By April a kind of hysteria had taken over the little town. Children, shepherdesses, even the town prostitute told of their visions, all wildly differing. One local woman began to throw fits, and declared herself a clairvoyant; besides the Virgin, she saw St Peter and another male figure who twirled his moustache.

Miracles could not be far behind. The first was bestowed on Louis Bouriette, a man who worked with Bernadette's father in a stable. Blind in one eye, he procured some mud from around the spring and made a compress of it, and regained his sight. Newspapers began to pick up on the story, and both the bishop of Tarbes and the authorities came to investigate. As soon as word got around, Lourdes became a very busy place.

Throughout the holy carnival that followed, Bernadette seemed to be the only one to keep her head. Always the very picture of sincerity and simplicity, she never encouraged any sensationalism or commercialization. She continued to have her visions, and described them politely to anyone who troubled to ask; that was all. Bernadette was a girl of few words. A famous sculptor came down to try and reproduce the Virgin as Bernadette saw her, and spent days talking with the girl, making sure he had the description down perfectly. When it was finished, he asked her if it was a good resemblance. 'Not at all,' was the reply.

Bernadette entered a convent up north in Nevers in 1866. By some accounts, she was forced into it – Lourdes had become big business, and there was always the chance she might say something the Church would find inconvenient. In Nevers she led a quiet, secluded life. Always subject to bouts of ill health, she died there in 1879, at the age of only 35. A movement for canonization sprang up almost immediately, though with the Church's accustomed deliberation it took 54 years to finally make Bernadette a saint.

As for her role in history and religion, her own wishes sum it up best: 'The less people say about me,' she once said, 'the better.'

The *Cité Religieuse*

When the pilgrims are in town, the **Boulevard de la Grotte** is the closest thing the Pyrenees can offer to a North African souk – jam-packed with people and vast heaps of glittering merchandise spilling out into the street from every shopfront. Every bit of that merchandise, though, is a holy souvenir: sea-shell shrines, medallions, Virgin Mary toaster-covers, gargantuan rhinestone rosaries, and gilt plastic-framed magic pictures that show Bernadette in the grotto when you look one way, and a smirking pope when you look the other. Though quality has been dropping off in recent years, for connoisseurs of kitsch this is still the next best thing to paradise.

After running the gauntlet, you'll cross the little bridge over the Gave de Pau and enter the '**Domaine de la Grotte**' – no shorts or beach clothes, no dogs, no smoking. Everything is impeccably organized, as it has to be, and there are guides, maps and signposts everywhere, along with visitors' centres that speak every language known to Catholicism. The Domaine begins with the pretty **Esplanade des Processions**, with room for 40,000 people – and it's often full in the evening when groups from all over the world parade up and down with their home-town banners. At the end of this stands the **Basilique du Rosaire**, built in 1883. Unlike the souvenirs, this bit of kitsch fails to amuse. The 'Romanesque-Byzantine' style, invented in 19th-century France, undoubtedly marks the low point of Christian sacred architecture, a degenerate parody of the medieval Age of Faith; Emile Zola found it 'ugly enough to make one cry'. The frescoes and mosaics within match the architecture perfectly, and may even surpass it.

Even when it was new the Basilica often proved too small to accommodate the crowds, but it was not until the 50s that a larger facility was built. The chilly **Underground Basilica Pius X**, to the left of the Esplanade, seats 20,000. Walk around the back of the Basilique du Rosaire to see where it all started, the little **Grotte de Massabielle**, and the adjoining spring, where the water that isn't poured into little bottles is channelled into pools to bathe the sick. Up above on the hillside, pilgrims trek a Calvaire made of giant bronze statues. Lourdes is starting to gear up for the 150th anniversary of the visions in 2008 – you have been warned.

Roadside Attractions and More Mysteries

Beyond the *cité religieuse* Lourdes has a formidable array of holy sites and dubious 'museums' to entertain its pilgrims. Among many others, there's the **Musée de Lourdes**, at the car park l'Egalité, with dioramas of little Bernadette's vision and village life in the 1850s. Of course there's also a branch of the **Musée Grévin**, with more of the same, along with Jesus and 12 pasty-faced Apostles

Musée de Lourdes
*t 05 62 94 28 00;
open April–Oct daily
9–12 and 1.30–6.30;
Nov–Mar daily 10–12
and 2–5; adm*

Musée Grévin
*87 Rue de la Grotte,
t 05 62 94 33 74; open
Easter–Oct Mon–Sat
9–12 and 1.45–6.30,
Sun 10–12 and
1.45–6.30; adm*

11

The High Pyrenees | Lourdes

Musée de la Nativité
*21 Quai St-Jean,
t 05 62 94 71 00; open
Easter–Oct daily 9–12
and 1.30–7; adm*

Musée du Petit Lourdes
*67 Av Peyramale,
t 05 62 94 24 36; open
Easter–Oct daily 9–12
and 1.30–7; adm*

Le Cachot
*t 05 62 94 51 30; open
May–Sept daily 9–12
and 2–7, Oct–April 3–5*

Aquarium
*34 Av François
Abadie, t 05 62 42
01 00; open April–Sept
10–12 and 2–6, Oct
Wed–Sun 2–6*

Musée Christi
*24 Rue de la Grotte,
t 05 62 42 25 65*

Pic du Jer caves
*t 05 62 94 00 41; open
Mar–Nov 10–6; adm*

Grottes du Loup
*t 05 62 94 20 91; open
Easter–Sept daily 9–7*

reproducing Leonardo's *Last Supper*. And if you can stand any more, there's the **Musée de la Nativité**, and the **Musée du Petit Lourdes**, with the village of Bernadette's time in miniature. On Rue des Petits-Fosses, a building that was once a prison and later the home of Bernadette's family can be visited: **Le Cachot**, 'the cell'.

For something different visit the **Aquarium de Lourdes** to see local river fish, and a 3D film of carp and pike in a lake, and you can tickle the sturgeon; and the **Musée Christi** is a museum on calligraphy and old PR methods.

Visitors also like to take trips up the mountains that fringe the town; you can ride to the top of the 3,081ft (940m) Pic du Jer on a **funicular railway**; there is a grand view, and caves to explore near the summit. More caves await atop the slightly shorter Le Béout.

If you want to see some stalactites without the trouble of going up into the mountains, there is the **Grottes du Loup**, near the Basilica on Chemin des Bottes.

Just west of town, off the D937, the **Lac de Lourdes** is one of the largest natural lakes of the Pyrenees, today a favourite picnic ground. Until recent times, however, its overgrown banks were a sinister place, seldom visited. Legends said that the lake could swallow up swimmers or boatmen and hold their souls for eternity. According to another story, there once was a city here, that sank under the waters as punishment for its sins; fishermen claimed they could sometimes hear its church bell ringing under the surface. In July and Aug you can rent a canoe and listen for yourself.

Bordering the lake to the north is a stretch of countryside around the village of Bartrès. This area, as far north as Pontacq and Ossun, was a major **necropolis** and perhaps a religious site in Neolithic times. Dozens of tumuli and standing stones can still be seen, a small fraction of the original total. Survivors include some of the largest mounds in the south of France – one over 170ft (52m) in diameter. Others have stone corridors inside with branching funeral chambers. In this lonely, haunted landscape, a little girl named Bernadette Soubirous used to spend long days alone, watching the sheep. Bernadette's family lived for a time in **Bartrès**, where both the family's house and the barn have been converted into shrines.

Market Days in Lourdes

Easter–early Oct: Daily, Place du Champ-Commun.

Where to Stay in and around Lourdes

In all France, only Paris has more hotel rooms. Nearly all of them close in winter. English, Spanish and German are spoken and most hotels accept pets and require half-board. In short, it's a factory; visitors aren't very demanding and nothing really stands out. Mid-range hotels crowd the Boulevard de la Grotte, just above or behind the souvenir shops. Away from the inferno, though, some quiet addresses may be found.

(i) **Lourdes >**
Place Peyramale,
t 05 62 42 77 40,
www.lourdes-
infotourisme.com; open
Jan–Mar and early
Oct–Dec Mon–Sat 9–12
and 2–6, closed hols;
April–June and July–
early Oct Mon–Sat
9–6.30, Sun 10–12.30,
hols 10–6

(i) **St-Pé-de-**
Bigorre
Place des Arcades,
t 05 62 41 88 10; open
Sept–June Mon–Fri 8–12
and 2–6; July and Aug
daily 9–12.30
and 2–6.30

Lourdes ✉ 65100

****Grand Hôtel de la Grotte**, 66 Rue de la Grotte, t 05 62 94 58 87, *www.hotel-grotte.com* (€€€–€€). A traditional grand hotel just below the château, with ringside rooms overlooking the basilica. Gastronomic restaurant and brasserie. *Open early April–early Nov.*

***Hotel Beauséjour**, 16 Av de la Gare, t 05 62 94 38 18, *www.hotel-beausejour.com* (€€€–€€). This fine old hotel opposite the station has a modern, glitzy interior; well-equipped, comfortable rooms. Although spacious, those at the front can be noisy due to the large volumes of traffic. *Menus €13–25. Open all year.*

***Moderne**, Av Bernadette Soubirous, t 05 62 94 12 32, *www.hotelmodernelourdes.com* (€€). Another real palace of the *belle époque. Open mid-April–mid-Oct.*

Hotel Majestic, 9 Chaussée Maransin, t 05 62 94 27 23 (€). A good option not far from the shrines, with very comfortable rooms and a terrace. *Open April–Oct.*

St-Savin, Rue des Pyrénées, t 05 62 94 06 07, *www.hotelsaintsavin-lourdes.com* (€). Neat rooms on a street where you might even find a parking place, a consideration in Lourdes. *Open all year.*

There are plenty of places on the periphery of town and in neighbouring villages, where life can be more peaceful.

Hotel Le Virginia, Adé, 5km north of Lourdes on the N21, t 05 62 94 66 18, *www.hotelvirginia-lourdes.com* (€). A motel with separate cottages and a restaurant. *Chalets €57. Menus €15–26. Open all year.*

Eating Out in Lourdes

Lourdes' pilgrims do not much concern themselves with cuisine either.

Le Magret, 10 Rue des 4 Frères-Soulas, t 05 62 94 20 55, *www.lemagret.com*. Worth a visit for good unpretentious local cuisine and southwest wines. *Menus €13–33. Closed Mon and Jan.*

Pizzeria da Marco, Rue de la Grotte. t 05 62 94 03 59, *http://perso.orange.fr/pizzeria.Da.Marco/index.html*. An inexpensive oasis for Italian pilgrims, with a menu, Italian pasta and wines. Eat for about €12, less at lunchtime. *Closed Sun and Mon except summer.*

A La Petite Bergère, Bartrès, t 05 62 94 04 28. It's worth travelling out to Bartrès for the food here. On the garden terrace, you can try lamb and chicken dishes, shad and salmon, prepared in often surprising ways. *Menus from €17. Open all year exc Wed eve.*

Tarbes

Almost half the 220,000 people of the Hautes-Pyrénées live in or around this grey, unfathomable toadstool of a departmental capital. There's precious little to see or do here; upon careful consideration, you might be inclined to agree that among all the cities of southern France, Tarbes is the one most sadly wanting in personality and character (Salon-de-Provence comes in a close second). It has long been a military town (like Salon), and do not doubt there is a connection.

History

According to legend, Tarbes was founded by an Ethiopian queen named Tarbis. Having been defeated in battle by the Pharaoh's army – commanded by none other than Moses – she offered Moses her hand and half her kingdom. When he refused, the queen was so distraught that she went off to the south of France with her

Getting to and around Tarbes

Tarbes-Ossun-Lourdes **airport** (*www.tarbes-lourdes.aeroport.fr*), halfway between the two Hautes-Pyrénées cities, has a daily flight from Paris on Air France. For information in Tarbes, ring **t** 05 62 32 92 22.

Another easy way to get into the region is the **TGV** from Paris to Tarbes; there are usually four a day, as well as night trains and motorail.

Tarbes is the hub for **bus** connections. Most buses start from the bus station at Place aux Bois, and some from in front of the train station; call SALT for further information (**t** 05 62 34 76 69). There are at least a dozen runs a day to Lourdes, and many continue on from there to Argelès, Arrens and Plerrefitte.

sister Lorda (who founded Lourdes). More likely, the city started out as a trading post for Aquitaine merchants on the Adour, *c.* 300 BC. It grew into a Roman town, and after being destroyed by the Normans in the 9th century reappeared under the leadership of its bishops. Being sited on a plain made defence difficult, and medieval Tarbes grew up in the odd form of six walled, self-contained *bourgs* strung in a row (nothing of these survives today). The counts of the Bigorre fixed their residence here, and Tarbes acquired its status as capital of the region. Slow but steady industrialization after the railroad arrived in 1859 made Tarbes what it is today. Among other things, Tarbes makes aeroplane parts, and the local Resistance won the Croix de Guerre for effectively sabotaging the plant in 1944.

For all its industry, and the fact that it is the administrative capital of the Hautes-Pyrénées, Tarbes is still really just a big market town, and its liveliest corner is still the Place Marcadieu, where the enormous Thursday farmers' market spreads out around the big metal *halles*, built in 1880. The *place* got its centrepiece about the same time: the Fontaine Duvignau. Four local sculptors combined to make this fountain, a complex allegory representing the four valleys that stretch up to the mountains from around Tarbes, dripping with cute allegorical maidens as well as bears, izards and other Pyrenean wildlife.

Besides the market, Tarbes is also an army town. There are large and stately barracks, belonging to a division of *hussards parachutistes* on the Allées Général Leclerc, and nearby, on Cours de Reffye, the **Haras Nationaux**, a cavalry stud farm founded by Napoleon. Despite the current lack of demand for cavalry, it's still in business, an elegant compound of Empire-style buildings with some lovely gardens and a **Maison du Cheval** to explain what it's all about. There is a guided tour of the stables, forge and saddlery, and a carriage ride.

Maison du Cheval
*t 05 62 56 30 80,
www.haras-nationaux.
fr; open school holidays
and summer visits at 2,
3 and 4, otherwise by
appointment; closed
mid-Nov–early Dec and
most of Jan; horses out
to stud Feb–July*

**Birthplace of
Maréchal Foch**
*t 05 62 93 19 02; open
Thurs–Mon 9–12 and
2–6.30; adm*

Just north of the Haras is the heart of the old town, with the **cathedral**, called here La Sède, an ungainly thing full of Baroque fripperies, begun in the 12th century and tinkered with ever since. Nearby, on Rue de la Victoire, you might explore another military connection by visiting the **birthplace of Maréchal Foch**. The Hero of the Marne's family furniture is present, along with mementoes from the war and some surprising gifts – a bizarre decorative helmet presented by the city of New York, and a beaded chief's belt from the Crow Indians .

The Jardin Massey

The only reason for stopping at Tarbes, though, is this remarkable, wrought-iron-fenced island of civility on the northern edge of town. Placide Massey was a wealthy botanist and naturalist who for years was in charge of the gardens at Versailles. Beginning in 1829, he turned his own 35-acre (14ha) estate at Tarbes into a lush, English-style park, and embellished it with trees and plants from around the world: everything from Californian sequoias and Lebanese cedars to an outlandish, gigantic Siberian elm and an avenue of rare, frost-resistant palm trees. When he died, Massey left the park to the city of Tarbes, along with his home and art collections, now a museum.

The most beautiful thing in the park is the delicate iron and glass **Orangerie**, full of palms and exotic cacti. All the foreign trees and shrubs along the park's walks are labelled for identification; there's a pretty lagoon full of ducks, baby deer and peacocks, a Victorian bandstand and a café. The most unexpected feature is an entire medieval **cloister**, reassembled here from St-Sever-de-Rustan. The 14th-century carving is first-rate, on some of the strangest capitals ever: besides more conventional scenes you'll notice birds pulling a woman's toes, swans killing a bear, and a fellow chasing a lady with a long knife. The peculiar building with the neo-Moorish tower near the Orangerie, once Placide Massey's home, now houses the **Musée Massey**. Most of the space is taken up with the Musée Internationale des Hussards. Tarbes' hussars may jump out of aeroplanes now, but this museum will remind you that the idea of 'hussars' as a flashy élite cavalry goes back to Hungary in the 15th century. Other countries, including France, developed corps of their own; with their élite training and fancy uniforms hussars were singularly effective in terrorizing natives in the colonies and rebellious workers at home. Most of the museum consists of paintings and empty uniforms on horseback and it's all very colourful. There is also a **Musée de la Déportation et de la Résistance**.

Musée Massey
t 05 62 36 31 49; closed for major restoration; no date set for reopening

Musée de la Déportation et de la Résistance
63 Rue Georges Lassalle, t 05 62 51 11 60; open Mon–Fri by appointment

Around Tarbes

The northernmost part of the Hautes-Pyrénées, very much a continuation of Béarn's Vic-Bilh, is a jumbled-up land of parallel river valleys only a few miles apart, full of innumerable tiny villages. If anything, the area is famous for beans, the *haricots tarbais* without which no *cassoulet* would be right. **Vic-en-Bigorre**, the only large village, could be Tarbes in a nutshell, built around its old market *halles* and 15th-century church. **Rabastens-de-Bigorre**, a 14th-century *bastide*, claims to be the national centre for milk-fed veal, most of which gets sent to Italy to make *scallopine* and *osso buco*. East on the D6, you can see what's left of the abbey at **St-Sever-de-Rustan**: the 12th-century abbey church, remodelled in the Renaissance, and the Pavillion des Hôtes from the 1700s.

(i) **Tarbes >>**
3 Cours Gambetta, t 05 62 51 30 31, www.tarbes.com; open all year Mon–Sat 9–12.30 and 2–7

Market Days around Tarbes

Tarbes: Thursdays.
Vic-en-Bigorre: Saturdays.

Where to Stay and Eat in Tarbes

As at Lourdes, you'll do better just outside town. Tarbes has plenty of accommodation for visiting salesmen; it's never crowded and rooms are generally much cheaper.

Tarbes ✉ 65000
★★★**Henri IV**, 7 Av Bertrand Barère, between the railway station and Place de Verdun, t 05 62 34 01 68 (€€). A good bargain, with helpful staff and very comfortable rooms. *Open all year.*
★★★**Hôtel l'Aragon**, Juillan, on the D921 towards Lourdes, t 05 62 32 07 07,

ⓘ **Vic-en-Bigorre**
*Centre Multimédia,
Place du Corps
Franc Pommiès,
t 05 62 33 74 00,
www.vic-bigorre.com*

www.hotel-aragon.com (€). A modern but gracious establishment set in spacious gardens. Even if you don't stay, try to drop in for dinner. The restaurant is run by Bernard Cazaux. It's popular, with a reputation for the best food around; try *filets de rougets et pinces de homard en bouillabaisse*. *Menus €32–52. Closed Sun eve, and 2 weeks in Jan and 2 in Aug.*

**Hôtel de l'Avenue, Av Bertrand Barère, t 05 62 93 06 36, www.hotel-de-l-avenue-tarbes.com (€). Basic. Open all year.

L'Ambroisie, 48 Rue Abbé, t 05 62 93 09 34, http://perso.wanadoo.fr/ambroisie. A popular local restaurant in an old presbytery, with a terrace

and garden. Tuna steak and beef roasted with Madiran wine are especially recommended. *Menus €34–70. Closed Sun and Mon.*

L'Asia, 77 Av Régiment-du-Bigorre, t 05 62 93 03 43, www.asia-restaurant.fr. As its name implies, this offers tasty specialities from China, Japan and elsewhere, including a Vietnamese fondue, plenty of seafood and dramatically flambéed fruits for dessert. *Menus €16–32. Closed for lunch exc Sun plus Sept.*

L'Isard, Av Maréchal-Joffre, near the railway station, t 05 62 93 06 60. Usually crowded at lunch time, with filling menus €12–20 and *à la carte. Closed Sun eve.*

Pyrenean Valleys: the Lavedan

This is the highest of the High Pyrenees, and the most famed for its scenic wonders. A trio of the chain's giants, Balaïtous, Vignemale and Monte Perdido, look down on a host of smaller fry – mere 7,500-footers (2,300m) – as well as the most astounding sight the mountains have to offer, the great natural wall of the Cirque de Gavarnie. The mountain views are never short of spectacular, a paradise for skiers and hikers, though beyond sports and activities there isn't a lot to do. The difficult terrain has always kept the Lavedan out of the mainstream of culture and history. Today, the valleys that run down from the heights get more than their share of tourists year-round. Cauterets and Gavarnie, in fact, were the first fashionable resorts in the Pyrenees, back in the early 19th century when mountain-touring first became popular.

Tourism remains the sum total of the Lavedan economy, though this was not always the case. Busy and heavily populated by a Gaulish tribe called the Levitani in ancient times, when mountain pasture-land was a greater asset than it is now, the Lavedan lived as a world in itself, where Romans and Franks were but distant nuisances who would come sniffing around for tax money. Charlemagne created a viscount of the Lavedan to do the job better, and his successors ruled the valleys as their private preserve up to the Revolution. All the while, people made a comfortable though never luxurious living from their cows and sheep, guiding them up to the heights in summer and back down again when the leaves started to turn. Because the Lavedan valleys provided a way into the mountains but not through them, the region has always been more isolated than the valleys to the west; proper roads were not built until the 18th century. You won't get trapped at a dead end at the

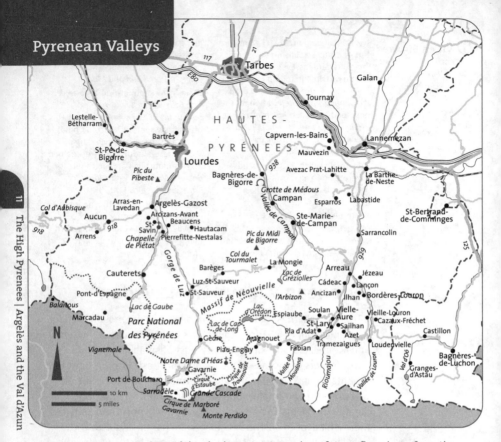

Spanish border, however. A number of rivers flow down from the highest peaks to form the Adour and the Gave de Pau, and there will be several chances to branch off along the way and follow them.

Argelès and the Val d'Azun

Heading south from Lourdes on the N21, the big mountain on your right is the **Pic du Pibeste**, a fine area for hiking, its slopes crisscrossed with trails. Herds of mouflons, deer, eagles and vultures are commonly sighted here. The next town is **Argelès-Gazost**, one of the main centres of mountain tourism. Argelès has a split personality: an attractive and well-kept medieval centre of stone houses and narrow alleys, and below that a spacious spa resort laid out in the 1890s. There's a **park of Pyrenean animals** on the Avenue des Pyrénées.

Parc Animalier Pyrénées
t 05 62 97 91 07,
www.parc-animalier-pyrenees.com

The Val d'Azun

From Argelès, there is a choice of roads: either straight down the D921 into the heart of the mountains, or a detour west on the D918 into the Val d'Azun. It's a lovely detour, passing through unspoiled medieval villages like **Arras**, with ruins of a castle and a Romanesque church that has a low Gothic *porte des Cagots*. From Arras, you can really get away from it all by detouring even further down the D103 (or the main Pyrenean hiking route, the GR 10, which parallels it) up the **Vallée d'Estaing**, an isolated region in the shadow of Moun Né (2,698m/8,853ft); the road ends at a pretty mountain lake, the Lac d'Estaing.

The D918 continues west to **Aucun**, with another Romanesque church; this one conserves truly unusual holy water stoups and baptismal fonts from its original equipment, covered with naïve carvings. Aucun also has a small museum, the Musée du Lavedan.

Musée du Lavedan
t 05 62 97 12 03; open daily in school hols, guided visit at 5pm; adm; rest of year by appt at weekends

Further west, there are more churches worth a look at **Arrens**: the 12th-century St-Pierre, with a stoup 'of the Cagots', and just south of the village **Notre-Dame-de-Pouey-Lahün**, called the 'Golden Chapel' because of its extravagant gilded wood-carved decoration inside; this chapel is a pilgrimage site much like Lourdes, commemorating an appearance of the Virgin to a shepherd long ago. From here the D105 will take you up to the slopes of **Balaïtous** on the Spanish border, a sparse region of mountain lakes created by dams; the big glacier that covers Balaïtous' northern face is the dominant sight. Go any further on the twisting, gear-grinding but exceptionally scenic road west from Arrens and you'll be approaching the Col d'Aubisque, gateway to the Vallée d'Ossau in Béarn (*see* p.238).

St-Savin and the Gave de Pau

South of Argelès, the D921 passes through one of the most densely inhabited valleys of the Pyrenees, dotted with tiny villages on both sides of the Gave de Pau. On the left bank of the Gave, beautifully sited on a shelf above the valley with a wonderful view, **St-Savin** goes back quite a way for a tiny village. Founded on the site of a Roman villa, it was sacked by the Arabs and Normans, and then rebuilt under Charlemagne. Later it became a *sauveté*, and the home of a Benedictine abbey favoured by the counts of Bigorre.

From this busy history only the **church** of St-Savin remains, but it is one of the medieval treasure houses of the western Pyrenees. The austere exterior is punctuated by 12 buttresses (to represent the Twelve Apostles, as the novices were no doubt told when they entered the abbey). Savin was a 6th-century hermit – or 8th-century, according to some; there's nothing definite known about him, though in the apse a painter of the 15th century did his best to portray Savin in fresco. Some odd Renaissance paintings can be seen around the altar: mythological figures, allegories of the liberal arts, a sun and moon and orrery. The abbot who commissioned them in 1546, an interesting character by the name of François de Foix-Candale, was a translator of the mystic books of Hermes Trismegistus, and also one of the first recorded mountain-climbers;

he made it up the Pic du Midi in the same year. Among the paintings are three carved grimacing faces, the '*barabouts*' – comically representing the three men it took to work the organ. Note the painted wooden *Crucifixion* from the same period; like many others of this popular Spanish genre, Christ seen from one side seems to be dead, while alive from the opposite angle. Note also the *bénitier des Cagots*, the holy water stoup reserved for the Cagots, carved with a rabbit's foot. Adjacent to the church, the chapter hall of the abbey also survives. The church treasure, housed here, contains some unique baubles, which include a Renaissance gold box holding the relics of St-Savin and two medieval statues of the Virgin Mary.

The beautifully forested slopes around St-Savin and on the opposite side of the Gave make one of the most delightful corners of this valley. Below the village, the chapel of **Notre-Dame-de-**

The Apotheosis of the Bean

Cassoulet might be the ultimate test for whether or not southwest France is your kind of place. Every proper Gascon (or Périgourdin or Languedocien) housewife serves it up every Wednesday or Thursday, depending on family custom. On the other hand, some of the southwest's great chefs present it with pride on their menus, and there is even an *académie* dedicated to the perfection and enjoyment of *cassoulet*. Though marvellously time-consuming, it's easy enough to make, if you have the right ingredients – but really, what sort of meat you use doesn't matter; *cassoulet* is infinitely adaptable. No two recipes for this formidable bean casserole are ever alike, and in practice a *cassoulet* often gets made when sausages and/or other miscellaneous pork parts start piling up in the fridge. Of course you would want to find the best *haricots tarbais* available, unless you come from east of Toulouse, in which case you know that beans from Castelnaudary in the Lauragais are obviously far superior.

Wherever you get your beans, put a half-kilo of them in warm water and let them soak a few hours, or preferably overnight. Then, wash them off and put them in a pot with cold water, and cook for a half-hour or so. Now, what meat do you have as leftovers, and what do you need to buy? The general principle is some pork and some duck or goose, altogether 1½ times as much meat as the beans (dry weight). The bulk of it should be pork shoulder and sausage (*saucisse de Toulouse*, or else chipolatas, or whatever you fancy). Along with that goes a few *confits* (duck or goose), which also provide the fat necessary for the operation. Other possible meats include 1) a big chunk of *jambon de Bayonne* or similar country ham, 2) a pig's foot, 3) an *andouille* (a sausage made from ground pork rinds), 4) *confits de gésiers* (duck gizzards – recommended if you can get them).

At about three in the afternoon, cut the pork, sausage and ham into large bits. Chop a big onion and an entire head of garlic – a big one – into endless tiny bits. In a large casserole, fry the pork and sausage in some of the fat from the *confits* for about 15 minutes, then add the onions and garlic, the *confits* and ham; keep stirring everything around until the onions are transparent. Dump in the beans and cover with water; add salt and pepper and maybe a little thyme; why not? Boil this on a high flame until the water starts to evaporate, then turn it all the way down, and cover. Let it continue until the beans are just done, which may take three hours or more. Sit back and relax for a while. Stir the mixture around a bit from time to time so that nothing sticks to the bottom. Add water if necessary; when the beans are done there should be very little liquid, though.

Now the thing's ready to go in the oven. Make sure that the beans cover the meat as much as possible, and give the top a good dusting of breadcrumbs. Many cooks like to put some grilled Toulouse sausage on top too. On a low heat (about gas mark 4) bake it, covered, for an hour or a little more. Serve with any old *vin de pays*: you can save the good stuff for another time.

Piétat stands on a height in a setting worthy of a jigsaw puzzle picture. From St-Savin, you can detour up the pretty D13 to **Arcizans-Avant**, with its 'Castle of the Black Prince' (that's the traditional name, though most of it dates from much later than Edward's day). It has been thoroughly restored and is now a chambre d'hôtes (*see* p.260). Continuing this route, you'll cross over back towards the Vallée d'Estaing (*see* above).

Down in the valley beneath St-Savin, stop for a minute as you pass through **Adast** to see the singular Romanesque portal on its church: a woman with a dragon, along with dancing figures. On the opposite side of the Gave de Pau, no fewer than 12 small villages occupy a strip of fertile mountain slope 8km long; in the Middle Ages, when the Pyrenees became densely populated, no bit of space went to waste. **Beaucens** was the old headquarters of the viscounts of Lavedan, and they left a well-preserved medieval **castle** to explore, now housing the **Donjon des Aigles**, a zoo for birds of prey, with eagles, kites, vultures, owls and such; in season they let them fly about. Nearby is the ski resort of Hautacam. At Pierrefitte-Nestalas, a sizeable village, the unlikely attraction is the **Aquarium Tropical du Haut Lavedan**, with coral and exotic specimens from the South Seas.

From Pierrefitte, you have the choice of heading right, towards Cauterets, or left, towards Luz-St-Sauveur and the Pays Toy.

Donjon des Aigles
t 05 62 97 19 59, www.donjon-des-aigles.com; open spring school holidays to end Sept daily 10–12 and 2.30–6.30; flights 3.30 and 5, Aug 3, 4.30 and 6; adm

Aquarium Tropical du Haut Lavedan
t 05 62 92 79 56; open Tues–Sun 9.30–12.30 and 2–6.30; closed Sun am; adm

11
The High Pyrenees | Argelès and the Val d'Azun

Market Days in Argelès and the Val d'Azun

Argelès-Gazost: Tuesdays and Saturdays.
Pierrefitte-Nestalas: Saturdays.

⭐ **Hôtel du Lac d'Estaing >>**

ⓘ **Argelès-Gazost >**
Grande Terrace, t 05 62 97 00 25, www.argeles-gazost.com; open daily 9–12 and 2–6.30

⭐ **Le Viscos >>**

Where to Stay and Eat in Argelès and the Val d'Azun

Argelès-Gazost ✉ 65400

**Bon Repos, Av des Stades, t 05 62 97 01 49, www.bonrepos.com (€€–€). Sometimes we take France for granted, but it's gratifying to think that nearly always, when you find a hotel with a name like this, the establishment is likely to provide just that. There are 18 rooms, a pool, a welcoming family and very reasonable rates. *Closed mid-Oct–April.*

**Beau Site, t 05 62 97 08 63, www.hotel-beausite-argeles.com (€). Typical old French inn, full of big flowery

wallpaper and old furniture. A bit shabby but comfortable none the less. *Menu €17. Closed mid-Oct–mid-Dec.*

*Victoria, on the N21, t 05 62 97 08 34 (€). The cheapest option to be found in town and quite acceptable if a bit scruffy. *Open all year.*

Estaing ✉ 65400

*Hôtel du Lac d'Estaing, t 05 62 97 06 25 (€€–€). Out by itself in the mountains, on the road to the lake, the hotel offers generous helpings of peace and quiet, nice rooms, and a restaurant worth the detour. There's a lunch menu, but it's worth going for the spectacular local charcuterie, river fish, and main courses such as the delicious stuffed *roulade d'agneau*. *Menus (lunch €16 up to €40). Open daily May–mid-Oct.*

St-Savin ✉ 65400

**Le Viscos, t 05 62 97 02 28, www.hotel-leviscos.com (€). On the edge of the village, with beautiful views over this exceptional corner of the valley, this hotel has functional rooms, but a

(i) **Pierrefitte-Nestalas**

Av Jean-Moulin, t 05 62 92 71 31, www.pierrefitte-nestalas.net; open Mon–Sat 10–12 and 2.30–6.30

restaurant you are bound to remember. M. Saint-Martin presents innovative dishes that are never over the top; everything seems just right, as in the *lotte* (monkfish) in a casserole with ham. Also wonderful are simple desserts such as tarts made with wild strawberries. *Menus €21–50. Restaurant closed Sun eve and Mon exc July and Aug.*

Arcizans-Avant ✉ 65400

**Le Cabaliros, t 05 62 97 04 31, *www.auberge-cabaliros.com* (€). You might not think of basing yourself in this out-of-the-way hamlet, but Arcizans has one sweet little hotel, offering 8 nice rooms with a view, and

dinner on the terrace. *Menus €18–50. Open early Feb–early Nov.*

Château du Prince Noir, Arcizans-Avant, **t** 05 62 97 02 79, *http://prince.noir.free.fr* (€). For a big gulp of history and amazing views at nearly 2,000 ft up this is the place to stay. The oldest part of this historic building dates back to before the prince's time, to 1120 (*see* p.259.) The ruin was bought and totally renovated by André Doyen in 1972. It now has 3 guest rooms and although they don't appear to have been decorated since he moved in, they're spacious and full of character. *Open Mar–Nov.*

Cauterets

The only real town close to the mountains owes its founding to the presence of mineral waters. This seems to be one spring the Romans missed, but one of the earliest documents concerning the Lavedan, from c. 950, records Count Raymond of Bigorre handing the property over to the abbot of St-Savin, in return for the monks building and running baths. Gaston Fébus, one of the first celebrity visitors, came here to try and cure his growing deafness. In the 18th century, Cauterets became fashionable among French aristocrats, and with the rediscovery of the beauties of nature in the Romantic era, people began to pour in from all over Europe, including Napoleon's brother, the 'King of Holland', with his Queen Hortense (the Bonapartes liked to keep everything in the family: Hortense was none other than Josephine de Beauharnais' sister, and the mother of Napoleon III). Cauterets remained fashionable for another century, drawing crowned heads and several presidents of France to take the waters.

Though most of the bath establishments have closed, Cauterets is still a major tourist centre, albeit one comfortably down at heel and in need of a lick of paint. The narrow valley and the steep mountain walls on both sides make it seem a bit claustrophobic at times, but Cauterets is still the essential base for seeing this corner of the Pyrenees. It has also become a ski resort. A *télécabine* and then a chairlift (running July–late Aug) go up the slopes to the crest of **Cirque du Lys**, tucked under 2,698m/8,853ft **Moun Né**, where an orientation table helps identify peaks and valleys.

In the old days, your introduction to Cauterets would have been the **railway station**, an 1890s wooden confection now used as a coach station. The other remarkable feature of the town is the

Gave de Cauterets and its rapids, flowing right through the centre with houses closely built up along both sides. Most of the old bath establishments have been closed, and you can see some once-glorious pavilions in the centre that have been converted into a cinema and shops. One of the old hotels, the Résidence d'Angleterre, has been turned into the **Musée 1900** with displays of 18th- and 19th-century costumes. The turn-of-the-19th-century grand hotels are in much better shape, along with the recently restored casino, on Boulevard Latapie-Flandrin.

If you're headed further into the mountains, an indispensable stop is the **Maison du Parc** on Place de la Gare. Run by the Parc National management, this includes a small museum, exhibitions on Pyrenean wildlife, and occasional films.

For children and bee lovers, the **Pavillion des Abeilles** offers a big glass beehive and guided tour through the world of bee-keeping . You can see how cheese is made and taste some at **Le Saloir**.

Still, the best thing to do here is to get up into the mountains. The road south of Cauterets will take you a difficult 8km further, as far as the locality called **Pont d'Espagne**. For hikers, the GR 10 follows the road on the opposite side of the Gave; from Pont d'Espagne it branches off into two paths: one for the **Vallée du Marcadau**, a lovely area forested with pines, and the other up to the Lac de Gaube and then on to the refuges for people scaling **Vignemale**. For determined hikers only, it continues from there around the northeastern face of the mountain, practically under an enormous glacier, and then descends into the Vallée d'Ossoue. To have a look at Vignemale the easy way, there is a **chair lift** from Pont d'Espagne up to the Lac de Gaube.

Musée 1900
*t 05 62 92 02 02;
open daily for summer
and winter hols 10–12
and 3–6.30*

Maison du Parc
*t 05 62 92 52 56;
open June–Sept daily
9.30–12 and 3–7*

Pavillion des Abeilles
*Av du Mamelon Vert;
t 05 62 92 50 66; open
July and Aug Mon–Sat
10.30–12.30 and 2.30–7
Sept–June Wed–Sat
2.30–7*

Le Saloir
*Rte de Pierrefitte, t 05
62 92 59 67; open daily*

Chair lift
*runs June–mid-Sept;
contact the tourist
office for further
information; adm*

Market Day in Cauterets

Thursdays, June–Sept.

Where to Stay and Eat in Cauterets

ⓘ **Cauterets >**
*Pl du Maréchal Foch,
t 05 62 92 50 50,
www.cauterets.com;
open Mon–Sat 9–12.30
and 1.30–7 in summer;
otherwise times vary;
a tourist train runs in
July and Aug from
Place Clémenceau*

Cauterets ✉ 65110

***Hotel Balneo Aladin, t 05 62 92 60 00, www.hotelbalneoaladin.com (€€€). Such luxury as Cauterets can provide is limited to this modern hotel, with a pool and gym. There are studios and apartments too. *Closed late Sept–mid-Dec and May.*

**Hôtel Edelweiss, 7 Bd, Latapie Flurin, t 05 62 92 52 75 or 06 81 61 08 26, www.edelweiss-hotel.fr (€). Pleasant, family-run hotel in the centre of town.

Light, airy bedrooms and a very reasonable restaurant; good value all round. *Menus from €15. Open mid-Dec–end of Sept.*

Hôtel César, 3 Rue César, t 05 62 92 52 57, www.cesarhotel.com (€). This hotel is conveniently situated for the thermes and ski lift alike, with a good traditional restaurant. *Menus €15–40. Closed Wed in winter plus May and first 3 weeks Oct.*

Lion d'Or, Rue Richelieu, t 05 62 92 52 87, www.hotel-lion-dor.net (€). This simple place, also a survivor from a bygone age, is on a thoroughly grim, narrow street that provides an interesting contrast to the Pyrenean glory to be found all around. The restaurant open to residents only. *Menus €19–25. Closed for several weeks in May, and Oct–mid-Dec.*

Gavarnie: the Route to the *Cirques*

The other road from Pierrefitte-Nestalas, the D921, will probably be a little busier. This is the road that leads up to the *cirques*, the most obviously spectacular and most-visited sites the Pyrenees have to offer. A *cirque* is a freak of erosion on a grand scale. The centre of the Pyrenees may be good hard granite, pushed up from below when the mountains were formed, but there are layers of mostly limestone to either side. In places like Gavarnie, these strata were pushed up almost vertically to form the highest peaks of the chain. In geological periods when the climate here was much warmer than today, rainfall on the northern face started to erode the soft limestone into something like its present form, and in the Ice Ages glaciers finished the job, leaving landforms that seem to have been gouged out by an ice-cream scoop, one several miles wide.

First, though, the road passes through the long Gorge de Luz, and arrives at **Luz**, the biggest village in the valley. This is a medieval-looking place of not much interest, except for its 14th-century church, **St-André**. Though often called the 'Templar church' by locals, it was really largely built by their Crusading rivals, the Knights Hospitaller (Knights of Malta); perhaps they picked up an earlier church on the site with the rest of the booty they acquired after the suppression of the Templars in 1307. Though a stout, fortified church, it has a touch of striking grace on its porch: a carved tympanum of *Christ and the four Evangelists*. Inside, some frescoes remain, as well as a church treasury that holds some fine works of medieval sculpture. Across the Gave de Gavarnie from Luz stands another spa: **St-Sauveur**, the younger half of the consolidated village of Luz-St-Sauveur. Here you can find sulphurous waters to fix your aching bones, and an impressive arched bridge embellished with imperial eagles, the gift of satisfied spa customer Napoleon III.

Continuing south toward the *cirques*, the D921 traverses more gorges, and then passes the Pyrenees' biggest hydroelectric plant, at Pragnères. From any high ground at **Gèdre**, the next village, you may catch a first glimpse of the Cirque de Gavarnie, along with the famous notch in the wall, the Brèche de Roland, over 10km away. Two roads go south from Gèdre, and both of them lead to *cirques* – there are three of them in a row, an almost continuous, thrice-indented wall almost 18km in length. The right turn is only a steep and very difficult track up to the Cirque de Troumouse, and if you have a car you'll be going the other way, to Gavarnie, the highest village in the Pyrenees and the traditional base for seeing the area.

Cirque de Gavarnie

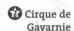 Cirque de Gavarnie

There are two ways to see the Cirque de Gavarnie: either walking (about 4hrs) or on the back of a donkey or horse. (The families with the donkeys have been serving as guides for generations. Usually they only take you one way; if you want them to wait for the trip back, make arrangements in advance.) Contact the tourist office for further information.

One of the oddities of seeing the *cirque* is reflecting that at the top of the wall lies Spain; the border follows the crests of all three of the *cirques*. The panorama takes in a view of almost 4km: 2,300m/7,547ft Pic des Tantes on the right, then fragments of the tremendous glacier that once covered all of Gavarnie. Near the centre, at an altitude of 2,781m/9,123ft, is the huge gash in the wall, the **Brèche de Roland**. In local legend, the hero smote at the mountain with his sword Durandal in futile rage when he was surrounded by the Saracens (never mind that the ambush happened at Roncesvalles, far to the west; relics of Roland, his horse's footprints and so on, turn up all over Europe). One of the most spectacular sights (if you can get close enough to it) is the **Grande Cascade**, the highest waterfall in Europe; the water drains out of semi-frozen marshes, high above on the Spanish side. On the eastern edge loom two formidable mountains: **Marboré** (which means 'marble' in Gascon) and behind it, visible from some angles, the second-tallest peak of the entire chain, 3,323m/10,904ft Monte Perdido, entirely on the Spanish side of the border.

It's hard to believe, looking up at it, but you can actually walk to the top of the *cirque* in the summer months. A trail leads up to the Sarradets *refuge*, and reaches the crest from there, though you'll have to cross some difficult patches of glacier to make it all the way. For one additional attraction, if you get to the top you can have a look inside some of the biggest and highest-altitude **ice caves** in the world, first explored by Norbert Casteret in the 1920s. All are on the slopes of Marboré and Monte Perdido, and unless you are an experienced spelunker it isn't wise to go too far into any of them – there are some surprise drops of hundreds of feet.

For another view of the *cirque*, there is a steep road (the D923) from Gavarnie village up to **Port de Boucharo** on the border, where it peters out into a hiking trail; this is the only reliable path into Spain in a stretch of some 40km. Along the way, you can get out and climb without too much difficulty up to the top of Pic des Tantes, for a grandstand seat that takes in the entire area.

The Cirque de Troumouse and Cirque d'Estaubé

Anywhere else, this would be a three-star attraction, but next to the more awesome Gavarnie the Cirque de Troumouse gets stuck with the role of little sister. Just as broad as Gavarnie, it is much lower, with neither a waterfall nor a *brèche* – but it may afford you a bit more peace and quiet in summer, when all the trails around Gavarnie are packed. To get there, take the D922 from Gèdre up the Gave de Héas. This passes a dammed lake, the **Lac des Gloriettes**, and the **chapel of Notre-Dame de Héas**, commemorating yet another apparition of the Virgin, back in 1349. The last part of the route is a toll road, but it leads up to a 1,981m/6,500ft peak for a grand view of the *cirque*.

Even less visited is the *cirque* in the middle, the Cirque d'Estaubé, smallest of the three. A hiking trail from the Lac des Gloriettes is the only way in.

Barèges and the Col de Tourmalet

On the way back, instead of returning to Lourdes, you can take a short-cut into the next valley, the **Vallée d'Aure**, by means of the D918 from Luz (or by the ubiquitous GR 10). This is big-time skiing country, beginning with **Barèges**, an old thermal resort (the highest one in France) that has successfully made the transition to concentrating on winter sports. Barèges and **La Mongie**, just down the road, have between them the biggest ski area and greatest number of pistes in the Pyrenees. This whole area is an *Aire Pastoral*, which means you quite often have to stop for the herds of sheep, cattle or horses that roam free. This just adds to the beauty of this breathtaking mountain pass, and makes the first glimpse of La Mongie and its concrete tower blocks quite jarring.

Further along the D918, the views take in a chain of big peaks to the north, culminating in the 2,838m/9,312ft **Pic du Midi de Bigorre**, and to the south, the **Massif de Néouvielle**, a huge region of lakes that is easily accessible only from the south (*see* p.278). Halfway to the Vallée d'Aure the road crosses over the Col de Tourmalet, where the waters of the Gave de Pau and those of the Adour divide. On the way you can see the **Jardin Botanique de Tourmalet**, a two-hectare garden which presents wild flowers of the Pyrenees in appropriate settings, from rocks to forest. Nearly every year, the Tour de France bicycle race is routed over this pass, providing the ultimate test of stamina for the riders (and filling all the hotels and blocking up the roads for everyone else, for a few days in mid-July). Along the route you'll notice the competitors' names, painted on the roads in huge letters, along with contributions from local graffiti artists and ETA supporters.

At the top of the Pic du Midi is a magnificent **observatory**, built by the University of Toulouse in 1881, which has one of the biggest telescopes in Europe. It has opened to the public as a **Musée des Etoiles** with splendid viewing platforms and observatories, terraces with spectacular views of the Pyrenees, and a restaurant. Access is

Jardin Botanique de Tourmalet
t 05 62 92 18 06; open mid-May–mid-Sept daily 9–7; adm

Musée des Etoiles
t 05 62 56 71 11, www.picdumidi.com; open June–Sept daily 9–7, Oct–May usually 10–5.30; sometimes closed Tues and other days

by *téléférique* from La Mongie. Further east, another cable car leads up to the EDF dam and its lake, the Lac de Greziolles; beyond the hairpin bend there's a favourite postcard subject, a waterfall called the **Cascade de Garet**.

Market Days around Gavarnie

Cauterets: Thursdays, from June through to September.

Luz-St-Sauveur: Mondays.

Arrens-Marsous: Sundays, in July and August.

Sports and Activities around Gavarnie

As far as activities go, as you would imagine in this busy area nearly everything is on offer, and all well-organized: nature walks, courses in rock-climbing and ornithology, children's activities, photo safaris, mountain lake fishing, telemark and cross-country skiing, paragliding, canoes and kayaks and so on.

All the local tourist information offices are well-informed, and worth writing to in advance if you have a special field of interest; both Luz and Argelès are particularly good.

Maisons du Parc

Besides the tourist offices, you can find out everything about the natural wonders of the area, plus information on hiking, sports, flora and fauna, at the Maisons du Parc, run by the administration of the Parc National des Pyrénées. They also have regular schedules of films, exhibitions and activities for all the family.

Cauterets: t 05 62 92 52 56.

Luz: t 05 62 92 38 38.

Gavarnie: t 05 62 92 49 10.

Where to Stay and Eat around Gavarnie

Luz-St-Sauveur ⊠ 65120

***Le Montaigu**, on the D172 to Vizos, t 05 62 92 81 71, *www.hotelmontaigu. com* (€€). This is a modern building in a traditional style. Rooms are spacious

and comfortable, some with balconies, all with a great view. A pleasant hotel in a beautiful setting. *Menus €15–25. Restaurant open eve only. Closed Oct and Nov.*

***Les Cimes**, in the centre of Luz, t 05 62 92 82 03 (€). A good choice.

****Hôtel-Restaurant Panoramic**, 30 Av Impératrice Eugénie, Quartier Thermal, t 05 62 92 80 14, *www.hotel-panoramic-luz.com* (€). A fine old family hotel that must have been quite grand in its day; though it is a bit faded now, the bedrooms are modern, clean and functional. The restaurant offers honest, regional cooking at €14. Excellent value with a pretty summer terrace overlooking the town. *Open end April–late Sept, and weekends and school holidays in winter.*

Gèdre ⊠ 65120

****Hôtel des Pyrénées**, t 05 62 92 48 51 (€€–€). Another lovely old establishment right in the centre of town. No restaurant. *Closed mid-Oct–mid-Dec.*

****Brèche de Roland**, t 05 62 92 48 54, *www.gavarnie.com/hotel-la-breche* (€). One of the famous old hotels of the Pyrenees, this is an old mansion, all mountain austerity outside but retaining many of its original furnishings and walnut panelling within. A sauna and a lift have recently been added. There is a garden and a restaurant with outdoor terrace, and the management helps arrange winter sports and helicopter rides. *Menus €16–32. Closed Oct–mid-Dec and several weeks in April.*

Gavarnie ⊠ 65120

If you're spending the day here and decide to stay in the town overnight, ensure you book early as every room is taken by hikers or skiers by about 5pm. Parking in a private hotel you will also avoid the exorbitant €4 (for 5 minutes or 5 hours), that is mandatory for public parking.

ⓘ **Gavarnie >>**
Rte Nationale, t 05 62 92 49 10, www.gavarnie. com; open daily 9–12 and 2–6

ⓘ **Luz-St-Sauveur >**
t 05 62 92 81 60/t 05 62 92 30 30, www.luz.org; open July and Aug Mon–Sat 9–7.30, Sun 9–12.30 and 4.30–7.30; Sept–June Mon–Sat 9–12 and 2–7.30

11

The High Pyrenees | Gavarnie: the Route to the *Cirques*

***Hôtel-Club Vignemale, t** 05 62 92 40 00, *www.hotel-vignemale.com* (€€€€). This hotel has little to justify its rates, but its restaurant is the best in the valley: mountain trout and *écrevisses*, and good desserts on a pretty outdoor terrace. Restaurant is open for residents only. *Open mid-May–mid-Oct.*

****Le Marboré, t** 05 62 92 40 40, *www.lemarbore.com* (€€). Set in a distinctive 19th-century building, with a sauna and gym. Like many French hotels recently, this lovely old building has been totally modernized inside. Still, it's clean and comfortable and at a good price. *Menus €21. Closed mid-Nov–mid-Dec.*

Hôtel Compostelle, t 05 62 92 49 43, *www.compostellehotel.com* (€). Very simple, more like a posh refuge. *Open 26 Dec–30 Sep.*

Refuge des Espuguettes, on the trail from Gavarnie to the Cirque d'Estaubé, **t** 05 62 92 40 63 (€). For hikers, this is the best base for a thorough exploration of the *cirques*. Be sure to book ahead, especially for July and August. *Open mid-June–mid-Sept.*

Barèges ✉ 65120

****Hôtel de l'Europe, t** 05 62 92 68 04 (€€). The games room is the highlight of this modern, functional and somewhat faceless hotel. *Menus €13–22. Closed Oct, Nov, April and May.*

Auberge du Lienz, just east, near the cable car up the Pic de l'Ayre, **t** 05 62 92 67 17. In an idyllic mountain setting, this lovely *auberge* has been a haven for hikers and skiers since 1905. Louisette is passionate about maintaining mountain traditions, and adamant (almost religious) about using only locally farmed produce. The only access in winter is by ski, and after being totally cut off for weeks once, she now bakes her own bread daily and smokes her own trout. *A la carte €30–40.*

Campsite La Ribère, on the road to Luz, **t** 05 62 92 69 01. This is a good site on the edge of town. Mobile homes to rent. *Closed late Oct–early May.*

*****La Grange aux Marmottes** and **Les Campanules** at Viscos 65120. On D149 off the D921, **t** 05 62 92 91 13, *www.grangeauxmarmottes.com*. Ancient stone and slate buildings joined together on different levels make up the two hotels oozing rustic charm. The restaurant is a member of Les Tables Gourmand. *Menus up to €40. Closed mid-Nov–mid-Dec.*

Hôtel Central, 11 Rue Raymond, Barèges, **t** 05 62 92 68 05, *www.central-tourmalet.com* (€). As the name implies, in the middle of town. A well-run modest hotel with a garden. *Menus €13–24. Closed early Oct–end Nov and Easter–end May.*

ⓘ **Barèges ›**
t 05 62 92 16 00, www.bareges.com; open July and Aug Mon–Sat 9–12 and 2– 6.30, Sun 10–12 and 4–6; Sept–June Mon–Sat 9–12 and 2–6.30

Bagnères and the Baronnies

Bagnères-de-Bigorre

Bagnères-de-Bigorre is a wonderful town for eating ice cream and turning your brain off. Sitting in the cafés, under the plane trees of the Allées des Coustous, the world seems far away. This is what Bagnères is for, and the city on the Adour has had centuries of practice as a resort to perfect its charm. The Romans, who liked nothing better than taking the waters, built the town of Vicus Aquensis ('Waterville'), and it has known the favours of rulers since, from Alaric the Goth to Napoleon III and Eugénie. Bagnères is also the only town in the Pyrenees to have a subatomic particle named for it (the hyperon, after the Boulevard de l'Yperon by the casino; the scientists of the Observatoire du Pic du Midi, who do a lot of work on cosmic rays, have their main laboratories here).

The old town extends westwards from a pretty square, the Allées des Coustous, on the site of part of the old town walls. In one corner, the church of **St-Vincent** has a good Renaissance portal. Other monuments can be found on the narrow streets that begin on the opposite side of the square: yet another Maison de Jeanne d'Albret, on Rue Daléas (rheumatic Jeanne was a frequent visitor), and around the corner the Gothic **Tour des Jacobins**, from a monastery now largely demolished.

Musée Salies
t 05 62 91 07 26;
open May–Oct
Wed–Sun 3–6, until 7 in
July and Aug; adm

Vallon de Salut
t 05 62 91 12 05; open
July–Aug Wed–Sun 3–6,
May, June and Sept,
Wed–Sat

**Musée du Vieux
Moulin**
t 05 62 91 07 33

The spa zone begins at the opposite side of the old town, at **Place des Thermes**, with the imposing neoclassical Etablissement Thermal, built in 1823, and the casino from the 1890s, with 70 slot machines if you want a flutter, a restaurant, a bar, concerts on Saturday night and dancing on Sunday. Next door, the **Musée Salies** has a small collection of 17th- and 18th-century ceramics and art from the Renaissance to modern times, including a work of the Dadaist Francis Picabia and drawings by Honoré Daumier.

Bagnères has another museum, devoted to marble and natural history at **Vallon de Salut** in an old spa building with the cabins and baths still in situ. There is also the **Musée du Vieux Moulin** on farm life and crafts.

Into the Baronnies

A beautiful country, and sometimes a sad country, the Baronnies is a *pays* in the foothills east of Bagnères: no great elevations, but plenty of cliffs and valleys, and tortuous narrow roads connecting a score of villages, most of which are nothing more than a handful of old stone houses. Many of these are either empty or restored holiday homes, for few places in all the depopulated rural areas of the Midi have lost so many people in the last century.

The Baronnies takes its name from the four little lords who divided the area amongst themselves. Tradition has it that they would meet once a year, at a spot in the Forêt des Baronnies where each of their domains met (south of Arrodets), and have a drink, each with one foot on his own land and one on his neighbour's. Its inhabitants always held themselves a bit apart from the other *pays* around them. In fact they were different – research on their blood types has established that the people of the Baronnies are of Basque origin, a pocket of the Basques who once inhabited all the Pyrenees; here, they managed to hold out in this backwater and resist assimilation much longer than the others. They scraped by on their sheep and cows for millennia, building distinctive houses out of the local limestone with heavy lauze roofs. But their land is too poor and too hilly for modern farming and, lacking thermal waters or any other tourist attractions, the *pays* has watched its people simply drain away.

From Bagnères, the main road across the Baronnies is the D938, a green and lovely drive that follows the River Luz. It crosses the river at the **Abbey of Escaladieu** the first Cistercian foundations in the Midi (and the mother house of Flaran, in the Gers). The church, built with the usual Cistercian austerity, nevertheless has a wonderful pavement of stones of different colours, arranged in geometric patterns. The chapter house also survives, along with some of the other buildings. The abbey is sometimes used for concerts and exhibitions during the summer. Just a few kilometres up the road stands **Mauvezin**, worth a stop for its **castle**, built in the 12th–14th centuries. Over the gate an odd inscription can be read: JAY BELLE DAME, 'I have a beautiful lady'. Southern scholars like to argue about it, and some claim it was put there by one of the castle's lords, none other than Gaston Fébus of Béarn. Whether true or not, the castle is currently occupied by the Escole Gaston Fébus, a literary society dedicated to keeping alive the Gascon language and culture. They maintain a large Gascon library here, and hold meetings and poetic competitions in the manner of the Félibres of Provence. The castle keep has a view over most of the Baronnies, and down in the court you can inspect some modern reconstructions of catapults and a number of other medieval engines of war.

Capvern-les-Bains, in the hills above Mauvezin, is a thermal spa with little of the glamour of Bagnères, though it too has been around since Roman times. North of the D938, where the Tarbes–Toulouse motorway breaks the stillness of the Baronnies, **Tournay** is a *bastide* founded in 1307 and the largest village in the *pays*.

Another very scenic road traverses the southern end of the Baronnies, the D84/D26, which also begins in Bagnères. The D84 passes over the **Col des Palomières**, with a lovely view, before entering the collection of tiny villages that make up the heart of the region. **Esparros**, a representative hamlet with only about 200 people, about a quarter of what it had a century ago, is a place that didn't go down without a fight. The village became famous, with annual appearances on the French television news for its *foire aux célibataires*, where the Baronnies' bachelors put themselves on display to try and attract some womenfolk, all for the worthy cause of repopulating the region. History doesn't relate why the village has given up these efforts. The lord of Esparros, one of the four old barons of the Baronnies, laid out **Labastide** with the same thing in mind, back in the 1300s. It never was much of a success, and Labastide is even smaller than Esparros. Near the village is a cave with colour paintings from the Palaeolithic era, discovered by Norbert Castaret, the **Gouffre d'Esparros**. Although he discovered them in 1938, the caves were not opened to the public until 2000; you'll see immense carpets of what looks like

Abbey of Escaladieu
t 05 62 39 16 39; open May–Sept daily 19.30–12.30 and 1.30–6.30; Oct–April 9.30–12.30 and 1.30–5

Mauvezin castle
t 05 62 39 10 27, www. chateaumauvezin.com; open daily 10–7

Gouffre d'Esparros
t 05 62 39 11 80; www. gouffre-esparros.com; open all year for hols and weekends 10–12 and 2–6; daily June–Sept; visit lasts for about 50 mins; call ahead; adm

delicate coral, and huge caves draped with impressive stalactites in a vast array of colours.

Around **Avezac** there is a straight line of 22 Neolithic burial tumuli but none are marked and unless you are an expert they are difficult to spot. At one time there were many more but they have long since been built over or otherwise vanished. The director at the tourist office in La Barthe de Neste is something of a specialist if you want to know more. However, there are plans to set up a museum in Avezac of the funerary objects, weapons and household items that were found in those tumuli that have been excavated – no date as yet for when it will open

South of Bagnères: the Vallée de Campan

Grotte de Médous
t 05 62 91 78 46, www.
grottes-medous.com;
open April–June and
Sept–mid-Oct 9–11.30
and 2–5, July–Aug daily
9–12 and 2–6; adm

Following the River Adour southwards, the D935 offers glimpses of the Pic du Midi de Bigorre and another giant that has strayed from the centre of the range, 9,285ft (2,830m) **L'Arbizon**, just behind it. Just south of Bagnères, signs point the way to the **Grotte de Médous**. Discovered only in 1948, it offers some magnificent sights, including a grotto of colourful formations called the 'Hall of Orchids' and a branch of the Adour that flows underground; they'll take you down it in a boat.

Campan, one of the prettier villages in this part of the mountains, is built around its wooden *halles* and a 16th-century fountain; many houses have half-timbering and corbelled second floors.

If you pass through this pretty village during the summer, at first glance you might think it's a very busy place – full of industrious little people up ladders cleaning windows, fixing cars, getting married or just hanging around chewing the fat. On closer inspection of course, you'll realize that they're all rag dolls (*mounaques*), about 4ft (121cm) high, stuffed with hay and fully dressed in various costumes. The custom comes from the old days, when folks in Campan did not take kindly to one of their girls marrying an outsider, especially if she was the heiress to a house or farm. When that happened, the young people of the village would demand a 'tribute' from the prospective bridegroom – enough money to throw a fête for the village. If he didn't come through, they would appear every night outside the girl's house with cowbells around their necks for mocking serenades. And on the wedding day, they would make sure that the procession had to pass under a pair of satirical effigies of the wedding couple – the origin of the *mounaques*. Nowadays, no such reason is needed; the locals just like the look of them decorating the village.

At Ste-Marie-de-Campan, the road meets the D918 from the Col de Tourmalet (*see* above); the only other alternative is to continue on eastwards, with another beautiful but taxing drive over the **Col d'Aspin**, and so into the valley of the Aure (*see* below).

ⓘ **Sarlabous**
Maison des Baronnies,
t 05 62 40 93 01, www.
si-des-baronnies.fr.; open
mid-June–mid-Sept

ⓘ **Tournay**
t 05 62 35 79 67

ⓘ **Capvern-les-Bains >>**
Pl de Thermes, t 05 62
39 00 46, www.ville-
capvern.com; open
Mon–Sat 9–12.30 and
3–6.30

ⓘ **Bagnères >**
3 Allées Tournefort,
t 05 62 95 50 71, www.
bagneresdebigorre-
lamongie.com; open
daily 9–12.30 and 2–6

Market Days in Bagnerès and the Baronnies

Bagnères: Saturdays.

Capvern-les-Bains: Tuesdays April–Oct.

Where to Stay and Eat in Bagnères and the Baronnies

Bagnerès ✉ 65200

More than just a stopover, this town is a good place to relax for a few days.

Le Trianon, Pl des Thermes, **t 05 62 95 09 34, *www.perso.wanadoo. fr/hotel.trianon* (€). Not quite up to the standard of its namesake palace at Versailles, but you won't find a more gracious hotel round here: set in a shady park, with pool, near the baths. *Open April–Oct.*

**Hôtel Les Vignaux, t 05 62 95 03 41 (€). This budget option is a good choice. *Menus €11–25. Closed Dec–Jan.*

Le Bigourdin, Rue Victor Hugo, **t** 05 62 95 20 20. This is a good stop for lunch in the centre, offering traditional treats, and also pasta. *Closed Sun eve and Mon.*

Capvern-les-Bains ✉ 65130

There are plenty of choices in town, which is good to know as you aren't going to find much in any of the Baronnies villages. Capvern being one of the more humble spa resorts, accommodation here tends to be modern and functional.

**Lemoine, t 05 62 39 02 18 (€). This is well-priced and pleasant enough for an overnight stay. *Menus €8–22. Closed late Oct–mid-April.*

The Lannemezan Plateau

Set on a high, flat, semi-arid plateau of reddish-brown rock and gravel dumped by a glacier in the Quaternary age, Lannemezan means the '*Lande du Milieu*' or 'Middle Moor'. Windswept or fog-bound much of the winter, covered with broom, heather and ferns, the Middle Moor has never been good for much, except perhaps for escaping the heat that can poach the surrounding valleys in the summer. It has long been a place to hurry through rather than stay in; the Neolithic salt road passed across it, as did age-old trans-humance trails from the mountains and the Roman road from Dax to St-Bertrand-de-Comminges. In the Middle Ages it was widely believed that witches gathered on the forlorn corners of the plateau for their Sabbaths, presided over by the devil himself in the form of a he-goat (*bouc* – hence Lannemezan's older name, the *lande de bouc*. Packs of wolves and large bands of bandits and ruffians terrorized the population. Once oak trees dotted the plateau, and accounts say they were never, never without a body or two hanging in the wind, under the plateau's famous *ciel d'airain* 'sky of bronze'.

For the last hundred years, the plateau has been tamed to provide a livelihood from the rearing and marketing of piglets and lambs. If snubbed by Mother Nature, the otherwise empty wastelands around Lannemezan are ideal for setting up hydro-electric plants, and chemical and fertilizer plants.

Founded as a *bastide* in 1270 to defend the surrounding area from bandits, **Lannemezan** is now the market town of the eastern

Hautes-Pyrénées: come if you can on a Wednesday, when the main square is packed with shoppers twanging away in Gascon, while in the nearby Halle du Nébouzan, broad-shouldered farmers mutter in their berets around the biggest sheep market in the Pyrenees. And once you've seen that, and the excellent **retable** (1703) in the choir of its church, you've seen the sights of Lannemezan. However, in the grounds of the electrochemical plant along the D939 to La-Barthe-de-Neste, you can see the large if low Neolithic **tumulus of Pierrehitte** crowned by an oak tree. The mound marks the old crossroads of the salt road and the ancient route to Spain through the Vallée d'Aure, a road known as the Ténarèze, and was originally crowned by a large stone that stood equidistant from the sources of the rivers Save, Gers and Baïse.

Heading north across the plateau of Lannemezan towards Armagnac on the D939, you can look in at the *bastide* of **Galan** (1318), which has kept much of the medieval character that Lannemezan has lost, with its half-timbered houses and fortified Gothic church. Further north, fortified **Trie-sur-Baïse** (founded in 1323), 'France's biggest piglet market', is similar, preserving its precise grid plan and arcaded central market square. Unusually, Trie built its largest church smack in the middle of the market square; this dates from the 15th century and has a Gothic portal.

East of Trie, on the River Gers, **Castelnau-Magnoac** was once the capital of its own little region, the Magnoac; it now boasts of rivalling Trie in piglet sales. It has a handsome collegiate church from the 15th century, but most of the piety in the Magnoac is concentrated to the south, where in 1520 the Virgin Mary appeared to a shepherdess and requested that a church be built on the site. And so it was, called the **Chapelle de Notre-Dame Garaison**. It drew its fair share of pilgrims in its day, and has pretty if provincial 16th- and 17th-century frescoes on the miracles of Our Lady of September.

Market Days on the Lannemezan Plateau

Lannemezan: Wednesdays.
Trie-sur-Baïse: Tuesdays.
Castelnau-Magnoac: Saturdays.

Where to Stay and Eat on the Lannemezan Plateau

Lannemezan ✉ 65300

**De La Gare, Av de la Gare, t 05 62 98 00 10 (€). This place is okay for a night, and open all year.

*Le Madrigal, 45 Rue du 8 Mai 1945, t 05 62 98 02 13 (€). Another unremarkable choice. There is also a restaurant. *Menus €12–16. Closed Fri and Sun eve.*

Castelnau-Magnoac ✉ 65230

Le Petit Château, 65130 Laborde, on D26 coming from Esparros, t 05 62 40 90 16, www.petitchateau.com. This beautiful white house set in its own park is a welcome contrast to the usual grey stone and slate of the Baronnies. The owners are very keen for all guests to have a wonderful, fun-packed holiday. Children are obligatory in July and Aug, but they'll take them off your hands for 25 hours

ⓘ **Cizos**
Maison du Magnoac, t 05 62 39 86 61; open July and Aug Tues–Sun 10–1 and 3–7; Sept–June closes at 5 and Sat pm

ⓘ **Lannemezan ›**
73 Rue Jean Jaques Rousseau, t 05 62 98 08 31, www.lannemezan.fr; open Mon–Fri 9–12.30 and 2–5.30, Sat 9–12.30

a week and entertain them with various themes; in the evening they'll set up a native American camp, a circus or Pyrenean folk dancing whilst the parents enjoy a candle-lit supper. There is also a full itinerary for the adults. *July and Aug weekly bookings only; €1,350 for 2 adults and 2 children, this includes half-board, wine and juice. Sept–June rooms €55.*

Moulin d'Ariès, 2km from Castelnau at Aries-Espenan, t 05 62 39 81 85, *www.poterie.fr.* (€). Five handsomely furnished *chambres d'hôte* have been installed in a lovingly renovated mill, with a pleasant garden and tennis court. *Evening meals €20. Closed Nov–mid-May.*

Hôtel-Restaurant du Mont d'Aure, 65250 Lortet, t 05 62 39 02 43, *www.baronnies.com* (€). Pleasant *auberge* on the river. The décor is a bit arty and a little scruffy, the bedrooms simple though comfortable. The restaurant offers generous portions of tasty regional cuisine, nicely presented. *Menu €10–20 and à la carte. Closed Wed.*

The Vallée d'Aure and the Vallée de Louron

The sunny mountains and valleys south of Lannemezan are sometimes called 'the Pyrenees of the Nestes of the Garonne' – not that the mighty River Garonne hatches out of bird's nests, but from *nestes*, the Gascon word for 'river'. Since the invasion of the Visigoths and Moors, the westernmost valleys and *nestes* (the Aure, Barousse, Basse-Neste and Magnoac valleys) have been collectively known as the **Pays des Quatre Vallées**, a province jointly administered by Bigorre, Comminges and Aragon.

Throughout the Middle Ages, the various lords of the Quatre Vallées adroitly maintained their independent political arrangements and pacts, and the region prospered perhaps more than most Pyrenean valleys, especially after 1492, when Spain's demand for wool for the uniforms of its troops in the Americas brought a small economic boom to the Pyrenees. All the private dealing, however, gradually ended between 1473 and 1715, when through marriages and treaties the four valleys were gobbled up by the French Crown. This had a dark side: France's wars with Spain cut off the valleys' natural political and economic outlets. The Industrial Revolution and the First World War only aggravated the decline, as people headed north in search of easier jobs and better pay.

During the Spanish Civil War, the population picked up a bit, most dramatically in June 1938 when the Republic's 43rd Brigade, trapped at Bielsa, was pushed over the border into the Vallée d'Aure, with hundreds of civilian refugees. During the Second World War, the traffic went the other way, as local shepherds, woodcutters and others helped Jews, German dissidents and escapees from French political prisons to flee over the mountains; in the Aure valley alone, an estimated 1,500 of the 2,000 who made the attempt survived to make it to Spain.

Getting around the Vallée d'Aure and the Vallée de Louron

All **trains** between Pau, Tarbes and Toulouse stop at Lannemezan, and from there **buses** continue south 3 or 4 times a day to Sarrancolin, Arreau and St-Lary. Once a day there's a direct connection between Tarbes and St-Lary.

For information, call SNCF buses on t 36 35 or the tourist office.

The Vallée d'Aure: Sarrancolin to St-Lary

Moulded by ancient glaciers into a giant fishhook around the formidable peaks of the Massif de Néouvielle, the Vallée d'Aure not only receives more sunshine than most French valleys, but is blessed by a warm Spanish wind, known locally as the *et bentthat*, which sweeps the surrounding peaks clear of clouds and mists. Perhaps because of its sunny disposition, the Vallée d'Aure was one of the first valleys, back in the 1950s, to reverse its decline by attracting tourists and skiers. Another feather in its cap is the recent opening of the Aragnouet–Bielsa tunnel, confirming the Aure's age-old links with Spain that began with the 'royal way' or Ténarèze (a peculiar Gascon word, apparently derived from the Latin words *in itinere* or itinerary), used at least from Neolithic times to link the valleys of the Garonne and hence the Atlantic with those of the Ebro and the Mediterranean.

Sarrancolin

From La Barthe-de-Neste (just south of Lannemezan and the A64) the D929 follows the route of the Ténarèze through rather dismal scenery to Sarrancolin. The Romans loved it for its red marble with grey veins, and in more recent years the quarries have been reopened to decorate Versailles and build the famous grand stair of the Paris Opéra. The medieval town was once heavily fortified, although today only a tower gate remains, the **Porte Ste-Quitterie**, carved with the arms of France. The lanes here, especially the picturesque Rue Noire, are lined with 15th- and 16th-century houses (note the dates on the marble lintels). The pride of Sarrancolin is the handsome church and bell tower of St-Ebons, begun in the 12th century in the form of a Greek cross. Inside, the relics of **St-Ebons** (or Ebontius, *d.* 1104), the first bishop of Roda de Isabena in Aragon after its reconquest from the Moors, are preserved in a magnificent 13th-century gold and copper enamel casket made in Limoges, decorated with medallions showing scenes from the New Testament and the figures of Christ, the Apostles, St Louis and St Ebon. Carefully preserved through centuries of troubles, the casket was stolen in 1911 and, to the dismay of Sarrancolin, given up for lost – until one dry year, when the waters in the Neste d'Aure were exceptionally low and it was spotted in the middle of the river where the thief had dropped it.

Also of interest are the 17th-century paintings on wood by the entrance and the carved choir stalls, where the usual funny faces seem to groan and grimace under the weight of the churchmen who once sat there.

Next to St-Ebons are the scant remains of a Benedictine **priory**, founded in 1032 by the abbot of Simorre in the Gers. Four centuries later it was used as the residence of the lovely but singularly unhappy Isabelle, made the 'Dame des Quatre Vallées' by Jean V, Count of Armagnac, her brother and husband. The story goes that Jean V had been separated from his sister until she turned 18, and when he saw her he fell passionately in love with her. So potent was this affection that he even found a bishop to try to justify their incestuous love to the pope, using the gods of Olympus as a precedent for their unnatural union. Isabelle bore him three children before he was assassinated (*see* p.148), then spent the rest of her life secluded at Castelnau-Magnoac, dying of a disease given to her by her brother. Her subjects in the Quatre Vallées apparently felt sorry for their lady, and never caused her any more trouble than she already had, but when she died they were quick to offer their allegiance to Louis XI rather than face one of her heirs.

Lastly, if you're in Sarrancolin and it's time for a picnic and just a view of the surroundings, take the steep *route forestier*, which winds 8km to the east up to the panoramic **Col d'Estivère** (1,217m/3,993ft).

Arreau

The main valley road continues 7km south to Arreau, the pretty capital of the Quatre Vallées, located at the meeting of the Aure and Louron rivers and various roads, including the route up to the Col d'Aspin (see p.269). Like the Aure itself, Arreau's name comes from the Celtic Arebaci, the original inhabitants of Pamplona, whom Pompey defeated and relocated here when re-founding the town in his own name. Now a popular base for walks, rafting, hang-gliding and skiing (at **Val-Louron**, 1,450–2,150m/4,757– 7,054ft), Arreau used to attract merchants and wheeler-dealers from all across the Pyrenees, who met in the centre of the village under the 17th-century *halles*. Just opposite, the most beautiful house in the village, the 16th-century **Maison des Lys**, is named after the fleurs-de-lys carved in the timber – a testimonial to local enthusiasm for distant French rule after the too-close-for-comfort Armagnacs. At the top of the Grand Rue, the parish church of **Notre-Dame** is worth a look for its elegant and colourful retable from the 18th century and the arm reliquary of St Exuperius. Exuperius (born in Arreau, died 411) was one of the first bishops of Toulouse, and a good friend and benefactor of St Jerome. He was famous for his generosity, sending food to the poor as far away as

Palestine and Egypt. The diminutive **Château des Nestes** contains the tourist office and an intriguing **Musée des Cagots**. Over the river, below the Château de Ségur (where there's convenient parking), stands the 16th-century **Chapelle St-Exupère**, with an octagonal bell tower and a Romanesque portal. By the entrance, an old *coffre* was set up for offerings, in the style of St Exuperius himself; if the chapel's open, note the fine 16th-century wrought-iron screen. There's also **Les Aigles d'Aure**, with flying displays of eagles and other birds of prey.

Musée des Cagots
open 9.30–12 and 2–6

Les Aigles d'Aure
t 05 62 40 10 35; call for times of flights

Around Arreau

The best church around, however, is 3km east of Arreau at **Jézeau**, beautifully set on the mountain flank over the medieval hamlet. Ask at the *mairie* (call ahead, mornings only) for the key before setting out because the interior is what you've come to see: when it was remodelled and enlarged in the 16th century, the church was given a magnificent brightly painted Renaissance retable, several polychrome statues and, on the wooden ceiling, vigorous, imaginative paintings by an unknown hand, including a remarkable *Last Judgement* that has inspired Jézeau's enthusiasts to call it 'The Sistine Chapel of the Pyrenees'.

Continuing up the Neste d'Aure from Arreau, **Cadéac-les-Bains** is a spa down on its luck since the Second Empire, with the 19th-century fountains and the donjon of a 13th-century castle built by Sancho of Aragon as its landmark. Next is **Ancizan**, an important textile centre in the 16th century, when many of the houses were built and the villagers plumped for the fine *mise au tombeau* in the parish church. You can discover what life was like around here not even a hundred years ago at the **Musée de la Vallée d'Aure** and there's a **museum on local cider-making**.

Musée de la Vallée d'Aure
Rte de St-Lary, t 05 62 39 97 75; open 2–6.30, closed early Nov–early Dec; guided visits available

For a mighty dose of scenery, turn up the D113 for the **Hourquette d'Ancizan** (1,538m/5,975ft), passing by way of **l'An Mil**, a fortified 11th-century village with heather-thatched roofs – constructed a few years back as a film set. Beyond Hourquette, the D113 continues to Payolle, where you can circle back to the Vallé d'Aure by way of the dramatic Col d'Aspin.

Museum of cider-making
t 05 62 39 97 61, www.cidrerieancizan65. com; open Dec–Oct daily 2–6.30

A by-road to Compostela passed through the Vallée d'Aure, but few traces remain of the pilgrims' passing; one is the **Chapelle d'Argos**, south of Guchen, all that survives of a hospital set up by the Knights Hospitaller. The next village south, **Vielle-Aure**, has a sweet little Romanesque church, with 15th-century frescoes inside and a gilded Renaissance retable, and many houses from the 16th to 18th centuries in the centre (and plenty of condominiums and pseudo-Pyrenean bungalows from the 20th century on the outskirts, part of the sprawl from St-Lary). The restored **manganese mines** are brought to life with a sound and light show.

Manganese mines
t 05 62 39 46 79, www.vielleaure.com; open summer daily 10–12 and 2–7, rest of year 10–12 and 2–7; closed mid-Nov–mid-Dec

Market Days in the Vallée d'Aure

Sarrancolin: Tuesdays and Saturdays.
Arreau: Thursdays.

Where to Stay and Eat in the Vallée d'Aure

Sarrancolin ✉ 65410

Jeanne Puchol's Chambres d'Hôte, Route du Tous, t 05 62 98 78 18 (€). Here there are two rooms in a typical Pyrenean house in the trees. *Open all year on reservation only.*

Marie Menvielle's Chambres d'Hôte, Quartier Porailhet, t 05 62 98 77 60 (€). Bed and breakfast place in a woodland setting. *Open all year.*

Arreau ✉ 65240

**Hôtel d'Angleterre, on the edge of town, t 05 62 98 63 30, http://hotel-angleterre-arreau.com (€€–€). A big comfortable country inn, with a garden terrace; the owners arrange rafting or hang-gliding excursions. Heated pool. The restaurant serves good hearty food – *garbure, confits* and regional dishes – perfect for high-altitude appetites. *Half-board obligatory mid-July–mid-Sept. No restaurant in winter. Closed Jan–Mar except weekends and school hols, April–mid-May, Oct–mid-Dec, and Mon May–Sept.*

**Hôtel de France, t 05 62 98 61 12 (€). On the main street, a traditional family hotel with a pleasant garden terrace. *Menus €12–20. Closed mid-Oct–mid-Dec and mid-April–mid-May. Restaurant closed Tues eves and all day Wed.*

**Hostellerie du Val d'Aure, just south of Arreau in Cadéac, t 05 62 98 60 63, www.hotel-valdaure.com (€€). Lovely family-run hotel set in some pretty woods with a pool. *Menu lunch €17–25. Closed Sun eve in winter, late Mar–late May and late Sept–26 Dec.*

ⓘ **Sarrancolin** ⟩
Rue de l'Hôtel de Ville,
t 05 62 98 79 88; open
during school hols

ⓘ **Arreau** ⟩
for Aure/Louron valleys:
Pl du Monument, t 05
62 98 63 15, www.vallee-aure.com; open 9.30–12
and 2–6

★ **Hôtel d'Angleterre** ⟩

Notre-Dame-de Bourisp
open periodically in
summer, and every
Sunday for Mass
at 10am

Even better are the murals in the church of **Notre-Dame-de Bourisp,** just to the east over the Neste d'Aure. In 1542, two painters named Jean Berneil and Jean Boé embellished the interior with scenes from the *Life of Christ* and *SS Stephen and Sebastian,* but when it came to painting the *Seven Deadly Sins* Berneil and Boé showed their misogynist colours – all the sins are represented by fashionably dressed women, riding beasts symbolic of their various vices (Pride on her lion, Avarice on what looks like a wolf). All are escorted by the most kindly, solicitous demons imaginable; each has three faces, butterfly wings, and stands lightly on the beast's hindquarters like a circus performer.

St-Lary

St-Lary claims (as do several other towns) to be nothing less than the biggest winter/summer sports resort in the Pyrenees. It certainly had a head start. Back in the 1950s, when all the workers who built the dams and hydroelectric plants in the valley had finished their tasks and gone home, St-Lary was left so empty and disconsolate that its bigwigs decided immediate action was called for. By 1957 the town had built its first aerial **cableway,** at the time the largest in the world, to the ski slopes of Pla d'Adet (these days it looks quite puny); most recently (1988) it built a deluxe modern spa at Soulan, to treat rheumatism and nose-ear-throat troubles in the hopes of attracting tourists in the dead periods of May, October and November.

Another recent project has been the restoration of the old core of St-Lary, including the 16th-century Maison Fornier in Place de la Mairie, now home to the **Maison du Parc National**, with audio-visual information on the fauna of the Pyrenees. There's also a **museum** to the Pyrenean bears with two real ones originally born in a circus. But it's the great outdoors that brings most people to St-Lary – in the winter, ice-skating and skiing on the 33 pistes at Pla d'Adet, where you can ride all the way up to the **Soum de Matte** (2,477m/8,174ft) for the eagle-eye views; in the summer, para-gliding, riding, rock climbing, canyoning and walking take over. The popular three-day trek known as the Tour de la Vallée d'Aure begins at **Vielle-Aure**, as does the D123 up to the old village of **Soulan** (annexed by St-Lary) and **Espiaube**, where during the winter the *téléférique* lifts people up to the stupendous **Col de Portet** (2,215m/7,309ft).

Maison du Parc National
t 05 62 39 40 91; open mid-Dec–end Oct Mon–Fri 9–12 and 2–6.30; plus Sat and Sun in July and Aug

Bear museum
t 05 62 39 50 83; open summer Wed–Sun 9–12.30 and 1.30–6.30; rest of year 9–12.15 and 1.45–5.30

Around St-Lary

Nearby **Ens** is a typical mountain village, with a Romanesque church in a superb setting. The unpaved but quite driveable D225 from Sailhan rises up to the remote old village of **Azet** with more grand views, then crosses the mountains for the Vallée de Louron to the east.

Continuing up the valley from St-Lary, the small village, sheer rock and ruined 11th-century castle of **Tramezaïgues** (from the Latin *inter ambas aquas*, 'between two waters' – the Neste d'Aure and the Torrent de Rioumajou) stand like an exclamation mark at the beginning of the deep green, arcadian 12km-long **Vallée du Rioumajou**. The driveable track that cuts up the middle is the heir of the Ténarèze; you can drive or walk this ancient route as far as the Hospice de Rioumajou (1,560m/5,118ft), and join the High Pyrenees trail (HPH) or continue south of the border from **Port d'Urdisseto** (2,403m/7,884ft). Daniel Defoe came this way in 1689, during one of the worst winters in history, and was lucky to come out uneaten by the ravenous wolves; he fictionalized the experience in a chapter of *Robinson Crusoe*. The next little valley, the **Vallée du Moudang**, was a favourite smugglers' route; a bad road braves it part of the way, from where it's an easy walk to a curious village of barns, the **Granges de Moudang**, where shepherds lodged in the summer.

The D929 continues to Fabian, the crossroads for the Routes des Lacs and the Réserve Naturelle de Néouvielle (*see* below), and then to Le Plan d'Aragnouet. Here a very photogenic Templars' chapel has a charming if unusual *clocher-mur* with windows at the top, although all attempts to find any esoteric meaning in it have fallen flat. At Le Plan a road branches off for **Piau-Engaly**, the highest and snowiest ski resort in the Pyrenees (1,400–2,500m/4,590–8,200ft), and certainly the most futuristic, with 40 pistes, 21 lifts and illuminated night skiing to prolong the thrills. There are a number of trails passing near the station, including a link up to the National Park and Gavarnie. The D929 continues to the **Tunnel de Bielsa** to Spain and the dry, wild mountains of Upper Aragon.

Tunnel de Bielsa
*tunnel open April–
Sept 24hrs; Oct–April
closes Sat–Thurs 11pm,
Fri 12am*

The Réserve Naturelle de Néouvielle: the Route des Lacs

In 1935, the great south-facing granite *massif* of Néouvielle became the first nature reserve in France; the French call it the Parc National *bis*. It's an especially good place for bird-watching, with golden eagles soaring high overhead. The reserve also has the highest growth of pines in Europe (the *massif* is wooded up to 2,400m/7,920ft), thanks to a sunny micro-climate that supports another 1,250 known species of plants, not a few of which are in and around its score of lovely lakes. Early July, when the rhododendrons burst into bloom, is the perfect time for a visit. Thank the French power monopoly, EDF, for the narrow road up from Fabian, which for a few months in the summer allows you (and half the population of St-Lary in August) to motor as far as the Lac d'Orédon and Lac de Cap-de-Long, both within easy striking distance of other lakes. There are several *refuges* and a wide range of easy to difficult and dangerous paths; an easy, classic circuit on the GR 10 and GR 10c includes most of the lakes and an overnight stay at Barstan; the main GR 10 continues west to Barèges (*see* p.264).

Refuges
www.gite-etape.com

Market Days in St-Lary

Saturdays.

Where to Stay and Eat in and around St-Lary

ⓘ St-Lary ›
Rue Principale, **t** *05 62
39 50 81,
www.saintlary.com;
open daily in school
hols; otherwise
Mon–Sat 9–12 and 2–7*

ⓘ Piau-Engaly
*Maison du Tourisme,
t 05 62 39 61 69, www.
piau-engaly.com; open
July–Aug Mon–Fri 9–12
and 2–7; peak winter
9–7; rest of year call first*

St-Lary-Soulan ✉ **65170**
In the town that helped inaugurate package ski holidays in the Pyrenees, there are no bargains. The restaurants in St-Lary, such as they are, are notoriously mediocre.

***La Pergola, 25 Rue Vincent Mir, **t** 05 62 39 40 46, *www.hotellapergola.fr* (€€€–€€). This hotel is set in a lovely park with peak views. Bedrooms are comfortable and have balconies or terraces facing the mountains. Some bathrooms have massage showers. There are two restaurants: one has traditional rustic décor and offers good regional fare; the other, *L'Enclos des Saveurs*, offers a gastronomic tour of *nouvelle cuisine*. *Menus €13–39 but change regularly; €10 for an excellent buffet breakfast.*

La Détente, 4 Rte Autun, **t** 05 62 39 53 09 (€€). This is the place to come for longer stays, with studio apartments with kitchenettes, sleeping 2 to 4, and a play area for the children. *Open all year.*

Pons 'Le Dahu', Rue de Couderes, **t 05 62 39 43 66, *www.hotelpons.com* (€€). An inexpensive and sunny choice. *Open all year.*

Hôtel de la Neste, **t 05 62 39 42 79, *www.hotel-delaneste.com* (€€–€). By the river, the hotel enjoys a grand view of the mountains; all rooms have bath, TV and mini-bar. A little over a kilometre from the village centre. Do not be put off by the ugly modern exterior. Clean, comfortable well-run hotel with a pool. The restaurant offers simple regional fare. *Menus €12–24. Closed Nov.*

**La Terrasse Fleurie, 21 Rue Principale, t 05 62 40 76 00, *www.la-terrasse-fleurie.com* (€). In the town centre, a pleasant and comfortable hotel with wooden balconies.

Chez Lulu, in Sailhan, t 05 62 39 40 89. Here you can dine pleasantly on the summer terrace. There are Gascon favourites on the menus and grills over an open fire. *Menus €13–22. Closed end of June and Nov.*

La Grange, Quartier d Autan St-Lary (on D118 on the outskirts, coming from Arreau), t 05 62 40 07 14. The chef is trying to get St-Lary on the gastronomic map with an ambitious menu. Try the *tatin de canard au chou* or the *foie frais poêlé et sa sauce aux morilles*. The décor is rustic and there is a summer terrace. *Menus €15–38. Closed Tues and Wed plus mid-Nov–mid-Dec and mid-April–early May.*

The Vallée de Louron

Arreau (*see* p.274) stands at the foot of the 25km-long Vallée de Louron, green and tranquil compared to its neighbours, the Vallée d'Aure to the west and the Vallée de Luchon to the east. It has a pair of ski resorts, at **Val-Louron** (2,260m/7,415ft) and **Peyresourde** (2,241m/7,352ft), and is increasingly a popular base for hang-gliding and paragliding daredevil adventurers; the 'altiport' at Peyragudes is unique in the Pyrenees. Water sports are another focus on the new large man-made **Lac de Loudenvielle**, a mirror under a 12th-century castle.

The Valley of Romanesque Churches

By the 16th century, the wool and cloth business in the Vallée de Louron was good enough for the inhabitants of its villages to pool their money to hire painters to decorate their churches.

Churches tour
the Maison du Tourism at Bordères offers afternoon tours on Thursdays, t 05 62 99 92 00; ring ahead

Unfortunately they are often locked; but **tours** are available. Heading up the valley, **Lançon** (take the D219 from Arreau) has a Romanesque church, not with murals but an unusual bell tower topped with a pepperpot roof; **Ilhan** just south has fine views of the valley. South of Bordères-Louron, **Vielle-Louron**'s church has both walls and ceilings covered with 16th-century paintings. From **Génos** you can take the road past the Val-Louron ski resort over the mountains to the Col de Peyrefitte (1,578m/5,177ft) for the majestic views, then descend down the unpaved road to St-Lary.

Loudenvielle, south of its large man-made lake, and the power station at **Tramezaïgues** 8km west, are the bases for walks in the upper Vallée de Louron. Other good Romanesque churches are just to the east: one at **Cazaux-Fréchet** and another at **Armenteule**, isolated and decorated with a curious carved frieze. **Mont** has the finest frescoes in the whole valley, painted in 1573 by one Melchior Rodiguis of St-Bertrand-de-Comminges, who decorated both the interior and exterior and the cemetery chapel with charming provincial Renaissance paintings on the *Lives of the Virgin, John the*

ⓘ **Bordères-
Louron**
*Maison du Tourism,
t 05 62 99 92 00,
www.lelouron.com;
open all year Mon–Sat
9–12.30 and 2–6, plus
Sun mornings July
and Aug*

Where to Stay in the Vallée de Louron

Vallée de Louron ✉ 65590

Le Relais d'Avajan, Avajan, t 05 62 99 67 08 (€€). A handful of reasonably priced rooms and a stout menu. *Menu* €12. *Open all year exc Wed in winter.*

Auberge des Isclots, overlooking the Lac de Loudenvielle at Aranvielle, t 05 62 99 66 21 (€€–€). Utterly

pleasant, with doubles, or cheaper *gîte d'étape* rooms in a dormitory. *Menus* €14–20. *Open all year.*

Accueil sans Frontière Pyrénées, Germ, t 05 62 99 65 27, www.germ-louron. com (€). A popular complex of well-furnished *gîtes* and hostel accommodation, with a camp site, good food, lovely swimming pool and loads of information and equipment for summer and winter sports in the area.

Baptist and Christ. Lastly, tucked off the main route, is a clean and pleasant little hamlet lost in nature called **Germ** (yes, really), named after a saint so obscure that he never made it out of the valley. Beyond the turn-off for Germ, the main D618 continues up to the **Col de Peyresourde**, with beautiful views back to the Vallée de Louron. If you don't want to backtrack, it continues down to Bagnères-de-Luchon (*see* p.292).

Into the Haute-Garonne: the Comminges

East of the Vallée de Louron extends the southernmost bit of the *département* of the Haute-Garonne, lodged between the Hautes-Pyrénées and the Ariège like an insistent jigsaw puzzle piece. Before the bureaucrats of the Revolution changed all the political contours, this bit of the puzzle was the county and bishopric of the Comminges, one of the most venerable provinces of Gascony.

Located exactly midway between the Atlantic and Mediterranean, the Comminges encompasses the upper valley of one of France's four great rivers, the Garonne, and has been inhabited, literally, since the cows (and bison and woolly mammoths) came home in the last Ice Age; one of the villages gave its name to the misty Aurignacian era. The Iberians, Celts and especially the Romans recognized its strategic and commercial importance as a natural crossroads. Although few places in the Pyrenees have as many proud relics of the prehistoric, Roman and medieval past, tourism is a fairly recent phenomenon in the region, with the exception of the grand old spa of Bagnères-de-Luchon.

Approaching the Comminges from the west on the N117, the first town is Montréjeau. From there we move south into the spiritual heart of the Comminges, at St-Bertrand, then continue into the Pyrenees; if you're going north from Montréjeau into the 'Petites Pyrénées', *see* p.297.

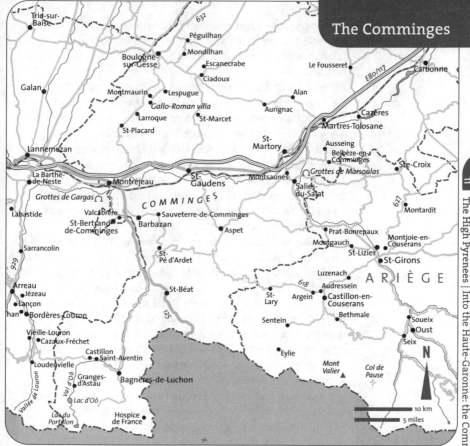

Montréjeau

At the confluence of the Neste and Garonne, Montréjeau stands on a natural terrace, where it was founded as a *bastide* in 1272, called Mont-Royal before Gascon tongues tried to fit around it. It has lovely views over to the Pyrenees from its two main squares, central arcaded **Place Valentin Abeille** and **Place Verdun**, with the market and public garden; on Bd de Lassus, skirting the edge of the plateau, an orientation table has been set up. Montréjeau's **church**, first built in the 12th century, has a handsome octagonal bell tower, typical of the hinterland of Toulouse. The **Château de Valmirande** is a fairytale castle designed by Louis Garros in the late 19th century, a folly of different façades with a Gothic chapel, all set in a park and formal gardens.

Château de Valmirande
Rte de Tarbes, t 05 61 95 80 11; guided tour daily at 3, July–mid-Aug; write to book at other times; adm

Grotte de Gargas
t 05 62 39 72 39, http://grottesdegargas. free.fr; open daily 10–12 and 2–5; numbers limited so reserve ahead

Grotte de Gargas

There's always an ineffable quality to prehistoric caves, perhaps because the thoughts and dreams of our remote ancestors can never be recaptured; no amount of study nor comparative science can really fathom the Palaeolithic mind or the meaning behind the often stunning, often inscrutable works left behind by humanity's first artists.

The Grotte de Gargas, south of Montréjeau on the D26, is even more uncanny and troubling than most. Gargas is one of the oldest-known decorated caves in France, dating from the Aurignacian era, the period of the first figurative art (*c.* 33,000 BC), and its oldest paintings and engravings of bison, horses, mammoths, bulls, deer and goats (and, unusually, two birds) are still rather awkward and archaic, compared to the more graceful and lively works of the Magdalenian era (*c.* 12,000 BC) made famous at Lascaux; a few examples here testify to millennia of use following the last Ice Age.

But what sets Gargas apart are its bizarre, **mutilated hands** – 231 pictures in different sizes and different colours (red ochre or black magnesium oxide), made by blowing paint through a tube around a hand. Nearly all the pictures are somehow deformed or missing parts of or whole fingers. Evidence of fingerprints in the clay seem to show that both living hands and amputated hands were used for models, and guesses are that they were damaged either through frostbite, disease, accidents or ritual mutilation. The painted outlines of hands are found everywhere in Upper Palaeolithic art, almost as if they were signatures, but rarely are any mutilated and nowhere else do they appear in such a large quantity. The only other cave where similar mutilated hands have been found is in the Grotte de Tibiran, the nearest cave to Gargas (*not open to visitors*).

Curiously enough, Gargas has long had a rather nefarious reputation. Its name is derived from the giant 'Gargas' who lived there, the precursor of Rabelais's giant, Gargantua. In the 18th century, the national newsapaper, the *Mercure de France*, claimed it was the abode of a cannibal named Blaise Ferrage, who ate a few dozen shepherds and local women and couldn't be caught because he also ate a certain magic plant called *herba Heraclea* that gave him jaws of iron. In the 19th century, tourists en route to Luchon would stop at Gargas for a *frisson* and were shown a bunch of bears' bones by the guides, who claimed they were the remains of Blaise's unnatural dinners. All along, no one 'saw' Gargas's pre-historic art: no one even imagined anything of the sort existed until the early 1900s.

As for Blaise the anthropophage, he was apparently based on a ruffian named Chaillet, who was condemned to death in 1782 in Toulouse for his crimes, although chewing up the local citizenry wasn't one of them.

St-Bertrand-de-Comminges

Until the Virgin Mary appeared at Lourdes, the religious centre of the central Pyrenees was St-Bertrand-de-Comminges. Magnificently placed on an isolated promontory where the River Garonne curls about a fertile plain, the massive Gothic church of **Ste-Marie** makes for an unforgettable sight, a kind of inland Mont-St-Michel, as the French like to say, with its nearly windowless walls, tower and buttresses rising up like an ocean liner, dwarfing the village below. The important remains of St-Bertrand's Roman predecessor and a fine Romanesque church nearby are added attractions, along with a unique restaurant that specializes in ancient Roman cuisine.

The Citadel of the Rising Sun

St-Bertrand was settled by Iberians from around the River Ebro, who built the first *oppidum* on the naturally fortified site of the cathedral. Their Celtic cousins, the Volcae Tectosages (the founders of Toulouse), gave it its name, Lugdunum, which can be literally translated as the 'Citadel of the Rising Sun'. A temple to Lug, the Celtic sun god, stood in the centre of the *oppidum*, and there may have been a market nearby – Iberian coins have been found in excavations under the square in front of the cathedral. By 76 BC, when Pompey was campaigning in Spain, the Iberians had been chased to the south and the region was largely empty except for various guerrilla tribes holding out against the joys of Roman rule. They were collectively known as the *convenii*, the 'robbers of souls', and they were determined and tough enough to make even a great general like Pompey think twice before taking to the hills to exterminate them. Rather than making war, he decided to win them over by kindness; he declared them to be Roman colonists and granted them the fertile region around Lugdunum, henceforth Lugdunum Convenarum.

The ferocious Convenii turned out to be excellent citizens. Set at the crossing of two major Roman roads, Lugdunum Convenarum grew by leaps and bounds: by the time of Augustus the town covered much of the plain, and the temple, the baths and forum were built. The great 1st-century-AD Jewish historian Josephus wrote that Lugdunum received the Tetrarch Herod and his family in 39 AD, when Caligula exiled them from Palestine (perhaps to keep company with Mary Magdalene and the other Marys, Martha, Veronica and Zaccheus and other New Testament characters who supposedly ended up in France). Local legend has it that one winter Herod's famously wicked stepdaughter Salome fell into a lake and drowned, so that only her head stuck out of the ice, as if on a great white platter – just as she had demanded John the Baptist's head in exchange for her dance. A square tower, known as Herod's tomb for as long as anyone can remember, stands by the Garonne on a rock known as the **Mail de Martrouilh**.

The first Christian basilica was built in the lower town shortly after the Comminges was annexed by the Visigoths of Toulouse in 410. But by then Lugdunum Convenarum was in decline; final disaster arrived in the form of Gondowald, the bastard son of Clotaire II, king of the Franks. Gondowald had been raised by Narses, the eunuch governor-general of Italy in the name of Byzantium. Always keen to undermine the pretensions of the pope in Rome, who was increasingly infringing on the rightful domain of the emperor of Constantinople, Narses sent his ward Gondowald to take power in Gaul. Waiting for a local uprising of the Gascons and an army from Spain, Gondowald holed up in the fortress of Lugdunum (585), but in the meantime the new king of the Franks, Childebert, allied with the king of the Burgundians, led a forced march on Lugdunum, hurled Gondowald over a precipice, and proceeded to vent their feelings about Byzantium on the town and its citizens in a murderous, fiery rampage. For centuries the once-rich town of Lugdunum Convenarum became a stone quarry for southwest France, while its statues fed the local limekilns.

The town next appears in the 11th century, in the biography of Bertrand de l'Isle-Jourdain, a cousin of the extraordinary count of Toulouse, Raymond IV, who fought with El Cid in Spain and led the First Crusade. Bertrand shared much of Raymond's energy and zeal; when appointed bishop of Comminges he rebuilt both the church and the town and presided there for 50 years, performing enough miracles to be canonized by popular demand in 1175. In the late 13th century, another Bertrand, Bertrand de Got of Bordeaux, was named bishop and replaced his predecessor's Romanesque church with the grand Gothic edifice that stands here today. When Bertrand de Got was elected Pope Clement V, he remembered his old see and confirmed the canonization of the first Bertrand in 1309, putting his bull of approval on the pilgrimage to his tomb and personally visiting to render homage before the saint's relics. Decline began with the Wars of Religion and quickened with the Revolution, when the episcopate was suppressed; today fewer than 300 people call St-Bertrand home.

Ste-Marie Cathedral

Cathédral Ste-Marie
t 05 61 89 04 91,
www.cathedrale-saint-bertrand.org; open
Feb–April Mon–Sat 10–12
and 2–6; May–Sept 9–7;
Oct 10–12 and 2–6;
Nov–Jan 10–12 and 2–5

When Bertrand de Got rebuilt St Bertrand's cathedral, he left the 100ft bell tower-cum-donjon and the rather severe façade intact; if you look carefully, you can see that a number of stones used in the construction were first cut as pagan tombstones. At the top of the well-worn marble steps, the richly decorated portal also dates from the 12th century, its tympanum carved with the Three Magi (and the future St Bertrand) paying their respects to the Virgin, seated

sacristy
(treasury)

tomb of
St-Bertrand

tapestries

altar

tomb of
Hugues
de
Châtillon

tomb of Vital
d'Ardengost

choir
stalls

Chapelle
Notre-Dame

cloister

organ

parish
altar

Pillar of the
Evangelists

bell

tower

portal

XI–XII-century	XV-century
XIV-century	Sacristy: XIV-century

on a throne holding a crowned Jesus the size of an 8-year-old child, an image known in the Pyrenees as 'the Seat of Wisdom'. Imaginary animals look down from the capitals, while on the left side of the door demons daintily drop sinners into the maw of hell. As you enter, don't miss the embalmed crocodile, hanging on the right over the parish altar; no one knows who left it here, but guesses tend towards a passing Crusader. Note, too, the fine altar front, made of Cordoba leather. On the left, columns support one of the most lavish **Renaissance organs** in France, known as 'the Third Wonder of Gascony', built in the 16th century and decorated with finely carved wooden panels representing the labours of Hercules. Although its 3,000 pipes were purloined in the Revolution, the organ was restored in the 1970s and still works a treat, as you can hear every Sunday at 10.30am.

The nave is closed off from the choir by an opulently carved Renaissance rood screen, but to continue any further down the nave you have to buy a ticket (tours are optional, but you have to at least tag along with one to get into the treasury). The delightful 12th–13th-century **cloister**, just to the right of the ticket desk, is another legacy of St Bertrand d'Isle-Jourdain; squeezed onto the edge of the promontory, it's small and irregularly shaped, and has an open gallery with a charming view over the wooded hillside. The west gallery is the oldest; among the carved capitals are fighting cockerels and Adam and Eve, while in the centre you'll find one of the cathedral's prizes, the **Pillar of the Evangelists**, carved with four column-like figures, the whole topped with a capital showing the Labours of the Months and signs of the Zodiac, although they're not easy to make out. Tombs, inscriptions and coats of arms line the walls, including one in the east gallery belonging to Canon Vital d'Ardengost, who died in 1334 and was given a pungent epitaph: *Hic jacet in tumba rosa mundi, non rosa munda, no redolet, set olet quod redolere solet.* (Here in the tomb lies a rose of the world, but no longer a rose intact. She no longer perfumes, but smells of what she should smell.)

The superb **choir stalls** were carved between 1523 and 1551 on the order of Jean de Mauléon, 52nd bishop of the Comminges. He hired a workshop of sculptors from Toulouse influenced by the Italian Renaissance. Inspired perhaps by the great choir stalls then under way at Auch, they expressed a large part of their humanistic view of the universe on the 66 stalls: wicked sins and somberly elegant religious and secular scenes intermingle with an imaginary bestiary. One of the most prominent stalls has an abbot caning a bare-bottomed monk. Along the top of the choir are the twelve Sibyls, prophets, Christian virtues, and knights (among them Roland and Oliver), and over the rood screen an intricate Tree of Jesse. Here and there you can make out Bishop Jean de Mauléon's motto, *Omnis amor tecum*, 'All my love is for you', addressed to his beloved cathedral. Behind the high altar, a small chapel holds the tomb of St Bertrand, decorated with folksy 15th-century paintings from his life. The last scene shows Pope Clement V venerating the saint's relics; because of his importance, the painters made him as big as the Jolly Green Giant.

Upstairs, still off the right side of the nave, is the sacristy with the cathedral **treasury**. The two exquisite medieval copes are believed to have belonged to Clement V, who also donated what was long the cathedral's most precious valuable, the *alicorne*, a horn from a *narwhal* that was long believed to come from a unicorn. Any water that passed through the *alicorne* was considered a sure-fire anti-dote for any poisoned food eaten by man or beast. Medieval popes put a lot of faith in such talismans, and as Clement lay dying in Avignon from a stomach ache he must have wished he had kept his unicorn horn. Centuries later, Catherine de' Medici, a deep believer in every kind of juju and hocus-pocus on the market, coveted St-Bertrand's *alicorne* and did all she could to get her son Charles IX to add it to the royal treasury, without success. In 1594 a band of Huguenots under Corbeyran d'Aure stole it along with much of the cathedral treasure, but even Corbeyran feared the vengeance of St Bertrand, and he returned the *alicorne* in exchange for a complete amnesty for his theft. And it's in the treasury to this day.

In the easternmost chapel are three surviving 15th-century stained-glass windows, while around the choir on the left side of the nave, the Gothic **Chapelle Notre-Dame** contains the finely sculpted **tomb of Hugues de Châtillon**, the bishop who designed the chapel in the 14th century. The bishop's alabaster effigy sits atop a black marble slab, itself finely carved with some 70 figures in a funerary procession.

Around the Town

There are a number of fine old buildings here and there around the upper town, still enclosed behind its three gates (you'll drive through one as you leave the village car park; if you're in a van or a Cadillac, don't even try to squeeze through it, but reverse out of the entrance). One of the prettiest buildings of all, the 15th-century **Maison Bridault**, now houses the local post office.

Lugdunum Convenarum

Lugdunum Convenarum

To visit the excavations of Roman Lugdunum Convenarum, first check the opening hours with the tourist office, and then follow the road for Valcabrère. Since 1913, large sections – although hardly all – of the Roman town have been revealed amid more recent buildings. In the centre of Lugdunum (opposite the school), the

Forum temple with its impressive podium was built *c.* 15 AD and is believed to have been dedicated to the cult of Rome and the Emperor. As evidence of Lugdunum's prosperity, originally a lavish covered portico, 24ft (7m) wide, enclosed the temple's *temenos* or sacred area. A courtyard separated the temple from the baths, or **Thermes du Forum**, built about the same period; you can make out the hot and cold rooms (*caldaria* and *frigidaria*) and much of the plumbing. Bathing in Roman times was hardly the quick private affair it is today, but a long-drawn-out afternoon social ritual, a place to meet friends and talk business and politics. Most private houses or apartments at the time were dark and poky, so people tended to spend as much time as possible in the airy, marble-clad public buildings of the forum.

Across the present D26 stood the commercial heart of Lugdunum, the **market**, or *macellum*, with 26 boutiques paved with black and white mosaics – a 1st-century AD covered shopping mall. Measuring over 500 square metres, it is among the largest and most opulent covered markets ever discovered in the western Roman Empire. It had an attached chapel or *sacellum*, probably dedicated to Mercury, god of commerce. Towards the car park, a raised circular sanctuary of uncertain import has recently been unearthed near what were the main crossroads of Lugdunum. The large **Thermes du Nord** were run by the city and perhaps were used as a spa as well; they included an early version of the sauna, as well as an open-air pool, a *palaestra* (an open-air exercise area), and a row of small shops.

South of the Macellum, near the chapel of St-Julien, Lugdunum's Palaeo-Christian **Basilica** dates from the mid-5th century and is larger than most; it has a pretty green, red and white mosaic floor, and, judging by the sarcophagi discovered here, the basilica escaped the sacking after the Frankish-Burgundian siege of Gondowald and was used at least into the 8th century. The little **theatre**, nestled in the hillside, was damaged when a road was run through the middle of it in the 18th century, although you can make out the entrances to the stands, which were originally covered with marble and sat perhaps 2,000 (making Lugdunum, though a metropolis in Gaul, still just a small market town by Roman standards). A **museum** near the site houses the numerous finds, including the handsome sculptural groups from an Augustan trophy discovered near the temple.

Valcabrère

On the left bank of the Garonne, on the eastern edge of Lugdunum Convenarum, the charming rural hamlet of Valcabrère, 'the valley of goats', is said to have got its name from a trick pulled by the Vandals in 407. When they found Lugdunum too well defended for their tastes, they gathered all the goats they could find and tied torches to their horns, and at night drove the herd towards the gate that once stood in Valcabrère. The defenders sounded the alarm, and as everyone rushed to ward off what seemed to be a massive attack, the other gates were left undefended for the Vandals to waltz in and overturn the wagons, break the windows and paint their names all over the walls.

Basilique St-Just
t 05 61 95 49 06;
open May–June daily
10–12 and 2–7, July–Sept
9–7, April and Oct 10–12
and 2–6; Nov–Mar
weekends and hols
only 2–5

The main attraction in Valcabrère is the delightful Romanesque **Basilique St-Just**, one of the most beautiful churches in the Pyrenees, isolated in a field 500 yards to the south and perfectly situtated for photographs with the tremendous cathedral at St-Bertrand looming behind its shoulder. Originally the site of a pagan necropolis, adapted by the early Christians, the basilica was built in the 11th or 12th century, primarily using stone and decorative bits cannibalized from Lugdunum; its importance yet relative isolation have led some scholars to guess that St-Just stands on the site of the first cathedral of Lugdunum, before St Bertrand arrived and built his new church on the other hill.

The square apse, with radiating polygonal chapels, is a lovely and unique essay in medieval geometry, as well as a veritable collage of Gallo-Roman bits; note the theatre mask embedded in the wall, and a relief of a supper party. The portal was inspired by the Roman models so near at hand, crowned with a tympanum showing Christ in majesty and the four Evangelists, while on the sides are marble column statues believed to represent SS Just and Pastor, brothers martyred in Spain under Diocletian, as well as St Stephen. The fourth, a woman holding a cross, is believed to be St Helen; the capitals over their heads show various forms of martyrdom with vigour and relish. The interior, beautiful in its simplicity, has fine acoustics (classical music concerts take place here in the summer Festival de Comminges); note the re-use of antique columns and Roman and Merovingian capitals. A parchment discovered in the masonry of the high altar dates its consecration to October 1200. The sarcophagus behind it, sheltered under a Gothic ciborium, perhaps originally held the relics of St-Just. Near the main entrance note the 4th-century Christian tombstone of a certain Valera Severa and two holy water stoups made from Roman columns.

Roman garden
t 06 61 95 04 79

Also in the village is a small **garden** with plants used in Roman times for cooking, medicine and perfumes.

South of St-Bertrand: along the Garonne

The glacial valley of the 'laughing' Garonne offers a few tempting stops along the way to the mighty mountains of the Haute-

Garonne. **Barbazan**, just across the river from Valcabrère, is an old spa trying to get back into the business; its water is rich in magnesium and calcium, and reputed for its digestive qualities. The Thermes building has recently been restored; see, too, the Baroque church with a lovely gilded interior. In nearby **Sauveterre-de-Comminges**, you can visit and take home a souvenir puppet from **L'Atelier des Marionnettes**.

L'Atelier des Marionnettes
t 05 61 88 36 04, ring ahead

More typically Pyrenean, perhaps, is the 11th-century church at **St-Pé-d'Ardet**, 15km south on the D33, decorated with excellent wall paintings by a 15th-century itinerant artist (if it's not open, the neighbour has the key). The altars to the right of the high altar were originally part of a Gallo-Roman temple. The road continues to the small lake of **Géry**, formed when the giant Gargas (*see* p.282) was walking through the valley and answered a gigantic call of nature.

St-Béat

Further south, squeezed in between the Cap det Mount and the Pic d'Ayre, St-Béat has long been known as the 'Key to France'; any army from Spain marching down the narrow defile of the Garonne from the Val d'Aran would have to beat its way past St-Béat and its citadel, so naturally well defended that it could be held with only a handful of men. Another nickname, although this one doesn't always look so good on the tourist brochure, is 'the shadiest town in the Pyrenees'. It was the home of the ancient Garunni, the tribe who gave their name to the River Garonne; in 75 BC Pompey founded a fort here, which he called Passus Lupi (Wolf Step). While in the area, he might have noticed that the two mountains that enclose St-Béat were made of white marble. One massive vertical excavation in the flank of Cap det Mount is said to have been carried off to Rome to become Trajan's column; an altar discovered nearby, guarded by two ancient marble quarrymen, was dedicated to the gods of the wood and mountain for allowing them to extract such a sizeable chunk without accident. Some of the mountain now decorates the garden of Versailles, but these days St-Béat can't keep up with the even whiter marble of Carrara. The tourist office can help if you want to visit the Roman quarries. There is a marble festival in July with sculpture in the streets and workshops.

Not surprisingly, much of St-Béat is built of marble, including the donjon (now the town clocktower), all that remains of its once nearly impregnable 11th-century castle, and the Romanesque **church**, from the same century. It has a portal with a sculpted tympanum and carved capitals, while inside is a small museum with some fine Renaissance statues and the relics of St-Privat. Nearby, note the houses overhanging the Garonne. Elsewhere in

St-Béat, the **Maison Consulaire** in Rue Galliéni dates from 1553; it inspired the balcony scene in Rostand's *Cyrano de Bergerac*. The street is named after Maréchal Joseph-Simon Galliéni, who was born here in 1849 and went on to serve the Third Republic's colonial ambitions in Indochina, Madagascar and Senegal, and who, as his last great act for *la patrie*, was instrumental in 1914 in rounding up Paris taxis to transport troops to the front in the Battle of the Marne; his statue stands on the right bank. At Cierp-Gaud, to the west of St-Béat, you will find a tree-top **adventure park** offering all sorts of exciting activities.

East of St-Béat, the **Col de Mente** sounds like a green drink but is actually a lovely pass (1,349m/4,425ft), reached by enough hairpin bends to make a ringlet. It is the perfect place to begin a walk for people who like easy strolls in the mountains; a sweet and easy shepherds' path begins by a *refuge* and leads up in an hour to a second shepherds' hut with superb views down to St-Béat, the Garonne valley and the peaks rimming the frontier around Luchon, including Maladetta, the highest of them all (3,404m/11,168ft). Rather than backtrack, you can make a scenic loop by taking the D618 back around over the Col des Ares.

Adventure park
t 05 61 94 08 36,
www.pyrenees-ho.com

Where to Stay and Eat South of the Garonne

ⓘ **Montréjeau >**
Pl Valentin Abeille,
t 05 61 95 80 22,
http://otimontrejeau.
ifrance.com; open
Sept–June Mon–Sat
9–12 and 2–6, July and
Aug 9.30–6.30

★ **Le Lugdunum >>**

ⓘ **St-Bertrand-de-Comminges >**
'Les Olivetains', next to
the cathedral, t 05 61 95
44 44; open July and
Aug 10–7, Sept–Dec and
Feb–June 10–5; guided
tours of the town

ⓘ **St-Béat**
t 05 61 79 45 98,
www.ot-st-beat.com;
open July and Aug
Mon–Sat 8.30–7.30, Sun
9–7; Sept–June Mon–Fri
10–12 and 2–6

Montréjeau ✉ 31210
Domaine de Jean-Pierre, 8km west in Pinas (✉ 65330), **t** 05 62 98 15 08, *www.domainedejeanpierre.com* (€). If you're after something with character, this choice has 3 very pretty rooms in a typical country house immersed in creepers, set in a large park. *Open all year book ahead in winter.*

St-Bertrand-de-Comminges ✉ 31510
L'Oppidum, up in the medieval town, **t 05 61 88 33 50 (€€–€). This pretty place has 15 comfortable rooms, some sleeping as many as four. The restaurant serves local specialities: stuffed trout, veal dishes and a delicious mousse with caramel and walnuts. *Menus €16–38. Closed mid-Nov–mid-Dec, restaurant closed Sun eves and all Mon except July and Aug.*
*Hôtel du Comminges, facing the cathedral, **t** 05 61 88 31 43 (€). An old ivy-covered building that was once a private house, this option has nicely furnished large rooms, and an interior garden to sit in as well as the terrace in front. *Closed Nov–Mar.*

Chez Simone, a street back from the cathedral, **t** 05 61 94 91 05. If you crave a good old stuffed Gascon chicken, ring Simone and have her cook one up to go with the home-made desserts and pretty views from the terrace. *Menus €15–18. Open every lunch and dinner for July and Aug; closed Christmas and Jan.*

Le Lugdunum, Valcabrère, **t** 05 61 94 52 05, *www.lugdunum-restaurant.com*. For something unique in France, book a table here and dine like Pompey himself. Here chef Renzo Pedrazzini (born locally of Italian parents) bases his dishes on the recipes compiled in the *Ten Books of Cooking* by the famous ancient gastronome Apicius in the 1st century. No Caesar salads or hummingbirds' tongues, but dishes such as partridge in cold sauce and young boar, served with spiced wines; a local herbalist supplies the authentic ingredients. The restaurant terrace has an equally delicious view of St-Bertrand. Mr Pedrazzini is very friendly and enthusiastic. *A la carte €40–50. Closed Sun eve–Tues out of season.*

(i) **Barbazan >**
*Parc Thermale, t 05 61
88 35 64,
www.tourisme-
barbazan.com; open
Mon–Sat 9–12 and 2–6*

Barbazan ✉ 31510

***Hostellerie des Sept Molles, on the D9 just east of Barbazan, in Sauveterre-de-Comminges, **t** 05 61 88 30 87, *www.hotel7molles.com* (€€€). The all-white hotel is perched on a high hill and offers luminous rooms and suites, spread out in several buildings, with a heated pool, tennis, and bubbling stream in the grounds. The restaurant has a lovely terrace for summer dining, or a roaring fire in the winter, and specializes in baby lamb with *mounjetado*, the local version of **cassoulet**. *Menus €30–47. Closed Tues and Wed mid-Sept–May.*

***L'Aristou, on road to Sauveterre, **t** 05 61 88 30 67 (€). Small and cosy, in a 19th-century house. There's also a good restaurant. *Menus €19–40. Closed Dec–mid-Feb; also restaurant Sun eve and Mon Sept–April.*

The Upper Comminges: Bagnères-de-Luchon and its Valleys

The 'Queen of the Pyrenees', Bagnères-de-Luchon, or just Luchon as everyone calls it, wears two different hats: as France's fourth (some say fifth) largest spa and as a favourite base for walking, canoeing, skiing, paragliding and a host of other sports in the mountains. Set in a sunny amphitheatre on the River One, surrounded by the highest peaks of the Pyrenees and a web of luscious emerald valleys, Luchon began its career under Tiberius in 25 AD as the Baths of Ilixo, named after the Celtic god of hot springs. It was not only the local spa for Lugdunum Convenarum (St-Bertrand-de-Comminges), but one whose hot springs, rich in sulphur and sodium, attracted rheumatic Romans from across the Empire. After the various invaders literally wiped it off the map, Luchon's hot waters went to waste for over 1,000 years until 1759, when Antoine Mégret, Baron d'Etigny and *Intendant* of Gascony, Béarn and Navarre, decided it was time to do as the Romans did and revive the genteel custom of taking the waters. He built the road down from Montréjeau and persuaded the governor of Languedoc, the influential Duke of Richelieu (great-nephew of the famous Cardinal), to take a cure. The duke found it simply marvellous, and especially liked picking out Roman artefacts that were then scattered about everywhere. He did the baron the supreme favour of telling everyone at Versailles what a good time he had had in Luchon, and before long an entire *Who's Who* of Europe had descended upon Luchon, from Flaubert and Louis Napoléon to Bismarck and Mata Hari.

Luchon

⭐ **Luchon**   Luchon (locally pronounced Lootch-ON) is a bustling modern town, but the gilded days when its spa hosted princes, politicians, literati and spies have left a burnished glow, especially along the elegant Allée d'Etigny, laid out in 1759 by the baron whose name it bears. Lined with lime trees, grand old hotels, restaurants and

Getting to and around the Upper Comminges

Both **trains** and **buses** pull in at the *gare*, just over the river from the centre. All come by way of Montréjeau, with connections to Lourdes, Tarbes and Toulouse. For information, call **t** 05 61 79 03 36.

cafés, it culminates in the lovely **Parc des Quinconces**, with its catalpas and tulip trees planted in quincunxes (like fives on a dice) and Luchon's **Thermes** (1849). In 1973, a natural cave sauna and hot pool called the **Vaporarium** was added to the baths complex; the vapours are apparently good for respiratory ailments, and singers, preachers and lawyers form a large part of the clientele. The sauna attracts thousands of *curistes* a day in the summer (as in Dax, French national health reimbursements have something to do with this). One of Baron d'Etigny's innovations at Luchon was having doctors on duty at the spa, but the first pioneering patients could hardly have felt like up-to-date Romans. In 1787 Arthur Young visited and wrote: 'The present baths are horrible holes; the patients lie up to their chins in hot sulphurous water, which, with the beastly dens they are placed in, one would think sufficent to cause as many distempers as they cure.' A French writer from the same period mentioned that the hot waters attracted hundreds of snakes, which were a bit of a nuisance slithering about when one was naked in the bath.

Luchon has a second public garden, the **Parc du Casino**, with exotic trees and shrubs and a lake; both of Luchon's gardens are famous for their large population of marble ladies and gents. When wallowing in pungent water, strolling past the statues and lounging around in the cafés begins to pale, you can take in the atmospheric municipal attic called the **Musée Pays de Luchon** and learn about the early days of mountaineering, speleology and *thermalisme* through old photos, memorabilia of celebrity visitors, traditional rural gear, a few Roman bits and bobs, a small hermaphrodite Celtic god, a display of the Romanesque churches in the surrounding valleys (the photos from the Vall d'Aran in Spain may well tempt you over the border for a closer look), stuffed animals and birds, and some of the tools used by the legendary Pyrenean explorer and speleologist, Norbert Casteret. There's also a **museum on aircraft** from 1934 until Concorde, including bits from planes that crashed in the Pyrenees during the Second World War.

Musée Pays de Luchon
18 Allée d'Etigny,
t 05 61 79 29 87; open daily 9–12 and 2–6; closed bank hols

Aircraft museum
at the aerodrome,
t 05 61 79 29 87; open April–Oct Tues, Thurs and Sat 3–6

The Valleys around Luchon

Exploring the majestic high-altitude scenery that surrounds Luchon can take up an entire holiday. Of the classic excursions, perhaps the most classic is to the Port de Venasque, beginning at the top of the superb Vallée de la Pique, lined with forests of silver firs and beech trees – unfortunately, many ill from the worst acid rain problem in the Pyrenees. From the end of the D125 it's a 30-min walk up to the **Hospice de France** (1,385m/4,570ft), founded by the Knights Hospitaller in the Middle Ages to shelter wayfarers or the occasional pilgrim who passed this way; these days it's a popular family picnic destination. To make it to the 2,448m/8,078ft **Port de Venasque** on the Spanish border and back, get to the Hospice early in the morning and count on at least a 6-hr march past forests, waterfalls and pastures. The reward: the unforgettable view from Port de Venasque of the looming rock-bound massif called **Maladetta**, the 'accursed mountains', a jagged, 6km-long, glacier-crowned spine, reaching 3,404m/11,168ft at Aneto, the highest peak in the Pyrenees. In the 19th century, visitors to Luchon thrilled to the dark legends surrounding Maladetta, said to be responsible for more deaths than any other mountain in the Pyrenees. One story relates how shepherds on Maladetta refused to help two poor pilgrims (Jesus and St Peter, in disguise) and were turned into stone with all their sheep – a story believed into the 18th century, the mayor of one village counting 7,000 'petrified people and sheep'. Others tell how countless other shepherds, working men and mountain guides have been entombed in its rocky embrace, under avalanches, or at the bottom of its lakes, lured there by *fadas* or sirens. The locals held the peaks of Maladetta in such awe that it fell to foreigners with piquant names (Wilhelm von Parrot and Platon de Tcihatcheff) to be the first to scale their highest peaks. Linguists, for their part, say the whole thing is baloney, that the *Mala* in its name is simply an old word for 'mountain'.

The Spanish village of **Venasque** (by road the easiest way to get there is via St-Béat) is so remote from the rest of Spain that during the Franco years it was the only place where you could hear the *Himno de Riego*, the national anthem of Republican Spain.

Branching off from the Vallée de la Pique, the D46 follows the Vallée du Lys (or more properly, the Bat de Lys, the 'valley of avalanches'), carved by glaciers with a rare symmetry; both sides of the valley are nearly equal in shape and size. Along the way you can peer down an abyss, the **Gouffre Richard**, then take the road up to the ski resort, **Superbagnères**, 18km from Luchon (take the D125 and D46), with superb views; there's an orientation table by the Grand Hotel. Best of all, continue up the main road past the hydroelectric plant to the **Cirque de Lys** and its **Cascade d'Enfer**, a waterfall splashing through a narrow cleft in the rocks that could pass for the gate of hell. The gentler, more pastoral Vallée d'Oueil northwest of Luchon (take the D618 and D51) has a church with colourful 15th-century murals at **Benque-Dessous-et-Dessus**. Further up the road, a belvedere called the Kiosque de Mayrègne offers a panoramic view and a chance for refreshments; **Cirès**, a charming mountain village, lies below **Bourg d'Oueil**, a cross-country ski resort.

One of the most popular excursions is up the Vallée d'Oô (take the D618 and turn on the D76), passing by way of St-Aventin, 5km from Luchon. Perched high onto its promontory, and a good 100-yard (90m) walk up a steep slope from the road, **St-Aventin** is a 12th-century gem with two beautiful bell towers and a tympanum carved with a *Christ in Majesty* and an excellent *Virgin and Child*. The capitals are finely carved as well, with the *Massacre of the Innocents*, the *Washing of the Feet* and, curiously, a bear; according to the story, Aventin, an 8th-century hermit, was a protector of bears, to the extent that they would come to him to have thorns removed from their paws. A number of Gallo-Roman blocks were reused to build the church, most strikingly the three monuments embedded in the south wall. Inside, the stoup is a remarkable pre-Romanesque work, decorated with the lamb of Christ, little fish (the newly baptized) and doves (the souls of the blessed). The lacy choir screen is a fine example of Pyrenean ironwork, and around Aventin's tomb are more sculpted capitals, one showing the saint helping a bear, the other showing him holding his head after the Moors lopped it off. The murals from the 12th century found under the plaster show St-Sernin, patron of Toulouse, with St-Aventin.

At Castillon, the road forks; take the left along the Neste (another word for 'river') d'Oô, which is drivable as far as the **Granges d'Astau** (1,139m/3,736ft). There you can pick up the GR 10, passing the silvery waterfall known as the Chevelure de Madeleine, for its resemblance to the Magdalene's flowing hair. The track continues up, taking about an hour in all, to the stunningly azure **Lac d'Oô**, the loveliest of a pocket of glacier lakes, set in nearly lunar surroundings. In the background, a 900ft (275m) waterfall from the lake of Espingo adds to the setting, and if you're feeling energetic, you can walk up to Espingo, or continue even further up to the spectacular Lac du Portillon; there are *refuges* at both lakes.

The Larboust and West towards the Vallée de Louron

West of Luchon, the **Vallée de Larboust** leads up to the Col de Peyresourde, one of the highest passes in the Pyrenees, linking the Comminges to the Vallée de Louron (*see* p.280). Larboust is still relatively densely populated for a high valley in the Pyrenees, and it was one of the final valleys to be inhabited by Cagots, the last of whom died in the early 20th century (*see* **Culture**, pp.37–9). Just after the turn-off for the Vallée d'Oô, on the D618, **Cazaux** has a church with a remarkable late medieval mural of the *Last Judgement*, discovered in the last century under the plaster by a local painter. The iconography is unique: the Christ is shown sitting atop a solid rainbow, not in stern triumph or majesty, but with the bleeding wounds of the Passion. On his right, the Virgin Mary pleads for mercy, but intercedes in a most unusual way: she bares her breasts and squirts milk on her son's wounds. Unfortunately, the church is usually locked because of a theft, but the Luchon tourist office may help you locate the key. A bit further on, high on the left-hand side of the road, there's another fine Romanesque chapel, **St-Pé**, made out of Roman tombstones. At the top of the Col de Peyresourde are two fairly ugly but excellent ski resorts, **Peyragudes** and **Les Agudes**.

Market Days in the Upper Comminges

Bagnères-de-Luchon: Wednesday and Saturday mornings, daily in July and August.

Where to Stay and Eat in the Upper Comminges

ⓘ Bagnères-de-
Luchon >
18 Allée d'Etigny,
t *05 61 79 21 21,*
www.luchon.com; open
daily 9–12 and 2–7;
July–Aug daily 9–7;
closed weekends
in Nov

Bagnères-de-Luchon ✉ 31110

Luchon claims two powerful specialities you may want to watch out for: *pétéram*, a stew made of ham and sheep's tripe and trotters, and *pistache*, mutton braised in wine and vegetables and 50 cloves of garlic.

Hotel d'Etigny, 3 Av Paul Bonnemasion, **t 05 61 79 01 42 (€€€–€). Opposite the baths, this is a solid, atmospheric, old-fashioned place with a restaurant. *Menus €16–43. Open May–mid-Oct.*

***Corneille, 5 Av A. Dumas, **t** 05 61 79 36 221, *www.hotel-corneille.com* (€€). At this handsome 19th-century hotel set in a lovely garden on the edge of Luchon, you'll find tranquil rooms and a restaurant. Has been taken over by Best Western chain. *Menus €18–31.*

Jardin des Cascades, near the church of Montauban-de-Luchon, east of Luchon, **t** 05 61 79 83 09 (€€–€). Here you'll find a few double rooms, enchanting views from the dining terrace and excellent preparations of traditional dishes, although they don't come cheap. The restaurant's always packed, so book. *Menus lunch €19 and about €38 for à la carte. Closed Oct–Mar.*

Hôtel des Neiges, 27 Rue Victor Hugo, **t** 05 61 79 00 02 (€€–€). This well-

priced option has a lovely garden. *Closed Nov.*

*Des Deux Nations, 5 Rue Victor-Hugo, **t** 05 61 79 01 71 (€). Quiet, yet central and an old favourite, this hotel-restaurant is run by a friendly family, who are also more than competent in the kitchen. *Menus €10–30. Restaurant closed Sun eves, and all day Mon in Nov, Dec, Jan and Mar.*

*François Ier, 1 Allée d'Etigny, **t** 05 61 94 89 89 (€). This is also a low-priced option and is open all year. Part of brasserie on the main boulevard.

*La Petite Auberge, 15 Rue Lamartine, **t** 05 61 79 02 88 (€). Also has a very reasonably priced restaurant. Rooms are bright, clean and comfortable with new bathrooms. *Menus €14. Closed late Oct–mid-Dec.*

La Lanette, just east of Luchon at Montauban-de-Luchon, **t** 05 61 79 00 38. This campsite is one of the best of the many in the area, with trees and lovely views. There are bungalows to rent.

Around Luchon ✉ 31110

Le Sapin Fleuri, Bourg d'Oueil, **t 05 61 79 21 90, *www.hotel-sapin-fleuri.com* (€). At 1,400m/4,620ft, this comfortable little chalet hotel is in a magnificent setting. *Menus €23–35. Closed 10 Oct–26 Dec.*

Auberge d'Astau, 4km from Oô, **t** 05 61 79 35 63, *www.astau-pyrenees.com* (€). Very simple *auberge* in a beautiful setting, ideally placed for the trek up to the Lac d'Oô. Bedrooms are in a modern annexe or there are cheaper, dormitory-style rooms.

Hostellerie des Spijeolles, Oô, **t** 05 61 79 06 05 (€). Situated in this quiet village, the hotel has a handful of rooms and a restaurant. Very simple. *Menu €15. Closed Nov.*

St-Gaudens and North of the Garonne: the Petites Pyrénées

For 90 per cent of people travelling in the region, bedazzled by the beauty of the Pyrenees, the area north and west of the Garonne of the baby mountains, or 'Petites Pyrénées', is *terra incognita*. Yet these rolling hills of the Comminges were beloved in antiquity and have seemingly changed little since: remarkably intact landscapes, unspoiled by billboards, subdivisions and all the other detritus of our times. The departmental roads are still lined on either side with ancient plane trees, rare in the rest of France, where one or both sides are sacrificed to road-widening schemes. Here there's not enough traffic to bother.

St-Gaudens

Busy St-Gaudens, with a population of 13,000 and the big factory of Cellulose d'Aquitaine, is the metropolis in these parts. It offers a striking contrast to the Petites Pyrénées and would be a perfect point of departure for visiting them, if you can manage to escape the infernal circle of its road system, which has been designed with inscrutable Gallic logic.

St-Gaudens is named after a 12-year-old shepherd boy, who (as the pious story says) met a band of Moorish cavalrymen who demanded that he convert to Islam. Like a good boy, young Gaudens asked his mother if it was all right, but she said no. The Moors then chopped off his head, but like so many regional saints his body still had the panache to pick it up, and with the wicked Moors in hot pursuit, he ran with it all the way to the safety of the nearest church. No wonder Gascons make such good rugby players. The most important church, however, is the **Collégiale St-Pierre-de-St-Gaudens**, in Place Jean-Jaurès, with a great square bell tower (containing the biggest carillon in the Midi-Pyrénées) and a flamboyant Gothic portal from the 17th century. Walk around the sides to see the modillons, the capitals from the cloister on the south end, and various Roman bits embedded in the walls. Along the nave, 18th-century tapestries from Aubusson illustrate the *Martyrdom of St Gaudens*, the *Transfiguration* and the *Triumph of Faith*, and the 17th-century choir stalls and organ are worth a glance. Best of all are the unusual sculpted capitals around the choir: bears fight, monkeys make faces, Adam seems to gag on the forbidden fruit, King Nebuchadnezzar is turned into a beast, and people queue up under the palms, perhaps to be baptized.

Just east of the Collégiale, the **Musée du Comminges** has an interesting ensemble of traditional tools, costumes and domestic items, local minerals, medieval manuscripts and memorabilia

Collégiale St-Pierre-de-St-Gaudens
open Mon–Sat 9–12 and 2.15–6, Sun 9–12

Musée du Comminges
t 05 61 89 05 42; open Tues–Sat 9–12 and 2–6

Getting to and around the Petites Pyrénées

St-Gaudens is the transport centre for the region, with **train** connections (t 05 62 00 78 73) to Toulouse and Luchon, and TER **bus** connections to Montréjeau, Lannemezan, Tarbes and Lourdes, as well as to Luchon and Martres-Tolosane.

related to the three great military men from the Pyrenees: Foch (from Tarbes), Joffre (from Rivesaltes, in the eastern Pyrenees) and Galliéni (from St-Béat). The three are also the subject of the **Monument des Trois Maréchaux**, near St-Gaudens's belvedere, located just across Boulevard Bepmale from the museum. Near here, in the Jardin Publique, the elegant twin-columned gallery once adorned the cloister of the abbey of Bonnefont (*see* below).

Montmaurin: Roman Indolence North of St-Gaudens

⭐ **Montmaurin**

Gallo-Roman Villa
t 05 61 88 74 73; open May–Aug daily 9.30–12 and 2–6, Sept–April Tues–Sun 9.30–12 and 2–5; adm includes entry to Montmaurin museum

It's 16km on the D9 north of St-Gaudens to the banks of the River Save and Montmaurin, where the well-preserved **Gallo-Roman Villa** stands in splendour on the crest of a hill – a setting little changed since Roman times. In the 1st century a rich man named Nepotianus, owner of the surrounding 7,000ha (17,000 acres) (*see* p.137 for an idea of how the other half lived in Roman Gaul), built himself a typical country estate, with all the farm outbuildings. At some point the Save flooded and covered it irredeemably in muck, but by the 4th century Nepotianus' heirs were ready to rebuild. Their pretensions had outgrown a mere agricultural manor: nothing would do but a white marble palace fit for a prince, or at least a Hollywood mogul, with 200 rooms, complete with its own private baths, shady porticoes, gardens, fountains, temple, swimming pool, heated dining rooms, summer and winter apartments with terraces and views. It's the largest and most luxurious Gallo-Roman villa ever discovered in France; the mountains of oyster shells the archaeologists turned up confirmed the *dolce vita* led by its residents. In the 5th century the villa burned down and was abandoned and buried in the mud. In the centre of Montmaurin

Montmaurin museum
open May–Aug daily 9.30–12 and 2–6, Sept–April Tues–Sun 9.30–12 and 2–5; adm

village, a **museum** in the *mairie* contains a scale model of the villa and a collection of Roman and prehistoric finds from the area, including a cast of the celebrated fat lady from the Aurignacian period, the Vénus de Lespugue, found in the nearby Grotte des Rideaux by the Countess of St-Périer in 1922, and now in the Musée de l'Homme in Paris.

Around Montmaurin: along the Save and Gesse Rivers

Anyone who has been along the River Vézère in the Dordogne will recognize the nearby **Gorges de la Save** along the D69c as just the kind of place to warm the cockles of prehistoric hearts, pocked with caves and natural rock shelters; a number of grottoes here have yielded not only the Venus but other interesting finds. At **La Hillère**, just outside Montmaurin, the cemetery chapel has a beautiful mosaic with a swastika – an ancient sun symbol – left over from a 4th-century sanctuary by a spring. **Lespugue** further down-river controlled much of this area; you can explore the striking ruins of its 13th-century castle, dramatically balanced on the lip of a ravine. In 1913 an experimental botanical forest, the **Forêt de Cardeilhac**, was planted east of Larroque, to see what sort of trees from around the world would adjust to the climate; part of it is now a public arboretum and a pretty place for a stroll.

Hill Towns of the Petites Pyrénées

North of Montmaurin, **Boulogne-sur-Gesse** began its career as a *bastide* in 1282, founded by the king and abbot of the nearby Cistercian abbey of Nizors, who named the new town after his university, Bologna. The main square is closed in by arcades and old houses, and the old *halles* in the centre is now the *mairie*.

Boulogne-sur-Gesse is only the largest of a fine set of *villages perchés* in this corner of the Petites Pyrénées, touching on the western confines of the Lannemezan Plateau. The most spectacular, **Mondilhan**, 9km to the northeast, sits on the highest hill around and enjoys an extraordinary, magical view of the big Pyrenees that on a clear day ranges 250km; the view from nearby **Péguilhan** is almost as good. Southeast of Boulogne and back over the Save, Ciadoux and Escanecrabe also crown the hills; **Ciadoux** has an excellent life-size 16th-century *mise au tombeau* in its church, the figures carved in stone (pick up the key at the café), while **Escanecrabe** offers a fortified 14th-century **church** with an octa-gonal tower typical of the region, and has another lovely panorama of the Pyrenees, with the River Save in the foreground. Lastly, follow the tree-lined D17 north along the Save to **L'Isle-en-Dodon**, another *bastide* town with an arcaded square, well worth a halt for its fortified red brick **church** and handsome octagonal bell tower, both from the 14th century, and gorgeous Renaissance stained-glass windows in the choir made by the school of Arnaud de Moles.

Northeast of St-Gaudens and into the Aurignacian Era

The St-Marcet natural gas field north of St-Gaudens, discovered back in 1939, was responsible for many of the jobs in the area. The gas has been sucked nearly dry now, but the pleasant village of **St-Marcet**, 10km north of St-Gaudens, carries on regardless, with one of the oldest *halles* in the region and ruins of the 12th-century castle of the Counts of Comminges sitting on a nearby hill.

When the counts were bored there they could hop over to the pretty medieval village of **Aurignac**, gathered around the skirts of another castle of theirs, built in 1240; you can climb up the surviving donjon for a view of the Pyrenees. The church has a flamboyant Gothic portal and porch, framed by twisted barley-sugar columns left over from a previous church; above are figures of the Virgin and Child from the 17th century, and one of Christ awaiting death from the 15th.

In 1852, a labourer digging along the road to Boulogne-sur-Gesse came upon a cache of skeletons tucked under a rock shelter. No one was too surprised; the locals had often found skeletons in their fields from the murderous Wars of Religion and the bones were dutifully gathered and reburied in the local cemetery. In 1870, a palaeontologist in the Gers, named Edouard Lartet, heard of the discovery and came over to investigate, and found enough bones and ancient tools to theorize that perhaps the traditional, biblical chronologies of the creation of man then current were not quite accurate. His hunch was confirmed in 1888, when railworkers at Cro-Magnon (near Les Eyzies) found similar skeletons, and since 1906, the first ten millennia of the Upper Palaeolithic era (30,000–20,000 BC) have been known as the Aurignacian era. Although Aurignac's most important finds are in the National Museum at St-Germain-en-Laye near Paris, the local **Musée de la Préhistoire** contains local finds, including animal bones and tools.

Musée de la Préhistoire
Rue Fernand-Lacorre,
t 05 61 98 70 06; open
July–Aug daily 10–12
and 2–6; Sept–June
Mon–Fri 9–12 and 2–6

Just because their cathedral was in St-Bertrand-de-Commingès, it didn't mean the bishops of Commingès had to spend all their time there. In 1270, they petitioned the Counts of Toulouse to let them build a winter palace halfway between St-Bertrand and Toulouse, at the old *bastide* hilltown of **Alan**, 5km east of Aurignac. The **Palais des Evêques de Commingès** remained a favourite residence over the next five centuries, although the building is marked most by the taste of Bishop De Foix-Grailly who, in 1470, converted a feudal castle into a flamboyant Gothic palace. The magnificent portal has a striking cow carved on the tympanum – the cow of Béarn from the bishop's own coat of arms, although it has always been known as the cow of Alan. Inside the portal, much of the palace has been carried off bit by bit by 20th-century antique collectors, but it's still impressive to see the scale to which a medieval bishop could aspire, and there are fine views from the top floor. In 1784, just before the Revolution and the end of the bishopric of the Commingès, Bishop du Bouchet built the handsome **Hôpital Notre-Dame-de-Lorette** (a kilometre away) to care for the people of the local parish. It's one of the rare French classical buildings in these parts, and usually open on Sunday afternoons if you want a look at its monumental stair, pharmacy, chapel and courtyard.

Palais des Evêques de Commingès
t 05 61 98 90 72; open
July–Sept Sat and Sun
3–6; Oct–June, by appt
only; adm

Down the Garonne: St-Gaudens towards Toulouse

Few towns in France have been inhabited as long as **St-Martory**, where human bones found in the caves and shelters go back 240,000 years. Although not the most exciting of towns, it produced Norbert Casteret (*see* p.293) and has a 12th-century medieval castle and **church** with a menhir and Gallo-Roman stele by its side, and a Romanesque door from the nearby Cistercian **abbey of Bonnefont**. This once-proud 12th-century abbey founded priories and *bastides* in France and Spain, and served as the burial place of all the Counts of Comminges. Nevertheless, after the Revolution Bonnefont was broken up in bits and auctioned off, its cloister divided between St-Gaudens, Nice and New York, while its chapterhouse was moved to the west end of St-Martory to be used as a *gendarmerie*, of all things. Now even the cops have vanished.

St-Martory has an attractive **18th-century bridge** over the Garonne, which you should take for **Montsaunes**, once the site of the most important commandery of the Knights Templar in southwest France. Nothing remains, although the fortified 12th-century brick Romanesque **church** they built has some excellent carvings over its north and west portals of scenes from the childhood of Christ, including one referring to an apocryphal story of the blind wife who miraculously regains her sight on washing the newborn infant – a common theme in Eastern church art, but one rarely seen in the West. There are paintings of holy and not-so-holy scenes, and symbols inside include six-pointed stars, wheels and crisscrossed circles. A bit further on, **Salies-du-Salat** is a little spa village in the Salat valley that enjoys an exceptionally sunny microclimate. Romans came to bathe in its salty waters, '*la plus minéralisée d'Europe!*', now installed in a curious Neo-Egyptian Art Deco spa building, built in 1898 and remodelled in 1924. A ruined donjon, all that survives of the 12th-century castle of the counts of Comminges, stands over the town like a big stone thumb.

There are famous views over the Pyrenees due north of **Belbèze-en-Comminges** and the hamlet of Ausseing; take the panoramic D83, which noodles back down to the Garonne and **Martres-Tolosane**, where the Petites Pyrénées give way to the great plain of the Garonne. In the old centre, the **Musée Archéologique Municipal** contains a large assortment of sculpture found in the Gallo-Roman villas that once surrounded Martres-Tolosane, most notably at Chiragan. The 14th-century brick **church**, dedicated to the town's patron, St-Vidan, has an octagonal bell tower, and among the marble sarcophagi inside is one belonging to the saint who was killed in combat against the Moors in the 8th century; the battle is annually reproduced with considerably pageantry on the first Sunday after Pentecost. Since the 16th century, **Martres** has been synonymous with ceramics, although the unique local style of decoration, known as 'meadow flowers', dates only from the 19th century. Two potteries still make it in Martres and welcome visitors during working hours. There is also a permanent exhibition of ceramics at the tourist office.

Musée Archéologique Municipal
Rue du Donjon,
t 05 61 98 66 41; open July–mid-Sept 10–12.30 and 1.30–5.30

ⓘ **Boulogne-sur-Gesse** >>
*Pl de l'Hôtel de Ville,
t 05 61 88 13 19,
www.ville-boulogne-
sur-gesse.fr; open
Mon–Sat 9.30–12 and
3–6.30, Sun 10–12.30*

★ **Ferme-Auberge du Péguilhan** >>

ⓘ **St-Gaudens** >
*2 Rue Thiers, t 05 61
94 77 61; open July–Aug
Mon–Sat 9–7;
Sept–June 9–12
and 1.30–6*

ⓘ **Aurignac** >>
*Rue des Nobles,
t 05 61 98 70 06,
www.aurignac.fr; open
July and Aug daily
9.30–12.30 and 2–6;
otherwise contact the
mairie, t 05 61 98 90 08*

ⓘ **Salies-du-Salat** >>
*Bd Jean-Jaurès, t 05 61
90 53 93, http://
salinea.free.fr/salies-
salat; open Oct–April
Mon–Thurs 10–12 and
2–6, Fri 10–12 and 2–5;
May–Sept Mon–Fri
10–12 and 3–6, Sat
10–12 and 3–5*

ⓘ **St-Martory** >>
*Rue des Ecoles, t 05 61
97 40 48, www.
petitespyrenees.com;
open June–Aug daily*

ⓘ **Martres-Tolosane**
*mairie, t 05 61 98
66 41; open May–Sept
daily 10–6, Oct–April
Mon–Sat 9.30–12.30
and 1.30–5.30*

Market Days in the Petites Pyrénées

St-Gaudens: Thursdays and Saturdays.
Boulogne-sur-Gesse: Wednesdays.
L'Isle-en-Dodon: Saturdays.
Aurignac: Tuesdays.
Salies-du-Salat: Mondays.

Where to Stay and Eat in the Petites Pyrénées

St-Gaudens ✉ 31800

***Hostellerie des Cèdres**, just outside St-Gaudens in Villeneuve de Rivière, t 05 61 89 36 00, www.hotel-descedres.com (€€–€). Set in a large park, the building formerly belonged to the Marquise de Montespan, Louis XIV's mistress. Rooms are elegantly furnished with antiques, and there is a pool, tennis courts and a fitness room. The restaurant specializes in various veal dishes of which the marquise would have approved. *Menus €30–60. Open all year. Closed Sun eve, restaurant closed Mon and Tues.*

****Pedussaut**, 9 Av de Boulogne, t 05 61 89 15 70 (€). Now renovated, this hotel has an excellent restaurant, serving good-value menus chock full of regional ingredients. *Menus €12–36. Restaurant closed Sun eve in winter.*

Restaurant de l'Abattoir, Bd Leconte de l'Isle, t 05 61 89 70 29. St-Gaudens is famous throughout France for its white veal, and it and any number of high-quality meats are prepared here at a genuine carnivore's oasis, located just opposite you know what. *Menus €12–25. Closed Sun and bank hols.*

Montmaurin ✉ 31350

Caso Nuosto, in the woods not far from the Roman villa, t 05 61 88 25 50 (€). This place offers three *chambres d'hôte* in a restored old farmhouse, with a pool and garden. *Table d'hôte* also available specializing in regional cuisine using the farm's produce. *Menus €14 and €16. Open all year.*

Boulogne-sur-Gesse ✉ 31350

Ferme-Auberge du Péguilhan, Péguilhan, t 05 61 88 75 78 (€€). Located in an old half-timbered farmhouse, this *chambres d'hôte*-restaurant serves delicious stuffed lamb shoulder, *poule au pot* and other tasty home-grown fare, and is one of the very few *ferme-auberges* to offer a vegetarian menu if you order ahead. There are also cookery courses on preparing duck. *Menus from €12. Open daily all year by reservation only.*

Restaurant La Ferme de Préville, on the road to Auch, t 05 61 88 23 12, www.preville.fr (€). Pleasant restaurant offering traditional, hearty menus at €14 for lunch and €20–39 in the evening. *Open lunch and Mon, Fri and Sun eve, closed Sat and last weekend of each month.*

Aurignac/Alan ✉ 31420

Notre-Dame de Lorette, Alan, t 05 61 98 98 84, www.notredamedelorette.com (€€). For something different, two magnificent *gîtes* for 4–6 have been installed in this 18th-century hospital, one in the old pharmacy, the other next to a fireplace large enough to roast a camel. Concerts and events organized.

****Le Cerf Blanc**, Aurignac, t 05 61 98 95 76 (€). The hotel is well-equipped and open all year round; it also has a good restaurant featuring regional cooking. *Menus €24–59. Restaurant closed Sun eves and Mon.*

Salies-du-Salat ✉ 31260

***Hotel Central**, 1 Av de la Gare, t 05 61 90 50 01 (€). This may be the only hotel-restaurant in town, but it's a pleasant little place. *Menus €11–28.*

St-Martory ✉ 31360

Ferme-Auberge Auzas, near the centre of the village, t 05 61 90 23 61. This restaurant is open all year, but by reservation only. It serves its own farm lamb, foie gras, *confits* and delicious home-made bread. Courses offered on preparing duck and baking bread. Can also provide simple *chambres d'hôte* for €42. *Menu €14.*

Toulouse

Toulouse, called 'La Ville Rose' for its millions of pink bricks, has 800,000 lively inhabitants, counting over 110,000 university students and 70 per cent of the industry in the Midi-Pyrénées region, much of it high-tech and related to aeronautics and space.

Toulouse should have been the rosy capital of a nation called Languedoc, but it was knocked out of the big leagues in the 1220s by the popes and kings of France. Spain, and in particular Barcelona, extends her cape here, distilling enough passion to give the heirs of medieval Toulouse's fat merchants a dose of madness. Toulouse is above all une ville d'émotion; listen to the Toulousains chant their national anthem at every possible occasion: 'O moun païs, Toulouse, Toulouse! O moun païs, Toulouse, Toulouse!' over and over again. There aren't any other verses; according to the natives, there's nothing else to say.

SPAIN

12

Don't miss

⭐ **Romanesque architecture**
Basilica of St-Sernin p.309

⭐ ***Pastel* palaces**
Hôtel de Bernuy p.314

⭐ **Not so new**
Pont Neuf p. 315

⭐ **Restaurant revolution**
Old Toulouse p.320

⭐ **Medieval art**
Musée des Augustins p.317

See map overleaf

BOULEVARD DE L'EMBOUCHURE

BOULEVARD DE LA MARQUETTE

Jardin Compans-Caffarelli

PLACE ARNAUD-BERNARD

BOULEVARD LASCROSSES

PL. DES TIERCERETTES

RUE LASCROSSES

ALLÉE DE BARCELONE

ALLÉE DE BRIENNE

Canal de Brienne

BOULEVARD MAL. LECLERC

BOULEVARD ARMAND DUPORTAL

Université des Sciences Sociales

RUE DES PUITS CREUSÉS

PLACE A. FRANCE

RUE DES AMIDONNIERS

AV. PAUL SEJOURNE

St-Pierre des Chartreux

RUE VALADE

EDF Bazacle

St-Pierre-des-Cuisines

RUE PARG

PONT DES CATALANS

PLACE ST-PIERRE

RUE LARREY

Garonne

QUAI LOMBARD

RUE DE L'ABATTOIR

PONT ST-PIERRE

Don't miss

⭐ Basilica of St-Sernin **p.309**
⭐ Hôtel de Bernuy **p.314**
⭐ Pont Neuf **p. 315**
⭐ Old Toulouse **p.320**
⭐ Musée des Augustins **p.317**

PLACE DES ABATTOIRS

Les Abattoirs

Hospice St-Joseph de la Grave

Hôtel-Dieu St-Jacques (Musée d'Histoire de la Médecine)

Ec Bea

PONT

ALLÉES

St-Nicolas

RUE RECLUSANE

Château d'Eau

PLACE LAGANNE

Centre Municipal de l'Affiche, de la Carte Postale, et de l'Art Graphique

RUE ADOLPHE COLL

CHARLES DE

PLACE ST-CYPRIEN

PLACE ROGUET

PLACE OLIVIER

RUE DE LA PLACE

REPUBLIQUE

RUE J. VIE

AV. ETIENNE BILLERES

FITTE

RUE TEINTURIERS

RUE COUPEFER

RUE LAGANNE DILLON

PRAIRIE DES FILTRES

COURS DILLON

Garonne

RUE DE CUGNAUX

N

RUE DES ARCS ST-CYPRIEN

RUE STE-LUCIE

PLACE DU FER-A-CHEVAL

PONT ST-MICHEL

250 metres
250 yards

Bus Station
(buses to airport)

Train Station

Canal du Midi

BOULEVARD DE BONNEPOS

BOULEVARD P. SEMARD

BOULEVARD DE

BOULEVARD D'ARCOLE

RUE DE LA CONCORDE

RUE MATABIAU

RUE RAYMOND IV

RUE DE BAYARD

PLACE DE BELFORT

PLACE JEANNE D'ARC

R. ARNAUD BERNARD

Lycée St-Sernin

Basilique du St-Sernin

PLACE ST-SERNIN

RUE ST-BERNARD

BOULEVARD DE STRASBOURG

RUE CAFFARELLI

ALLÉES JEAN JAURES

RUE DE LA CHAINE

Musée St-Raymond

RUE DE PERIGORD

PLACE DU PEYROU

RUE DES LOIS

RUE DU TAUR

RUE DE REMUSAT

RUE LORRAINE

PLACE VICTOR HUGO

RUE DE L'INDUSTRIE

RUE GABRIEL PERI

BOULEVARD DE

Chapelle des Carmélites

RUE RIVALS

R. PORT SALDANE

RUE AUSTERLITZ

RUE MAURY

Clocher des Cordeliers

RUE DEVILLE

Nôtre-Dame du Taur

Post Office ✉

RUE DE LA COLOMBETTE

RUE CASTELLANE

RUE ROMIGUIERES

RUE MIREPOIX

Hôtel de Ville

RUE LA FAYETTE SQ CH. DE GAULLE

PLACE WILSON

BOULEVARD LAZARE CARNOT

RUE D'AUBUISSON

LA GARE

AMINIERES

PLACE DES JACOBINS

PLACE DU CAPITOLE

Tourist Information ℹ

RUE LAPEYROUSE

RUE ST-ANTOINE DU T.

RUE M. FONVIELLE

RUE RIQUET

LAKANAL

Les Jacobins

RUE GAMBETTA

Théâtre du Capitole

RUE DE LA POMME

PLACE OCCITANE

Hôtel de Bernuy

RUE ST-URSULE

Musée du Vieux Toulouse

R. DES GESTES

RUE ST-ROME

RUE CHALANDE

RUE D'ALSACE

PLACE ST-GEORGES

RUE DU REMPART ST-ETIENNE

PLACE DE LA DAURADE

R. DU MAY

PLACE DES PUITS-CLOS

RUE CANTEGRIL

RUE PEYROLIERES

Nôtre-Dame -la-Daurade

R. PEYRAS

PLACE DE LA BOURSE

RUE DES

Musée des Augustins

RUE DES ARTS

Fondation Bemberg/ Hôtel d'Assézat

RUE DE LA BOURSE

PLACE ESQUIROL

RUE DE METZ

RUE FERMAT

PLACE DUPUY

R. DU PORT GUITHEMERY

Q. DE LA DAURADE

PLACE DU PONT NEUF

RUE DE METZ

PLACE DE LA TRINITE

PLACE ST-ETIENNE

RUE DES POTIERS

École des Beaux-Arts

PONT NEUF

AV. DE TOUNIS

RUE DES COUTELIERS

RUE DES PARADOUX

RUE DES FILATIERS

R. DE LA TRINITE

RUE CROIX BARAGNON

Cathédrale St-Etienne

RUE DES POTIERS

ST ETIENNE

RUE DU COQ D'INDE

Préfecture

Halle aux Grains

ALLÉES F. VERDIER

RUE SAUVEUR

QUAI DE TOUNIS

Nôtre-Dame la Dalbade

PLACE DES CARMES

RUE LANGUEDOC

PLACE MAGE

Musée Paul Dupuy

RUE NINAU

PORT SAINTE

Canal du

R. PONT DE TOUNIS

RUE DE LA DALBADE

Hôtel de Malte

Halles

Hôtel d'Ulmo

ALLEE P. SABATIER

Hôtel de Pierre

RUE ST ROMEY

RUE PHARAON

RUE DU

RUE MAGE

R. PLEAU

R. PERCHEPINTE

AVENUE M. HAURIOU

RUE DE LA FONDERIE

Hôtel du Vieux Raisin

RUE NAZARETH

RUE OZENNE

Grand Rond

Midi

Institut Catholique

PLACE DU SALIN

Jardin Royal

ALLEE DES SOUPIRS

PLACE DU PARLEMENT

Palais de Justice

ALLEES J. GUESDE

Théâtre Sorano

Jardin des Plantes

ALLEE F. MISTRAL

ALLEE P. FEUGA

RUE ALFRED DUMERIL

Musée d'Histoire Naturelle

RUE MONPLAISIR

To Musée Labit

RUE DES MARTYRS DE LA LIBERATION

Monument à la Gloire de la Résistance

Getting to Toulouse

By Air

Toulouse's international **airport** is at Blagnac, 10km from the centre, **t** 05 61 42 44 00, *www.toulouse. aeroport.fr*. Airlines include Air France (**t** 08 20 82 08 20), British Airways (**t** 08 25 82 54 00), BMI, Flybe and easyJet (*see* p.60). The **airport bus**, **t** 05 34 60 64 00, *www.navettevia-toulouse.com*, departs from Toulouse's SNCF station every 20mins from 5am–8.20pm daily, and from the airport to central Toulouse every 20mins 7.35am–12.30am. Ticket price is €4 one way. The ticket booth at the airport is outside Hall 1.

By Train

Trains run from Paris-Austerlitz through Gourdon, Souillac, Cahors and Montauban to Toulouse in 6hrs 30mins; TGVs from Paris-Montparnasse do the same in around 5hrs – by way of Bordeaux. The slow trains to Bordeaux take 2hrs 30mins and stop in Montauban, Castelsarrasin, Moissac, Agen and Aiguillon. Other connections include Albi (1hr) and Castres (1hr 30mins), Auch, Carcassonne, Nice, Lyon and Lille (TGV, 7hrs).

By Bus

The **bus station** is next to the railway station at 68 Bd Pierre Semard, **t** 05 61 61 67 67; there are buses to Foix, Albi, Gaillac, Auch, Nogaro and Montauban, and also to London, Madrid and Barcelona on Eurolines, **t** 05 61 26 40 04 (buy tickets in advance from a travel agent).

History

Toulouse grew up at a ford in the Garonne, a natural strategic crossroads at the centre of what the ancient Greek geographer Strabo called the 'Gallic isthmus' between the Mediterranean and the Atlantic. When the Romans found it, its inhabitants were the Tectosage Gauls, a tribe that had grown rich from mining and the wine trade. After first forcing them into an alliance, the Romans crushed them in 107 BC, gobbling up the Tectosages' fabulous treasure – 100 tons of gold and silver hidden at the bottom of a swamp. As a refounded Roman colony, Palladia Tolosa enjoyed five centuries of peace and quiet, developing into a modest provincial city of some 20,000. The Visigoths took over in 420 AD, but instead of a sacking and burning, Tolosa got a surprising new role to play – as capital of a new Visigothic Kingdom, under warrior king Ataulf and his loving bride, the Roman imperial princess Galla Placidia.

That kingdom lasted only until 507, when Clovis's Franks decisively defeated the Visigoths. They moved over the Pyrenees to found a new kingdom in Spain, while under Clovis's 'do-nothing' Merovingian successors, Toulouse and the rest of the southwest was largely left to itself. And by its own efforts, the city repelled an attack by the Arabs in 721, a decade before Charles Martel chased them out of Gaul for good. After that, the new Carolingian dynasty enjoyed a nominal rule over the southwest, and to hold onto it they set up a branch of the family as Counts of Toulouse, governing a vast territory extending from the Rhône to the Garonne and from the Pyrenees to the Dordogne.

Most of these counts were named Raymond, and over the next two centuries they would become a powerful dynasty, retaining most of these lands and ruling them more as independent princes

Getting around Toulouse

By Métro and City Bus

In 1993 Toulouse proudly opened its first métro line, running northeast to southwest from Joliment, the railway station and the Capitole to the Mirail; this has now been extended several kilometres beyond Joliment. A new line, running north to south, should be operational by 2007. The métro and city buses are run by TISSEO, which has an information office at 7 Place Esquirol, t 05 61 41 70 70, www.tisseo.fr.

There is a free bus that runs around the historic quarters of the city. Find a red line – stick your arm out and the bus should stop (runs Mon–Sat 9–7). A tramway is due to be built to the west of the city and should be operational by 2009.

A **tourist train** trundles around the main sites, departing from in front of the Post Office, Rue Lafayette, daily June–Sept.

By Taxi

If you can't find one cruising around or at a taxi stand, try t 05 61 42 38 38, or t 05 34 25 02 50. There are also tourist taxis – the driver providing commentary (about €40 an hour, t 05 34 25 02 50).

By Car

The most convenient pay car parks are at Place du Capitole, Allée Jean Jaurès, Place Victor Hugo and Place St-Etienne; but it is quite expensive, over €1 an hour. Alternatively, you can battle to find a space in the free parking areas such as Place St-Sernin and Allées Jules Guesde (near the Grand Rond), trawl the streets looking for a free spot (easiest in the summer when people leave the city for the coast) or park at Joliment or Gramont and take the métro in – the price of parking is included in the métro ticket price, but head out early, the car parks fill up during the week.

By Bicycle and Motorcycle

You can hire bikes at **Movimento** – there are kiosks at the bus station and near the tourist office, t 05 34 30 03 00, www.movimento.coop. You can be driven around rickshaw-like on an electric tricycle (t 06 67 71 17 22, June–Sept).

By Boat

The system of aqueducts that enabled the people to paddle around the city in the 6th century is sadly long gone, but you can still see some of the nicest corners of Toulouse by river. In summer, Toulouse Croisières (t 05 61 25 72 57, www.toulouse-croisieres.com) offers trips on the Garonne from Quai de la Daurade, daily except Monday, at 10.30, 4.30 and 6, and other times. There are also night cruises in July and Aug, to show off the city's illuminated river banks.

---

than vassals of the French king. Toulouse's golden age began in the 11th century, under such mighty counts as Raymond IV, who built the great basilica of St-Sernin and led the Christian armies in the First Crusade in 1095. Raymond V, a princely troubadour, granted the city of Toulouse a large degree of self-rule, and did his best to fight off that eternal troublemaker Richard the Lion-Heart, who invaded his domains in the 1190s.

Under its governing *capitouls*, Toulouse grew wealthy and fat, with one of the biggest grain-milling industries in Europe. But more troubles would soon be coming from outside. Raymond VI, who became count in 1195, was a modern, tolerant soul; the new religion of the Cathars was making great advances in his lands, and Raymond defended them against the powers of the Church. That resulted in a powerful coalition against him, led by Innocent III, strongest of all the medieval popes, and the King of France. The 'Albigensian Crusade', as the attack on the Cathars came to be known, was in reality a massive grab for land and power at Toulouse's expense. A northern army under Simon de Montfort invaded the county in 1209. In 1213, the crushing defeat of Raymond and his Aragonese allies at Muret, just outside Toulouse, ensured the end of Languedoc's independence, and also of southern culture and prosperity. Simon de Montfort entered Toulouse as its new count two years later, while Bishop Folquet de Marseille, a former troubadour who became the most rabid bigot of them all, presided over a grisly Inquisition. Toulouse revolted successfully two years later, and de Montfort died besieging it, but the last two Raymonds of the line were only able to hold out a little longer. King Louis VIII himself led another bloody invasion in 1229, and the county reverted to the French crown when the last count, royal appointee Alphonse de Poitiers, died childless in 1271.

Under French rule, Toulouse gradually lost its rights and privileges, and over the next three centuries it would decline to an economic and cultural backwater. The city was lucky to avoid the calamities of the Hundred Years War, and it even enjoyed a period of prosperity after 1560 thanks to *pastel*, a locally grown crop much in demand across Europe for dyeing. Indigo from the Carolinas put an end to *pastel's* prominence in the 1660s, but at the same time, a new engine of prosperity was taking shape – the Canal du Midi (1666–81), a locally planned and financed effort that linked the Atlantic and the Mediterranean by way of the Garonne, and brought Toulouse a considerable amount of new wealth and trade.

Still, compared to its medieval heyday Toulouse remained little more than a sleepy provincial city; even with the coming of the railroad in 1856. What proved to be the turning point for modern Toulouse literally fell from the sky. The city's surprising aerial adventures began with pioneer aviator Clément Ader, who managed to get a steam-powered plane off the ground in the 1890s. By the First World War Toulouse had an aircraft factory, and afterwards it served as the hub of France's first big air mail service. Another local firm, nationalized in the 1930s, grew to become Aérospatiale. In the 50s the government decided to concentrate all its air and space efforts here, and the last few giddy decades have seen France's City of the Air give birth to the Ariane rockets and Hermès, the European space shuttle, as well as Caravelle, Concorde and Airbus jets. Today, many visitors' startling introduction to the city will be the vast complex of factories, research centres and industrial parks that surrounds the airport at Blagnac.

The new Toulouse has become the fourth-largest city in France, and the capital of the Midi-Pyrenees region, giving it a political role, albeit a limited one, for the first time since the Middle Ages. New building and improvements are everywhere, including a shiny new metro. At times Toulouse may seem all business, but a lively population that includes the descendants of the wave of refugees from the Spanish Civil War and *pieds noirs* from Algeria, along with hordes of students at the bustling University, keeps it one of the most engaging cities of the Midi.

Place du Capitole

This dignified front parlour of Toulouse dates from 1850, when the 200-year-long tidying away of excess buildings was completed and the edges rimmed with neoclassical brick façades. As a permanent memorial to the southern kingdom of nevermore, the centre of the pavement is marked by an enormous **Cross of Languedoc**. This same golden cross on a red background hangs proudly from Toulouse's city hall, the **Capitole**, or 'capitolium' as it reads, bowing to a 16th-century story claiming that ancient Rome got its Capitol idea from Toulouse's temple of Capitoline Jupiter.

Théâtre du Capitole
t 05 61 22 29 22; open Mon–Fri 9–5

The portal on the right belongs to the **Théâtre du Capitole**, while over the central door eight pink marble columns represent the eight *capitouls*; the extravagant pompous historical rooms upstairs were decorated in the 1800s with busts of famous Toulousains and a painting by Henri Martin of *Jean-Jaurès on the banks of the Garonne*. Behind the great façade, the Cour Henri IV gives on to Square Charles de Gaulle, defended by the Donjon of 1525, where the *capitouls* kept the city archives. The building, well restored by Viollet-le-Duc, now houses the city tourist office.

The Basilica of St-Sernin

⭐ Basilica of St-Sernin
t 05 61 21 80 45; open Oct–May 8.30–11.45 and 2–5.45, Sun 8.30–12.30 and 2–7; June 8.30–12.30 and 2–6.15, Sun 8.30–12.15 and 2–7; July–Sept 8.30–6.15, Sun 8.30–7

Running north from Place du Capitole, narrow **Rue du Taur** was the road to Cahors in Roman times. The Taur in its name means 'bull', which features in the life of the city's first saint, Sernin, who died here in the 240s. Sernin (a corruption of Saturnin) was a missionary from Rome who preached in Pamplona and Toulouse. One day, runs the legend, he happened by the temple of Capitoline Jupiter, where preparations were under way for the sacrifice of a bull to Mithras. The priests ordered him to kneel before the pagan idol and, when Sernin refused, a sudden gust of wind blew over the statue of Mithras, breaking it to bits. In fury the crowd demanded the sacrifice of Sernin instead, and he was tied under the bull, which, maddened by the extra weight, dragged his body through the city streets.

After turning Sernin to pulp, the bull left his body where the 14th-century **Notre-Dame-du-Taur** now stands, replacing an oratory built over Sernin's tomb in 360. Its 135ft/41m *clocher-mur* looks like a false front in a Wild West town; the nave is surprisingly wide, and has a faded fresco of the *Tree of Jesse* along the right wall. Sernin's tomb attracted so many pilgrims and Christians who desired to be buried near him that in 403 a *martyrium* was built

300 yards (275m) to the north. An imperial decree permitted the removal of the saint's relics to this spot, and over the centuries tombs lined the length of Rue de Taur, as in the Alyschamps in Arles. In 1075, just as the pilgrimage to Compostela was getting under way, Count Guilhem decided Sernin deserved something more grand. The construction of the **Basilique de St-Sernin** was continued by his famous brother Raymond IV, and of such import that in 1096 Pope Urban II, on tour that year preaching the First Crusade, came to consecrate its marble altar.

In 1220 St-Sernin was finished – at 380ft (116m) the largest surviving Romanesque church in the world (only the great abbey church of Cluny, destroyed in the Revolution, was bigger). It was begun at the same time, and has the exact same plan as the basilica of St James at Compostela: a cross, ending in a semi-circular apse with five radiating chapels. In the 19th century the abbey and cloister were demolished, and in 1860 Viollet-le-Duc was summoned to restore the basilica. He spent 20 years on the project – and botched the roof so badly that rainwater seeped directly into the stone and brick. A century later the church was found to be in danger of collapse – hence a 22 million-franc 'de-restoration' project to undo Viollet-le-Duc's mischief. Off came all his neo-Gothic ornamentation and heavy stone, to be replaced with tiles handcrafted in the 13th-century manner.

The Exterior

The apse of St-Sernin (seen from Rue St-Bernard) is a fascinating play of white stone and red brick, a crescendo culminating in the octagonal bell tower that is Toulouse's most striking landmark. New York had its war of skyscrapers in the 1930s; 13th-century Toulouse had its war of bell towers: St-Sernin's original three storeys of arcades were increased to five for the sole purpose of upstaging the bell tower of the Jacobins. The most elaborately decorated of the basilica's portals is an odd, asymmetrical one on the south side, the **Porte Miège-ville**. It faces Rue du Taur; apparently this street, called Miège-ville or 'mid-city' in medieval times, ran right through the spot before the basilica was built. Devotees of medieval Toulousain arcana – a bottomless subject – say that this portal is the real cornerstone of the kingdom of Languedoc that the 11th-century counts were trying to create; books have been written about its proportions and the symbolism of its decoration, even claiming that it is the centre of a geomantic construction, with 12 lines radiating from here across the counts' territories, connecting various chapels and villages and forming Raymond IV's twelve-pointed Cross of Languedoc. The tympanum was carved by the 11th-century master Bernard Gilduin, showing the *Ascension of Christ*, a rare scene in medieval art, and one of the most choreographic: Christ surrounded by dancing angels, watched by the Apostles on the lintel. On the brackets are figures of David and others riding on lions; the magnificent capitals tell the story of the Redemption (*Original Sin, Massacre of the Innocents, Annunciation*), all from the expressive chisel of Gilduin. The north transept door, now walled up, was the royal door; the south transept door, the **Porte des Comtes**, is named after several 11th-century counts of Toulouse who are buried in Palaeo-Christian sarcophagi in the deep *enfeu* nearby. The eight capitals here, also by Gilduin (*c.* 1080), show the torments of hell, most alarmingly a man having his testicles crushed and a woman whose breasts are being devoured by serpents, both paying the price for Lust.

The Interior

Begun in 1969, the 'de-restoration' of the barrel-vaulted interior stripped the majestic brick and stone of Viollet-le-Duc's ham-handed murals and fiddly neo-Gothic bits. In the process, some fine 12th-century frescoes have been found, especially the serene angel of the Resurrection in the third bay of the north transept, which also has some of the best capitals. In the south transept, the shrine of St Jude, the patron saint of lost causes, blazes with candlelight in July – when French students take their exams.

Ambulatory
*open July–Sept
Mon–Sat 10–6,
Sun 2–6; rest of year
Mon–Sat 10–11.30 and
2–5.30, Sun 2–5.30*

For a small fee you can enter the **ambulatory** and make what the Middle Agers called 'the Circuit of Holy Bodies', for the wide array of saintly anatomies stashed in the five radiating chapels. In the 17th century, bas-reliefs and wood panels on the lives of the saints were added to bring the relics to life, and although these were removed in the 1800s they were restored and replaced in 1980. Opposite the central chapel are seven magnificent marble bas-reliefs of 1096, carved and signed by Bernard Gilduin.

The Holy Bodies circuit continues down into the upper crypt, with the silver shrine of St Honoratus (1517) and the 13th-century reliquaries of the Holy Cross and of St-Sernin, the latter showing the saint under the hooves of the bull. The lower crypt contains, more bodily, two Holy Thorns (a present from St Louis), 13th-century gloves and mitres, and a set of six 16th-century painted wooden statues of apostles. In the choir an 18th-century baldachin shelters St-Sernin's tomb, remade in 1746 and supported by a pair of bronze bulls. In the south transept, note the big feet sticking out of a pillar, all that remains of a shallow relief of St Christopher effaced by the hands of centuries of pilgrims.

Around Place St-Sernin and Quartier Arnaud-Bernard

At No.3, the Lycée St-Sernin occupies the **Hôtel du Barry**, built by Louis XV's pimp, the Roué du Barry. Du Barry married his charming lover, Jeanne de Bécu, to his brother and then in 1759 introduced her to the king. His pandering earned him the money to build this mansion in 1777; it would later earn the Comtesse du Barry the guillotine in the Terror. (The word *roué*, incidentally, was first used in the 1720s, to describe the bawdy companions of the regent, the Duke of Orléans; it was invented by some disapproving soul who thought they should have been broken on the wheel.)

On the south side of the square stood a pilgrims' hostel, founded in the 1070s by a chanter of St-Sernin named Raymond Gayard, who was canonized for his charity to the poor. His hostel was succeeded by the **collège** of St-Raymond (1505) for poor university students, and now by the rich archaeological collections of the

Musée St-Raymond
*t 05 61 22 31 44;
open daily 10–6;
June–Aug 10–7*

Musée St-Raymond. This is the antiquities museum of Toulouse, with some exceptional pieces. The top floors concentrate on finds from the Roman region of Narbonnaise and one of its biggest towns, Tolosa, ancient Toulouse. One of the most interesting exhibits is the section of a relief depicting two Amazons in combat, one clearly with the upper hand over a man: this would have formed part of a temple or major monument. The collection of outstanding busts is small compared to the avenue of heads of emperors, men, women and children on the floor below: all found, with the other exhibits here, at Chiragan in Martres-Tolosane, 60km to the south of Toulouse. Don't miss the splendid marbles depicting the *Labours of Hercules*. Digs carried out in the basement of the museum have revealed the presence of a Christian necropolis dating from the 4th century which grew up around the tomb of St-Sernin. Several of the tombs have been left not far from where they were found, close to a large, circular 5th-century lime kiln. Ornate sarcophagi from southwest France and other funerary objects are also on display. There are also vestiges of walls from an 11th-century hospital and a 13th-century college. Temporary

Musée St-Raymond Library
11 Rue des Trois Renards; Mon–Fri 10–6, Sat and Sun 10–1 and 2–6

exhibitions allow the public to see other museum artefacts, principally from the Iron Age through to the Middle Ages. The museum's specialist **library** is open to the public.

Just south of St-Sernin in Rue du Périgord, the southern Gothic **Chapelle des Carmélites** (1643) owes its existence to Anne of Austria, wife of Louis XIII. The walls are covered with paintings, and vaulting has been restored to bring out its lavish ceiling, with an unusual allegory on the *Glory of Carmel* by Jean-Baptiste Despax.

This northernmost medieval neighbourhood, the lively **Quartier Arnaud-Bernard**, has been the city's Latin Quarter ever since 1229, when the **University of Toulouse** was founded in Rue des Lois (part of it now occupies the old seminary of St-Pierre-des-Chartreaux to the west). Although forced down Toulouse's throat by Paris (*see* 'History', above), the university enjoyed a certain prestige in the Middle Ages; among its alumni were three popes, Montaigne and Rabelais.

The three principal squares of the quarter – Place du Peyrou, Place des Tiercerettes and Place Arnaud-Bernard – became the centre of immigrant life in the 20th century; today they are quickly being gentrified, but are still quite lively after dark. North of the boulevard, the neighbourhood's 'lung', the **Jardin Compans-Caffarelli**, was laid out in 1982 with exotic plants, a Japanese garden and tearoom.

Les Jacobins

Les Jacobins
t 05 61 22 23 82;
open daily 9–7;
adm for the cloister

Just west of Place du Capitole stands the great Dominican mother church, Les Jacobins, the prototype for Dominican foundations across Europe and one of the masterpieces of southern French Gothic. The Spanish priest Domingo de Guzmán had tried hard to convert the Cathars before the Albigensian Crusade; by 1206 he had reconverted enough women to found a convent, which became the germ of his Order of Preaching Friars, established in Toulouse in 1215. Confirmed by the pope in 1216, the new Dominican order quickly found adherents across Europe. In 1230, the Dominicans erected this, their third convent in Toulouse, which took the name of the Jacobins from the Dominicans' Paris address, in Rue St-Jacques (the very same convent where the fanatical party of Robespierre would later meet, hence the *Jacobins* of the French Revolution – a fitting name in light of the Dominicans' role as Inquisitors). The magnificent Jacobins in Toulouse so impressed the popes that they made it the last resting place of the greatest Dominican of them all, St Thomas Aquinas (*d.* 1274). After it was confiscated in the Revolution, Napoleon requisitioned the church and convent as a barracks for his artillery, which built an upper floor in the nave. When Prosper Mérimée, inspector of historic monuments, visited Toulouse in 1845, he found the mutilated complex occupied by 500 horses and cannoneers. In 1865 the military was finally convinced to leave the Jacobins to the city, and Toulouse spent a hundred years on its restoration.

The church is the perfect expression of the 13th-century reaction to Rome's love of luxury, which made the great preaching orders, the Dominicans and Franciscans, so popular in their day. Gargoyles are the only exterior sculpture in this immense but harmonious brick pile of buttresses, alternating with flamboyant windows; its octagonal bell tower of brick and stone crowned with baby towers is one of the landmarks of the city skyline. The interior is breathtakingly light and spacious, consisting of twin naves divided by seven huge columns, crisscrossed by a fantastic interweaving of ribs in the vault, reaching an epiphany in the massive flamboyant *palmier* in the apse. The painted decoration dates from the 13th to the 16th century, but only the glass of the rose windows on the west side is original.

A small door leads out into the lovely garden **cloister** (1309), with brick arcades and twinned columns in grey marble. The east gallery gives on to the large **chapter house**, supported by a pair of slender marble columns. The walls of the adjacent **Chapelle St-Antonin**, the funerary chapel, were painted in the early 1300s with scenes from the life of St-Antonin, while the ceiling is decorated with southwest France's favourite vision from the Apocalypse: the 24 Elders and angels glorifying Christ. In Rue Pargaminières, the **Refectory**, nearly 200ft (61m) long, houses temporary exhibitions, often on historical and cultural themes.

Les Jacobins Refectory
open daily 9–7

West of Les Jacobins, near the Garonne's hog-backed bridge, Pont St-Pierre, are Toulouse's two churches dedicated to St Peter. **St-Pierre-des-Cuisines**, a little Romanesque priory associated with Moissac, is named after its kitchens, where a person's bread could be baked at cheaper rates than at the counts' ovens. St-Pierre-des-Chartreux, to the north in Rue Valade, was founded in the 17th century and, if open, has some fine works from the 17th and 18th centuries.

St-Pierre-des-Cuisines
t 05 61 22 31 44; open July Mon 10–1 with guided tour at 11, Aug daily 10–12 and 2–7, guided tour at 4

Pastel Palaces

Just south of Les Jacobins, to the south end of Rue Gambetta, is one of the city's most splendid residences, the **Hôtel de Bernuy**, built in 1504 by a *pastel* merchant from Burgos, Don Juan de Bernuy, a Spanish Jew who fled Ferdinand and Isabella's Inquisition and became a citizen – and *capitoul* – of Toulouse. Although Gothic on the outside, inside his master mason Loys Privat designed an eclectic fantasy courtyard, a mix of Gothic, Plateresque and Loire château, topped by a lofty tower rivalling those of all the other *pastel* nabobs. De Bernuy had a chance to repay France for the fortune he made by paying the ransom for King François I when he was captured at the battle of Pavia by Emperor Charles V. In his distress the king had promised an *ex voto* to St-Sernin if he survived, and in the ambulatory you can still see the black marble statue he donated when he came in 1533 to thank the saint and de Bernuy for his generosity.

⭐ **Hôtel de Bernuy**

Not long after de Bernuy's time the Jesuits converted his *hôtel particulier* into a college, now the **Lycée Pierre de Fermat**, named after its star pupil, the brilliant mathematician (1595–1665) who left his last theorem as a challenge to subsequent generations of mathematicians. Just to the east, a 16th-century *hôtel particulier* houses the **Musée du Vieux Toulouse** with a fascinating collection from the city's history and its former porcelain industry, as well as paintings and etchings. Rue du May gives on to Rue St-Rome, decorated with 16th-century mansions built by the *capitouls* and wealthy merchants. At its south end don't miss the triangular **Place de la Trinité**, with a 19th-century fountain supported by bronze

Musée du Vieux Toulouse
7 Rue du May, t 05 62 27 11 50; open mid-May–mid-Oct Mon–Sat 2–6; guided tours Wed and Fri at 3pm

mermaids. Near here, you can examine the popular artistic pulse of Toulouse in the ever-changing murals along Rue Coq-d'Inde.

One of the finest private residences built in Toulouse, the **Hôtel d'Assézat,** is just west, off Rue de Metz. The *hôtel* was begun in 1555 by another *pastel* magnate, Pierre d'Assézat, who had a near monopoly on the dye in northern Europe. Designed by Nicolas Bachelier, Toulouse's master architect-sculptor-engineer, it consists of two buildings around a large square court, and a curious tower crowned with an octagonal lantern and dome that served the merchant as an observation post over the Garonne, enabling him to keep an eye on his fleet. Facing the street, an Italianate loggia has seven brackets decorated with *pastel* pods. Inside, the Fondation Bemberg has a collection of art, specializing in Renaissance and modern French paintings.

Fondation Bemberg
t 05 61 12 06 89, www.fondation-bemberg.fr; open Tues–Sun 10–12.30 and 1.30–6; nocturnal visits Thurs 9pm, themed visits Thurs 7pm; adm

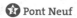 **Pont Neuf**

Along the Garonne

Rue de Metz continues to Toulouse's oldest bridge, which, as in Paris, is rather confusingly known as the new, or **Pont Neuf**. This Pont Neuf, with its seven unequal arches of brick and stone and curious holes (*oculi*), took from 1544 to 1632 to build, and links Gascony – the Left Bank – with the medieval province of Languedoc. Just down the quay stands the **Ecole des Beaux-Arts**, its façade larded with allegorical figures (1895). Hidden under the icing is a 17th-century U-shaped monastery connected to **Notre-Dame-la-Daurade**. Only the name recalls what was for centuries one of the wonders of Toulouse, the 10-sided, domed, 5th-century palatine chapel of the Visigothic kings, known as the Daurade ('the golden one') after its shimmering mosaics. Similar to the churches of Ravenna, it was destroyed in 1761, when the nitwitted monks who owned it decided to replace it with a reproduction of the Vatican, completed in the mid-19th century. The paintings in the choir are by Ingres's master, Roques.

One of the finest views of the Pont Neuf and river front is to the south along the **Quai de Tounis**. Rue du Pont de Tounis, built in 1515 as a bridge over the Garonnette (a now covered tributary of the Garonne), leads back to the original riverbank and **Notre-Dame-la-Dalbade** (Our Lady the Whitened, after its medieval whitewash, in contrast to the Golden One). This church too has taken some hard knocks. It was rebuilt in the Renaissance with a 280ft (85m) spire, to show up St-Sernin's bell tower. At 31 Rue de la Fonderie, the **Catholic Institute** has put together an archaeology museum that includes a fragment of the Gallo-Roman ramparts and funerary artefacts.

Catholic Institute
t 05 61 36 81 00, www.ict3.cp.asso.fr/musee; open 1 Sun afternoon each month, call in advance

The Quartier du Jardin

At the south end of Rue de la Dalbade/Rue de la Fonderie in Place du Salin stood the fortified residence of the counts of Toulouse, the celebrated Château Narbonnais; it was also the site of the *parlement*, established in Toulouse in 1443. The whole complex was demolished in the 19th century for the **Palais de Justice**, with only the square brick tower, the 14th-century royal treasury (converted into a Protestant church), as a memory. In the adjacent Place du Parlement is an old house built on the Roman wall, donated to Domingo Guzmán for his new preaching order, and later converted to the use inscribed over the door: 'Maison de l'Inquisition.'

South of the Place du Parlement, Allées Jules Guesde replaces the walls torn down in 1752. At No.35 is Toulouse's fascinating **Musée d'Histoire Naturelle**. The **Jardin Royal** was planted outside the walls and, in the 19th century, Toulouse's prettiest park, the **Jardin des Plantes**, was added. The garden's grand 16th–17th-century portal on Allée Frédéric-Mistral was salvaged from the original Capitole; just south of this is the **Monument à la Gloire de la Résistance**, with a crypt aligned to be illuminated by the sun's rays on 19 August, the anniversary of the Liberation of Toulouse. If you are interested in the Resistance, look out also for the **Musée Départemental de la Résistance et de la Déportation** at 52 Allées des Demoiselles.

There is one last museum in this quarter, and one not to be missed if you're fond of Egyptian, Coptic, Indian and Far Eastern Art. This is the **Musée Georges Labit**, in a neo-Moorish villa. Labit was a 19th-century traveller with plenty of money and a good eye, who accumulated a choice Oriental collection, considered the best in France after the Guimet Museum in Paris.

Place du Salin to the Cathedral of St-Etienne

The parliamentarians liked to build themselves distinguished houses in the homogenous quarter between the old *parlement* and the cathedral: all uniform pink brick, with light grey shutters and black wrought-iron balconies. In this mesh of quiet lanes, there are a few to pick out during a stroll, such as the sumptuously ornate **Hôtel du Vieux Raisin** (1515), 36 Rue du Languedoc, built by another *capitoul* in love with Italy. Another *hôtel* houses the **Musée Paul Dupuy**, named after the obsessed collector who left to Toulouse his hoard of watches, automata, guns, coins, fans, faïence, pharmaceutical jars and gems.

Rue Perchepinte and Rue Fermat, lined with antique shops, lead up to Place St-Etienne, with Toulouse's oldest fountain (1546) and the massive archbishop's palace (1713), now used as the Préfecture. All are overpowered by the **Cathédrale St-Etienne**, begun in the 11th century by Raymond IV, but completed only in the 17th century. Fashions and finances rose and fell in the three major building campaigns, resulting in a church that seems a bit drunk. Have a good look at the façade: in the centre rises a massive brick bell

---

Musée d'Histoire Naturelle
closed for renovation; due to reopen in 2007

Monument à la Gloire de la Résistance
open Mon–Fri 10–12 and 2–5; closed hols

Musée Départemental de la Résistance et de la Déportation
t 05 61 14 80 40

Musée Georges Labit
43 Rue des Martyrs-de-la-Libération, off Allée Frédéric-Mistral, t 05 61 22 21 84; open 10–5, till 6 in summer; closed Tues and hols

Musée Paul Dupuy
13 Rue de la Pleau, t 05 61 14 65 50; open 10–5, until 6 in summer; closed Tues and hols

tower with a clock, over the Romanesque base. To the right is a worn, asymmetrical stone Gothic façade, where the portal and rose window are off-centre; to the left extends the bulge of the chapel of Notre-Dame, a small church in itself stuck onto the north end. It's even tipsier inside. In 1211, Raymond VI inserted the oldest known representation of the Cross of Languedoc as the key in one of the vaults, just before 1215, when Bishop Folquet rebuilt most of Raymond IV's church in the form of a single nave 62ft (19m) high and 62ft (19m) wide, with ogival crossings, a style that went on to become the model for southern Gothic. In 1275, Bishop Bertrand de l'Isle-Jourdaine decided Bishop Folquet's bit of the cathedral was hardly grandiose enough for Toulouse's dignity and came up with a plan based on northern French Gothic that involved realigning the axis of the church. The choir was built, a fine example of flamboyant Gothic, with beautiful 14th-century glass on the west side, but the vaults, designed to be 132ft (40m) high, were cut short at 90ft (27m) due to limited funds. Money and energy ran out completely when Bishop Bertrand died, leaving a curious dogleg where his choir meets Raymond IV and Bishop Folquet's nave, marked by the massive Pilier d'Orléans, one of four intended to support the transept; it bears a plaque marking the tomb of Pierre-Paul Riquet, father of the Canal du Midi. Although many of the cathedral's best decorations are now stowed away in the Musée des Augustins, there are tapestries, faded into negatives of themselves, from the 15th and 16th centuries, and some interesting grotesques in the choir.

Musée des Augustins

⭐ Musée des Augustins
t 05 61 22 21 82,
www.augustins.org;
open 10–6,
till 9 on Wed; closed
Tues and hols

Rue Croix Baragnon, opposite the cathedral, has two beautiful Gothic houses, especially No.15, decorated with a band of stone carvings. But the greatest medieval art in this part of town is in the Musée des Augustins, a block north at the corner of Rue de Metz and Rue d'Alsace-Lorraine. The museum, one of the oldest in France, is housed in a 14th-century Augustinian convent, beauti-fully restored in 1950.

The nave of the convent church is devoted to religious paintings (Van Dyck's *Christ aux anges* and *Miracle de la mule*, Rubens' *Christ entre deux larrons* and *San Diego en extase* by Murillo) and reliefs by Nicolas Bachelier. Best of all are the Romanesque works, most of them rescued from demolished cloisters: from St-Sernin, there's a capital sculpted with the *War of Angels* and an enigmatic bas-relief from the Porte des Comtes showing two women looking at one another, one holding a lion in her arms, the other a ram, an image that also appears on the main portal at Compostela. Other capitals stylistically related to those of Moissac come from the Romanesque cloister of the Daurade; the most beautiful of all are from Raymond IV's 11th-century cloister of St-Etienne – note especially the delicate, almost fluid scene of the dance of Salome and the beheading of John the Baptist.

The first floor of the convent is devoted to paintings, including two portraits of *capitouls*; one of their oldest prerogatives was the *droit d'image* – the right to have their portraits painted. In the 13th and 14th centuries this was exceptional: kings, emperors, the doge of Venice and the pope were among the few allowed to leave their likenesses for posterity. Other paintings include a 15th-century Florentine hunt scene, an extremely unpleasant *Apollo flaying Marsyas* by the 'Divine' Guido Reni and works by Simon Vouet, Philippe de Champaigne, Van Dyck, Rubens (in the Augustins' church), the two Guardis, Delacroix, Ingres, Manet, Morisot, Vuillard, Maurice Denis and Count Henri de Toulouse-Lautrec.

Toulouse's Left Bank

Although the Left, or Gascon, bank of the Garonne has been settled since the early Middle Ages, the periodic rampages of the river dampened property values until the end of the 19th century, when flood-control projects were completed. The main reason for visiting is just over the Pont Neuf: the round brick lighthouse-shaped tower of a pumping and filtering station, built in 1817 to provide pure drinking water to the city. In 1974 this found a new use as the **Galerie Municipale du Château-d'Eau**. The hydraulic machinery is still intact on the bottom level, while upstairs you can visit one of Europe's top photographic galleries; exhibits change 15 times a year. An annexe has been installed in a dry arch of the Pont Neuf. There is also a reference **library** on the history of photography.

Opposite the water tower is the **Hôtel-Dieu St-Jacques**, a medieval pilgrimage hospital rebuilt in the 17th century. The grand Salle St-Jacques and Salle St-Lazare have magnificent ceilings, while down on floor level the hospital now houses a **Musée d'Histoire de la Médecine**, and a **museum of medical instruments** from the city's hospitals from the second half of the 19th century until today. Each of France's four great rivers has a nickname, and the Garonne is 'the Laughing'. Often enough, the joke has been on Toulouse. St-Cyprien, the original dedicatee of the Left Bank's parish church (behind the Hôtel-Dieu), proved to wield so little celestial influence over the water that when his church was rebuilt in 1300 he was sacked in favour of **St-Nicolas**, patron of sailors and protector of the flooded. The church is a small southern Gothic version of the Jacobins and boasts a grand 18th-century altar painted by Despax.

More visual arts, this time in the form of graphics, posters, ads and postcards from the 17th century to the present, are the subject

Galerie Municipale du Château-d'Eau
t 05 61 77 09 40, www.galerie chateaudeau.org; open Tues–Sat 1–7; closed hols; adm

Photography Library
open Mon–Fri 1.30–6 and 1st Sat of month

Musée d'Histoire de la Médecine
t 05 61 77 84 25; open Wed–Sun 1–6

Museum of Medical Instruments
t 05 61 77 82 72; open Thurs and Fri 1–5

Centre Municipal de l'Affiche, de la Carte Postale et de l'Art Graphique
58 Allée Charles de Fitte, t 05 61 59 24 64, St-Cyprien métro; open Mon–Fri 9–12 and 2–6; commercial collection by appt only; adm

Les Abattoirs
76 Allée Charles de Fitte, t 05 34 51 10 60, www.lesabattoirs.org; open Tues–Sun 11–7

ⓘ **Toulouse**
Donjon du Capitole, Rue Lafayette, behind the Capitole, t 05 61 11 02 22, www.ot-toulouse.fr

ⓘ **Midi-Pyrénées**
Comité Régional du Tourisme Midi-Pyrénées, 54 Bd de l'Embouchure, t 05 61 13 55 55 (ring first), www.tourisme-midi-pyrenees.com; Maison Midi-Pyrénées, 1 Rue Rémusat, near Pl du Capitole, open Mon–Fri 10–7

of the changing exhibits at the **Centre Municipal de l'Affiche, de la Carte Postale et de l'Art Graphique**; there's an extensive book, film and record library and, most popular of all, French commercials – those that used to be shown in the cinemas – from 1904 to 1968, on video cassettes (open to the public by appointment). Just up the road is **Les Abattoirs**, dedicated to modern art. The prize exhibit, displayed on and off throughout the year, was created just outside the timeframe for most of the work: a stage curtain for the play *14 Juillet* by Romain Rolland, painted by Luis Fernandez in 1936 on the request of Pablo Picasso, and copied from the great man's gouache of the corpse of a Minotaur in the costume of a Harlequin.

Tourist Information in Toulouse

The **tourist office** offers a range of themed guided tours, some in English. If you plan to be around for a while buy an 'En Liberté' card from the tourist office (€10 or €13) providing discounts on tours, entrance fees, activities, accommodation and restaurants.

For information on the whole Midi-Pyrénées region, stop by the **Comité Régional du Tourisme Midi-Pyrénées** or the **Maison Midi-Pyrénées**.

Markets and Shopping in Toulouse

There are regular covered **markets** at **Place des Carmes** (*daily exc Mon*) and at **Les Halles** in Bd Victor Hugo (*Tues–Sun 6am–1pm*). On Tuesday and Saturday mornings, **Place du Capitole** has a lively organic produce market. There is a good fruit and veg market (*daily exc Mon*) along **Boulevard de Strasbourg**, starting near Place Jeanne d'Arc, and Sun (and to a lesser extent Sat) morning sees a huge flea market around **St-Sernin** and along the length of the boulevards, the 'relics' of modern Toulouse that draw thousands of 'pilgrims'.

With many of the major French department stores, the Pink City is the shopping capital of the southwest. You can obtain superb **chocolates** at Maison Pillon, at 2 Rue Ozenne, which won the prize for the best in France in 1996.

The Bookshop, 17 Rue Lakanal, t 05 61 22 99 92, has **books** in English. For **posters** and reprints, try the shop in the Centre Municipal de l'Affiche.

If you fancy tasting some of the best **cheese** that France has to offer, head for Betty, 2 Place Victor Hugo; you smell it from fifty paces. There are 200 different types from all over the country, some of them quite special, such as the Vieux Salers, made in just one village in the Cantal and given a minimum of one year to mature.For fine **preserves** and French classics such as **olive oil** and very dark chocolate, go to La Boutique des Saveurs at 1 Rue Ozenne, t 05 61 53 75 21, a delightful shop that bombards you with tantalizing smells. Toulouse's flower is the **violet** – visit the violet barge on the Canal du Midi near the station. It is run by a woman potty about the flower – she has soaps, sweets, liqueur, mustard and so on.

Sports and Activities in Toulouse

At the time of writing, the **Toulouse Football Club** (T.F.C., pronounced 'tayfessay') plays in France's second division. The city hosted matches in the 1998 World Cup, but the city's heart lies with its rugby team, the **Stade** (*www.stadetoulousain.fr*), over a hundred years old, and frequent champion of France (and champion of Europe in 1996, 2003 and 2005). You can buy tickets online or at some of the big supermarkets. The stadium is at Sept Deniers.

You can swish out a figure of eight at the Patinoire Olympique de Blagnac, an **ice rink** at 10 Av du Général de Gaulle, **t** 05 62 74 71 40 (buses 66 or 70). *Open Wed–Fri afternoons and evenings, all day Sat and Sun.*

Where to Stay in Toulouse

Toulouse ✉ 31000

Toulouse has chain hotels galore for its numerous business visitors as well as a short list of reliable independent establishments in the historic centre. Try to avoid the cheap fleabags near the station. Book early, especially in conference season, and check hotel websites for special deals, particularly at weekends and during the summer.

****Grand Hôtel de l'Opéra, 1 Place du Capitole, **t** 05 61 21 82 66, *www.grand-hotel-opera.com* (€€€€€–€€€). This, the most beautiful hotel in Toulouse, has 50 luxurious rooms and three suites set in a former convent, with sumptuous Italianate rooms, indoor pool, fitness room and a magnificent restaurant.

***Grand Hôtel Capoul, 13 Place Wilson, **t** 05 61 10 70 70, *www.hotel-capoul.com* (€€€€–€€€). Large, light, air-conditioned rooms, a Jacuzzi and an excellent bistro, now part of Holiday Inn.

★ Old Toulouse >>

***Hôtel des Beaux Arts, 1 Place Pont-Neuf, **t** 05 34 45 42 42 (€€€€–€€). Set in a picturesque 18th-century hôtel, this is charming with pleasant, cosy, soundproofed rooms overlooking the Garonne.

***Mermoz, 50 Rue Matabiau, **t** 05 61 63 04 04, *www.hotel-mermoz.com* (€€€). Delighful air-conditioned rooms overlooking inner courtyards and one of the best breakfasts to be found in Toulouse.

★ Les Jardins de l'Opéra >>

***Brienne, 20 Bd du Maréchal Leclerc, **t** 05 61 23 60 60, *www.hoteldebrienne.com* (€€). Ultra-modern with well-equipped rooms, many with balconies. Good value.

Arnaud-Bernard, Pl des Tiercerettes, **t 05 61 21 37 64 (€€). In the centre of Toulouse's lively popular quarter near St-Sernin; has well-renovated rooms.

Castellane, 17 Rue Castellane, **t 05 61 62 18 82, *www.castellanehotel.com* (€€). Down a quiet street off Bd Carnot: light and spacious rooms with the usual facilities. Private parking for a nightly fee and the breakfast area is pleasant.

Grand Hôtel d'Orléans, 72 Rue de Bayard, **t 05 61 62 98 47 (€€–€). Near the station. Plenty of character, with its interior galleries, garden and satellite TV too.

Relais Blanhac, 200m from the airport, **t 05 61 71 93 93 (€€–€). Good bet for those early flights; motel-like rooms sleep up to four. OK restaurant. *Menus* €14–29. Luggage trolleys available, but make sure to book for a weekday stay.

*Anatole France, 46 Place Anatole France, **t** 05 61 23 19 96 (€). Near the Capitole, with some of the nicest cheap rooms in Toulouse, all with showers and phones.

*Hôtel des Arts, 1 bis Rue Cantegril, **t** 05 61 23 36 21 (€). A friendly place near lively Place St-Georges: good rooms with showers.

Eating Out in Toulouse

Toulouse, and in particular its restaurant quarter, Old Toulouse, has enjoyed a restaurant revolution that has trickled down from *les grandes tables* to the corner bistro. Yet along with this leap in the quality of food, the city hasn't quite forgotten its key place in the southwest bean belt, and claims to make a *cassoulet* that walks all over the cassoulets of rivals Carcassonne and Castelnaudry. Note: many restaurants close in August.

Very Expensive–Expensive (€€€€– €€€)

Les Jardins de l'Opéra, 1 Place du Capitole, **t** 05 61 23 07 76, *www.lesjardinsdelopera.com*. Toulouse's finest gastronomic experience is also one of the most beautiful restaurants in the southwest, a cool, refreshing glass-covered oasis overlooking a garden pool. The food matches the setting, orchestrated by the excellent Dominique Toulousy. *Menus* €42–98. *Closed Sun, Mon, Aug and first week in Jan.*

Le Pastel, 237 Rue de St-Simon, in a villa at Mirail, **t** 05 62 87 84 30. Make the extra effort to book lunch for some of the finest, most imaginative gourmet food in Toulouse at some of the kindest prices. *€30–95. Closed Sun and some of Aug.*

Expensive–Moderate (€€€– €€)

Au Pois Gourmand, 3 Rue Emile Heybrard, **t** 05 34 36 42 00, *www.pois-gourmand.fr*. In a handsome old manor house with wooden galleries in Casselardit (just off the *rocade*, or ring road around the city). The perfect atmosphere for the refined and original cuisine that comes out of the kitchen. *Menus €23–64. Closed Sat and Mon lunch, and Sun, and several weeks in Aug.*

Le Bibent, 5 Place du Capitole, **t** 05 61 23 89 03. One of the most beautiful *brasseries* in Toulouse, strategically located, with a grand dining room last remodelled in the Roaring Twenties, and a terrace; excellent shellfish selection and southwest favourites. *Menus €20–25.*

⭐ Chez Emile ›

Chez Emile, 13 Place St-Georges, **t** 05 61 21 05 56, *www.restaurant-emile.com*. Something of a city institution, preparing some of the very finest seafood in Toulouse or a *confit de canard*, or other meat; in warm weather, there are worse things to do than sit out on the terrace. *Menus €18–48. Closed Sun and Mon, just Sun and Mon lunch in summer.*

Grand Café de l'Opéra, 1 Place du Capitole, **t** 05 61 21 37 03, *www.brasserieopera.com*. Excellent versions of the classics with a particular emphasis on seafood, but there's meat, too, in a cosy brasserie atmosphere – the original was burnt to the ground before being rebuilt exactly as it was. *Closed Sun and most of Aug.*

Les Ombrages, 48 bis Route de St-Simon, **t** 05 61 07 61 28. A bit hard to find (taking a taxi is recommended) but worth the effort for its fresh, sunny cuisine, immaculately prepared. *Menus €20–40. Closed Sun eve, Mon and 2 weeks in Aug.*

⭐ Sept Place St-Sernin ›

Sept Place St-Sernin, 7 Place St-Sernin, **t** 05 62 30 05 30. A large ivy-covered house in a perfect spot opposite the cathedral. The menus are delightful and varied: try *foie gras de canard aux figues et salade d'herbes. Menus €18–60. Closed Sat lunch and Sun.*

Moderate (€€)

La Bascule, 14 Av Maurice-Hauriou, **t** 05 61 52 09 51, *www.restaurantlabascule.com*. A popular *brasserie* a bit out from the centre and on a busy corner, but set back enough that you can eat on the terrace lined with bamboo. Good selection of fish including oysters, and traditional meat dishes plus some a bit different such as *gigot d'agneau des Pyrénées en croûte avec jus d'estragon. Menus €15–23. Closed Sat lunch, Sun and Mon.*

Les Beaux-Arts-Flo, 1 Quai Daurade, **t** 05 61 21 12 12, *www.brasserielesbeauxarts.com*. On the Garonne, this handsome *belle époque brasserie* offers well-prepared favourites: seafood platters, roasted fish, *cassoulet*, good desserts. *Menus €20–30.*

Le Belvédère, 11 Bd des Récollets, **t** 05 62 26 69 14. Southwest classics in a modern setting south of the centre, to accompany its grand views over Toulouse. *Closed Sun and Aug.*

Le Bon Vivre, 15 Place Wilson, **t** 05 61 23 07 17. This place packs them in with its authentic southwestern cooking: *confits, magrets*, et al. *Menus €20–25.*

Moderate–Inexpensive (€€– €)

Benjamin, 7 Rue des Gestes (off Rue St-Rome), **t** 05 61 22 92 66. Positioned right in the centre of old Toulouse, here you will find the likes of fennel and courgette terrine and steak with *cèpes* – and all for some of the friendliest prices in town.

Caves de la Maréchale, 3 Rue Jules-Chalande, **t** 05 61 23 89 88. Set in the immense cellar of a 13th-century Dominican priory off Rue St-Rome, and populated with copies of classical statues. *Closed Sat, Sun and Mon lunch.*

Inexpensive (€)

The first floor of the **Marché Victor Hugo** has a number of cheaper places to eat that daily attract Toulousains of every ilk for lunch (*exc Mon*). *Open Tues–Sun.*

A la Truffe du Quercy, 17 Rue Croix-Baragnon, **t** 05 61 53 34 24. The same family has been dishing out southwestern home-cooking for three generations. Spanish options too. *Formule menu €10, delicious regular menu for a bit more. Closed Sun, Mon eve and Aug.*

Cafés, Bars and Wine Bars in Toulouse

L'Ancienne Belgique, 16 Rue de la Trinité. Try a pint or two from their big selection, 10 beers on tap and 80 bottled.

Bar Florida, Place du Capitole, **t** 05 61 23 94 61. The place in central Toulouse to sit outside on a warm day with a drink in hand and watch the world go by. Some tourists, but plenty of Toulousains too. Champagne, cocktails, spirits, beer or coffee on offer. *Open 7am–2am.*

Le Père Louis, 45 Place des Tourneurs, between Rue Peyras and Rue de Metz, **t** 05 61 21 33 45. The most resolutely traditional bar in Toulouse has drawn Toulouse's *quinquina* drinkers for over a century. *Open 8.30am–3 and 5pm–10.30.*

Gay bars are clustered around Rue de la Colombette, east of Place Wilson.

Entertainment and Nightlife in Toulouse

The weekly *Flash*, available at any newsstand, will tell you what's on in Toulouse; also pick up *Toulouse Culture*, edited by the *mairie* (free).

Zénith, Av Raymond Badiou, **t** 05 62 74 49 49, is the biggest stage and performance venue in the area and hosts a range of events from displays of Basque sports to pop concerts, and more besides.

Theatre, Music and Dance

La Cave Poésie, 71 Rue du Taur, **t** 05 61 23 62 00. For a listen to the current state of French poetry, *chanson* and theatre.

Sorano Théâtre, 35 Allées Jules-Guesde, **t** 05 34 31 67 87. Puts on some of the finest plays in Toulouse.

Théâtre du Capitole, Place du Capitole, **t** 05 61 22 31 31. From October to June, this theatre presents a series of opera and dance.

Concerts and exhibitions of dance are also given in the renovated auditorium of the old church of **St-Pierre-des-Cuisines**, Place St-Pierre, **t** 05 61 22 31 44.

Cinema

Toulouse likes its fair share of movies as well; the **Cinémathèque**, 69 Rue du Taur, **t** 05 62 30 30 10, *www.tacinemathequedetoulouse.com*, is the second most important in France, and often shows films in V.O. (*version originale*), as does **ABC**, 13 Rue St-Bernard, **t** 05 61 29 81 00.

Clubs

L'Aposia, 9 bis Rue Jean Rodier, **t** 05 05 71 84 11. Huge club with several different rooms.

El Barrio Latino, 144 Av de Muret, **t** 05 61 59 00 58. Good Latin music venue. *Closed Sun to Wed.*

Puerto Habana, 12 Port St-Etienne, **t** 05 61 54 45 61, *www.puerto-habana.com*. Good venue for a lively night out. *Closed Sun.*

Shanghaï Club, 12 Rue de la Pomme, **t** 05 61 23 37 80. Central and one of the oldest discos in Toulouse, something of an institution.

The Ariège, Andorra and the Eastern Pyrenees

Once the proud, remote and independent Comté de Foix, the Ariège occupies several frontiers: obviously Spain and Andorra over the Pyrenees, but also the more subtle division between Gascony (west of the River Ariège) and the Mediterranean-facing region of Languedoc. The region has its full share of grand Pyrenean scenery to offer: high mountains and beautiful valleys to explore, although their hamlets often seem haunted due to a drastic drop in the population since the 1850s.

SPAIN

13

Don't miss

⭐ Underground river-boating
Labouiche **p.344**

⭐ The Alamo of the Cathars
Château de Montségur **p.345**

⭐ An intriguing multi-layered church
Vals **p.351**

⭐ Fabulous monster caves
Tarascon-sur-Ariège **p.353**

⭐ Palaeolithic artistry
Grotte de Niaux **p.355**

See map overleaf

Don't miss

🟡 Labouiche **p.344**

🟡 Château de Montségur **p.345**

🟡 Vals **p.351**

🟡 Tarascon-sur-Ariège **p.353**

🟡 Grotte de Niaux **p.355**

The difference between Gascony and Languedoc was most acute between the 12th and 14th centuries, when the Cathar heresy thrived on the Languedoc side and Montségur, the Cathars' famous temple-cum-fortress, defied the Albigensian Crusaders from the north. The Ariège has another distinction, magnificent on at least one level, even if it's subterranean: it has more caves than any *département* in France, including 13 that were decorated in prehistoric times (one, Niaux, has the best art of any cave that's readily open to the public). Just as prehistoric are the *mérens* of the Ariège, a sturdy breed of black horses with a pedigree as old as Magdalenian times – now stables hire them out for mountain treks. The wilder tributaries of the Ariège river are one of the last habitats of the timid *desman*, the aquatic web-footed mole, not to mention the last place in France where you can pan for gold.

Because of the decline of the traditional mining and textile industries, few *départements* have suffered such drastic drops in population. Among the 136,500 people who still call it home are scores of refugees from French cities, and increasingly from the UK and the Netherlands, in search of an alternative, rural life; they run most of the mohair goat farms and little bed-and-breakfast places. If the rest of the Ariège is a rather sleepy, get-away-from-it-all place, the departmental tourist office in Foix is a veritable pamphlet-spewing dynamo: contact them for their detailed lists of campsites, mountain *refuges*, *gîtes*, *gîtes d'étape* and trail guides.

The Western Ariège: the Couserans

During the Revolution, when old feudal boundaries were erased and new, neatly numbered *départements* were created to take their place, the Couserans, once a vassal of the Comminges, Gascon and solidly Catholic, was surprised to find itself lumped together with a pair of old vipers' nests of heretics – the Cathars of Foix and the Protestants of the lower Ariège. Surprised, but far too isolated in its own little world to change. But if it is the emptiest corner of the Ariège, the Couserans is also the most beautiful: two rivers, the Lez and the Salat, and their tributaries, literally cascading down from the tremendous frontier range, form its heart. Its valleys, especially the Biros and Bethmale, are renowned among students of folklore for their astonishing costumes. In those days the mines were still open and the forests were cut to feed the iron forges in the Ariège and Catalonia; since the 18th century, most of the trees have been turned into cigarette papers, a local speciality, along with cheese.

St-Lizier and St-Girons

Prettily piled on its hill like a Tuscan hill town, St-Lizier is the age-old capital of the Couserans, one of the chief cities of Gallo-Roman Novempopulanie. Its founding father, Pompey, called it Lugdunum Consoranum, a mouthful the inhabitants soon changed to Austria, and then to St-Lizier, after a 7th-century Portuguese priest who defended the town against the Visigoths. After being thoroughly sacked in 1130 by Count Bertrand III of Comminges, the population trickled down to a new town, St-Girons, located at the confluence of the Salat and the Lez, leaving lofty St-Lizier alone with its bishop. The Revolution not only gave him his walking papers, but forced St-Lizier and St-Girons to join together as one *commune*.

There's no reason to loiter in St-Girons; instead make your way up to St-Lizier by way of the D117, passing a 13th-century **bridge** built from cannibalized Roman stones, including an altar to Belisama, the Gallo-Roman goddess of wisdom. Roman stone also went into the quirky **Cathédrale St-Lizier**, begun in the 11th century; the name of the architect is unknown, but anyone who knows their nursery

Getting around the Western Ariège

Buses link St-Girons to Toulouse, Martres-Tolosane and St-Martory; others descend daily to Seix and Aulus-les-Bains (**t** 05 61 66 08 87), while one or two go to Castillon-en-Couserans and Sentein (**t** 05 61 66 26 56).

rhymes will recognize the hand of the crooked man who built the crooked house. From the outside it looks fairly normal, sporting a stout, straight octagonal bell tower, good modillons around the apse and a Gothic brick portal. Cross this threshold and everything's a bit fishy: the nave and choir are built on different axes, the left wall is at a tilted angle, the columns with little faces and carvings peering out from the bases don't match up and the transepts are of uneven length. The walls of the apses are 6ft (2m) thick, and may have originally been defensive towers. Rare, faded 12th-century frescoes of the *apostles*, the *Annunciation* and the *Epiphany* decorate the arches, while in the apse there's a 14th-century po-faced *Christ Pantocrator*, with rosy cheeks and a stern, startled expression (doubtless a comment on the architecture). The oak choir stalls and gilded *Pietà* date from the 17th century; don't miss the richly coloured 15th-century stained glass near the entrance.

The pretty yet simple two-storey 12th-century **cloister** is to the right, its arcades of marble columns crowned with carved capitals, some with interlacings, others with figures of imaginary beasts and demons. St-Lizier's **trésor** (open only with the guided tour, *see* tourist information p.329) is full of precious things that somehow escaped the usual robbers, Protestants and anti-clerical *sans-culottes*: a 14th-century reliquary bust of St-Lizier, made of silver and semi-precious stones, a 12th-century bishop's mitre of white silk, a 13th-century painted wooden chest, and much more. The tour also includes a visit to the intact 18th-century hospital **pharmacy** in the former Hôtel Dieu (now a retirement home), with its lovely woodwork, shelves of pharmaceutical jars made in Martres-Tolosane and an armillary sphere the doctors would consult to calculate the most auspicious time for an operation.

While strolling the narrow streets of St-Lizier, look out for traces of ancient Austria's 3rd-century **walls** and dozen **towers**, some of which have melded with later buildings. The road from the cathedral square leads up to the garden terrace and the massive 1660 **Palais des Evêques** that dominates the skyline; it incorporates three semi-circular Roman towers and the Gothic cathedral of Notre-Dame-de-la-Sède (12th–15th centuries; under restoration until 2010), and has excellent views over the Couserans. Housed in the palace is the **Musée Départemental de l'Ariège**, with the anthropological collections of Jacques Bégouen and Chaubert Mader, focused particularly on the Valley of Bethmale.

Palais des Evêques
*t 05 61 04 81 86,
www.sesta.fr; winter
school holidays 2–6,
April and May Tues–Sun
2–6, June and Sept
10–12 and 2–6, July and
Aug Tues–Sun 10–7,
Oct–early Nov Wed–Sun
2–6; guided visits mid-
June–mid-Sept at 11, 3
and 4.30*

13

The Ariège, Andorra and the Eastern Pyrenees | St-Lizier and St-Girons

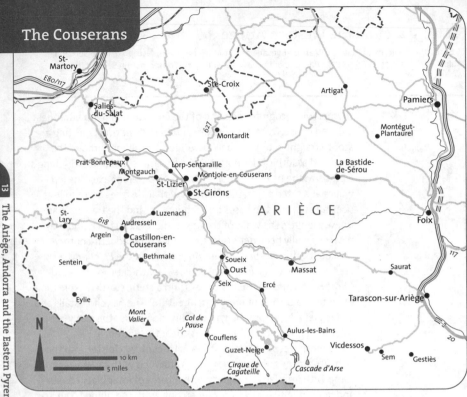

Around St-Lizier

Just east of St-Lizier, a narrow road climbs up to 14th-century **Montjoie-en-Couserans**, a tiny fortified town with a massive warlike church, built on the site of a temple dedicated to Jupiter. North, the pretty D627 leads to **Montardit**, where the charming little **chapel** of Notre-Dame-de-la-Goutte was built by the local abbé using only pebbles and stones from the River Volp. Further north, the luxuriant fir **Fôret de Ste-Croix** is a botanical oddity, at only 350m altitude instead of the cool 1,400 or so metres that the species usually prefers – an odd pocket of trees that found the microclimate convivial after the retreat of the glaciers in the last Ice Age, 15,000 years ago.

The D33 leads west of St-Lizier to the charming Romanesque church of **Montgauch**, containing medieval frescoes by an itinerant Catalan artist. The road continues around to **Prat-et-Bonrepaux**, a largish town under a 13th-century castle belonging to the Counts of Comminges. Its Renaissance decoration dates from its occupation by Jean de Mauléon, the art-loving bishop of Comminges.

The D117 heads west of St-Lizier to **Lorp-Senteraille** and its **museum** on paper, posters and printing including some old printing presses. North of St-Lizier at **Barjac** is an open-air **snail farm**.

Lorp-Senteraille museum
t 05 61 66 13 97;
open Sat afternoon,
call for other times

Snail farm
t 05 61 96 41 27;
open Sat 3–5

ⓘ **St-Lizier**

Pl de l'Eglise, t 05 61 96 77 77, www.ariege. com/st-lizier; daily tours in July and Aug, the only way you can see the cathedral treasure and hospital pharmacy; call for times; book ahead for guided tours in winter

★ **Eychenne** >

ⓘ **St-Girons** >

Pl Alphonse-Sentein, t 05 61 96 26 60, www.ville-st-girons.fr; open July and Aug Mon–Sat 9.30–6.30 plus Sun 10–1; Sept–June Mon–Sat 9–12 and 2–6

Market Days in St-Girons

St-Girons: Saturday and the second and fourth Monday of each month.

Where to Stay and Eat in St-Lizier and St-Girons

St-Girons ✉ 09200

***Eychenne**, 8 Av Paul-Laffont, t 05 61 04 04 50, *www.ariege.com/hotel-eychenne* (€€€–€€). Built as St-Girons's post house, it has been in the same family for six generations. Over the decades they have made it into a wonderfully comfortable inn with a heated pool and garden. The vast old-fashioned dining room has a menu of classic French specialities and one of the Ariège's best wine lists. *Menus €23–55. Closed Dec and Jan.*

***La Clairiere**, Av de la Résistance, t 05 61 66 66 66, *www.ariege.com/la-clairiere* (€€–€). A modern, wood-shingled hotel and restaurant just outside St-Girons, with a garden, swimming pool and a pretty good

restaurant. *Menus €19–64, vegetarian menu €20. Hotel closed Nov. Restaurant closed Sun eve and Mon and Nov.*

**Hôtel de l'Union, 1 Pl du Champ-de-Mars, t 05 61 66 09 12 (€). A reasonable hotel in an old building beside the river. There's a jazz bar and brasserie. *Open all year.*

La Maison Blanche, t 05 61 66 48 33, *http://home.tele2.fr/lamaisonblanche* (€). In Lorp, west of St-Lizier. Three bed-and-breakfast rooms for non-smokers only. *Meals for guests €15. Open all year.*

Le Relais d'Encausse, 1.5km outside St-Girons, at Saudech, t 05 61 66 05 80, mornings t 05 61 96 21 03 (€). A beautifully restored old country inn with four rooms, and a salon with a fireplace. *Open all year.*

Restaurant Le Pâtre Gourmand, 14B Av A. Berges, ✉ 09190 Lorp Senteraille. On D117, direction Salies. 5.5km from St Girons, t 05 61 66 54 49. Excellent food, good value, friendly and efficient service. The management also runs the **Château de Beauregard** (*same phone*). *Menus €15–31. Closed Mon and Tues from Oct–May and several weeks in June and Oct.*

Fromagerie Le Moulis

Moulis, t 05 61 66 09 64; Fri–Wed visits from 2.30

Le Moulin Gourmande

Engomer, t 05 61 96 83 38, open Mon–Fri 10–12

Le Bamalou

Castillon, t 05 61 96 76 19; open summer, weekends and school hols, demonstration of cheese-making Tues–Fri

Fromagerie Jean Faup

Caumont, t 05 61 66 01 63; visits July and Aug Mon–Fri at 10am; phone for rest of year

The Valleys of the Couserans

For centuries cut off from the mainstream, the magnificent high valleys of the Couserans are now almost deserted. But life, if very colourful, was always hard here. The women hired themselves out as wet nurses, the men as miners, woodcutters or shepherds; they brought ice down the mountains to Toulouse, or trained dancing bears. While travelling in the region, you may want to consider a Couserans cheese-tasting tour; four *fromageries* with their ripening caves welcome visitors.

Up the Vallée du Lez

South of St-Girons, the D618 follows the torrential River Lez to **Aubert**, an otherwise nondescript hamlet with marble quarries that produced stone used for Napoleon's tomb in the Invalides (he's boxed in seven sarcophagi, all of different materials, to make sure he never gets out again). The next hamlet, **Luzenac**, has a pretty Romanesque church, with mullioned windows in its bell tower and a unique undulating façade. **Audressein** is one of many villages in the Couserans with a very nasal 'ein' ending, believed to go back to the Iron Age language of the Pyrenees. It has a remarkable pilgrimage church, the Gothic **Notre-Dame-de-Tramezaygues** (from the Latin *inter-amabas-aquas*, 'between two waters'), built in the 13th century. Murals cover its porch: SS James and John the Baptist, pilgrims with candles and a whole series of vivid *ex-votos* from the 1400s and 1500s thanking the Virgin for assistance rendered in all aspects of life, from stopping nosebleeds to cushioning falls out of trees (note the flagrant lack of underwear!). One man in his *ex- voto* seems to be thanking the Mother of God for a successful murder.

If all this is too cosmopolitan, there's the **Vallée de la Bellongue** west of Audressein, lined with beech and fir forests and twelve tiny hamlets, including **Argein**, which are the best places to stay and eat in the Couserans. Further up the valley, **Castillon-en-Couserans** was the local seat of the Counts of Commminges, although the castle was demolished by Cardinal Richelieu, leaving only the **Chapelle de St-Pierre**, with a large wooden porch and a pretty door with marble columns, sculpted capitals and a very old statue of St Peter. There's a big hydroelectric plant at **Bordes-sur-Lez**, standing at the confluences of the Biros and Bethmale valleys; nearby, the teeny tiny hamlet of **Ourjout** has a quaint old bridge and a quaint old church from the 11th century.

The Vallées de Biros and Mont Valier

Francis Bacon's 'One triumphs over nature only by obeying its rules' is the slogan of the enchanting Biros valley, with its peaceful, rural landscapes frozen in time, lush green in the spring and shimmering with a golden patina in early autumn. It is one of the finest places for walks in the Pyrenees, with the majestic backdrop of **Mont Valier** (2,839m/9,369ft), which is also a popular and easy ascent if you think you may be up to a bit of mountain climbing. Named after the first man to scale it, the 5th-century bishop of the Couserans, St Valerus, the mountain was long thought to be the highest of the Pyrenees; its abrupt east flank, rising 1,700m/5,577ft (including 800m/2,500ft of sheer rock wall), holds the record for the highest rock face in the range, and Valier's glacier is the easternmost in the Pyrenees. In St Valerus' day, the forests were full of wolves and bears; these days the mountain is a *Réserve de Chasse*, where you're quite likely to see izards springing from rock to rock. The classic route up Valier is to drive up the Riberot valley (south of Bordes-sur-Lez) to the car park, then make the four-hour walk up to the **Refuge des Estagnous**, leaving the remaining two-hour ascent until the next morning.

Refuge des Estagnous
*t 05 61 96 76 22,
www.ariege.com; open
June–Sept daily plus
May and Oct weekends
only, €*

The capital of the Biros valley, **Sentein**, has a very old church built in the 15th century, once fortified and still defended by three square towers (a fourth was lopped off). One forms the base for an octagonal bell tower with a jauntily tilted weathervane; frescoes inside depict the *Tree of Jesse* and the *Last Judgement*. A fairly easy one-day's walk from Sentein leads up to the **chapelle d'Isard**, where until recently pilgrim shepherds would spill sheep's milk offerings over the rocks; if you weren't already, the beautiful setting is enough to make you religious.

Serious walkers can continue on the route for the two-day hike up the GR 10 to the **Pic de Crabère** (2,629m/8,676ft). If you make it to the top you are rewarded by some wonderful views west over Maladetta. South of Eylie, at the end of the Biros valley road, you can take an even more difficult path right up to the frontier at the **Port d'Urets** (2,512m/ 8,290ft), which is at the foot of the local landmark, the rounded Pic de Maubermé, a two-day trek; contact the Sentein tourist office, which has all the details and maps.

The Vallée de Bethmale

Bordes-sur-Lez stands at the entrance to the most famous valley of the Couserans, the Vallée de Bethmale, celebrated for both its natural beauty and its delightful red and black costumes. The men's costumes are remarkably similar to those once worn in the Peloponnese (these days they're only taken out of the closets for holidays; 15 August is a good time to see them). The striking physical differences between the natives of the Biros and Bethmale valleys has often been commented on. While the people of Biros are short, those in Bethmale are tall and famous for their exceptional good looks. Local stories account for the difference and the costumes: one, that a Bethmale man named Soulan led a colony of Irish to Greece, but they were eventually evicted and ended up back here; another, perhaps slightly less outlandish, tells how a 17th-century merchant made his fortune in Greece, came back with a harem of a dozen wives and repopulated the valley with his progeny. The most extraordinary part of the Bethmale costume is the pointy, scimitar-shaped clogs decorated with copper nails and hearts. Wonderfully bizarre, they are remarkably similar to the footwear featured in that 1989 Finnish film classic, Aki Kaurismäki's *Leningrad Cowboys Go America*. In the old days, the clogs would be carved out of walnut wood by a man for his fiancée; the points are said to have shielded tender toes from the mountain rocks. If seeing is believing, go to **Aret-en-Bethmale** where they're still made, displayed and sold by one of the two last clog-makers in the Ariège (there are only 10 left in the whole of France), or *sabotiers* (the word 'sabotage' comes from disgruntled French workers hurling their *sabots* into factory machinery; a Bethmale *sabot* could stop a tank).

Other sights in the valley are slightly less pointed, including a 7ft (2m) menhir, **Peyro-Quillado**, near Ayet. The most traditional village,

ⓘ **Castillon-en-Couserans**
t 05 61 96 72 64, www.ot-castillon-en-couserans.fr; open Mon–Sat 9–12 and 2–6

⭐ **L'Auberge d'Audressein >>**

ⓘ **Sentein**
t 05 61 96 10 90, http://otbiros.free.fr; open July and Aug Mon–Sat 2–6.30; winter Mon–Fri 9–12 and 1.30–5.30, Sat 9–12

Ayet-en-Bethmale
t 05 61 96 78 84; open all year, July and Aug 3–7; otherwise call first

Canoe hire at Seix
t 05 61 66 92 00 or t 05 61 55 84 88

Where to Stay and Eat in the Valleys of the Couserans

Accommodation is a bit scarce on the ground in the Couserans. Even so, it is not the most frequented of areas and you may have it all to yourself, except in July and August when it is wise to book in advance.

Argein ✉ 09800

**La Terrasse, t 05 61 96 70 11 (€€). Charming, with 10 comfortable rooms. The restaurant has good local specialities on the menu, including fresh trout and wild boar with chestnuts. *Menu €20. Closed Nov–Easter.*

*L'Auberge d'Audressein, 3km from Argein, t 05 61 96 11 80, *www.auberge-audressein.com* (€). An old stone house beside a stream; a good place to book a table for a special meal. Some of the most delicately prepared dishes in the whole département are served in the cosy dining room; try *tournedos de bœuf aux girolles, jus de Gigondas.* There is also a handful of rooms available. *Closed mid-Nov to mid-Feb; Sun eve and all Mon except July and Aug. Menus €16–85.*

Ayet-en-Bethmale, is also the starting point for the valley's prettiest walk, to the romantic **Lac de Bethmale** (about two hours, there and back). At the top of the valley, the D17 continues east over the beautiful Col de la Core to Seix and the Vallée de Salat (*see* below).

The Valleys of the Salat

If you're not riding over the Col de la Core, the main approach to the Couserans' eastern river from St-Girons is on the D3, through the Gorges of Ribaouto and the Kercabannac tunnel. Following this and the Salat to the south, the first village is **Soueix**, where the Romanesque chapel of St-Sernin has some pretty capitals. The main centre is **Seix**, a convivial old cheese-making village, with houses overlooking the Salat and places to **hire canoes** or kayaks for thrills and spills. By car you can continue straight up the Salat river gorge to **Couflens**: if your brakes are in perfect working order, you can twist and turn up the zigzagging D703 to the **Col de Pause** (1,527m/5,039ft) for the breathtaking view of Mont Valier just to the west. If you're very adventurous, you can continue up the even more hair-raising and hairpin extension to the **Port d'Aula** (3,360m/7,458ft) for a look into the wildest corner of Spain. The much more sedate D8 south of Seix runs up the bucolic, pastoral **Vallée d'Ustou** and over to Aulus-les-Bains.

From the north, the approach to Aulus is down the equally beautiful **Vallée du Garbet** (take the D32 between Soueix and Seix). **Vic d'Oust**, the first hamlet, is a pretty little place, built around a Romanesque church with a charmingly painted ceiling and a 16th-century manor house. In the 19th century the next hamlet, **Ercé**, was famous for its **Bear School**. As far as anyone knows the first bears were trained to dance, perform tricks and simulate mock fights in the 12th century. If a cub was captured young (the fiercely protective mother bear invariably had to be killed first), it could be as easily domesticated as a dog, raised to play with the children and fed with milk. The rest of the dancing bear's life was tough, beginning with rigorous training, with far more stick than carrot. When the year's graduating class of bears was ready, they would be brought into Ercé's main square and bound tightly to the trees, soon to be roaring with agony as white-hot irons were driven through their muzzles for the nose rings they would wear for the rest of their lives. By the 1850s, bears were so rare that the Ariégeois trainers had to import them from Russia or Hungary; they were so prized that a local bride could have a bear as her dowry (which is a bit more exciting than the typical dowry of a country maiden in the Gers: a bag of pigeon droppings). There is a permanent **bear exhibition** in the Foyer Municipal on the trainers and their bears, with documents and eye-witness accounts.

Bear exhibition
t 05 61 66 86 00;
open June–Aug
Mon–Sat 3–7

Aulus-les-Bains

At the top of the narrow valley of the Garbet, surrounded by a *cirque* of wild rocky walls and waterfalls, Aulus-les-Bains, the spa of the Couserans, enjoys one of the most spectacular settings of any town in the Pyrenees. Until recently dismissed as a rather fuddy-duddy old place for people with digestive and urinary ailments, Aulus has built itself a brand-new glass and wood **Thermes** worthy of its lovely surroundings, with a pool open to the general public. The most popular day excursion from Aulus is on the GR 10 to the absolutely gorgeous triple waterfall with an irresistible name, the **Cascade d'Arse**; from there circle back to Aulus by way of the Etang de Guzet. Other beauty spots are the **Col d'Escot**, along the D68 above Aulus, and the ski resort of **Guzet-Neige** (there are buses in the winter from Aulus); both overlook the bewitching **Cirque de Cagateille**, one of the most beautiful in the Pyrenees.

The Green Valleys

The drive east of Aulus to the **Vallée de Vicdessos** on the D18 is just as spectacular, passing by way of the **Col d'Agnes** (1,570m/5,181ft), with its excellent views of the Andorran frontier chain, and the lake and waterfalls of **Lers** (or Lhers). Lers sits in luscious emerald scenery; the lake lent its name to lherzolite, the curious green volcanic rock formations you see along its banks. At the lake, a secondary road leads north to **Massat**, former capital of the viscounts of the Couserans and today the centre of the Vallées Vertes, a region if anything even quieter and more forgotten than the rest of the Couserans. Massat itself is a handsome old village, with plenty of room to spare, surrounded by chestnuts, beech and pine forests; there's a stable of *mérens* for riding tours, and good cross-country skiing in the winter. Just outside Massat, beside the river is an 18th-century **watermill** turned museum. In its past it has been a flour mill, saw mill and has produced electricity. East of Massat the scenic D618 leads eventually down to Tarascon, or you can cut across the mountains at Caougnous (a short but very steep road) for the D17, the beautiful 'Route Verte' where one enchanting view follows another all the way down to Foix.

Watermill
open July and Aug daily 5–7, rest of year Sat and Sun 5–7, and by appt

Aulus-les-Bains >>
www.aulus-les-bains.com; call Seix

Market Days in the Valleys of the Salat

Seix: first and third Thursday each month, and second and fourth Wednesday July–mid-Sept.
Castillon: Tuesday in July and Aug.
Sentein: Friday in July and Aug.

Where to Stay and Eat in the Valleys of the Salat

Accommodation is scarce here. Even so, it is not the most frequented of areas and you may have it all to yourself, except in July and August when it is wise to book in advance.

★ **Hostellerie de la Poste >**

Oust ☒ 09140
Hostellerie de la Poste, Rue Principale, **t 05 61 66 86 33, *www.ariege.com/hoteldelaposte* (€). In an old village house with a garden, pool and rooms with terraces. The restaurant is a local favourite for Sunday lunch, especially for the *confit de canard et ses pommes de terres rustiques. Menus €21–38. Closed Jan–early Feb and early Nov–mid-Dec.*

ⓘ **Massat >>**
t 05 61 96 92 76, www.ariege.com/massat; open July and Aug Mon–Sat 10–1 and 2–6, Sun 10–1

ⓘ **Seix >**
t 05 61 96 00 01, www.haut-couserans.com; open all year daily 9.30–12.30 and 2.30–6.30

Seix ☒ 09140
*Auberge des Deux Rivières, t 05 61 66 83 57, *www.ariege.com/auberge2rivieres* (€). In a pretty former post house, with a terrace overlooking the river and good local cooking. *Menus €15–30. Closed mid-Nov–Jan.*

*Auberge du Haut Salat, t 05 61 66 88 03 (€). A simple but comfortable hotel. *Closed mid-Nov–mid-Dec.*

Auberge des Ormeaux, Trein d Ustou, Seix (on D8), **t** 05 61 96 53 22, *www.ariege.com/aubergedesormeaux* (€). Pleasant *auberge* with pretty

bedrooms. Restaurant serves local cuisine. *Menus €13–22. Closed Wed except July and Aug plus 2 weeks in Nov.*

Aulus-les-Bains ☒ 09140
***Hostellerie La Terrasse, in the main street, **t** 05 61 96 00 98, *www.ariege.com/hostellerie-de-la-terrasse* (€€). The most delightful place to stay and eat in Aulus, with a terrace over the Garbet and an interior furnished with antiques. Try one of the specialities of the house such as *tourte aux foie gras. Menus €20–40. Closed mid-Sept–mid-June.*

**Les Oussaillès, t 05 61 96 03 68, *www.ariege.com/les-oussailles* (€). Mock-Gothic turrets and balconied rooms. You can feast on delicious salads, trout or veal, or ask for a picnic basket to take away. *Menus €20–31. Open all year.*

Massat ☒ 09320
Le Globe, in the centre, **t 05 61 96 96 66 (€). A comfortable old inn with a garden. There's a café serving breakfast and sandwiches. *Open all year.*

**Hostellerie des Trois Seigneurs, t 05 61 96 95 89 (€). A chalet-style *auberge* with a terraced restaurant, comfortable salon and garden. Good country cooking includes delicious *coq au vin* and river perch with sorrel. *Menus €15–20. Open mid-April–early Nov.*

Ferme-Auberge Las Trinquades, Boussenac, **t** 05 61 96 95 39, *www.trinquades.com* (€). In a peaceful village in the middle of nowhere, 6km east of Massat. Superb location, isolated in the mountains. Very comfortable lodging is available in four chalets for 2–5 people during July and August, and at weekends the rest of the year. For a meal based on lamb, book a table here. *Menus €15–20.*

East of St-Girons and the Lower Ariège

The northeast corner of the Ariège has for its centrepiece the Grotte du Mas-d'Azil, a cave with a record-breaking occupancy rate for more millennia than tongue can tell. It occupies the green hilly *piedmont* area where the mountains meet the plain, but where far too often the traditional free spirit of the mountains collided head on with less tolerant central powers, especially in the Wars of Religion, when most of the Basse-Ariège belonged to the Protestant camp.

Le Mas-d'Azil: the Cave and the Village

It sounds like something you'd expect in California: a drive-through prehistoric cave. But there it is – the D119 winds right through the yawning 214ft (65m) mouth of the **Grotte du Mas-d'Azil**, running alongside the cave-tunnel's architect, the River Arize. The first human inhabitants settled here in the Aurignacian era (30,000 BC) and stayed on through the Solutrean (18,000 BC) and the Magdalenian (12,000 BC). At the end of the Ice Age (8000 BC), the cave still had its inhabitants, and gave its name (Azilian) to their culture, one of the chief links between Upper Palaeolithic and Neolithic civilizations. In the Azilian era, the glaciers slowly retreated, along with the reindeer that Palaeolithic hunters had depended on, forcing them to make the change from hunting to pastoral and agricultural pursuits. The first persecuted Christians in the region, in the 3rd century, worshipped in the cave; in the 9th century the Benedictines built an abbey here. Every possible band of Pyrenean fugitives – Moors, Cathars and Protestants – took refuge at Le Mas-d'Azil at some point.

Cave Galleries
t 05 61 69 97 71; open July and Aug Tues–Sun 10–6; Sept–June, call for times

Some of the **galleries** on the right bank may be visited. There are three upper floors; the lowest one, unfortunately not open, is named after the great prehistorian Henri Breuil, who discovered its Magdalenian-era **etchings**. The next level has the **Salle du Temple**, where the Protestants worshipped in 1625 while holding out against the Catholic army (*see* below), and on top is the **Galerie des Ours**, full of bones and teeth left behind by the enormous but now extinct cave bears. A discovery made here in 1961, of the skull of a girl with carved bones simulating eyes stuck in the sockets, is remarkable as the only known example of a Palaeolithic skull prepared in any ritual way; some scholars see it as proof of a Stone Age belief in the afterlife. Tools from the Azilian technological revolution and other finds are exhibited here, while others have been deposited in the **Musée de la Préhistoire**, in the village of

Musée de la Préhistoire
t 05 61 69 97 71; open July and Aug Tues–Sun 11–1 and 2–7; April–June and Sept Tues–Sun 2–6; Mar Sun 2–6; Oct and Nov Sun and school hols 2–6; call ahead

Le Mas-d'Azil, just opposite the 17th-century church with a bulbous dome. Artistically, the Azilian era was marked by abstract designs in pebbles painted red with iron pyroxide. These aren't nearly as arresting as earlier Magdalenian-era pieces: the ivory carved animals and casts of two masterpieces from Le Mas-d'Azil (both now in the National Prehistory Museum in St-Germain-en-Laye), the expressive *Protome de Cheval*, carved from a reindeer's antler, and the *Faon aux Oiseaux*, a throwing stick topped with a remarkable carving of a fawn bent over to unburden itself of a large turd, which has two birds sitting and pecking on it. As other items decorated with the same motif have been found around the Pyrenees, the fawn and birds may have had a secret meaning, or it could just be that French cavemen had the same scatological sense of humour as their descendants. On the museum's top floor

Market Days in Le Mas-d'Azil

Le Mas-d'Azil: Fair on 2nd and 4th Wednesday of the month, otherwise a simple market.

Where to Stay and Eat in Le Mas-d'Azil

Le Mas-d'Azil >
*opposite the church,
t 05 61 69 99 90,
www.citaenet.com/le-mas-d'azil; open all year
Mon–Fri 9.30–12.30 and
2–6, plus Sat 9.30–12.30
in May–Sept*

Le Mas-d'Azil ✉ 09290

**Hôtel Gardel, on the main square, t 05 61 69 90 05 (€). Pleasantly old-fashioned. The restaurant features freshwater fish and Ariégeois cheeses. *Menus €15–28, vegetarian options. Closed mid-Nov–mid-Mar; restaurant closed Sun eves (Sept–May).*

Le Jardin de Cadettou, St-Féréol, t 05 61 69 95 23, www.cadettou.fr (€). Just outside the centre, serving the best food in Le Mas-d'Azil. The top-notch restaurant specializes in an unusual variety of *confits* – potted duck, pork, lamb, rabbit and pigeon; the pork served with an onion *confiture* is especially good. Also try their famous *profiteroles de foie gras aux cepes*. Three rooms provide accommodation. *Menus €15–35. Closed Jan plus all Mon, Tues, Sat lunch and Sun eves exc July and Aug.*

Auberge des Traouques, Montfa, t 05 61 69 85 79 (get there by way of Sabarat and Les Bordes-sur-Arize, then take the D114 west). The local favourite for a long afternoon outing. There is no accommodation but the cuisine is cheap and copious, and there's a pool for a dip, before or after the meal (make sure you leave enough time to digest the meal). You'll need to reserve a table if you want to eat on the terrace. *Menu €21. Open daily June–mid-Sept, the rest of the year closed Mon–Fri lunch.*

Dinosaur Park
*t 05 61 60 03 69,
www.ariege-dinosaures.com;
open all year*

there's an exhibition on the Ariège's **glass industry** – now as extinct as its bears. Also, for the kids, there's a **dinosaur park** with reconstructions of the giant reptiles, bones, their environment and a dig.

Le Mas-d'Azil itself is a pleasant *bastide* town founded in 1286. It was the main Protestant centre in the area in the 16th century; legends say Calvin himself preached here. The ubiquitous Jeanne d'Albret sent money for the town to turn its remarkable cave into a remarkable fortress and, defended by only a thousand Protestants, it stood up in 1625 to a royal army of 14,000 troops for five weeks before they retreated. Not surprisingly, Cardinal Richelieu put it at the top of his castle demolition list. The Neolithic salt road passed by here, and there are several dolmens close by: the best one, **Cap del Pouech**, is some 2km up a narrow country road. It's in better shape than the weird abandoned hillside calvary a few kilometres down the D119, in Raynaude.

Around Le Mas-d'Azil

The region around Le Mas-d'Azil is known as the **Montagnes du Plantaurel** – mountains that are hardly mountains at all, but gentle green hills, real golf-course and horse country. North at **Sabarat** is an **observatory**, regularly open to the public, that instructs in the ways of the stars and the universe. La Bastide-de-Sérou, along the main D117 between St-Girons and Foix, supplies

Observatory
see www.observatoire-sabarat.com for the programme of events

both: the 18-hole Golf Club de l'Ariège and the Centre National du Chevel des Mérens, where the black horses of the Ariège are bred. Note the *halles* in the centre of the village, with its original grain measure intact. West along the D117 at **Castelnau-Durban** the **Asinerie de Feillet** produces donkey milk that they make into cosmetics and soap.

Asinerie de Feillet
*t 05 61 96 38 93,
www.asinus.fr; open in
summer; call for times*

Northeast, at **Montégut-Plantaurel**, you can visit the *Sculpture Monumentale d'Amnesty International*, designed by Christian Lovis. Plaques with the names of political prisoners cover the walls, and are removed whenever the prisoner is freed – and replaced by the name of another prisoner of conscience. The sphere in the centre of the sculpture is to be rebuilt on the day (don't hold your breath) when there are no more plaques to put up.

North of Le Mas-d'Azil, **Carla-Bayle** is a pretty village on a hill crest with a fine panoramic view of the Pyrenees and a beautiful man-made **lake**, where you can swim. It was called Carla-le-Comte until the Revolution, when it chopped the Comte off and replaced him with Carla-le-Peuple; in 1879 it decided to change once more, dismissing the people and adding Bayle in honour of its most famous son, philosopher-writer Pierre Bayle, a brave soul who fought his own battles against intolerance. Born in 1647, Bayle, a Protestant, lived and died in exile in Rotterdam; his most famous works, an analysis of superstitions (*Pensées sur la comète*) and his *Dictionnaire historique et critique*, were among the main precursors of the 18th-century encyclopedists. You can learn more in the **Musée Pierre-Bayle** in the village.

Musée Pierre-Bayle
*t 05 61 68 53 53; open
winter Mon, Wed, Fri
and Sat 9–12 and 1–6;
summer until 7, but
check first*

East of Carla-Bayle, **Artigat** was the scene of one of the most haunting stories to come out of the 16th century, when a man returning from war convinced most of the village and his 'wife' that he was really who he said he was, even if he bore only a faint resemblance to Martin Guerre. When the real Martin Guerre returned, there was big trouble. The impostor's trial in Toulouse was diligently recorded by Jean de Coras, whose account was used as the basis for *The Return of Martin Guerre* – the book by Natalie Zemon Davis and the movie with Gérard Depardieu, filmed in lushest Ariège.

Le Fossat, further north, has a row of old houses and a powerful fortified church, but more geometrically memorable is **St-Martin-d'Oydes**, to the east, its houses built as a solid circle wall around the fortified **church**; until 1880, the only entry into the round central square was through a corridor 'for the living and the dead' in one of the houses. The church, quirkily modified in the 19th century, still has four baby crenellated towers sprouting out from the bell tower and a few frescoes about a local saint, Anasthase, who was tending plague victims when he collapsed in exhaustion outside the round walls of St-Martin. Satan, who just happened to be passing by, offered to cure Anasthase in exchange for a bowlful of his blood. But the bowl had a leak, and as the saint grew even weaker, he seized his stick and threatened Satan, who beat a hasty retreat; the stick fell in the spilled blood and at once a miraculous spring gurgled up. Washing himself with the water, Anasthase was cured and entered St-Martin, healed a number of people, died on 16 October 1085, and was buried in the church. In May there's a popular pilgrimage to the spring.

Lastly, **Lézat-sur-Lèze**, the northernmost village of the Ariège, is worth a stop for its church of **St-Jean**, with an octagonal bell tower and steeple and a Romanesque portal; inside are a few frescoes and a beautiful 16th-century *Mise au tombeau*.

Pamiers

Pamiers, 'Gateway to the Pyrenees' (if you're coming from Toulouse) and home of flat green beans called *haricots cocos*, is a square peg in the round Ariège, but a successful square peg that has long outgrown Foix and was most upset in the 18th century when the backward old seat of the counts got to be departmental capital. Originally known as Frédèlas after a 5th-century prince of Toulouse, the town and its *pays* were annexed to the Comté de Foix in 1111; when the count returned from the First Crusade, he renamed it Castrum Apamée (after Apamea in Syria), hence 'Pamiers'. If the rest of the *comté* was tempted by Catharism, Pamiers stayed orthodox Catholic; its bishop-inquisitor, Jacques Fournier, became Pope Benedict XII (see p.358). The Protestants savaged the town so thoroughly in the Wars of Religion that there's little left to see outside of the central Place du Mercadel and the **St-Antonin Cathedral** (the Romanesque door and carved capitals, and the octagonal brick bell tower with a carillon that plays songs every Sunday morning at 9.45). A second church, **Notre-Dame du Camp**, has a high, austere windowless façade and twin watchtowers; like the cathedral it was mostly rebuilt after the Wars of Religion.

The low rolling agricultural lands of the Basse-Ariège around Pamiers offer a few attractions if you're passing through. In the spirit of intolerance that has scarred this region, it was a choice area for concentration camps: there was one at Mazères, another at Villeneuve du Paréage, but the biggest and longest-lasting (1939–44) was just north of Pamiers at **Le Vernet**. Prisoners from many countries were locked up at Le Vernet, including a number of important figures in Resistance movements across Europe. Those who never left are buried in Le Vernet's international cemetery. There is now a **memorial** there to the prisoners.

North of Le Vernet, **Saverdun**, in spite of being the birthplace of Benedict XII (there are 17th-century frescoes of his life in the

Concentration camp memorial
for a guided visit call the mairie, **t** *05 61 68 36 43*

13

The Ariège, Andorra and the Eastern Pyrenees | Around Le Mas-d'Azil church), was and still is the main Protestant stronghold in the Ariège. The troops of the Duke of Wellington used the bell tower of the Romanesque church in nearby **Canté** as target practice, so only half of it stands; if it's open, don't miss the Gallo-Roman **statue** disguised as a holy water stoup. Just west, **Mazères** is an interesting *bastide* founded in 1252, with a beautiful *halles*. It was once one of the most important towns in the Ariège: in 1390, Gaston Fébus entertained Charles VI of France in the Palace of Mazères; part of the welcoming committee was a huge herd of Béarn cows with blue painted horns.

Mazères was also the land of the powerful **abbey of Boulbonne**, founded in 1129 by Roger IV of Foix and used for many generations as the pantheon of the Counts; both the palace and abbey were razed to the ground by the Huguenots. The abbey was rebuilt massively in brick in 1652 and still stands rather forlornly near Calmont. The story is all re-told at the **Musée du Vieux Mazères**, housed in a grand 16th-century *pastel*-merchant's residence, the Hotel d'Ardouin.

Musée du Vieux Mazères
t 05 61 69 42 04; call for times

Market Days around Le Mas-d'Azil

Pamiers: Tuesday, Thursday and Saturday.
Mazères: Thursday.
Saverdun: Friday and Sunday.

Where to Stay and Eat around Le Mas-d'Azil

La Bastide-de-Sérou ✉ 09240
Le Cent-Dix-Sept, t 05 61 64 50 26 (€). Convenient for the golf course and close to Le Mas-d'Azil. *Menus from €12. Open all year.*
Château Rhodes, 3.5km from Bastide, on D117, **t** 05 61 03 24 50, *www.chateaurhodes.com*. This is a truly lovely place set majestically in its own park. It has been renovated and decorated beautifully throughout, crammed with antiques but with the additional benefit of all mod cons. There is a pool, Jacuzzi, billiards, and tennis, and all bedrooms have Internet access and cable TV. You can no longer rent any of the 10 individual rooms, only the whole château. The kitchen is used to prepare your meals. Housekeeping is included in the price (call for a quote).

Lanoux/Artigat ✉ 09130
Farm Thibaut, 1km from Artigat, **t** 05 61 68 58 45 (€). Handy if you want to stay in the *pays de Martin Guerre*. *Table d'hôte €15. Closed Dec–Mar.*

Pamiers ✉ 09100
Hôtel de France, 5 Cours J. Rambaud (near the Hôpital Loumet), **t 05 61 60 20 88, *www.hoteldefrancepamiers.com* (€). A bit too cute for its own good but has comfortable rooms and good meals. *Menus €16–35.*
Hotel de la Paix, 4 Place Albert Tournier, **t 05 61 67 12 71, *http://hoteldelapaix-pamiers.com* (€). An old post house with original Empire decoration. Serves hearty traditional cuisine featuring foie gras, and also good fish dishes. *Menus €22–24.*
Le Roi Gourmand, 21 Rue P. Sémard, Hotel-restaurant, **t** 05 61 60 12 12, *http://hotel-roigourmand09.com*. Now well-established, this restaurant serves local delicacies with a twist, including *magret de canard* with *vin d'orange*, and fish roasted with *Banyuls*. *Menus €20–35. Open all year.*

Carla-Bayle ✉ 09130
Auberge Pierre Bayle, Rue Principale, **t** 05 61 60 63 95. Bar and restaurant with views of the Pyrenees. It serves simple local cuisine such as warm

ⓘ **Pamiers »**
Bd Delcassé, t 05 61 67 52 52, www.ot-pamiers.fr; open July and Aug Mon–Sat 9–12 and 2–5; May, June, Sept and Oct Mon–Fri 9–12 and 2–6, Sat 9–12 and 2–5; Nov–April Mon–Fri 9–12 and 2–5, Sat 9–12

ⓘ **La Bastide-de-Sérou ›**
t 05 61 64 53 53; open all year Mon–Fri 9–12 and 2–6 plus Sat 10–12

ⓘ **Carla-Bayle »**
www.carla-bayle.com

chèvre salad with honey. *Menus* €18–33. Closed Wed.

Mazères ✉ 09270
Auberge de l'Hers, Faubourg St-Louis, t 05 61 69 45 22. Terrace restaurant

beside the river, serving local delights such as duck stuffed with foie gras, *cassoulet* and *azinat* (Ariégeois cabbage soup). *Menus* €11–35. Closed Mon and Tues eves.

Foix

Foix may be among the tiniest departmental capitals in France, but it's one of the most striking, a wing of a town tucked between the Arget and Ariège rivers, crowned with a triple tiara of towers on top of its immense rock. This was once the base of the Counts of Foix, who made Foix famous throughout France and Italy, especially when they were named Gaston.

The first Fuxéens, as they're called, lived in the Magdalenian era around the big rock. The Romans planted a military camp here, although the first reference to the town's name (Castro Fuxi) only appears on a Merovingian coin. Not long after, a Carolingian abbey was founded here, joined in the 11th century by a castle when the lord of Foix was made a count. Together with the great lords of Languedoc – the Counts of Toulouse and Carcassonne – the Counts of Foix protected the Cathars and fought for their independence against the northern French invaders in the Albigensian Crusade (*see* 'Montségur', p.345). Their defeat discouraged the Counts for about five minutes. Throughout the 13th century their power and influence spread over the Pyrenees; in 1278 they were made co-princes of Andorra; in 1290 Count Roger Bernard III inherited the country of Béarn through his wife. This juicy prize made the dynasty's fortune, especially under the leadership of Gaston de Foix, better known as Gaston Fébus (*d.* 1391) who made himself one of the most powerful lords in the 14th century and came close to creating a new Pyrenean state (*see* pp.221). His descendant, Catherine de Foix, Queen of Navarre, married Jean d'Albret, and their son, another Gaston de Foix, made his reputation in Flanders and the wars of Italy, as the Renaissance's 'perfect knight', before he was killed in the Battle of Ravenna.

Foix had already lost much of its importance in the 14th century, when its counts abandoned it to reside in Béarn. In 1663 it lost its bishopric and administrative roles to Pamiers, and was well along the way to sinking into even greater obscurity when the deputies of the Revolution gave it a new lease of life as the capital of the new *département* number 09 – the Ariège.

A Walk around Medieval Foix

Although ringed by 19th-century development, the narrow winding street plan of old Foix is still intact, closed in by its rivers

342

Getting to and around Foix

Foix is on the Toulouse–Barcelona **rail** line, with connections to Pamiers, Tarascon-sur-Ariège, Ax-les-Thermes and L'Hospitalet (with **bus** connections to Pas de la Casa and Andorra). The station is on Av Pierre Semard, t 05 61 02 03 60; information and tickets t 08 36 35 35 35.

Several of the runs are taken by SNCF buses; all depart from the station at the north end of town off Cours Irenée-Cros. SALT buses, t 05 61 65 08 40, www.saalt.fr, link Pas de la Casa and Toulouse; Denamiel buses, t 05 61 66 24 37, run from Foix to St-Girons; and Sovitours, t 05 61 01 02 35, link Pamiers, Foix, Lavelanet, Mirepoix and Perpignan.

---

and the mighty rock of the castle. The town wall has been replaced by busy Cours Gabriel Fauré, named after the musician and composer (1845–1924) who was born in Pamiers but spent much of his early life in Foix; it's the easiest place to park as well. Behind the Hôtel de Ville, half-timbered houses from the 14th to 16th centuries lean out, especially over Place Parmentier, Place Lazema, Rue des Chapeliers (note No.30, the house of De Téville, captain of the Mousquetiers under Louis XII) and Rue de la Faurie, the street of the blacksmiths. Where Rue de la Faurie meets Rue des Marchandes, a bronze relief of a swan decorates the lovely if misnamed 19th-century **Fontaine de l'Oie**.

Down at the bottom of Rue des Marchandes you'll find Foix's cosy **market square** and its church, **St-Volusien**, begun in the 11th century by the counts, and mostly rebuilt in the 17th century. St-Volusien, who lived in the 5th century, doesn't exactly get a lot of churches. A senator of Tours, married to a famous nagging shrew, Volusien managed to stay out of his wife's way by becoming one of the most powerful, high-ranking supporters of Clovis, king of the Franks. He was made bishop of Tours in 488, but was exiled to Toulouse by the Visigoth King Alaric II for his refusal to support the Arian heresy. When Clovis killed Alaric II in 507 and besieged Toulouse, the Visigoths under their new king, Amalric, made a run for Spain with their hostages, including Volusien, who died of exhaustion along the road, somewhere between Pamiers and Foix. After thumping the Visigoths, Clovis brought the remains of his regretted supporter here, where the monks of the abbey that sheltered his reliquary invented a more exciting decapitation-martyrdom and plenty of miracles to make Volusien a bit more interesting to the parish. Only the portal and part of the transept survived destruction in the Wars of Religion, while the rebuilt interior is reminiscent of Catalan Gothic churches, with a spacious, wide and lofty nave unhindered by aisles. The painted capitals and frieze around the choir apses are imitation Gothic, but the excellent 16th-century terracotta painted *Mise au tombeau* in the easternmost chapel is the real McCoy. The 17th-century choir stalls were originally in Toulouse's St-Sernin. The Romanesque crypt, rebuilt in the 16th century, no longer houses either the relics or the casket of the unfortunate Volusien; the Huguenots chucked them from the castle rock into the River Arget.

Château des Comtes de Foix
www.sesta.fr; open July and Aug 9.45–6.30; June and Sept daily 9.45–12 and 2–6; Oct–May daily 10.30–12 and 2–5.30 exc Mon Nov–Mar, and weekdays in Jan; guided visits possible, one a day in English in July and Aug; adm

The **Château des Comtes de Foix** has seen its share of action, especially under Count Raymond Roger, the arch-enemy of the Albigensian Crusaders from the north. After the disastrous defeat of the southern cause at the Battle of Muret near Toulouse (1213), Simon de Montfort, the fiendishly efficient leader of the Crusaders, came down to Foix, vowing to 'make the Rock of Foix melt like fat and grill its master in it'. When he couldn't capture the castle or its count even after four tries, Montfort burned the rest of Foix to the ground, and in 1215 Raymond Roger gave in and surrendered the castle to the Papal Legate. Still unbowed, he made the obligatory journey to Rome, where he boasted to the Lateran Council: 'No Catholic who fell into my hands or those of my followers failed to have his eyes, hands or feet chopped off.' Yet as soon as Simon de Montfort was killed trying to recapture Toulouse in 1219, the castle was returned to the count.

Although the Counts of Foix, along with all the other barons of the south, were officially reconciled with the Church in Montpellier in 1223, they were not too chastened; the pride and independence of Roger Bernard 'the Great' brought King Philip the Fair down to Foix in person in 1272. Rather than smoke out the Count, the king set his men to dig the rock out from under him, before he surrendered and swore to be a good vassal.

The castle isn't all quite as old as it seems. The square tower on the end is from the 11th century, but the most feudal-looking tower, in the middle, was reconstructed in the 19th century; the great round tower, generally attributed to Gaston de Foix, actually dates from the 15th century. The lower, lightless floor served as a royal prison from the 17th century until 1864; the walls are scratched with pathetic graffiti in several languages. In the old days the prison guards had an easy time of it, thanks to the fierce and reliable Pyrenean sheepdogs who patrolled the enclosure between the towers, ready to rip the throat out of anything that moved. These days instead of prisoners, the Château de Foix houses the **Musée Départemental du Château de Foix**. Exhibitions today are mainly aiming to recreate Foix at the time of the counts and include buildings and building techniques during the Middle Ages, images of medieval times and people, Foix then and now, the castle as a prison, and Henri IV.

For the best view the other way, towards Foix and the surrounding Pyrenees, climb up the steep and rocky path to the **Croix-de-St-Sauveur**, beginning in the Rue St-Sauveur. The few ruins on top belonged to a hermit who used to enjoy the same fabulous view; now it's lorded over by a giant cement cross, put up there as some kind of heretic-detector.

Around Foix

Les Forges de Pyrène
t 05 34 09 30 60; open June and Sept daily 10–6; July and Aug daily 10–7; Oct–May Tues–Sun 1.30–6

🟊 Rivière Souterraine de Labouiche
t 05 61 65 04 11; open July and Aug daily 9.30–5.15; April–June and Sept daily 10–11.15 and 2–5.15; Oct and Nov daily 2–4.30; the boat journey lasts about 75mins

Just outside Foix, at Montgailhard, is **Les Forges de Pyrène**, a new museum based on one of the great iron forges of the region. You can see the restored forge in operation, a collection of old tools and equipment, and artisans demonstrating crafts and techniques from the past, from bread-making to panning for gold.

Six kilometres northwest of Foix on the D1 is the entrance to the chief curiosity around Foix, the **Rivière Souterraine de Labouiche**, nothing less than 'Europe's Longest Subterranean River Open to the Public'. There are two waterfalls, several levels of galleries, streams and sinkholes; Norbert Casteret said it was 'the most sensational of all underground excursions', and having done nearly every possible one himself, it must be true.

Down the Ariège, just north of Foix, **St-Jean-de-Verges** is a striking Romanesque church, once part of a priory founded by Foix's abbey of St-Volusien. In 1229 Count Roger Bernard came here to make his submission to the Church and king. It has a pretty apse, with windows and capitals decorated with carvings.

Market Days in Foix

Place St-Volusien, Friday. Fair on the 1st, 3rd and 5th Monday.

Where to Stay and Eat in and around Foix

ⓘ Foix >
29 Rue Delcassé, t 05 61 65 12 12, www.ot-foix.fr

Foix ✉ 09000
***Audoye-Lons**, Pl Duthil, t 05 34 09 29 00 (€€–€). Former post house near the Ariège river. A comfortable place to stay, with a terrace restaurant. *Menus €14–26. Closed Sat lunch in winter, plus mid-Dec–mid-Jan.*
***Hôtel Pyrène**, Rue Serge-Denis, Le Vignoble (2km north on the N20), t 05 61 65 48 66, www.hotelpyrene. com (€€–€). Up-to-date furnishings, a pool and garden. *Closed mid-Dec–Jan.*
Barbacane, Av de Lérida, t 05 61 65 50 44 (€€–€). One of the nicer places to stay in the centre of town, in a grand bourgeois mansion. *Closed mid-Nov–Mar.*
Ferme de Caussou, 2km from Foix at Cos, t 05 61 65 34 42 (€). A renovated old farm with rooms with views over the château and the Pyrenees, and small kitchens. *Menus from €16 for guests, €23 for others. Open all year.*

Le Phoebus, 3 Cours Irenée-Cros, t 05 61 65 10 42. Popular local restaurant with a balcony facing the château. They serve local produce with a rich twist; try duck liver with caramelised apples. There's a good wine list. *Menus €17–48. Closed Sat lunch and Mon from mid-July–mid-Aug.*
Le Ste-Marthe, 21 Rue Noel Peyrévidal, t 05 61 02 87 87. A restaurant serving classics such as *cassoulet*, but also inventive dishes such as a *tart of boudin noir* with *champignons* and salmon with vanilla. *Menus €22–51. Closed Wed exc July and Aug.*
Sud Asie, 36 Cours Irenée Cros, just up the Toulouse road, t 05 61 02 82 61. A sensation in Foix; a rather austere-looking Vietnamese restaurant with a large selection of delicious soups, starters and main courses (get there early if you want a table). *Menus €16. Closed Sat, Sun and Mon lunch.*

Around Foix
Auberge des Myrtilles, on the D17 (head west of Foix up to the Col de Marrous), t 05 61 65 16 46 (€€). Little timbered mountain *auberge*, tucked away in the forest. Comfortable rooms with full bathrooms plus indoor pool, sauna and Jacuzzi. The restaurant specializes in grills, local

trout, duck sausage and, naturally, *tarte aux myrtilles* (mountain bilberries). *Menus €16–24. Closed Tues and Wed lunch out of season, and Nov–early Feb.*

La Barguillère, St-Pierre-de-Rivière, on the D17, **t 05 61 65 14 02 (€€–€), is a fine little Logis de France hotel with an excellent restaurant. There are a number of fish dishes on the menu,

which is rare in the heart of the mountains. *Menus €12–38. Closed Tues eve, Wed, Nov–mid-Dec and mid-Jan–early Feb.*

Le Château de Bénac, Bénac, **t** 05 61 02 65 20 (€), 6km west of Foix. Six tranquil rooms overlooking the lawn, with good views over the Vallée de la Barguillère. *Menu €18. Closed mid-Nov–1 Feb.*

East of Foix: Montségur and Mirepoix

The haunting memories evoked by Montségur attract thousands of pilgrims each year. If you're approaching from Foix and have a little extra time, don't take the main Lavelanet road, the D117, but rather climb the scenic D9, passing by way of another Cathar citadel, built in the 13th century high on an eyrie above the village of **Roquefixade**, its walls blending in with rocky crags around it. Simon de Montfort didn't even try to bag it, but after the Comté de Foix was subdued by Philip the Bold, it was annexed by the Crown.

Montségur: the Cathars' Last Stand

② Montségur castle and museum
t 05 61 01 06 94, www.citaenet.com/ montsegur; Château open April, Sept and Oct daily 9.30–6; May–Aug 9–7.30, Nov 10–5.30, Mar 10–5, Dec–Feb 10–4; closed Jan and in bad weather; Museum open June–Aug daily 10–12.30 and 2–7, May 10.30–12.30 and 2–7, Sept 10.30 and 2–6, April and Oct 2–6, Mar and Nov 2–5, Dec and Feb 2–4.30; closed Jan

The castle of Montségur, hovering spectacularly high on a rocky outcrop (or *pog* in Occitan) at the edge of the St-Barthélemy massif, is the special shrine and Alamo of the Cathars, a magnet for anyone fascinated by the virtuous heretics, or 'goodmen' as they called themselves. But for both sentimental and activist southerners, Montségur symbolizes more than religion, something like the lost soul of an aborted nation: the tolerant, sophisticated nation of southern France, or Occitania, where Cathars and Catholics had lived as neighbours until the king of France and the pope made its demise and annexation the goal of a war of northern conquest officially known as the Albigensian Crusade. Human beings are easier to kill than ideas: *Occitania Indépendente!*, scrawled on the big rock under Montségur castle, is a sentiment shared by many these days, when the Occitan/Provençal language of the troubadours is being revived across the south (if mostly on a literary level) and contacts between nationalistic Occitans and Catalans have already begun to create a cross-border cultural union – an eastern counterpart to the relationship between French and Spanish Basques. One last attraction of Montségur, especially for lovers of the occult and esoteric, are the persistent legends that identify it as the Castle of Montsalvage, the home of the Holy Grail.

The Castle and Siege of Montségur

In 1204, just as St Dominic began his preaching mission, the Cathars asked Raymond de Péreille, one of their supporters, to

Getting around East of Foix

Public transport is pretty thin on the ground here, although there are **bus** connections from Toulouse to Lavelanet and Mirepoix (SALT buses, **t** 05 61 65 08 40), and from Foix to Lavelanet on Sovitour buses, **t** 05 61 01 02 35.

rebuild his castle at Montségur ('Mount Safety' in French, for the site is nearly impregnable). It became their chief stronghold, the seat of their church and their bishop Bertrand Marty. While the Cathars' other castles fell easily, the besiegers found Montségur impossible to seal up tightly and starve out, even with 6,000 men. It held out for ten months, into the difficult winter; impatiently, Hugues des Arcis hired mercenaries from the surrounding villages, who in the dead of night led the Crusaders up to the east end of the *pog*, where they killed the defenders and captured a tower within catapult range of the castle. The Cathars held out another two months in the snow, but on 2 March, as food ran low and all chances of relief were eliminated, the commander of the Montségur garrison, Pierre Roger de Mirepoix, opened talks with Hugues des Arcis. The Cathars were given two weeks' respite: they would then be freed if they became Catholics, and burnt at the stake if not. The soldiers who defended them would also be freed, once they had appeared before the Inquisition. The Cathars spent the two weeks receiving the sacrament of the *consolament* and giving away their worldly goods to the soldiers. A number of the soldiers themselves decided to become Cathars, even though they knew what awaited them.

At the beginning of the path up to the fortress, a stone memorial erected by the Society for Cathar Studies marks the **Camp des Crémats**, the burning field, where a stockade full of firewood was set alight as the archbishop of Narbonne arrived to take possession of Montségur and all the souls who converted to Catholicism. Not a single one took up the offer; all 225 *perfecti* and *perfectae* climbed the ladders and jumped into the flames rather than abjure their religion. The inscription reads: ALS CATARS/ALS MARTIRS DEL PUR AMOR CRESTIAN 16 MARS 1244. The castle itself has been partially rebuilt: after the Cathars' hecatomb, the present village of Montségur reused much of the castle's stone for its houses. A curious feature of the castle are two lateral openings in its triangular walls, perfectly aligned to the rising of the sun on the summer solstice, fuelling considerable speculation about the castle as a solar temple, if not for the benefit of the Cathars, for the masons who originally built it; special cele-brations are held every 21 June. Archaeological excavations around the castle have uncovered wells, cellars and stairways from the Cathar village.

The Good, the Bad and the Inquisition

For years now I have brought you words of peace. I have preached, I have implored, I have wept. But as the common people say in Spain: if a blessing will not work, then it must be the stick. Now we shall stir up princes and bishops against you, and they, alas, will call together nations and peoples, and many will perish by the sword. Towers will be destroyed, walls overturned, and you will be reduced to slavery. Thus force will prevail where gentleness has failed.

Domingo Guzmán (later St Dominic), to the Cathars

Few beliefs have had the staying power of dualism, a doctrine first expounded by the Greek Gnostics in the first three centuries of the Christian era. Good and Evil were explained as eternal opposing forces, Good residing somewhere beyond the stars, while Evil was here and now – in fact all of creation was Evil, the work not of the God of the Old Testament but of a fallen spirit, identifiable with Satan. Our task on earth was to seek purity by having as little to do with creation as possible.

In the 3rd century, a Persian holy man named Mani came up with a popular revision of the Gnostic dualism that spread like wildfire as far as southern Gaul. Although the Church in Rome condemned his doctrines as the 'Manichaean heresy' and stomped them out along with many other alternative beliefs in those early years, dualism continued to attract adherents in the East, making an organized revival in the 9th century with the 'Bogomils' in the Balkans. By the 11th century it had spread through much of Europe, its adherents known as Bulgars or Paterenes, Cathars or Albigensians. The Church in Italy and northern France massacred and burned as many of the heretics as it could catch, but in southern France, the faith attracted many merchants, craftsmen, poor people and members of the nobility. In 1167, Occitan Catharism was organized into a proper church at a council at St-Félic-de-Caraman.

The Cathars believed that their faith was a return to the heroic virtue and simplicity of the early Church. Their teaching encouraged complete separation from the Devil's world; feudal oaths were forbidden, and believers solved differences between themselves by arbitration rather than going to the law. Some features were quite modern: Cathars promoted vegetarianism and non-violence; marriages were by simple agreement, not a sacrament – enhancing the freedom of women by doing away with the old Roman paternalist traditions and laws. Two other points made Catharism especially attractive to an increasingly modern society. It had a much more mature attitude towards money and capitalism than the Roman Church, with no condemnation of loans as usury, and no church tithes. This earned it support in the growing cities; like the later Protestants, many Cathars were involved in the textile trades. And Cathar simplicity, and its lack of a big Church organization, made a very favourable contrast with the bloated, bullying and thoroughly corrupt machinery of the Church of Rome.

Best of all, Catharism had a very forgiving attitude towards sinners. If creation itself was the Devil's work, how could we not err? Cathars were divided into two levels: the mass of simple believers, upon whom the religion was a light yoke indeed – no Mass and few ceremonies, no money-grubbing, easy absolution – and the few *perfecti*, those who had received a sacrament called the *consolament* and were thenceforth required to lead a totally ascetic life devoted to faith and prayer. Most Cathars conveniently took the *consolament* on their deathbeds.

In 1203, a Spanish monk named Domingo Guzmán embarked on a mission to save the souls of the heretics of Occitania, founding along the way a preaching Order that would become the Dominicans. The Order was more successful than its founder's attempts to herd the Cathars back to the fold; by 1209, the papacy, the behaviour of which has always been a strong argument for the basic tenet of dualism, saw enough of a threat to its power to require a policy of genocide. The terror, enforced by French arms (and fuelled by the promise that all the lands of lords who tolerated the Cathars would be given to good Catholics), was overseen at first by local bishops. When many of these failed to kill enough Cathars, the Church decided to entrust the task to specialists – the followers of Dominic. The first group of Inquisitors, led by Guillaume Arnaud, was based in Toulouse and torched so many people in mass *auto-da-fés* that the Toulousains rioted and expelled them in 1235. But they were back the next year, worse than before, leaving a swathe of blood across the south. In May 1242, knights from Montségur murdered Guillaume Arnaud and his court of 11 Inquisitors. The Inquisitors were quickly beatified by the pope and the next year 6,000 men under Hugues des Arcis, seneschal of Carcassonne, began their siege of Monségur, where some 350 Cathars lived, protected by a garrison of 150 men.

The 'Treasure' of the Cathars and Parzifal

An incident that happened in the last two weeks before the final surrender of Montségur has intrigued people for centuries. As the Crusaders knew that the Cathars had a spotless record for honesty and integrity, they didn't stand a very close guard over the castle once Pierre Roger de Mirepoix brokered the surrender agreement. Yet by a special request of Bishop Marty, four Cathars were secretly lowered by ropes over the cliffs on the night of 15 March. They made their way over La Peyre pass to a cave, where they picked up a treasure hidden three months earlier by two other *perfecti*. From there they travelled east to the Castle of Usson, where they met one of the *perfecti*, who hid the treasure and then disappeared from history.

What the Cathars''Treasure' might have been, according to a number of writers, was the Holy Grail, as in Wolfram Von Eschenbach's great Arthurian romance, *Parzifal*, a poem completed around 1212. The Grail – a precious jewelled cup with divine powers – had already neatly made the voyage from Celtic mythology to Christian thanks to the 12th-century Welsh stories of Parzifal brought to France through the court of Eleanor of Aquitaine and the Plantagenets. According to the various versions of the legend, the Grail is either the cup used by Christ in the Last Supper or the cup in which Joseph of Arimathea collected the blood of Christ on the cross (hence the presumed etymology of Holy Grail from San Graal or Sang Real – 'Holy Blood'). Wolfram always claimed he got the story of his masterpiece from a certain Kyot, a singer or magician from Provence, and there is certainly an uncanny resemblance between some of the places and names in *Parzifal* and those of the Cathars, suggesting that the romance could be read as an allegory of the Albigensian Crusade: Montségur means the same thing as Wolfram's Munsalvaesche, where the Grail ceremony takes place; the mother of Parzifal, Herzeloyde, who was first married to Castis, could be Adélaïde, wife of King Alphone the Chaste, who was alive at the time; the Vicomte Raymond Trencavel of Carcassonne, a knight errant and protector of the Cathars, has in a number of aspects been identified with Parzifal (his contemporaries certainly didn't shy from comparing him to Christ himself, especially after his betrayal and death at the hands of Simon de Montfort). Perhaps another argument in favour of the Cathar interpretation is the fact that Wolfram's only other surviving epic, *Willehalm*, concerns the same geographical era, dealing with the 8th-century knight, Count William of Toulouse, who fought the Saracens with Charlemagne's son, Louis the Pious.

Legends of treasure in the Pyrenees are certainly old hat. One was discovered by the Visigoths in the Grotte de Pyrène, that included a fabulous chalice and an emerald table. This was taken to Spain when the Franks invaded Aquitaine; with the conquest of Spain by the Moors, the Visigoths' treasure was taken by the Omayyads to Syria, whence during the Crusades the Genoese brought it back to Genoa, where you can see it to this day in the Cathedral Treasury, labelled the 'Chalice of the Last Supper'.

This hardly satisfies some people. The weirdest of all modern Europe's occultist sects, the Nazis, were obsessed with the Cathars. After their occupation of the south in 1942, they sealed off all the important Cathar sites and cave refuges in the Pyrenees, and Nazi high priest Alfred Rosenberg sent teams of archaeologists to dig them up amidst the utmost secrecy. In 1944, not long before liberation, a group of local Cathars sneaked up to Montségur for an observance to commemorate the 700th anniversary of their forebears' last stand. A small German plane with a pilot and a passenger appeared and circled the castle. The Cathars, expecting the police, watched in amazement as the plane, using skywriting equipment, traced a strange eight-branched cross over their heads, and then disappeared beyond the horizon.

A steep road winds down to the small village of Montségur, a cute little place built in tiers on the hillside with more footpaths than streets. Here **L'Occitadelle** offers an audio-visual on the history of the Cathars and the Albigensian Crusade. Montségur's little **Musée Archéologique** has finds from excavations and a model of the château.

Musée Archéologique
*t 05 61 01 06 94;
opening times vary:
calling ahead is
recommended*

Around Montségur: the Pays d'Olms

This region east of Foix has its full share of minor curiosities and enough altitude to support a ski resort, **Les Monts d'Olmes**, south of Montségur. If, however, you continue east of Montségur village, the D9 leads to the Hers, the most important river in these parts. A narrow road follows the Hers up as far as the savage **Gorges de la Frau** (the Gorge of Fear), where you can pick up the trail to Montaillou. Along the road from Fougax-et-Barrineuf to **Bélesta** and its lovely forest, stop to see the 'mad fountain', the **Fontaine Intermittente de Fontestorbes**, famous since Roman times; a subterranean river comes flowing out of a cave – at variable intervals (from mid-July to August, it flows for a few minutes every half-hour or so). This is because the fairies, or Encantadas, who live in a subterranean palace, are washing and rinsing their laundry – at least that's as good an explanation as any.

Lavelanet is the industrial power of the Pays d'Olms, an important manufacturer of carded wool and textiles. Until the invention of plastic, it had another more unusual, specialized craft – the manufacture of combs from horn and boxwood. Established all along the Hers valley by Protestants after Henry IV's Edict of Nantes (1598), the horn comb industry once employed over a

13

The Ariège, Andorra and the Eastern Pyrenees | East of Foix: Montségur and Mirepoix

Musée du Textile et du Peigne en Corne
65 Rue Jean-Jaurès,
t 05 61 03 01 34; open mid-June–mid-Sept Mon–Sat 2–6

Art Mony
t 05 61 01 11 09; call to visit

Abbey at Camon
contact the tourist office, t 05 61 68 88 26

Mirepoix local history museum
t 05 61 01 38 64; open Jan–Nov daily 2–6

thousand workers. You can learn about them in the **Musée du Textile et du Peigne en Corne** or watch how it's done at **Art Mony**, the last horn comb factory in the region, at Lesparrou, 7km to the east. West of Lavelanet, **Montferrier** has a curious Neolithic monument known as the **sacrificial rock of Peyregade** (up the Touyre stream).

Mirepoix

Mirepoix, centre of the little sister *pays* north of the Pays d'Olme, is one of the prettiest villages in the Ariège. A few detours may tempt you off the main D625 from Lavelanet: the *bastide* village of **Léran**, for instance, has a well-preserved castle of the dukes of Lévis-Mirepoix, the descendants of Gui de Lévis, right-hand man of Simon de Montfort. The vast artificial **lake of Léran-Montbel** has become a focus of summer leisure activities and bird-watching in the area. Further north along the Hers, picture-postcard **Camon** is a little fortified village that grew up under the protection of its 10th-century **abbey**; its cloister, church and frescoed oratory are open for guided tours.

An inventory showed 600 Cathars living in Mirepoix in 1209, when Simon de Montfort deposed its lord, Pierre-Roger de Mirepoix, and replaced him with Gui de Lévis. In 1279, a dam holding the waters of the Hers burst and flooded Mirepoix so badly it had to be abandoned. Jean de Lévis rebuilt it as a regular *bastide* on higher ground; in 1355, during the Hundred Years War, the Black Prince sacked and pillaged it, and a band of *routiers* burned it down again a decade later. But little has happened since; Mirepoix looks very much as it did at the end of the 14th century, with its half-timbered houses, its arcaded square on wooden pillars and 13th-century **Maison des Consuls**, the ends of its beams carved with heads of people and monsters. The Maison des Consuls is now a stylish hotel (*see* p.352). One of its fortified **gates**, the Porte d'Aval, survives at the west end of town.

In 1317, the Avignon Pope John XXII elevated Mirepoix to a bishropic as part of his scheme to bring danger zones of heresy back into the fold. The Lévis, who had already paid to build a new church in Mirepoix, began its enlargement into the **Cathédrale St-Maurice**; work was more or less completed when Philippe de Lévis was bishop in the 15th century. Southern Gothic in style, the cathedral seems designed for a much larger town than Mirepoix; its octagonal bell tower stands 190ft (58m) high, and behind its handsome Gothic portal the church stands 79ft (24m) high and measures 158ft (48m) long and 73ft (22m) across, making it the second widest single nave in Europe. There's a **museum** to local history and traditions near the cathedral.

The Vertical Church of Vals

Lastly, towards Pamiers are a pair of Romanesque **churches** well worth a detour, but do check at the Mirepoix tourist office before setting out to make sure the one at Vals is open. The church at **Teilhet** is fortified with a *clocher-mur*, sculpted with a knight on his horse (just under the bell); the portal has beautifully carved capitals and a frieze of grotesques. Two kilometres further on, the unique church at **Vals** is a local version of Rome's San Clemente.

⭐ Church at Vals

The huge rock it stands on had a sacred spring and was first inhabited in the Bronze Age; in Gallo-Roman times it supported a temple to the Celtic god Rahus. The entrance itself is uncanny, a tunnel and stair that follows a natural fault in the rock. It leads to the original 8th-century church: a nave measuring 35ft (10m), excavated from the living rock. To this, a vaguely Mozarabic apse was added in the 11th century; in the 12th century it was beautifully frescoed by Catalan artists with the *Life of Christ*, the paintings rediscovered under the plaster in 1956. The original nave came to resemble a crypt when a second, upper nave was added, dedicated to the Virgin Mary (restored in 1887); above that, orientated sideways, there's a 12th-century chapel of St-Michel, built into a *clocher-mur* that looks just like a castle keep. The idea was that the archangel would act as the protector of the gentle Virgin.

13 The Ariège, Andorra and the Eastern Pyrenees | East of Foix: Montségur and Mirepoix

Market Days East of Foix

Lavelanet: Wednesday and Friday.
Mirepoix: Thursday and Monday.
Laroque d'Olme: Thursday and Saturday.

Where to Stay and Eat East of Foix

Montségur and Environs
✉ 09300

**Costes, t 05 61 01 10 24 (€). A pleasant creeper-covered old hotel with a garden in the middle of town. It has an excellent restaurant serving omelettes with *cèpes* and other southwestern delicacies. *Menus* €19–30. *Closed Jan.*

Hôtel Couquet, 81 Rue Principal, **t** 05 61 01 10 28. This is an old place; some of the plumbing is out of the ark, but it's well kept and cheap.

L'Occitadelle, t 05 61 01 21 77. Well-prepared dishes such as perch in sorrel sauce. *Menus* €15–22. *Closed Fri exc July and Aug plus mid-Nov–Jan.*

Les Sapins, Conte, 09300 Nalzen. On the D117, direction Lavelanet, **t** 05 61 03 03 85. Cuisine of the Ariège served with care. *Menus* €13–42. *Closed Sun and Wed eves plus all Mon.*

Léran ✉ 09600

Bon Repos, t 05 61 01 27 83 (€). An isolated country farm 3km from the lake of Léran-Montbel. You can sleep peacefully in the comfortable rooms here. Home-cooked meals are available on request. *Menu* €18. *Open all year.*

Camon ✉ 09500

Domaine de Couchet, Peyrefitte-du-Razès on the road from Mirepoix to Limoux, **t** 04 68 69 55 06, *www. domainedecouchet.com* (€€). A lovely 18th-century *maison particulier* with grand bedrooms. *Menu* €25. *Open all year by reservation only.*

Bergerie, t 05 61 68 81 96. Restaurant that serves a famous *agneau en croûte*. *Menus* €12–31. *Closed Wed exc July and Aug plus Jan.*

ⓘ **Lavelanet >**
Foyer Municipal,
t *05 61 01 22 20,*
www.paysdolmes.org;
open July and Aug
Mon–Sat 9–12 and 2–7,
Sun 9–12; Sept–June
Mon–Sat 9–12 and 2–6

ⓘ **Montségur >**
t *05 61 03 03 03,*
www.montsegur.org;
open July and Aug daily
10.30–12 and 1.30–6.30;
Sept–June call for times;
closed Jan

ⓘ **Montferrier**
t *05 61 01 14 14; open*
all year Mon–Sat 9–12
and 2–6

(i) Mirepoix >
*t 05 61 68 83 76,
www.ot-tourisme-
mirepoix.com; open
Mon–Fri 10–12 and 3–6*

Mirepoix ✉ 09500

***La Maison des Consuls**, 6 Place Couvert, **t** 05 61 68 81 81, *www.maisondesconsuls.com* (€€). Stylish hotel in the Maison des Consuls, an arcaded building with wonderful carved beams. Rooms overlook the medieval streets. *Open daily all year.*

****Commerce**, Cours Docteur-Chabaud, **t** 05 61 68 10 29, *www.chez.com/lecommerce* (€). The nicest place in town, with a welcome shady garden and good restaurant. *Menus €12–35.*

Closed Sat, exc July and Aug, plus Jan and some weeks in Oct.

Roquefixade ✉ 09300

Le Relais des Trois Châteaux, Palot, **t** 05 61 01 33 99, *www.troischateaux.com* (€). A prettily decorated hotel and restaurant, which offers a changing menu according to season; try combinations such as eel with shrimps, kidneys with *cèpes*, or frogs' legs with grapes. *Menus €15–48. Closed Sat lunch and Sun eve plus Tues and 3 weeks Jan–Feb.*

Tarascon-sur-Ariège and its Caves

Up the River Ariège from Foix, the main N20 passes the twin-towered '**Devil's Bridge**' at Mercus-Garrabet (famous for tele-waterskiing if you like being dragged across the water) and the river-rafting centre at **Bompas** before reaching Tarascon-sur-Ariège, one of the main crossroads of the *département*. Tarascon held a similar status in the dawn of time: today it's the proud capital of prehistory in the Pyrenees.

Tarascon-sur-Ariège

Tarascon-sur-Ariège (like the Tarascon in Provence) was first settled by the Tarusques, a Ligurian tribe mentioned in Pliny's *Natural History*. It has an isolated baby mountain for its landmark, crowned by a round clock tower, the Tour du Castella – all that remains of the castle that once stood here. In 1702, Tarascon was consumed by a fire, and never really recovered its former importance. Recently, however, a group of historically minded gourmets in Tarascon has revived the distillation of *Hypocras*, the favourite chugalug of Gaston Fébus himself. Named after Hippocrates, the Father of Medicine, it was regarded in the Middle Ages as a panacea and aphrodisiac; Gaston Fébus attributed all his prowess to drinking the elixir every day. Based on an infusion of mountain herbs, Malvasy wine, cinnamon, ginger, cloves and cardamon, the recipe of 'sweet and savage Hypocras' has been the subject of long research. Elyane and Michel Séguélas at Tarascon's **Caves du Castella** are the official producers; if you don't see it in the shop, ring them up.

Caves du Castella
*t 05 61 05 60 38,
www.hypocras.com*

**Parc Pyrénéen de
l'Art Préhistorique**
*on the route to
Banat, t 05 61 05 10 10;
open April–early Nov
10–6; adm*

Also new and old at the same time, Tarascon's **Parc Pyrénéen de l'Art Préhistorique** opened in August 1994 to console the many visitors turned away from the Grotte de Niaux; among its attractions are perfect replicas of the paintings of Niaux, a 'sonar labyrinth', a circular diorama of a Magdalenian-era hunt, a meadow planted with Pyrenean plants and flowers, and a picnic area.

Really Big Caves: Bédeilhac and Lombrives

From Tarascon it's 5km up the D618 to Mt Soudour and its **Grotte de Bédeilhac**, marked by a huge porch. The first scientists in the Pyrenees in the 18th century remarked that Bédeilhac was a typical large Pyrenean stalactite cave with a kilometre-long gallery, famous for its formations (among them the 'tomb of Roland', a fallen stalagmite the size of a sequoia), but it was the Abbé Henri Breuil, the indefatigable 'father of prehistory', who discovered the Palaeolithic art inside in 1906: deer, horses, bison, mountain goats and mysterious symbols painted on the wall, and four bison modelled out of clay with a pubic triangle inscribed above them, very similar to those found by Norbert Casteret in the cave of Montespan in the Haute-Garonne, and perhaps moulded by the same 'sorcerers' college'. After the Magdalenian artists departed, the cave was inhabited until the Iron Age. The Neolithic skeleton of a man aged between 30 and 40 years, but only 4ft 6in (1.3m) tall, was found near the entrance of the cave, before it was spoiled by the Germans, who installed an aircraft factory here during the last war.

Saurat, just up the valley from Bédeilhac, is the last place in France where whetstones are mined and polished, by **Sylvain Cuminetti**. The D618 continues over the spectacular Col de Port with splendid scenery to Massat (*see* p.333). The next valley south, the beech-wooded **Vallée de la Courbière**, is especially fine walking country, especially beyond **Rabat-les-Trois-Seigneurs**, a magnificently set village where the Cathars took refuge in the castle Roche des Irretches.

If you think Bédeilhac is a monster of a cave, a few kilometres south of Tarascon on the N20 is the **Grotte de Lombrives**, the biggest cave in Europe open to the public, but you'll still only see a fraction of the whole. A little train takes you up to the entrance. Among the stalactite and stalagmite formations is the remarkable *Mammoth*, the *throne of King Bébrix*, and the *sepulchre of Pyrène*, his daughter, the lover of Hercules and namesake of the mountains that became her funerary monument. Lombrives goes on and on – it's said to have subterranean links to Niaux – and has upper galleries, 150ft (45m) up, accessible only by ladders. Numerous skeletons, nearly all women and children, were found up there; in his Gallic Wars, Caesar wrote how the Romans snuffed out many Pyrenean tribes by walling them up in their cave refuges, but in Lombrives all the legionnaires had to do was take away the ladders. Another cave nearby, the **Grotte de Bethléem**, was apparently used by the Cathars for initiation ceremonies of the *consolament*; no one knows what kind of mumbo-jumbo they got up to, but there's a very Pythagorean pentangle deeply engraved in the wall.

Lombrives is in the small spa town of **Ussat-les-Bains**. Ussat became fashionable after 1807 when Napoleon's brother Louis Bonaparte, king of Holland, came here to soak in the relaxing tepid, sulphuric (but not smelly) waters, recommended for nervous disorders. The pretty arcaded thermal establishment was built in 1850, and in 1982 reopened for patients stressed out by modern life. Above Ussat, the **church of Ornolac** is a model of Romanesque simplicity, but has two curious bends in the axis of its nave, commonly interpreted as an attempt by the architect to represent the contortions of Christ on the Cross. Not a few people come to see the grave of the famous 19th-century poisoner, Madame Lafarge, who was pardoned by Napoleon III and came to Ussat to recover her health, but died anyway in 1852.

The Grotte de Niaux and up the Vallée de Vicdessos

In the old days the region around Tarascon was called the **Sarbates**, a name that lives on in the Pechiney-Sabart aluminum factory and the tiny 11th- and 12th-century church of **Notre-Dame de Sarbates** at the entrance of the Vicdessos valley (take the D8 just southwest of Tarascon). According to legend, the first church on this site was founded by Charlemagne after he defeated the Saracens. A brief apparition of Mary in a halo of light had accompanied the victory; the day after, Charlemagne brought his army to the spot, where a bronze statue of the Virgin on a stone altar was found. Charlemagne tried to send the precious statue to the abbey of St-Volusien in Foix, but the statue kept mysteriously disappearing and reappearing on this site, so a church was built here. It was burnt down by the Huguenots in 1568 and rebuilt from the ruins; the statue of the black Virgin draws her share of pilgrims on 8 September.

Niaux is one of Abbé Breuil's 'six giants' of prehistoric mural art and justly attracts most of the attention around Tarascon. But do slot in a little extra time to see the fascinating **Musée Pyrénéan de Niaux**, just below the cave, housing a private collection of over 2,000 artefacts assembled by Max and Denise Déjean, experts on rural life and traditions in the Pyrenees. There are unique pieces among the ingenious tools and widgets that made the harsh life in the mountains a bit easier and sometimes just a little more fun.

Musée Pyrénéan de Niaux
t 05 61 05 88 36; open July and Aug daily 9–8, other times 10–12 and 2–6; adm

The Grotte de Niaux
The most beautiful prehistoric art in all the Pyrenees and, according to many, the best after Lascaux and Spain's Altamira, is in Niaux, discovered in 1906 in the cliffs of the Cap de la Lesse. A

Prehistoric Postmodernism

Part of the wonder and magic of Niaux and the other decorated prehistoric caves (nearly all are in southwest France or northwest Spain) is that they uncannily achieve many of the aims of art in the late 20th and early 21st century – they suggest far more than they actually show and invite the viewer to participate actively in their meaning; they admirably make use of their environment and the palette presented by nature; they are not bound as compositions into the artificial rigours of a canvas, or limited by ideas of up and down or north and south – a cave is a perfect three-dimensional installation. Most of all, the painted caves beautifully combine form, function and meaning, so that even if their exact nature may never be discovered, their art leaves a strong and poignant impression even after thousands of years.

⭐ Grotte de Niaux

open July and Aug Tues–Sun 9–5.45; mid-April–June and Sept 9.45–5; Oct–early Nov and mid-Feb 10.15–4.15; early Nov–mid-Feb 11–4.15; only 20 people (including babies and children) admitted at a time; reservations essential, t 05 61 05 88 37, www.sesta.fr; some visits in English; arrive 15mins before your departure time; the walk in the cave is nearly 2km and somewhat hard, and not advised for anyone who has difficulty walking; bring something warm, as the temperature is a fairly chilly 12°C/54°F

winding road leads up to its spectacular gaping mouth, marked by a 'porch' – a modern metal prow-like structure extending into space over the cliff. Mysterious signs are painted in red and black on the walls near the entrance, reminiscent of the symbols of Joan Miró, and reach a remarkable intensity and complexity at the cave's natural crossroads; they appear to bear some hidden message about the topography, perhaps directing Magdalenian-era visitors to the superb **Salle Noir**, an immensely powerful and poetic composition of charcoal line-drawings, dated at around 10,500 BC. Bison, horses and lively mountain goats are beautifully rendered, a few superimposed over one another but all wonderfully clear, making expert use of the natural contours and formations of the walls. Here is Niaux's famous stag, exquisitely posed, graceful and noble, and a spontaneous finger engraving of a salmon, preserved in the mud. Whether you believe in the traditional school of prehistoric art historians that the Magdalenian artists were motivated by hunting magic, or in Leroi-Gourhan's more recent theories that another kind of ritual language and meaning was communicated through the drawings, the Salle Noir was certainly a sanctuary, where a lost and unfathomable civilization kept its secrets.

Grotte de la Vache

t 05 61 05 95 06, www.grotte-de-la-vache.org; booking is obligatory all year; July and Aug 10–5.30, Sept–June open 2.30–4 in school hols

The people who painted caves such as Niaux never lived in them, whereas just opposite the valley, in the **Grotte de la Vache**, in Alliat, palaeontologists have unearthed a regular Magdalenian hunters' camp – but no paintings. Here the **Salle Monique** stands out, where, 13,000 years ago, pebble walls were built to divide the households, and flint tools and bones from their meals were found. The cave yielded engraved bones, ivory and antlers – movable art, or *art mobilier*, as it's called. Some of it looks like idle scratching; other works seem to have a deeper meaning.

Up the Vallée de Vicdessos

Beyond Niaux and Alliat, the D608 continues up the Vicdessos valley; there are turn-offs for **Miglos**, crowned with a ruined castle, and for **Siguer**, site of a Renaissance house said to have been a hunting lodge of Gaston Fébus. Some fine Romanesque paintings decorate the chapel of **St-Nicolas**, just outside the hamlet of **Gestiès**.

(i) **Auzat**

Maison du Tourisme,
t 05 61 64 87 53,
www.pays-du-
montcalm.com; open all
year Mon–Sat 9–12 and
2–6, plus Sun in July
and Aug

(i) **Tarascon-
sur-Ariège >**

BP 33, Centre
Multimedia, Av des
Pyrénées, t 05 61 05
94 94, www.
paysdetarascon.com;
open summer Mon–Sat
9–1 and 2–6; winter
Mon–Sat 9–1

Market Days around Tarascon-sur-Ariège

Tarascon-sur-Ariège: Wednesday and Saturday.
Vicdessos: Thursday.

Where to Stay and Eat around Tarascon-sur-Ariège

Tarascon-sur-Ariège ✉ 09400

**Hostellerie de la Poste, 16 Av V. Pilhes, t 05 61 05 60 41 (€€–€). A terrace over the river and a restaurant. *Menus €13–35. Restaurant closed Mon lunch and Wed lunch except school hols.*

**Le Confort, 3 Quai A. Sylvestre, t 05 61 05 61 90, *www.paysdetarascon. com* (€). Small and nice, overlooking the Ariège. *Closed Jan.*

Hôtel-Restaurant Le Bellevue, 7 Pl Jean-Jaurès, t 05 61 05 52 06 (€). An adequate small hotel with a decent restaurant, serving local specialities such as *azinat*, Ariège's famous filling cabbage soup. *Menus €15–23.*

Ornolac/Ussat-les-Bains ✉ 09400

**Hôtel Thermal du Parc, t 05 61 02 20 20, *www.thermes-ussat.com* (€). The biggest hotel in Ussat, with a pool. *Menus €14–32. Closed mid-Nov–early Feb.*

Up the Vicdessos ✉ 09220

Hivert, t 05 61 64 88 17, *www. hotelhivert.com* (€). The only hotel in Vicdessos, but it's open all year and has a restaurant. *Menus €12–20. Closed Oct–mid-Nov.*

Relais d'Endron, Goulier (5km from Vicdessos), t 05 61 03 87 72 (€). In an old school building, now part inn, part dormitory. They also serve filling home-cooked meals (€13–25), perfect for tired cross-country skiers. *Closed mid-Oct–mid-Nov.*

Further up, **Vicdessos** is the biggest village in the valley with all of 700 people. Nearby **Sem** has a massive dolmen known as the **Palet de Samson**. It differs from most megalithic monuments; this one was made by Mother Nature, the giant table-top stone deposited atop two other rocks by an ancient glacier. In the summer you can walk around the top of an old iron mine, worked from antiquity until 1929. **Auzat**, at the top of the valley, looks over the 'roof of the Ariège', the Pic de Montcalm (3,077m/10,154ft). The upper valleys of Vicdessos and Auzat are dotted with dry-stone *orrys*, built by shepherds since Neolithic times and used for shelter, cheese-making, storage or even dog houses. The GR 10 weaves between them and a string of lakes that Montcalm and the Andorran range wear like blue brooches across their stony bosoms.

Up the Ariège: Ax-les-Thermes and Around

There are two ways to continue southeast of Tarascon to Ax-les-Thermes. The main valley road, the N20, is often busy with all the extra traffic trundling to and from Spain by way of the duty-free republic of Andorra (*see* p.360). The alternative, the longer, twisting and more scenic D20/D2 or Route des Corniches, follows the upper rim of the valley, beginning 3km north of Tarascon at Bompas.

Getting around Ax-les-Thermes and Environs

The **railway** between Tarascon-sur-Ariège, Ax-les-Thermes and L'Hospitalet is one of the highest in Europe and was a great engineering feat when it opened in 1888. For train information in Hospitalet, ring **t** 05 61 05 20 78.

Tarascon to Ax-les-Thermes

If you do opt for the longer, slower Route des Corniches, the views over the Ariège valley are complemented by the discreet charm of the little Romanesque churches along the way. The first one is in **Verdun** above Les Cabannes, and the next one, at **Axiat**, once belonged to Cluny. Just beyond, the ruined 11th-century **castle** at **Lordat** towers 1,300ft (400m) over the river below; it was one of the largest owned by the Counts of Foix, and after the fall of Montségur the last die-hard Cathars took refuge here. In 1582 Henry IV ordered the castle knocked down, but received the plaintive message from his governor: 'The castle of Lordat is too big to be destroyed', which Henry must have found amusing enough to let the issue slide. Time has since accomplished much of the governor's task. A path leads up from the village to the top of the hill for a huge view. These days Lordat makes its living from its mountain of baby powder, excavated from the **Carrière de Talc de Trimouns**, a huge blinding white scar carved from the Montagne de Tabe, that yields 8 per cent of the world's supply.

Carrière de Talc de Trimouns
t 05 61 64 68 05. open mid-May–Oct Mon–Fri; site closed during bad weather; sunglasses essential; call first

One of the best Romanesque churches in the whole of the Ariège is at **Unac**, another gift from the Counts of Foix to Cluny, with a lovely bell tower, exquisitely chiselled windows in the apse, and fine capitals and friezes inside. Unac also has a donkey farm, **La Ferme aux Anes**, with sweet little beasts ready to carry your children or up to 40kg of supplies on treks of one or several days. Along the main N20, Les Cabannes marks the crossroads to the **Plateau de Beille**, excellent cross-country skiing territory.

La Ferme aux Anes
t 05 61 64 44 22, www.la-ferme-aux-anes.com

Ax-les-Thermes

Nestled in green mountains, Ax has a long history, but unfortunately a long record of fires to go with it. Although commonly presumed to be named for its waters (*aquae*) like Aix-en-Provence and Aix-la-Chapelle, another school of thought derives its name from the Iberian word *ats*, meaning 'stinker', after the pungent smell of its highly sulphurous waters that gush out of the earth at 77°C/170°F. One of the first people since the Romans to exploit Stinker-les-Thermes's medicinal possibilities was St Louis, who in 1260 built a hospital here for his Crusaders who had caught leprosy in the Holy Lands. All that survives is the Bassin des Ladres, in Place du Teich; if the waters didn't heal leprosy, they proved handy for melting the ice off the streets in the winter. As elsewhere in the Pyrenees, the spa is undergoing a revival, specializing in rheumatism and respiratory diseases.

Ax is the best base for exploring the highest mountains of the Ariège; the tourist office has a detailed list of all the walks and *refuges* in the environs, many taking less than a day. There is excellent, exciting skiing up at **Ax-Bonascre**, 8km south on the D820, 2,305m/7,562ft up – some of the pistes are over 3km long – and at the smaller **Ascou-Pailhères**, 13km east.

Around Ax

Northeast of Ax on the D613, **Montaillou** is synonymous with Emmanuel LeRoy Ladurie's now classic study of a 14th-century village. Even after the fall of Montségur (*see* pp.345–9), Catharism continued to exist in pockets, especially in the mountains of the Ariège and Catalunya; in spite of the threat of the Inquisition, there was even a heresy revival in 1300 until 1326, when the last Cathars were all rounded up, burned at the stake, imprisoned, or made to wear a big yellow cross sewn on their backs. Ladurie owed the amazing detail in his *Montaillou: The Promised Land of Error* to the zeal of the head Inquisitor, Jacques Fournier, Bishop of Pamiers, who painstakingly had every word of his inquiries recorded and translated into Latin. Born in 1280 in Saverdun, the incorruptible, ascetic Fournier so distinguished himself for his diligence in catching heretics (and enforcing the new, much resented decrees of tithes paid to the Church), that he was made cardinal and, in 1334, elected Pope Benedict XII. (During his pontificate, Benedict XII amassed so much loot for the papacy that he was believed to have found the priceless 'treasure of the Jews'; he began the building of the great papal palace at Avignon, imported the best Italian painters to decorate it, and still died with a full till.) Only a handful of souls live in Montaillou now, but in the 1970s Ladurie looked through the telephone directory and found the same surnames common 650 years ago.

Refuge
t 05 61 64 61 88

La Maison des Loups
t 05 61 64 02 66,
www.maisondesloups.
com; open July–Aug
daily 10–7; April–June
daily 10–5.30, Sept–Oct
Wed–Sun 11–5

Southeast of Ax, the forests of the **Réserve Naturelle d'Orlu** once fed the big iron forge at Orlu, still rusting under the sharp shadow of the Dent d'Orlu. In 1975 the valley was set aside to increase its herd of izards, until 2010 at least, when it's supposed to reopen to hunters. The best place to see them, as well as marmots, boar and golden eagles, is by the **Etang de Beys**, a lovely mountain lake with a *refuge*; you can make a circuit beginning at the end of the Orlu valley, then return by way of the Etang de Naguilles.

There is also a wolf reserve, **La Maison des Loups**, at Les Forges d'Orlu, with wolves from Europe and Canada, part of the European programme for the breeding and the preservation of endangered species. You can observe the wolves in the wild from specially constructed observatories.

Further east, the D25 from Ax takes you to the thrilling 15km drive up the D22 to the **Col du Pradel** for a tremendous view (1,680m/5,544ft); meanwhile the D25 continues east over the Port de Pailhères pass (2,001m/6,603ft; closed in winter) to the rugged **Donézan**. On the map it looks like a big toe stuck in the *départements* of the Aude and Pyrénées Orientales; in the 19th century, because of its isolation, it tried to secede from the Ariège and join up with Perpignan. **Mijanès** is the prettiest village, and opens up its handful of drag lifts whenever there's enough snow. **Quérigut** is the main village, with its stumpy ruined castle of Donézan, where Cathars held out for a decade after Montségur.

The nearby fierce if crumbling **château at Usson** was built by the Counts of Foix to defend their lands from the king of France; it was the place where the four Cathars from Montségur brought their treasure before vanishing from history. There is now a museum in the stables on the history of Donézan. Note that it is a 15-minute walk up to the castle from the car park.

On the road to Andorra, **Mérens-les-Vals** is named after the small, sure-footed black horses believed to be the direct descendants of the horses painted at Niaux. Further south, **L'Hospitalet**, once the site of a pilgrims' hostel, stands at the southernmost end of the Ariège, at the entrance into Andorra and Spain; the latter has been made much easier to access since the opening of the tunnel of Puymorens in 1994.

Château de Quérigut
www.donezan.com

Château at Usson
t 04 68 20 41 37; open July–mid-Sept daily 10–1 and 3–7; winter and Easter school hols 2–5

---

13 The Ariège, Andorra and the Eastern Pyrenees | Around Ax

Where to Stay and Eat in and around Ax-les-Thermes

ⓘ **Luzenac**
office for the Vallées d'Ax, t 05 61 64 60 60; open all year Mon–Sat 9–12 and 2–6

ⓘ **Ax-les-Thermes >**
La Résidence, 6 Av Théophile Délcassé, t 05 61 64 60 60, www.vallees-ax.com; open mid-June–mid-Sept Mon–Sat 9–12 and 2–7; mid-Sept–mid-June 9–12 and 2–6

★ **L'Orry Le Saquet >**

Unac ✉ 09250
Jean-Claude Berde, t 05 61 64 45 51 (€) runs a bed-and-breakfast in his typical Ariègeois house. *Meals €16.*

Ax-les-Thermes ✉ 09110
*** L'Orry Le Saquet, t 05 61 64 31 30, www.auberge-lorry.com (€€), just south of Ax. Nice rooms, a garden, a terrace, and a fireplace in winter. They also have a refined kitchen that keeps travellers coming back year after year. Inventive cuisine. You can learn some of the chef's secrets on one of their cookery courses, 2 Saturdays a month. *Menus €23–45. Restaurant closed Tues and Wed.*

**Le Grillon, Rue St-Udaut, t 05 61 64 31 64, www.hotel-le-grillon.com (€). Lovely views, a garden and pretty panelled rooms, making it the nicest place to stay in Ax. The restaurant is excellent. *Menus €15–18. Closed mid-April–May and mid-Oct–early Nov.*

L'Auzeraie, Av Delcassé, t 05 61 64 20 70, www.auzeraie.com (€€–€). Central and also good, with a decent restaurant. *Menus €19–38. Closed mid-Nov–mid-Dec and restaurant closed Tues lunch except school hols.*

Le Chalet, Av Turrel, Ax, t 05 61 64 24 31, www.le-chalet.fr (€). Clean, bright bedrooms and a very good restaurant. *Menus €21–44. Closed Sun eve and Mon, exc school hols and mid-Nov–mid-Dec.*

L'Hospitalet ✉ 09390
*Puymorens, t 05 61 05 20 03 (€). A simple choice (*open all year*).

Andorra

The little **Principat de les Valles de Andorra**, as it's officially known, is an independent historical oddity in the style of Grand Fenwick and the Marx Brothers' Fredonia, a little Catalan-speaking island of mountains measuring 468 square kilometres that has managed to steer clear of the French and Spanish since its foundation by Charlemagne. Its name is apparently a legacy of the Moors, derived from the Arabic *Al-gandûra* – 'the wanton woman' – though unfortunately the story behind the name has been forgotten. Andorra has two 'co-princes', the President of France (as the heir of the Count of Foix) and the Bishop of La Seu d'Urgell in Catalunya. According to an agreement spelled out in 1278, in odd-numbered years the French co-prince is sent 1,920 francs, while in even-numbered years the Spanish co-prince receives 900 pesetas, twelve chickens, six hams and twelve cheeses. Napoleon thought it was quaint and left it alone, he said, as a living museum of feudalism.

Being Catalan, the Andorrans were always most adamant about preserving their local privileges, which they did through the **Consell de la Terra**, founded in 1419, one of Europe's oldest continuous parliaments. The citizens also claim to be the only people in the world who have avoided warfare for 800 years (surely a claim for 'small is beautiful'), though there was a close call in 1934, when a White Russian count proclaimed himself King Boris I of Andorra and declared war on the bishop at Seu – a war the bishop ended after two weeks by sending four Guardias Civils, who escorted King Boris to Barcelona and thence out of Spain.

Until the 1940s Andorra remained isolated from the world, relying on dairy-farming, tobacco-growing, printing stamps for collectors, and more than a little smuggling. This peaceful Ruritania began to change with the Spanish Civil War, with an influx of refugees and a new popular sport called 'downhill skiing'. And then came the great revelation: why bother smuggling when you can get the consumer to come to you? For many Andorrans, it was simply too much of a good thing; their traditional society, already swamped by emigrants (32,000 Spaniards, 4,000 French; only 12,000 native Andorrans) all but disappeared under a wave of over 6 million visitors a year, most of whom were only passing through to purchase tax-free petrol, electronics, booze and American smokes, imported tax-free by Philip Morris and Reynolds, who ran the native tobacco-growers out of business. In 1993, Andorra even gave up feudalism and voted for a constitution – although the co-princes still get their cash and cheese.

Outside the summer and peak ski seasons, however, Andorra slows down considerably; even in the summer a stout pair of walking shoes and a reasonable amount of energy can take you far

Getting to Andorra

By air: There is no airport but there is an aero-taxi helicopter that can get you from Toulouse airport to Andorra for a cool €1,800, (*www.hola-andorra.com*).

By train and bus: SNCF trains on the Toulouse–Perpignan–Barcelona line (**t** 05 61 05 20 78, *www.voyages-sncf.com*) get as close as L'Hospitalet, with bus connections the rest of the way (Pas de la Casa is only 12km). Other buses to Andorra depart from Toulouse train station and airport twice a day (**t** 00 376 80 37 89, *www.andorrabybus.com*). The website gives information on times, routes, including to and from Barcelona and Girona, and you can book online. There is a bus from Foix to Pas de la Casa, see *www.saalt.fr*.

away from the congestion, sophisticated sport complexes, high-rise hotels and discos to some breathtaking scenery, a storybook land of green meadows and azure lakes, waterfalls and minute hamlets with stone houses drying tobacco on their south walls, clustered below Romanesque churches, with mountains towering overhead, the silence broken only by the tinkling of cowbells.

Andorra la Vella

Andorra la Vella ('Europe's Highest Capital') and the former villages of **Les Escaldes-Engordany** have melded into a vast arena of conspicuous consuming. Worth a visit, however, is the old stone **Casa de la Vall**, the seat of the Counsell de la Terra since 1580, and home of the famous **Cabinet of the Seven Keys**, containing Andorra's most precious documents, accessible only when representatives from each of the country's seven parishes are present. A folklore museum (*not open to the public*) has been installed on the top floor. You can visit the main hall and kitchen. The latter is where the parish meetings used to take place – the councillors would walk long distances in the cold to come here, and then would warm up by the stove and eat at the table there, discussing parish business. There is also a dovecote, a fountain, ornamental gardens and a monument by Pujol. If there is a session going on you won't be allowed to visit.

Casa de la Vall
*C/ de la Valle,
t (376) 829 129; free guided tours by appt May–Oct Mon 3–6.30, Tues–Sat 9.30–1.30 and 3–6.30; Nov–April Mon–Fri 9.30–1.30 and 3–6.30, Sat 9.30–1.30*

Around Andorra

Andorra is famous for its Romanesque churches and bell towers: a 40-minute walk south of Andorra la Vella will take you to the best one, the 11th-century **Santa Coloma**, with a unique, round bell tower and Visigothic arches. A winding road from Escaldes (or ride on the *telecabina* from Encamp to the north) ascends to the isolated 11th-century **Chapel of Sant Miquel d'Engolasters**. Its fine frescoes, now in the Museu Nacional d'Art de Catalunya in Barcelona, have been replaced by copies, and its three-storey *campanile*, as often in Andorra, totally dwarfs the church. Beyond the chapel lies a forest and the pretty **Lago d'Engolasters** ('lake swallow-stars'), where an old tradition states that all the stars in the universe will one day fall. It's a good place for walking or fishing.

13

The Ariège, Andorra and the Eastern Pyrenees | Andorra

Exploring the hidden corners of old Andorra can be difficult if you're not walking or don't have a car to zigzag up the narrow mountain roads. Buses ply the two main roads through Andorra every couple of hours towards El Serrat, and more frequently towards Soldeu. **La Cortinada**, en route to Soldeu, is a good tranquil base, with only one very reasonably priced hotel, excellent scenery, and some of Andorra's oldest houses. In a 1967 restoration of its parish church, **Sant Martí**, some of the original Romanesque frescoes were uncovered. **El Serrat** is more touristy but worth a visit in the summer for the gorgeous panorama of snow-clad peaks from the **Abarstar de Arcalís** (via the ski resort). Another branch of the road from El Serrat leads to the three stunning mountain lakes of **Tristaina** in Andorra's loveliest and least developed northwestern corner, and site of its finest ski resort, Ordino-Arcalis.

Areny-Plandolit Museum

visits by appt, t (376) 836 908; open July and Aug Tues–Sat 9–8, Sun and hols 10–2

There's also a museum of note in Ordino town, the **Areny-Plandolit Museum**. It is the ancestral home of a long line of local nobility and has three floors; the oldest part of the building dates from 1613.

Another destination reached by bus (on the Soldeu road) is **Meritxell**, the holy shrine of Andorra – an old Romanesque church standing in ruins since a devastating fire in 1972, and next to it, a new sanctuary housing a copy of the 11th-century *Virgen de Meritxell*, designed in 1976 by Barcelona's overrated superstar architect Ricardo Bofill. The Andorrans have their doubts about this gruesome hybrid of their traditional architecture with the modern, which may explain why the principality decided against going ahead with a Bofill-designed ski resort near Andorra la Vella. The lovely 12th-century church **Sant Joan de Caselles** is located on a hillside on the north edge of Canillo (the big village in these parts), its interior adorned with a Gothic retable, painted wooden ceiling, and Romanesque paintings; the bell tower has fine mullioned windows in the Lombard style.

Tourist Information in Andorra

(i) **Andorra la Vella**

C/ Dr. Vilanova, t (376) 82 02 14, www. andorra.com and www.turisme.ad; open summer 9–1 and 3–7, winter 10–1 and 3–7, Sun and hols 10–1 only

(i) **Andorra Delegation**

63 Westover Rd, London SW18, t (020) 8874 4806

The **Syndicat d'Initiative** sells a map of Andorra's camp sites and mountain refuges (*refugios* and *cabanas*). Two trails (*sentiers de grande randonnée*) pass through Andorra: GR 7 and GR 75.

Telephones

If you're dialling an Andorran number from France, dial 00, wait for the tone, and then dial the prefix t 376 and the number.

Entry Formalities

Entry formalities are very simple, though you will find that there are checks at both French and Spanish customs and you may well be stopped twice.

Currency and Shopping

Although **Catalan** is the official language of Andorra, both **French** and **Spanish** are well understood. Local currency is the euro. **Credit cards** are widely accepted in this region. Andorra's agreement with the EU on **customs allowances** has considerably increased the permitted value of goods that can be bought in Andorra and taken back to EU countries; check *www.tourisme-andorre.net* for a clear description of allowances.

Skiing in Andorra

Andorra has abundant snow from December to April, combined with clear, sunny skies – a skier's heaven. It has six major installations. See *www.skiandorra.ad*.

High season, when everywhere is extra busy, includes the following religious holidays: 4–10 December (4–12 in Ordino), 23–7 Jan, 3 Feb–4 Mar, 12–16 April, and weekends.

Pas de la Casa-Grau Roig (2,050–2,600m), just within the border with France, **t** 80 10 60, *http://pas_grau. andorramania.com*. The oldest (1952), with 55 pistes, 28 ski lifts, 427 snow cannons, a slalom course, and several slopes for beginners as well as the advanced, night skiing (floodlit, on the Font Negre run), two medical centres; 31 lifts, six cafés and restaurants and 40 hotels.

Ordino Arcalís (1,940–2,600m), 17km from town and 4km from El Serrat, **t** 85 01 21, *www.vallnord.com*. Served by half-hourly buses from Andorra la Vella. Perhaps the most dramatically beautiful and the best place to ski in Andorra. It has 25 pistes and 12 lifts, a medical centre, eight cafés, restaurants and hotels in Ordino itself.

Soldeu-El Tartar (1,710–2,560m), near Canillo, **t** 85 11 51, for piste condition. The biggest and most popular complex, 850 hectares, with 90km of slopes including 52 runs (some especially for children), 25 lifts, 427 snow cannons, a 2km cross-country course, a surf park, a new snowboard school and snowpark, three medical centres, four cafés and restaurants, 25 hotels and five self-catering apartment blocks. (Soldeu and Pas de la Casa have also joined forces but as they are from two different parishes the join is not as complete as Arinsal-Pal).

Arinsal-Pal, **t** 73 70 00, *www.vallnord. com*. The Arinsal and Pal resorts linked up in the 2000/2001 winter season for the first time. They have joint services and share lift connections, and you can get a combined pass. There's a snow park for snowboarders, 63km of runs, monoskiing, big foot, alpine, snowboarding, heliskiing and 350 snow cannons.

La Rabassa (2,050m), near Sant Julià de Lòria, **t** 32 38 68, *www.larabassa. com*. A cross-country skiing station and features 15km of pistes through meadows and forests, separate pistes for snowmobiles, 3km of runs, 17 snow cannons, 13 lifts, 2km for snow shoes, a children's snow park complete with snow slides, sleds and the like, a sports centre with pool, gym, sauna, etc, and horse-riding. There are rooms, and a café and restaurant at the refuge which is approached by a good road.

Note that Andorra's high altitude and reasonably even terrain make it especially good for ski trekking, or *ski randonnée*, with overnight accommodation in *refuges* around the rim of Andorra.

Other Andorran Sports

There are a number of sports complexes and facilities all over Andorra, providing an inescapable chance for holiday-fitness.

Andorra la Vella

Andorra's **sports complex**, **t** 80 45 60, is used for indoor sporting events and has a shiny multi-purpose court with stands for over 4,000 people.

Mercure health centre, Ctra la Roda, **t** 87 36 02, *http://hotelmercure. andorre.net*, is part of the Mercure hotel but is open to non-residents and offers saunas, swimming pool, gym, solarium, mini-golf, Jacuzzi and, most usefully, pre-ski warm-up programmes and après-ski relaxation.

Serradells swimming pool, Ctra de la Comella, **t** 87 41 00. An Olympic-size pool. This complex has both indoor and outdoor pools, a shallow learning pool, gym, sauna, tennis courts, squash court and a snack bar. *Open all year, Mon–Fri 7–10.45, Sat and Sun 10–9*.

Canillo

Palau de Gel, Ctra General, **t** 80 08 40, *wwww.palaudegel.ad* is a giant skating-rink (*patinaje*): in addition there is a 25m swimming pool, gym, sauna, games room and much more. Would-be skaters can book up for lessons for both ice-hockey and normal/'artistic' skating.

Encamp

Encamp's **sports centre**, t 83 28 30, has the usual facilities (squash, tennis, swimming, gym, etc), plus some surprising ones, such as a library, exhibition hall, table-tennis, billiards, martial arts and dancehall. *Open weekdays 7.30–11pm plus Sat and Sun 9–8.*

La Massana

In nearby Anyós the **sports centre**, t 73 71 73, *www.anyospark.com* includes a shooting gallery, solarium, massage rooms, sunbeds, jacuzzis, Turkish baths and saunas as well as swimming pools, squash and tennis courts. *Open 8am–11pm.*

A few kilometres north in L'Aldosa, the **sports complex**, t 83 72 75, has both indoor and outdoor facilities along with its saunas, Jacuzzis, vertical sunbed. *Open 10am–10pm. Open school hols only.*

Sant Julià de Lòria

La Rabassa Shooting Range, t 84 37 47, *www.santjulia.ad*, is a nice, new outfit with six semi-automatic posts, Olympic and universal pits, an armoured gun room and, comfortingly, a first-aid room. There's also archery and paintball. *Open all year, 10–sunset.*

Escaldes-Engordany

Caldea, an impressive hydrotherapy centre and spa near the centre of town at Parc de la Mola 10, t 80 09 99, *www.caldea.ad*. This is the largest spa centre in southern Europe and perfect for après-ski. A modern, mirrored, pyramidal structure with thermal water facilities (60°C), air baths, indoor and outdoor jacuzzis, hydromassage and many, many more watery things all within luxurious, aquatic surroundings; there is even a chocolate treatment! As expected, the treatments are expensive and you need to book in advance. There are also a number of other facilities that you might not expect at a spa: a shopping centre, restaurant, bars, a cinema, and a nursery for children up to 5 years.

Where to Stay in Andorra

Andorra ✉ 61699

Andorra now has some 300 hotels, the vast majority of them spanking new. The Association of Hoteliers can help (t 80 96 02, *uhotelera@uha.ad*). Also refer to the government website *www.turisme.ad*.

****Roc Blanc**, Plaça de Co-Prínceps 5, Escaldes, t 87 14 00, *www.rocoblanchotels.com* (€€€€€). In terms of glamour, this takes the cake, with a five-storey atrium lobby and a glass elevator, sauna and a thermal spa with a number of treatment programmes offered, including two weeks of magnetotherapy to realign your electrons. The Roc Blanc's two restaurants, *El Pi* and *El Entrecôt*, feature a very good selection of French, Spanish and Catalan dishes. *Menus €25–50.*

****Andorra Park**, 24 C/ de les Canals, Andorra la Vella, t 87 77 77 (€€€€€–€€€€). A charming little palace set in a park with a beautiful rock-cut pool, croquet lawn, driving range and tennis court. Its smart restaurant is one of the best in Andorra, with tasty fresh pasta dishes and excellent Spanish and Chilean wines.

*****Plaza**, María Pla 19, Andorra la Vella, t 87 94 44, *www.plazaandorra.com* (€€€€–€€€). Ultra-contemporary, elegant and classy, if right in the centre of the hubbub. The **Cupula** restaurant has a reasonably priced set menu, with *à la carte* around €50; the pizzeria has pizzas for €7, and there's also a grill.

Crown Plaza Holiday Inn, Prat de la Creu 88, t 87 44 44 (€€€). Well-equipped, with two restaurants and a cafeteria.

****Pitiusa**, C/ d'Emprivat 4, Andorra la Vella, t 86 18 16, *www.hotelpitiusa.com* (€€), is modern and quiet, on the edge of town.

***Marfany**, Av Carlemany 99, Escaldes, t 82 59 57 (€). Long-established and comfortable, though only 24 rooms have baths; the rest come with a shower.

Hostal del Sol, Plaça Guillemó, Andorra la Vella, t 82 37 01 (€). Outside the capital hub there are numerous alternatives, which are especially convenient for skiers.

Eating Out in Andorra

La Borda de l'Avi, on the Arinsal road, t 83 51 54. Typical Andorran meals roasted in front of you on a wood fire, as well as fresh fish, foie gras, *magrets* or snails. *Menus €36–120.*

La Guingueta, on the Rabassa road, in Sant Julià de Lòria, t 84 29 41.

Restaurant offers unexpected dishes like roast dove with foie gras and charcoal-grilled sea bass with home-cured ham in its rustic interior. It specializes in French and Mediter-ranean cuisine. *Menu €50. Closed Sun eve and Mon.*

Versailles, Cap. del Carrer 1, Andorra la Vella, t 82 13 31. *A la carte* only for about €30.

Topic, on the main road in Ordino, t 73 61 02, serves Belgian beer and a selection of fondues alongside. *Pizzas. €10–31.*

The Pyrénées Orientales

The southeastern corner of the Pyrenees, or the Pyrénées Orientales, belong to the old province of Roussillon. You'll notice that some malcontents have decorated the yellow diamond 'priority road' signs with four red stripes, making them into little escutcheons of the long-ago Kingdom of Aragon. On your restaurant table, sweet wines and peculiar desserts will appear, and you may begin to suspect that you are not entirely in France any more.

As in Andorra, you are among the Catalans, in the corner of Catalunya that was destined to become part of France. Like the other captive nations of the Hexagon, most of Roussillon's people have rationally decided that being French isn't so terrible after all. Catalan is spoken by relatively few, and this culturally passionate people stays in close touch with the rest of Catalunya, and in the squares of many villages they still do a weekly *sardana*, the dance and symbol of Catalan solidarity.

Perpignan is the capital; around it stretches the broad Roussillon plain, crowded with the dusty, introverted villages that make all that sweet wine. The city is the best base for trips into the valleys that climb up into the eastern Pyrenees.

There are two important valleys: the **Conflent** (the valley of the River Têt) and the **Vallespir** (of the River Tech), sloping in parallel lines toward the Spanish border. Don't think that this end of the Pyrenees consists of mere foothills; in between the two valleys stands snow-capped **Canigou**, not the highest (a mere 9,134ft/2,784m) but certainly one of the most imposing peaks of the chain, jauntily wearing a cap of snow until late spring. The *muntanya regalada*, 'fortunate mountain' of the Catalans, is one of the symbols of the nation, the subject of one of the best-known Catalan folksongs. Every summer solstice Catalans from both sides of the frontier ceremoniously light a huge bonfire on its summit, the signal for surrounding villages to light their own, all at the exact

Getting around the Pyrénées Orientales

The **coach** and **train** service is probably better here than in any other rural region in this book – only it won't help you see rural monuments like St-Michel or Serrabone. Using Perpignan as a base, it's possible to see quite a bit of the Conflent and Vallespir; from the *gare routière* there are 10 or 12 **buses** a day to Prades and Villefranche-de-Conflent, and a few of these continue on to Font-Romeu and Latour-de-Carol. At Villefranche you can pick up **Le Petit Train Jaune** (see *www.trainstouristiques-ter.com/train_jaune.htm*), a scenic narrow-gauge train that runs twice a day into the Cerdagne, practically unchanged since 1910. One of the most unlikely railways in France, it was entirely a political project, meant to bring some new life into the mountain valleys. It has kept puffing ever since – only tourism has saved it from closing: while checking the schedule make sure you don't choose one of the departures taken over by buses. The last station is Latour-de-Carol, where you can pick up a bus to Andorra and Spain, or a train to Toulouse. For the Vallespir, there are frequent, convenient daily buses to Arles-sur-Tech and Amélie-les-Bains-Palada, with a few pressing on further up the valley to Prats-de-Mollo.

moment. Legends and apparitions abound on Canigou. Fairies and 'ladies of the waters' are said to frequent its slopes, and King Pedro of Aragon climbed it in 1285, and met a dragon near the top.

The Eastern Pyrenees

Perpignan

'PERPIGNAN DEAD CITY' is the slogan the local anarchists write on the walls, and if that's slightly premature, you can't help wondering about a town named after a reactionary murderer, and one that has let its most beautiful Gothic building become a restaurant.

There's a little craziness in every Catalan soul. In *Perpinyà* (as its residents call it), this natural exuberance was rather suppressed by French centralization but as Europe's frontiers melt away, the electricity of Barcelona seems to be again galvanizing it along with the rest of greater Catalunya. Look around at all the new building works. The king of kookiness himself, Salvador Dalí, set off the first sparks when he passed Perpignan's train station in a taxi, and 'it all became clear in a flash: there, right before me, was the centre of the universe!' The otherwise ordinary Gare SNCF has been a hot

Getting to and around Perpignan

By Air

Perpignan's **airport** is 7km northwest of the city and linked by shuttle bus *navettes* from the station an hour before each flight (info from the airport on **t** 04 68 52 60 70). There are connections with Paris Orly on Air France (*www.airfrance.co.uk*), Ryanair has a daily no-frills cheap flight to Perpignan from London Stansted (*www.ryanair.com*), BMIbaby has flights from Manchester (*www.bmibaby.com*) and Flybe goes from Southampton and Birmingham (*www.flybe.com*).

By Train

The train station is at the end of Avenue du Général de Gaulle and has frequent services to the Spanish border at Port Bou and a new TGV that cuts the journey to Paris to 6 hours. An early morning SNCF bus from Perpignan's station links up with the *Le Petit Train Jaune* into the Cerdagne, departing from Villefranche-Vernet-les-Bains; call the tourist office on **t** 04 68 66 30 30 for more information.

By Bus

The *gare routière* is to the north, on Avenue du Général Leclerc, **t** 04 68 35 29 02 (see *www.cg66.fr/ institution/transport/bus/index.html* for information on all bus routes and timetables).

Car and Bike Hire

You can **hire a car** at the airport, or from Europcar, SNCF station, Pl Salvador Dali, **t** 04 68 34 89 80, or Avis, 13 Bd du Conflent, **t** 04 68 34 26 71. **Bike hire** is available at Cycles Mercier, 20 Av Gilbert-Brutus, **t** 04 68 85 02 71.

destination for surrealist pilgrims ever since; the street leading to the station, Av du Général de Gaulle, has undergone a *traitement dalinien*, which includes the installation of benches shaped like Mae West's lips and a Dalinien railway carriage suspended in front of the station.

History

Perpignan is named after Perperna, a lieutenant of the great 1st-century BC populist general, Quintus Sertorius. While Rome was suffering under the dictatorship of Pompey, Sertorius governed most of Spain in accordance with his astonishing principle that one should treat Rome's provinces decently. The enraged Senate sent out five legions to destroy him, but his army, who all swore to die if he were killed, defeated each one until the villainous Perperna invited his boss to a banquet in the Pyrenees and murdered him.

In 1197, Perpignan became the first Catalan city granted a municipal charter, and governed itself by a council elected by the three estates or 'arms'. Its merchants traded as far abroad as Constantinople, and the city enjoyed its most brilliant period in the 13th century when Jaime I, king of Aragon and conqueror of Majorca, created the Kingdom of Majorca and County of Roussillon for his younger son Jaime II. This little kingdom was absorbed by the Catalan kings of Aragon in the 14th century, but continued to prosper until 1463, when Louis XI's army came to claim Perpignan and Roussillon as payment for mercenaries sent to Aragon.

Besieged, the Perpignanais ate rats rather than become French, until the King of Aragon himself ordered them to surrender. In 1493 Charles VIII, more interested in Italian conquests, gave Perpignan back to Spain. But in the 1640s Richelieu pounced on the first available chance to grab back this corner of the mystic Hexagon, and French possession of Roussillon and the Haute Cerdagne was cemented in the 1659 Treaty of the Pyrenees.

Le Castillet

When most of Perpignan's walls were destroyed in 1904, its easy-going river-cum-moat, La Basse, was planted with lawns, flowerbeds, mimosas and Art Nouveau cafés. The fat brick towers and crenellated gate of **Le Castillet** in Place Verdun were left upright, for memories' sake; built in 1368 by Aragon to keep out the French, it became a prison once the French got in, especially during the Revolution. In 1946, a mason broke through a sealed wall in Le Castillet and found the body of a child, which on contact with the air dissolved into dust; from the surviving clothing fragments the corpse was dated to the end of the 18th century. And ever since, people have wondered: could it have been Marie-Antoinette's son, the dauphin Louis XVII? After all, the child buried in the Temple in Paris was known to be a substitute, and there have always been rumours that the Revolutionaries used the Dauphin as a secret bargaining chip in dealing with his Bourbon relatives in Spain.

Along with this mysterious ghost, Le Castillet houses a cosy museum of Catalan art and traditions, the **Casa Pairal**, with items ranging from casts of Pau (Pablo) Casals's hands to a kitchen from a Catalan *mas*, complete with a hole in the door for the Catalan cat. **Place du Verdun**, by Le Castillet, is one of Perpignan's liveliest squares, while just outside the gate, the **Promenade des Platanes** is lined with rows of magnificent plane trees.

Casa Pairal
t 04 68 35 42 05; open May–Sept 10–6.30;Oct–April 11–5.30; closed Tues

Loge de Mer to the Musée Rigaud

From Le Castillet, Rue Louis Blanc leads back to Place de la Loge, where the cafés provide a grandstand for contemplating Aristide Maillol's voluptuous bronze *Venus* and Perpignan's most beautiful building, the Gothic **Loge de Mer**, or **Llotja**, built in 1397 by the king of Aragon to house the exchange and the Consolat de Mar, a branch of the Barcelona council founded by Jaime I to resolve trade and maritime disputes. This proud and noble building of ochre stone, with its Venetian arches and loggia and ship-shaped weathercock, fell on hard times – there's now a restaurant on the ground floor.

The neighbouring 13th-century **Hôtel de Ville** has been spared the Llotja's humiliation, probably because it still serves its original purpose: on Saturday mornings, its courtyard fills with blushing brides posing for photos by Maillol's allegory of the Mediterranean (as a naked woman, of course). The Hôtel de Ville is built of rounded river pebbles and bricks in the curious layer-cake style of medieval Perpignan; three bronze arms sticking out of the façade are said to symbolize Perpignan's three estates, or *bras*.

To the right, the **Palais de la Députation Provinciale** (1447) is a masterpiece of Catalan Renaissance, formerly the seat of Roussillon's parliament and now housing dismal municipal offices. Rue Fabrique d'en Nabot, opposite the palace, was once the street of drapers: note the **Hôtel Julia** (No.2), a rare survival of a 1400s town house, with a Gothic courtyard.

Musée Rigaud
t 04 68 35 43 40; open May–Sept 12–6.30; winter 11–5.30; closed Tues; adm

South of the Députation, in Rue de l'Ange the **Musée Rigaud** is named after Perpignan native Hyacinthe Rigaud (1659–1743), portrait painter to Louis XIV. Hyacinthe, master of raising the mediocre and unworthy to virtuoso heights of rosy-cheeked, debonair charm and sophistication, is well represented, but all the hyper-sensitive alarms, however, are around the *Retable de la Trinité* (1489) by the Master of Canapost, painted for the 100th anniversary of the Consolat de Mar and showing, underneath, a fanciful scene of the sea lapping at the base of the Llotja. Works by Picasso, Dufy, Maillol, Miró and a score of others, are upstairs.

Cathédrale de St-Jean and the Dévôt Christ

Just east of Place de la Loge unfolds Place Gambetta, site of Perpignan's pebble-and-brick cathedral, topped by a lacy 19th-century wrought-iron campanile. Begun in 1324 but not ready for use until 1509, the interior is a success because the builders stuck to the design provided in the 1400s by Guillem Sagrera, architect of the great cathedral of Palma de Majorca. Typical of Catalan Gothic, it has a single nave, 157ft (48m) long, striking for its spacious width rather than its soaring height.

The chapels, wedged between the huge piers, hold some unique treasures, the oldest of which is a mysterious marble **baptismal font** (first chapel on the left). Pre-Romanesque, perhaps even Visigothic in origin, and carved from the drum of a Roman column to look like a tub bound with a cable, it bears a primitive face of Christ over an open book. Further up the left aisle, the massive organ was decorated in the 15th century with painted shutters and sumptuous carvings. On the pendentive under the organ note the **Moor's head** – a common Catalan conceit symbolizing wisdom, taken from the Templars, who exerted a powerful influence over the kings of Aragon. The jaw was originally articulated, to vomit sweetmeats on holidays; now it's stuck, gaping open.

The cathedral is proudest of its exquisite **retables**: on the high altar, the marble *Retable de St-Jean*, carved in a late Renaissance style in 1621 by Claude Perret; at the end of the left crossing, the *Retable des Stes Eulalie et Julie* (1670s); in the apsidal chapels, the painted wood *Retable de St-Pierre* (mid-1500s) and to the right, the lovely, luminous *Notre-Dame de la Magrana* (1500) – its name 'of the pomegranate' comes from an earlier statue of the Virgin, which held a pomegranate, symbolic of fertility.

A door in the right aisle leads out to a 16th-century chapel constructed especially to house an extraordinary wooden sculpture known as the **Dévôt Christ**. Carved in the Cologne region in 1307, this wasted Christ, whose contorted bones, sinews and torn flesh are carved with a rare anatomical realism, is stretched to the limits of agony on the Cross. Almost too painful to behold, it comes straight from the gloomy age when Christendom believed that pain, contemplated or self-inflicted, brought one closer to God.

Nearby in Place Gambetta is the entrance to the cathedral's Campo Santo (1302), the only cloister-cemetery of its kind of France, the tombs decorated with fine bas-reliefs; this being Perpignan, until the late 1980s it was used as offices by the local Gendarmerie. A door from the cloister leads into the striking 15th-century **Salle Capitulaire**, its complex ogival vaulting attributed to Guillem Sagrera. To the left of the cathedral's façade is Perpignan's oldest church, **St-Jean-le-Vieux** (1025), converted into an electrical generating station in 1890. Its Romanesque portal offers a very different view of Jesus from the German *Dévôt Christ*: the imperious and typically Catalan *Majestat* (Christ in Majesty).

Campo Santo
open Oct–Mar
Tues–Sun 11–5;
April–Sept 12–7; closed
July and Aug

Quartier St-Jacques

The piquant neighbourhood south of the cathedral, built on the slopes of Puig des Lépreux (Lepers' Hill) was once the *aljama*, or Jewish quarter of Perpignan. In its happiest days, in the 13th century, it produced a remarkable body of literature – especially from the pen of the mathematician and Talmudic scholar Gerson ben Salomon (author of the philosophical *Gate of Heaven*), as well as rare manuscripts and calligraphy, all now in Paris.

After the Jews were exiled, the quartier was renamed St-Jacques. The 12th–14th-century church of **St-Jacques** is opulent and rich inside: there's a 'Cross of Insults' as in Elne, a statue of St James in Compostela pilgrimage gear (1450) and more fine retables, especially the 15th-century *Notre-Dame de l'Espérance*, featuring a rare view of the pregnant Virgin. In the early 1400s, while the fire-eating Dominican preacher St Vincent Ferrer was in Perpignan to advise in the dispute between Antipope Benedict XIII and Rome, he founded in this church the confraternity of the Holy Blood (*de la Sanch*) to bring religious comfort to prisoners condemned to death. As in Seville, the confraternity reaches a wider audience during Holy Week, when it dons spooky Ku Klux Klan-like hoods and bears a procession of holy floats (the *misteri*) while singers wail dirges from the crowd.

The Palace of the Kings of Majorca

Palais des Rois de Majorque
entrance in Rue des Archers, **t** 04 68 34 48 29; open June–Sept daily 10–6; Oct–May 9–5; adm

Enclosed in a vast extent of walls, originally medieval and later enlarged by Vauban, the **Palais des Rois de Majorque** is the oldest royal palace in France, begun in the 1270s by Jaime the Conqueror and occupied by his son Jaime II after 1283. Yet for all its grandeur, only three kings of Majorca were to reign here before Roussillon, Montpellier, the Cerdagne and the Balearic islands were reabsorbed by Aragon in 1349. A rectangle built around a mastodonic but elegant Romanesque-Gothic courtyard, the palace is now a favourite venue for events, exhibitions and dancing the sardana, the Catalan national dance. The **Salle de Majorque**, or throne room, with its three vast fireplaces, and the double-decker chapels in the **donjon**, with the queen's chapel on the bottom and the king's on top, both offer hints at the exotic splendour of the Majorcan court.

The sacristy was the entrance to a network of underground passageways that connected the palace to its enormous 147ft- (45m) deep wells, which also afforded Jaime II an escape from his fierce and unwelcome older brother, Pedro III of Aragon.

A few traces remain to the right of the mightiest tower, the **Tour de Homage**. The narrow grid of streets around the church of St-Mathieu, were designed by the Templar tutors of Jaime the Conqueror, although most buildings date from the 18th century.

Cabestany

Of all the villages ingested by Greater Perpignan, none is as celebrated as Cabestany (*Cabestanh*), 4km to the southeast. It produced a highly original Romanesque sculptor known as the Master of Cabestany who worked as far afield as Tuscany, and left his hometown church a tympanum of the *Dormition and Assumption of the Virgin*, and a scene of the Virgin in heaven, handing her girdle to St Thomas. Cabestany was also the home of the troubadour Guilhem de Cabestanh, who wrote some of the most popular love poems of the Middle Ages.

(i) **Perpignan >**
Palais des Congrès, Pl Armand-Lanoux, **t** 04 68 66 30 30, www.perpignantourisme.com; open mid-June–mid-Sept Mon–Sat 9–7 plus Sun 10–4; mid-Sept–mid-June Mon–Sat 9–6 plus Sun 10–1

(i) **Cabestany**
www.cabestany.com

Market Days in Perpignan

Tues–Sun in Pl de la République; daily in Pl Cassanyes.

Where to Stay in Perpignan

Perpignan ✉ 66000
****La Villa Duflot**, 109 Av Victor Dalbiez, **t** 04 68 56 67 67, www.villa-duflot.com (€€€€–€€€). Perpignan's only luxury hotel is near the Perpignan-Sud-Argelès motorway exit, in the middle of an industrial zone! However, you can pretend to be elsewhere in the comfortable air-conditioned rooms and garden, or in the popular restaurant overlooking the pool. Menus €31–41. Open all year.

***Hôtel de la Loge**, 1 des Rue Fabriques-Nabot, **t** 04 68 34 41 02, www.hoteldelaloge.fr (€). Nicest in the centre, in a 16th-century building, this has pretty rooms, some with TV and air conditioning, and a lovely inner courtyard. Open all year.

***Le Park**, 18 Bd Jean-Bourrat, near the tourist office, **t** 04 68 35 14 14, *www.parkhotel-fr.com* (€). Plush, air-conditioned, soundproofed rooms with an old Spanish feel and flair. *Open all year.*

****Le Helder**, Av du Général de Gaulle, **t** 04 68 34 38 05 (€). *Open all year.*

***Le Berry**, 6 Av du Gén. de Gaulle, **t** 04 68 34 59 02 (€). *Closed Jan and Feb.*

Auberge de la Jeunesse, Av de Grande-Bretagne, **t** 04 68 34 63 32 (€). A small youth hostel; bed and breakfast €12. *Closed 20 Dec–20 Jan.*

Eating Out in Perpignan

Le Chapon Fin, Park Hôtel (*see* above). This has been Perpignan's finest restaurant for years, as well as one of the prettiest in the area with its Catalan ceramics. But it's the *tartare de saumon* and ravioli stuffed with scallops that keep its clients coming back for more, even all the way from Spain. *Menus €55–100, à la carte €35–45.*

Casa Sansa, 3 Rue Fabriques Couvertes, near Le Castillet, **t** 04 68 34 21 84. Lively, with excellent food in a 14th-century cellar – from Catalan escargots to rabbit with *aïoli* – occasional live music and wine-tasting, and more than its share of Catalan flair (book Fri and Sat nights). *Menus €36. Closed Sun and Mon lunch.*

Les Antiquaires, Pl Desprès, **t** 04 68 34 06 58. This is a local favourite for reliable classic French cooking. *Menus €21–38. Closed Sun eve and Mon plus 1–20 July.*

Les Trois Sœurs, 2 Rue Fontfroide, **t** 04 68 51 22 33. Fashionable trendy restaurant with stylish modern bar and terrace tables on cathedral square. Fine Catalan cooking with an extra dash of invention, like monkfish with *mousserons* (tiny wild mushrooms), sea bass with sesame seeds, lamb with honey and spiced pears. *Menus €20. Closed Sun and Mon lunch.*

Le Vauban, 29 Quai Vauban, **t** 04 68 51 05 10. This restaurant is well situated in the centre of town with a flowery summer terrace. It's a sure bet, and has well-prepared *plats du jour*. *Menus €16–32. Closed Sun and Tues eve, mid-Sept–mid-June.*

Brasserie l'Arago, Place Arago, **t** 04 68 51 81 96. Packed day and night; good food and pizza – not always a strong point locally. *Menus €9–26.*

Les Expéditeurs, 19 Av du Général Leclerc, **t** 04 68 35 15 80. The classic €12 lunch with wine; Catalan cooking and paella. *Menus €12 and à la carte. Open lunchtime only, closed Sun.*

Entertainment and Nightlife in Perpignan

On evenings from June to September in Place de la Castillet, the Perpignanais come to dance sardanas, the national Catalan circle dance. Nightlife is mostly concentrated on students.

Le Zinc, 8 Rue Grand-des-Fabriques, **t** 04 68 35 08 80. Jazz and cocktails; specially animated during the Perpignan Jazz Festival in Oct.

Every year in September, Perpignan is host to Visa pour Image, *www.visapourimage.com*, the annual world festival of photojournalism, with exhibitions from top photographers in venues from churches to shops, all over the city.

Cinemas

Cinema Castillet, 1 Bd Wilson, **t** 08 92 68 01 29.

The Valley of the Conflent

Thuir cellars
t 04 68 53 05 42, www.byrrh.com; tours April–Oct 9–11.45 and 2.30–5.45; July and Aug 10–11.45 and 2–6.45; adm

From Perpignan to Ille-sur-Têt

The fish-filled Têt, before passing through Perpignan, washes a wide plain packed full of vineyards and fat villages. The fattest, Thuir, puts up signs all over Roussillon inviting us over to see the

Castelnou
www.castelnou.com

Cerdagne castle
t 04 68 53 22 91; open most of the year 10–7, July and Aug until 7.30, winter 2–5; weekends only in Jan; adm

Centre d'Art Sacré
t 04 68 84 83 96; open mid-June–Oct Mon–Fri 10–12 and 2–7, Sat and Sun 2–7; Oct–Nov and Feb–mid-June Wed–Mon 2–6; closed Dec and Jan

Orgues
t 04 68 84 13 13; open Nov–Jan 2–5; Feb and Mar 10–12.30 and 2–5.30; April–June and Sept 10–6.30; July and Aug 9.30–8; Oct 10–12.30 and 2–6; adm

Château-Musée
t 04 68 84 55 55

Castle
open mid-June–mid-Sept daily 2–7; mid-Sept–mid-June 2–5.30, closed Tues and Sat

Serrabonne church
t 04 68 84 09 30; open daily 10–6; adm

World's Biggest Barrel, in the cellars of the famous apéritifs Byrrh and Dubonnet – wine mixed with quinine, invented here a little over a century ago. After a few apéritifs, head 6km west for golden-hued **Castelnou**, a perfectly preserved medieval village on winding, pebble-paved lanes and steps under the 10th-century **castle** of the Counts of Cerdagne.

The narrow D48 wiggling west of Castelnou is unabashedly beautiful: if you have a couple of hours to spare, you can circle around to the Prieuré de Serrabonne (*see* below) by way of the D2 to Caixas, Fourques, then on to the D13 for Llauro, and **Prunet-et-Belpuig**, where the ruins of the Château de Belpuig offer a superb view and the 11th-century Chapelle de la Trinité has sculpture by the same school as Serrabonne; in Boule d'Amont just up the road, there's another church from the same century.

At **Ille-sur-Têt**, an attractive old village at the gateway to the mountains, neglected art from the 11th to 19th centuries from churches all over Roussillon has been assembled in a 16th-century hospital, the **Centre d'Art Sacré**, with exhibitions on various themes and periods, changing every six months or so.

The D2 northwest of Ille to Montalba-le-Château takes you very quickly to some surprising scenery: orange eroded 'fairy chimneys' called the **Orgues**, with a ruin of the 12th-century **tower** perched on top, the Pyrenees forming a magnificent backdrop.

The fortified church of **Régleille** (from Ille, take the D2 over the river, and after one kilometre turn right on a little road) looks like a castle at first sight – a typical example of a monastic church, in an area without any castles, that grew into a fortress to protect not only the monks, but the population of the village; Ille was located here before its population drifted to the present site.

Six kilometres north on the D21, in little **Bélesta**, is the **Château-Musée**, which holds the treasure found in a Neolithic tomb in 1983 and the superbly restored **castle**, itself a 13th-century work built by Saint Louis.

Prieuré de Serrabonne

Seeing the finest medieval sculpture in Roussillon requires dedication: even the most direct route (for others, *see* above) requires 13km of hairpin turns on a road where you dread oncoming traffic, starting from the D618 at Bouleternère, just west of Ille, and ending in a lofty, remote, barren spot on the slopes of a mountain called Roque Rouge. The solemn, spare shape and dark schist of Serrabonne's **church** are not promising, making the surprise inside that much the greater. The best efforts of the 12th-century Catalan sculptors were concentrated in the single gallery of the cloister and especially in the *tribune*, in rose marble from Canigou. Perfectly preserved in its isolated setting, this includes a fantastical bestiary, centaurs, a grimacing St Michael, reliefs of the four evangelists and more.

Prades, St-Michel-de-Cuxa and Canigou

Prades is known around the world in connection with the music festival founded in 1951 by Pablo Casals, but few people could place it on a map. Casals, in exile after the Spanish Civil War, spent much of the 1940s and 50s here, in the one safe corner of his beloved Catalunya. From the beginning his festival (late July–early August) attracted many of the world's greatest musicians. Otherwise Prades is a rather typical, stolid Catalan town. There are a couple of things to see: the **Musée Pablo Casals** has a section dedicated to Casals – photos, his piano and pipes, records, letters, etc. At the moment it is in the new Médiathèque but it should be moving to Casals's old residence shortly. The Médiathèque also has space dedicated to locally born artist Martin Vivès (1905–91) who was pally with Picasso, and an exhibition on local prehistoric finds. In the heart of Prades, the church of St-Pierre has a fine Romanesque bell tower with a pyramid crown and inside, an operatic Baroque retable in full 17th-century fig by Catalan chisel virtuoso Joseph Sunyer and an exhibition of church treasures.

Best of all, it's only a few kilometres from Prades up through orchards to **St-Michel-de-Cuxa**, one of the most important monasteries of medieval Catalunya. Even in its reduced, semi-ruined state, the scale is impressive; this was one of the great monastic centres from which medieval Europe was planned and built.

The coming of the French Revolution found St-Michel already in a state of serious decay. Looted and abandoned, the abbey suffered greatly in the last century. One of the two bell towers collapsed, and much of the best sculptural work went 'in exile' as the Catalans put it, carted off to the Cloisters Museum in New York. Now restored, St-Michel is occupied once again by a small community of Benedictine monks from Montserrat, the centre of Catalan spiritualism and nationalism.

While much of the inspiration for early medieval architecture in Languedoc came from north Italy or France, Roussillon was heavily influenced by nearby Spain. Here the obvious Spanish feature is the more-than-semicircular 'Visigothic' arches in the nave. This style, which goes back almost to Roman times, never became too popular in Christian Europe, though the Muslims of Spain adopted it to create the architectural fantasies of Seville and Granada. Other notable features of St-Michel include the massive and extremely elegant **bell tower**, and an unusual circular **crypt**, built in the 11th century under a building that was later demolished. The crypt is covered by toroid barrel-vaulting, with a mushroom-like central column almost unique in medieval architecture. Antonio

Musée Pablo Casals
Médiathèque, t 04 68 96 28 55; open July and Aug Tues–Fri 9–1 and 2–5, Sat 9–1; Sept–June Tues and Thurs 10–12 and 3–7, Wed 10–7, Fri 3–7, Sat 10–1

St-Michel-de-Cuxa
t 04 68 96 15 35, www.cuxa.org; open 9.30–11.50 and 2–6, to 5pm in winter; closed Sun am; adm

13 The Ariège, Andorra and the Eastern Pyrenees | The Valley of the Confent

Gaudí used similar columns in his work in Barcelona – a fascinating piece of Catalan cultural continuity; Gaudí could not have got the idea here, since the crypt was discovered and excavated only in 1937. In the **cloister**, you can see the galleries and capitals that didn't go to Manhattan.

If **Canigou**'s magnetism is working its juju on you, don't resist the call. You can make two-thirds of the climb – 7,053ft/2,150m – by car, on a forest road that begins on the east end of Prades. This leaves you at the **Chalet-Hôtel des Cortalets** *refuge*. From here it's a fairly easy three–four-hour walk to the summit, requiring only a decent pair of walking shoes and windbreaker. There's a second, even more hair-raising forest road up to the *refuge* from the D27, practical only in a four-wheel drive. The Prades tourist office has a list of operators; leave the driving to them.

Chalet-Hôtel des Cortalets
open May–Sept; call t 04 68 96 36 19 to book a bed; bed €14, meals €15

Vernet-les-Bains and St-Martin-du-Canigou

The D27, the narrow road that snakes around the lower slopes of Canigou, is an exceptional drive through the mountain forests, with grand views of the big mountain itself; after St-Michel-de-Cuxa, it meets **Vernet-les-Bains**, a bustling modern spa with most of the accommodation in the area, and hot sulphuric waters that are good for your rheumatism and respiratory problems. Three kilometres further up, **Casteil**, a little wooded resort with a small museum of mountain life and plenty of picnic grounds, is the base for visiting Canigou's other great medieval monument, the abbey of **St-Martin-du-Canigou** – a taxing though lovely 40-minute walk up from the town.

St-Martin-du-Canigou
t 04 68 05 50 03; open Mon–Sat 10–12, Sun 10–12.30; closed Tues Oct–mid-April; call for times of tours; adm

A monkish architect named Sclua designed this complex, begun in the early 11th century by a count of the Cerdagne named Guifred Cabreta. Sclua was a designer ahead of his time; he made his monastery a rustic acropolis, spectacularly sited with views around Canigou and the surrounding peaks, and arranged as a series of courtyards and terraces on different levels. The church, with its immense, fortress-like bell tower, has two levels, an upper church dedicated to St-Martin and a lower crypt for a certain obscure subterranean Virgin Mary: Notre-Dame-sous-Terre. Some good white marble capitals can be seen in the cloister, heavily restored in the early 1900s, and medieval tombs, including Count Guifred's, survive in the upper church. But on the whole St-Martin, damaged by an earthquake in 1428, abandoned after the Revolution, restored between 1952–71 and reinhabited, retains relatively few of its former glories.

To complete the tour of Romanesque Canigou, there is another 11th–12th-century **church** in the village of **Corneilla-de-Conflent**, a former Benedictine priory full of good sculpture. Side roads to the west, in the valley of the Rotja, can take you to several more, including rare 10th-century churches in the tiny villages of **Fuilla** and **Sahorre**. Not all the area's attractions are on Canigou.

Five kilometres northeast of Prades, in the empty, largely forested Pyrenean foothills, **Eus**, 'one of the most beautiful villages in France', is an ambitious place; it also claims to have 'the most sunshine of any *commune* in France'. Spilling down its steep hillside, as you see it from the Têt valley, it makes an elegant composition. The parish church has some elaborate 17th-century polychrome retables. Heading up from Prades in the Castellare valley, on the D14, **Molitg-les-Bains**, on a hill in the forest, has been a spa (specializing in skin disorders) since the *belle époque*, with a suitably grand hotel with a lake, river and lovely gardens open to the public. Beyond Molitg the road climbs up to the Col de Jau, a pass with stunning views, once the border between France and Spain, and a route to the Aude valley. On the way you pass the fortifed village of Mosset, a little haven of artists and potters, where there is a beautifully restored Romanesque chapel, the *capelletta*, in the old village.

Villefranche-de-Conflent

Ramparts
*t 04 68 96 22 96;
open July and Aug daily
10–8.; June and Sept
10–7; Feb and Nov
10.30–12.30 and 2–5;
Mar–May and Oct
10.30–12.30 and 2–6;
Dec 2–5; closed Jan*

Fort Liberia
*t 04 68 96 34 01;
open 9–8
in summer, 10–6 daily
in winter; adm*

Grotte des Canalettes
*t 04 68 05 20 20;
open July and Aug
10.30–5; adm*

Grotte des Grandes Canalettes
*www.grotte-grandes-canalettes.com and
www.3grottes.com;
open April–mid-June
and mid-Sept–Oct 10–6,
mid-June–mid-Sept
10–6.30, Nov–Mar Sun
and hols 2–5; adm*

Some villages have their own ideas for welcoming visitors. This one casually points cannons down at you as you pass along the N116, by way of an invitation to drop in. Villefranche, the most logical place from which to defend the Têt valley, has had a **castle** at least since 1092. In the 17th century it took its present form, as a model Baroque fortress-town, rebuilt and re-fortified by Vauban. Almost nothing has changed since, and Villefranche remains as a fascinating historical record, a sort of stage set of that era. Tours of Vauban's **ramparts** with their walkway built through in the wall are offered and if you have sufficient puff and military curiosity, there's a steep climb up the remarkable 1,000 subterranean rock hewn steps (at the end of Rue St-Pierre) to **Fort Liberia**, another Vauban opus, further fortified by Napoleon III, dominating the valley and long used as a prison where you can 'meet the villainous female prisoners' (don't be alarmed – they're made of wax). There's a bus up from Villefranche's Café Canigou if you're feeling lazy.

A survivor from the pre-Vauban Villefranche, the church of **St-Jacques** is a fine 12th-century building with the familiar capitals from the workshop of St-Michel-de-Cuxa; inside there's another retable by Sunyer and, by the door, note the measures engraved in the stone, used by drapers who had market stalls in the square. Vauban built its walls and tower into his wall to help with the defence. For all its grim purpose, Villefranche is a lovely town. A kilometre up the Vernet road, some of the Pyrenees' most peculiar stalactites await your inspection at the **Grotte des Canalettes** and the **Grotte des Grandes Canalettes**.

ⓘ **Ille-sur-Têt**
Av Pasteur, t 04 68 84 02 62, www.ille-sur-tet.com; open Sept–June Mon–Fri 9–12 and 2–6 (5 on Fri), closed Wed; summerMon–Sat 9–12 and 2–6 plus Sun am

ⓘ **Prades >**
4 Rue des Marchands, t 04 68 05 41 02, www.prades-tourisme.com; open June–Aug 9–12 and 2–6.30, Sept–May 9–12 and 2–5

★ **Jardin d'Aymeric >**

ⓘ **Vernet-les-Bains >>**
6 Pl de la Mairie, t 04 68 05 55 35, www.ot-vernet-les-bains.fr; open June–Sept Mon–Fri 9–12.30 and 2–6.30, Sat 9–12 and 3–6, Sun 10–12.30, Oct–May Mon–Fri 9–12 and 2–6

ⓘ **Villefranche-de-Conflent >>**
Pl de l'Eglise, t 04 68 92 22 96; open July and Aug daily 10–7.30; June and Sept 10–6.30; Oct–May 2–5 plus school hols 10–12 and 2–5; closed Jan

★ **Château de Riell >**

Market Days in the Valley of the Conflent

Ille-sur-Têt: Wednesday and Friday.
Prades: Tuesday.

Where to Stay and Eat in the Valley of the Conflent

Although until recently this area has been a gastronomic desert, prospects are improving, with imaginative treatment of Catalan cuisine and excellent fish and seafood.

Prades ✉ 66500

**Les Glycines, 129 Av Général de Gaulle, t 04 68 96 51 65 (€). Tucked away in a quiet courtyard, with comfortable rooms and a restaurant. *Menu €31. Restaurant only open July and Aug.*

*Hostalrich, 156 Av Général de Gaulle, t 04 68 96 05 38 (€). A big neon sign makes it easy to find the **Hostalrich**, where all rooms have TV and showers and some have balconies from which to observe the throbbing street life below. Avoid the restaurant if you can; the food served is simple to the point of dullness (although there is a wonderful chestnut-shaded garden). **Jardin d'Aymeric**, 3 Av Général de Gaulle, t 04 68 96 53 38. The best bet for stylish regional cooking, though the excess of neon detracts from the atmosphere. *Menus €20–34. Closed Sun eve and Mon; and Wed eve in winter, plus 2 weeks June–early July, 2 weeks in Feb and 1 in Nov.*

L'Hostal de Nogarols, Chem Nogarols, on the way to St-Michel-de-Cuxa, t 04 68 96 24 57. A good stop before music concerts, serving excellent wood-fired pizzas, as well as Catalan classics like *petit gris* snails and rabbit, in an airy dining room or pretty shady garden. *Menus €20–35.*

Molitg-les-Bains ✉ 66500

****Château de Riell, t 04 68 05 04 40 (€€€€€–€€€). Molitg may have only 180 inhabitants, but it can claim Roussillon's top luxury hotel, the sumptuous Relais et Châteaux

Château de Riell. This Baroque folly from the turn of the 19th-century is in a theatrically Baroque setting, perched on a rock with exquisite views of Canigou; it has elegant, luxurious Hollywoodian rooms – a contrast with the medieval oubliettes, which you can visit – and two pools, including one on top of the tower, perhaps the best place in the world to watch the Catalan bonfires go up on the equinox. Lots of extras, and a restaurant worthy of the décor. *Menus €43. Closed Nov–Mar and lunch Mon–Fri.*

Grand Hotel Thermal, t 04 68 05 00 50 (€€€–€€). Less pricey, but almost as splendid, with marble spa rooms, swimming pool and marble terrace, glorious views and also a very good-value restaurant. *Menus €26. Closed Dec–Mar.*

Mas Lluganas, just outside Mosset, t 04 68 05 00 37, www.maslluganas.com (€). Offers rooms and *chambre d'hôte* meals based on its own produce of ducks, guinea fowl, veal and foie gras. The same family also offers inexpensive *chambre d'hôte* accommodation at **La Forge**, a peaceful retreat by the river (t 04 68 05 04 84). *Meals €16.*

Vernet-les-Bains ✉ 66820

***Le Mas Fleuri, 25 Bd Clemenceau (the road up to St-Martin), t 04 68 05 51 94, www.hotellemasfleuri.fr (€€€–€€). At the top of the list, this century-old hotel is set in a pretty park, with a pool; rooms are air-conditioned. A modern annexe for bedrooms has been added. (No restaurant). *Closed Nov–Mar.*

**Princess, Rue Lavandières, t 04 68 05 56 22, www.hotel-princess.com (€€–€). A pleasant Logis de France with a better-than-average restaurant. *Menus €16–31. Closed Dec–mid-Mar.*

Villefranche-de-Conflent ✉ 66500

**Auberge du Cèdre, Domaine Ste-Eulalie, outside the walls, t 04 68 96 05 05 (€). Ten comfortable rooms, an adequate restaurant and two fat, friendly ginger cats in the garden. *Evening meal €21. Closed early Nov–early Dec.*

Auberge St-Paul, Place de l'Eglise, t 04 68 96 30 95, *www.auberge. stpaul.free.fr, http://perso.orange.fr/ auberge.stpaul*. The chef at this lovely restaurant fetches from Canigou the basic ingredients for mountain surprises like *filet mignon de sanglier* (boar) and beef with morel mushrooms. *Menus €20–85. Closed Mon plus Sun eve and Tues early Oct–Easter.*

Au Grill, 81 Rue St-Jean, t 04 68 96 17 65. Solid traditional cuisine. *Menus €17–25. Closed Tues and Wed, and mid-Oct–mid-Nov.*

The Valley of the Cerdagne

The lofty plateau of the Cerdagne (*Cerdanya* in Catalan) was an isolated and effectively independent county in the Middle Ages; from the 10th century its counts gradually extended their power, becoming eventually Counts of Barcelona – the founders of the Catalan nation. In spite of this heritage, the Cerdagne was split between Spain and France in the 1659 Treaty of the Pyrenees. The building of the Little Yellow Train, in 1911, brought the French Cerdagne into the modern world; skiing has made it rather opulent today. And besides skiing, you can see some good Romanesque churches, warm up at the world's largest solar furnace, visit the highest railway station in France – and circumnavigate Spain in less than an hour.

To Mont-Louis and the Capcir

After Villefranche, the main N116 climbs dramatically into the mountains. There are a few possible stop-offs on the way: at **Olette**, you can turn off to explore nearly abandoned old mountain villages like **Nyer** and **Evols**. A bit further up, at **Thuès-entre-Valls**, you can stretch your legs in the beautiful **Gorges de la Carança**, then soak your weary bones in the natural hot-springs jacuzzi at **St-Thomas-les-Bains** at Fontpedrouse, where no matter the weather you can take a dip outside.

Climb, climb, climb and at last you'll reach the gateway to the Cerdagne, **Mont-Louis**, another work of Vauban's and the highest fortress in France (5,250ft/1,600m), named after Louis XIV. The army still resides here, though only to look after a pioneer **solar furnace**, built in 1953 and used, not for generating power, but for melting substances for scientific experiments. A 7km detour up into the mountains will take you to tiny **Planès** and its equally tiny and unique triangular 11th-century church. Like the seven-sided model at Rieux-Minervois, this one has occasioned much speculation; some have claimed it as the centre of a network of ley-lines.

The road to Planès is a dead end, but there are better choices from the big crossroads at Mont-Louis. To the north, D118 carries you to the isolated **plateau of the Capcir**. It's a perfect place to get away from it all – after a road was built into the Capcir in the 19th century, almost the entire population deserted it, tired of

St-Thomas-les-Bains
t 04 68 97 03 13, www.bains-saint-thomas.com; open daily 10–8, till 9 in summer; adm

Solar furnace
t 04 68 04 14 89, www.four-solaire.fr; open for guided visits mid-June–mid-Sept 10–6, mid-Sept, Oct and Feb–mid-June 10–4; adm

scratching a living from land that would only support a few cows. They left behind beautiful pine forests, and a score of little lakes carved out long ago by Pyrenean glaciers. Skiing has brought the Capcir back to life since the 1960s, and the government has transformed the landscape with a number of dams and artificial lakes.

On your way into the Capcir, don't miss the church of **St-Vincent** in **La Llagonne**, only 3km from Mont-Louis. The centuries have left it in peace, with a remarkable collection of medieval art, including an altarpiece and painted baldachin (12th- and 13th-century) and an excellent polychrome Majestat. Further north, Les Angles, Matemale and Formiguères are the main ski centres. **Les Angles** has, as well as some 29 ski pistes, a **Parc Animalier**, a free-range zoo with native fauna of the Pyrenees, both current and past residents, including bears, reindeer, wolves and bison. **Formiguères** (not the ski station, but the village, 4km away) is one of the prettiest and best preserved in the region, hardly changed since the days when the kings of Majorca sojourned here to relieve their asthma. This region is great for hiking. The best parts lie to the west, on the slopes of the 9,580ft/2,921m **Pic Carlit**; there you will find the sources of the Têt and Aude (above the D60, in the Forêt de Barrès).

Parc Animalier
*t 04 68 04 17 20,
www.faune-pyreneenne.com; open daily summer 9–6 and winter 9–5*

Font-Romeu

The western road (D618) will take you through more pine forests to Font-Romeu; along with its new satellite towns, **Super-Bolquère** and **Pyrénées 2000**, this is one of the biggest ski resorts in France. Font-Romeu grew up after 1910, around a now-closed 'Grand Hôtel'; it prospers today partly by its excellent sports facilities, often used for training France's Olympic teams. Stamped from the same mould as every other continental ski resort, it has plenty of fake Alpine chalets, innumerable pizzerias, and 260 snow machines to help out when the weather isn't co-operating. But no other resort has the **World's Largest Solar Furnace**, 'stronger than 10,000 suns!', the successor to the one in Mont-Louis. With its curved mirror, covering an entire side of the nine-storey laboratory building, it reflects the Pyrenees beautifully while helping scientists work out all sorts of high-temperature puzzles. Above the town, the pilgrimage chapel of **Notre-Dame-de-Font-Romeu** has an exuberant altarpiece by Joseph Sunyer and a 12th-century statue of the Virgin. There's also a golf course.

World's Largest Solar Furnace
t 04 68 30 77 86; open daily 10–12 and 2–5.15; adm

Another solar experiment can be seen at **Targasonne** west of Font-Romeu on the D618; this big mirror was built to generate electricity, but hasn't quite worked as well as intended. The glaciers that reshaped the Capcir were busy here too, leaving a strange expanse of granite boulders called the **Chaos**. The Cerdagne is famous for its Romanesque churches and chapels, testimony to the mountain Catalans' prosperity and level of culture even in the very early Middle Ages. One of the best of the churches is **St-André**, at **Angoustrine**, west of Targasonne, with fragments of 13th-century frescoes representing the months of the year. To the west, **Dorres** is a lofty *village perché* with another church, this one from the 11th century, with another Romanesque Virgin inside and a chance to soak in a granite **hot tub** with a sulphurous pong.

Hot tub at Dorres
t 04 68 04 66 87;
open daily 9–6

The Vallée du Carol

From the village of **Ur** (with yet another richly decorated Romanesque church), you can make a northern detour into the Vallée du Carol, the western edge of Roussillon. **Latour-de-Carol** is a romantic name for another great border rail-crossing most of us have blinked at in the dark; the name does not come from Charlemagne, as most people think, but the Carol river. Latour's church has more work by Joseph Sunyer. The best church in the area, however, is the Chapelle St-Fructueux in the minuscule village of **Yravals**, above Latour-de-Carol – with a wealth of medieval art inside, and a magnificent mid-14th-century altarpiece of St Martha. Further up this scenic valley, you'll pass the tower of the ruined 14th-century castle that gives Latour its name. The trees give out as the tortuous road climbs to the pass of Puymorens. From here, if you have a sudden hankering for some tax-free Havanas, or a new phonograph, it's only 40km to the Pyrenean Ruritania, the Principality of Andorra (*see* p.360).

Llivia, Llo and Eyne

Bourg-Madame, 'the same latitude as Rome, but sunnier' as its brochure claims, is the crossing point for Spain; just across the border lies **Puigcerdà**, with a 14th-century church and the best ice-hockey squad on the Iberian peninsula. The N116 will take you northeast from here, back to Mont-Louis, completing your circumnavigation of Spain – or at least the tiny Spanish enclave of **Llivia**, left marooned by accident in the Treaty of 1659. The treaty stipulated that Spain must give up the villages of the Cerdagne, and everyone had forgotten that Llivia had the legal status of a *ville*; it had been a Roman *municipium*, the capital of the Cerdagne in ancient times. Llivia's historic centre is clustered around a 15th-century fortified **church**; opposite, in the **Musée Municipal**, the unlikely attraction is a 16th-century pharmacy, one of the oldest and best-preserved in Europe.

Musée Municipal
open Tues–Sat 10–1
and 4–7, Sun 10–2

East of Bourg-Madame, more Catalan Romanesque churches can be visited: at **Hix**, an impressive edifice of 1177, built when the town was the residence of the counts of the Cerdagne, and containing a majestic Romanesque Virgin, with a little kingly Christ child on her lap, and at **Caldégas**, where the frescoes include a hunting scene with falcons. Further east, along the N116, road signs will startle you with town names like Llo and Err; linguists say they're Basque, evidence that the Basques lived here in remote times. **Llo** has a church with a lovely sculptured portal and an exceptionally sweet cemetery in nearby **Ste-Léocadie** (home of the highest vineyard in Europe). You can visit the **Musée de Cerdagne** in a 17th-century farm, dedicated to the pre-ski trades of the great plateau – shepherding and farming. There are opportunities for hiking, southwards into the narrow **Gorges du Sègre**. Even better, come to nearby **Eyne** in May, late enough to avoid the skiers from the resort called Eyne 2600, and just in time for spectacular wild flowers and medicinal herbs in the Vallée d'Eyne, climbing up to the Spanish border. Contact the **Réserve Naturelle d'Eyne** for day or half-day guided tours in July and August through the Réserve as well and a **Balade Archéologique** to the village's menhirs and dolmens.

Musée de Cerdagne
t 04 68 04 08 05; open July–Sept, guided tours 10, 11.30, 2.30, 4 and 5.30

Réserve Naturelle d'Eyne
t 04 68 04 77 07

ⓘ **Les Angles**
2 Av de l'Aude, t 04 68 04 32 76, www.les-angles.com; open all year daily 9–7

ⓘ **Bourg-Madame**
Pl de Catalagne, t 04 68 04 55 35; open July and Aug daily 9–8; winter 9–12 and 2–6

★ **La Vieille Maison Cerdane >>**

ⓘ **Mont-Louis >**
Rue Lieutenant Pruneta, t 04 68 04 21 97, www.mont-louis.net; open July and Aug daily 10–12 and 2–6; Sept–June 10–12 and 2–5, closed Sun

ⓘ **Font-Romeu >**
38 Av E.-Brousse, t 04 68 30 68 30, www.font-romeu.fr; open daily 9–12 and 2–6; summer and school hols 8.30–7

Market Day in the Valley of the Cerdagne

Puigcerdà: Sunday morning, the best market in the area.

Where to Stay and Eat in the Valley of the Cerdagne

Olette ✉ 66360

La Fontaine, 3 Rue de la Fusterie, t 04 68 97 03 67, www.hotelrestaurant-lafontaine.com (€€). Sweet little hotel in a mountain village on the route to Font Romeu, with pleasant rooms and hearty meals. *Menus €12–45. Closed Tues eve, Wed lunch and Jan.*

Mont-Louis ✉ 66210

**Le Clos Cerdan, t 04 68 04 23 29, www.lecloscerdan.com (€€). Get a room with a view at this grey stone hotel on a cliff overlooking the valley; modern but comfortable. *Menu €14–22. Closed early Nov–mid-Dec.*

Lou Roubállou, Rue des Ecoles-Laïques, t 04 68 04 23 26 (€). In the village, by the ramparts, the family-run Lou Roubállou operates now only as a *chambre d'hôte*.

Font-Romeu ✉ 66120

**Clair Soleil, Rte Odeillo, t 04 68 30 13 65, www.hotel-clair-soleil.com (€). With a view, pool and restaurant. *Menus €20–32. Closed mid-Oct–mid-Dec and mid-April–mid-May.*

Cal Xandera, Angoustrine, 8km away, t 04 68 04 61 67, www.calxandera.com (€). Completely different – a beautifully restored 18th-century farmhouse serving traditional mountain cuisine, with *gîtes d'étape* (dormitory accommodation). *Menu €17. Open all year if booked ahead.*

Llo and Saillagouse ✉ 66800

***L'Atalaya, Llo, t 04 68 04 70 04 (€€€). A rare example of a country inn unconcerned with the skiing business; tranquillity is assured, close to the wild flowers of the Vallée d'Eyne, with a pool and an excellent restaurant. *Menus €31–35. Closed Nov–20 Dec and mid-Jan–Mar.*

**La Vieille Maison Cerdane, Pl des Comtes-de-Cerdagne, Saillagouse, t 04 68 04 72 08 (€). This restaurant has been going since 1895; the dining room, with its huge fireplace, is a great place to settle down to a plate of Catalan anchovies. *Menus €22–44. Closed early Nov–mid-Dec and 2 weeks in Mar.*

Planotel, Rue de la Poste, t 04 68 04 72 08, www.planotel.fr (€). Run by the same family that runs **La Vieille Maison Cerdane**. *Open June–Sept and school hols.*

Valcebollère ✉ 66340

Les Ecureuils, t 04 68 04 52 03 (€€€–€). Friendly mountain *auberge* offering charming rooms and well-cooked local produce. Guided mountain walks. *Menus €19–52. Closed early Nov–early Dec.*

The Valley of the Vallespir

The valley of the Tech, the southernmost valley of Roussillon, and of France, winds a lonesome trail around the southern slopes of Canigou. Known for its mineral waters since Roman times, it traditionally made its living from these and from ironworking, the basis of Catalan prosperity in the Middle Ages. When the iron gave out, there was smuggling. Today, as smugglers have become superfluous, the Vallespir lives by tourism, with some income on the side from cherries and cork oak.

Le Boulou and St-Martin-de-Fenollar

From Perpignan, you reach the Vallespir by the A9, getting off at **Le Boulou**, a truck-stop known to every European TIR jockey. The ancient Roman teamsters knew it too. Le Boulou has been fated by geography as an eternal transit point; just coincidentally it has a fine Romanesque church with a superb white marble tympanum sculpted by the Master of Cabestany, portraying the *Resurrection of the Virgin*. The cornice shows scenes of the Nativity, the Christ Child's first bath (also rarely depicted in art), the *Shepherds, Magi* and *Flight into Egypt*. There's also a casino here. East of Le Boulou, **St-Génis-des-Fontaines** was one of the important early medieval monasteries of Roussillon. Its church has a remarkable carved lintel dated 1020, with a *Majestat* and stylized apostles shaped like bowling-pins; the cloister was dismantled and sold off in 1924, one of the final scandals of France's traditional lack of concern for its medieval heritage. In 1988 it was rebuilt as it was, with originals and copies. At the neighbouring village of St-André there's a 12th-century Romanesque Church and the **Musée Transfrontalier d'Art Roman** with reproductions of sculpture from the abbey.

The A9 and N9 continue south into Spain, passing **St-Martin-de-Fenollar** and its 9th-century **church**, with some of the most unusual and best-preserved 12th-century frescoes in the Midi. Nine-tenths of all early medieval painting is lost to us, and this is a rare example of the best of what is left: brilliant colours and a confident stylization, with an imagery untroubled by the dogma of later religious painting, as in the *Nativity*, where Mary lies not in a stable but in a comfortable bed under a chequered baldachin. **Maureillas-las-Illas** is also known for its **cork museum** – you often see cork oaks along the roadside here, partially stripped.

Hannibal entered Gaul through **Le Perthus**, the last, or first stop in France. As a fitting bookend to this long volume, archaeologists have recently uncovered, at Panisars, a monumental pedestal, identified as belonging to the **Trophée de Pompée**. This monument was erected by a victorious Pompey in 71 BC on the Gallo-Hispanic frontier. Part of the stone was used to build a priory in 1011 (the

St-Génis-des-Fontaines
t 04 68 89 84 33; open May–Sept daily 10–12 and 3–7, Oct–May Mon–Fri 9.30–12 and 2–5

Musée Transfrontalier d'Art Roman
t 04 68 89 04 85, www.saint-andre66.fr, open mid-June–mid-Sept 10–12 and 2.30–7, closed Mon; otherwise 10–12 and 3–6, closed mid-Nov–mid-Mar

Church of St-Martin-de-Fenollar
t 04 68 87 73 82; open mid-June–mid-Sept Tues–Sun 10.30–12 and 3.30–7; mid-Sept–mid-June, Wed–Sun 2–5; adm

Cork museum
t 04 68 83 48 00; open Wed–Mon

13

The Ariège, Andorra and the Eastern Pyrenees | The Valley of the Vallespir

Fort de Bellegarde
*t 04 68 83 60 15;
open June–Sept
10.30–6.30; adm*

**Musée d'Art
Moderne**
*8 Bd du Maréchal
Joffre, t 04 68 87 27 76;
www.musee-ceret.com;
open mid-June–mid-
Sept daily 10–7; mid-
Sept–mid-June 10–6;
closed Tues from
Oct–April; adm*

**Maison de
l'Archéologie in
the Tour Port
d'Espagne**
*t 04 68 87 31 59; open
July and Aug daily 10–12
and 1–6; Sept–June
Mon–Fri 10–12 and 2–5*

Musée de la Poste
*t 04 68 39 34 90;
open May–Sept Tues–Fri
10–12 and 2–6.30, Mon
and Sat 2–6.30; mid-
Feb–April and Oct–mid-
Dec Tues–Fri 10–12 and
2–5.30, Mon and Sat
2–5.30; adm*

ruins are nearby); the rest was quarried by Vauban in the 17th century to build the **Fort de Bellegarde**.

Céret: the 'Mecca of Cubism'

Back in the valley of the Tech, the D115 streaks from Le Boulou to Céret, centre of the optimal cherry-growing region suspended between the Pyrenees and the sea. Amid the orchards, Céret is a laid-back town under enormous plane trees, with perfect little squares (especially the **Plaça dels Nous Raigs**), medieval gates, the biggest Baroque church in Roussillon, **St-Pierre**, a war memorial by Maillol and an elegant 14th-century **bridge** over the Tech.

Have a look around Céret before visiting the **Musée d'Art Moderne** and you'll be surprised at how many scenes you'll recognize. Céret found its artistic destiny at the turn of the 19th century, thanks to Picasso, Braque, Gris, Manolo, Matisse, Soutine, Kisling, Masson, Tzara, Lhote, Marquet and others who spent time here up until 1940, and whose works fill the rooms. Best of all are the works donated by Picasso in 1953, among them 28 little plates painted in a five-day spurt of energy, all with variations on the *corrida* under a blasting sun. Although not as dazzling, the **Maison de l'Archéologie in the Tour Port d'Espagne** has well-arranged Neolithic, classical and medieval finds from the Vallespir.

Amélie-les-Bains and Arles-sur-Tech

Sulphurous waters, good for your rheumatism, have been the fortune of **Amélie-les-Bains** since ancient times; a Roman swimming pool with a vaulted roof has been uncovered, and the spa, rising on either side of the River Tech, still does a grandstand business. Amélie's pretty medieval ancestor, **Palalda**, is piled on a nearby hill, and offers a small **Musée de la Poste** for snail-mail nostalgia from the days of Louis XI to 1900; there's a collection of stamps, and telephones, too.

Just west, **Arles-sur-Tech**, the ancient capital of the Vallespir, is a curious village built on a maze of lanes. It offers some even more curious hagiography in its 11th- and 12th-century church of Ste-Marie, originally the centre of an important monastery. Dark Age Arles-sur-Tech got by with an anonymous saint – an empty 4th-century sarcophagus known as *Sainte-Tombe* – until the dreaded *simiots* came to town, ape-like monsters that trampled the crops and violated the women. In despair, the abbot went to the pope asking for some holy relics. This was in 957, when demand for saints' bones was at its peak, and the best the pope could offer was a pair of Persian martyrs named Abdon and Sennen. The abbot brought them back in a false-bottomed water-barrel, to fool the Venetians and Germans and any other relic thieves, and they dealt with the *simiots* as efficiently as if they had been the bones of

St Peter himself. The story is portrayed in a 17th-century retable, in the chapel where the relics are kept. The *Sainte-Tombe* itself, once a major pilgrimage attraction, is kept in a little enclosure outside the front door. It fills continually with perfectly pure water – some 500 to 600 litres a year, ceremoniously pumped every 30 July.

Arles-sur-Tech is the home of Tissages Catalans, where they've been making cloth since 1900: you will find a little **museum** on Rue des Usines; and it was the last redoubt of the valley's famous medieval iron industry; the last working mine in Roussillon, up at Batère, closed in the early 1990s. There's an iron museum with rocks and minerals; call the tourist office for times. Two kilometres northwest along the D44 you can go through the World's Narrowest Gorge, the **Gorges de la Fou**, a giant crack in the rock with sides towering 650ft (200m), with waterfalls and caves along the mile-long walkway.

Continuing up the valley, just south of the D115, the hill-top village of **Serralongue** has a church dating from 1018, with a fine portal and one of the only surviving examples of a Catalan *conjurador*; this is a small, square pavilion with a slate roof and statues of the four Evangelists facing the four cardinal directions. When a storm threatened, the priest would go up to the *conjurador* and perform certain rites facing the direction of the storm to avert its wrath.

A detour further south, on the D3, will uncover **St-Laurent-de-Cerdans**, famous for making espadrilles, and **Coustouges**, which has a lovely early 12th-century fortified church with a slate roof and two carved portals, one inside the other.

Some towns just ask for it. As if having a name like **Prats-de-Mollo** wasn't enough, this tiny spa advertises itself as the 'European Capital of Urinary Infections'. The baths are really at **La Preste**, 8km up in the mountains; Prats-de-Mollo itself is an attractive old village. Don't miss the whale bone stuck in the church wall. This is as far as we go; the Spanish border is 14km away.

Arles-sur-Tech museum
t 04 68 39 10 07; open April–Oct Mon–Fri 10–12 and 2.30–5.30, July and Aug Mon–Fri 10–12 and 2.30–5.30, Sat 2–5.30

Gorges de la Fou
t 04 68 39 16 21; open April–Nov daily 10–6

13

The Ariège, Andorra and the Eastern Pyrenees | The Valley of the Vallespir

Market Days in the Valley of the Vallespir

Céret: Saturday.
Arles-sur-Tech: Wednesday.

Where to Stay and Eat in the Valley of the Vallespir

Céret ✉ 66400
Le Mas Trilles, Pont de Reynes, on the Céret–Amélie-les-Bains road, t 04 68 87 38 37, www.le-mas-trilles.com (€€€€–€€€). A tastefully renovated *mas* with a heated pool and a charming garden overlooking a trout stream. No restaurant but they can provide light meals. *Closed Oct–April.*

****Terrasse au Soleil, Rte Fontfrède, t 04 68 87 01 94, www.la-terrace-au-soleil.com (€€€). A restored, modernized *mas* on a hill above Céret, with a view, a heated pool and tennis court (a bit dear, especially on full board). Restaurant **Cerisaie** has menus from €31 and there's also a brasserie in summer. *Closed Dec–Feb.*

⭐ **Terrasse au Soleil >>**

ⓘ **Céret >**
Av Clemenceau, t 04 68 87 00 53, www.ot-ceret.fr; open all year Mon–Sat 9–12 and 2–6

ⓘ Prats-de-Mollo

Pl le Foiral, t 04 68 39 70 83, www. pratsdemollolapreste. com; open Mon–Sat 9–12 and 2–6

ⓘ Arles-sur-Tech >>

mairie, t 04 68 39 11 99, www.tourisme-haut-vallespir.com; open Mon–Sat 9–12 and 2–6, Sun 2–5

**Les Arcades, 1 Pl Picasso, t 04 68 87 12 30, *www.hotel-arcades-ceret.com* (€). Artistically decorated, with balconies overlooking the market square and the old town walls. You can hire rooms with a kitchenette by the week in July and Aug (€360). *Open all year.*

*Vidal, 4 Pl du 4 Septembre, t 04 68 87 00 85 (€). In a charming, if quirky, listed building. There's a restaurant. *Menus €15–33. Open all year.*

Les Feuillants, 1 Bd Lafayette, t 04 68 87 37 88. Catalan cooking with *haute cuisine* ambitions and modern art on the walls. *Menus €25–55. Closed Sun and Mon.*

Le Pied dans le Plat, Pl des 9 Jets, t 04 68 87 17 65. For something a tad simpler, with tables out in the pretty square. *Menus €10–16. Closed Sun.*

Amélie-les-Bains ✉ 66110

**Castel Emeraude, Rte de la Corniche, t 04 68 39 02 83, *www. lecastelemeraude.com* (€€–€). This is the place to get away from it all: a big white manor on the banks of the river, with a good restaurant. *Menus €17–36. Closed mid-Nov–mid-Mar.*

Arles-sur-Tech ✉ 66150

Les Glycines, Rue Jeu de Paume, t 04 68 39 10 09 (€). Named for the ancient wisteria that shades the garden terrace, **Les Glycines has modernized rooms and a wonderful restaurant where the chef defies every snide remark we've made about Catalan cuisine with the best menu for miles: try his aubergine *tian* and delectable *panaché* of Mediterranean fish; lunch is cheaper. *Menus €15–28. Closed mid-Nov–mid-Feb.*

Language

In France a certain level of politeness is expected: use *monsieur*, *madame* or *mademoiselle* when speaking to everyone (and never *garçon* in restaurants!). *See* Food and Drink, pp.43–52, for a menu vocabulary.

Pronunciation

Vowels

a, à, â between a in 'bat' and 'part'
é, er, ez at end of word as a in 'plate'
   but a bit shorter
e at end of word not pronounced
e at end of syllable or in one-syllable word
   pronounced weakly, like er in 'mother'
i as ee in 'bee'
o as o in 'pot'
ô as o in 'go'
u, û between oo in 'boot' and ee in 'bee'

Vowel Combinations

ai as a in 'plate'
aî as e in 'bet'
ail as i in 'kite'
au, eau as o in 'go'
ei as e in 'bet'
eu, œu as er in 'mother'
oi between wa in 'swam' and u in 'swum'
oy as 'why'
ui as wee in 'twee'

Nasal Vowels

Vowels followed by an n or an m have a nasal sound.
an, en as o in 'pot' + nasal sound
ain, ein, in as a in 'bat' + nasal sound
on as aw in 'paw' + nasal sound
un as u in 'nut' + nasal sound

Consonants

Many French consonants are pronounced as in English, but there are some exceptions:

c followed by e, i or y and **ç** as s in 'sit'
c followed by a, o or u as c in 'cat'
g followed by e, i or y as s in 'pleasure'
gn as ni in 'opinion'
j as s in 'pleasure'
ll as y in 'yes'
qu as k in 'kite'
s between vowels as z in 'zebra'
s otherwise as s in 'sit'
c followed by e, i or y and **ç** as s in 'sit'
w except in English words as v in 'vest'
x at end of word as s in 'sit'
x otherwise as x in 'six'

Stress

The stress usually falls on the last syllable except when the word ends with an unaccented **e**.

Useful Words and Phrases

General

hello/good evening *bonjour/bonsoir*
goodbye/goodnight *au revoir/bonne nuit*
yes/no *oui/non*
good/bad *bon (bonne)/ mauvais(e)*
please/thank you *s'il vous plaît/merci*
excuse me *pardon, excusez-moi*
Can you help me? *Pourriez-vous m'aider?*
My name is... *Je m'appelle...*
How are you? *Comment allez-vous?*
Fine *Ça va bien*
I don't understand *Je ne comprends pas*
I don't know *Je ne sais pas*
Speak more slowly *Pourriez-vous parler plus lentement?*
Help! *Au secours!*
Where is (the railway station)? *Où se trouve (la gare)?*
Is it far? *C'est loin?*
left/right *à gauche/à droite*
straight on *tout droit*
entrance/exit *l'entrée/la sortie*

open/closed *ouvert/fermé*
WC *les toilettes*
men's/ladies *hommes/dames* or *femmes*
doctor *le médecin*
hospital *un hôpital*
emergency room *la salle des urgences*
police station *le commissariat de police*
How much is it? *C'est combien?*
Do you have...? *Est-ce que vous avez...?*
It's too expensive *C'est trop cher*
bank *une banque*
money *l'argent*
change *la monnaie*
post office *la poste*
stamp *un timbre*
shop *un magasin*
central food market *les halles*
tobacconist *un tabac*
pharmacy *la pharmacie*
aspirin *l'aspirine*
insect repellent *l'anti-insecte*
sun cream *la crème solaire*
tampons *les tampons hygiéniques*

Transport

airport *l'aéroport*
aeroplane *l'avion*
bicycle *la bicyclette/le vélo*
mountainbike *vélo tout terrain, VTT*
bus/bus stop *l'autobus/l'arrêt d'autobus*
coach station *la gare routière*
railway station *la gare*
train *le train*
date-stamp machine *le composteur*
left-luggage locker *la consigne automatique*
car/taxi *la voiture/le taxi*
subway *le métro*
ticket/ticket office *le billet/le guichet*
single to... *un aller* (or *aller simple*) *pour...*
return to... *un aller et retour pour...*
What time does the ... leave?
   A quelle heure part...?

Accommodation

single room *une chambre pour une personne*
twin room *une chambre à deux lits*
double room *une chambre pour*
   deux personnes
bed *un lit*
blanket *une couverture*
cot (child's bed) *un lit d'enfant*
pillow *un oreiller*

soap *du savon*
towel *une serviette*
booking *une réservation*
I would like to book a room
   Je voudrais réserver une chambre

Months

January/February *janvier/février*
March/April *mars/avril*
May/June *mai/juin*
July/August *juillet/août*
September/October *septembre/octobre*
November/December *novembre/décembre*

Days

Monday/Tuesday *lundi/mardi*
Wednesday/Thursday *mercredi/jeudi*
Friday/Saturday *vendredi/samedi*
Sunday *dimanche*

Numbers

one/two/three *un/deux/trois*
four/five/six *quatre/cinq/six*
seven/eight/nine *sept/huit/neuf*
ten/eleven/twelve *dix/onze/douze*
thirteen/fourteen *treize/quatorze*
fifteen/sixteen *quinze/seize*
seventeen/eighteen *dix-sept/dix-huit*
nineteen/twenty *dix-neuf/vingt*
twenty-one *vingt et un*
twenty-two *vingt-deux*
thirty/forty *trente/quarante*
fifty/sixty *cinquante/soixante*
seventy *soixante-dix*
seventy-one *soixante-onze*
eighty *quatre-vingts*
eighty-one *quatre-vingt-un*
ninety *quatre-vingt-dix*
hundred/two hundred *cent/deux cents*
thousand *mille*

Time

What time is it? *Quelle heure est-il?*
month/week *un mois/une semaine*
day *un jour/une journée*
morning/afternoon *le matin/l'après-midi*
evening/night *le soir/la nuit*
today *aujourd'hui*
yesterday/tomorrow *hier/demain*
day before yesterday *avant-hier*
day after tomorrow *après-demain*

Glossary

abbaye abbey

arrondissement city district

auberge inn

aven natural well

bastide fortified new town founded in the Middle Ages, usually rectangular, with a grid of streets and an arcaded central square, or sometimes circular in plan

cardo a north–south street in a Roman *castrum*; a street running east–west was called a *decumanus*

castelnau village, often planned, that grew up around a *seigneur*'s castle (often the parish church will be on the edge of a *castelnau* instead of at its centre)

castrum rectangular Roman army camp, which often grew into a permanent settlement

cave cellar

château mansion, manor house or castle. A strictly military castle is a *château fort*

chemin path

chevet eastern end of a church, including the apse

clocher-mur west front of a church that rises high above the roofline for its entire width to make a bell tower; a common feature in medieval architecture in many parts of southwest France

cloître cloister

commanderie local headquarters of a knightly order (such as the Templars or Knights Hospitaller), usually to look after the order's lands and properties in an area

commune in the Middle Ages, the government of a free town or city; today, the smallest unit of local government, encompassing a town or village

cornière arched portico surrounding the main square of a *bastide*

cour d'honneur principal courtyard of a palace or large *hôtel*

couvent convent or monastery

Croquant 'teeth grinder', a peasant guerrilla in the anti-French revolts of the 17th and 18th centuries

écluse canal lock

église church

enfeu niche in a church's exterior or interior wall for a tomb

étang lake

fontaine source

gare station

gave river

gisant sculpted prone effigy on a tomb

halles covered market

hôtel (particulier) originally the town residence of the nobility; by the 18th century the word became more generally used for any large, private residence

lauze heavy grey stones used for making steep roofs, now mostly replaced by machine-made tiles; the rare *lauze* roofer these days manages to do about a square metre a day

lavoir communal fountain, usually covered, for the washing of clothes

mairie town hall

marché market

mas (from Latin *mansio*) large farmhouse, or manor, or hamlet

mascaron ornamental mask, usually carved on the keystone of an arch

modillon stone projecting from the cornice of a church, carved with a face or an animal figure

neste river

oppidum Roman town

orry small dry-stone building with a corbelled dome or vault for a roof; many were built as shepherds' huts, others as refuges for villagers in plague times, also called *bories, gariotes, caselles* or *cabannes* in different parts of the Midi

Parlement French juridical body, with members appointed by the king; by the late *ancien régime, parlements* exercised a great deal of influence over political affairs

pays region, or village

pech hill

plan d'eau artificial lake

port mountain pass

puy hill

quartier In the Landes, a division of land in a *commune*; each had 6–12 *quartiers*

retable carved or painted altarpiece, often consisting of a number of scenes or sculptural ensembles

rez-de-chaussée (RC) ground floor

sauveterre village or town founded under a guarantee against violence in wartime, agreed to by the Church and local barons; *sauveterres'* boundaries are often marked by crosses on all the roads leading into them

serre serrated ridge

tour tower

transi in a tomb, a relief of the decomposing cadaver

trumeau column between twin doors of a church portal, often carved with reliefs

tympanum semicircular panel over a church door; often the occasion for the most ambitious ensembles of medieval sculpture

village perché hilltop village

Index

Main page references are in **bold**. Page references to maps are in *italics*.

About the Updater

Linda Rano, her husband and two children, have been living near Toulouse for nine years. Linda writes regularly for a number of publications in particular on tourism and the property market in southwest France.

Fifth edition published 2007

Cadogan Guides
2nd Floor, 233 High Holborn,
London WC1V 7DN
info@cadoganguides.co.uk
www.cadoganguides.com

The Globe Pequot Press
246 Goose Lane, PO Box 480, Guilford,
Connecticut 06437–0480

Copyright © Dana Facaros and Micahel Pauls
1995, 2001, 2004, 2006, 2007
Updated by Linda Rano

Cover photographs: © DAVID NOBLE
PHOTOGRAPHY / Alamy and Tim Mitchell
Introduction photographs: © Tim Mitchell
Maps © Cadogan Guides, drawn by
Maidenhead Cartographic Services Ltd

Art Director: Sarah Gardner
Managing Editor: Antonia Cunningham
Editor: Claire Strange
Assistant Editor: Nicola Jessop
Proofreading: Daphne Trotter
Indexing: Isobel McLean

Printed in Italy by Legoprint
A catalogue record for this book is available
from the British Library
ISBN: 978-1-86011-360-4

The author and publishers have made every effort to ensure the accuracy of the information in this book at the time of going to press. However, they cannot accept any responsibility for any loss, injury or inconvenience resulting from the use of information contained in this guide.

Please help us to keep this guide up to date. We have done our best to ensure that the information in this guide is correct at the time of going to press. But places and facilities are constantly changing, and standards and prices in hotels and restaurants fluctuate. We would be delighted to receive any comments concerning existing entries or omissions. Authors of the best letters will receive a Cadogan Guide of their choice.

Gascony, Toulouse &
the Pyrenees touring atlas

E72

Caudecoste
Dunes
Auvillar
St-Roch
Moissac
TARN-ET-GARONNE
Réalville
Caussade
St-Antonin-
Noble-Val
Aveyron
Berrac
Ste-
Mère
Rouillac
Valence
d'Agen
Flamarens
Lachapelle
Castelsarrasin
Belleperche
Montbeton
La Ville-Dieu-
du-Temple
Négrepelisse
Montricoux
Penne
Bruniquel
Miradoux
Escatelens
Montauban
Vaïssac
Lectoure
Gramont
St-Créac
Beaumont-
de-Lomagne
Montech
Terraube
St-Clar
Avezan
St-Sardos
TARN
Fleurance
Bouillac
Verdun-sur-
Garonne
Fronton
Roquelaure
Mauvezin
Lavaur
Montaut-les-
Crénaux
Auch
Gimont
L'Isle Jourdain
Blagnac
Tarn
Garonne
124
632
Saramon
Caumont
St-Lys
Le Mirail
TOULOUSE
Seissan
Samatan
Rieumes
Muret
Masseube
Simorre
Lombez
HAUTE
Montmaur
L'Isle-en-Dodon
GARONNE
Nn13
632
Péguilhan
Mondilhan
Escanecrabe
Le Fousseret
Carbonne
Lézat-sur-
Lèze
Port-Lauragais
Baraigne
Belflou
Boulogne-
sur-Gesse
Ciadoux
Lespugue
Alan
E80/117
Montesquieu-
Volvestre
Canté
Saverdun
Mazères
Montmaurin
Larroque
St-Marcet
Aurignac
Cazères
Martres-Tolosane
Le Fossat
Le Vernet
E09
St-Placard
St-
Martory
Ausseing
Belbèze-en-
Comminges
Ste-Croix
Carla-Bayle
St-Martin-
d'Oydes
Artigat
Pamiers
Vals
Teilhet
St-
Gaudens
Montsaunes
Salles-
du-Salat
627
Le Mas
Montardit
Grotte du
Mas-d'Azil
Montégut-
Plantaurel
COMMINGES
Sauveterre-de-Comminges
La Bastide-
de-Sérou
Barbazan
Aspet
Prat-Bonrepaux
St-Lizier
Montjoie-en-Couserans
St-Jean-
de-Verges
alcabrère
St-Pé d'Ardet
Montgauch
ARIÈGE
Foix
Roquefixade
Lavelanet
St-Béat
Luzenach
Audressein
St-Girons
Dm1
Montferrier
125
618
St-
Lary
Castillon-en-Couserans
Saurat
Grotte
Soudour
Montségur
Sentein
Bethmale
Soueix
Massat
Bédeilhac
Bompas
Les Monts
d'Olmes
Eylie
Oust
Ercé
Tarascon-sur-Ariège
Ornolac
Seix
Grotte de Lombrives
Verdun
Lordat
Bagnères-de-Luchon
Mont
Valier
Col de
Pause
Couflens
Aulus-les-Bains
Grotte de Niaux
Les Cabannes
Unac
spice
ance
Guzet-Neige
Cirque de
Cagateille
Vicdessos
Cascade d'Arse
Sem
Gestiès
Ax-les-Thermes

20